Fodor's upCLOSE

NEW YORK CITY

the complete guide, thoroughly up-to-date

SAVVY TRAVELING: WHERE TO SPEND, HOW TO SAVE

packed with details that will make your trip

CULTURAL TIPS: ESSENTIAL LOCAL DO'S AND TABOOS

must-see sights, on and off the beaten path

INSIDER SECRETS: WHAT'S HIP AND WHAT TO SKIP

the buzz on restaurants, the lowdown on lodgings

FIND YOUR WAY WITH CLEAR AND EASY-TO-USE MAPS

FODOR'S TRAVEL PUBLICATIONS
NEW YORK • TORONTO • LONDON • SYDNEY • AUCKLAND

www.fodors.com

Second Edition

ISBN 0–679–00384–3

ISSN 1098–6235

FODOR'S UPCLOSE NEW YORK CITY

Editor: Donna Cornachio

Editorial Contributors: Stephanie Adler, Hannah Borgeson, Jennifer D'Angelo, John J. Donohue, Dori Fern, Melisse Gelula, Anto Howard, Melissa Klurman, Christina Knight, Andrea Lawlor, Heather Lewis, Lauren Myers, Helayne Schiff, Kristen Schurr

Editorial Production: Brian Vitunic

Maps: David Lindroth Inc., Eureka Cartography, *cartographers;* Rebecca Baer, Robert Blake, *map editors*

Design: Fabrizio La Rocca, *creative director;* Allison Saltzman, *cover and text design;* Jolie Novak, *photo editor*

Production/Manufacturing: Robert B. Shields

Cover Photograph: © Berenholtz/The Stock Market

SPECIAL SALES

Fodor's upCLOSE Guides and all Fodor's Travel Publications are available at special discounts for bulk purchases for sales promotions or premiums. Special editions, including personalized covers, excerpts of existing guides, and corporate imprints, can be created in large quantities for special needs. For more information, contact your local bookseller or write to Special Markets, Fodor's Travel Publications, 201 East 50th Street, New York, NY 10022. Inquiries from Canada should be directed to your local Canadian bookseller or sent to Random House of Canada, Ltd., Marketing Department, 2775 Matheson Boulevard East, Mississauga, Ontario L4W 4P7. Inquiries from the United Kingdom should be sent to Fodor's Travel Publications, 20 Vauxhall Bridge Road, London SW1V 2SA, England.

PRINTED IN THE UNITED STATES OF AMERICA

10 9 8 7 6 5 4 3 2 1

CONTENTS

I. BASICS *1*

2. EXPLORING NEW YORK CITY 26

3. WHERE TO SLEEP 141

4. FOOD 155

5. SHOPPING 197

6. AFTER DARK 212

7. THE ARTS 228

8. SPORTS AND OUTDOOR ACTIVITIES 246

INDEX 254

ON-LINE SURVEY

Tell us what you think of this guide and get a free Fodor's How to Pack *guidebook. Our on-line reader survey can be found at* **www.fodors.com/ upclose/upclosesurvey.html**

TRAVELING
UPCLOSE

Take the subway. Stay in a B&B. Try a hostel. Relax at an outdoor concert. Picnic in Central Park. Prowl the flea markets. Go to a festival. Memorize the symphony of the streets. And if you want to experience the heart and soul of New York City, whatever you do, don't spend too much money. The deep and rich experience of New York City that every true traveler yearns for is one of the things in life that money can't buy. In fact, if you have it, don't use it. Traveling lavishly is the surest way to turn yourself into a sideline traveler. Restaurants with white-glove service are great—sometimes—but they're usually not the best place to find the perfect knish or slice of pizza. Doormen at plush hotels have their place, but not when your look-alike room could be anywhere from Dusseldorf to Detroit. Better to stay in a more intimate place that truly gives you the atmosphere you traveled so far to experience. Don't just stand and watch—jump into the spirit of what's around you.

If you want to see New York City up close and savor the essence of the city and its people in all their charming, stylish, sometimes infuriatingly arrogant glory, this book is for you. We'll show you the local culture, the offbeat sights, the bars and cafés where tourists rarely tread, and the B&Bs and other hostelries where you'll meet fellow travelers—places where the locals would send their friends. And because you'll probably want to see the famous places if you haven't already been there, we give you tips on losing the crowds, plus the quirky and obscure facts you want as well as the basics everyone needs.

OUR GANG

Stephanie Adler was weaned on *A Chorus Line*—her first words were "Dance 10, Looks 3"—so perhaps it was inevitable that one day she'd take on the attitude of high-brow poetry readings and the altitude of Broadway's cheapest seats to update the Arts chapter of this book. These days, Stephanie finds herself at the Angelika far more often than the Shubert—that is, of course, when she's not hard at work as an editor for Fodor's.

Hannah Borgeson leads many free bike rides throughout the year and participates in countless others—she gave up taxis years ago. A freelance editor and full-time New York City–buff, she's pursuing a graduate degree in urban history and is a docent at the Museum of the City of New York.

When **Jennifer D'Angelo,** a reporter and editor at the *Queens Tribune,* isn't pounding the pavements of that borough in search of a story, she can be found at New York Sports Club, leading a grueling Ki Bo workout. But her favorite thing to do? "Curl up in bed with a novel written before 1900," says the former NYU English major.

John J. Donohue is the Night Life editor of *The New Yorker* magazine and his fourteen-hour days begin around noon. He prowls the streets below 14th Street pursuing his hobbies of eating, drinking, and sleeping.

Dori Fern is a proud—and polite—native New Yorker who disputes the idea that the city's indigenous folk are rude. When not offering up opinions on any number of subjects, or dyeing her hair strange colors, this freelance food writer loves nothing more than to walk miles in search of a great meal.

When it comes to shopping, **Melisse Gelula** has a knack for distinguishing the well-worth-its from the worthless, even if a label carries caché. When not scavenging the showrooms and salesfloors of the Big Apple, or reaching bravely into piles of secondhand rags for the prize at the bottom, she's updating or editing Fodor's books and weeping over the popular demise of millinery.

Dublin native **Anto Howard** (christened Anthony; Dubliners have a bad habit of abbreviating perfectly good names) has lived in NYC for the last six years where he has worked as a travel writer and editor. He has written sections of *Fodor's Ireland 2000* and *UpClose Ireland,* and edited *UpClose Central America* and *Rome 2000.*

Melissa Klurman stepped into the heat of Hell's Kitchen and the hip streets of Chelsea to prove that Midtown really can be cool if you just know where to look. When not updating the Exploring and Dining sections of this book, Melissa is an editor at Fodor's and has also contributed to the *Cityguide New York* and *Washington, D.C.,* books.

Brooklyn's Park Slope gave **Christina Knight** its last affordable apartment and a safe place to ride her bike and ignore fashion trends. From her kitchen window, the Fodor's editor keeps time by her beloved landmark, The Williamsburgh Savings Bank's clock tower.

Andrea Lawlor agreed to update the Bronx section of this book primarily so that she would have an excuse to spend entire afternoons gawking at the miniature cheese animals that live in Belmont cheese shop windows. She has lived in tiny apartments in three boroughs–Manhattan, Brooklyn, and the Bronx.

When not updating for Fodor's, **Heather Lewis** writes novels and explores her latest neighborhood, the Far East Village, where she lives with her cat Whoopie. After 15 years in the city, she almost considers herself a native.

Fodor's editor **Lauren Myers,** who lives on the Upper East Side, came away from her work on that neighborhood's dining and exploring section with refined crowd-dodging skills, not to mention a healthy respect for Museum Mile's colossal and diverse art scene. Her dining excursions were guided in part by a quest for that elusive fluffy-yet-crunchy New York bagel.

Helayne Schiff has very happily lived her adult life below 23rd Street. When she's not updating for Fodor's, she's busy writing plays, performing, and taking full advantage of what only this truly amazing city has to offer. Her plays have been read and produced uptown as well as downtown.

Kristen Schurr freelances for the New Press, an independent book publisher, tends bar in a dive downtown, and studies the politics of revolution. She worked as a staff writer for the *Seattle Weekly* covering all things music, and continues to publish in independent music magazines. She is a contributor to the upcoming tome, *The History of Northwest Music* (Sasquatch Books).

A SEND-OFF

Always call ahead. We knock ourselves out to check all the facts, but everything changes all the time, in ways that none of us can ever fully anticipate. Whenever you're making a special trip to a special place, as opposed to merely wandering, always call ahead. Trust us on this.

And then, if something doesn't go quite right, as inevitably happens with even the best-laid plans, stay cool. Missed your train? Stuck in the airport? Use the time to study the people. Strike up a conversation with a stranger. Study the newsstands or flip through the local press. Take a walk. Find the silver lining in the clouds, whatever it is. And do send us a postcard to tell us what went wrong and what went right. You can e-mail us at: editors@fodors.com (specify the name of the book on the subject line) or write the New York City editor at Fodor's UpClose, 201 East 50th Street, New York, NY 10022. We'll put your ideas to good use and let other travelers benefit from your experiences. In the meantime, bon voyage!

INTRODUCTION

I n recent years, the city of New York has been hanging banners around town proclaiming that it's the Capital of the World. And despite the claims to fame of other cities—Tokyo has more banks, Seattle has more musicians, Vancouver is the new darling among moviemakers, and Kuala Lumpur, Malaysia, now has the world's tallest skyscraper—New York can still lay claim to the most grand-championship titles. It's home to the United Nations and is a longtime nucleus of such varied fields as advertising, art, publishing, classical music, fashion, cuisine, finance, law, and headline-grabbing corporate takeovers. Though naysayers the world over have been predicting New York's demise for decades, it still seems you can't turn on the TV or read a magazine without getting the impression that at least half of everything in the United States happens in New York. And if you were to ask someone in Bangkok or Berlin or Bujumbura to sketch an American city, it's at least even money that the Empire State Building or the Statue of Liberty would appear in the picture.

Which leads to another thing New York City is the capital of: attitude. True, Parisians are probably equally, um, brusque, but you'll find few other places on earth where people so clearly bear the imprint of their hometown. After a few days walking Manhattan streets you'll really know your New Yorkers. Be they foppish like Eustace Tilley, Rea Irvin's famed *New Yorker* cartoon cover model, or tough and street savvy as DeNiro in *Taxi Driver,* whether they're newly immigrated cabbies or megalomaniac financiers, all seem to possess a real whoop-de-do enthusiasm (and wardrobe heavy on black clothes) for living here. Maybe it's survivor's mentality: The journalist Edward Hoagland once jokingly noted that annually the city's 7.3 million residents probably "see more death than most soldiers do."

Whatever the reason for the in-your-face attitude of New Yorkers, you'll have plenty of opportunities to mix and mingle with (or at least stand behind velvet ropes and stare at) this peculiar breed of urban dweller. For this is one of few American cities where people prefer to walk rather than drive (not surprising, given that traffic crossing Midtown averages 5.3 mi an hour), where face-to-face interaction has not been obliterated by cruise control and car pool lanes. New York sidewalks attract around 10,000 pedestrians per hour, making them some of the busiest on earth. By all means, take advantage of its 722 mi of convenient subway lines while you're visiting, but don't forget to get out and walk a few blocks; it's the best way to discover the city's 400 art galleries, 17,000 restaurants, 150 museums, and 200 skyscrapers—as long as you don't mind dodging the piles of doggie doo and, in the winter, crusty, black drifts of snow.

But long before these subways and skyscrapers were even a glimmer in New Yorkers' eyes, before the city became "the nation's thyroid gland," as Christopher Morley once described it, New York City was the tiny town of New Amsterdam, settled at the southern tip of Manhattan by the Dutch in 1624. In an astounding episode of flimflammery, the settlers had purchased Manhattan from the Indians for trinkets worth $24. This 22-square-mi island with the bargain-basement price exhibited an "anything goes" vibe from the get-go. When a missionary visited in 1643, he found an already cosmopolitan community of 500 settlers speaking 18 different languages. From its very inception, it was clear that New York would never become another lost-in-the-woods Roanoke.

Except for a decade or so break for the Revolutionary War (we won), the city, blessed with a commodious natural harbor, expanded into the corners of Manhattan Island and inched outward to swallow Brooklyn, the Bronx, Queens, and Staten Island. Canals and railroads built in the first half of the 19th century brought trade—and money—by the bushel, and the city soon became the largest and richest in the hemisphere, eclipsing its old rival, Philadelphia. But it wasn't until the second half of the 1800s that the city really started to percolate. With America as a whole, and New York in particular, shining as a beacon of prosperity for the rest of the world (Europe was suffering through a devastating famine), immigrants poured in, and then poured in some more. The melting pot that we alternately glorify and curse today took shape as some 16 million Italian, African, Irish, Jewish, and German immigrants arrived over the next six decades. All told, over 120 different nationalities now live here, including a new wave of immigrants from Central America and Southeast Asia, and each has left their mark on the city, whether it's an innovative cuisine or a special festival.

No one knows for sure, but the name Manhattan may have come from the Munsee Indian word "manahactanienk," meaning "place of general inebriation."

Ironically, as the teeming masses fled Europe for New York in the 19th century, the city's wealthiest residents were striving to re-create the splendor of a European capital right here at home. The upper crust made no secret of their envy of Paris when they lobbied city officials to create Central Park in the 1850s. Throughout the century, city planning and private philanthropy gave birth to powerhouse institutions like the Metropolitan Opera, the Metropolitan Museum of Art, the New York Public Library, and the American Museum of Natural History. This self-aggrandizing spirit continued through the next century, producing, among other things, the Museum of Modern Art, the Studio Museum in Harlem, and Lincoln Center for the Performing Arts. Of course, you can't have world-class cultural institutions without world-famous artists, writers, and performers. The city's literary giants include Walt Whitman and Herman Melville in the 19th century; Marianne Moore, e.e. cummings, and Dorothy Parker in the 1920s; and Ralph Ellison, Carson McCullers, and Allen Ginsberg at mid-century. New York was the spot where "modern art" from Europe was introduced to an outraged public in 1913, and it's been synonymous with the avant-garde ever since—from abstract expressionists like Franz Kline to the pop art masters of the 1960s. Georgia O'Keeffe, Jackson Pollock, Mark Rothko, Agnes Martin, and Andy Warhol have all called the city home.

As much as New York can trumpet its economic, social, and cultural success, it also boasts an impressive array of things that don't work quite as well: It's crowded, dirty, expensive as hell, and yes, occasionally dangerous. Newt Gingrich rightfully received flak for dissing New York as a "culture of waste" in 1995, but the fact is, organized crime, bloated bureaucracy, mounting debt, and crumbling infrastructure *are* ongoing problems here. Add to that the crash of the go-go '80s—which clipped the wings of many a high-rolling Wall Streeter—and the subsequent recession of the early '90s—which sent many big corporations scurrying for low-rent New Jersey—and you'll see why many people seem ready to kick New York in the kidneys and turn out the lights. But do you really think it'd be that easy? As the millennium approaches, the city seems to be once again springing back to life and cleaning up its act: FBI records show that violent crime rates in NYC fell dramatically from 1988 to 1998. Notoriously sleazy XXX-filled Times Square is being cleaned up and turned over to Disney; parks like Bryant and Tompkins Square have been reclaimed from drug peddlers; and farmers' markets and neighborhood cafés are flourishing. Better still, the city's transportation department swears it's got a handle on the 60,000 or so potholes that show up annually, and they've just finished adding air-conditioning to 99% of the city's subway cars. Whether or not you agree that New York deserves to be called Capital of the World, you can't dispute that it's one hell of a town.

BASICS

contacts and savvy tips to make your trip hassle-free

I f you've ever traveled with anyone before, you know that there are two types of people in the world—the planners and the nonplanners. Travel brings out the worst in both groups. Left to their own devices, the planners will have you goose-stepping from attraction to attraction on a cultural blitzkrieg, while the nonplanners will invariably miss the flight, the bus, and maybe even the point. This chapter offers you a middle ground; we hope it provides enough information to help you plan your trip to New York without nailing you down. Keep flexible and remember that the most hair-pulling situations turn into the best travel stories back home.

AIR TRAVEL

BOOKING YOUR FLIGHT

When you book **look for nonstop flights** and **remember that "direct" flights stop at least once.** Try to avoid connecting flights, which require a change of plane.

CARRIERS

MAJOR AIRLINES • Within the United States: **American** (tel. 800/433–7300). **America West** (tel. 800/235–9292). **Continental** (tel. 800/525–0280). **Delta** (tel. 800/221–1212). **Northwest** (tel. 800/225–2525). **TWA** (tel. 800/221–2000). **United** (tel. 800/241–6522). **US Airways** (tel. 800/428–4322). From Canada: **Air Canada** (tel. 800/776–3000). **Delta** and **US Airways** also serve New York from Canada. From the United Kingdom: **Air India** (tel. 020/8745–1000). **American** (tel. 0345/789–789). **British Airways** (tel. 0345/222–111). **Continental** (tel. 0800/776–464). **El Al** (tel. 020/7957–4100). **Kuwait Airways** (tel. 020/7412–0007). **United** (tel. 0800/888–555). **Virgin Atlantic** (tel. 01293/747–747). From Down Under: **Qantas** (tel. 800/227–4500 in the U.S., 02/9957–0111 in Australia). **United** has service from Australia and New Zealand to all three airports in the NYC area.

SMALLER AIRLINES • **Midway** (tel. 800/446–4392). **Midwest Express** (tel. 800/452–2022).

CHECK-IN & BOARDING

Assuming that not everyone with a ticket will show up, airlines routinely overbook planes. When that happens, airlines ask for volunteers to give up their seats. In return these volunteers usually get a certificate for a free flight and are rebooked on the next flight out. If there are not enough volunteers, the airline must choose who will be denied boarding. The first to get bumped are passengers who checked in late and those flying on discounted tickets, so **get to the gate and check in as early as possible,** especially during peak periods.

Always **bring a government-issued photo I.D. to the airport.** You may be asked to show it before you are allowed to check in.

CUTTING COSTS

The least-expensive airfares to New York must usually be purchased in advance and are nonrefundable. It's smart to **call a number of airlines, and when you are quoted a good price, book it on the spot**—the same fare may not be available the next day. Always **check different routings** and look into using different airports. Travel agents, especially low-fare specialists (*see* Discounts & Deals, *below*), are helpful.

LOCAL RESOURCES • If you're in New York and shopping for a ticket out, you'll find dozens of companies advertising unbelievably cheap flights in the *Village Voice* and in the Sunday travel section of the *New York Times*. Most are legit, but call around, and check with the **Better Business Bureau** (tel. 212/533–6200) before you purchase. A couple to try: **Travel Abroad, Inc.** (47 W. 34th St., at Broadway, Suite 546, tel. 212/564–8989) or **ABS Travel, Inc.** (347 5th Ave., between 33rd and 34th Sts., Suite 406, tel. 212/447–1717).

Consolidators are another good source. They buy tickets for scheduled international flights at reduced rates from the airlines, then sell them at prices that beat the best fare available directly from the airlines, usually without restrictions. Sometimes you can even get your money back if you need to return the ticket. Carefully read the fine print detailing penalties for changes and cancellations, and **confirm your consolidator reservation with the airline.**

When you **fly as a courier** you trade your checked-luggage space for a ticket deeply subsidized by a courier service. There are restrictions on when you can book and how long you can stay.

CONSOLIDATORS • **Cheap Tickets** (tel. 800/377–1000). **Discount Airline Ticket Service** (tel. 800/576–1600). **Unitravel** (tel. 800/325–2222). **World Travel Network** (tel. 800/409–6753).

Airfare Busters (5100 Westheimer, Suite 550, Houston, TX 77056, tel. 713/961–5109 or 800/232–8783, fax 713/961–3385). **Globe Travel** (507 5th Ave., Suite 606, New York, NY 10017, tel. 212/843–9885 or 800/969–4562, fax 212/843–9889). **United States Air Consolidators Association** (925 L St., Suite 220, Sacramento, CA 95814, tel. 916/441–4166, fax 916/441–3520). **UniTravel** (1177 N. Warson Rd., St. Louis, MO 63132, tel. 314/569–2501 or 800/325–2222, fax 314/569–2503). **Up & Away Travel** (347 5th Ave., Suite 202, New York, NY 10016, tel. 212/889–2345 or 800/275–8001, fax 212/889–2350).

ENJOYING THE FLIGHT

For more legroom **request an emergency-aisle seat.** Don't sit in the row in front of the emergency aisle or in front of a bulkhead, where seats may not recline. If you have dietary concerns, **ask for special meals when booking.** These can be vegetarian, low-cholesterol, or kosher, for example. On long flights, try to maintain a normal routine, to help fight jetlag. At night **get some sleep.** By day **eat light meals, drink water** (not alcohol), and **move around the cabin** to stretch your legs.

HOW TO COMPLAIN

If your baggage goes astray or your flight goes awry, complain right away. Most carriers require that you **file a claim immediately.**

AIRLINE COMPLAINTS • U.S. Department of Transportation **Aviation Consumer Protection Division** (C-75, Room 4107, Washington, DC 20590, tel. 202/366–2220). **Federal Aviation Administration Consumer Hotline** (tel. 800/322–7873).

AIRPORTS & TRANSFERS

Three major airports—**John F. Kennedy International, La Guardia,** and **Newark International**—serve New York City, though Newark is actually in the state of New Jersey.

John F. Kennedy International is the largest of New York's three airports, with five terminals located about 15 mi southeast of Manhattan, in Queens. There's a currency-exchange booth on the second floor of the JFK International building and one in the Delta terminal. Luggage storage (tel. 718/656–8617) facilities are in the International building (Building 4E/4W), between Gates 10 and 11 and between 33 and 34. Rates are $3.50–$5 per bag, per day. There are information booths in the east and west wings of the International building, on the first floor. Each terminal has its own parking lot. Six lots are for long-term parking with a 30-day maximum stay at a cost of $8 per day.

La Guardia Airport is the smallest New York airport, 8 mi northeast of Manhattan, in Flushing, Queens. There are currency-exchange windows on the upper level between the American and United terminals, and at the US Airways terminal. Luggage storage (tel. 718/478–1690) facilities are in the US Airways terminal on the departure level next to the food court and in the main terminal between the American and United ticket counters. Rates are $1.50–$3.50 per bag, per day. Parking costs $4 for the first two hours and $2 per hour after that, maxing out at $24 per day. Reduced-rate long-term parking is available for $24 for the first 24 hours, and $2 per hour with a maximum of $10 per day thereafter.

Newark International Airport is about 16 mi southwest of New York City, in New Jersey. Newark has half a dozen currency-exchange windows; those in Terminal A are open daily 7 AM–8:30 PM, those in Terminal B, daily 7 AM–9 PM. Terminal B has a buy-back counter on the arrivals level between doors five and six (open daily noon–8) and a regular exchange counter on the concourse level. Terminal C also has an exchange center on the concourse level next to the bank and one on the ticketing level by door four; both are open daily 7 AM–8:30 PM. Luggage storage (tel. 201/961–4720) at Newark is at Terminal B on the ground-floor level, open daily 7 AM–9 PM. Rates are $1.50–$5 per bag, per day. Parking is divided into hourly, daily, and long-term lots. Hourly parking is $4 for the first two hours and then $4 per hour after that. Daily parking costs $24 for 24 hours, with a maximum stay of three days. Long-term is the farthest lot from the airport, though there is a free shuttle bus for passengers. Long-term costs $8 per 24 hours.

AIRPORT INFORMATION • JFK International Airport (tel. 718/244–4444). **La Guardia Airport** (tel. 718/533–3400). **Newark International Airport** (tel. 973/961–6000).

TRANSFERS

Call the Port Authority's **Air Ride hot line** (tel. 800/247–7433) for detailed, up-to-the-minute recorded info on how to reach your destination from New York's three major airports via car, private bus, shuttle service, or public transportation. The cheapest option is the public transit system, although what you save in dollars you'll pay for with time and effort, since routes can take an hour or more and may involve transferring between bus and subway. Private shuttle services travel between all three airports and many Manhattan hotels. Taxis and car services are the most expensive option, with fares running as high as $35 one-way, plus $3–$4 in bridge tolls. When all is said and done, you'll find that one of the easiest and most reasonable ways to get to and from the airport is with a bus service—either NJ Transit to and from Newark or Gray Line Air Shuttle to and from La Guardia, JFK, and Newark (*see* Shuttle Buses, *below*).

JFK INTERNATIONAL • Taxis and Car Service: There is now a flat $30 fee (plus tolls) for travel from JFK to Manhattan (*not* from the city to the airport) for taxis and private car services. On average, car service to JFK costs about $33 plus tolls and tip. Taxis cost a bit more.

Shuttle Buses: The **Gray Line Air Shuttle** (tel. 212/315–3006 or 800/451–0455) picks up outside all JFK terminals every 20–30 minutes between 6 AM and 11 PM and stops in Manhattan at the Port Authority Bus Terminal (W. 42nd St. at 8th Ave.), Grand Central Terminal (E. 42nd St. at Park Ave.), and major hotels between 23rd and 63rd streets. The ride costs $14 from JFK and takes anywhere from 45 minutes to an hour, depending on traffic. Outbound Gray Line buses (from Manhattan to JFK) operate 365 days a year and are more expensive ($19 one-way to JFK). Make reservations at the airport's transportation center.

Public Transport: Taking the subway to JFK is fairly simple and cheap ($1.50). Take the A train to the Howard Beach Station, from where you can catch a free shuttle run by the Port Authority. The shuttle makes the trip to JFK every 10 minutes and takes about 20 minutes to reach the terminals. All told, it's about a 70-minute trip from Midtown.

LA GUARDIA • Taxis and Car Service: On average, taxi and car service to La Guardia costs $22–$29, plus tolls and tip.

Shuttle Buses: The **Gray Line Air Shuttle** (tel. 212/315–3006 or 800/451–0455) costs $13 one-way from La Guardia and stops at any major hotel between 23rd and 63rd streets. Make reservations at the airport's ground transportation center or use the courtesy phone.

Public Transport: The **Triboro Coach Corp.** (tel. 718/335–1000) runs its Q-33 line from the airport to the Jackson Heights subway stop in Queens every 10 minutes during peak morning and evening hours. Its Q-47 line services the Marine Air Terminal at La Guardia. The ride costs $1.50, and the buses run daily 4 AM–2 AM. The **MTA** runs its M60 line to La Guardia; catch it in Manhattan on 118th Street at Broadway. The route follows 125th Street across town and runs every half hour. The fare is $1.50.

NEWARK • Taxis and Car Service: On average, car or taxi service to Newark is about $34–$38, plus tolls and tip.

Shuttle Buses: Olympia Trails Airport Express (tel. 212/964–6233, 718/622–7700, or 908/354–3330) picks up every 15–30 minutes, between 6:15 AM and midnight, outside all Newark terminals and stops at Grand Central Terminal, Port Authority, Penn Station, and the World Trade Center. The ride takes 25–45 minutes and costs $10. The **Gray Line Air Shuttle** (tel. 212/315–3006 or 800/451–0455) costs $14 one-way from Newark and stops at any major hotel between 23rd and 63rd streets (the price is $19 from Manhattan to Newark). Make reservations at the airport's ground transportation center or use the courtesy phone.

Public Transport: You can take New Jersey Transit's Airlink buses, which leave every 20 minutes from 6:15 AM to 2 AM, to Penn Station in Newark. The ride takes about 20 minutes and costs $4 (exact change). From there, the cheapest option ($1) is a PATH train from Newark to various stops in Manhattan (for more info *see* Regional Train Services *in* Train Travel, *below*).

BUS TRAVEL TO AND FROM NEW YORK CITY

All long-distance bus companies depart from the **Port Authority Bus Terminal** (625 8th Ave., at W. 41st St., Midtown, tel. 212/564–8484. Subway: A, C, or E to W. 42nd St.), open 24 hours. This huge terminal, which services more than 35 bus companies and nearly 200,000 people a day, is in a somewhat squalid neighborhood. For New York City buses going uptown, board the M10 on the east side of 8th Avenue; board the downtown M11 on 9th Avenue across the street from the south wing entrance; board the cross-town M42 on 42nd Street at 8th Avenue. You are expected to tip the terminal's Red Caps if they help you haul your 200-pound suitcase to a ticket window.

GREYHOUND

Bus service in North America can be grungy and depressing—but it is cheap. **Greyhound-Trailways** (tel. 212/971–6300 or 800/231–2222) has routes throughout the United States, including service between New York and Boston (4½ hrs, $34), Philadelphia (2½ hrs, $19), Washington, D.C. (4½ hrs, $34), Chicago (18 hrs, $91), Atlanta (21 hrs, $69), San Francisco (2½ days, $126), and Los Angeles (3 days, $135). You can order tickets by mail with a credit card or buy your ticket at the station up to one hour before the bus leaves. Cheapest fares are offered during the low season (January–June) and advance-purchase specials. You're allowed two carry-on and two checked pieces of luggage.

GREYHOUND PASSES • Greyhound's Ameripass, valid on all U.S. routes, can be purchased in advance in cities throughout the States; spontaneous types can also buy it up to 45 minutes before the bus leaves the terminal. The pass allows purchasers unlimited travel within a limited time period: seven days ($199), 15 days ($299), 30 days ($409), or 60 days ($599). Foreign visitors get slightly lower rates.

REGIONAL BUS SERVICES

For bus travel into and around New Jersey, contact **New Jersey Transit** (tel. 201/762–5100 or 800/772–2222). **East Coast Explorer** (tel. 718/694–9667 or 800/610–2680) runs backroad trips to Boston ($29 one-way) and Washington, D.C. ($32), with stops at places of natural, historical, and cultural interest—like Newport, Rhode Island, and the Pennsylvania Amish country. Buses depart New York for Boston on Monday and for Washington, D.C., on Thursday; returns are on the following day and travel a different route.

BUS TRAVEL WITHIN NEW YORK

Though New York's subway system is amazingly comprehensive and quick, there are a few reasons to venture above ground and onto a city bus. For one thing, it's a good way to sightsee while you travel, and you'll probably feel a great deal more cheery if you're not spending all your time in a dark, dank, subterranean tunnel. Second, buses provide better door-to-door service if you just want to go a few blocks and can't find (or don't want to pay for) a cab. Say you want to skip from the Metropolitan Museum (5th Ave. at 82nd St.) to Sak's Fifth Avenue (5th Ave. at 50th St.) for some shopping; that's a 15-minute bus ride, but it'd be 40 minutes or more of walking and waiting and climbing stairs if you wanted to go by subway. You'll find that in some neighborhoods where subway lines are scarce—like the Upper East Side, Chelsea west of 8th Avenue, and the East Village—you'll be practically forced to grab a bus to quickly move from point A to B. Ditto for crossing Central Park. A final reason, valid only in summer: All buses are air-conditioned (subway cars are air-conditioned, too, but subway platforms are typically sweltering hot). Keep in mind that during rush hours all the nice things we've told you about buses will still make for a pleasant trip—but not if you're in any kind of hurry. Manhattan's snarled traffic makes for slow going weekday mornings and evenings.

In Manhattan, buses run along virtually every north–south avenue, with several lines running up heavily used routes like 5th Avenue, Madison Avenue, and Broadway. Crosstown buses run at least every 10 blocks, and across Central Park at 66th, 72nd, 79th, 86th, and 96th streets. Stops are every two or three blocks on north–south avenues and every block on crosstown streets. Bus stops are indicated by a red, white, and blue sign on a pole, plus a yellow-painted curb. You'll also find a route schedule and map posted at each stop (you can pick up a map detailing *all* of the Manhattan bus routes at any subway station). During rush hours, buses run about every seven minutes (although you may have to let a too-crowded bus go by and wait for the next one), but at other times, and in bad weather, you can easily end up waiting 10–15 minutes or more. At night many bus routes run less frequently (or not at all); check the posted route schedule for info.

FARES & SCHEDULES • Bus fare is $1.50 per person, just like the subway, and buses accept subway tokens. You can also pay the fare with coins—but not pennies or dollar bills. But remember: Drivers will not make change, ever, even if you rend your clothing and weep loudly. Don't forget to ask for your free transfer ticket after you've paid. It's good on one intersecting bus route (from a list on the back of the ticket) and must be used within two hours. You can use the MetroCard (*see* Subway Travel, *below*) on all New York City Transit buses in Manhattan, which now enables you to transfer free from bus to subway, subway to bus, or bus to bus for up to two hours.

For schedule information, *see* Transportation, *below*.

BUSINESS HOURS

Business hours in New York are roughly 9–5, though some Wall Streeters are up with the crows and long past suppertime. Lunch varies, but usually lasts about an hour, somewhere between 12–2.

MUSEUMS & SIGHTS

Most museums and other sites open at 10 and close around 5; though several remain open late one or two nights a week. The majority of museums are closed Mondays.

SHOPS

Most shops are open from 10 to 6 with a late-night closing at the major department stores usually on Thursdays.

CAMERAS & PHOTOGRAPHY

PHOTO HELP • Kodak Information Center (tel. 800/242–2424). *Kodak Guide to Shooting Great Travel Pictures,* available in bookstores or from Fodor's Travel Publications (tel. 800/533–6478; $16.50 plus $4 shipping).

EQUIPMENT PRECAUTIONS

Always **keep your film and tape out of the sun.** Carry an extra supply of batteries, and **be prepared to turn on your camera or camcorder** to prove to security personnel that the device is real. Always **ask for hand inspection of film,** which becomes clouded after successive exposures to airport X-ray machines, and **keep videotapes away from metal detectors.**

CAR RENTAL

Renting a car in New York might make you think that it's cheaper just to buy one and drive it home. Rates in New York City begin at $52 a day and $316 a week for an economy car with air-conditioning, automatic transmission, and unlimited mileage. This does not include tax on car rentals, which is 13¼%. On summer weekends, cars can be scarce, so reserve one in advance.

LOCAL AGENCIES • Allstar Rent A Car (325 W. 34th St., between 8th and 9th Aves., Midtown, tel. 212/563–8282), open Monday–Thursday 7:30–6:30, Friday 7:30–8, Saturday 8–6, Sunday 8–2. **Amcar Discount Car Rentals** (315 W. 96th St., between West End Ave. and Riverside Dr., Upper West Side, tel. 212/222–8500), open weekdays 7:30–7:30, weekends 9–5. **Elite Car Rental** (1041 Coney Island Ave., between Foster and 18th Aves., Brooklyn, tel. 718/859–8111), open Monday–Thursday and Sunday 8–7, Friday 8–5). **Rent-A-Wreck** (tel. 800/535–1391) specializes in cheaper, older, and uglier cars, sometimes undercutting the national companies on rates—but make sure the lower cost is not eclipsed by added mileage charges. **Thrifty** (tel. 800/367–2277).

MAJOR AGENCIES • Alamo (tel. 800/327–9633; 020/8759–6200 in the U.K.). **Avis** (tel. 800/331–1212; 800/879–2847 in Canada; 02/9353–9000 in Australia; 09/525–1982 in New Zealand). **Budget** (tel. 800/527–0700; 0144/227–6266 in the U.K.). **Dollar** (tel. 800/800–4000; 020/8897–0811 in the U.K., where it is known as Eurodollar; 02/9223–1444 in Australia). **Hertz** (tel. 800/654–3131; 800/263–0600 in Canada; 0990/90–60–90 in the U.K.; 02/9669–2444 in Australia; 03/358–6777 in New Zealand). **National InterRent** (tel. 800/227–7368; 0345/222525 in the U.K., where it is known as Europcar InterRent).

CUTTING COSTS

To get the best deal **book through a travel agent who will shop around.** Also **price local car-rental companies,** although the service and maintenance may not be as good as those of a major player. Remember to ask about required deposits, cancellation penalties, and drop-off charges if you're planning to pick up the car in one city and leave it in another. If you're traveling during a holiday period, also make sure that a confirmed reservation guarantees you a car.

Do **look into wholesalers,** companies that do not own fleets but rent in bulk from those that do and often offer better rates than traditional car-rental operations. Payment must be made before you leave home.

WHOLESALERS • Auto Europe (tel. 207/842–2000 or 800/223–5555, fax 800/235–6321).

INSURANCE

When driving a rented car you are generally responsible for any damage to or loss of the vehicle as well as for any property damage or personal injury that you may cause. Before you rent see what coverage your personal auto-insurance policy and credit cards already provide.

For about $15 to $20 per day, rental companies sell protection, known as a collision- or loss-damage waiver (CDW or LDW), that eliminates your liability for damage to the car. New York has outlawed the sale of the CDW and LDW altogether. In New York you pay only for the first $100 of damage to the rental car.

In most states you don't need a CDW if you have personal auto insurance or other liability insurance. However, **make sure you have enough coverage to pay for the car.** If you do not have auto insurance or an umbrella policy that covers damage to third parties, purchasing liability insurance and a CDW or LDW is highly recommended.

REQUIREMENTS & RESTRICTIONS

In New York you must be 18 to rent a car. You'll pay extra for child seats (about $3 per day), which are compulsory for children under five, and for additional drivers (about $2 per day). Non-U.S. residents will need a reservation voucher, a passport, a driver's license, and a travel policy that covers each driver, in order to pick up a car.

SURCHARGES

Before you pick up a car in one city and leave it in another **ask about drop-off charges or one-way service fees,** which can be substantial. Note, too, that some rental agencies charge extra if you return the car before the time specified in your contract. To avoid a hefty refueling fee **fill the tank just before you turn in the car,** but be aware that gas stations near the rental outlet may overcharge.

CAR TRAVEL

The biggest mistake you could make while living in or visiting New York is driving a car—New Yorkers typically only use cars to *leave* the city, not drive around in it. So consider this: If the city's Department of Transportation doesn't get you (with unfilled potholes and outdated signs), a car thief might get your car. Reports of grand larceny (or vehicles stolen when the driver was not around) totaled 18,289 in 1998, for example. Also keep in mind that traffic in New York is simply awful: On a good day, it can take 30 minutes to travel 30 blocks during the rush-hour commute. Though it is possible to see Manhattan by car, you should definitely get to know the city a little before committing to the four-wheel experience.

BRIDGE & TUNNEL TOLLS

New York City has dozens of bridges and tunnels. Tolls are levied one-way only, usually on traffic headed into Manhattan. Bridges leading into Manhattan and charging a toll are the George Washington Bridge ($4), which connects New York with New Jersey, and the Triboro Bridge ($3.50), which leads from the Bronx and Queens into Harlem. Around a dozen other bridges connect the outer boroughs and charge tolls ranging from $1.50 to $4. Tunnels leading into Manhattan include the Brooklyn Battery Tunnel

($3.50), Holland Tunnel ($4), Lincoln Tunnel ($4), and Queens Midtown Tunnel ($3.50). For more info, contact the Triborough Bridge and Tunnel Authority (tel. 212/360–3000) or the Port Authority of New York and New Jersey (tel. 212/435–7000).

EMERGENCIES
Dial 911.

GASOLINE
Gas stations are clustered on the far west and east sides of Manhattan, and gas (like the rest of New York) does not come cheap. If you happen to take a day trip into New Jersey, fill up there.

PARKING
Whether you opt for a garage or take your chances parking on the street, you'll have a few headaches to contend with. The first is price: Parking lot and garage rates vary from neighborhood to neighborhood, but you should expect to pay upwards of $6–$14 per hour or $25–$31 per day. Among the highest rates are those on the Upper East Side and in Midtown; the cheapest garages are on the Lower East Side. Or you can make the long trek north on the B or C trains to **WD Lot** (304 W. 135th St., at Amsterdam Ave., Harlem), which offers rock-bottom prices: $3 an hour or $10 a night.

If you want to conserve cash you can park on the streets for free—if you can find a legal space, that is. New Yorkers also contend with a boggling number of posted parking restrictions, including the dreaded alternate side of the street system—which means moving your car across the street to make way for street sweepers. The moral here is always read curbside signs, and if you're serious about parking on the street, call 212/225–5368, a 24-hour automated help line, to find out about when alternate side of the street parking is suspended, and to get the skinny on other parking regulations. To speak to a live human being, call between 7 AM and 7 PM.

CHILDREN IN NEW YORK
If you are renting a car don't forget to **arrange for a car seat** when you reserve.

FLYING
If your children are two or older **ask about children's airfares.** As a general rule, infants under two not occupying a seat fly at greatly reduced fares or even for free. When booking **confirm carry-on allowances** if you're traveling with infants. In general, for babies charged 10% of the adult fare, you are allowed one carry-on bag and a collapsible stroller; if the flight is full the stroller may have to be checked or you may be limited to less.

Experts agree that it's a good idea to use safety seats aloft for children weighing less than 40 pounds. Airlines set their own policies: U.S. carriers usually require that the child be ticketed, even if he or she is young enough to ride free, since the seats must be strapped into regular seats. Do **check your airline's policy about using safety seats during takeoff and landing.** And since safety seats are not allowed just everywhere in the plane, get your seat assignments early.

When reserving, **request children's meals or a freestanding bassinet** if you need them. But note that bulkhead seats, where you must sit to use the bassinet, may lack an overhead bin or storage space on the floor.

LODGING
Most hotels in New York allow children under a certain age to stay in their parents' room at no extra charge, but others charge for them as extra adults; be sure to **find out the cutoff age for children's discounts.**

CONCIERGES
Concierges, found in many hotels, can help you with theater tickets and dinner reservations: a good one with connections may be able to get you seats for a hot show or prime-time dinner reservations at the restaurant of the moment. You can also turn to your hotel's concierge for help with travel arrangements, sightseeing plans, services ranging from aromatherapy to zipper repair, and emergencies. Always, **always tip** a concierge who has been of assistance (*see* Tipping, *below*).

CONSUMER PROTECTION

Whenever shopping or buying travel services in New York, **pay with a major credit card** so you can cancel payment or get reimbursed if there's a problem. If you're doing business with a particular company for the first time, **contact your local Better Business Bureau and the attorney general's offices** in your state and the company's home state, as well. Have any complaints been filed? Finally, if you're buying a package or tour, always **consider travel insurance** that includes default coverage (*see* Insurance, *below*).

LOCAL BBBS • Council of Better Business Bureaus (4200 Wilson Blvd., Suite 800, Arlington, VA 22203, tel. 703/276–0100, fax 703/525–8277).

CUSTOMS & DUTIES

When shopping, **keep receipts** for all purchases. Upon reentering the country, **be ready to show customs officials what you've bought.** If you feel a duty is incorrect or object to the way your clearance was handled, note the inspector's badge number and ask to see a supervisor. If the problem isn't resolved, write to the appropriate authorities, beginning with the port director at your point of entry.

IN AUSTRALIA

Australia residents who are 18 or older may bring home $A400 worth of souvenirs and gifts (including jewelry), 250 cigarettes or 250 grams of tobacco, and 1,125 ml of alcohol (including wine, beer, and spirits). Residents under 18 may bring back $A200 worth of goods. Prohibited items include meat products. Seeds, plants, and fruits need to be declared upon arrival.

INFORMATION • Australian Customs Service (Regional Director, Box 8, Sydney, NSW 2001, tel. 02/9213–2000, fax 02/9213–4000).

IN CANADA

Canadian residents who have been out of Canada for at least 7 days may bring home C$500 worth of goods duty-free. If you've been away less than 7 days but more than 48 hours, the duty-free allowance drops to C$200; if your trip lasts 24–48 hours, the allowance is C$50. You may not pool allowances with family members. Goods claimed under the C$500 exemption may follow you by mail; those claimed under the lesser exemptions must accompany you. Alcohol and tobacco products may be included in the 7-day and 48-hour exemptions but not in the 24-hour exemption. If you meet the age requirements of the province or territory through which you reenter Canada, you may bring in, duty-free, 1.14 liters (40 imperial ounces) of wine or liquor *or* 24 12-ounce cans or bottles of beer or ale. If you are 16 or older you may bring in, duty-free, 200 cigarettes and 50 cigars. Check ahead of time with Revenue Canada or the Department of Agriculture for policies regarding meat products, seeds, plants, and fruits.

You may send an unlimited number of gifts worth up to C$60 each duty-free to Canada. Label the package UNSOLICITED GIFT—VALUE UNDER $60. Alcohol and tobacco are excluded.

INFORMATION • Revenue Canada (2265 St. Laurent Blvd. S, Ottawa, Ontario K1G 4K3, tel. 613/993–0534; 800/461–9999 in Canada).

IN NEW ZEALAND

Homeward-bound residents 17 or older may bring back $700 worth of souvenirs and gifts. Your duty-free allowance also includes 4.5 liters of wine or beer; one 1,125-ml bottle of spirits; and either 200 cigarettes, 250 grams of tobacco, 50 cigars, or a combination of the three up to 250 grams. Prohibited items include meat products, seeds, plants, and fruits.

INFORMATION • New Zealand Customs (Custom House, 50 Anzac Ave., Box 29, Auckland, New Zealand, tel. 09/359–6655, fax 09/359–6732).

IN NEW YORK

Visitors age 21 and over may import the following into the United States: 200 cigarettes or 50 cigars or 2 kilograms of tobacco, 1 liter of alcohol, and gifts worth $100. Prohibited items include meat products, seeds, plants, and fruits.

IN THE U.K.

From countries outside the EU, including the United States, you may bring home, duty-free, 200 cigarettes or 50 cigars; 1 liter of spirits or 2 liters of fortified or sparkling wine or liqueurs; 2 liters of still table wine; 60 ml of perfume; 250 ml of toilet water; plus £136 worth of other goods, including gifts and souvenirs. If returning from outside the EU, prohibited items include meat products, seeds, plants, and fruits.

INFORMATION • HM Customs and Excise (Dorset House, Stamford St., Bromley Kent BR1 1XX, tel. 020/7202–4227).

IN THE U.S.

Non-U.S. residents ages 21 and older may import into the United States 200 cigarettes or 50 cigars or 2 kilograms of tobacco, 1 liter of alcohol, and gifts worth $100. Meat products, seeds, plants, and fruits are prohibited.

INFORMATION • U.S. Customs Service (inquiries, 1300 Pennsylvania Ave. NW, Washington, DC 20229, tel. 202/927–6724; complaints, Office of Regulations and Rulings, 1300 Pennsylvania Ave. NW, Washington, DC 20229; registration of equipment, Registration Information, 1300 Pennsylvania Ave. NW, Washington, DC 20229, tel. 202/927–0540).

DINING

The restaurants we list are the cream of the crop in each price category. In few other cities has the notion of dining out evolved into an art form as New York. Our advice: you can scrimp on the hotel, but you owe it to yourself to have at least one blow-out meal in the Big Apple.

RESERVATIONS & DRESS

Reservations are always a good idea: we mention them only when they're essential or are not accepted. Book as far ahead as you can, and reconfirm as soon as you arrive. We mention dress only when men are required to wear a jacket or a jacket and tie.

WINE, BEER & SPIRITS

The legal drinking age in New York state is 21. It's unevenly enforced, and corner stores ("bodegas" in New York lingo) are likely to sell beer to anyone who looks like they've graduated junior high. Most bars and clubs do not ask for ID, which translates into lots of college freshmen getting tanked in bars on the weekends. However, if you're underage and you're caught drinking, you may be fined and/or prosecuted. Likewise, despite the fact that people from Wall Streeters to derelicts can be seen drinking in public, the punishment—spending a few hours in a holding tank—is not worth the thrill.

DISABILITIES & ACCESSIBILITY

Although New York was largely built decades before the watershed Americans with Disabilities Act, most of the major sights, museums, and parks are accessible to those who use wheelchairs. Hotels, hostels, restaurants, bars, and clubs are a different story: Generally, only the newest and most recently renovated are fully accessible. If you're in doubt about accessibility at a particular destination, your best bet is to call ahead.

LOCAL RESOURCES • Hospital Audiences, Inc., now staffs the **HAI Hotline** (tel. 888/424–4685) weekdays 9–5, offering information on transportation, hotels, restaurants, and cultural venues. **Big Apple Greeters** (1 Center St., Suite 2035, 10007, tel. 212/669–8159) offers tours of New York City tailored to visitors' personal preferences and will provide guides with a knowledge of accessibility in the city, as well as guides for visitors with hearing and vision impairments.

PUBLICATIONS • The bible for New York visitors with disabilities is ***Access for All*** ($5), published by Hospital Audiences, Inc. (220 W. 42nd St., New York, NY 10036, tel. 212/575–7663, TDD 212/575–7673). It lists theaters, museums, and other cultural institutions that offer wheelchair access and services for people with hearing or vision impairments. The free ***I Love New York Travel Guide*** and ***Big Apple Visitors Guide,*** describing access to the city's major sights, is available from the New York State Division of Tourism (1 Commerce Plaza, Albany, NY 12245, tel. 518/474–4116 or 800/225–5697). The Andrew Heiskell Library for the Blind and Physically Handicapped (40 W. 20th St., between 5th and 6th Aves., Midtown, tel. 212/206–5400, TDD 212/206–5458) has a large collection of Braille, large-print, and recorded books, from city history to current fiction.

LODGING

When discussing accessibility with an operator or reservations agent **ask hard questions.** Are there any stairs, inside *or* out? Are there grab bars next to the toilet *and* in the shower/tub? How wide is the doorway to the room? To the bathroom? For the most extensive facilities meeting the latest legal specifications **opt for newer accommodations.**

TRANSPORTATION

Of the 469 subway stations in New York, a paltry 23 have elevators—and even those aren't very dependable. City buses are more convenient: All 3,700 buses kneel to the curb, 95% are equipped with wheelchair lifts, and drivers will announce stops for riders with vision impairments. People with disabilities are eligible for reduced fares on public buses and subways with proper ID; call 212/878–7294 for info on obtaining a disability ID card. The Transit Authority's **Accessibility Hotline** (tel. 800/734–6772) has 24-hour recorded info regarding subway elevators and escalators, or you can speak directly to a Transit Authority representative about accessibility by calling 718/596–8585 daily 6 AM–9 PM. Take note: Taxi drivers tend to avoid passengers who might cause them inconvenience or delay, while drivers for car services (which charge a per-trip flat rate) are more accommodating.

COMPLAINTS • Disability Rights Section (U.S. Department of Justice, Civil Rights Division, Box 66738, Washington, DC 20035-6738, tel. 202/514–0301; 800/514–0301; 202/514–0301 TTY; 800/514–0301 TTY, fax 202/307–1198) for general complaints. **Aviation Consumer Protection Division** (*see* Air Travel, *above*) for airline-related problems. **Civil Rights Office** (U.S. Department of Transportation, Departmental Office of Civil Rights, S-30, 400 7th St. SW, Room 10215, Washington, DC 20590, tel. 202/366–4648, fax 202/366–9371) for problems with surface transportation.

TRAVEL AGENCIES

In the United States, although the Americans with Disabilities Act requires that travel firms serve the needs of all travelers, some agencies specialize in working with people with disabilities.

TRAVELERS WITH MOBILITY PROBLEMS • Access Adventures (206 Chestnut Ridge Rd., Rochester, NY 14624, tel. 716/889–9096), run by a former physical-rehabilitation counselor. **CareVacations** (5-5110 50th Ave., Leduc, Alberta T9E 6V4, tel. 780/986–6404 or 877/478–7827, fax 780/986–8332) has group tours and is especially helpful with cruise vacations. **Flying Wheels Travel** (143 W. Bridge St., Box 382, Owatonna, MN 55060, tel. 507/451–5005 or 800/535–6790, fax 507/451–1685). **Hinsdale Travel Service** (201 E. Ogden Ave., Suite 100, Hinsdale, IL 60521, tel. 630/325–1335, fax 630/325–1342).

TRAVELERS WITH DEVELOPMENTAL DISABILITIES • New Directions (5276 Hollister Ave., Suite 207, Santa Barbara, CA 93111, tel. 805/967–2841 or 888/967–2841, fax 805/964–7344). **Sprout** (893 Amsterdam Ave., New York, NY 10025, tel. 212/222–9575 or 888/222–9575, fax 212/222–9768).

DISCOUNTS & DEALS

Be a smart shopper and **compare all your options** before making decisions. A plane ticket bought with a promotional coupon from travel clubs, coupon books, and direct-mail offers may not be cheaper than the least expensive fare from a discount ticket agency. And always keep in mind that what you get is just as important as what you save.

DISCOUNT RESERVATIONS

To save money **look into discount-reservations services** with toll-free numbers, which use their buying power to get a better price on hotels, airline tickets, even car rentals. When booking a room, always **call the hotel's local toll-free number** (if one is available) rather than the central reservations number—you'll often get a better price. Always ask about special packages or corporate rates.

AIRLINE TICKETS • tel. 800/FLY–4–LESS. tel. 800/FLY–ASAP.

HOTEL ROOMS • Accommodations Express (tel. 800/444–7666). **Central Reservation Service (CRS)** (tel. 800/548–3311). **Hotel Reservations Network** (tel. 800/964–6835). **Quickbook** (tel. 800/789–9887). **Room Finders USA** (tel. 800/473–7829). **RMC Travel** (tel. 800/245–5738). **Steigenberger Reservation Service** (tel. 800/223–5652).

PACKAGE DEALS

Don't confuse packages and guided tours. When you buy a package, you travel on your own, just as though you had planned the trip yourself. Fly/drive packages, which combine airfare and car rental, are often a good deal. In cities, ask the local visitor's bureau about hotel packages that include tickets to major museum exhibits or other special events.

EMERGENCIES

Heaven help you if you should get sick or injured in New York and not have insurance—low-cost care is really hard to come by. Fortunately, most hospitals take credit cards. On the other hand, New York is filled with some of the best hospitals and doctors in the world. If you need health care, call a referral service (*see below*) or try one of the following hospitals.

DOCTORS & DENTISTS • The **Dental Referral Service** (tel. 800/917–6453) gives referrals to standard-rate private practices.

EMERGENCY SERVICES • Dial 911 for **police, fire,** and **ambulance.**

HOSPITALS • **Bellevue** (462 1st Ave., at E. 27th St., Gramercy, tel. 212/562–4141 or 212/562–4344 for emergency room). **Cabrini** (227 E. 19th St., between 2nd and 3rd Aves., Gramercy, tel. 212/995–6000). **St. Vincent's** (170 W. 12th St., at 7th Ave., West Village, tel. 212/604–7000).

24-HOUR PHARMACIES • Need a prescription filled? Try a **Duane Reade** discount drugstore. Of their 50 stores citywide, several are open 24 hours: 57th Street and Broadway (tel. 212/541–9708), 47th Street and Lexington Avenue (tel. 212/682–5338), 91st Street and Broadway (tel. 212/799–3172), and 74th Street and 3rd Avenue (tel. 212/744–2668). A few pharmacies even deliver; try **CVS** (East Village, tel. 212/254–1454; West Village, tel. 212/255–5054; or **McKay Drugs** (Upper East Side, tel. 212/794–7000).

PHYSICIAN REFERRAL SERVICES • Referral services can usually refer you to doctors offering sliding-scale fees, meaning that you pay based on your ability to pay. To use a referral service is absolutely free, so try calling around to a few of the following hospital referral lines if you're worried about getting a giant doctor's bill: **Beth Israel** (tel. 800/420–4004); **Columbia-Presbyterian** (tel. 212/305–5156); **Cornell** (tel. 800/822–2694); **Lenox Hill** (tel. 212/434–2046); **Mount Sinai** (tel. 800/637–4624); **New York University** (tel. 212/263–5000); or **St. Luke's–Roosevelt** (tel. 212/876–5432).

HOTLINES • If you are the victim of an assault or rape, call the 24-hour **Sex Crimes Hotline** (tel. 212/267–7273) to report it and get help. The office is staffed by female investigators of the New York Police Department. The 24-hour **Crime Victims Hotline** (tel. 212/577–7777) provides over-the-telephone counseling and referrals. A few other numbers you'll hopefully never need: the **New York City Department of Health AIDS Hotline** (tel. 212/447–8200); **Poison Control Center** (tel. 212/764–7667 or 212/340–4494; 212/836–3667 for Spanish speakers); **Substance Abuse Information Line** (tel. 800/522–5353); and the **Sexually Transmitted Disease Hotline** (tel. 212/788–4415).

GAY & LESBIAN TRAVEL

GAY- AND LESBIAN-FRIENDLY TRAVEL AGENCIES • **Different Roads Travel** (8383 Wilshire Blvd., Suite 902, Beverly Hills, CA 90211, tel. 323/651–5557 or 800/429–8747, fax 323/651–3678). **Kennedy Travel** (314 Jericho Turnpike, Floral Park, NY 11001, tel. 516/352–4888 or 800/237–7433, fax 516/354–8849). **Now Voyager** (4406 18th St., San Francisco, CA 94114, tel. 415/626–1169 or 800/255–6951, fax 415/626–8626). **Skylink Travel and Tour** (1006 Mendocino Ave., Santa Rosa, CA 95401, tel. 707/546–9888 or 800/225–5759, fax 707/546–9891), serving lesbian travelers.

HOLIDAYS

Banks close on the following national holidays: **New Year's Day** (January 1), **Martin Luther King Jr.'s Birthday** (third Monday of January), **Presidents' Day** (third Monday of February), **Memorial Day** (last Monday in May), **Independence Day** (July 4), **Labor Day** (first Monday of September), **Columbus Day** (second Monday in October), **Veteran's Day** (November 11), **Thanksgiving** (fourth Thursday in November), and **Christmas** (December 25). Buses and trains follow weekend schedules on holidays. Most stores are closed only on New Year's Day, Thanksgiving, and Christmas.

INSURANCE

The most useful travel insurance plan is a comprehensive policy that includes coverage for trip cancellation and interruption, default, trip delay, and medical expenses (with a waiver for preexisting conditions).

Without insurance you will lose all or most of your money if you cancel your trip, regardless of the reason. Default insurance covers you if your tour operator, airline, or cruise line goes out of business. Trip-delay covers expenses that arise because of bad weather or mechanical delays. Study the fine print when comparing policies.

British and Australian citizens need extra medical coverage when traveling overseas.

Always **buy travel policies directly from the insurance company**; if you buy it from a cruise line, airline, or tour operator that goes out of business you probably will not be covered for the agency or operator's default, a major risk. Before you make any purchase **review your existing health and home-owner's policies** to find what they cover away from home.

TRAVEL INSURERS • In the U.S. **Access America** (6600 W. Broad St., Richmond, VA 23230, tel. 804/285–3300 or 800/284–8300), **Travel Guard International** (1145 Clark St., Stevens Point, WI 54481, tel. 715/345–0505 or 800/826–1300). In Canada **Voyager Insurance** (44 Peel Center Dr., Brampton, Ontario L6T 4M8, tel. 905/791–8700; 800/668–4342 in Canada).

INSURANCE INFORMATION • In the U.K. the **Association of British Insurers** (51–55 Gresham St., London EC2V 7HQ, tel. 020/7600–3333, fax 020/7696–8999). In Australia the **Insurance Council of Australia** (tel. 03/9614–1077, fax 03/9614–7924).

LAUNDRY

Finding a Laundromat is no problem in New York; they're on practically every block. Self-service machines typically cost $1.50 per wash and 75¢–$1.50 for 10 or 15 minutes of dryer time. Most machines only accept quarters. Drop-off service (where you leave your stinky stuff in the morning and pick it up clean and folded at the end of the day) costs 60¢–$1.50 per pound. Bleach and softener cost an additional 50¢ each. Dry cleaning will set you back $3–$6 per pair of pants, or $4 each for blouses and shirts. At **Ecowash** (72 W. 69th St., between Columbus Ave. and Central Park W, Upper West Side, tel. 212/787–3890) you can clean your clothes without hurting the planet.

LODGING

The lodgings we list are the cream of the crop in each price category. We always list the facilities that are available—but we don't specify whether they cost extra: When pricing accommodations, always ask what's included and what costs extra. Assume that hotels operate on the European Plan (EP, with no meals) unless we specify that they use the Continental Plan (CP, with a Continental breakfast daily), Modified American Plan (MAP, with breakfast and dinner daily), or the Full American Plan (FAP, with all meals).

APARTMENT RENTALS

If you want a home base that's roomy enough for a family and comes with cooking facilities **consider a furnished rental.** These can save you money, especially if you're traveling with a group. Home-exchange directories sometimes list rentals as well as exchanges.

INTERNATIONAL AGENTS • **Hometours International** (Box 11503, Knoxville, TN 37939, tel. 423/690–8484 or 800/367–4668). **Rental Directories International** (2044 Rittenhouse Sq., Philadelphia, PA 19103, tel. 215/985–4001, fax 215/985–0323). **Rent-a-Home International** (7200 34th Ave. NW, Seattle, WA 98117, tel. 206/789–9377 or 800/964–1891, fax 206/789–9379). **Hideaways International** (767 Islington St., Portsmouth, NH 03801, tel. 603/430–4433 or 800/843–4433, fax 603/430–4444; membership $99).

For complete lodging listings, including hostels and B&Bs in New York City, *see* Chapter 3.

HOME EXCHANGES

If you would like to exchange your home for someone else's **join a home-exchange organization,** which will send you its updated listings of available exchanges for a year and will include your own listing in at least one of them. It's up to you to make specific arrangements.

EXCHANGE CLUBS • **HomeLink International** (Box 650, Key West, FL 33041, tel. 305/294–7766 or 800/638–3841, fax 305/294–1448; $93 per year). **Intervac U.S.** (Box 590504, San Francisco, CA 94159, tel. 800/756–4663, fax 415/435–7440; $83 for catalogues).

HOSTELS

No matter what your age you can **save on lodging costs by staying at hostels.** In some 5,000 locations in more than 70 countries around the world, Hostelling International (HI), the umbrella group for a number of national youth-hostel associations, offers single-sex, dorm-style beds and, at many hostels, couples rooms and family accommodations. Membership in any HI national hostel association, open to travelers of all ages, allows you to stay in HI-affiliated hostels at member rates (one-year membership is about $25 for adults; hostels run about $10–$25 per night). Members also have priority if the hostel is full; they're eligible for discounts around the world, even on rail and bus travel in some countries.

ORGANIZATIONS • Australian Youth Hostel Association (10 Mallett St., Camperdown, NSW 2050, tel. 02/9565–1699, fax 02/9565–1325). **Hostelling International—American Youth Hostels** (733 15th St. NW, Suite 840, Washington, DC 20005, tel. 202/783–6161, fax 202/783–6171). **Hostelling International—Canada** (400–205 Catherine St., Ottawa, Ontario K2P 1C3, tel. 613/237–7884, fax 613/237–7868). **Youth Hostel Association of England and Wales** (Trevelyan House, 8 St. Stephen's Hill, St. Albans, Hertfordshire AL1 2DY, tel. 01727/855215 or 01727/845047, fax 01727/844126). **Youth Hostels Association of New Zealand** (Box 436, Christchurch, New Zealand, tel. 03/379–9970, fax 03/365–4476). Membership in the U.S. $25, in Canada C$26.75, in the U.K. £9.30, in Australia $44, in New Zealand $24.

HOTELS

All hotels listed have private bath unless otherwise noted.

TOLL-FREE NUMBERS • Best Western (tel. 800/528–1234). **Choice** (tel. 800/221–2222). **Clarion** (tel. 800/252–7466). **Comfort** (tel. 800/228–5150). **Days Inn** (tel. 800/325–2525). **Doubletree and Red Lion Hotels** (tel. 800/222–8733). **Forte** (tel. 800/225–5843). **Four Seasons** (tel. 800/332–3442). **Hilton** (tel. 800/445–8667). **Holiday Inn** (tel. 800/465–4329). **Howard Johnson** (tel. 800/654–4656). **Hyatt Hotels & Resorts** (tel. 800/233–1234). **Inter-Continental** (tel. 800/327–0200). **Marriott** (tel. 800/228–9290). **Le Meridien** (tel. 800/543–4300). **Nikko Hotels International** (tel. 800/645–5687). **Omni** (tel. 800/843–6664). **Quality Inn** (tel. 800/228–5151). **Ramada** (tel. 800/228–2828). **Renaissance Hotels & Resorts** (tel. 800/468–3571). **Ritz-Carlton** (tel. 800/241–3333). **Sheraton** (tel. 800/325–3535). **Westin Hotels & Resorts** (tel. 800/228–3000). **Wyndham Hotels & Resorts** (tel. 800/822–4200).

MEDIA

New York is a news- and gossip-intensive town—not surprising for this home of international movers and shakers. What other city in the country has three daily papers? The city also has its own 24-hour cable TV news station, **New York One** (Channel 1), with local and international news announcements around the clock and daily recaps at 6:30, 9:30, 10, and 11 PM. City weather reports are broadcast "on the ones" (1:01, 1:11, 1:21, etc.).

CYBER NEW YORK

A few cool New York–specific sites to browse include the New York Public Library at www.nypl.org; mega–New York dance club Webster Hall at www.webster-hall.com; MovieFone 777–FILM Online at www.777film.com; and Columbia University's Web Music Archive at www.columbia.edu/~hauben/music.

Of New York's many webcams, the **UpperWestSide Cam** at www.zietgeist.com/camera and its view of Columbus and 72nd may be the most famous. The **Village Voice** at www.villagevoice.com and **New York Sidewalk** at newyork.sidewalk.com offer comprehensive, searchable events listings. The **New York Subway Finder** at www.krusch.com/nysf.html provides subway directions between any two New York addresses.

NEWSSTANDS

The best newsstands for browsing include **Hotaling's** (142 W. 42nd St., near 6th Ave., Midtown, tel. 212/840–1868), around since 1905 and great for foreign publications and obscure titles; **Nikos Magazine & Smoke Shop** (462 6th Ave., at W. 11th St., West Village, tel. 212/255–9175), which stocks some 2,500 titles, from scholarly stuff and literary journals to 'zines like *Paranoia: The Conspiracy Reader*; and **Universal News Ltd.** (676 Lexington Ave., at E. 56th St., Midtown, tel. 212/750–1855), which amasses some 4,000 foreign and domestic rags. The citywide café/newsstand chain **News Bar** (*see* Cafés and Coffee Bars *in* Chapter 4) is also great for a CNN fix or if you want to browse a rack of more than 400 foreign and domestic publications.

NEWSPAPERS & MAGAZINES

The tabloid-style *New York Daily News* bills itself as "New York's Hometown Newspaper." Look for lots of slang and lurid headlines. *Tel. 212/210–2100. Cost: 50¢. Published Mon.–Sun.*

New York Observer. The city's peach-colored weekly covers the New York arts, media, and political scenes, with an often pretentious, though tongue-in-cheek tone. Its "Eight-Day Week" is a quirky listing—equal parts uptown society and downtown hip. *Tel. 212/755–2400. Cost: $1. Published Wed.*

New York Post. World War III–size headlines bark out the "news" in Rupert Murdoch's cheap, gritty tabloid that's way more in line with most New Yorkers than the *Times*. It's got the quick and dirty on local murders and national scandals, plus "Page Six," the city's premier gossip column. *Tel. 800/552–7678. Cost: 50¢. Published Mon.–Sun.*

New York Press. This free weekly rag features some of the most acerbic writing in all of New York. Plus there are comprehensive restaurant, film, art, theater, and music listings. *Tel. 212/941–1130. Published Tues.*

New York Times. The nation's newspaper of record features quality writing and in-depth reporting you simply can't find anywhere else. Special sections include Sports (Monday); Science (Tuesday); Dining In and Out (Wednesday); Circuits (Thursday) and two Weekend sections on Friday. The Sunday paper, bigger than a Britannica, is required reading for most New Yorkers. *Tel. 800/631–2500. Cost: 75¢. Mon.–Sat. 60¢, Sun. $2.50.*

Village Voice. For political coverage that's strongly left of center, arts coverage that tends toward the avant-garde, and personal ads so hot they seem to smoke on the printed page, pick up the weekly bible for the downtown set. Must-reads include "Voice Choices," for unbeatable cinema, music, and club listings, and gifted gossip columnist Michael Musto's "La Dolce Musto." *Tel. 800/875–2997. Cost: Free ($1.25 outside Manhattan). Published Wed.*

Wall Street Journal. This business-only paper (it's published by Dow Jones & Company) won't familiarize you with New York beyond the world of Wall Street mergers and acquisitions. *Tel. 800/778–0840. Cost: 75¢. Published weekdays.*

MAGAZINES

New York. This glossy magazine delivers weekly reports on city politics and endless looks at how the monied "other half" lives. Its "Cue" section is great for arts listings and reviews, its "Best Bets" and "Sales & Bargains" required reading for shopaholics. *Tel. 800/535–1168. Cost: $2.95.*

The New Yorker. The nation's revered literary weekly, founded in 1925, has shaken off its penchant for timeless, quirky ruminations in favor of trendier topics, though you'll still find the famous cartoons. Its "Goings On About Town" is a critical listing of theater, gallery shows, readings, dance, film, and classical music concerts. *Tel. 800/825–2510. Cost: $2.95.*

Paper. This monthly is a great resource for what's happening on the downtown art/music/club scene. *Cost: $3.*

Time Out. A relatively new arrival in New York (other versions thrive in London and Amsterdam), the weekly *Time Out* offers the city's most comprehensive and easy-to-read listings and reviews for theater, music, film, readings, sports, art exhibitions, you name it. It's hip, but not intimidating. *Tel. 212/539–4444 or 800/457–4364. Cost: $1.95.*

RADIO & TELEVISION

Here's a sampling of what's going out over the FM airwaves in New York City: WNYU (89.1), whatever's cool at New York University; WKCR (89.9), whatever's cool at Columbia University; New York's infamous "shock jock" Howard Stern broadcasts live weekday mornings from WXRK (92.3); WNYC (93.9), National Public Radio; WQXR (96.3), classical music; WQHT (97.1), the phattest hip-hop jams; WRKS (98.7), soul; WBAI (99.5), cutting-edge music of all sorts; WHTZ (100.3), alternative rock and Top-40; WCBS (101.0), oldies; WNEW (102.7), classic rock; and WAXQ (104.3), lots of '80s rock.

MONEY MATTERS

New York is, was, and will always be one of the most expensive cities in the United States. Stores and restaurants usually accept traveler's checks but prefer cash, and a few turn up their noses at credit cards. At least there are plenty of banks.

In New York it's easy to get swept up in a debt-inducing cyclone of $50 dinners, $40 theater tickets, $25 club covers, $10 cab rides, and $100 hotel rooms. Don't do it. Get around on the subway, check out

Off-Broadway performances, and take advantage of lunch specials at restaurants and no-cover nights at clubs and bars. In this case, you'll have a fabulous time for about $50 per day.

ACCOMMODATIONS • Hostels are the best deal for solo travelers, with dorm beds for $22–$25. Singles and doubles cost $40–$90 at even the cheapest (and, predictably, skankiest) hotels, though groups of three or more can find decent hotels offering triples, quads, and suites for a bargain $75–$125. Note: Temperatures really soar in New York during summer, so you might want to plunk down a few extra dollars to stay at a hotel or hostel that offers rooms with air-conditioning; many (but not all) do.

FOOD • It's easy to gorge yourself at a cool restaurant in the East Village for under $10, but in many other neighborhoods you'll probably spend twice that. That said, many restaurants cut prices drastically for their "lunch specials" (typically weekdays 11 AM–6 PM). Hot dogs, falafel sandwiches, tacos, pizza slices, and bagels are easy to find, and all cost under $2. The city's many Greenmarkets (see Chapter 4) also offer inexpensive, fresh produce.

ENTERTAINMENT & NIGHTLIFE • This is where you can go broke fast. Cover charges for nightclubs can hit $20 or more, not including drinks ($2–$10 each). Tickets to Les Miz or Rent are $25–$100 a pop. A beer in a bar usually costs $2–$3.50, though some Manhattan bars serve $1 pints during weekday "happy hours." Movies are a ridiculous $9.50 most places. Crazy, huh? If you steer clear of the big names you can find live music and dance clubs with covers under $10, Off-Broadway shows with tickets for $5–$25, and, especially in summer, tons of concerts and performances for free.

Prices throughout this guide are given for adults. Substantially reduced fees are almost always available for children, students, and senior citizens. For information on taxes, see Taxes, below.

ATMS

Virtually all U.S. banks belong to a network of card-slurping, cash-expectorating ATMs. Before leaving home, **make sure that your credit cards have been programmed for ATM use.**

ATM LOCATIONS • **Cirrus** (tel. 800/424–7787). **Plus** (tel. 800/843–7587).

CREDIT CARDS

Throughout this guide, the following abbreviations are used: **AE,** American Express; **D,** Discover; **DC,** Diner's Club; **MC,** MasterCard; and **V,** Visa.

CURRENCY EXCHANGES

You'll have no trouble finding currency-exchange services in Manhattan—**try touristy areas** like the South Street Seaport, World Trade Center, Herald Square, Times Square, or Grand Central Terminal. All three airports also offer currency exchange. Currency-exchange offices are less common in the outer boroughs, so **try a bank**; they have good rates but short hours (they typically close at 3 PM on weekdays and shut down entirely on weekends).

Chase Foreign Currency Department has more than a dozen offices throughout Manhattan, plus branches in Queens and the Bronx. Each offers a multilingual staff. **Chequepoint USA** has four branches in Midtown. The main office is open daily from 8 AM to 11:30 PM. **Thomas Cook Currency Services** has five offices throughout Manhattan, including one at Grand Central Terminal.

EXCHANGE OFFICES • **Chase Foreign Currency Department** (tel. 212/935–9935). **Chequepoint USA** (Main office: 22 Central Park S, at 5th Ave., tel. 212/750–2400). **Thomas Cook Currency Services** (Main Office: 1590 Broadway, at W. 48th St., tel. 800/287–7362).

PACKING

Keep in mind that New York is a fashionable city, and residents do not—as "Seinfeld" would have you believe—wear white Reeboks and windbreakers. Though it's important to pack pragmatically (bring comfortable, easy-to-clean clothes) you may feel awkward if you're always dressing down. It's better to have one decent shirt you can wear every other day than a whole slew of tacky T-shirts. Summers are gruesomely hot, so bring lightweight clothes, as well as a sweater or jacket for overly air-conditioned subway cars and museums. In winter, you'll need a coat and shoes that can handle snow, sleet, and ice, plus a hat, gloves, and a scarf to protect you from those –10° winds. And you should be prepared for rainfall any time of year.

In your carry-on luggage **bring an extra pair of eyeglasses or contact lenses** and **enough of any medication you take** to last the entire trip. You may also want your doctor to write a spare prescription using the drug's generic name, since brand names may vary from country to country. In luggage to be checked, **never pack prescription drugs or valuables.** To avoid customs delays, carry medications in their original packaging. And don't forget to copy down and carry addresses of offices that handle refunds of lost traveler's checks.

CHECKING LUGGAGE

How many carry-on bags you can bring with you is up to the airline. Most allow two, but not always, so make sure that everything you carry aboard will fit under your seat, and get to the gate early. Note that if you have a seat at the back of the plane, you'll probably board first, while the overhead bins are still empty.

If you are flying internationally, note that baggage allowances may be determined not by piece but by weight—generally 88 pounds (40 kilograms) in first class, 66 pounds (30 kilograms) in business class, and 44 pounds (20 kilograms) in economy.

Airline liability for baggage is limited to $1,250 per person on flights within the United States. On international flights it amounts to $9.07 per pound or $20 per kilogram for checked baggage (roughly $640 per 70-pound bag) and $400 per passenger for unchecked baggage. You can buy additional coverage at check-in for about $10 per $1,000 of coverage, but it excludes a rather extensive list of items, shown on your airline ticket.

Before departure **itemize your bags' contents** and their worth, and label the bags with your name, address, and phone number. (If you use your home address, cover it so that potential thieves can't see it readily.) Inside each bag **pack a copy of your itinerary.** At check-in **make sure that each bag is correctly tagged** with the destination airport's three-letter code. If your bags arrive damaged or fail to arrive at all, file a written report with the airline before leaving the airport.

PASSPORTS & VISAS

U.K. CITIZENS • U.S. Embassy Visa Information Line (tel. 01891/200–290; calls cost 49p per minute, 39p per minute cheap rate) for U.S. visa information. **U.S. Embassy Visa Branch** (5 Upper Grosvenor Sq., London W1A 1AE) for U.S. visa information; send a self-addressed, stamped envelope. Write the **U.S. Consulate General** (Queen's House, Queen St., Belfast BTI 6EO) if you live in Northern Ireland. Write the **Office of Australia Affairs** (59th fl., MLC Centre, 19-29 Martin Pl., Sydney NSW 2000) if you live in Australia. Write the **Office of New Zealand Affairs** (29 Fitzherbert Terr., Thorndon, Wellington) if you live in New Zealand.

PASSPORT OFFICES

The best time to apply for a passport or to renew is during the fall and winter. Before any trip, check your passport's expiration date, and, if necessary, renew it as soon as possible.

AUSTRALIAN CITIZENS • Australian Passport Office (tel. 131–232).

NEW ZEALAND CITIZENS • New Zealand Passport Office (tel. 04/494–0700 for information on how to apply; 04/474–8000 or 0800/225–050 in New Zealand for information on applications already submitted).

U.K. CITIZENS • London Passport Office (tel. 0990/210–410) for fees and documentation requirements and to request an emergency passport.

REST ROOMS

For travelers with tiny bladders, New York is a cold and stingy town. In Midtown, there are clean, pleasant rest rooms at **Bryant Park** (W. 42nd St. between 5th and 6th Aves.), decent ones in **Grand Central Terminal** (E. 42nd St. at Park Ave.), and grit-your-teeth options at the **Port Authority Bus Terminal** and **Penn Station.** Downtown near City Hall you'll find a single, high-tech, coin-operated toilet kiosk modeled after those on the streets of Paris. There are rest room facilities in a few subway stations, but you're better off staying away from them. You can discreetly visit the bathrooms in public buildings, diners, cafés, and hotels such as the **St. Regis,** on 55th Street and 5th Avenue; the **Plaza,** on 59th Street and 5th Avenue; or the **Stanhope,** at 81st Street and 5th Avenue. Department stores are also a good bet. The plush, unguarded rest rooms at **Bloomingdale's** (3rd Ave. at E. 59th St.), for example, are no secret to shoppers. If you're looking for the ultimate bathroom read, check out *Where To Go: A Guide to Manhattan's Toilets,* by Vicki Rovere. It's available at most city bookstores. Come to think of it, Barnes & Noble isn't a bad bathroom experience either.

SAFETY

Crime in New York has dropped like a rock in recent years: The overall crime rate in New York City is down 54% since 1994, and is at the lowest level in 30 years. This has a lot to do with the increasing vigilance of New York's cleaned-up cop force. Petty offenses like public drinking or urination or even jaywalking won't get the nudge-and-a-wink treatment these days, and the biggies will land you in jail for sure. Drug possession and/or consumption warrants arrest and fines. Stay on the right side of the law unless you want your vacation to include a stay on Riker's Island (you don't).

WOMEN IN NEW YORK

Solo women travelers often have to put on a tough and surly facade to avoid unwelcome advances. You can take some comfort in knowing that some 1.1 million single women call New York home, but you'll still need to take some precautions, especially at night. Obviously, **avoid situations where you're alone** with a stranger—in a subway car, for example, or at an ATM machine. On city streets, **walk briskly and with confidence,** even if you're lost; you can duck into a café or shop to discreetly check your map. Your best bet is to hook up with fellow travelers whom you feel you can trust, then enjoy exploring the city together.

RESOURCES • Young Women's Christian Association (YWCA; 610 Lexington Ave., at E. 53rd St., tel. 212/755–4500) offers social-service programs and accommodation referrals for women. **National Organization for Women** (NOW; 105 E. 22nd St., Suite 307, New York, NY 10010, tel. 212/627–9895) offers regular meetings, support groups, lectures, and referrals.

SENIOR-CITIZEN TRAVEL

To qualify for age-related discounts **mention your senior-citizen status up front** when booking hotel reservations (not when checking out) and before you're seated in restaurants (not when paying the bill). When renting a car ask about promotional car-rental discounts, which can be cheaper than senior-citizen rates.

EDUCATIONAL PROGRAMS • Elderhostel (75 Federal St., 3rd fl., Boston, MA 02110, tel. 877/426–8056, fax 877/426–2166).

STUDENTS IN NEW YORK CITY

STUDENT IDS & SERVICES • Council on International Educational Exchange (CIEE, 205 E. 42nd St., 14th fl., New York, NY 10017, tel. 212/822–2600 or 888/268–6245, fax 212/822–2699) for mail orders only, in the U.S. **Travel Cuts** (187 College St., Toronto, Ontario M5T 1P7, tel. 416/979–2406 or 800/667–2887) in Canada.

YMCA

Y's Way International is a network of YMCA overnight centers offering low-cost accommodations (average overnight rate of $40) in New York City (224 E. 47th St., New York, NY 10017, tel. 212/308–2899), around the United States, and around the world to travelers of all ages. Its booklet, "The Y's Way," details locations, reservation policies, and package tours.

SUBWAY TRAVEL

New York's subway system is amazing—it covers Manhattan and the outer boroughs thoroughly, it's quick and easy to use, and it's air-conditioned (on the trains). The city's 714-mi system operates 24 hours a day and is used by over 3.5 million people daily, but it's safest to avoid deserted subway platforms and cars late at night.

A quick orientation for the first-time straphanger: Express trains only stop at major stations and transfer points, while local trains stop at every station. You can transfer to another subway line free of charge at many express stations—just follow the easy-to-read signs from platform to platform. Also, maps are posted at every subway station and inside most cars. Subway station entrances are often specific to uptown or downtown trains; be sure you enter on the correct side. If there's a green globe light outside the station, that means the station is open and there's a transit clerk inside. A red globe means the entrance is closed. All stations have off-hours waiting areas (usually near the staffed booth), designated by bright yellow signs. If you're at all concerned about your safety, wait in one of these areas rather than wandering off alone.

FARES & SCHEDULES

Subway fare is $1.50, although reduced fares are available for senior citizens and people with disabilities during nonrush hours. If you're just taking a few trips, you should pay with tokens (available at token booths in the subway). It's better to **buy more than one token at a time to avoid waiting in lines later.** To enter the subway, simply drop a token into the turnstile; you can now ride anywhere you want and transfer as many times as you wish before exiting. For four or more trips, you may find it easier to use the MetroCard, a plastic card with a magnetic strip; swipe it through the reader on the turnstile, and the cost of the fare is automatically deducted. You can buy a card for a minimum of $3 and a maximum of $80. More than one person can use the same card. The MetroCard also enables you to transfer free from bus to subway, subway to bus within two hours. But, if you lose your MetroCard, you've lost all the credits you paid for, so keep it in a safe place.

SUBWAY INFORMATION • For general city bus and subway travel info, call the **MTA/New York City Transit hotline** (tel. 718/330–1234), staffed daily 6 AM–9 PM, or the **Multilingual Transit hot line** (tel. 718/330–4847), staffed daily 6 AM–9:30 PM.

TAXES

ROOM TAX

The tax for hotel rooms in New York City is 13.25%.

SALES TAX

The sales tax in New York City is 8.25%. This tax applies to meals in restaurants, too.

TAXIS & CAR SERVICES

The only real difference between taxis and car services is that a taxi is yellow and a car-service sedan is not. Taxis run on a meter (charging by the amount of time a trip takes) while car services charge a flat fee based on distance, no matter how long the trip takes. Most of the time, the price ends up being about the same. The only times car services come in handy are when you're going crosstown (which tends to be slower going), when you're traveling during commuter-hour traffic (especially to and from the airports), or when you're in the outer boroughs late at night and can't find a taxi.

There are 12,053 yellow cabs and 30,000 private cars (including limos) for hire in the city. The **New York City Taxi and Limousine Commission** (TLC; tel. 212/692–8294) calculates that there are about 30,000 "gypsy" taxi drivers out there as well; these drivers are not licensed by the taxi commission and often do not even have a driver's license, much less insurance. Licensed private cars must display a decal in the shape of a diamond on the right-hand side of their windshields—look for it. There is now a flat $30 fee for travel from JFK to Manhattan (*not* from the city to the airport) for taxis and private car services.

TAXIS

With the exception of rainy days, when everyone wants a cab, all you have to do is stick out your arm and about four taxis should come careening toward you for the fare. (There are fewer available cabs on rainy days.) Taxis cost $2 for the first ⅕ mi, 30¢ for each ⅕ mi thereafter, 20¢ for each 90 seconds in standing traffic, plus a 50¢ surcharge daily 8 PM–6 AM. There is no surcharge for additional people or luggage. Still, taxi fare adds up pretty quickly, so unless you're rich, stick with public transportation—unless it's late at night or you don't feel safe in a particular neighborhood. Because a taxi's meter calculates time as well as distance, the meter should click, adding another 30¢ about every four blocks while you're moving at a good clip. In slow traffic, or when you're traveling crosstown, the meter may click as often as every block. Sadly, drivers have been known to manipulate their meters in all kinds of crafty ways to speed them up and stick you with a higher fare—like the one chap who connected his meter to the radio, so that every time he turned up the volume, his meter increased the rate.

Be sure to ask for, and save, your receipt so if you have a complaint about a taxi, or wish to compliment the driver, or if you leave something in the car, the Taxi Commission can locate the car and driver easily.

CAR SERVICES

In order to use a car service, you must call ahead. Most companies have a flat-rate chart they consult for different distances and for different times of the day. The rate per mile is about $2. Some charge extra for large luggage and additional passengers. A few reliable services include **Carmel** (tel. 212/666–6666), **Highbridge Car Service** (tel. 212/927–4600), and **Tel-Aviv** (tel. 212/777–7777).

TELEPHONES

AREA CODES

The area codes for Manhattan are 212, 646, and 917. Any call from Manhattan to another area code must be dialed like so: 1 + (area code) + (seven-digit number). The Bronx, Brooklyn, Queens, and Staten Island are in area code 718. Most cellular phones and pagers in New York City use area code 917.

COLLECT CALLS

Charges for collect calls are higher than for normal long-distance calls, so if you want to keep your friends, give them your number so they can call you back. (Not all pay phones accept incoming calls, so read the fine print on the phone before trying this.) Station-to-station is the standard collect call; anyone answering at the number you dial can accept the charges. Less common, and even more expensive, is a person-to-person call, which authorizes only the person whose name you give to the operator to accept the charges. On the upside, you won't be charged if the person you want to reach is out. Collect calls can be made by dialing 0 + the number.

Anything can happen on New York subways, from meeting the love of your life to being accosted by some freak claiming to be from Jupiter. The underground network is a city of its own, a place to buy flowers, catch some live music, or have your shoes shined.

DIRECTORY AND OPERATOR ASSISTANCE

For local directory assistance, dial 411. For long-distance help, dial the area code plus 555–1212. If you don't know the area code or need help with a local call, dial 0 for the operator; for long-distance or international calls, dial 00. To find out if a particular business has an 800 number, call 800/555–1212.

INTERNATIONAL CALLS

Calls to Canada can be dialed as regular long-distance calls. To reach any other country, dial 011, the country code, the city code (dropping the initial zero if there is one), then the actual number. The country code for Great Britain is 44, Ireland 353, New Zealand 64, and Australia 61. Rates vary widely, depending on the hour of your call; ask a long-distance operator for exact rates.

PUBLIC PHONES

There are more than 58,000 public telephones in New York, which translates to one on almost every street corner. Of those that work (probably about half), most allow you to place international calls and use a calling card. Not all pay phones are alike. Look for Bell Atlantic pay phones, to avoid rip offs and inconvenience. Pay phones should charge 25¢ for the first three minutes of a local call (this includes calls between 212 and 718 area codes); an extra deposit is required for each additional minute. Local directory-assistance calls are free.

CALLING LONG DISTANCE

AT&T, MCI, and Sprint long-distance services make calling home relatively convenient and let you avoid hotel surcharges. In the United States, you typically dial an 800 number.

At the **AT&T Public Calling Center,** on the Main Concourse level of Grand Central Terminal (E. 42nd St. and Park Ave., Midtown), you can make long-distance calls in relative quiet using a credit card or calling card. It's open weekdays 7 AM–9 PM.

TIPPING

The customary tipping rate is 15% for taxi drivers and waiters. You can do the math quickly in restaurants by just doubling the tax noted on the check—it's 8¼% of your bill—and rounding up or down. Bartenders should get between 50¢ and $1 per drink, or more if you're sloshed. Hotel maids and porters should be tipped about $1. Tip $1 per coat checked.

Depending on the service rendered (last-minute restaurant reservations, tickets to that "sold-out" Broadway hit), a hotel concierge expects a tip of $3 to $5.

TOURS & PACKAGES

On a prepackaged tour or independent vacation everything is prearranged so you'll spend less time planning—and often get it all at a good price.

BOOKING WITH AN AGENT

Travel agents are excellent resources. But it's a good idea to collect brochures from several agencies because some agents' suggestions may be influenced by relationships with tour and package firms that reward them for volume sales. If you have a special interest **find an agent with expertise in that area**; ASTA (*see* Travel Agencies, *below*) has a database of specialists worldwide.

Make sure your travel agent knows the accommodations and other services of the place they're recommending. Ask about the hotel's location, room size, beds, and whether it has a pool, room service, or programs for children, if you care about these. Has your agent been there in person or sent others whom you can contact?

Do some homework on your own, too: Local tourism boards can provide information about lesser-known and small-niche operators, some of which may sell only direct.

BUYER BEWARE

Each year consumers are stranded or lose their money when tour operators—even large ones with excellent reputations—go out of business. So **check out the operator.** Ask several travel agents about its reputation, and try to **book with a company that has a consumer-protection program.** (Look for information in the company's brochure.) In the United States, members of the National Tour Association and United States Tour Operators Association are required to set aside funds to cover your payments and travel arrangements in case the company defaults. It's also a good idea to choose a company that participates in the American Society of Travel Agent's Tour Operator Program (TOP); ASTA will act as mediator in any disputes between you and your tour operator.

Remember that the more your package or tour includes the better you can predict the ultimate cost of your vacation. Make sure you know exactly what is covered, and **beware of hidden costs.** Are taxes, tips, and transfers included? Entertainment and excursions? These can add up.

TOUR-OPERATOR RECOMMENDATIONS • American Society of Travel Agents (*see* Travel Agencies, *below*). **National Tour Association** (NTA, 546 E. Main St., Lexington, KY 40508, tel. 606/226–4444 or 800/682–8886). **United States Tour Operators Association** (USTOA, 342 Madison Ave., Suite 1522, New York, NY 10173, tel. 212/599–6599 or 800/468–7862, fax 212/599–6744).

PACKAGES

The companies listed below offer vacation packages in a broad price range.

AIR/HOTEL • Continental Vacations (tel. 800/634–5555). **Delta Dream Vacations** (tel. 800/872–7786, fax 954/357–4687). **United Vacations** (tel. 800/328–6877). **US Airways Vacations** (tel. 800/455–0123).

CUSTOM PACKAGES • Amtrak's Great American Vacations (tel. 800/321–8684).

HOTEL ONLY • Globetrotters MTI (139 Main St., Cambridge, MA 02142, tel. 800/333–1234).

FROM THE U.K. • Americana Vacations Ltd. (11 Little Portland St., London W1 5ND, tel. 020/7637–7853). **Jetsave** (Sussex House, London Rd., East Grinstead, West Sussex RH19 1LD, tel. 01342/312033). **Key to America** (1–3 Station Rd., Ashford, Middlesex, TW15 2UW, tel. 01784/248–777). **Premier Holidays** (Westbrook, Milton Rd., Cambridge CB4 1YQ, tel. 01223/516–688). **Trailfinders** (42–50 Earls Court Rd., London W8 6FT, tel. 020/7937–5400; 58 Deansgate, Manchester M3 2FF, tel. 0161/839–6969). **Travelpack** (Clarendon House, Clarendon Rd., Eccles, Manchester M30 9AL, tel. 0990/747–101).

THEME TRIPS

CULTURAL TOURS • **IST Cultural Tours** (225 W. 34th St., New York, NY 10122-0913, tel. 212/563–1202 or 800/833–2111, fax 212/594–6953).

PERFORMING ARTS • **Dailey-Thorp Travel** (330 W. 58th St., #610, New York, NY 10019-1817, tel. 212/307–1555 or 800/998–4677, fax 212/974–1420). **Keith Prowse Tours** (234 W. 44th St., #1000, New York, NY 10036, tel. 212/398–1430 or 800/669–8687, fax 212/302–4251). **Sutherland Hit Show Tours** (370 Lexington Ave., #411, New York, NY 10017, tel. 212/532–7732 or 800/221–2442, fax 212/532–7741).

SPAS • **Spa-Finders** (91 5th Ave., #301, New York, NY 10003-3039, tel. 212/924–6800 or 800/255–7727).

TENNIS • **Championship Tennis Tours** (7350 E. Stetson Dr., #106, Scottsdale, AZ 85251, tel. 602/990–8760 or 800/468–3664, fax 602/990–8744). **Dan Chavez's Sports Empire** (Box 6169, Lakewood, CA 90714-6169, tel. 310/920–2350 or 800/255–5258). **Esoteric Sports Tours** (2005 Woods River La., Duluth, GA 30155, tel. 770/622–8872 or 800/321–8008, fax 770/622–8866). **Spectacular Sport Specials** (5813 Citrus Blvd., New Orleans, LA 70123-5810, tel. 504/734–9511 or 800/451–5772, fax 504/734–7075). **Steve Furgal's International Tennis Tours** (11828 Rancho Bernardo Rd., #123–305, San Diego, CA 92128, tel. 619/675–3555 or 800/258–3664).

TRAIN TRAVEL

Unlike the rest of this car-obsessed country, people on the East Coast actually rely on trains to get from city to city or commute from home to work. Departures are frequent and fares are cheap. New York City has two major railroad stations: **Pennsylvania Station** (W. 31st–34th Sts. between 7th and 8th Aves.; Subway A, C, E, 1, 2, 3, or 9 to W. 34th St.) and **Grand Central Terminal** (W. 42nd–45th Sts. at Park Ave.; Subway 4, 5, 6, or 7 to Grand Central). Trains bound for Grand Central also stop at the tiny 125th Street Station (125th St. at Park Ave.; Subway 4, 5, or 6 to E. 125th St.).

AMTRAK

Amtrak (tel. 212/582–6875 or 800/875–7245) is the only passenger rail service in the United States. It's also a damn fine way to travel to New York; you get a dining car, a smoking lounge (if you're so inclined), and lots of pretty scenery. Trains arrive daily at Pennsylvania Station (*see above*) from Boston (5 hrs, $43 one-way), Philadelphia (1½ hrs, $36), Washington, D.C. (3½ hrs, $60), Chicago (18 hrs, $141), Seattle (2¾ days, $259), Los Angeles (3 days, $259), and many other American cities. Fares fluctuate according to time of the year and other factors (they're generally higher on Fridays and holidays), so call ahead for the latest ticket info. At presstime, Amtrak planned to begin its new 150-mile-an-hour high-speed express service between Washington and Boston, reducing the trip between New York and Boston to just 3 ½ hours.

RAIL PASSES • Amtrak's **All-Aboard America Fare,** actually a booklet of tickets, allows riders special rates for three stops made in 45 days of travel. Ticket agents need to know your dates of travel and intended destinations for ticketing, so reserve in advance. Cost is $198–$378, depending on the season and the number of regions traveled. Amtrak's **USARail Pass** is terrific for the foreign budget traveler (it's not available to U.S. or Canadian citizens) because it allows unlimited travel on any of Amtrak's U.S. routes, with no formal itinerary required. A 15-day pass costs $355 ($245 September–May), a 30-day pass $440 ($350). You can buy one at a travel agency in your home country before you leave or from an Amtrak office in the States. A passport and visa are required for purchase, and reservations are recommended several months in advance.

REGIONAL TRAIN SERVICES

Whether you're a freshman at Yale or a visitor crashing at your aunt's house in Greenwich, Connecticut, there's a train to take you into New York City. One-way fares from most destinations cost less than $12; purchase your ticket before you board to avoid a $1–$3 lazy person's surcharge. The **Metro-North Commuter Railroad** (tel. 212/532–4900) serves New York's northern suburbs and southwestern Connecticut, terminating in New Haven. The **Long Island Railroad** (LIRR; tel. 718/217–5477) runs through Long Island, smarty. **New Jersey Transit** (tel. 201/762–5100) offers service from towns in northern and central New Jersey, including Princeton. In Manhattan, Metro-North trains stop at Grand Central Terminal and at 125th Street; the LIRR and New Jersey Transit lines terminate at Pennsylvania Station.

PATH

The **PATH** (tel. 800/234-7284) trains run between New York City and terminals in New Jersey (including Hoboken, Jersey City, and Newark). In Manhattan, PATH stations are at the World Trade Center; on Christopher Street (at Greenwich Street); and along 6th Avenue at West 9th, 14th, 23rd, and 33rd streets. Trains run 24 hours and depart every 10-30 minutes. The fare is $1.

TRANSPORTATION AROUND NEW YORK CITY

The **Metro Transit Authority** (MTA) publishes excellent fold-out maps that show all the subway and bus routes and stops; ask for one in any subway station. You might also want to request the MTA's booklet, "Token Trips: New York City Subway and Bus Travel Guide," which lists every conceivable attraction in the city with easy-to-follow travel directions. The tiny "Transitwise NY Metropolitan Commuter Rail Map" ($6.95) is worth purchasing if you don't want to advertise your tourist status, because it shows all Manhattan subways and buses, but tri-folds to fit in a pocket. It's available at bookstores and newsstands. For info on ferry service to the Statue of Liberty, Ellis Island, and Staten Island, *see* Chapter 2.

TRAVEL AGENCIES

A good travel agent puts your needs first. Look for an agency that has been in business at least five years, emphasizes customer service, and has someone on staff who specializes in your destination. In addition **make sure the agency belongs to a professional trade organization.** The American Society of Travel Agents (ASTA), with 27,000 agents in some 170 countries, is the largest and most influential in the field. Operating under the motto "Integrity in Travel," it maintains and enforces a strict code of ethics and will step in to help mediate any agent-client disputes if necessary. ASTA also maintains a Web site that includes a directory of agents. (Note that if a travel agency is also acting as your tour operator, *see* Buyer Beware *in* Tours & Packages, *above*.)

LOCAL AGENT REFERRALS • American Society of Travel Agents (ASTA, tel. 800/965-2782 24-hr hot line, fax 703/684-8319, www.astanet.com). **Association of British Travel Agents** (68-271 Newman St., London W1P 4AH, tel. 020/7637-2444, fax 020/7637-0713). **Association of Canadian Travel Agents** (1729 Bank St., Suite 201, Ottawa, Ontario K1V 7Z5, tel. 613/521-0474, fax 613/521-0805). **Australian Federation of Travel Agents** (Level 3, 309 Pitt St., Sydney 2000, tel. 02/9264-3299, fax 02/9264-1085). **Travel Agents' Association of New Zealand** (Box 1888, Wellington 10033, tel. 04/499-0104, fax 04/499-0786).

VISITOR INFORMATION

TOURIST INFORMATION • Contact the New York City visitors information offices below for brochures, subway and bus maps, a calendar of events, listings of hotels and weekend hotel packages, and discount coupons for Broadway shows. For a free "I Love New York" booklet listing New York City attractions and tour packages, contact the New York State Division of Tourism.

CITY INFORMATION • New York Convention and Visitors Bureau (810 Seventh Ave., New York, NY 10019, tel. 212/484-1200, fax 212/484-1280), weekdays 9-5; **New York City Visitors Information Center** (tel. 212/397-8222).

STATEWIDE INFORMATION • New York State Division of Tourism (1 Commerce Ave., Albany, NY 12245, tel. 518/474-4116 or 800/225-5697).

VOLUNTEERING

A variety of volunteer programs are available. Council (*see* Students, *above*) is a key player, running its own roster of projects and publishing a directory that lists other sponsor organizations, *Volunteer! The Comprehensive Guide to Voluntary Service in the U.S. and Abroad* ($12.95 plus $1.50 postage). Service Civil International (SCI), International Voluntary Service (IVS), and Volunteers for Peace (VFP) run two- and three-week short workcamps; VFP also publishes the *International Workcamp Directory* ($12). WorldTeach programs, run by Harvard University, require that you commit a year to teaching on subjects ranging from English and science to carpentry, forestry, and sports.

RESOURCES • **SCI/IVS** (5474 Walnut Level Rd., Crozet, VA 22932, tel. 804/823–1826). **VFP** (43 Tiffany Rd., Belmont, VT 05730, tel. 802/259–2759, fax 802/259–2922). **WorldTeach** (1 Eliot St., Cambridge, MA 02138-5705, tel. 617/495–5527 or 800/483–2240, fax 617/495–1599).

WEB SITES

Do **check out the World Wide Web** when you're planning. You'll find everything from up-to-date weather forecasts to virtual tours of famous cities. Fodor's Web site www.fodors.com, is a great place to start your online travels. For more information specifically on New York City, visit the official tourism site of the **New York City Convention and Visitors Bureau,** at www.nycvisit.com; **New York Public Library** at www.nypl.org offers wonderful historical information; **MovieFone 777–FILM Online** at www.777film.com is one-stop shopping for movie previews and tickets; the **Village Voice** at www.villagevoice.com and **New York Sidewalk** at newyork.sidewalk.com offer comprehensive listings; the **New York Subway Finder** at www.krusch.com/nysf.html provides subway directions to any New York address.

WHEN TO GO

Because New York is so awfully hot in summer, many locals get the hell out June–August, when the streets are quieter, the bars are less crowded, and the ratio of tourists to locals jumps way up.

Without a doubt, fall and spring are the best times of year to visit New York, both in terms of the weather and the scenery. In fall the city's parks turn golden, and there's something about the smell of roasting chestnuts carried on a crisp autumn breeze that makes you feel at peace with the world. In spring, usually by early April, the snow melts for good, flowers start blooming, and the birds start singing—ah, sylvan Manhattan.

CLIMATE

If you don't like the weather in New York, goes the old joke, wait a minute. Temperatures not only fluctuate dramatically from season to season, they often change from balmy to miserable and back again in a single afternoon. In winter, lows can hit 15°F (-9°C), with or without wicked winds and blizzards of snow. Summers bring hotter-than-hell temperatures coupled with 99.9% humidity.

FORECASTS • Weather Channel Connection (tel. 900/932–8437), 95¢ per minute from a Touch-Tone phone.

The following chart shows the average highs and lows in Manhattan:

Jan.	41°F	5°C	May	70°F	21°C	Sept.	76°F	24°C
	29	−2		54	12		61	16
Feb.	43°F	6°C	June	81°F	27°C	Oct.	67° F	19°C
	29	−2		63	17		52	11
Mar.	47°F	8°C	July	85°F	29°C	Nov.	56° F	13°C
	34	1		70	21		43	6
Apr.	61°F	16°C	Aug.	83°F	28°C	Dec.	43° F	6°C
	45	7		68	20		31	−1

FESTIVALS

Every month of the year finds some kind of celebration or happening, whether it's a daylong parade up 5th Avenue or a summer-long series of performances. The huge diversity of people in New York adds plenty of spice to the mix—a wild proliferation of events celebrating different groups and all kinds of ethnic holidays, from the huge St. Patrick's Day parade to the Festival of San Gennaro in Little Italy. For more festival info ask at the NYCVB (*see* Visitor Information, *above*) for a calendar of events or get a copy of the *Village Voice, Time Out, The New Yorker,* or the Friday edition of the *New York Times.* For info on free summer concerts and music festivals, *see* Summer Arts *in* Chapter 7.

JANUARY • For **New Year's Eve** you have two very different options: Hang out with drunken out-of-towners on Times Square and watch the famous ball drop at midnight, or catch a free midnight fireworks display in Central Park. On New Year's Day the Polar Bear Club takes its annual swim in the frigid Atlantic, at Coney Island.

The **Winter Antiques Show** (tel. 718/292–7392), held near the end of the month at the Seventh Regiment Armory (Park Ave. at E. 67th St.), is one of the nation's largest. It sounds dull, but it's actually pretty cool if you like antiques.

FEBRUARY • Chinatown hails the **Chinese New Year,** on the first full moon after January 21, with processions and a dragon parade. The main parade starts on Mott Street in Chinatown and continues down Canal Street and East Broadway.

It's a dog-eat-dog world (not literally) at Madison Square Garden, as Schnauzers, Rottweilers, and Afghan hounds compete for the title of champion at the **Westminster Kennel Club Dog Show.** Believe it or not, this is a big deal in New York. The show is usually held the second Monday and Tuesday of February. *Tel. 212/682–6852.*

MARCH • The gargantuan **Art Expo** (tel. 216/826–2858 or 800/827–7170), at the Jacob K. Javits Convention Center, includes cultural performances from around the world. For blooms, check out Bronx's New York Botanical Gardens' **Spring Flower Show** (tel. 718/817–8700). The Sunday **Easter Parade** is all about people in extravagantly odd hats sauntering along 5th Avenue from 49th to 59th streets.

The **St. Patrick's Day Parade** is the city's biggest event, held every March 17 on 5th Avenue between 44th and 86th streets. The four-hour parade features lots of beer, green hats, and woozy marchers. In the past few years it's also featured an unsanctioned band of Irish gays and lesbians protesting their exclusion from the official ceremonies. *Tel. 212/484–1200.*

MAY • The **Cherry Blossom Festival,** held at the Brooklyn Botanic Garden, includes haiku readings, taiko drumming, the ancient tea ceremony, and exhibits of Japanese art. *Tel. 718/622–4433. Free with paid admission to garden ($3).*

On the first Sunday after May 17, Brooklyn's thriving Scandinavian community parties down at the annual **Norwegian Constitution Day Parade** in Bay Ridge. The **Loisada Street Fair** takes place on the last weekend in May, celebrating those hip and funky inhabitants of the Loisada (Lower East Side).

The Brooklyn Academy of Music (*see* Arts Centers *in* Chapter 7) hosts the largest annual gathering of African-American dance companies in the States for **Dance Africa.** Accompanying the performances are classes, discussions, and a bazaar with African-American crafts and foods.

Navy ships from the United States and abroad are joined by Coast Guard ships during **Fleet Week** for a parade up the Hudson River, then a docking in Manhattan during which ships are open to the public. It all happens at the *Intrepid* Air, Sea, and Space Museum (*see* Museums and Galleries *in* Chapter 2) during the week before Memorial Day.

Ninth Avenue, site of the most varied ethnic foods in the city, closes to traffic between West 34th and West 57th streets when it hosts the **Ninth Avenue International Food Festival** for an entire weekend so chefs can show off their stuff. *Tel. 212/581–7217 or 212/581–7029.*

New York's Ukrainian community whoops it up at the **Ukrainian Festival,** an East Village affair, held on the weekends between Mother's Day and Memorial Day. *E. 7th St. between 2nd and 3rd Aves., tel. 212/674–1615.*

At the **Washington Square Art Show,** artists display their work around this Village park on Memorial Day weekend and the following weekend, and then again during the first two weekends of September. *5th Ave. at Washington Sq. North, West Village, tel. 212/982–6255.*

JUNE • East Broadway between Rutgers and Montgomery streets is the site of the **Lower East Side Jewish Spring Festival,** held on the second Sunday in June.

New York's **Gay Pride Parade,** held on the last Sunday in June, commemorates the 1969 Stonewall riots—considered by many the birth of the gay rights movement. *Tel. 212/807–7433.*

The wild and wacky **Mermaid Parade** along the Coney Island boardwalk celebrates the summer solstice; marching bands and antique cars share the procession with people dressed like creatures of the sea. *Tel. 718/372–5159.*

During the annual **Museum Mile Festival,** 5th Avenue from 82nd Street to 104th Street is closed to traffic 6–9 PM. Admission to the Mile's museums is either free or greatly reduced. *Tel. 212/606–2296 or 212/397–8222.*

During the raucous **Puerto Rican Day Parade,** flag-waving Puerto Ricans jam the streets for an exuberant celebration of one of New York's biggest immigrant groups. Join the crowds on 5th Avenue between 44th and 86th streets. *Tel. 212/484–1200.*

For two weeks the Italian **St. Anthony of Padua Feast** is held on Sullivan Street from Spring to Houston streets in SoHo; carnival rides, street vendors, and joviality climax in a grand pageant. *Tel. 212/777–2755.*

JULY • On American **Independence Day** (July 4), the city explodes with illicit and legit fireworks (the East Village sounds like a war zone). And keep an eye out for the **African Street Festival** in Brooklyn's Bedford-Stuyvesant neighborhood, a weeklong block party celebrating African-American culture.

AUGUST • The **Caribbean Cultural Center** produces Carnival (tel. 212/307–7420), held the first weekend in August and celebrating people of the African diaspora. The last Sunday in August sees **Fiesta Folklorica,** a Latin American festival in Central Park. Harlem celebrates its heritage with **Harlem Week** (tel. 212/427–7200), a weeklong bash of cultural events.

SEPTEMBER • New York's biggest German-American event is the **German-American Steuben Parade** along 5th Avenue from 64th to 86th streets on the third weekend in September (tel. 516/239–0741). Mulberry Street in Little Italy is the site of the hugely popular **Festival of San Gennaro,** an Italian street carnival—the entire street is lined with arcade games, sellers of Italian kitsch, and stands selling greasy snacks or cotton candy.

The three-day **New York is Book Country** festival, in mid-September, celebrates books of all kinds. On one afternoon, 5th Avenue from 48th to 57th streets is closed and handed over to publishers, book-stores, and small presses displaying their wares. *Tel. 212/207–7242.*

The **New York Film Festival,** held late September–early October, is the premier showcase for dozens of films from around the world—and your best bet for seeing directors and actors at the opening of their films. The **New York Video Festival** runs concurrently. *140 W. 65th St., at Broadway, tel. 212/875–5050.*

OCTOBER • The **Columbus Day Parade** (tel. 212/249–9923), the second-largest in New York after St. Paddy's Day, is held around October 12 on 5th Avenue between 44th and 86th streets. The Cathedral of St. John the Divine (Amsterdam Ave. at W. 112th St., tel. 212/316–7540) is the site of the **Feast of St. Francis** on the first Sunday in October, featuring a Blessing of the Animals. The **International Expressions Festival** is a monthlong affair highlighting Caribbean and African-diaspora cultures (tel. 212/307–7420).

NOVEMBER • The **New York City Marathon,** in early November, is one of the world's most prestigious, featuring racers from around the world. Starting at the Verrazano-Narrows Bridge in Staten Island, the race proceeds through Brooklyn, Queens, and the South Bronx before finishing at Tavern on the Green in Central Park. *Tel. 212/860–4455.*

Macy's **Thanksgiving Parade** takes place on Thanksgiving Day, beginning at Central Park West and 77th Street, heading down to Columbus Circle, and then snaking down Broadway to 34th Street. The night before finds many New Yorkers watching the whole shindig being prepared—somebody's gotta blow those balloons up—on Central Park West from 77th to 88th streets. *Tel. 212/695–4400.*

DECEMBER • In the first week of December a Christmas tree is lit up at **Rockefeller Center** (5th Ave. at 50th St., tel. 212/632–3975). The scene is *very* New York. With the annual **Christmas Spectacular** (tel. 212/247–4777), Radio City Music Hall puts on its Christmas bash through January 4; expect rap-ping elves and lots of lasers. The hyper-consumptive 5th Avenue is closed to traffic on the two Sundays before Christmas so people can go berserk with their credit cards. **Kwanzaa,** an African-American holi-day, celebrates the "first fruits of the harvest" (as the name means in Swahili) and includes various cul-tural events and fairs at the Jacob K. Javitz Convention Center.

EXPLORING NEW YORK CITY

UPDATED BY JENNIFER D'ANGELO, DORI FERN, ANTO HOWARD, MELISSA KLURMAN, CHRISTINA KNIGHT, ANDREA LAWLOR, HEATHER LEWIS, LAUREN MYERS, HELAYNE SCHIFF, AND KRISTEN SCHURR

On returning from a visit, Charles Dickens once described New York City as "a vast amount of good and evil intermixed and jumbled up together." Though he pissed off a great number of his American readers, he made an excellent point. The premium of space and time in this city makes for a bit of unpleasantries, and as you're rudely muscled aside during rush hour, you may even discover your own inner-aggressor. But many of the setbacks of city life affect us all, which does bring out simple moments of camaraderie and acknowledgment that we're in this mess together.

New York is full of distractions that will loosen any tightly planned itinerary, so if you get lost or miss a show-time, relax—it's the things you come across by accident here that are often the most memorable. Do persevere on the long lines to the top of the World Trade Center or the Empire State Building—one of the few places on earth where you can get views so vertigo-inducing. And budget some time to stray off the beaten path: Hop on the subway to Fort Tryon Park, stay up until 5 in the morning to see the fishmongers close shop at the Fulton Fish Market, or spend the afternoon in a Hell's Kitchen Irish pub drinking Guinness with regulars who probably have been glued to their bar stools for the past four decades. The outer boroughs have major attractions, too: The mammoth Brooklyn Museum of Art, the world-famous Bronx Zoo, and the New York Botanical Gardens are just a few examples, and all are certainly worth day trips.

Wherever you go, you'll find New York's subway system extremely convenient, and aside for some weekends when trains get rerouted, they'll often speed you to your destination faster than a cab will—especially during rush hour. That said, moving around Manhattan by bus or, better yet, on your own two feet is the ideal way to get a real feel for the city. New York's street life—its glamour, its frenetic pace, even its occasional hints of evil—is an important element of any visit.

GUIDED TOURS

If you were planning to skip this section because you bristle at the thought of being led around by the nose like a show pony, stop and reconsider. Not all guided tours will treat you like you're on a fourth-grade field trip. Indeed, if you're new to New York and unfamiliar with its offerings, doesn't it make sense to turn to an expert? Many of the museums, historical buildings, parks, and other attractions described in this chapter offer guided tours that will give you a rare, behind-the-scenes look at how they operate, or enchant you with historical tidbits and lore. Best of all, many of these tours are absolutely free once you've paid your admission (if any). Some of the most fascinating tours include those at **Lincoln Center,** the **New York Stock Exchange, Carnegie Hall, Times Square,** the **American Museum of Natural History,** the **United Nations,** the **Fulton Fish Market,** the **Brooklyn Botanical Garden,** the **Federal Reserve Bank,** and the **Historic Orchard Street Bargain District,** but of course there are dozens of others. For times and locations, *see below.*

NBC Studio Tour. What could be better for a TV junkie than a one-hour tour ($8.25) of the sets of the *Today Show, Saturday Night Live,* or *Dateline NBC.* (Don't set your heart on seeing a particular show's set, however—it may not be available that day.) Plus, you'll peek at behind-the-scenes stuff like tons of technical gizmos, and look at all of NBC's broadcast milestones. There's also a demonstration of the three elements of TV: light, sound, and action. Tours depart weekdays every 15 minutes (during January and February and September and October every half hour) between 9:30 and 4:30, but arrive early because tickets are usually sold out before noon. *30 Rockefeller Plaza, at 6th Ave., Midtown, tel. 212/664–7174. Subway: B, D, F, or Q to W. 47th–50th Sts./Rockefeller Center.*

WALKING TOURS

Walking tours are one of the best ways to learn about New York and make new friends, all at the same time. And they're not just for tourists: Longtime New Yorkers rely on walking tours to get into some of New York's most inaccessible places, and into places they might not feel comfortable going to on their own. For a guide, you'll usually get some sort of expert, like a professor, graduate student, historian, or author. Most walking tours are held on weekends year-round and require reservations. Walking tours are listed in the "Above and Beyond" section of *The New Yorker's* "Goings On About Town" listings, the "Around Town" section of *Time Out,* and *New York's* "Cue" pages.

There are two types of must-see attractions in New York: those that lifelong New Yorkers dismiss with "never been there," and the kind over which they gush, "you must go there first." Do them both.

Several museums offer walking tours focusing on their particular neighborhood or area of expertise. For tours focusing on New York history, check out the **Cooper-Hewitt Museum** (tel. 212/849–8380), which charges $15–$25, or the **Museum of the City of New York** (tel. 212/534–1672, ext. 206), where you can join a tour for $10 and up. The **New-York Historical Society** (tel. 212/873–3400) asks for a donation of $5 for walking tours relating to their exhibits. If you want out of Manhattan, try the **Brooklyn Historical Society** (tel. 718/624–0890), which offers tours of historic Brooklyn neighborhoods for about $12 for nonmembers. The **Brooklyn Center for the Urban Environment (BCUE)** (tel. 718/788–8500) covers Brooklyn with nature, history, and architecture tours. The $8 tours offered on weekends by the **Lower East Side Tenement Museum** (90 Orchard St., tel. 212/431–0233) focus on the history and culture of Lower East Side immigrant groups—Chinese, Latino, Italian, Irish, German, and Jewish. The **New York Transit Museum** (tel. 718/243–3060) offers tours most weekends through spooky, abandoned New York City subway tunnels. Tours are $15–$20; reservations are required. For more details on each museum, *see* Museums and Galleries, *below.*

92nd Street Y. The Y's excellent tours range from two hours to a full day, and can take in anything from "Chinatown's Herb Markets" and "The Planning and Architecture of the Great Central Park" to a look inside the Harvard Club or a walk through artists' studios. Tickets range from $20 to $55. *1395 Lexington Ave., New York, NY 10128, tel. 212/996–1100. Tours given year-round; call for schedule. Reservations recommended.*

Adventure on a Shoestring. For a bargain $5 you get a 1½-hour tour of the city's less-touristed neighborhoods, like Hell's Kitchen; Astoria, Queens; the Carnegie Hill area on the Upper East Side; Chelsea; or Roosevelt Island. Tours of ethnic neighborhoods end with lunch (not included in ticket price). *300 W. 53rd St., New York, NY 10019, tel. 212/265–2663. Tours given weekends.*

Big Onion Walking Tours. Grad students pursuing degrees in American history are your enthusiastic guides to attractions such as the Brooklyn Bridge or New York's Revolutionary War sites. There's also a multiethnic eating tour of the Lower East Side, taking in Chinatown, Little Italy, and the Jewish Lower East Side. The 2½-hour tours are $10–$15. *Cherokee Station, Box 20561, New York, NY 10021, tel. 212/439–1090. Most tours given weekends at 1 PM.*

Harlem Your Way! These 2½- to three-hour tours explore Harlem's historic districts and landmarks, like Sugar Hill, Hamilton Grange, and the Apollo Theater. On Sundays, the tour takes in a gospel church service. Cost is $25. *129 W. 130th St., near Adam Clayton Powell Jr. Blvd., New York, NY 10027, tel. 212/690–1687 or 800/382–9363. Tours given Mon.–Sat. at noon, Sun. at 10:30 AM. Reservations required.*

THE FIVE BOROUGHS

Newark International Airport ✈

Goethals Bridge

Bayonne Bridge

Newark Bay

Pulaski Skyway

Lincoln Tunnel

Liberty I.

Ellis I.

Holland Tunnel

Kill Van Kull

STATEN ISLAND

Staten Island Zoo ■

Snug Harbor Cultural Center

Garibaldi-Meucci Museum ■

ST. GEORGE

St. George Ferry Terminal

Ferry Terminal

Staten Island Institute of Arts and Sciences

Statue of Liberty

ROSEBANK

Alice Austen House ■

Battery Tunnel

Brooklyn Battery Bridge

Verrazano-Narrows Bridge

M A

East River

Manhattan Bridge

Williamsburg Bridge

GREENPOINT

WILLIAMSBURG

BAY RIDGE

Queens Expwy.

SUNSET PARK

BOROUGH PARK

PARK SLOPE

COBBLE HILL

BROOKLYN HEIGHTS

BROOKLYN FORT HEIGHTS GREENE

CLINTON HILL

BEDFORD-STUYVESANT

QUEENS

BENSONHURST

Belt Pkwy.

Green-Wood Cemetery ■

Prospect Park

FLATBUSH

Brooklyn Museum of Art and Botanic Gardens ■

Eastern Pkwy.

Atlantic Ave.

CROWN HEIGHTS

CANARSIE

BROOKLYN

Ocean Pkwy.

Flatbush Ave.

Linden Blvd.

Jackie Robinson

CONEY ISLAND

BRIGHTON BEACH

MANHATTAN BEACH

SHEEPSHEAD BAY

NY Aquarium ■

Marine Park

Floyd Bennett Field

Gateway National Recreation Area

Jamaica Bay Wildlife Refuge

Cross Bay Blvd.

Southern Pkwy.

J.F.K. International Airport ✈

Rockaway Inlet

Jacob Riis Park

Rockaway Beach ■

ATLANTIC OCEAN

28

NEW JERSEY

Meadowlands
Sports Complex

3

17

80

46

95

4

5 km

5 miles

Palisades Pkwy.

Hudson River

Spuyten Duyvil

Wave Hill ■
RIVERDALE

Van Cortlandt
Park

Woodlawn
Cemetery

WESTCHESTER

George
Washington
Bridge

MANHATTAN

Central
Park

Fordham ■
University

Bronx
Park

FORDHAM

BELMONT

Bronx Zoo and New York
Botanical Garden

THE BRONX

Pelham Bay
Park

Orchard
Beach ■

Long Island
Sound

Grand Concourse

Harlem R.

Yankee
Stadium ■

Bronx Museum
of the Arts ■

Crotona
Park

95

Queens-
Midtown

Queensboro
Bridge

LONG ISLAND
CITY

Triborough
Bridge

Grand Central Pkwy.

ASTORIA

Northern Blvd.

JACKSON
HEIGHTS

La Guardia
Airport

East

Whitestone Bridge

Eastchester
Bay

Eastchester City I.

Little Neck
Bay

FOREST
HILLS

Queens
Museum ■

Flushing Meadows-
Corona Park

Shea
Stadium ■

USTA Nat'l
Tennis Center ■

Queens
Botanical ■
Garden

FLUSHING

River

Throgs Neck
Bridge

Clearview Expwy.

Long Island Expwy.

Cross Island Pkwy.

Van Wyck Expwy.

Grand Central Pkwy.

JAMAICA

Alley
Pond
Park

NASSAU

SIGHTSEEING ON THE CHEAP

If you want a motorized overview of Manhattan but don't want the perky commentary, save some cash by joining New York's cranky commuters on a standard city bus. On a hot summer day, it's particularly pleasant in the air-conditioning. You won't get the tape-recorded rundown on the sights, but your daily or weekly Metro Card gets you on as many of the following routes as your time allows:

Bus M1: Battery Park, the World Trade Center, Wall Street, SoHo, Union Square, the New York Public Library, Rockefeller Center, Central Park, the Metropolitan Museum of Art, Museum Mile.

Bus M4: Empire State Building, Central Park, Columbia University, Harlem, the Cloisters Museum, and Fort Tryon Park.

Bus M10: Central Park West, the American Museum of Natural History, Times Square, Chelsea, the West Village, and the World Trade Center.

Bus M11: West Village, Chelsea, Hell's Kitchen, Lincoln Center, the Upper West Side, Columbia University, Riverbank State Park.

Bus M101: City Hall, Chinatown, Little Italy, the East Village, Gramercy, Murray Hill, Grand Central Terminal, the Upper East Side, Martin Luther King Jr. Boulevard in Harlem, and Washington Heights.

Municipal Art Society. The Municipal Art Society's "Discover New York Tours" focus on architecture, history, and urban planning, with offerings like "Merchants, Mayors and Magnificence: Manhattan's Civic Center" or "Times Square and How It Got That Way." Tours are 1½ hours and cost $12–$15. *Tel. 212/935–3960 or 212/439–1049 for recorded information on tours. Tours given year-round. Reservations recommended for some tours.*

Wildman Steve Brill. The Wildman leads four-hour tours of Greater New York's parks, on which you'll learn how to identify, harvest, and prepare edible and medicinal plants, including berries, mushrooms, roots, herbs, seeds, seaweed, and greens. Suggested donation is $10. *143–25 84th Dr., Apt 6C, Jamaica, NY 11435, tel. 718/291–6825. Tours given weekends and holidays Mar.–1st weekend in Dec.; send SASE for schedule. Reservations required.*

BUS TOURS

Bite the bullet, because you're going to be branded a tacky, cheesy tourist the second you board a tour bus. That said, an air-conditioned bus ride is one of the better ways to explore the city during the summer heat (keep in mind that most double-decker buses don't have air-conditioning). Tours generally zip around on one of 10–20 different routes, stopping for a quick look-see from ground level before hustling off to the next big attraction.

Gray Line Tours. Gray Line aims to please: They offer two types of tours. Double-decker buses follow uptown and downtown loops; armed with a two-day pass, you can get on and off at your leisure, stopping at blockbusters like the Metropolitan Museum of Art, Central Park, the Empire State Building, the World Trade Center, and Chinatown. Gray Line also offers six- to nine-hour motor-coach tours. Reservations for either type of tour are unnecessary; just call for the day's schedule and show up at one of the Gray Line terminals (in the Port Authority bus terminal, 42nd Street and 8th Avenue, 42nd Street entrance, street level or at the new Times Square Visitors Center, 1560 Broadway, between 46th and 47th streets) 30 minutes before departure. They'll also show you New York by helicopter ($44–$79) and Central Park by trolley car. *Port Authority bus terminal, 42nd St. and 8th Ave., Midtown, tel. 212/397–2600; Times Square Visitors Center, 1560 Broadway, between 46th and 47th Sts.; for information and brochures, write to 1740 Broadway, New York, NY 10019. Subway: A, C, E, 1, 2, 3, or 7 to 42nd St. or N or R to Times Square. Tickets: Double-decker tours $19–$36, motor-coach tours $41–$54. Tours daily 8:30–6:30.*

Harlem Spirituals, Inc. These multilingual tours of Harlem and other uptown neighborhoods include stops at Hamilton Grange, the neighborhood of Sugar Hill, and a Baptist church service. The jazz tour ($75) includes dinner and club cover charge. *690 8th Ave., at 43rd St., Midtown, tel. 212/391–0900. Tickets: $30–$75.*

The Hasidic Discovery Welcome Center Tours. A Hasidic rabbi leads this tour through Hasidic Williamsburg and Crown Heights. Visit a synagogue and private library, see a scribe writing a Torah, browse in a Judaica shop, and lunch at a kosher deli (cost included). You must make reservations; the tour is on Sunday, 9:30–1:30. *Meet in front of the New York Public Library, 42nd and Fifth Ave., tel. 800/838–8687. Tickets: $36.*

New York Apple Tours. Want to ride around New York in an authentic London double-decker? Here's your chance. These big, bright-red buses run daily 9–6 on three loops: uptown, downtown, and along the Hudson River. The "Full City Tour" allows for two days of their regular hop-on, hop-off service in Manhattan and Brooklyn. There's also a 15-stop Brooklyn tour and several theme tours. A two-day pass with unlimited stops is $39 for all three loops and $25 for the downtown route (there is no pass for the river route only). They also offer nighttime "city lights" tours late May through early October. You can pick up buses at 8th Avenue at 53rd Street, Rockefeller Center, or 7th Avenue at 41st Street. **New York Doubledecker Tours** (Empire State Bldg., 34th St. and 5th Ave., tel. 212/967–6008) offers similar services. *Tel. 212/944–9200 or 800/876–9868.*

BOAT TOURS

One of the best, and cheapest, ways to see New York by boat is aboard the Staten Island Ferry (*see* Staten Island *in* the Outer Boroughs, *below*); and it's free. From Pier 16 at the South Street Seaport (*see* Lower Manhattan *in* Manhattan Neighborhoods, *below*) you can take a two-hour voyage ($20) to New York's past aboard the 1885 iron cargo schooner ***The Pioneer*** (212/748–8786; reservations recommended), or one-hour sightseeing tours ($12) of New York Harbor and Lower Manhattan with **Seaport Liberty Cruises** (tel. 212/425–3737). For info on ferry service to the Statue of Liberty and Ellis Island, *see* Major Attractions, *below.*

Circle Line. More than 40 million passengers have steamed around Manhattan on the eight 165-ft Circle Line yachts since the cruises were inaugurated in 1945. It's one of those true New York experiences—Conan O'Brien and crew even taped an episode of *Late Night* from the deck of a moving Circle Line ship in 1995. Once you've finished the three-hour, 35-mi circumnavigation of Manhattan (60- and 90-minute tours are also available), you'll have a good idea of where things are and what you want to see next, and your hair will possess that sought-after windblown quality. *Two locations: Pier 83, 12th Ave. at W. 42nd St., Midtown. Subway: A, C, or E to W. 42nd St. (Port Authority). South Street Seaport, Pier 16, 207 Front St., Lower Manhattan. Subway: 2, 3, 4, 5 to Fulton, A, C to Broadway-Nassau or 1 to World Trade Center. Tel. 212/563–3200. Fare: $18–22, Seaport one-hour tour $12. Call for schedule.*

HORSE-DRAWN CARRIAGE TOURS

Whether it's a frosty, crisp winter morning or a warm summer night, one of the most romantic ways to see the city is by horse-drawn cab. Carriages occasionally go as far as Times Square, but a spin through the southern stretch of Central Park is perfect. Carriages line up on Grand Army Plaza (at the corner of 5th Avenue and 59th Street), and along 59th Street between 5th and 7th avenues. The cost is city-regulated at $34 for the first half hour, $10 for each quarter hour after that; the fare is calculated by time, not per passenger. In recent years, PETA (People for the Ethical Treatment of Animals) and other animal-rights groups have agitated for better working conditions for the city's carriage horses. Reforms mean the horses are treated better than they have been in the past, but the question of whether or not to ride is ultimately yours to answer.

MAJOR ATTRACTIONS

It takes months, or even years, to really get to know New York, but if you're only in town for a few days you'll want to check out the city's "bests"—its top museums, tallest skyscrapers, most stirring monuments, and best-loved park. Just don't try to do them all in one afternoon.

EMPIRE STATE BUILDING

The Empire State Building may no longer be the world's tallest building (it currently ranks fifth), or even the tallest building in New York, but it's certainly one of the world's most famous skyscrapers. More than 3.8 million visitors a year make the trip up to its observatory decks on the 86th and 102nd floors, where they gawk and snap photos and speculate about whether a penny dropped from this height would really bore a hole through the skull of someone on the sidewalk below. So, you ask, what's to love about a 1,250-ft-tall skyscraper? For one, the building's stats are pretty impressive: Approximately 20,000 people fill its offices (which includes the state's largest sperm bank), and its 73 elevators cruise 7 mi of shafts at speeds ranging from 600 to 1,200 ft per minute. In its framework you'll find 60,000 tons of steel, enough to lay tracks from New York City to Baltimore, and on its top you'll find the world's greatest TV tower, which reaches eight million television sets in four states. Then there are the windows, all 6,500 of them, which are continuously being hand-washed by people who we can only presume are unafraid of heights. Beyond size, the Empire State Building, a New York City and National Landmark, is a real beauty: Zoning laws of the 1930s required that its design include numerous setbacks to allow sunlight to reach the street, and this steplike effect is a delight to the eye. With its graceful art deco embellishments, it's 10 times more attractive than the boxy World Trade Center. No wonder the Empire State Building has appeared in more than 100 movies during its lifetime, including 1933's unforgettable *King Kong,* as well as the 1957 romantic classic *An Affair to Remember* and its modern-day update *Sleepless in Seattle,* both of which culminate in romantic rendezvous atop the skyscraper.

Hard to imagine, isn't it, that the whole thing started with a pencil. Yes, the design of the most imitated building in the world was inspired by a large pencil one of the principal architects noticed sitting on his desk. Construction started in March 1930 and was completed in April 1931 at a cost of $41 million. The framework rose at a rate of 4½ stories per week, making the Empire State Building the fastest-rising major skyscraper ever built. Of course, the Great Depression put a damper on opening day ceremonies, and for the next few decades New Yorkers referred to it as the "Empty State Building." To further sour things, the original plan to make the building into a mammoth blimp mooring pad was a total failure. Two blimps briefly made contact in 1931, but barely. Eventually, the 102nd floor (where the blimps were to moor) and the 86th floor (where the blimp ticket agencies and baggage rooms were to be situated) were turned into observation decks.

The blimp world's loss is a tourist's gain, because the views from the two observation decks are absolutely incredible. The better is on the 86th floor, with amazing *plein air* views of the city and far, far beyond. On a clear day you can see as far as 80 mi, which means you've got stellar views of not just New York City, but also parts of New Jersey, Pennsylvania, Connecticut, and Massachusetts. Another thing to look for: In certain atmospheric conditions, the 86th floor's outdoor deck experiences enormous buildups of static electricity, and quite a few couples have experienced "shocking" kisses. Unless you're a fiend for high spots, don't bother with the extra wait at the elevators to go up 200 more ft to the smaller, cramped 102nd floor observatory; you really won't see much more, and you'll have to look out through badly vandalized windows at that. It's worth timing your visit to the Empire State Building for early or late in the day, when the sun is low on the horizon and the shadows are deep across the city. Morning is the least crowded time, while at nighttime the views of the city's lights are absolutely dazzling.

You'll probably notice that the top 30 floors of the Empire State Building are lit up at night with seasonal colors. What started in 1976 with red, white, and blue lights for the American bicentennial has grown to include: Christmas (red and green lights); Easter (white and yellow); Thanksgiving (red and orange); Martin Luther King Jr. Day (red, black, and green); Valentine's Day (red and white); Pulaski Day (red and white); Columbus Day (red, white, and green, the colors of the Italian flag); and of course, the Fourth of July (red, white, and blue); plus a rainbow of colors for almost every special occasion during the year.

350 5th Ave., at 34th St., Midtown, tel. 212/736–3100. Subway: 6 to E. 33rd St. or B, D, Q, or F to W. 34th St./Herald Sq. Admission $6. Open daily 9:30 AM–11:30 PM.

NEW YORK SKYRIDE • The Empire State Building's other attraction may be the hairiest eight minutes you'll have in New York outside a cab. After being subjected to a Comedy Central video laced with subliminal messages (e.g., "Buy your kid NY stuff") and a *Blade Runner*–like "preflight" briefing in English and Japanese, strap yourself into the cramped flight seats and look up at the two-story-tall movie screens for a bucking, rough ride through New York City. It's not recommended for anyone who has trouble with motion sickness; pregnant women are not admitted. *Tel. 212/279–9777. Admission $11.50 for skyride, $14 for Skyride and Observatory. Open daily 10–10.*

STATUE OF LIBERTY

The Statue of Liberty is one of America's most potent icons—the thing Batman rappelled off in *Batman Forever,* that Charlton Heston viewed with rising dread (well, the crown part, anyway) in *Planet of the Apes,* and that author David Foster Wallace fancied as a product spokesmodel (holding aloft Tucks medicated pads and Whoppers instead of a torch) in his epic *Infinite Jest.* Of course, to New Yorkers, this great monument is practically a cliché. But France's gift to America, officially entitled *Liberty Enlightening the World,* still impresses even the most jaded. The only way you could avoid a rush of patriotism as you chug through New York harbor toward this great green toga-covered lady is if you've gotten so seasick you're stuck in the ferry's loo.

Immigrants who have passed through Ellis Island include Charles Atlas, Irving Berlin, Frank Capra, Claudette Colbert, Marcus Garvey, Samuel Goldwyn, Bob Hope, Al Jolson, Bela Lugosi, Rudolph Valentino, and Maria von Trapp and her singing family.

Behind every 151-ft-tall, 225-ton woman, of course, stands a much smaller man. For Ms. Liberty that's Frédéric-Auguste Bartholdi, a renowned 19th-century French sculptor. An odd fellow ruled by strong passions (after a trip to the Sphinx and Great Pyramids he became infatuated with the idea of building a Suez Canal colossus, which Egypt's king squelched), Bartholdi executed the statue as a monument to French–American solidarity. During a trip to New York he chose tiny, uninhabited Bedloe Island, where "people get their first view of the New World," as the perfect spot to display his work. Bartholdi made a few sketches with his mother as model, and 15 years later, on October 28, 1886, the statue was unveiled to an adoring public. Of course, the man wasn't acting entirely alone. The framework inside the statue was designed by Alexandre-Gustave Eiffel, of Eiffel Tower fame. The 89-ft-tall pedestal on which the statue stands was completed thanks to the efforts of Joseph Pulitzer, publisher of the *New York World.* In a savvy marketing coup, Pulitzer promised the working poor of New York that he would publish in his paper the name of every contributor, no matter how small the donation. The money for the pedestal was raised and Pulitzer increased the *World*'s circulation by 50,000. Inscribed on a bronze plaque attached to the statue's base is the sonnet *The New Colossus* ("Give me your tired, your poor, your huddled masses . . ."), written by the radical socialist Emma Lazarus.

Once you've strolled around Liberty Island, you have two choices at the ground-floor entrance of the monument: You can take an elevator 10 stories to the top of the pedestal, or, if you've got the cardiovascular strength of a Himalayan sherpa, you can climb 354 steps to the crown (visitors are not allowed to climb into the torch). It usually takes two or three hours to walk up to the crown because of the long lines, and the trip is not recommended for claustrophobes. Exhibits on the ground floor illustrate the statue's history, including videos of the view from the crown for those too wimpy to make the ascent. There's also a model of the statue's face for the blind to feel. *Tel. 212/363–3200. Admission free. Open daily 9–5.*

COMING AND GOING • The ferry to the Statue of Liberty and Ellis Island (*see below*) departs from Castle Clinton in **Battery Park** (*see* Lower Manhattan *in* Manhattan Neighborhoods, *below*), at the southern tip of Manhattan. The ferry ride is one loop; you can get off at Liberty Island, visit the statue, then reboard any ferry and continue on to Ellis Island, boarding another boat once you are ready to return. Ferries depart every 30 minutes 9:30–3:30, with more frequent departures and extended hours in summer. *Tel. 212/269–5755 for ferry info. Subway to Battery Park: 1 or 9 to South Ferry; also 4 or 5 to Bowling Green. Round-trip fare to Statue of Liberty and/or Ellis Island: $7.*

ELLIS ISLAND

From 1892 to 1924 some 16 million immigrants—men, women, and children—took their first steps on U.S. soil at Ellis Island in New York harbor. In all, by the time the island's federal immigration facility closed for good in 1954, it had processed the ancestors of more than 40% of Americans living today. Now, after many years of restoration, this 27½-acre island has become a museum devoted to immigration. Even if your ancestors didn't arrive here, the visit leaves a powerful impression. At its heart is the **Registry Room,** where inspectors once attempted to screen out "undesirables," like polygamists, criminals, poor people, and people suffering from contagious diseases. The cavernous **Great Hall,** where immigrants were registered, has amazing tiled arches by Rafael Guastavino; white-tiled dormitory rooms overlook this grand space. The **Railroad Ticket Office** at the back of the main building houses exhibits on the "Peopling of America," recounting 400 years of immigration history, and "Forced Migration," focusing on the slave trade. The old kitchen and laundry building has been stabilized, rather than restored, so that you can see what the whole place looked like just a few years ago.

The most moving exhibit is outdoors to the west of the Main Building: the **American Immigrant Wall of Honor,** a circular wall covered in stainless steel and engraved with the names of 420,000 immigrants of all stripes and colors. The names include Miles Standish, Priscilla Alden, George Washington's grandfather, and Irving Berlin; they include people who came to the South on slave ships, to San Francisco on Chinese junks, and to Plymouth, Massachusetts, on the *Mayflower*. A $100 fee was charged for each name on the wall, to pay for Ellis Island's restoration. Guided 30-minute tours of the island are given daily. For info on ferries to Ellis Island, *see* Coming and Going, *above. Tel. 212/363–3200 for recorded info. Admission free. Open winter, daily 9–5; summer, daily 9–6.*

WORLD TRADE CENTER

In a city where practically everything is described in superlatives like "biggest" and "most," the mammoth World Trade Center—which boasts the two tallest buildings in the city and the fourth-tallest in the entire world—is the *maxi-plus-ultra*-most. It's more like a miniature city than an office complex, really, with a daytime population of 130,000 (including 50,000 employees and 80,000 visitors); several train stations; dozens of restaurants; an 800-room hotel; and a huge performance space. Hey, it's even got its own blood bank and the world's largest air-conditioning system. The World Trade Center's "twin" towers are actually different heights. One World Trade Center is 1,368 ft tall, and Two World Trade Center is 1,362 ft tall. Besides those famous twin towers, it has five other buildings arranged around an enormous plaza, modeled after Venice's St. Mark's Square. Below that, you'll find a giant subterranean shopping mall. There's lots to explore, but what you're really here to do is ride one of the warp-speed elevators to the Observation Deck (*see below*) on the 107th floor of Tower Two.

Unlike some of the city's other skyscrapers—the Empire State Building, the Chrysler Building in Midtown, or the Flatiron Building in Gramercy—the Trade Center towers are more an engineering marvel than architectural masterpiece. Completed in 1976, they've since been criticized as being nothing more than boring glass-and-steel boxes. But something about their brutalist design and sheer magnitude gives them the beauty of modern sculpture, and at night, when they're lit from within, they dominate the Manhattan skyline. Where the towers differ most radically from other office buildings is hidden inside; they were engineered so that each of the nearly 1-acre floors is completely open, free of beams, pillars, and other visible means of support. Think about this for a minute and you might wonder how the whole thing keeps from collapsing like a house of cards. Don't worry. Structurally, the towers are capable of withstanding sustained winds of over 100 mi per hour. It probably would take a nuclear bomb to level them.

Of course, anyone who watches CNN knows that the World Trade Center is not invincible. On February 26, 1993, a Ryder van loaded with explosives detonated in one of the underground parking garages, killing six and injuring thousands. Today, the damage has been fixed and the main suspects are serving life sentences in prison. The only reminders are the metal detectors that all employees and visitors must now pass through before entering the center, and a small, granite **memorial** imbedded in the sidewalk of the outdoor plaza.

VISITOR INFO • The New York Visitor Information Center, on the mezzanine of Two World Trade Center, is an excellent place to begin your visit. Helpful if eccentric little old ladies will furnish you with an abundance of info on the Trade Center and other Big Apple sights. On the same level, you'll find the ticket booth for the Trade Tower's observation deck and the downtown branch of **TKTS** (*see* Chapter 7), your one-stop shop for cheap theater tickets. *Subway: C or E to World Trade Center; also 1 or 9 to Cort-landt St. Open weekdays 9–5; also Sat. 9–4:30 in summer.*

OBSERVATION DECK • The best views in Manhattan are from the newly renovated observation deck at Two World Trade Center. And if you look at the line of tourists waiting to buy tickets at the mezzanine-level office, you'll see that this is no big secret (the line is shortest weekday mornings and evenings). The elevator ride alone is worth the price of admission, as you hurtle a quarter-mile into the sky in only 58 seconds. Once you reach the top you can, if you dare, press your nose to the glass of the floor-to-ceiling windows and look out upon the entire island of Manhattan, or across the New York Bay to the Statue of Liberty and Ellis Island (the view potentially extends 55 mi, although signs at the ticket window disclose how far you can see that day). Brand-new additions include three helicopter simulation theaters with moving seats and a nightly laser-light show. There's a café here as well as a Central Park–themed dining room. The prices are elevated to correspond with the height. A can of Coke costs $2, sandwiches $7.50. On nice days you can ride up another few floors to the **Rooftop Observatory,** the world's highest outdoor observation platform. It's offset 25 ft from the edge of the building and surrounded with a barbed-wire electric fence, to thwart spontaneous hurlers of bowling balls. Notice that planes and helicopters are flying *below* you. *Tel. 212/323–2340. Admission $12. Open June–Sept., daily 9:30 AM–11:30 PM; Oct.–May, daily 9:30 AM–9:30 PM.*

COMMODITIES EXCHANGE • At Four World Trade Center, one of those other, shorter Trade Center buildings, you can spy on the capitalist equivalent of circus clowns: commodities traders, who roll up their sleeves and then sweat, shout, and shove their way through a day handling millions of dollars worth of petroleum, livestock, precious metals, and agricultural products (the exchange started in 1886 as the New York Butter and Cheese Exchange). Pick up a pass (free) from the security checkpoint at the southeast corner of the Trade Center's Mall. Warning: You'll be exposed to an endlessly repeating tape—espousing the glory of the free market—that only a Young Republican could love. *Open weekdays 10:30–3.*

Enough aluminum was slapped onto the World Trade Center to side 7,000 homes, and enough concrete was poured for the foundations to build a 5-ft-wide sidewalk from New York to D.C.

CENTRAL PARK

Central Park is probably America's best-loved and best-known park, an 843-acre rectangle of green smack in the middle of Manhattan. You've probably spied it in Absolut Vodka ads, various episodes of *Seinfeld,* and countless movies old and new. If you care, it's the reason behind "Central Perk," the name of the café in *Friends,* the place where Robin Williams danced nude in *The Fisher King,* and where Holden Caulfied in *Catcher in the Rye* spent his late night driving around in a taxi cab. On the flip side, it's also made national headlines as the place where teenage gangs go "wilding," though these days the park is pretty safe—so long as you don't go wandering around its northern woods after dark.

Conceived in 1853, Central Park was America's first landscaped public park. Wealthy New Yorkers lobbied hard for its creation so that they'd have as pretty a place for carriage rides as their rivals in London and Paris, and also because they felt it would get the working classes out of the saloons. Besides, the stretch of land between 59th and 110th streets was at the time a swampy no-man's-land filled with squatters and roving packs of wild pigs and dogs. Leading the campaign was *New York Post* editor and part-time writer of nature poetry William Cullen Bryant, who later got a fine park named after himself in Midtown (*see* Parks and Gardens, *below*). Ultimately, master landscape architects Frederick Law Olmsted and Calvert Vaux (*see box* They Built This City, *below*) were teamed to draw up its design. The two met at night, walking over every acre of the land as they drew up plans to reconfigure it. What resulted, called the "Greensward Plan," cultivates the impression of rural English countryside, with wide sweeps of forest and lawn interspersed with beautiful cast-iron bridges and elaborate fountains. It took 15 years to mark out the park and another 40 for the trees to grow and fill in the outline. Over the decades the park has continued to grow, and it now includes 22 playgrounds, 26 ball fields, 30 tennis courts, and 58 mi of paved pedestrian paths.

You'll probably want to start your exploration at the south end of the park. Between Center and East Drives is the first of a few small bodies of water in the park, **The Pond** and **Hallett Nature Sanctuary.** The area between 59th and 65th streets is largely devoted to children: The **Conservatory Water** is a small pond usually cluttered with model boats and their child captains. Races and regattas are held here every week-

Jacqueline Kennedy Onassis
Reservoir

85th St. Transverse

W. 87th St.
B,C
W. 86th St. **S**
W. 85th St.
W. 84th St.
W. 83rd St.
W. 82nd St.
B,C
W. 81st St. **S**

W. 77th St.
W. 76th St.
W. 75th St.
W. 74th St.
W. 73rd St.
B,C
W. 72nd St. **S**
W. 71st St.
W. 70th St.
W. 69th St.
W. 68th St.
W. 67th St.
W. 66th St.
W. 65th St.
W. 64th St.
W. 63rd St.
W. 62nd St.
W. 61st St.
W. 60th St.

E. 87th St.
E. 86th St.
E. 85th St.
E. 84th St.
E. 83rd St.
E. 82nd St.
E. 81st St.
E. 80th St.
E. 79th St.
E. 78th St.
E. 77th St.
E. 76th St.
E. 75th St.
E. 74th St.
E. 73rd St.
E. 72nd St.
E. 71st St.
E. 70th St.
E. 69th St.
E. 68th St.
E. 67th St.
E. 66th St.
E. 65th St.
E. 64th St.
E. 63rd St.
E. 62nd St.
E. 61st St.
E. 60th St.
E. 59th St.
E. 58th St.
E. 57th St.

0   200 yards
0   200 meters

N

Great Lawn

Turtle Pond

79th St. Transverse

West Dr.

East Dr.

The Ramble

The Lake

Bow Bridge

Conservatory Water

Central Park West

Sheep Meadow

65th St. Transverse

Heckscher Playground

Cedar Dr.

West Dr.

East Dr.

The Pond

Columbus Circle

Central Park South

Grand Army Plaza

Broadway

Seventh Ave.

Sixth Ave.

Fifth Avenue

W. 58th St.
W. 57th St.

KEY
i Tourist Information
S Subway

*A,B,C,D,
1,9*

S

N,R **S**   B,Q **S**

S N,R

American Museum of Natural History and Hayden Planetarium, **1**

Belvedere Castle (tourist info), **5**

Bethesda Fountain and Terrace, **11**

Chess and Checkers House, **17**

Cleopatra's Needle, **6**

Croquet Grounds and Lawn Bowling Greens, **12**

The Dairy (tourist info), **18**

Delacorte Theater, **4**

Friedsam Memorial Carousel, **15**

Hallett Nature Sanctuary, **20**

Literary Walk, **16**

Loeb Boathouse, **10**

The Mall, **14**

Metropolitan Museum of Art, **8**

The Ramble, **7**

Shakespeare Garden, **2**

Strawberry Fields, **9**

Swedish Cottage/ Marionette Theater, **3**

Tavern on the Green, **13**

Tisch Children's Zoo, **22**

Wildlife Conservation Center (Zoo), **21**

Wollman Rink, **19**

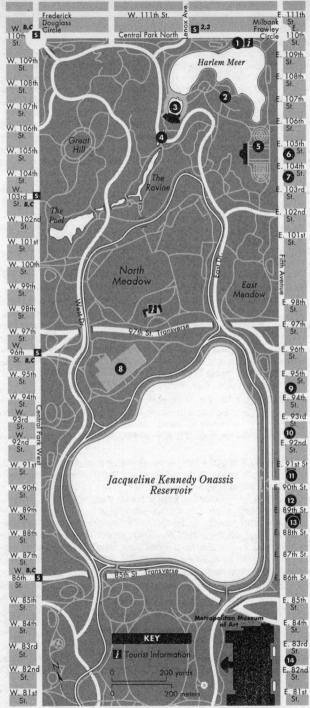

Conservatory
Garden, **5**

Huddlestone
Bridge, **4**

Charles A. Dana
Discovery Center, **1**

Lasker Rink
and Pool, **3**

McGowan's Pass, **2**

Tennis Courts, **8**

Museum Mile

Cooper-Hewitt
National Design
Museum, **11**

El Museo del
Barrio, **6**

Goethe House, **14**

Solomon R.
Guggenheim
Museum, **13**

International Center
of Photography
(ICP)–Uptown, **9**

The Jewish
Museum, **10**

Museum of the City
of New York, **7**

National Academy
of Design, **12**

KEY

ℹ️ Tourist Information

0   200 yards
0   200 meters

end. On the west end of the basin is a statue of **Hans Christian Andersen** with his pet goose; on the north end, saddling a huge mushroom, sits **Alice in Wonderland** with a few of her eccentric friends. The park's **Children's Zoo** was recently redesigned into a more naturalistic setting for its animal residents. At 79th Street, the landscape jogs upward to the top of **Vista Rock,** which forms the foundation for playful **Belvedere Castle** (*see below*). Just off to the left is the **Shakespeare Garden,** a beautiful plot crammed with flowering plants immortalized by the bard. East of the garden is the **Swedish Cottage,** where the **Marionette Theater** (tel. 212/988–9093) performs year-round Tuesday–Friday at 10:30 AM and noon; Saturday at 11 AM and 1 PM. Tickets are only $5 but reservations are required. At the edge of the park at 5th Avenue and 82nd Street is the grand **Metropolitan Museum of Art** (*see below*). Above 86th Street things start getting a little wilder, partly due to the original design, which called for footpaths through small rocky gorges and along creek beds, and partly due to lapsed supervision, although this area is undergoing a cleanup. While you're up here, look for the stone **Blockhouse,** the oldest building in the park. It dates from the War of 1812; you can still see gun ports in its decaying walls. Take a breather alongside the recently spruced up **Harlem Meer.** This idyllic, shady spot is usually thronged with Spanish families picnicking and napping in hammocks they truss between trees.

Public rest rooms are scattered throughout the park: at Bethesda Terrace, the Loeb Boathouse, the North Meadow Recreation Center, the Conservatory Garden, the Charles A. Dana Discovery Center, and north of the Reservoir near the tennis courts. For food, there's a restaurant/café at the Loeb Boathouse and the Ice Cream Café at the Conservatory Water. During summer, the park is home to numerous free arts performances, including the enormously popular **Summerstage** and **New York Shakespeare** festivals; for more info *see* Summer Arts *in* Chapter 7. Year-round, the park draws all sorts of sporting enthusiasts for rock-climbing, tennis, horseback-riding, softball, you name it, including winter ice-skating on its famous **Wollman Rink;** for more info, *see* Ice-Skating and Ice Hockey *in* Chapter 8. *Tel. 212/360–3456 for park events (tel. 800/281–5722 for TDD). Park open daily 30 mins before sunrise–1 AM.*

THE DAIRY • If you're planning to make a day of exploring Central Park, make this charming Victorian-style cottage your first stop. Back in the 19th century, when cows grazed on what's since become an ice-skating rink, the cottage was a dairy selling milk by the glass. It now houses the **Central Park Reception Center,** where you can pick up maps and info on park events, or check out exhibits on the park's history and wildlife. The striped-brick **Chess and Checkers House,** a short walk south of the Dairy, is perched atop a large rock named the *Kinderberg,* or "children's mountain." You'll find plenty of chess tables; with a $20 deposit, you can pick up pieces to play with at the Dairy. *Mid-park at 65th St., tel. 212/794–6564. Subway: N or R to 5th Ave. Open Tues.–Sun. 11–5 (shorter hrs in winter).*

FRIEDSAM MEMORIAL CAROUSEL • This turn-of-the-century carousel was brought to the park from Coney Island (*see* Brooklyn *in* the Outer Boroughs, *below*) in 1951. Its 58 beautiful, hand-carved jumping steeds, three-quarters the size of real horses, go 'round to music by a wheezy but cheerful pipe organ. *Mid-park at 65th St., just west of Center Dr., tel. 212/879–0244. Admission $1. Open weekdays 10–5:45, weekends 10–6:15.*

WILDLIFE CONSERVATION CENTER (ZOO) • The Zoo has given itself a snappy new eco-friendly name and labored long and hard to give its small collection of furred and feathered residents more natural habitats, like in the **Tropic Zone,** where birds and reptiles cavort among jungle vines and palm fronds. There's also **Temperate Territory** for monkeys, and **Edge of the Ice Pack** for a flock of penguins. But there's been trouble in the **Polar Circle,** where Gus, the 700-pound polar bear, was diagnosed as suffering from depression; like every other New Yorker, he now has a therapist. The new **Tisch Children's Zoo** (free with zoo admission) enchants the under-6 crowd. Just outside the Zoo's gates look for the **Delacorte Musical Clock.** Every hour its six-animal band circles around and plays a tune while monkeys on the top hammer their bells. *E. 64th St. at 5th Ave., tel. 212/861–6030. Subway: N or R to 5th Ave. Admission $3.50. Open year-round, weekdays 10–5, weekends 10:30–5:30.*

SHEEP MEADOW • Look around Sheep Meadow on a sunny summer Sunday and you'll see 15 acres full of sunbathers and Frisbee players. Unlike at the park's other grassy fields, team sports are prohibited here, so it's the perfect place to picnic or fly a kite. And, as you might have guessed from the name, the meadow was indeed once home-sweet-home to a woolly flock, evicted in 1934. Around that time the nearby sheepfold was turned into a glitzy restaurant, **Tavern on the Green** (Central Park W at W. 67th St., tel. 212/873–3200), which is expensive but just the tiniest bit tacky, with lots of trees wrapped in twinkling lights and deer antlers on the walls. Just north of Sheep Meadow are the manicured **Croquet Grounds** and **Lawn Bowling Greens.** You must have a permit ($30) to play on them; call 212/360–8133 for info. *Mid-park between 65th and 69th Sts.*

THE MALL • Sorry, this isn't the kind of "mall" that has a Gap and a food court. It's a wide avenue shaded by tall elms and made for strolling; pretend you're in a painting by Seurat. At its southern end is the **Literary Walk,** so named because statues of dead white scribes like William Shakespeare, Robert Burns, and Sir Walter Scott line the path. One welcome addition was **The Indian Hunter,** sculpted in 1869 by John Quincy Adams Ward; this was the first piece of made-in-America sculpture to stand in the park. *Mid-park between 66th and 72nd Sts.*

BETHESDA FOUNTAIN AND TERRACE • Not many New York views are more romantic than the one from the top of the magnificent stone staircase that leads down to Bethesda Fountain. And it makes an excellent place to meet when the weather's nice—you can either sit on the fountain's edge and let preteens soak you with their splashings, or choose one of the benches scattered around the elaborately patterned terrace. The fountain itself was created in 1873 and named for the biblical pool in Jerusalem that was supposedly given healing powers by an angel. The four figures around Bethesda Fountain's base symbolize Temperance, Purity, Health, and Peace. Beyond the terrace stretches the Lake (*see* Loeb Boathouse, *below*), filled with drifting swans and amateur rowboat captains. *Mid-park at 72nd St.*

LOEB BOATHOUSE • At the Loeb Boathouse, on the eastern side of the park's 18-acre **Lake,** you can rent a dinghy (or the one authentic Venetian gondola) for $10 per hour (plus $30 deposit), or pedal off on a bicycle for $8–14 per hour. There's also an open-air café-bar that's packed with a crowd of tipsy professionals on summer evenings. *Mid-park at 74th St., near East Dr., tel. 212/517–2233 for boat rentals and café or 212/861–4137 for bike rental. Subway: 6 to E. 77th St. Rental shop open daily 9–6; café closed fall–spring.*

STRAWBERRY FIELDS • Also known as the International Garden of Peace, Strawberry Fields is a memorial to the late John Lennon, donated by wife Yoko Ono. Every year on December 8, Beatles fans gather around the star-shaped, black-and-white tiled IMAGINE mosaic set into the sidewalk to mourn Lennon's 1980 murder, which took place across the street at the Dakota apartments (*see box* Don't You Wish You Lived Here?, *below*), where he lived. The curving paths, well-tended shrubs, and orderly flower beds of this small garden are supposed to look a bit British. *W. 72nd St. near Central Park W.*

THE RAMBLE • Yearning for romantic, Gothic wilderness? The Ramble comprises 37 acres of narrow footpaths that snake through thickets of trees, wind around a tiny stream, and even lead to a secret cave. It's one of the best parts of the park to wander (or ramble) because you're absolutely, positively guaranteed not to encounter any Rollerbladers. The Ramble is particularly popular with bird-watchers—and among some of the city's gay men, who come here to do something besides looking for titmice and warblers. The **Urban Park Rangers** lead bird-watching tours here; call 212/360–1406 for more info. *Mid-park between 74th and 79th Sts.*

BELVEDERE CASTLE • What park would be complete without a fanciful turreted castle? The Belvedere's a mishmash of styles—Norman, Gothic, Moorish—and deliberately built small so that when it was viewed from across the nearby lake, the lake would seem bigger. Now that the trees have grown you can't see the lake at all. Since 1919 the castle has housed a U.S. Weather Bureau station—look for twirling meteorological instruments on top of its tower. Inside is a **visitor information bureau** and some geology exhibits. *Mid-park at 79th St., tel. 212/772–0210. Subway: B or C to W. 81st St. Open Tues.– Sun. 10–5 (shorter hrs in winter).*

CLEOPATRA'S NEEDLE • Over the centuries this sturdy relic has really racked up the mileage: It began life as a giant obelisk in Heliopolis, Egypt, around 1600 BC, was eventually carted off to Alexandria by the Romans in 12 BC, passed a little time hither and yon, and was ultimately presented to the city of New York by the khedive of Egypt on February 22, 1881. Ironically, a century in New York has done more to ravage the Needle than millennia of globe-trotting, and the hieroglyphics have sadly worn away to a *tabula rasa.* Thank Ra it wasn't the Rosetta Stone. *Mid-park at 81st St., behind Metropolitan Museum of Art.*

JACQUELINE KENNEDY ONASSIS RESERVOIR • This 106-acre reservoir (named for the former First Lady after her death in 1994) takes up most of the center of the park, from 86th to 97th streets. Around its perimeter is a 1.58-mi track popular with runners year-round. Even if you're not training for the New York Marathon, it's worth visiting for the stellar views of surrounding high-rises and the stirring sunsets. *Mid-park between 86th and 97th Sts.*

CONSERVATORY GARDEN • The formal, symmetrical Conservatory Garden (laid out during the Depression as a WPA project) is a nice contrast to the rustic wilderness of the rest of Central Park. It's a favorite with couples and mournful poets. The **Central Garden** is bordered by flowering crab-apple trees (beautiful in spring), and has a reflecting pool and wisteria arbor. The **North Garden,** built around a

THEY BUILT THIS CITY

FREDERICK LAW OLMSTED (1822–1903), a farmer from Staten Island, and CALVERT VAUX (1824–95), a young architect from England, first teamed up in 1853 to design Central Park. Together the dynamic landscape architects went on to create Morningside Park, Prospect Park, Eastern Parkway, and many others. Their designs tended to be naturalistic rather than formal, re-creating the look of the English countryside, for example, with rustic stone walls, wide lakes, and scattered groves of trees. Eventually, the partnership dissolved in 1872 as Olmsted became antagonistic toward city politicians he felt were cramping his style; he bitterly opposed city-mandated additions to his parks by McKim, Mead & White (see below). Insanity forced his retirement in 1895. Vaux continued and worked on the Metropolitan Museum of Art and American Museum of Natural History with architect Jacob Wrey Mould. As the years passed he became increasingly bitter over the lack of recognition for what he considered his greatest works—Central Park and Prospect Park—and drowned under mysterious circumstances.

Just about every landmark beaux arts and neo-Renaissance building in town dating from 1880 to 1915 was designed by the architecture firm of McKim, Mead & White. Most notably: the Tiffany showroom, the Plaza Hotel, the Harvard Club, the Brooklyn Museum, J. P. Morgan's private library (now the Pierpont Morgan Library), City Hall's Municipal Building, portions of the Metropolitan Museum of Art, and all of Columbia University. WILLIAM RUTHERFORD MEAD (1846–1928) had a fairly low profile, but STANFORD WHITE (1853–1906) and CHARLES MCKIM (1847–1909) led busy lives outside the firm. White, lover of Italian Renaissance design, was solo designer for the triumphal Washington Square arch, Striver's Row houses in Harlem, and the original Madison Square Garden. He met an ironic end at a party on the roof of the Garden when he was shot point-blank by one Harry K. Thaw. White had been having an affair with Thaw's showgirl wife since she was 16. Meanwhile, White's partner, Charles McKim, was regarded as the most talented and influential architect of his day; he designed many beautiful New York mansions but lived alone in a modest rented flat. He suffered a nervous breakdown when White was shot and died at the home of White's widow.

pleasant fountain, explodes with some 20,000 tulip blossoms in spring and 5,000 chrysanthemums in fall. The **South Garden,** dedicated to *The Secret Garden* author Frances Hodgson Burnett, offers 175 kinds of perennials marshaled into proper British rows. Those impressive wrought-iron gates you passed through to enter the garden from 5th Avenue once graced the mansion of Cornelius Vanderbilt II. *5th Ave. between E. 103rd and 106th Sts. Subway: 6 to E. 103rd St. Open daily 8 AM–dusk.*

HUDDLESTONE BRIDGE • If you're exploring the north end of the park, take a few minutes to look at Huddlestone Bridge, made from boulders weighing up to 100 tons. No mortar was used in its construction—instead, the sheer weight of the rocks "huddling together" keeps it from falling apart. Head southwest on one of the footpaths and you'll pass several small waterfalls before arriving at the **Pool,** a romantic spot surrounded by weeping willows and clusters of tall reeds. *Mid-park at 105th St., just south of Lasker Rink and Pool.*

HARLEM MEER AND THE CHARLES A. DANA DISCOVERY CENTER • First, before you ask: *Meer* is the Dutch word for lake. This particular meer has been recently spruced up and stocked with 50,000 bluegills, largemouth bass, and catfish, which you're allowed to catch and release (what would you do with a dead fish at your hotel anyway?). Pick up fishing poles and bait (free) at the **Charles A. Dana Discovery Center** (tel. 212/860–1370), disguised as a petite Swiss chalet; the center is closed Mondays. Just south of the meer is **McGowan's Pass,** through which American troops fled from the British on September 15, 1776, and returned victoriously at the end of the Revolutionary War led by General Henry Knox. *Near 5th Ave., between E. 106th and 110th Sts. Subway: 6 to E. 110th St.*

In the Early Dynasty gallery of the Egyptian wing, look for the Met's unofficial mascot, William: a turquoise-colored statuette of a chubby hippo.

BROOKLYN BRIDGE

"The complete work, when constructed in accordance with my designs, will not only be the greatest bridge in existence, but it will be the greatest engineering work on this continent, and of the age." So wrote John Augustus Roebling, the visionary architect, legendary engineer, metaphysical philosopher, fervid abolitionist, and unabashed egotist who practically willed the Brooklyn Bridge into existence in the mid-1800s. At a length of 6,016 ft, it was four times longer than the longest suspension bridge of its day. Its twin Gothic-arched towers rise 268 ft from the river below, while the roadway is supported by a web of human-size steel cables, hung from the towers and attached to block-long anchorages on either shore. From roadway to water is about 133 ft, high enough to allow the tallest ships to pass. Though it is hardly the longest suspension bridge in the world anymore, the Brooklyn Bridge is still one of New York's noblest landmarks, testimony to the 19th century's potent mix of ambition and technology.

John Roebling first conceived of the bridge on an icy winter's day in 1852, when the ferry he wanted to catch had as much chance of crossing the frozen East River as the proverbial snowball in hell. Roebling spent the next 30 years designing, raising money for, and building the bridge. Tragically, two years into construction, a falling timber crushed his foot, and the stubborn visionary died of gangrene a week later. Roebling's son Washington rose valiantly to the task, only to suffer extensive nerve damage during the underwater phase of construction and end up in a wheelchair. Ultimately, the job of foreman fell to another Roebling, Washington's wife. In 1883, under her supervision, the bridge was finally completed. The public was so captivated by the long struggle to build this mighty bridge that it was quickly crowned the "Eighth Wonder of the World."

A walk across the **Great Bridge promenade,** a wooden pedestrian walkway and bike path elevated slightly above the roadway, is a New York experience on par with the Statue of Liberty trip or the Empire State Building ascent. It's a 40-minute walk from Manhattan's civic center to the heart of residential Brooklyn Heights (*see* the Outer Boroughs, *below*). Most days the promenade is busy with camera-toting tourists and a variety of New Yorkers speeding by on foot, bike, or 'blades. (When it comes to bikes, "speeding" hardly does justice to how fast some cyclists zoom across the bridge, so *absolutely* obey the lane markings: pedestrians keep to the north half of the promenade, bicyclists to the south.) At dusk the views of Manhattan's twinkling skyline are a ravishing feast for even the most jaded been-there-done-thatters. A last note: It's fine to zip across on a bike after the sun goes down (provided you're equipped with lights and reflective gear), but if you're on foot, don't plan to linger up here—especially if you're alone. *Subway: 4, 5, or 6 to Brooklyn Bridge/City Hall (Manhattan); also A or C to High St./Brooklyn Bridge (Brooklyn).*

METROPOLITAN MUSEUM OF ART

The Met, as it's known to New Yorkers, is a gargantuan treasure trove of art from around the world. It's a collection to end all collections (not bad, considering we had a late start). In fact, it's not really a single museum at all, but instead a vast network of many museums all under one roof. In its permanent collections are nearly three million works of art, from a reconstructed Egyptian temple to delicate Han dynasty dishes, spanning time from the good old Paleolithic days right up to the present. At any given time, only a quarter of the Met's permanent collection is on display. This is hardly surprising, considering holdings include thousands of European paintings and drawings, an equal number of American paintings and statues, 4,000 medieval objects, a comparable group of musical instruments, and a million prints. Add to that more than 30 special exhibitions each year and you'll see why even longtime city residents answer evasively when asked if they've seen everything in this 1½-million-square-ft megamuseum.

Despite the size and breadth of its collection, the Met does have its detractors. Its reputation as a bastion of Eurocentric art was only slightly improved back in 1969, when oil magnate Nelson Rockefeller donated significant cash to improving the collections of art from Africa, Oceania, and the Americas. Lately, however, attempts to diversify the collections have been picking up speed. In early 1996, the new African Gallery opened, with a focus on sculpture from the Kingdom of Benin (Nigeria). The spring of 1997 was especially good for the Chinese art collection; the newly expanded galleries reopened just in time to display a tremendous gift of 11 paintings, including "The Riverbank," a 10th-century silk scroll that is one of the most important landscape paintings in the world. In 1998, the Met renewed its commitment to expand and enrich its Asian Art collection, creating the Arts of Korea Gallery—devoted to Korean painting, ceramics, sculpture, metalwork, and lacquerware spanning 1,500 years. Special exhibitions are also looking farther afield; shows planned for 2000 include collections of ancient Egyptian panel portraits and Chinese ornamental rocks. And, as with any time-honored institution, the Met has to fight the fuddy-duddy demon. While it's not going to invest in Jeffrey Koonz anytime soon, it did receive a quick transfusion in late 1995—a major gift of 20th-century art by the likes of Picasso, Modigliani, and Brancusi, not to mention the museum's first Juan Gris painting.

It's hard to believe that the whole thing began in 1870 at a building south of its present location with a modest 174 works of art. The Met moved to its current home along posh 5th Avenue, in Central Park, a decade later, and there it began to grow. The first permanent building was designed by architects Calvert Vaux and Jacob Wrey Mould; most of this has since been swallowed up by additions (if you look just inside the Robert Wood Johnson, Jr., Gallery you can see one of the original pointed Gothic archways). Some of New York's most noted architects have had a hand in the Met's expansion, including R. M. and R. H. Hunt, and McKim, Mead & White. Beginning in the '70s, the museum's separate buildings were unified by bridging the spaces between them with huge glass-and-grid walls and roofs. Unlike most things from that style-challenged decade, this has resulted in some of the museum's most exuberant spaces. Finally, the huge stone steps out front, which had for decades terrorized those wanting in youthful energy (and to some embodied the museum's attitude toward its public), were redesigned to include landings where climbers could stop for rest. These days you'll find the steps crowded with citizens from all over the world, resting their weary feet and watching cabs jockey on 5th Avenue.

The biggest mistake you can make at the Met is to try to see everything (or even most things) in one visit. You should really focus on two to four sections rather than attempting the whole shebang. Because of reduced funding and ongoing renovations, some galleries are closed on a rotating schedule; inquire at the Information Desk (*see below*) when you pick up your trusty museum map. *1000 5th Ave., at 82nd St., Upper East Side, tel. 212/879–5500. Subway: 4, 5, or 6 to E. 86th St. Open Sun. and Tues.–Thurs. 9:30–5:15, Fri.–Sat. 9:30–8:45.*

PRACTICALITIES

The $10 admission is only a suggested amount, so if you're really broke, you can pay less—do as your conscience tells you. Your admission here also entitles you to a free same-day visit to the Cloisters (*see* Museums and Galleries, *below*), the Met's annex for medieval art. But that's a whole lot of art to absorb in one day.

The museum's **Information Desk** is in the center of the Great Hall—you can't miss it. You'll want to pick up a Floor Plan (without this you'll never make it out alive) and the calendar of special programs. Ask about the scheduled walking tours or pick up a bulletin posted on one of the columns as you enter the museum; the tours are usually free with your museum admission. The **International Visitors Desk** (tel. 212/879–5500, ext. 2987), also in the Great Hall, assists those speaking Chinese, French, German, Italian, Japanese, or Spanish. For info on **services for visitors with disabilities,** call 212/535–7710 or TTY 212/570–3828.

There is also an **audio tour** (tel. 212/396–5089) focusing on the highlights of particular wings and galleries, as well as major special exhibitions. The tour is self-guided and unstructured—you can skip from work to work and room to room, learning about only the pieces that interest you. It's available in six languages and rents for $5 from the Audio Tour Desk in the Great Hall and at the entrance to selected exhibits.

Special exhibits scheduled for 2000 include: "Tilman Riemenschneider: Master Sculptor of the Late Middle Ages" (Feb.–May); notable acquisitions in the American Wing from 1980–1999 (Nov. 99–Nov. 2000); Walker Evans and African Art, 1935 (Feb.–Aug.); and paintings from the School of Paris (Mar.–Dec.). Lectures, films, and panel discussions take place in the **Grace Rainey Rogers** and **Uris Center** auditoriums on topics as diverse as the collections; for schedule info, call 212/570–3949. Classical music concerts are also regularly scheduled at the Met; *see* Music *in* Chapter 7.

COLLECTION HIGHLIGHTS

The **20th-Century Art** galleries (first and second floors) span everything from Grant Wood's *The Ride of Paul Revere* to totally abstract stuff like gigantic Clyfford Still canvases of black and red, and Ellsworth Kelly's *Spectrum V,* symmetrical rectangles in an array of colors spanning an entire wall. If you're into Jasper Johns, be on the lookout for *White Flag;* recently acquired by the museum, this is the first painting by the artist to enter the museum's collection. In the **Islamic Art** galleries (second floor) you'll find a reconstructed room from an Ottoman Empire upper-class home, complete with a gurgling fountain. Also check out the 16th-century Persian rugs and the exquisite 17th-century tile wall mosaic from the royal garden of Isfahan. Nearby are the **Ancient Near Eastern Art** galleries, where you'll see the famous Assyrian reliefs from the palace of Ashurnasirpal II. A narrow hallway is all that is devoted to **Drawings, Prints, and Photographs**; if you're interested in photography, you're better off heading to the Museum of Modern Art (*see below*).

Don't miss the Met's collection of vintage baseball cards, on display in the American Wing. They date from the late 1800s to the 1950s.

AMERICAN WING • The American Wing offers room after reconstructed room of early American interiors and some of the museum's best-known paintings. If you enter the wing from the European painting galleries, you'll find yourself in a huge glass-roofed atrium; there's an indoor terrace on the first floor level. Taking up an awful lot of wall space in Gallery 223 is Emanuel Leutze's *Washington Crossing the Delaware,* the size and noble aspect of which should stir a patriotic feeling or two...never mind the glaring historical inaccuracies.

If you like portraits, rooms 217 and 218 are right up your alley; you'll find oodles of portraits of wealthy 18th- and early 19th-century colonial families, among them a nonchalant and almost jovial portrait of George Washington by Charles Willson Peale and a bust of Benjamin Franklin by Frenchman Jean-Antoine Houdou. A couple of rooms are devoted to the artists of the Hudson River School; in Frederic Edwin Church's 1859 masterwork *The Heart of the Andes,* look for Church's signature "carved" into a tree. Winslow Homer is well represented; his 1866 work *Prisoners from the Front* makes for an interesting character study of a handful of Confederate POWs. Turn-of-the-century paintings range from the pistol-packing cowboys of Frederic Remington to the genteel beauties of John Singer Sargent portraits. You'll also find a room from one of Frank Lloyd Wright's Prairie-style homes. *1st and 2nd floors.*

EUROPEAN SCULPTURE AND DECORATIVE ARTS • This warren of rooms includes sculpture, glass, porcelain, and jewelry that date from the 16th to 20th centuries. There are also scores of reconstructed interiors, including an 18th-century French bedroom that would be at home in Versailles. If all the ormolu is getting to you, look for the plain, carved wooden door with a brass knocker—it's a French storefront from 1775, complete with a small hanging sign. The number and shape of these galleries make it easy to get lost; if you're waking up a guard for directions, ask about the Carroll and Milton Petrie European Sculpture Court while you're at it. The court makes a great rest stop (you can buy a drink near the windows onto the park), and you can see part of the museum's original 1888 carriage entrance facade. *1st floor.*

COSTUME INSTITUTE • One floor below the Great Hall, you'll find the Costume Institute, a relatively small suite of rooms that exhibits a rotating array of items from the Met's huge collection of fashions—everything from 19th-century royal wedding gowns to see-through plastic dresses. *Ground floor.*

LEHMAN PAVILION • The **Robert Lehman Collection** was one of the Met's greatest acquisition coups; the mind-bogglingly large and diverse selection covers 18th-century French furniture, Renaissance paintings, a smattering of Renoirs, even a stained-glass dome from Lehman's home. However, the donation came with a hefty string attached—Lehman insisted the collection be housed together. As the pavilion shows, he got his way; the works are arranged around a skylit courtyard. At the center of the courtyard is a 15th-century Florentine fountain with an unhappy provenance: It was commissioned by a merchant who lost his life trying to snuff out a rival family, and his unhappy heirs ended up hawking it to pay the bills. *1st and ground floors.*

THE EGYPTIAN WING • The Met owns one of the most comprehensive collections of Egyptian Art outside Cairo, with objects from every facet and era of Egyptian life: crumbly yellow household linens, stone tools dating back some 6,000 years, an enormous walk-in tomb dating from 2415–2375 BC, and even a mummified gazelle that was once the pet of a royal court singer. It may be swamped with schoolkids, but it's also got scads of helpful information, from historical and geographical background to hieroglyph translations. Adjacent to the Egyptian Collection is the magnificent **Temple of Dendur,** an ancient temple donated by the Egyptian government. The whole shebang was transported here block by giant block. *1st floor.*

PRIMITIVE ART • In the Michael C. Rockefeller Wing you'll find the somewhat sparse galleries devoted to the **Arts of Africa, Oceania, and the Americas.** The sculptures, ritual objects, and everyday artifacts span 3,000 years. Michael Rockefeller had a special interest in the Asmat people of New Guinea, hence the respectively rich numbers of their artifacts, including shaggy woven body masks and a canoe that's almost 50 ft long. The Jan Mitchell Treasury gallery lures people in with shining gold masks and ornaments from Central and South America. *1st floor.*

ARMS AND ARMOR • The Arms and Armor galleries hold some impressive European armor—for both men and their horses. The decoration of both the weapons and armor is so finely worked it can be hard to keep their grisly purpose in mind. (It brings a whole new meaning to the phrase "going out in style.") To one side of the main hall is a wild collection of Japanese instruments of destruction; to the other are swords, shields, and early guns, including an original Colt percussion revolver (check out the portrait of George Washington on the cartridge cylinder). *1st floor.*

MEDIEVAL ART • The galleries housing art from the Dark Ages are dimly lit, appropriately enough, and home to a towering wrought-iron choir screen from Spain's Cathedral of Valladolid. (The annual museum Christmas tree and crèche are put up in front of the screen.) In the cavernous sculpture hall, built to resemble a church, there's a strikingly natural *Madonna and Child*; the baby is getting his mother's attention by playing with the pages of the book on her lap. *1st floor.*

GUBBIO STUDIOLO • Between the medieval art galleries and the arms and armor exhibit is this phenomenal little room, opened in May 1996 after almost a decade of restoration. One of only two surviving 15th-century *studioli* (private studies), this was originally made for the duke of Urbino. Using tiny pieces of differently colored wood, the artist covered the walls with trompe-l'oeil benches, shelves, and latticed doors; in the "cupboards" are books, musical instruments, even the count's coat of arms. Tear your eyes away from this amazing feat of perspective and look at the polychrome carved ceiling too. *1st floor.*

GREEK AND ROMAN ART • The Greek and Roman art galleries house dazzling displays of gold and silver tableware, ceremonial vessels, and Grecian urns. Take a walk through the new and improved 140-foot-long Greek central gallery; formerly a dark and dreary place, the gallery is illuminated by enormous skylights, and its once haphazardly displayed works are now artfully arranged. Don't miss the wonderful series of Roman portrait busts, known for their striking realism, and a display case explaining the uses for various Attic vases. *1st and 2nd floors.*

ASIAN ART GALLERIES • If you enter the Asian Art wing from the Great Hall Balcony, head straight to the newly expanded, much lauded Chinese art galleries. Right up front you'll see Dong Yuan's monumental landscape, *The Riverbank*, along with other silk scrolls and fans covered with didactic illustrations, bird-and-flower paintings, and poetry (almost always translated). The other works aren't too shabby either—dazzling jade, textile, and metal work from the eighth through the 20th century. The smooth mahogany columns and soft light—thank the renovation team—could almost make you forget you're in the Met. Take an uptight friend up to the third floor rooms and watch him swoon over the infinitesimally detailed lacquer carvings. An unassuming round entryway leads to the Zen-like peace of the Astor Court, modeled on the 16th-century Garden of the Master of the Fishing Nets in Soochow. This in turn leads to the Ming Scholar's Retreat, whose lattices, columns, and roof are all held together by joinery (look ma, no nails!). The exhibits in the Japanese art galleries rotate more frequently than those in the Chinese rooms, but you could see a beautifully spare, re-created *shoin* (study) or a turn-of-the-century sumo wrestler's ceremonial outfit. And don't miss the new Arts of Korea Gallery, sandwiched between the Chinese and South Asian galleries. *2nd floor.*

EUROPEAN PAINTINGS • Straight ahead as you come up the main staircase are the European paintings (pre–19th century, that is). These galleries necessarily cover a lot of art-historical ground, including some crisp works by Jacques-Louis David, the mercilessly pink cheeks done by Rococo pets Fragonard and Boucher, a few clear-as-a-bell portraits by Hans Holbein the Younger, and the violently lit paintings of El Greco. There are some mesmerizing canvases by Goya, such as *Majas on a Balcony* (who *are* those shady characters in the background?). Sixteenth-century Italian painters are headed by Veronese, Titian, and Bronzino (whose subject in *Portrait of a Young Man* could surely stare down the haughtiest member of New York society). Pieces by Flemish painter Peter Paul Rubens include a portrait of the artist, his second wife, and one of their children—a proverbial May–December marriage, he was 53, she 16. Velázquez's portrait, *Juan de Pareja,* was one of the museum's greatest acquisitions; ever since its creation, it's been compared to truth itself. Galleries 11–15 are devoted to Dutch painters such as Johannes Vermeer, Frans Hals, and Gerard Ter Borch—and there are 19 (count 'em, 19) Rembrandts. *2nd floor.*

MUSICAL INSTRUMENTS • This collection, featuring an extraordinary array of world instruments, is a must-see, even if you failed fifth-grade music class. There are curious (read: obsolete, and often unpronounceable) instruments at every turn: ophicleides, shawms, African lamellaphones, a clavicytherium, a double virginal, and Polynesian courtship instruments. There's even a barrel organ (*sans* monkey). *2nd floor.*

The MoMA continues to grapple with questions of relevancy and the true meaning of "modern art" as many of its original pieces turn 100 years old.

19TH-CENTURY EUROPEAN PAINTINGS AND SCULPTURE • These beaux arts galleries are one of the glories of New York. They also draw the biggest crowds. The long sculpture hall has an impressive number of Rodin works. Branching off of this are the galleries where you'll find painting after world-famous painting by Corot, Courbet, Delacroix, Millet, Turner, Pissarro, Degas, Gauguin, Seurat, and many others. There are several flushed-looking Renoirs, some creamy-skinned portraits by Manet, and more than half-a-dozen works by van Gogh, including a double-sided piece (on one side is a self-portrait, on the other a study of a woman peeling potatoes). In the room devoted to Cézanne you can catch hints of the cubist theory. And there's the whole gamut of Monet, from haystacks to Rouen Cathedral to lilypond. During the latter half of every year some of the galleries showcase *TV Guide*–magnate Walter Annenberg's collection of impressionist and postimpressionist masterpieces; upon Annenberg's death the installation becomes permanent. *2nd floor.*

SCULPTURE GARDEN • If you've made it this far, then you owe it to yourself to visit the **Iris and B. Gerald Cantor Roof Garden,** generally open May through October. From atop the museum, you'll have a millionaire's view of Central Park.

MUSEUM OF MODERN ART (MOMA)

The Museum of Modern Art, or MoMA, has long been the world's premier showcase for modern art. Opening on the heels of the 1929 stock-market crash, the museum's first exhibition, *Cézanne, Gauguin, Seurat, van Gogh,* was revolutionary—those now-famous artists were, at the time, unknowns in the United States, and their postimpressionist style had few admirers. Fortunately, scholar and founding director Alfred H. Barr, Jr.'s aesthetic agenda found an enthusiastic audience in New York City, and as the collections grew the museum expanded several times. It moved to its current location in 1939, and its gallery space was doubled in 1984. In 1997, the museum announced plans for a major overhaul, to be designed by Yoshio Taniguchi. The reconfiguration will incorporate the site of the former Dorset Hotel at 30 West 54th Street and will provide the MoMA with significantly more exhibition space by 2001. Currently, the museum is able to show only a fraction of its vast collection at any given time—but what a fraction it is. Among its pivotal permanent works are several huge canvases of Monet's *Water Lilies,* and van Gogh's *Starry Night.* Drawings, prints, books, film, video, and design are also well represented. And you'll find a few surprises, like a helicopter, lamps, and models of landmarks in modern architecture such as Frank Lloyd Wright's "Falling Water." Photography, too, has long been richly acknowledged by the MoMA, well before it acquired fine-art status, and its collection is one of the best around—for instance, it has the only complete set of *Untitled Film Stills* by Cindy Sherman. In fall 1999 the museum launched *MoMA2000,* an 18-month series of exhibitions that explores modern art from a variety of perspectives. During this time, many of the Museum's best known works will be incorporated into the show, but the exhibition will *not*, as the MoMA is quick to point out, be a greatest hits sort of display. So come with an open mind, and don't pin all your hopes on seeing one particular piece of work. *11 W. 53rd St., near 5th Ave., Midtown, tel. 212/708–9480. Subway: E or F to 5th Ave. Admission $8.50 (pay what you wish Fri. 4:30–8:30). Open Sat.–Tues. and Thurs. 10:30–6, Fri. 10:30–8:30.*

PRACTICALITIES

Brown bag lunch lectures (tel. 212/708–9795 or 212/333–1117) happen Tuesday and Thursday from 12:30 to 1:15; pay the $5 and learn while you eat. **Gallery talks** are conducted daily and are free with admission. Other programs include **Conversations with Contemporary Artists** (Friday at 6:30, entrance $5, free for students) and **Special Exhibition Programs**; for more information call 212/708–9795 or 212/708–9798. **MoMA INFORM** ($4) self-guided audio tours can be used for the painting and sculpture collections. Any galleries may be temporarily closed while new or changing exhibitions are installed.

COLLECTION HIGHLIGHTS

LOWER LEVEL/THEATER LEVEL • The **René d'Harnoncourt Galleries** and the **Theater Gallery** house temporary exhibitions. The **Roy and Niuta Titus Theaters** 1 and 2 are among the finest venues in the city for foreign, independent, and classic films. Tickets (free) are distributed in the main lobby; for more info, *see* Movies and Video *in* Chapter 7.

GROUND FLOOR • Besides the information desk, checkroom, and bookstore, you'll find two galleries showing temporary exhibitions on the ground floor: the **International Council Galleries** and the small **Projects Gallery**. **Jazz at the MoMA** is live and free on Friday evenings from September through May. Groups play in the **Garden Café** where decent cafeteria food ($3.50–$9.50) is served in a pleasant setting, while **Sette MoMA** (tel. 212/708–9710) serves up really pricey but excellent and authentic Italian food and usually requires reservations. Outside is the serene **Abby Aldrich Rockefeller Sculpture Garden**; this wonderful courtyard was planned by Philip Johnson to be an outdoor "room," with trees, fountains, pools, and (of course) sculpture. Juilliard Music School students perform free concerts in the garden during summer; for more info *see* Music *in* Chapter 7.

UPPER FLOORS • For 18 months, from the fall of 1999 through the winter of 2001, the three upper floors of the MoMA will be completely taken over by *MoMA2000,* an innovative attempt to explore three distinct historical periods in modern art (1880–1920, 1920–1960, and 1960–2000), using works culled from the Museum's extensive collection.

MANHATTAN NEIGHBORHOODS

Regardless of who you are or what you're after, New York City has a neighborhood to fulfill your every whim. Virtually all of the major "touristy" sights are in **Midtown,** including the Theater District, Rockefeller Center, and Times Square. If museums are what you want, the **Upper East Side's** Museum Mile has more than enough for even the most energetic art lover, while the **Upper West Side,** home to Lincoln Center, holds all the cards when it comes to the performing arts. If you're looking for a little boho culture, you might want to spend your time in the bar- and café-crowded **East Village** or **Chelsea.** There's great people-watching in the **West Village,** home to New York University students, the city's gay community, and a bunch of aging Beat poets. **SoHo** and **TriBeCa** have long been the haunts of artists and the people who profit from them, and both are packed with art galleries. For a vicarious taste of the good (or at least expensive) life, head to the ritzy blocks of **Gramercy, Union Square,** and up-and-coming **Flatiron District.** The **Lower East Side, Harlem, Little Italy,** and **Chinatown** are miniature cities in their own right, having been settled by Jewish, African, Italian, and Asian immigrants respectively. If you're interested in New York's legal and financial institutions, make your way to **Lower Manhattan.**

UPPER WEST SIDE

If you can believe it, the Upper West Side was actually a bunch of small villages until the late 1860s, an area the Dutch referred to as Bloemendael (Vale of Flowers). In those days wealthy islanders would take sleigh and carriage trips to Bloemendael and crash for the night in mansions converted into guest inns.

Broadway

Columbia
University

HARLEM

*Marcus Garvey
Park*

*Randall's
Island*

W.116th St.

E.116th St.

**MORNINGSIDE
HEIGHTS**

*Morningside
Park*

E.110th St.

Riverside Dr.

Amsterdam Ave.

*Ward's
Island*

Henry Hudson Pkwy.

**Museum
Mile**

**UPPER
WEST SIDE**

Central Park West

Central Park

**UPPER
EAST SIDE**

W.86th St.

E.86th St.

Hudson River

Columbus Ave.

**Metropolitan
Museum of Art**

E.79th St.

**Museum of
Natural History**

E.72nd St.

West End Ave.

Park Ave.

Lexington Ave.

QUEENS

W.72nd St.

E.65th St.

FDR Dr.

Roosevelt Island

**Lincoln
Center**

E.59th St.

Eleventh Ave.

Tenth Ave.

Ninth Ave.

Amsterdam Ave.

Fifth Ave.

**Queensboro
Bridge**

W.57th St.

E.57th St.

**Rockefeller
Center**

**Museum of
Modern Art**

**THEATER
DISTRICT**

**Times
Square**

**Grand
Central
Terminal**

**United
Nations**

W.42nd St.

E.42nd St.

**Queens-Midtown
Tunnel**

Lincoln Tunnel

**Port Authority
Bus Terminal**

MIDTOWN

Madison Ave.

Third Ave.

Second Ave.

First Ave.

**HELL'S
KITCHEN**

W.34th St.

**Madison
Square Garden**

**Empire
State
Building**

Eighth Avenue

Seventh

Ave. of the Americas

Madison
Sq.

**MURRAY
HILL**

W.23rd St.

CHELSEA

E.23rd St.

GRAMERCY

Broadway

W.14th St.

Union
Sq.

East River

E.14th St.

Tompkins
Sq.

**GREENWICH
VILLAGE**

Washington
Sq.

**EAST
VILLAGE**

**New York
University**

E. Houston St.

West Side Hwy.

W. Houston St.

SOHO

**LITTLE
ITALY**

Williamsburg Bridge

Canal St.

**LOWER
EAST SIDE**

Holland Tunnel

Hudson River

**TRI-
BECA**

**CHINA-
TOWN**

Manhattan Bridge

West St.

Broadway

Chambers St.

W. St.

**Civic
Center**

Wall Street

Brooklyn Bridge

**NEW
JERSEY**

**World Trade
Center**

**South Street
Seaport**

**LOWER
MANHATTAN**

BROOKLYN

N

0   440 yards

TO
STATUE OF LIBERTY
AND ELLIS ISLAND

*Battery
Park*

Brooklyn-Battery
Tunnel

0   400 meters

The main thoroughfare was tree-lined Bloomingdale Road, which connected "urban" Manhattan (that is, everything below 23rd Street) to Bloomingdale Village (around 114th Street). Though Central Park West quickly developed into a fashionable address, many of the area's pig farms and slaughterhouses to the west were converted into low-income apartments. By the end of World War II, the area west of Broadway was a slum ridden with drugs and prostitution. The government poured tons of money into building large plots of low-rent housing during the 1950s and '60s, but it wasn't until the building of Lincoln Center (see below) and the Fordham University campus that the area cleaned up its act. Today, famous folk like Madonna, Yoko Ono, Barbra Streisand, Paul Simon, John MacEnroe, and Liam Neeson live in the Upper West's giant luxury apartment buildings. Less hyped are the methadone clinics and soup kitchens between 90th and 110th streets.

In an attempt to confuse you, some streets change their name at 59th Street, the southern boundary of the neighborhood: 8th Avenue becomes **Central Park West,** 9th Avenue becomes **Amsterdam Avenue,** 10th Avenue becomes **Columbus Avenue,** and 11th Avenue becomes **West End Avenue.** The main drag on the Upper West Side is **Broadway,** and the main cross streets are 72nd, 79th, 86th, and 96th streets. Amsterdam, Columbus, and Broadway are crammed with funky bars, restaurants, and boutiques. Near **Riverside Park** (see Parks and Gardens, below), there's little action or excitement on the primarily residential streets of West End Avenue and Riverside Drive.

COLUMBUS CIRCLE

At all hours of the day and night, traffic zooms around Columbus Circle, where West 59th Street, Broadway, Central Park West, and 8th Avenue intersect. At all hours of the day and night, traffic zooms around Columbus Circle, where West 59th Street, Broadway, Central Park West, and 8th Avenue intersect, acting as a sort of gateway from Midtown to the Upper West Side. At the center of the circle (atop a marble pillar, gift of the city's Italian Americans) stands an 1894 sculpture of Mr. Round Earth himself, Christopher Columbus. Speaking of the earth, at the north end of the circle, thanks to Donald Trump, there's now a miniature chrome, much-tackier rendition of the 380-ton globe built for the 1939 World's Fair in Queens. Subway: A, B, C, D, 1, or 9 to W. 59th St./Columbus Circle.

BROADWAY

Broadway is home to one of the city's greatest food shrines—namely **Zabar's** (see Markets and Specialty Shops in Chapter 4), which stocks everything from reasonably priced deli items to expensive Belgian chocolates. It's always packed with New Yorkers who shop like they're stocking up for Armageddon. The massive **Sony IMAX Theater** (1998 Broadway, between W. 67th and 68th Sts., tel. 212/336–5000) is a ten-plex movie theater and "urban entertainment center" where you can see 3-D movies on eight-story-high screens (with the aid of heavy plastic viewing helmets), or movies of the usual 2-D variety.

A few "parks" along Broadway offer benches where you can munch sandwiches and rubberneck at careening taxis: Across from Lincoln Center, **Dante Park** is a tiny triangle named for the Italian poet; **Sherman Square** (south of W. 72nd St. subway station) is a tiny triangle named for the Civil War general; **Verdi Square** (north of W. 72nd St. subway station) is a tiny triangle named for the Italian opera composer—but was better known as "Needle Park" during the height of its popularity with drug dealers in the '70s. You're better off heading a few blocks east to Central Park or west to Riverside Park.

COLUMBUS AVENUE

Columbus Avenue, once just a street where residents of Central Park West stopped to pick up a few pints of Haagen-Däzs, has blossomed in the last decade as a tony stretch of cafés, boutiques, and restaurants. Watch for your favorite soap star or news anchor from the sidewalk facing the headquarters of the **American Broadcasting Company (ABC)** (56 W. 66th St., between Columbus Ave. and Central Park W); for info on getting tickets to tapings of some of its TV shows, see box Your Own 15 Minutes of Fame, below. Nearby are two museums: the **Museum of American Folk Art** and the mammoth **American Museum of Natural History** (for both, see Museums and Galleries, below), which has over 36 million artifacts, including a newly renovated dinosaur exhibit on the cutting edge of exhibition design. If you're around on a Sunday, check out the flea market/greenmarket on the corner of West 77th Street and Columbus Avenue.

CENTRAL PARK WEST

The real Central Park West has very little to do with that soapy, sleazy, failed Fox TV series Central Park West. It's basically just a quiet residential street bordering Central Park, where multimillionaires raise their families in peace and quiet. Besides the famous **Dakota** (see box Don't You Wish You Lived Here?, below),

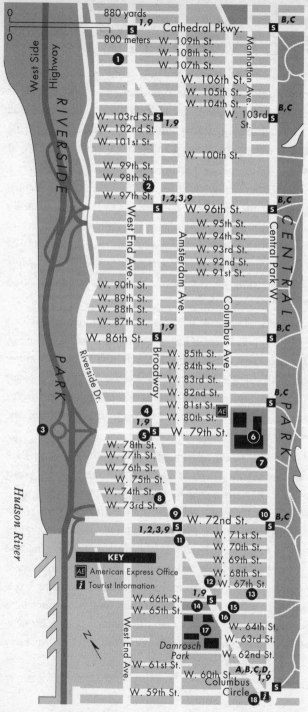

American
Broadcasting
Company (ABC), 13

American Museum
of Natural History/
Hayden
Planetarium, 6

The Ansonia, 8

Apthorp
Apartments, 5

Boat Basin, 3

The Dakota, 10

Dante Park, 16

Julliard School, 14

Lincoln Center for
the Performing
Arts, 17

Lotus Garden, 2

Museum of
American Folk
Art, 15

New-York Historical
Society, 7

New York
Convention and
Visitors Bureau, 18

Nicholas Roerich
Museum, 1

Sherman
Square, 11

Sony IMAX
Theater, 12

Verdi Square, 9

Zabar's, 4

Cathedral Pkwy.
W. 109th St.
W. 108th St.
W. 107th St.
W. 106th St.
W. 105th St.
W. 104th St.
W. 103rd St.
W. 103rd St.
W. 102nd St.
W. 101st St.
W. 100th St.
W. 99th St.
W. 98th St.
W. 97th St.
W. 96th St.
W. 95th St.
W. 94th St.
W. 93rd St.
W. 92nd St.
W. 91st St.
W. 90th St.
W. 89th St.
W. 88th St.
W. 87th St.
W. 86th St.
W. 85th St.
W. 84th St.
W. 83rd St.
W. 82nd St.
W. 81st St.
W. 80th St.
W. 79th St.
W. 78th St.
W. 77th St.
W. 76th St.
W. 75th St.
W. 74th St.
W. 73rd St.
W. 72nd St.
W. 71st St.
W. 70th St.
W. 69th St.
W. 68th St.
W. 67th St.
W. 66th St.
W. 65th St.
W. 64th St.
W. 63rd St.
W. 62nd St.
W. 61st St.
W. 60th St.
W. 59th St.

West Side Highway
RIVERSIDE PARK
Hudson River
West End Ave.
Riverside Dr.
Broadway
Amsterdam Ave.
Columbus Ave.
Central Park W.
Manhattan Ave.
CENTRAL PARK
Damrosch Park
Columbus Circle

880 yards
800 meters

KEY
AE American Express Office
i Tourist Information

49

DON'T YOU WISH
YOU LIVED HERE?

For the last century or so, the Upper West Side has competed with the Upper East Side for that rather limited pool of New Yorkers able to afford apartments equipped with live-in maid's quarters, grand ballrooms, and wall-to-wall priceless antiques. Although recently it was dubbed the Gold Coast, satisfying every Westsider's one-up competitive streak with the always posh East Side. A few of the West's best:

The Ansonia. This beaux arts beauty, built in 1904, has turrets, ornamented balconies, and rooftop gargoyles; live seals once played in the entrance hall's enormous fountain. Soundproof walls have made it especially attractive to musicians, like Enrico Caruso, Igor Stravinsky, and Arturo Toscanini, as well as theater producer Florenz Ziegfeld and writer Theodore Dreiser. More recently it served as the setting for the movie Single White Female. 2108 Broadway, between W. 73rd and 74th Sts.

The Apthorp Apartments. Designed to look like a pumped-up Italian Renaissance palazzo, this giant complex has shown up in a half-dozen films, including The Cotton Club and The Money Pit. It was built in 1908 by major New York landowner William Waldorf Astor (think Astor Place and Waldorf Astoria Hotel). New Yorkers in the know envy its rent-controlled apartments whereby enormous spaces are still renting for 1920s prices. 2101–2119 Broadway, between W. 78th and 79th Sts.

The Dakota. Most famous of all the apartment buildings along Central Park West is the Dakota. Squint at it and it looks like a dark, spooky castle (although, slightly less so since its incredible cleaning a couple of years ago). The design is by Henry Hardenbergh, who later did the famous Plaza Hotel; Singer sewing-machine heir Edward S. Clark ponied up the cash. When it was finished in 1884 it was so far uptown that it was jokingly described as being "out in the Dakotas." Ha, ha, ha—it rented anyway. A 10-room apartment originally cost $250 per month, which included service by the building's 150-person staff. In December 1980 resident John Lennon was fatally shot by a deranged fan on the sidewalk outside. Yoko Ono still keeps an apartment here, and Lennon is memorialized across the street in Central Park's Strawberry Fields. 1 W. 72nd St., at Central Park W.

there's an abundance of stately apartment buildings dating back to the late 19th century. Also here is the **New-York Historical Society** (*see* Museums and Galleries, *below*).

LINCOLN CENTER FOR THE PERFORMING ARTS

Lincoln Center, the largest performing arts center in the United States, is the year-round home for ballet, opera, musical, and drama performances of all kinds—some are even free. When it was conceived of in the late 1950s to meet "some of the needs of an anxious age," the idea of a single city center for the arts was considered pretty radical; neighbors protested the construction of the $165-million complex as disruptive, while the literati pronounced its design boring and limited. At its completion in the mid-'60s a critic for the *New York Times* sniffed that the halls "are lushly decorated, conservative structures that the public finds pleasing and most professionals consider a failure of nerve, imagination, and talent." Nonetheless, it's responsible for transforming the Upper West Side from urban ghetto to gourmet ghetto. For the complete scoop, consider one of the daily hour-long guided tours ($8.25) led by excitable Carol Channing look-alikes. For more info on various Lincoln Center activities, *see* Walter Reade Theater, and just about everything in Chapter 7. *W. 62nd to 66th Sts. between Columbus and Amsterdam Aves., tel. 212/546–2656. Subway: 1 or 9 to W. 66th St./Lincoln Center.*

Stand on Columbus Avenue, facing the central court with its huge fountain (where, incidentally, Cher and Nicolas Cage cavorted in *Moonstruck*). The three concert halls on this plaza are all made of pale travertine marble. To your left is the **New York State Theater** (tel. 212/870–5570), home to the New York City Ballet and the New York City Opera. The interior, designed to look like a jewel box, is covered in red plush with diamondlike light fixtures. In the lobby is a $20-million Jasper Johns creation, *Numbers.* Straight ahead, at the rear of the plaza, is the grand **Metropolitan Opera House** (tel. 212/362–6000), where the Metropolitan Opera and American Ballet Theatre perform. Its crystal chandeliers were a gift of the Austrian government; the brilliantly colored tapestries seen through the windows are by Marc Chagall. To your right, abstract bronze sculptures distinguish **Avery Fisher Hall** (tel. 212/875–5030), host to the New York Philharmonic Orchestra. The hall was originally plagued with sound problems; technicians struggled with bizarre makeshift solutions like hanging giant sheets of metal around the stage. In 1976 stereo-maker and philanthropist Avery Fisher donated a large sum and the problem was fixed for good.

On Thanksgiving eve, thousands of New Yorkers crowd the blocks around the American Museum of Natural History to watch giant balloons (now slightly less gargantuan due to a recent windy mishap) like Bart Simpson and the Cat in the Hat being inflated for the annual Macy's Thanksgiving Day parade.

Wander through the plaza, then head left past the Opera House into **Damrosch Park,** where summer open-air festivals like "Mostly Mozart" are often accompanied by free concerts at the Guggenheim Bandshell. Walk right from the plaza, between the Opera House and Avery Fisher, and you'll come to the North Plaza and a reflecting pool with a massive reclining sculpture by Henry Moore. To the rear is the **Library and Museum of the Performing Arts,** scheduled to reopen after renovation in the spring of 2000. Visitors can listen to any of their 50,000 records and tapes, or check out its four galleries. Next to the library is the **Vivian Beaumont Theater,** officially considered a Broadway house. Below it is the smaller **Mitzi E. Newhouse Theater,** where many award-winning plays have originated.

An overpass leads from the North Plaza across 65th Street to the world-renowned music and theater school, **The Juilliard School** (tel. 212/769–7406), alma mater of Robin Williams, Christopher Reeve, Itzhak Perlman, and other famous folk far too numerous to mention. There's usually something going on at its theater and recital hall. To the left is Lincoln Center's newest venue, the **Walter Reade Theater** (tel. 212/875–5600), screening avant-garde films. Take the elevator down to street level to find **Alice Tully Hall** (tel. 212/875–5050), home to the Chamber Music Society (tel. 212/875–5788) and the New York Film Festival.

COLUMBIA UNIVERSITY AND MORNINGSIDE HEIGHTS

The neighborhood of **Morningside Heights** covers the highest hill in Manhattan. To the east, Harlem sprawls below you; to the west is **Riverside Park** (*see* Parks and Gardens, *below*) and the mighty Hudson River. These days, the neighborhood is 99% geared toward serving the students of Columbia Uni-

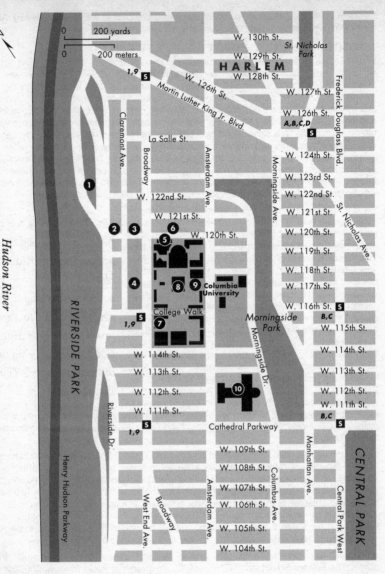

COLUMBIA UNIVERSITY AND MORNINGSIDE HEIGHTS

Hudson River

W. 130th St.
W. 129th St.
St. Nicholas Park
HARLEM
W. 128th St.
W. 127th St.
W. 126th St.
W. 126th St.
A,B,C,D S
W. 124th St.
W. 123rd St.
W. 122nd St.
W. 121st St.
W. 120th St.
W. 119th St.
W. 118th St.
W. 117th St.
W. 116th St. S
B,C
W. 115th St.
W. 114th St.
W. 113th St.
W. 112th St.
W. 111th St.
B,C S
Cathedral Parkway
W. 109th St.
W. 108th St.
W. 107th St.
W. 106th St.
W. 105th St.
W. 104th St.

W. 126th St.
Martin Luther King Jr. Blvd.

1,9 S

La Salle St.
W. 122nd St.
W. 121st St.
W. 120th St.

Claremont Ave.
Broadway
Amsterdam Ave.
Morningside Ave.
Frederick Douglass Blvd.
St. Nicholas Ave.

College Walk
Morningside Park
Morningside Dr.

1,9 S

W. 114th St.
W. 113th St.
W. 112th St.
W. 111th St.

1,9 S

Columbia University

RIVERSIDE PARK
Riverside Dr.
Henry Hudson Parkway
West End Ave.
Broadway
Amsterdam Ave.
Columbus Ave.
Manhattan Ave.
Central Park West

CENTRAL PARK

0 — 200 yards
0 — 200 meters

Columbia University
Barnard College, **4**
Low Memorial
Library, **8**
Pupin Hall, **5**
St. Paul's Chapel, **9**
School of
Journalism, **7**
Teachers College, **6**

Morningside Heights
Cathedral of St.
John the Divine, **10**
Grant's Tomb, **1**
Manhattan School
of Music, **3**
Riverside Church, **2**

versity. The area's main thoroughfares—Broadway and Amsterdam Avenue—are more a conglomeration of résumé services, textbook exchanges, and all-night diners than any kind of community. But before it became a college town, Morningside Heights was the sight of a pivotal victory (1776) for General Washington's forces during the American Revolution, in a buckwheat field since replaced by the all-women Barnard College (*see* Columbia University, *below*).

Besides Columbia University, several theological institutions are based here, as well as the respected **Manhattan School of Music** (*see* Music *in* Chapter 7). Cut into the steep gorge beneath the Morningside cliffs is **Morningside Park** (Morningside Dr. between W. 110th and 123rd Sts.), an overgrown and littered lot that was once a prime piece of greenery designed by Central Park's Frederick Law Olmsted and Calvert Vaux.

COLUMBIA UNIVERSITY

Founded by British royal charter in 1754 as King's College (the name changed after the Revolutionary War), Columbia University is the fifth-oldest institution of higher learning in the United States and the oldest in New York state. It's also wealthy, private, and a member of the Ivy League. Their only blight is their football team. Original alumni include John Jay, the first Chief Justice of the Supreme Court, and Alexander Hamilton, the first Secretary of the Treasury. The university's current campus was designed by McKim, Mead & White (*see box* They Built This City, *above*) and completed in 1897. Yes, its neoclassical and Renaissance-style buildings are covered with ivy, as you'd expect; they've also got copper roofs, used specifically because they'd turn green with oxidation over the years and create the illusion of vegetation (grass being fairly sparse then, as now). The university's underground tunnel system—third-largest in the world, after the Kremlin and the Massachusetts Institute of Technology—was closed indefinitely, due to "mischievous goings-on."

The ornate stone carvings on the facade of St. John the Divine feature the usual saints and biblical scenes, plus a few modern details—like a tiny Manhattan skyline.

Start your exploration of Columbia in the central quad at the **Low Memorial Library.** Outside, it's styled to look like the Greek Parthenon; inside is the spectacularly domed, templelike Reading Room. At the visitors center (Room 213, tel. 212/854-4900) you can pick up maps, or hook up with one of the free, student-led campus tours, given at 11 AM and 2 PM daily. Low's steps, presided over by the statue *Alma Mater* (designed by Daniel Chester French, who also did the statue of Abraham Lincoln in Washington, D.C.'s Lincoln Memorial), were a rallying point for students during the riots of '68. East of the library is the exquisite Byzantine-style **St. Paul's Chapel,** with a student-run art gallery (tel. 212/854-1953) on the ground level. Friday and Saturday nights the gallery hosts poetry readings and musical performances. At the north edge of campus is **Pupin Hall,** where the world's first successful splitting of a uranium atom took place on January 22, 1939—launching the Manhattan Project and ultimately leading to the development of the atom bomb. The university's renowned **School of Journalism,** founded by Joseph Pulitzer, holds classes in the building just south of the campus's west gates.

Across Broadway from Columbia is its sister institution, **Barnard College,** established in 1889. One of the former Seven Sisters of women's colleges, Barnard has steadfastly remained a single-sex institution and maintained its independence from Columbia, although its students can take classes there. Follow Broadway north to 120th Street, where you'll see the redbrick Victorian building of Columbia's **Teachers College,** founded in 1887 and today still the world's largest graduate school in the field of education.

CATHEDRAL OF ST. JOHN THE DIVINE

Someday, the Cathedral of St. John the Divine will be the largest cathedral in the world. But first they have to finish it: Construction has been off and on since 1892. Still unbuilt are three towers, the transept, and a "bioshelter," a plant-filled skylight that will create the effect of stained glass. What is done is the mammoth, soaring nave, the length of two football fields and with enough space for 5,000 worshipers. It's bigger than the nave in St. Peter's in Rome. Lining either side of the nave are small chapels dedicated to American history, the arts, people with AIDS, even lawyers. In some of the niches you'll find very unchurchly things like a 2,000-pound quartz crystal, a menorah, and a 100-million-year-old fossilized sea creature. The great front doors, called the Portal of Paradise, are opened only twice a year; once at Easter, and once on the first Sunday in October so that elephants and chihuahuas can walk the main aisle for the Blessing of the Animals. Other festivities include Halloween (with silent horror flicks and ghouls rappelling from the ceiling) and summer solstice (with ringing of a giant bronze gong). Tours ($3) of the cathedral are offered every day but Monday), and, on the first and third Saturday of each month, the cathedral offers vertical tours ($10), which allow you to climb around its towers and other tall parts. Next door, the **Children's Sculpture Garden** features a giant statue of a gruesome-looking angel triumphing over the devil, with surrounding inscriptions by Georgia O'Keeffe, John Lennon, Ray Charles, and Gandhi. *Amsterdam Ave. and W. 112th St., tel. 212/316–7540 or 212/932–7347 for tour reservations. Subway: 1 or 9 to W. 110th St. Open Mon.–Sat. 7–5, Sun. 8–5.*

RIVERSIDE CHURCH

Riverside Church has a gargoyle-encrusted neo-Gothic exterior modeled after the cathedral in Chartres, France, plus vaulted ceilings and archways so pretty they'll make you weep. Its congregation is nondenominational, interracial, extremely political, and socially conscious; live music and theatrical productions are a big thing here year-round (*see* Music *in* Chapter 7). If you're here on Sunday, take the elevator ($2) to the top of the 22-story, 356-ft tower, topped with a 74-bell carillon—the largest in the world. *Riverside Dr. and W. 120th St., tel. 212/870–6700. Subway: 1 or 9 to W. 116th St. Open Mon.–Sat. 9–5, Sun. noon–4.*

GRANT'S TOMB

The final resting place of Ulysses S. Grant, Civil War general and 18th U.S. president, and Julia Dent Grant, his wife, is a white-marble rotunda influenced by the tomb of King Mausolus at Halicarnassus, the tomb of Roman Emperor Hadrian, and Napoléon's tomb in the Hôtel des Invalides. It's the second-largest mausoleum in the western hemisphere (try to imagine what this place would look like if he'd been elected to a second term). Inside are various Civil War artifacts and, of course, his-and-hers black marble sarcophagi. Tours are given on request, and occasionally the staff here wear Civil War costumes. Recently cleaned and restored, the monument is resplendent in fresh paint and buffed statuary. *100 W. 122nd St., at Riverside Park, tel. 212/666–1640. Subway: 1 or 9 to W. 116th St. Open daily 9–5.*

HARLEM

Harlem is the birthplace of what was once a purely American art form—jazz. It also has a reputation for being a haven of crime and poverty. Nonetheless, Harlem remains a neighborhood deserving of exploration. Many areas in Harlem, from the main commercial spine of **Martin Luther King Jr. Boulevard** (125th Street) to the residential enclaves along **St. Nicholas Avenue**, are experiencing a commercial and civic renaissance. Rastafarian and Senegalese restaurants overflowing with customers, Dominican families listening to *musica* on their front stoops—these are some of the sights of Harlem today. Note that the city's numbered north–south avenues acquire different names up here, commemorating heroes of black history: 6th Avenue becomes **Malcolm X Boulevard** (formerly Lenox Avenue); 7th Avenue is **Adam Clayton Powell Jr. Boulevard**; and 8th Avenue is **Frederick Douglass Boulevard.** Many people still use the streets' former names, but street signs (and this book) use only the new names.

Harlem's sights are clustered together, making exploring easy: The majority are along Martin Luther King Jr. Boulevard. Farther north are the historic and affluent neighborhoods of **Sugar Hill** (Edgecomb Ave. between W. 145th and 155th Sts.; Subway: A, B, C, or D to W. 145th St.) and **Striver's Row** (*see below*), and, at **155th Street**, a cluster of museums and a spacious riverside park. East of Park Avenue is the predominantly Puerto Rican neighborhood of **East Harlem** (a.k.a. el barrio).

MARTIN LUTHER KING JR. BOULEVARD

Once a vacant strip, Martin Luther King Jr. Boulevard is fast becoming a lively, engaging street. At its intersection with Malcolm X Boulevard you'll find two worthwhile museums: The **Studio Museum in Harlem** (*see* Museums and Galleries, *below*) features exhibitions on African, Caribbean, and African-American art, while one block to the north, the **Black Fashion Museum** (*see* Museums and Galleries, *below*) has over 3,000 pieces in its collection—including all the costumes from *The Wiz*.

Across Malcolm X Boulevard from the Fashion Museum is the famed **Sylvia's Restaurant** (*see* Chapter 4), a nearly 40-year-old institution run by the self-proclaimed "Queen of Soul Food." Incidentally, the intersection of Malcolm X Boulevard with Martin Luther King Jr. Boulevard is also called **Africa Square.** A block away is the **National Black Theater** (*see* Theater *in* Chapter 7), which produces new works by contemporary African-American writers.

APOLLO THEATER

When it opened in 1913 this was a burlesque hall for white audiences only, but after 1934 music greats such as Billie Holiday, Ella Fitzgerald, Duke Ellington, Count Basie, James Brown, and Aretha Franklin

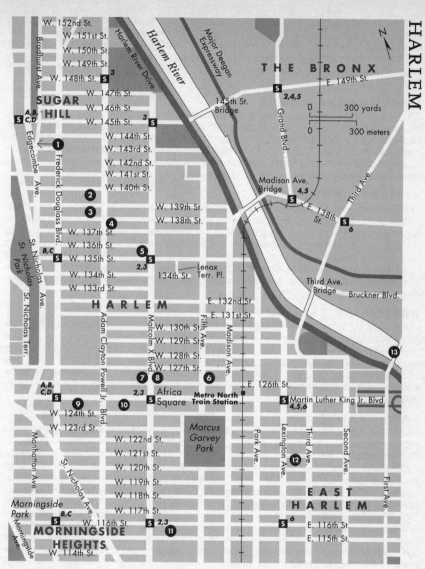

W. 152nd St.
W. 151st St.
W. 150th St.
W. 149th St.
W. 148th St. **S** *3*

**SUGAR
HILL**

Bradhurst Ave.
Edgecombe Ave.

S *A,B,
C,D*

W. 147th St.
W. 146th St.
W. 145th St. *3* **S**

W. 144th St.
W. 143rd St.
W. 142nd St.
W. 141st St.
W. 140th St.

❶

Frederick Douglass Blvd.

❷

❸

W. 139th St.
W. 138th St.

St. Nicholas Ave.
St. Nicholas Park
St. Nicholas Terr.

❹

W. 137th St.
W. 136th St.
W. 135th St.
W. 134th St.
W. 133rd St.

S *B,C*

❺ **S**
2,3

— Lenox
134th St. Terr. Pl.

H A R L E M

Adam Clayton Powell Jr. Blvd.
Malcolm X Blvd.

E. 132nd St.
E. 131st St.

W. 130th St.
W. 129th St.
W. 128th St.
W. 127th St.

Fifth Ave.
Madison Ave.

❼ ❽
S *2,3*
❿

Africa
Square

❻

**Metro North
Train Station**

E. 126th St.

S *A,B,
C,D*

❾

W. 124th St.
W. 123rd St.

Manhattan Ave.
St. Nicholas Ave.

S Martin Luther King Jr. Blvd
4,5,6

W. 122nd St.
W. 121st St.
W. 120th St.
W. 119th St.
W. 118th St.
W. 117th St.

*Marcus
Garvey
Park*

Park Ave.
Lexington Ave.
Third Ave.
Second Ave.
First Ave.

❶2

**EAST
HARLEM**

*Morningside
Park*

S *B,C*

W. 116th St. **S** *2,3*

❶❶

**MORNINGSIDE
HEIGHTS**

Morningside Ave.

W. 114th St.

S *6*
E. 116th St.
E. 115th St.

THE B R O N X

E. 149th St.

Harlem River Drive
Harlem River
Major Deegan Expressway

S *2,4,5*

Grand Blvd.
Third Ave.

145th St.
Bridge

Madison Ave.
Bridge *4,5*

S

E. 138th St.
S *6*

Third Ave.
Bridge

Bruckner Blvd.

❶3

N

0 ——————— 300 yards
0 ——————— 300 meters

55

Abyssinian Baptist
Church, **4**

Apollo Theater, **9**

Black Fashion
Museum, **7**

Harlem Court
House, **12**

Malcolm Shabazz
Mosque, **11**

National Black
Theater, **6**

Riverbank State
Park, **1**

St. Nicholas
Historic District, **2**

Schomburg Center
for Research in
Black Culture/
American Negro
Theatre, **5**

Striver's Row, **3**

Studio Museum
in Harlem, **10**

Sylvia's
Restaurant, **8**

Willis Avenue
Bridge, **13**

performed (or even got their first break) here. After falling on hard times in the '70s it roared back to life in 1986 and is now a TV studio. The regular Wednesday "amateur night" (7:30 PM) is as wild and raucous as it was in the theater's heyday. Tourists and locals flock to the show every week ($13–$21 for tickets). A poetry slam is also held here every second Monday at 7:30 PM. *253 MLK Jr. Blvd., between Adam Clayton Powell Jr. and Frederick Douglass Blvds., tel. 212/749–5838. Subway: A, B, C, or D to MLK Jr. Blvd. (W. 125th St.).*

MARCUS GARVEY PARK

Though this rocky, terraced park has fallen into disrepair, it offers spectacular views of the surrounding old Victorian homes and neoclassical churches, part of a designated historical district. Look for the park (renamed in 1973 for the Jamaica-born black nationalist leader of the 1920s) just south of Martin Luther King Jr. Boulevard. Farther south is the onion-domed **Malcolm Shabazz Mosque** (102 W. 116th St., near Malcolm X Blvd.), a former casino turned Black Muslim temple; in the '60s it rang with the preachings of Malcolm X. Several stores operated by Muslims are nearby.

STRIVER'S ROW

The handsome set of town houses known as Striver's Row was designed by powerhouse turn-of-the-century architects like Stanford White, who did the north side of West 139th Street. Since 1919, they've been the homes of African-American professionals and entertainers, including musicians W. C. Handy ("The St. Louis Blues") and Eubie Blake ("I'm Just Wild About Harry"). And that's how they got their name: Less affluent Harlemites felt its residents were "striving" to become well-to-do. The surrounding quiet, tree-lined streets of the **St. Nicholas Historic District** are a remarkable reminder of the Harlem that used to be. *W. 138th and W. 139th Sts., between Adam Clayton Powell Jr. and Frederick Douglass Blvds. Subway: B or C to W. 135th St.*

ABYSSINIAN BAPTIST CHURCH

One block east of Striver's Row is the Gothic-style Abyssinian Baptist Church. Founded in 1808, it's New York's oldest black church. Adam Clayton Powell, Jr., the first black U.S. congressman, once preached here; you'll find a tribute to him (including photos of him with Dwight D. Eisenhower, John F. Kennedy, and Lyndon B. Johnson) on the second floor. Stop in on Sunday at 9 or 11 AM to hear the gospel choir and a fiery sermon by Rev. Calvin O. Butts, III. A few blocks farther south is the **Schomburg Center for Research in Black Culture** (*see* Museums and Galleries, *below*). *132 W. 138th St., at Adam Clayton Powell Jr. Blvd., tel. 212/862–7474.*

EAST HARLEM

East of Park Avenue and north of 96th Street, all the way to the East River, is **el barrio,** a district with a radically different past from that of central Harlem. Historically home to some of New York's poorest, East Harlem has never known stately brownstone mansions or drawn wealthy inhabitants. In the 1880s, East Harlem's population was two-fifths foreign born: Working-class Germans, Jews, Irish, and enough Italians to earn it the nickname "Italian Harlem" lived in shoddy tenements in the shadow of the elevated railroads (the "El"). Immigration patterns shifted after World War II; by 1990 half of East Harlem's residents were Latin American, and the neighborhood became known as "Spanish Harlem." Housing projects, empty lots (some converted to carefully tended community gardens), burned-out buildings, and graffiti murals eulogizing victims of crack or gang violence all bear testimony to the neighborhood's struggles with chronic unemployment and capital flight. Even locals claim that many of the corner bodegas survive by peddling drugs. It's not the safest neighborhood in the city, but if you show respect to the residents you'll likely be treated with the same.

Most of el barrio's action is along **East 116th Street,** where tiny Puerto Rican cafés with blaring salsa music do quick business in deep-fried *orejas* (pigs' ears), and delicious *jugas tropicales* like *horchata* (a sweet rice drink). Botánicas sell herbs and objects for religious ceremonies. The intersection of East 116th Street with Lexington Avenue was Fiorello La Guardia's "lucky corner," where the beloved progressive mayor (and the first ever Italian-American elected to Congress, in 1923) always held his election-eve rallies. *Subway: 6 to E. 116th St.*

North of 116th Street, the sturdy **Harlem Court House** (170 E. 121st St., between Lexington and 3rd Aves.), built in 1891, is the area's most handsome structure and its only designated landmark. For views of East Harlem and the Bronx, cruise up the pedestrian lane of the **Willis Avenue Bridge** (E. 125th St. at 1st Ave.), spanning the Harlem River.

WASHINGTON HEIGHTS

Washington Heights, a.k.a. "Little Santo Domingo," is a mostly Latino neighborhood at the northern tip of Manhattan; its boundary with Harlem is West 155th Street. While wealthy New Yorkers built fanciful country estates here in the 19th century, in the 20th the area has been plagued with urban woes like poverty and drugs: In 1992 several days of rioting followed the shooting of a drug dealer by the police. In the past century, immigrant Greeks, Irish, Jews, Africans, Puerto Ricans, and Cubans have called the Heights their first American home. Presently, the largest Dominican population in the United States—plus a growing number of Salvadorans—live here. Though it won't win a prize as the nicest neighborhood in Manhattan, it's safe to visit Washington Heights during the day. Wander up **Broadway** and you'll find Spanish music blaring, discount merchandisers hawking cut-rate belts, shoes, or electronics, and random pay phones ringing off the hook.

The main attraction here is **The Cloisters** (*see* Museums and Galleries, *below*), the Metropolitan Museum's amazing collection of medieval European art and artifacts. It's housed in an imposing, atmospheric "castle" at the center of **Fort Tryon Park,** which offers inspiring views of the Hudson River. **Fort Washington Park,** near the George Washington Bridge, and **Inwood Hill Park,** much farther north, also offer open space and greenery rare in the rest of Manhattan.
For more on all three parks, *see* Parks and Gardens, *below.*

Harlem Renaissance author Langston Hughes lived at 20 E. 127th Street for the last two decades of his life.

The **Audubon Ballroom** (W. 165th St. and Broadway) is where Malcolm X was assassinated February 21, 1965, during a rally of his Organization of Afro-American Unity. It's now been swallowed up by a Columbia University biotechnology research facility, and only portions of the original facade and ballroom remain. Nearby is the oldest standing house in Manhattan, the **Morris-Jumel Mansion** (*see* Museums and Galleries, *below*). On Broadway at West 178th Street is the 14-lane **George Washington Bridge,** which links Manhattan with New Jersey. When it opened in 1931 it was the longest suspension bridge in the world. *Subway: A to W. 175th St.*

AUDUBON TERRACE

At Harlem's northern boundary stands Audubon Terrace, which houses the underappreciated museums of the **Hispanic Society of America** and the **American Numismatic Society** (for both, *see* Museums and Galleries, *below*). The **American Academy of Arts and Letters** (tel. 212/368–5900), also here, opens its doors to the public three months a year to exhibit sculpture, painting, and prints by promising young American artists; call for dates. The whole beaux arts compound was built on the former game preserve of artist/naturalist John James Audubon by a turn-of-the-century railroad magnate turned student of Hispanic culture. In the courtyard are a bas-relief of Don Quixote on his emaciated horse and a monumental sculpture of El Cid on his more muscular steed; both are works of the founder's wife. *W. 155th St. and Broadway. Subway: 1 to W. 157th St. Open Mar., May, and Nov., Thurs.–Sun. 1–4.*

TRINITY CEMETERY

Across the street from Audubon Terrace, Trinity Cemetery was established in the 19th century by Wall Street's venerable Trinity Church. Famous long-term residents include fowl-lover John James Audubon; rapacious real-estate magnate John Jacob Astor; and Alfred Dickens, son of the late, great British author. Pick up a free map of famous burial sites at the cemetery office (W. 153rd St. and Broadway; open daily 8 AM–9:30 PM). A bit farther west along the Hudson River, **Riverbank State Park** (*see* Parks and Gardens, *below*) has plenty to offer sports fanatics and view seekers. Who would guess such a gorgeous park and recreation complex was situated above a sewage treatment plant? *W. 153rd–155th Sts. between Amsterdam Ave. and Riverside Dr., tel. 212/368–1600.*

ST. FRANCIS XAVIER CABRINI CHAPEL

This is the final resting place of Mother Cabrini, clothed in her habit and lying in a crystal casket. Her smiling face is a wax replica; her real head is locked away somewhere in Rome. According to legend, a lock of the saint's hair supposedly cured a blind infant who grew up to be a priest in Texas. *Ft. Washington Ave. and W. 190th St. Subway: A to W. 190th St.*

YESHIVA UNIVERSITY

Founded in 1886, Yeshiva University is the oldest and largest Jewish studies center in the country. On campus you'll find a small **museum** displaying Hebrew treasures from around the world. The main building, Tannebaum Hall, has a fun-to-look-at facade combining modernist touches with Middle East-

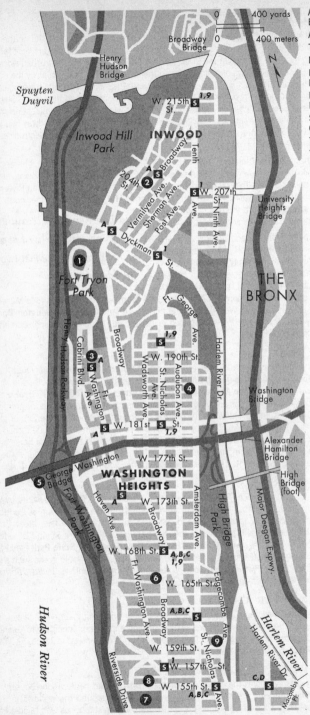

ern fancies like turrets, minarets, and pointy arches. *2520 Amsterdam Ave., at W. 185th St., tel. 212/960–5390. Subway: 1 or 9 to W. 181st St. Museum admission $3. Open Sept.–July, Tues.–Thurs. 10:30–5, Sun. noon–6.*

UPPER EAST SIDE

For most of its recent history the Upper East Side has been the domain of the super-rich, from old-money types, like the Rockefellers, whose names pop up on buildings all over town, to *nouveau riche* types like the Trumps and Hollywood celebrities. Luxury co-ops and condominiums, immaculate fin de siècle mansions and town houses, private schools, posh galleries, world-class museums, five-star restaurants, and international shops fill its blocks. You may find the people who live and work in this neighborhood a bit snobbish compared with other New Yorkers, but take it in stride—they treat everybody that way.

On **5th Avenue** (which borders Central Park) and **Park Avenue** are the homes of the wealthy and beyond wealthy: **998 5th Avenue,** at East 81st Street, was one of the city's first giant luxury apartment buildings, built in 1910. Prior to that, rich folk scraped by in giant mansions like the one that now houses the Polo/Ralph Lauren (*see* New Clothes *in* Chapter 5) store. Quite a few of the grandiose apartment buildings you'll see were designed in the 1920s and '30s by Rosario Candela, a Sicilian-born son of a plasterer; check out the most fantastic ones at 720, 740, 770, and 778 Park Avenue, and 834 and 960 5th Avenue. And if you're around in spring, stop to admire the tulips planted along the median of Park Avenue—the Metro-North Railroad's tracks run underneath it after they dip underground at 96th Street. Sandwiched between Park and 5th avenues is **Madison Avenue,** kingdom of couture, where slews of designer clothes give the *Vogue* editors something to do. For the best of the lot, *see box* Window-Shopping as an Art *in* Chapter 5. Showy reputation aside, between 75th and 83rd Streets there are some great bookstores, such as Crawford Doyle Booksellers (1082 Madison Ave., tel. 212/288–6300) and Archivia (944 Madison Ave., between 74th and 75th Sts., tel. 212/439–9194), where browsing can be as good as hitting a mini–antiquarian book fair.

Fifth Avenue on the Upper East Side as it runs along Central Park, between 59th and 110th streets, is also known as **Museum Mile** for its astounding concentration of, well, museums. In addition to the museums listed below, this area includes the unparalleled **Metropolitan Museum of Art** (*see* Major Attractions, *above*). The **Whitney Museum of American Art** (*see* Museums and Galleries, *below*) is one block east on Madison Avenue, which means it isn't technically part of Museum Mile, but it's easy to include in your afternoon museum orgy. If you're in town in June, check the local listings for the **Museum Mile festival,** when, for three brief hours one weekday evening, the museums along 5th Avenue throw open their doors, and the strip between 82nd and 104th streets becomes a festival for art lovers.

While the blue bloods and their debutante children dominate the blocks immediately adjoining Central Park, walk east all the way to the river and you'll find squat brownstones, cheap diners, and lots of Rollerbladers on their way to brunch. **Lexington Avenue** tends to show a little grit, while 3rd, 2nd, and 1st avenues are lined with moderately upscale restaurants and bars frequented by missed-the-'80s yuppies.

86TH STREET

A major crosstown artery, 86th Street used to be the center of the neighborhood's German and Austrian immigrant populations. One of the few holdouts in this area, called Yorkville, is **Schaller & Weber** (1654 2nd Ave., at 86th St., tel. 212/879–3047), a German market with a telltale window display of sausages and beer steins. Almost outnumbering the remaining German establishments are the Hungarian markets a few blocks farther south on 2nd Avenue; if you see a red-white-and-green awning along this stretch, chances are it's not a pizza parlor. At the east end of 86th Street is **Carl Schurz Park** and the mayor's home, **Gracie Mansion** (for more on both, *see* Parks and Gardens, *below*), where the sounds of birds replace the roar of traffic. It's a sweet place to be, even if the view across the river is of industrial zones. At East End Avenue and 86th Street is **Henderson Place Historic District,** a delightful (but partially amputated) enclave of 1880s brick Queen Anne houses.

ISLAMIC CULTURAL CENTER

This postmodern mosque, built in 1991 on a lawn that looks too good for the likes of Manhattan, was the first Islamic building in New York. If you conform to Islamic dress standards (long pants and shirt for men, neck to ankle *and* hair coverage for women), you can take a short free tour of the interior. *E. 96th St. at 3rd Ave., tel. 212/722–5234. Subway: 6 to E. 96th St. Open daily 9–4.*

E. 106th St.

KEY

AE American Express Office

E. 104th St.

E. 102nd St.

S 6

E. 101st St.

E. 100th St.

E. 99th St.

E. 98th St.

E. 97th St.

E. 96th St. S 6

E. 95th St.

E. 94th St.

E. 93rd St.

E. 92nd St.

E. 91st St.

E. 90th St.

E. 89th St.

E. 88th St.

Lexington Avenue

Third Ave.

YORKVILLE

E. 87th St.

4,5,6 S

E. 86th St.

E. 85th St.

E. 84th St.

First Ave.

E. 83rd St.

Madison Ave.

Park Ave.

E. 82nd St.

E. 81st St.

E. 80th St.

E. 79th St.

Carl Schurz Park

East End Ave.

E. 78th St. 6

E. 77th St. S

E. 76th St.

E. 75th St.

E. 74th St.

Second Ave.

York Ave.

E. 73rd St.

E. 72nd St.

E. 71st St.

E. 70th St.

E. 69th St.

E. 68th St.

6 S

E. 67th St.

E. 66th St.

E. 65th St.

First Ave.

East River

E. 64th St.

B,Q

AE S

E. 63rd St.

E. 62nd St.

E. 61st St.

E. 60th St.

Roosevelt Island Tramway

E. 59th St.

Queensboro Bridge

N,R

S

440 yards

400 meters

N,R 4,5,6

E. 58th St.

E. 57th St.

FDR Dr.

Central Park

998 Fifth Avenue, **14**

Abigail Adams Smith Museum, **24**

Asia Society, **20**

China House Gallery, **21**

Cooper–Hewitt National Design Museum/Smithsonian Institution, **6**

El Museo del Barrio, **1**

The Frick Collection, **17**

Goethe–Institut, **13**

Gracie Mansion, **10**

Henderson Place Historic District, **11**

International Center of Photography (ICP)—Uptown, **4**

Islamic Cultural Center, **3**

The Jewish Museum, **5**

Metropolitan Museum of Art, **12**

Museum of American Illustration, **22**

Museum of the City of New York, **2**

National Academy of Design, **8**

Polo/Ralph Lauren, **16**

Roosevelt Island, **25**

Solomon R. Guggenheim Museum, **9**

Whitney Museum of American Art, **15**

Galleries

James Danziger Gallery, **18**

M. Knoedler, **19**

Stone, **7**

Throckmorton, **23**

COOPER-HEWITT NATIONAL DESIGN MUSEUM, SMITHSONIAN INSTITUTION

The former mansion of steel magnate Andrew Carnegie provides the setting for the Cooper-Hewitt, one of the few museums in the country dedicated solely to design. Constructed in 1902 when this stretch of 5th Avenue was still all squats and tenements, the mansion—all 64 rooms of it—was built according to Carnegie's simple directive: To have "the most modest, plainest, and most roomy house in New York." OK, so his idea of "modest" is a bit different than yours. In this ornate space (albeit without Carnegie's original furnishings), you'll find brilliant temporary exhibitions covering all aspects of design: graphic, industrial, architectural, urban, decorative, etc. The museum has an extensive private collection of furniture, drawings and prints, textiles, and wallcoverings that can be seen by appointment only; however, as of early 2001 this collection will be displayed in rotating exhibits on the first floor. Don't miss the gardens, found by walking straight through the main hall from the entrance. If you notice that the benches around the perimeter seem a little mismatched, there's good reason—they're old city park benches from different eras. The Cooper-Hewitt also sponsors a number of educational programs, including tours, lectures, seminars, and workshops; for information call the Education Department at 212/849–8380. *2 E. 91st St., at 5th Ave., tel. 212/849–8400. Subway: 4, 5, or 6 to E. 86th St. Admission $5 (free Tues. 5–9). Open Tues. 10–9, Wed.–Sat. 10–5, Sun. noon–5.*

EL MUSEO DEL BARRIO

The northern outpost of 5th Avenue's Museum Mile is this museum dedicated to the art of Latin America. In a portion of the Heckscher Building (1921), El Museo really *is* in el barrio (*see* Harlem, *above*), which begins at about 96th Street—though el barrio is less evident along 5th Avenue than just a block east. The exhibition space provides over 8,250 square ft of simple white-walled galleries.

Millionaire industrialist Henry Clay Frick sought aesthetic and spiritual harmony in his collection, and apparently he found it—the Frick museum is often cited as one of the most peaceful spaces in New York City.

When El Museo was founded in 1969, it comprised only a single classroom in East Harlem. Since then, it has shifted locations several times as it assembled a permanent collection that today includes nearly 8,000 pieces of art, from pre-Columbian objects to contemporary videotapes. The museum also produces numerous temporary exhibitions, drawing from its rotating permanent collection as well as borrowed works; several shows are staged each year. Hour-long **gallery tours** are given by appointment only. For information, call the education department (212/831–7272, ext. 13). *1230 5th Ave., at 104th St., tel. 212/831–7272. Subway: 6 to E. 103rd St. Suggested donation $4. Open Wed.–Sun. 11–5 (May–Sept., Thurs. 11–8).*

THE FRICK COLLECTION

How did an uneducated American industrialist who made a million bucks in coke (the kind used for steel manufacturing) attain by his 30th birthday the cultural sophistication of a European aristocrat? He bought it, of course. Henry Clay Frick (1849–1919) began amassing his fabulous personal collection of paintings, sculptures, and decorative arts after his first trip to Europe in the 1890s, and continued up until his death. The elegant 5th Avenue mansion (built in 1914) where he lived was converted to a museum in 1935—yet it still looks like a home. Rather than echoing halls with sterile display cabinets, you get rooms decorated with 18th-century European furnishings, velvet- and wood-paneled walls, and art hung exactly as the industrialist hung it, brazenly mixing styles and schools and times, so that an ancient Chinese vase rests on a 19th-century French cabinet.

The collection itself (one-third of which was added by trustees after Frick's death) is a remarkable if Eurocentric sampling from the early Renaissance through the late 19th century: masterworks by Bellini, Constable, Gainsborough, Goya, Holbein, Rembrandt, Renoir, Titian, Turner, Van Dyck, and Velázquez (to name just a few), surrounded by exquisite candlesticks, tables, vases, and bronze and marble sculpture. In particular, look for the El Grecos, Vermeers, and Fragonards; Hans Holbein the Younger's luminous painting, *Sir Thomas More;* Rembrandt's mysterious *Self-Portrait;* Michelangelo Buonarroti's 16th-century bronze study, *Samson and Two Philistines;* and *Symphony in Flesh Colour and Pink* and *Harmony in Pink and Grey,* two bewitching portraits by Whistler, one of the few American artists included in the collection.

In keeping with the home-rather-than-museum effect, none of the art carries detailed labels, so consider picking up the *Guide to Works of Art on Exhibition* ($1) before you start exploring; or, better yet, take advantage of ArtPhone. This free, hand-held, digital audio guide (offered in a variety of languages) lets

READ 'EM AND WEEP

The members of the New York Landmarks Preservation Foundation have their work cut out for them on the Upper East Side. Every half block there's a notable building worth pointing out. Throughout the neighborhood, particularly between Park and 5th avenues, look for maroon signs on the lampposts—these are a sort of Cliff's Notes for the area's architecture and history.

you learn all about the works that interest you and skip the ones that don't; just punch in the number of the piece you want (look for the numbers on the walls) and listen to one of the museum's curators tell you fascinating tidbits about the artist, the work, and the history of its acquisition. There is also an excellent free introductory video that shows in the Music Room at half-past the hour from 10:30 to 4:30 Tuesday–Saturday and 1:30 to 4:30 on Sunday. The museum's downstairs galleries house temporary exhibitions and concerts are often hosted in the Music Room and piped into the Garden Court; for more info, *see* Music *in* Chapter 7.

If you're in need of a serious research library, you came to the right place: The **Frick Art Reference Library** (10 E. 71st St., tel. 212/288–8700) is right behind the museum. Free and open to scholars and art professionals, the Frick library contains an archive of over 900,000 photographs of works of art; 210,000 books, exhibition catalogs, and pamphlets; and 70,000 art-auction sale catalogs. *1 E. 70th St., at 5th Ave., tel. 212/288–0700. Subway: 6 to E. 68th St. Admission $7. Children under 10 not admitted. Open Tues.–Sat. 10–6, Sun. 1–6.*

GOETHE-INSTITUT

As the home of the German Cultural Center, the Goethe-Institut exhibits art relating to the German experience in its two small galleries. There's also a library open to the public, as well as language, lecture, and film programs. *1014 5th Ave., between 82nd and 83rd Sts., tel. 212/439–8688. Subway: 4, 5, or 6 to E. 86th St. Admission free. Open Tues. and Thurs. 10–7, Wed. and Fri. 10–5, Sat. 12–5.*

INTERNATIONAL CENTER OF PHOTOGRAPHY (ICP)–UPTOWN

Housed in a 1915 neo-Georgian mansion that was once home-sweet-home to the founder of the *New Republic,* the ICP features photographic installations culled from its collection of 45,000 works, as well as special exhibitions that change on a regular basis. You'll easily work your way through the modest, paneled galleries in a couple of hours. (Don't zip past the small, circular space just to the right as you enter the museum; there are often some astounding pieces inside.) For information about the ICP's photography education programs, call 212/860–1776, ext. 156. *1130 5th Ave., at 94th St., tel. 212/860–1777. Subway: 4, 5, or 6 to E. 86th St. Admission $6 (pay what you wish Fri. 5–8). Open Tues. and Thurs. 10–5, Fri. 10–8, weekends 10–6.*

THE JEWISH MUSEUM

Found in a French Gothic 5th Avenue mansion built in 1908, this museum assembles Jewish art and artifacts in a beautifully designed interior. The wonderfully conceived permanent exhibition, "Culture and Continuity," tracing the 4,000-year history of Judaism, begins on the fourth floor and continues on the third. You can take a free audio tour, narrated by Dustin Hoffman, that takes you progressively through each room, highlighting the historical and cultural significance of key artifacts (albeit a bit cursorily at times). Before heading down to the third floor, stop in at the "interactive Talmud" computer station; here you can ponder questions posed by the authors of the Talmud; then, watch Jewish scholars engage in Talmudic debates about topics such as begging, allocation of time, and the start of human life. Also not to be missed is the "audio café," where you can listen to reenacted conversations of Jews confronting modernity in cities such as New York, Vienna, Fez, and Tel Aviv. The first two floors carry changing exhibitions, displayed amidst the setting of the original mansion's interior. A small kosher café is on the bottom floor. *1109 5th Ave., at 92nd St., tel. 212/423–3230. Subway: 4, 5, or 6 to 86th St. Admission $8 (free Tues. 5–8). Open Sun.–Thurs. 11–5:45 (Tues. until 8).*

MUSEUM OF THE CITY OF NEW YORK

One of the best ways to start any visit to this daunting metropolis is with a visit to the Museum of the City of New York. Set in a Colonial Georgian mansion built in 1930, the museum illuminates the city's rich history and aspects of contemporary urban life. The museum—the first in America dedicated to a city's history—was founded in 1923 and was then housed in Gracie Mansion (now the mayor's residence).

Depending on the installation, the galleries occupy four to five spacious floors. The permanent exhibitions include several reconstructed New York residential interiors (sadly, no working-class rooms are shown), toys (with original stickball equipment, and of course, *Eloise* paraphernalia), decorative arts, and a survey of Broadway productions. You can walk along some docklike planking in the **Marine Gallery** to see models, dioramas, and paintings of early New York port life. There's also the **Fire Gallery,** which has one of New York's first water pipes—made from a hollowed-out pine log–and fire engines dating from the 1830s to the 1850s. In addition, the museum produces nearly a dozen excellent temporary exhibitions every year, which tend to be more intriguing than the permanent installations. The museum has an extensive **program schedule,** including various tours of New York, performances, film screenings, continuing education opportunities, and symposia. *1220 5th Ave., at 103rd St., tel. 212/534–1672. Subway: 6 to 103rd St. Suggested admission $5. Open Wed.–Sat. 10–5, Sun. noon–5.*

NATIONAL ACADEMY OF DESIGN

The Academy has a tradition of art exhibition and instruction that goes back more than 170 years. At its location in a 1914 mansion (which in this case makes the layout occasionally confusing), the Academy shows off its permanent collection of 19th- and 20th-century American art and architecture, including works by Richard Diebenkorn, Mary Cassatt, I. M. Pei, and John Singer Sargent. In addition to changing installations highlighting its permanent collection, the museum also presents loan exhibitions of all sorts, from Old Masters to contemporary artists. The Academy also produces a small number of lectures, tours, and performances; call for information. If you're in town in March or April, stop in at the **Annual Exhibition**; the whole museum is devoted to displaying its member artists' works and, though pricey, everything is for sale. *1083 5th Ave., at 89th St., tel. 212/369–4880. Subway: 4, 5, or 6 to 86th St. Admission $8 (pay what you wish Fri. 5–6). Open Wed.–Sun. noon–5 (Fri. 10–6).*

SOLOMON R. GUGGENHEIM MUSEUM

The Frank Lloyd Wright building housing the Guggenheim (opened in 1959) is a controversial work of architecture—even many who love its assertive six-story spiral rotunda will admit that it does not result in the best space in which to view art. Inside, under a 92-ft-high glass dome, a quarter-mile-long ramp spirals down past changing exhibitions of modern art. The Wright way to see the Guggenheim (if you'll pardon the pun) is to take the elevator to the top floor and walk *down* the spiral. Otherwise, it's quite a hike. It's best to get here early in the day in order to avoid the thronging crowds and absorb enough art to almost make you forget the museum's hefty admission. Originally conceived as the Museum of Non-Objective Painting, the Guggenheim has especially strong holdings in Wassily Kandinsky, Paul Klee, and Pablo Picasso; the oldest pieces are by the French Impressionists. A (non-round) annex called the Tower Galleries opened in June 1992, creating an additional 20,000 square ft of gallery space to display parts of the Panza di Buomo collection of minimalist art, and touching off frenzied yapping among artworld critics. In its defense, the uninspired 10-story annex was based on Wright's original designs, and accommodates the extraordinarily large art pieces that the Guggenheim owns but previously had no room to display.

The Guggenheim is unlike other museums in that most of its permanent collection is made up of several great private collections, rather than individually selected works. Besides the di Buomo acquisition, one of the museum's major buttresses is the Thannhauser collection, with works by Cézanne, Picasso, and van Gogh. The photography holdings got a late but impressive start with the 1992 gift of over 200 Mapplethorpe pieces from the Robert Mapplethorpe Foundation; in 1998 this collection received another boost—a gift of 531 photographs by George Platt Lynes.

Several **gallery talks and tours** are offered on exhibitions and the building itself. Inquire at the information desk or call 212/423–3600. Recorded **audio tours** are available for some major exhibitions. On Ramp 2, through a keyhole-shaped entrance, is the **reading room,** a good place to relax while perusing museum publications. The small **museum café** is miles ahead of most in both food and decor; sandwiches run about $7–$8 (but we're not talking soggy grilled cheese), and there are City Bakery signature tarts. Stop by if only to view the hung photos of the museum under construction. *1071 5th Ave., at 88th St., tel. 212/423–3500. Subway: 4, 5, or 6 to E. 86th St. Admission $12 (pay what you wish Fri. 6–8). Open Sun.–Wed. 10–6, Fri.–Sat. 10–8.*

THE MUSEUM THAT FRANK BUILT

As much a piece of modern art itself as the works it was designed to house, Frank Lloyd Wright's Guggenheim Museum can be a startling sight to unwary tourists strolling up 5th Avenue toward 88th Street—it's like a huge, bright-white child's spiral top. Wright's design for the museum was more than 15 years in the planning and wasn't fully completed until a few years after the architect's death in 1959. Much later the Guggenheim became the obvious inspiration for the Pavilion of Japanese Art, designed by Bruce Goff, at the Los Angeles County Museum of Art.

ROOSEVELT ISLAND

In the middle of the East River, straddled by the Queensborough Bridge, looms Roosevelt Island. For many years it was called Blackwell Island, after the English farmer who bought the property in the 18th century (and whose 1796 home still stands here). It was renamed Welfare Island in 1921, and finally Roosevelt Island in 1973. For much of its history, the island has been a repository for lunatics, criminals, smallpox victims, the elderly, and studying nurses. New York's first municipal asylum, the Octagon, was built here; with double the allotted number of patients, it was ripe for an exposé by the time newshound Nellie Bly came along in 1887. After going undercover as an inmate, Bly wrote scathing articles that resulted in much-needed reforms. Still, the island was quite a swinging place throughout the early decades of this century; among briefly incarcerated notables were Mae West and Tammany Hall honcho Boss Tweed. Prisoners pretty much ran their own coops and narcotics trafficking was rampant, until a penal crackdown sent the troublemakers off to Riker's Island. For a few decades the island's buildings lay empty; not until the 1970s did savvy developers move in to create one of the most successful high-density areas in the city, one that consciously mixes persons of all incomes in a postmodern idyll. The composition designed by Philip Johnson and John Burgee is strikingly pleasant: The winding, brick-paved **Main Street,** despite being flanked by some rather huge apartments, feels perfectly welcoming. And cars are mercifully kept all in one place, in an attractive parking structure (forgive the oxymoron) near the bridge that connects the island to Queens.

A walk north from the tram stop will lead you through the island's main residential area, past an 1889 Victorian Gothic chapel, and to the island's lighthouse, designed by James Renwick, Jr., the architect who designed St. Patrick's Cathedral. There's also a small, serene park at the north end. To visit Roosevelt Island, take the B or Q subway to Roosevelt Island. Or better yet, pay $1.50 and take the **Roosevelt Island Tram** (tel. 212/832–4543), which runs parallel to the Queensborough Bridge. Board the trams at 2nd Avenue and East 60th Street; they run every 15 minutes. A brochure describing the island and its history is available for 25¢ at the Manhattan tram station, or on the island at 591 Main Street.

MIDTOWN

If Manhattan has a heart, it is in Midtown, where nearly everything you think of as New York is found: the Empire State Building, Times Square, Rockefeller Plaza, the glitzy stretch of 5th Avenue and schmaltzy length of Broadway, the United Nations, and skyscrapers, by God, like you've never seen before. Fifth Avenue in the 50s looks like one obscenely posh mall, where tourists with fat wallets spend up a storm. Sixth Avenue is America's corporate heartland, a menacing tunnel of skyscrapers. Seventh and Eighth avenues in the 50s—and Broadway, which cuts the block between them—is tourist hell, where souvenir shops mix with expensive restaurants and the crowds heading to Times Square can sweep you away.

The west side of Midtown has long had a dicey reputation; its neighborhood name Hell's Kitchen is apropos of just what the place was really like. But new life has been breathed into the now friendly neighborhood around 9th Avenue in the 30s, 40s, and 50s. The new Hell's Kitchen is populated by a comfortable mélange of ethnic eateries, shops, and small apartments populated by twentysomethings looking for the last bastions of affordable housing in Manhattan. For info on the veritable buffet of cheap ethnic restaurants in this area, *see* Midtown West of 5th Avenue *in* Chapter 4.

One last note: Even though they're all in Midtown, we've covered the **Empire State Building** and the **Museum of Modern Art (MoMA)** *above,* in Major Attractions. You'll find reviews of Midtown's myriad museums in Museums and Galleries, *below*: the **American Craft Museum, *Intrepid* Air, Sea, and Space Museum, Japan Society, Museum of Television and Radio, Pierpont Morgan Library,** and **Sony Wonder Technology Lab.** Midtown's only good-sized park, **Bryant Park,** is in Parks and Gardens, *below.*

GRAND ARMY PLAZA

What was once a splendid public plaza, Grand Army Plaza is now the scene of intolerable traffic and tourist trappings—note the drivers of horse-drawn cabs (*see* Guided Tours, *above*) jockeying for potential fares. On the north half of the plaza is a massive gilded statue of Civil War general William Tecumseh Sherman and an unnamed, lithe Nubian; the southern half is dominated by the Pulitzer Memorial Fountain, now in a state of disrepair. Appropriately enough for this ritzy area, the lady on top is *Pomona,* the goddess of abundance. The palatial **Plaza Hotel** (768 5th Ave., at 59th St., tel. 212/759–3000), at the western edge of the plaza, is New York's grandest hotel building, home to Frank Lloyd Wright when he was in town building the Guggenheim Museum. It's difficult to believe that the architect who dreamed up the sinister-looking Dakota apartments (*see* Don't You Wish You Lived Here?, *above*), Henry Hardenbergh, could have concocted this confection with white-glazed brick and copper-and-slate roof. The hotel has been featured in notable films like *Plaza Suite* and *North by Northwest,* as well as less notable ones like *Crocodile Dundee* and *Home Alone 2.*

Diego Rivera's original murals in Rockefeller Center's GE building were removed because of his sympathetic depiction of socialism.

Next to the plaza, the **General Motors Building** (767 5th Ave., between 58th and 59th Sts.) is a much-maligned, 50-story tower of white Georgia marble and glass, recently bought by uber-developer Donald Trump. Spoil your inner child by going into the building's mammoth **FAO Schwarz** (*see* Specialty Stores *in* Chapter 5) for an $8,000 teddy bear or similarly extravagant toy. Beware of overly enthusiastic employees who feel the need to make you "play," tossing balloons or balls in your direction as you descend the stairs. If your inner grown-up is screaming for attention, don't forget about nearby **Bergdorf Goodman** (754 5th Ave., at 58th St., tel. 212/753–7300), where outrageously expensive clothing and housewares are sold by employees with an attitude. For more info on the shrines to consumerism that start here and stretch to the north, *see* Chapter 5.

NEWSEUM/NY

The only branch of the popular Newseum in Arlington, Virginia (which has the honor of being the sole interactive museum of news), this free photojournalism gallery uses rotating exhibits, lectures, and films to focus attention on journalism and First Amendment issues such as freedom of speech and freedom of the press. Recent exhibits have included looks at Tibet's struggle to survive and photographs from the Magnum news organization of civil unrest around the world during 1968. *580 Madison Ave., between 56th and 57th Sts., tel. 212/317–7596. Subway: N, R, B, Q to 57th St.*

CARNEGIE HALL

New York's premier concert hall, Carnegie Hall, has been hosting musical headliners since 1891, when its first concert was conducted by no less than Tchaikovsky. Audiophiles the world over have a lot to say about the hall's acoustics—though no two seem to be saying the same thing: Some have always said that it's a rare example of an acoustically perfect space. Others say that this has been true only since the 1995 discovery and removal of several tons of cement below the stage. Still others say the removal damaged the acoustics. And don't get them started on the effects of the 1990–1991 centennial renovations. Judge for yourself. At least one positive outcome of the earlier renovation was the increased size of the lobby that made room for the small **Rose Museum,** a trove of mementos from the hall's illustrious history, including Benny Goodman's clarinet and Arturo Toscanini's baton. The museum is free and is open Thursday to Tuesday, 11–4:30, and at intermission during concerts. For information on Carnegie Hall performances and tickets, *see* Music *in* Chapter 7, or consider taking a one-hour tour ($6) of the building. Tours are given Monday, Tuesday, Thursday, and Friday at 11:30, 2, and 3 (performance schedule permitting). *W. 57th St. at 7th Ave., tel. 212/247–7800 for tours. Subway: N or R to W. 57th St.*

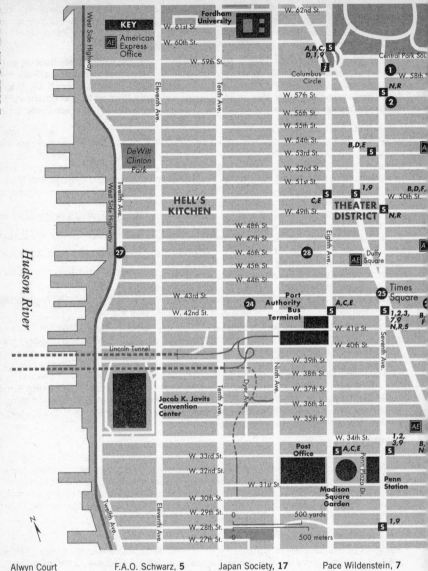

MIDTOWN

KEY

AE American Express Office

Fordham University

HELL'S KITCHEN

DeWitt Clinton Park

THEATER DISTRICT

Times Square

Port Authority Bus Terminal

AE Duffy Square

Hudson River

West Side Highway

Twelfth Ave.

Eleventh Ave.

Tenth Ave.

Ninth Ave.

Dyer Ave.

Eighth Ave.

Seventh Ave.

Penn Plaza Dr.

Jacob K. Javits Convention Center

Lincoln Tunnel

Post Office

Madison Square Garden

Penn Station

Columbus Circle

Central Park South

W. 62nd St.
W. 61st St.
W. 60th St.
W. 59th St.
W. 57th St.
W. 56th St.
W. 55th St.
W. 54th St.
W. 53rd St.
W. 52nd St.
W. 51st St.
W. 50th St.
W. 49th St.
W. 48th St.
W. 47th St.
W. 46th St.
W. 45th St.
W. 44th St.
W. 43rd St.
W. 42nd St.
W. 41st St.
W. 40th St.
W. 39th St.
W. 38th St.
W. 37th St.
W. 36th St.
W. 35th St.
W. 34th St.
W. 33rd St.
W. 32nd St.
W. 31st St.
W. 30th St.
W. 29th St.
W. 28th St.
W. 27th St.

A,B,C,D,1,9
N,R
B,D,E
1,9
B,D,F
C,E
N,R
28
24
A,C,E
25
1,2,3,7,9 N,R,S
B,F
1,2,3,9
A,C,E
B,N
1,9

0 ___ 500 yards
0 ___ 500 meters

Seagram
Building, **12**
Sony Wonder
Technology Lab, **8**
Theater Row, **24**
Times Square, **25**
United Nations, **18**
Urban Center, **16**

A block north and worth a look is the **Alwyn Court Apartments** (180 W. 58th St., at 7th Ave.), an example of what happens when architects get ahold of some terra-cotta and cheap labor. Built in 1909, this was the ultimate luxury apartment house of the time, with up to 34 rooms per apartment. Abandoned by the 1930s, it was renovated in 1985 as three- to five-room apartment units.

ROCKEFELLER CENTER

When movies and TV shows are set in Manhattan, they often start with a shot of Rockefeller Center. To many, this glitzy, 19-building complex *is* New York City. Begun during the Great Depression by John D. Rockefeller (who made his fortune in oil by age 26), Rockefeller Center occupies nearly 22 acres of prime real estate between 5th and 7th avenues and 47th and 52nd streets. At the time, it was the largest urban design project ever undertaken in the city. At its center is the 850-ft tall RCA Building—now the **GE Building,** and also called "The Slab"—which borrowed from Le Corbusier's "tower in the park" concept. But the real genius of its design was its intelligent use of public space: plazas, concourses, and street-level shops that create a sense of community for the nearly 250,000 human beings who use it daily. Headquartered here are such giants as NBC, Time-Warner, RCA, Simon & Schuster, General Electric, and the Associated Press (for more info on NBC, *see* Guided Tours, *above,* and *box* Your Own 15 Minutes of Fame, *below*).

Take a stroll through the **Channel Gardens** (5th Ave. between 49th and 50th Sts.), so named because they separate the British building to the north from the French building to the south. Artists, floral designers, and sculptors give the flower beds a fab new look monthly. At the foot of the gardens is the center's most famous sight, the gold-leaf statue of **Prometheus** (more familiarly known as "Leaping Louie"), surrounded by 50 jets of water and flags from the United Nations and United States. He's sprawled above a sunken plaza that holds an open-air café in summer and a romantic ice-skating rink (*see* Ice-Skating and Ice Hockey *in* Chapter 9) in winter. This is where they set up the enormous Christmas tree; the tree-lighting ceremony (tel. 212/632–3975) during the first week of December draws huge crowds. Inside and around all the center's buildings are innumerable art deco flourishes and artwork: The buff bronze *Atlas* stands guard outside the International Building (5th Ave. between 50th and 51st Sts.). Walking-tour brochures and maps for Rockefeller Center are available in the lobby of the GE Building (30 Rockefeller Plaza). *Subway: B, D, F, or Q to W. 47th–50th Sts.*

THE RAINBOW ROOM • On the 65th floor of the GE Building is the restaurant The Rainbow Room, which was bought in late 1998 by the Italian Cipriani restaurant clan. Unfortunately, they've decided to use the art deco gem as a private party space and only open it to the public on Friday nights and for Sunday brunch. If you decide to fight the crowds celebrating anniversaries and birthdays at the super-expensive restaurant or swanky bar, you'll be rewarded with beautiful views of Midtown and a taste of New York the way you're grandparents experienced it when they visited the city decades ago. Of course, gents need to wear coat and tie. *30 Rockefeller Plaza, tel. 212/632–5000.*

RADIO CITY MUSIC HALL • This 6,000-seat art deco jewel is the largest indoor theater in America. When it originally opened in 1932, the opulent interior was used to show first-run movies in conjunction with live performances by the legendary Rockettes. There still are singing elves at Christmastime, but during the rest of the year there's a pretty interesting lineup of major performers—oh, and a dancing rabbit at Easter too. What more could you want? Behind-the-scenes tours, offered daily, are $13.75 and leave every 30 minutes Monday to Saturday 10 to 5, and Sunday 11 to 5. *1260 6th Ave., between W. 50th and 51st Sts., tel. 212/247–4777 for events or 212/632–4041 for tours.*

ST. PATRICK'S CATHEDRAL

Across from Rockefeller Center, St. Patrick's Cathedral is an anatomically incorrect Gothic cathedral of sorts; it's got the ornate white spires, but totally lacks flying buttresses. Even so, as the Roman Catholic Cathedral of New York, it is the site of countless society weddings. If you can get past the limos and Armani-clad throngs, take a spin around the interior. Among the statues in the alcoves around the nave is a striking modern interpretation of the first American-born saint, Mother Elizabeth Seton. The corner-stone was laid in 1858, but the cathedral didn't achieve its present form until 1906, when the Lady Chapel (behind the altar) was built. *5th Ave. between 50th and 51st Sts., tel. 212/753-2261. Subway: B, D, F, or Q to W. 47th–50th Sts.*

SEAGRAM BUILDING

Built in 1958 by Bauhaus founder Ludwig Mies van der Rohe, the Seagram Building is the high point of high modernism. Its austerity set the tone for dozens of skyscrapers that followed in New York and other cities, though few have come close to the perfection of details in the Seagram. High priest of modern architecture Philip Johnson eats lunch daily at the Four Seasons restaurant (*see box* Serious Splurges *in* Chapter 4) off the main lobby, which he designed. The stark plaza out front—which works around New York's setback zoning laws—became an oft-copied model for high-rise buildings. By setting the base of their building back from the street, architects were free to construct a uniform glass box with sheer, unbroken sides. Free tours of the Seagram Building are given every Tuesday at 3 PM; meet in the lobby. *375 Park Ave., between 52nd and 53rd Sts. Subway: 6 to E. 51st St.*

URBAN CENTER

Housed inside a wing of the Villard Houses, an 1884 complex of some of New York's ritziest brownstones that now serves as the entrance to the New York Palace, the Urban Center acts as the locus of the urban design arts. New York's premier architectural preservation and education organization, the **Municipal Arts Society** (*see* Walking Tours, *above*) has its headquarters here; so too the **Architectural League** (tel. 212/753–1722) and the **Parks Council** (tel. 212/838–9410). The Center has three **galleries** that feature exhibitions focusing on contemporary planning, design, and preservation issues. Panel discussions and lectures are scheduled throughout the year. The Center also houses a library of clippings, leaflets, and books on New York City, open to the public weekdays from 11 to 5 (closed Thurs.). *457 Madison Ave., between 50th and 51st Sts., tel. 212/935–3960. Subway: E or F to 5th Ave./53rd St.*

The United Nations' site on the East River was an industrial slum district until oil magnate John D. Rockefeller gave $8.5 million to help build the high-modernist complex we know, fronted on days that the General Assembly is in session by the flags of all the member nations, neatly lined up, from Afghanistan to Zimbabwe. The buildings of this "workshop for peace" were finished in 1962, the collaborative product of 11 international architects led by Wallace Harrison. By running FDR Drive underneath the grounds, the architects created one of the most peaceful riverfront portions of Manhattan, including a large grassy expanse from which sunbathers and picnickers are banned.

Founded in 1945, the U.N. occupies land that is the domain of no nation—when you're there, you aren't really here in New York. Rather, you'll be on land that belongs to the U.N.'s 185 member states and has its own police force and fire department.

Though it seems every tourist makes a trip to the U.N., a visit can be disappointing. The main visitor attraction is the hour-long guided tour. On an ideal day, you'll get to see the General Assembly Hall, the Security Council Chamber, the Trustee Council Chamber, and the Economic and Social Council Chamber, though some rooms may be closed to the public on any given day if a meeting is in session. Still, a visit to one room is like a visit to any of them: They all look more or less like a big auditorium. The **tour,** offered in 20 languages, takes you through several fascinating installations that, unfortunately, are not accessible to those not on a tour. You'll see some terrifying artifacts of the atomic bombing of Hiroshima and Nagasaki, and displays on war, nuclear energy, and refugees, but you'll have little time to absorb it all. The tour guides give you their spiel, hurry you along, and dutifully deposit you in the lower-level gift-shop area. Besides the usual bric-a-brac with the U.N. logo on it, there's the **U.N. Postal Administration** (stamps and postcards bought here *must* be mailed from this post office), a decent coffee shop, and a bookstore that sells travel books and some of the U.N.'s technical publications.

Even if you decide not to take the tour, you can still visit the shops and the main General Assembly lobby. Its luminous north wall and long curving balconies make it one of New York's great modernist interiors. If you want to have an out-of-the-ordinary but pricey ($21.50) lunch of international delicacies often prepared by visiting chefs from around the world, the Delegates' Dining Room offers an international, tax-free buffet in a window-lined room that overlooks the East River. In the plaza outside, check out Carl Fredrik Reutersward's twisted gun sculpture, perhaps the best antiwar statement of them all. And if the weather's nice, stroll over to the river for a look at Queens and Roosevelt Island. *1st Ave. and E. 46th St., tel. 212/963–7713. Subway: 4, 5, 6, or 7 to Grand Central. Admission free. Tours $7.50. Open weekdays 9–5, weekends 9:15–5.*

CHRYSLER BUILDING

Although the Chrysler Corporation itself moved out a long time ago, the art deco Chrysler Building is a New York icon. The stainless-steel frills, a decorative band emblazoned with cars, and a lobby practically paved in African marble are just a few highlights of William Van Alen's 1930 tour de force. The 480 fluorescent tubes on the spire were added only recently; apparently, technology of the '30s wasn't up to Van Alen's designs for the illumination back then. *405 Lexington Ave., at 42nd St. Subway: 4, 5, 6, or 7 to Grand Central.*

GRAND CENTRAL TERMINAL

More than just a train station, Grand Central Terminal is an architectural jewel, one of the world's greatest public spaces. It stands as a masterpiece of urban design, a 1913 beaux arts shrine to space and transportation. Its main concourse is a billowing, reverberating hall where the sound of street musicians mixes smoothly with the bustle of commuters taking the Metro-North to Westchester County.

Grand Central recently underwent a four-year, $175-million restoration, which was completed in 1998. A major cleaning, on par with that given to the Sistine Chapel, restored the brilliance of the celestial map on the 120-ft ceiling, while part of the lower level was converted to a unique food and gift market. The building was also outfitted with air-conditioning and complete wheelchair access. Free **tours** of the terminal are given Wednesdays at noon by the Municipal Art Society (*see* Walking Tours, *above*); meet at the Chemical Bank Commuter Express on the main concourse. *E. 42nd St. at Park Ave., tel. 212/439–1049. Subway: 4, 5, 6, or 7 to Grand Central.*

One of the niftier additions to the terminal's Main Concourse is the **New York Transit Museum Gift Shop** (tel. 212/682–7608), adjacent to Vanderbilt Hall, formerly the Main Waiting Room. If you love the subways but can't make it to the New York Transit Museum in Brooklyn (*see* Museums and Galleries, *below*), at least come here to check out the books, T-shirts, and ephemera relating to the magnificent subway system. On the terminal's lower level is the famous, ancient **Oyster Bar and Restaurant** (tel. 212/490–6650), an eatery that seems far too tony to be in a train station. The scallops will set you back a cool $25, the bouillabaisse $26. The interior is cavernous and really cool, except for some nasty 1970s renovations. The take-out counter, found up the ramp from the main entrance, has sandwiches for about $7. Hours are weekdays 11:30–9:30.

Just south of Grand Central Terminal is the perfect al fresco dining area, **Pershing Square Park.** Just show up on the south side of Park Avenue (between E. 41st and 42nd Sts.) on summer weekdays from 11 to 3; the city provides the tables, chairs, umbrellas, and live music, and all you need to bring is the food. As you dine among the suits, get a load of the Park Avenue viaducts routing auto traffic above you—how oddly pleasing.

NEW YORK PUBLIC LIBRARY

A research and exhibition facility rather than a lending library, the **New York Public Library,** built in 1911, is rarely matched in beaux arts splendor anywhere in the city. Surely you've seen those two crouching marble lions—dubbed "Patience" and "Fortitude" by Mayor Fiorello La Guardia—on TV before? Tours of the building, beautifully restored in the 1980s, start in Astor Hall and are given for free Monday through Saturday at 11 AM and 2 PM; sign up in advance at the Information Desk. If you're going it on your own, be sure to peek into the Periodicals Room, decorated with trompe l'oeil paintings by Richard Haas commemorating New York's importance as a publishing center; and the Rose Main Reading Room, magnificent after a recent $15 million restoration. For information on current exhibits and events at the library, call 212/869–8089. If it's a nice day, though, you'd probably just enjoy sitting on the library's steps, an even livelier stage than those at the Metropolitan Museum of Art 40 blocks to the north. For the real scene, though, go behind the library to **Bryant Park** (see Parks and Gardens, below). 5th Ave. between 40th and 42nd Sts., tel. 212/930–0800. Subway: B, D, F, or Q to W. 42nd St. Open Mon. and Thurs.–Sat. 10–6, Tues.–Wed. 11–7:30.

INTERNATIONAL CENTER OF PHOTOGRAPHY—MIDTOWN
The Midtown branch of the ICP (the main one is on the Upper East Side) features both rotating exhibits and selections from the outstanding permanent collection. Admission to either ICP location includes a free pass for the other location valid for one week. 1133 Ave. of the Americas at 43rd St., tel. 212/768–4682. Subway: B, D, F, or Q to W. 42nd St. Admission $6. Open Tues.–Thurs. 10–5, Fri 10–8, Sat.–Sun. 10–6.

TIMES SQUARE
While it may not exactly be the Crossroads of the World, as it is often called, Times Square is one of New York's white-hot energy centers. Hordes of people, mostly tourists and the pickpockets who prey on them, crowd it day and night to gawk and walk. Though it's called a "square," it's actually two triangles formed by the angle of Broadway slashing across 7th Avenue at 42nd Street—and the roadways are so wide here that it can be hard to tell where that darned "square" really is. However, the former Times Tower, clad in white marble and called **One Times Square Plaza,** should be immediately obvious. When the New York Times moved into this, its new headquarters, on December 31, 1904, it publicized the event with a fireworks show at midnight. Fireworks of a different sort have since taken place every New Year's Eve at Times Square. Drunk and rowdy revelers mob the intersection below, and when the 200-pound illuminated ball being lowered down the flagpole hits bottom on the stroke of midnight, pandemonium ensues (savvy New Yorkers stay far away).

Times Square is hardly more sedate on the other 364 nights of the year, mesmerizing visitors with its zillion kilowatts of flashing neon, a mammoth digital display offering world news and stock quotes, a 42-ft-tall bottle of Coke, and the occasional way, way larger-than-life Calvin Klein billboard of a 16-story-tall waif in nothing but panties. Could it get any glitzier? Possibly. The city has made quite an effort in recent years to eradicate Times Square's sex shops, porn palaces, and other elements of XXX sleaze to make the area more palatable to tourists (and maybe even New Yorkers). Times Square's redevelopment has new stores opening up almost every month, replete with blazing neon signs that are required by the city for all new businesses here. The hype started with the April 1996 opening of the Virgin Megastore Times Square (see Records, Tapes, and CDS in Chapter 5), a 75,000-square-ft shrine to pop culture consumerism. Then came a Disney Store on 42nd Street and 7th Avenue as well as a state-of-the-art virtual reality and interactive video arcade. And now, well, there's so many mega-emporiums it almost feels like a mall—almost. Free walking tours of Times Square are given Friday at noon; meet at the Times Square Visitors Center (7th Ave. and W. 42nd St.). Subway: N, R, 1, 2, 3, 7, or 9 to Times Sq.

THEATER DISTRICT
Near Times Square, about 30 major Broadway theaters are clustered in an area bounded roughly by 6th and 9th avenues and 41st and 53rd streets. (At 47th St. and Broadway you'll find **TKTS** (see Chapter 7), where you can pick up half-price tickets on the day of the show.) Just a few short years ago, there weren't too many reasons to spend time here, unless you were on your way to a show or looking to buy an inflatable doll. But with the Giuliani administration's crackdown on porn and the influx of new stores, big name—Condé Nast (the magazine giant) and BMG (the record and publishing bigwig), just to name two—businesses, restaurants, and Disney-bankrolled productions, Times Square has become downright tourist friendly.

The bulk of live theater of 42nd Street is provided by a group of thriving Off-Broadway playhouses, called **Theatre Row,** between 9th and 10th avenues. Peek into No. 330, between 8th and 9th avenues, behind the Port Authority Bus Terminal. Originally the McGraw-Hill building, it was designed in 1931 by Raymond Hood, who later worked on Rockefeller Center. The lobby is an art deco wonder of opaque glass and stainless steel. More than 20 restaurants crowd block-long **Restaurant Row** (see Midtown West of 5th Avenue in Chapter 4) on 46th Street between 8th and 9th avenues, but most are pricey and cater to an upscale theatergoing crowd.

CHELSEA

The hip neighborhood of Chelsea (bounded by 14th Street to the south, 30th Street to the north, 5th Avenue to the east, and the Hudson River to the west) was not named after its equally hip counterpart in London but after the Chelsea Royal Hospital, an old soldiers' home in that British city. The area was at one time the country estate of one very lucky Clement Clarke Moore, a clergyman and classics professor better known for writing 'A Visit from St. Nicholas in 1822. Moore saw the city moving north and, intuitive urban planner that he was, decided to divide his land into sub-lots in the 1830s. He dictated a pattern of development that ensured street after street of graceful row houses. Manhattan's first elevated railroad was built on 9th Avenue in 1871—look for its remains around 10th Avenue at West 17th Street. The motion picture industry flourished briefly in Chelsea before heading west to Hollywood around World War I. And during the Depression, drama of a different sort flourished on the Chelsea waterfront: Longshoremen and ship owners went head-to-head in some vicious conflicts.

With the 1990s came gentrification: **8th Avenue** between West 14th and 23rd streets now rivals Christopher Street in the Village as the city's main gay street, with a slew of trendy restaurants, bars, cafés, gyms, and shops. The action continues on many side streets, particularly **West 18th Street.** Wander east on 18th Street to the block between 5th and 6th avenues to find a number of new bookstores (*see* Chapter 5). The stretch from **20th to 29th streets** between 10th and 11th avenues is where you'll find galleries displaying art so new the paint is still wet; the **Dia Center for the Arts** and the **Paula Cooper Gallery** are among the places worth checking out (*see* Museums and Galleries, *below*). Shopaholics should head to **6th Avenue,** between 18th to 22nd streets, where several grand old cast-iron buildings have been transformed into upscale discount stores (*see* Ladies' Mile, *above* Chapter 5). For a taste treat, head to the **Chelsea Market,** 9th Avenue between 15th and 16th streets, where a renovated warehouse is now home to more than a dozen gourmet wholesale storefronts (*see* Chelsea *in* Chapter 4). Tenth through 12th avenues is the land of warehouses, with a sprinkling of dance clubs; use caution when exploring around here at night. If you're here on a weekend, check out the **Annex Antiques Fair and Flea Market** (*see* Flea Markets *in* Chapter 5), the city's longest-running outdoor market with more than 300 vendors of treasure.

CHELSEA PIERS SPORTS AND ENTERTAINMENT COMPLEX

Way back in 1910, the Chelsea Piers was the launching point for a new generation of ocean liners. For the past few decades, the piers were pretty much abandoned, but in 1995 the old pier buildings along the Hudson River were turned into a sports lover's dream come true: a 1.7-million-square-ft state-of-the-art facility with two year-round indoor ice-skating rinks; a field house for gymnastics, soccer, field hockey, lacrosse, basketball, and batting practice; two outdoor in-line and roller-skating rinks; and the city's only year-round outdoor golf driving range. There's also a huge Sports Center containing the world's longest indoor running track, the largest rock-climbing wall in the Northeast, three basketball courts, and a 25-yard pool. The Maritime Center, the city's largest marina, has a 1.2-mi walking esplanade, and Spirit Cruises, which provides sightseeing around New York Harbor. Consider ending your day at one of Chelsea Piers' several restaurants with river views, including the Crab House and the Chelsea Brewing Company, or by pampering yourself with a well-deserved massage at the Origins Spa. *Piers 59–62 on the Hudson River from 17th to 23rd Sts.; entrance at 23rd St., tel. 212/336–6666. Subway: E to W. 23rd St.*

CHELSEA HISTORIC DISTRICT

In Chelsea's historic district—West 19th to 23rd streets between 8th and 10th avenues—you'll find examples of all of Chelsea's architectural periods, dating back to the days of Clement Clarke Moore. The houses of **Cushman Row** (406–418 W. 20th St., at 9th Ave.) are some of the country's most perfect examples of Greek Revival town houses. Look for the plaque between Nos. 412 and 414. **St. Peter's Episcopal Church** (344 W. 20th St., between 8th and 9th Aves.) "welcomes all faiths and uncertain faiths." Its fieldstone building is one of New York's earliest examples of Gothic Revival architecture, and its brick Victorian Gothic parish hall is home to the Atlantic Theater Company. Check out **467 West 21st Street,** at 10th Avenue; its live-in landlord was the late Anthony Perkins, of *Psycho* fame. Built in the 1930s, **London Terrace** (W. 23rd and 24th Sts. between 9th and 10th Aves.) is a 1,670-unit apartment complex that isn't revival-anything. It's just big—really, really big. The theme-crazed management used to dress up the doormen as London bobbies.

CHELSEA HOTEL

Chelsea's most famous landmark is the Chelsea Hotel, a slightly seedy redbrick building with lacy wrought-iron balconies. Though the street it stands on is half run-down, when the Chelsea opened in

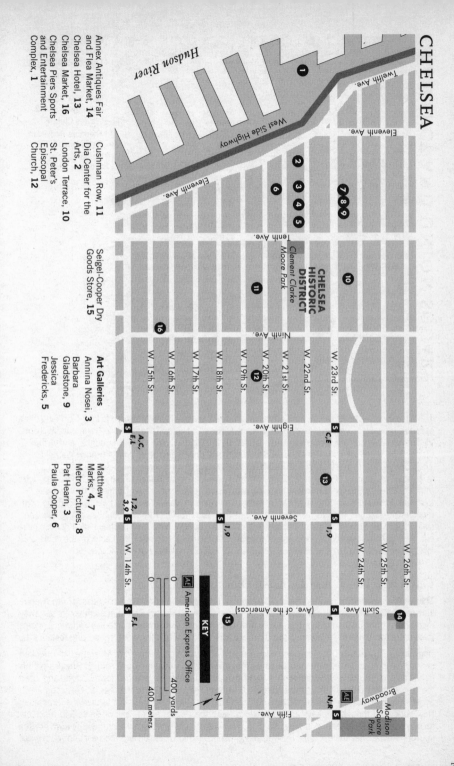

Annex Antiques Fair
and Flea Market, **14**
Chelsea Hotel, **13**
Chelsea Market, **16**
Chelsea Piers Sports
and Entertainment
Complex, **1**

Cushman Row, **11**
Dia Center for the
Arts, **2**
London Terrace, **10**
St. Peter's
Episcopal
Church, **12**

Seigel-Cooper Dry
Goods Store, **15**

Art Galleries
Annina Nosei, **3**
Barbara
Gladstone, **9**
Jessica
Fredericks, **5**

Matthew
Marks, **4, 7**
Metro Pictures, **8**
Pat Hearn, **3**
Paula Cooper, **6**

Hudson River

West Side Highway

Twelfth Ave.

Eleventh Ave.

Eleventh Ave.

Tenth Ave.

Clement Clarke
Moore Park

**CHELSEA
HISTORIC
DISTRICT**

Ninth Ave.

W. 15th St.
W. 16th St.
W. 17th St.
W. 18th St.
W. 19th St.
W. 20th St.
W. 21st St.
W. 22nd St.
W. 23rd St.

Eighth Ave.

Seventh Ave.

W. 24th St.
W. 25th St.
W. 26th St.

Sixth Ave.
(Ave. of the Americas)

Fifth Ave.

Broadway

Madison
Square
Park

W. 14th St.

KEY

AE American Express Office

N

0   400 yards
0   400 meters

S A,C.
E,L.

S C,E

S 1,2,
3,9

S 1,9

S 1,9

S F,L

S F

N,R.

S

AE

73

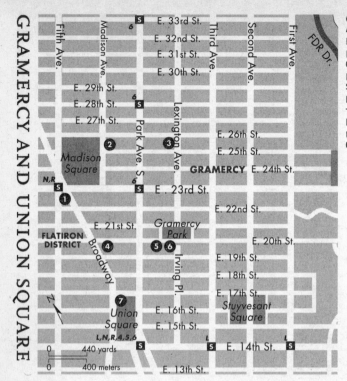

69th Regiment Armory, **3**

Flatiron Building, **1**

National Arts Club, **5**

New York State Supreme Court, **2**

Players Club, **6**

Theodore Roosevelt Birthplace, **4**

Union Square Greenmarket, **7**

1884 this was the center of New York's theater industry. It has traditionally catered to long-term (and often eccentric) tenants, including Mark Twain, Eugene O'Neill, O. Henry, Thomas Wolfe, Tennessee Williams, Vladimir Nabokov, Mary McCarthy, Arthur Miller, Dylan Thomas, William S. Burroughs, and Arthur C. Clarke (who wrote the script for *2001: A Space Odyssey* while living here). In 1966 Andy Warhol filmed *The Chelsea Girls* in artist Brigid Polk's Chelsea Hotel room. More recently, the hotel was seen on screen in *I Shot Andy Warhol* (1996) and *Sid and Nancy* (1986), a dramatization of the true-life Chelsea Hotel murder of Nancy Spungen, who was allegedly stabbed to death here by her boyfriend, drugged Sex Pistols punk rocker Sid Vicious. The shabby aura of the Chelsea Hotel is part of its allure. Read the commemorative plaques outside and then step into the lobby to see the 10-floor-high, skylighted open stairwell and the artwork, some of it donated in lieu of rent by residents down on their luck. For a hip haircut, Suite 303 is the salon of choice for downtown rockers (there's no sign, just knock on the door). *222 W. 23rd St., between 7th and 8th Aves., tel. 212/243–3700. Subway: 1 or 9 to W. 23rd St.*

GRAMERCY AND UNION SQUARE

The wealthy residential neighborhood of Gramercy (roughly defined as everything east of 5th Avenue between 14th and 30th streets) has a few quiet streets near Gramercy Park that allow you to get away momentarily from Manhattan's fast pace. The blocks along **Broadway,** particularly where it meets bustling Union Square, are home to some of New York's most happening bars, shops, and restaurants.

Originally, 17th-century Dutch settlers called this part of Manhattan island *Krom Moerasje* (little crooked swamp), and much of the area remained marshy swampland until developer Samuel Ruggles got his hands on it in 1831. Ruggles drained the swamp, replaced it with 66 beautiful town houses, and lured the rich with the promise of a private garden, **Gramercy Park** (E. 20th to 21st Sts. at Lexington Ave.), accessible only with a golden key. Over 150 years later it's still one of the most exclusive addresses in New York. And though the keys are no longer golden, the private park is still off-limits and residents fiercely guard this privilege (ironically, the park is frequently empty). Original 19th-century town houses in Greek Revival, Italianate, Gothic Revival, and Victorian Gothic styles still face the west and south sides of the park. The **Players Club** (16 Gramercy Park S) is an exclusive actor's club with notable alumni, including Mark Twain, Lionel Barrymore, Irving Berlin, Winston Churchill, Sir Laurence Olivier, Frank Sinatra, Walter Cronkite, and—the David among these Goliaths—Richard Gere. Next door, the **National Arts Club** (15 Gramercy Park S) was once the home of 19th-century New York governor Samuel Tilden; today this national historic landmark has free art exhibits open to the public and literary readings sponsored by the Poetry Society of America (*see* Spoken Word *in* Chapter 7).

UNION SQUARE

During the Civil War, Union troops paraded around, were reviewed in, and embarked from Union Square. History buffs will also recall that Union Square was the home of America's labor, socialist, and anarchist movements. In fact, a list of Union Square's former tenants reads like a who's who of America's radical left; the newspaper *Socialist Call,* the *Daily Worker,* the ACLU, the International Ladies Garment Workers' Union, and the League for Peace and Democracy all had their headquarters here. If that fails to interest you, at least come to Union Square to pay homage to an event that paved the way for a three-day weekend: On September 21, 1882, the Knights of Labor, a union that even during the 19th century included women and minorities, held a rally here. This rally was later commemorated as Labor Day.

During the early 20th century, demonstrations became increasingly large, and often violent, as city officials started calling in the heavy-handed NYPD to bash heads. At a vigil on the night that scapegoat anarchists Sacco and Venzetti were to be executed, National Guardsmen manned machine guns from the roofs of surrounding buildings. If you dropped by the square in the 1940s, you'd find big banners draped across the Communist party headquarters, urging DEMONSTRATE AGAINST IMPERIALIST WAR! FOR DEFENSE OF THE SOVIET UNION!

The Union Square Greenmarket (see Chapter 4) is the place where New York's finest chefs come to purchase farm-fresh produce, bread, cheese, and fruit.

By mid-century, the left left and Union Square became an entertainment center, full of bars and movie houses—a working-class Times Square (back before it became a den of sleaze). During the '60s, Andy Warhol had his famous Factory off Union Square, and Marcel Duchamp, expatriate French dada-ist, lived a block away. Today it's home to some of the city's finest restaurants, including **Union Square Cafe** (*see* box Serious Splurges *in* Chapter 4). At the southwest corner of the square, note the statue of Gandhi, surrounded by lovely flowers during spring and summer. Just north of Union Square is a mini-neighborhood, the **Persian Rug District,** where many shops hang richly patterned rugs in their windows. Check out every New Yorker's favorite store, **ABC Carpet and Home** (*see* Chapter 5), which arranges its expensive goodies in big jumbles like in grandma's attic. *Subway: N, R, 4, 5, or 6 to Union Sq.*

FLATIRON BUILDING

Christened the Fuller Building, this dramatic neo-Renaissance building was popularly called the Flatiron Building because of its resemblance to the clothes-pressing device popular at the time. Built on a triangular wedge of land in 1902, it rose 286 ft (20 stories), a height unprecedented at the time; it is often considered the world's first skyscraper. Its internal steel frame structure was revolutionary, allowing for taller and taller buildings (Otis's elevator also helped). Its unusual shape also had the effect of creating unusually strong winds at its tip at 23rd Street. Dirty old men (and young ones, too) would gather to watch the wind raise the ankle-length skirts of passing women. To these men policemen gave the warning "23-skidoo." *175 5th Ave., between 22rd and 23rd Sts. Subway: N or R to E. 23rd St.*

South of the Flatiron Building, between 5th Avenue and Park Avenue South, lies the **Flatiron District,** where some of the trendiest higher-priced restaurants and boutiques in New York have recently been popping up.

MADISON SQUARE

Most days this 7-acre park is full of activity: children playing, bums snoozing, and talent agents and internet start-up execs rushing to lunch. Statues in the park include Admiral David G. Farragut, Civil War hero, and one of those patently forgettable presidents, Chester A. Arthur. More important is the park's history: On this spot in 1842, a group of men calling themselves the Knickerbockers started playing a game known as New York ball—which was later to be known as baseball. By 1845, they had codified the rules that were later to become standard across the country. If you're a dog lover, head to the northwest corner of the park, where you'll find beloved pets scampering about in an area called James Dog Run.

Right off the park, between East 26th and 27th streets—where the New York Life Building now stands—was where the original incarnation of **Madison Square Garden** stood (it's since moved a few blocks farther northwest). Designed by Stanford White, an illustrious architect who helped design much of Columbia University, the Garden was the place where New York society gathered for hedonistic post-theater revelries. During a boisterous party at the Garden, White was shot through the head by Harry K. Thaw, a partner in White's firm. For the sordid details of White's "affairs," *see box* They Built This City, *above. E. 23rd to 26th Sts. between 5th and Madison Aves. Subway: N or R to W. 23rd St.*

Right across the street from Madison Square Park is the Appellate Division of the **New York State Supreme Court** (27 Madison Ave. at 25th St.), a gem of a courthouse, built on the heels of the City Beautiful movement in 1900. Flanking the portal are figures representing "Wisdom" and "Force"; among the other figures on the building are "Peace" and "Justice." Go inside to see the exhibitions in glass cases of New York historical ephemera (including a share in the stock of the City Lunatic Asylum) and the attractive murals. If it seems like there's a statue missing from the balustrade, there is: In the 1950s, the statue of Mohammed was removed at the request of local Islamic groups, as Islamic law forbids the representation of humans in sculpture or painting.

69TH REGIMENT ARMORY

Today, the only crowds moving in and out of the ugly, warehouselike 69th Regiment Armory are uniformed National Guardsmen. But over 85,000 New Yorkers caught the controversial 1913 Armory Show, which brought modern art by Picasso, Duchamp, and other artists to the American public for the first time. The stuffy American press roundly criticized the show: The European art was labeled subversive, and the American art too derivative of the European art. *E. 26th St. at Lexington Ave. Subway: 6 to E. 23rd St.*

Just north of the Armory, on Lexington Avenue between 27th and 29th streets, you'll find a number of Indian restaurants and grocery stores, where you can purchase exotic spices.

WEST VILLAGE

The West Village is also known as **Greenwich Village,** or sometimes just **The Village.** Greenwich Village used to encompass everything between 14th Street and Houston Street, from the Hudson to the East River. Nowadays, east of Broadway is considered the East Village, and everything west is the West Village. The Village really did begin life as its own little village, named Grin'wich, in the early 1700s. The people of New York City (who then lived much farther south, at the tip of Manhattan) regarded this as a resort town. When a series of nasty smallpox and yellow fever epidemics struck the city from 1799 to 1822, residents fled north to Grin'wich. Eventually, the area became a neighborhood of blue bloods who built lofty Greek Revival and Italianate style homes (some of which still survive) before continuing their migration north.

By the start of the 20th century, the Village had earned a pretty dicey reputation. The area around **Washington Square** (*see below*) became known as "Frenchtown" and was site of the city's highest concentration of brothels and rough bars. Writers and artists moved into its ornate brownstones anyway, because rent was cheap. Some former Village residents include: in the 19th century, Henry James, Edgar Allan Poe, Mark Twain, Walt Whitman, and Stephen Crane; at the turn of the century, O. Henry, Edith Wharton, Theodore Dreiser, and Hart Crane; and during the 1920s and '30s, John Dos Passos, Norman Rockwell, Sinclair Lewis, Eugene O'Neill, Edward Hopper, Margaret Sanger, and Edna St. Vincent Millay. In the late 1940s and early '50s, the Abstract Expressionist painters Franz Kline, Jackson Pollock, Mark Rothko, and Willem de Kooning congregated here, as did the Beat writers Jack Kerouac, Allen Ginsberg, and Lawrence Ferlinghetti. The 1960s brought folk musicians and poets, notably Bob "Positively 4th Street" Dylan and Peter, Paul and Mary. In the 1970s a burgeoning gay community helped make this the crucible for a national gay-rights movement. Today the area is still a center for liberal politics and tolerant attitudes, a home to writers, video artists, and AIDS activists—and a place where the elderly First Bohemians mingle in cafés with those newly minted at **New York University** (*see below*).

Bleecker Street is one of the Village's main drags. Where it intersects with **MacDougal Street** (*see below*) it's jammed with cafés, jazz clubs, and bars. Between 7th Avenue and Abingdon Square you'll find a more mellow Bleecker Street, with cozy little restaurants and purveyors of everything from Japanese furniture to African art. Consider making a detour off Bleecker Street to visit **18 West 11th Street**; the radical group The Weathermen had their bomb-making factory here until they accidentally blew it up in 1970. (At the time, Dustin Hoffman lived next door—he was seen on TV news frantically trying to rescue his possessions.) Or follow Bleecker Street east of 7th Avenue, to **Leroy Street,** to find an old Ital-

WEST VILLAGE

KEY

i Tourist Information

N

0 _____ 200 yards
0 _____ 200 meters

Hudson River

77

ian neighborhood that's a lot livelier than Little Italy these days: Italian butchers, bakers, and pizza-pie makers abound. To the west, Bleecker Street ends at **Hudson Street,** which has a lot of small, slick restaurants and a handful of lesbian bars and clubs. Beyond that, way over on **West Street,** you'll find druggies and prostitutes hanging out by the piers.

In addition to the must-sees listed below, be sure to check out the **Forbes Magazine Galleries** (*see* Museums and Galleries, *below*) and **Hudson River Park** (*see* Parks and Gardens, *below*). The Village is also home to the outrageous Halloween Parade and monthlong Gay Pride festivities; for more on these, *see* Festivals *in* Chapter 1.

WASHINGTON SQUARE

At the heart of the Village is Washington Square. Before it became a public park in 1827, this was a cemetery for victims of yellow fever, a military parade ground (bad idea—the heavy artillery kept collapsing into old graves), and finally a site of public executions during the late 18th and early 19th centuries. Quite a few citified desperadoes met their maker at the **Hanging Elm,** which stands at the park's northwest corner. These days, the square is a maelstrom of playful activity, shared by a truly bizarre mix of people: earnest-looking NYU students, ruthless chess players, businesslike drug dealers, homeless hippie folk singers, bongo-drum players, joggers, skateboarders, vociferous protesters—and people like you, sitting on benches, witnessing the grand opera of it all. At the center of the square is a perpetually broken and waterless **fountain**: It's the New York City equivalent of Speaker's Corner in London, a theater in the round for musicians, magicians, and ranting amateur politicians. Dominating the square's northern end is the triumphal **Washington Arch,** beyond which lies the start of glorious 5th Avenue. Originally, a wood-and-plaster arch was erected in 1889 to celebrate the 100th anniversary of George Washington's presidential inauguration; it proved so popular that a Tuckahoe marble version (designed by the irrepressible Stanford White) was thrown up in 1895. Below it you'll find two pollution-corroded statues of the president who hated to pose for portraits and such because it meant wearing those dreadful wooden teeth: "Washington at Peace," sculpted by Alexander Stirling Calder, and the Ying to Calder's Yang, "Washington at War," by Hermon MacNeil. Bodybuilding legend Charles Atlas was the model for "Peace." *Between Waverly Pl. and W. 4th St. at 5th Ave. Subway: A, B, C, D, E, F, or Q to W. 4th St. (Washington Sq.).*

Most of the striking old buildings bordering Washington Square belong to **New York University** (*see below*). The **Row,** a line of well-preserved, Federal-style town houses lining the north side of the square between 5th Avenue and University Place, now serves as offices and housing for lucky NYU faculty. Ditto for **Washington Mews** (half a block north), a cobblestone private street lined on one side with the former stables of the residences on the Row. Because Washington Square has long been considered tony real estate, it's had its share of famous residents: Author Willa Cather once lived at 60 Washington Square South, and Henry James's grandmother made her home at 18 Washington Square North (now demolished); James used it as the setting for his creatively titled, bodice-ripping novel *Washington Square.* Eugene O'Neill wrote *The Iceman Cometh* between trips to the pub from his home at 38 Washington Square South.

The **Judson Memorial Church,** a Romanesque Revival masterwork built in 1890 by McKim, Mead & White, is known as much for the social activism of its congregation as its impressive stained glass and marble reliefs: The American Baptist church has supported AIDS research and abortion rights. The church was also home to the famous avant-garde Judson Dance Theater in the '60s. The art world has never been the same since. The building's 10-story campanile makes it easy to identify. *55 Washington Square S, at Thompson St.*

MACDOUGAL STREET

Pick up MacDougal Street on the west side of Washington Square to watch Village people do their thing. South of the Square, between West 3rd and Bleecker streets, you'll find a row of ancient cafés that all claim to have been the Beats' "favorite" hangout (*see* Cafés *in* Chapter 4). The intersection with Bleecker Street is a major bar scene—well, for the bridge-and-tunnel crowd, anyway. North of Washington Square you'll find the **Provincetown Playhouse** (133 MacDougal St.), recently purchased by NYU, which provided a venue for showcasing the works of the great playwright Eugene O'Neill; the gracious Federal homes at **127–131 MacDougal Street** were once owned by former vice president and unfortunately accurate marksman Aaron Burr. Fiorello La Guardia, the enormously popular mayor of the 1930s and '40s who passed major social reforms (and also read "Dick Tracy" comic strips over the radio) was born at **177 Sullivan Street,** a block east of MacDougal Street. MacDougal Street ends to the north at **West 8th Street,** a.k.a. "The Shoe Street." It's filled with discount footwear boutiques.

NEW YORK UNIVERSITY

New York University was founded in 1831 by a group of prominent citizens fed up with what they saw as a ridiculous infatuation with Greek and Latin among the colleges of their day. NYU, they proclaimed, would cater to the common person. Today, it's the largest private university in the United States, offering over 2,500 courses (including Greek and Latin) and 25 degrees to both graduate and undergraduate students. Almost all of the programs at NYU are among the top in the nation, but its film school—which has graduated the likes of Spike Lee, Martin Scorsese, and Ang Lee—is perhaps the most famous one. Most of the buildings you'll see around Washington Square belong to the school—just look for the purple flags.

The **Elmer Holmes Bobst Library** (70 Washington Sq. S, at La Guardia Pl.) is a repository of some 2.5 million books. In the 1960s, well-intentioned but aesthetically impaired university officials planned (with aid of architects Philip Johnson and Richard Foster) to reface *all* its Washington Square buildings in ugly red sandstone, just like this one. Thankfully, cost proved prohibitive and they soon abandoned the plan. Next door, the **Loeb Student Center** (566 La Guardia Pl., at Washington Sq. S, tel. 212/998–4900) stands on the site of a famous boardinghouse, nicknamed the House of Genius for the talented writers who lived there over the years—Stephen Crane, O. Henry, and Theodore Dreiser, to name a few. Check its North Lobby for flyers about happenings around NYU. Pop by the university's Main Building (entrances at 100 Washington Sq. E and 33 Washington Pl.) to check out the exhibits, usually of contemporary art, at **Grey Art Gallery** (*see* Museums and Galleries, *below*). For maps and such, stop by **NYU information,** on the first floor of Shimkin Hall (50 W. 4th St., at Washington Sq. E, tel. 212/998–4636). It's open weekdays 8:30–8, weekends 10–4. On weekdays during the school year, **free tours** of the university are given several times daily. Tours depart from the Office of Undergraduate Admissions (22 Washington Sq. N, tel. 212/998–4524). Reservations are not necessary. *Subway: N or R to E. 8th St. or A, B, C, D, E, F, or Q to W. 4th St. (Washington Sq.).*

The Church of St. Luke-in-the-Fields (487 Hudson St., between Christopher and Barrow Sts.), a simple chapel built in 1821, has a small garden area that is open to the public during the day. It's a pleasant spot for a picnic lunch.

BROADWAY

The Great White Way turns incredibly unglamorous around NYU. It's lined by modern university highrises, fast-food joints, and mallish clothing stores. Two shops are worth checking out: The **Strand** (*see* Used and Rare Books *in* Chapter 5) overflows with some 8 mi of books, and a few steps north on the same block, Forbidden Planet (*see* Specialty Bookstores *in* Chapter 5) claims the title of world's largest comic book and sci-fi store. And Tower Records (*see* Records, Tapes and CDs *in* Chapter 5) is simply just big.

GRACE CHURCH • Seeing this ornate Gothic church on an undistinguished block of Broadway is a bit like spying a wedding dress in a rack of poly-blend T-shirts. James Renwick, Jr., a parishioner with a very odd hobby (some people collect model trains, he drew cathedrals) designed it for free; when it opened for business 1846, it was the first Gothic-style church in the United States. During the 19th century its flock was incredibly rich. Step inside and admire the glorious English stained-glass windows that bathe the interior in an otherworldly glow. Free brochures at the back of the church point out some of the church's architectural highlights. Classical music concerts (usually around $15) are held here throughout the year. *802 Broadway, between 10th and 11th Sts., tel. 212/254–2000. Admission free. Open weekdays 10–5:30, Sat. noon–4.*

WEST OF 6TH AVENUE

If you've been navigating Manhattan's efficient, numbered grid and just crossed over 6th Avenue into the heart of the Village, you're in for a shock: Its tree-lined streets are short and narrow, and cross each other at unfathomable angles. But don't let this vex you. It's one of the most beautiful neighborhoods in the city, with rows of ivy-covered brick town houses and nary a skyscraper in sight. Spend the afternoon wandering, then park yourself in one of its woodsy taverns (many former speakeasies) for a drink.

JEFFERSON MARKET LIBRARY • The triangle formed by West 10th Street, 6th Avenue, and Greenwich Avenue originally held a meat market, an all-women jail, and the magnificent 1877 courthouse that is now the Jefferson Market Library (a branch of the New York Public Library system). It's another fine design by the ubiquitous Calvert Vaux and Frederick Clarke Withers. A group of architects voted it one of the "ten most beautiful buildings in America" in 1885, but critics often have a hard time

JUSTICE IS DONE

At the corner of Greene Street and East Washington Place, one of New York City's great tragedies took place. Owners of the Triangle Shirtwaist Company, employers of about 500 women, felt the easiest way to keep workers at their sewing machines was to lock all the doors. When a fire broke out on March 25, 1911, there was no escape; 146 women perished, some by leaping to their deaths from the 10th floor. Families of 23 victims sued for damages and won, sort of, when a court ordered the company to pay each $75. The real victory came when the state passed 56 new laws regarding workers' safety.

describing it. Some say it's "Venetian," others call it "High Victorian Gothic." Villagers, noting the alternating wide bands of red brick and narrow strips of white granite, dubbed it the "Lean Bacon Style." *425 6th Ave., at W. 10th St., tel. 212/243–4334. Subway: 1 or 9 to Christopher St. (Sheridan Sq.). Open Mon. and Thurs. 10–6, Tues. and Fri. noon–6, Wed. noon–8, Sat. 10–5.*

Around the corner you'll find two tiny, charming courtyards, **Patchin Place** (off W. 10th St., between Greenwich Ave. and 6th Ave.) and **Milligan Place** (off 6th Ave., just north of W. 10th St.). Both were built in the 1850s for the waiters (mostly Basques) who worked at posh 5th Avenue hotels. **No. 4 Patchin Place** was the onetime home of e. e. cummings. Also worth a quick look is the gourmet wonderland **Balducci's**, which began decades ago with the lowly vegetable cart of the late Louis Balducci, and **Bigelow's Pharmacy** (414 6th Ave., between W. 8th and 9th Sts., tel. 212/533–2700), which looks the same as the day it opened in 1838, right down to the wooden display cases.

GAY STREET • This short, crooked lane is lined with small row houses circa 1810. It was once a black neighborhood and later a strip of speakeasies. Ruth McKenney wrote *My Sister Eileen* (based on experiences with her sister and her brother-in-law, Nathanael West) in the basement of **No. 14 Gay Street**. *Between Christopher St. and Waverly Pl., just west of 6th Ave.*

SHERIDAN SQUARE • In 1863 this was the site of one of the nastiest riots in American history; a mob outraged with the Civil War draft turned against the city's freed slaves and some 125 people were killed. You'll find a statue of the mighty and heavily mustached military man for whom the square is named, Civil War general Philip "Little Phil" Sheridan, near the north end. *7th Ave. S at intersection of Christopher, W. 4th, and Grove Sts. Subway: 1 or 9 to Christopher St. (Sheridan Sq.).*

Southwest of Sheridan Square is **Christopher Street,** chock-full of gay bars and shops and strolling gay couples. Whatever your sexual orientation, you should stop by the **Li-Lac Chocolate Shop** (120 Christopher St., tel. 212/242–7374) for homemade chocolate and buttercrunch. The national gay-rights movement was born not far from Sheridan Square in 1969, when riots broke out over a police raid of the now-defunct gay club, **Stonewall Inn,** which was at 51 Christopher St. The Inn is long gone, but a plaque marks the site (a gay bar, called Stonewall, is next door to the site of the original). In tiny **Christopher Park** (Christopher St., north of Sheridan Sq.) you'll find statues by sculptor George Segal of a lesbian couple sitting on a bench and gay male partners standing nearby.

BEDFORD STREET • The narrowest house in the Village is at **75½ Bedford Street,** a scant 9½ ft wide. It led a fine life as an alley until soaring real-estate prices inspired someone to put it to good use in 1873. Pulitzer-winning poet Edna St. Vincent Millay lived here in the 1920s. Next door, **77 Bedford Street** is the oldest house in the Village (1799), while **86 Bedford Street** was the site of a Prohibition-era speakeasy. The bar that stands here now, **Chumley's** (*see* Chapter 6), keeps up the tradition by leaving its entrance unmarked; for decades, it was a meeting place for writers, including John Steinbeck, Ernest Hemingway, and Jack Kerouac. At the intersection with Grove Street, look for the chaletlike 1835 house that Villagers call **Twin Peaks** (102 Bedford St.).

COMMERCE STREET • Walk two blocks south of Grove Street on Bedford Street to find the homes of more famous dead folk: Aaron Burr at **17 Commerce Street,** Washington Irving at **11 Commerce**

Street. The two identical brick houses separated by a garden are popularly known as the **Twin Sisters** (39–41 Commerce St.). Local legend has it that they were built by an indulgent sea captain for his two spoiled daughters, who loathed each other. The **Cherry Lane Theater** (38 Commerce St., tel. 212/989–2020) is one of the city's very first Off-Broadway houses and site of American premieres of works by O'Neill, Beckett, Ionesco, and Albee.

ST. LUKE'S PLACE • St. Luke's Place (the proper name for Leroy Street between Hudson Street and 7th Avenue South) is *the* place to go to check out classy 1850s town houses with famous pasts: Poet Marianne Moore lived at **No. 14**; Jimmy Walker, mayor of New York during the '20s and one of its most colorful political figures, lived at **No. 6** (the lampposts out front are special "mayor's lamps"); **No. 12** was shown as the Huxtables' home on *The Cosby Show* (although the family ostensibly lived in Brooklyn); and **No. 4** was the setting of the Audrey Hepburn movie *Wait Until Dark. Subway: 1 or 9 to Houston St.*

MEAT-PACKING DISTRICT

Believe it or not, New York City was the largest center of beef production in America during the mid-1800s. But with the advent of refrigeration, most meat packers quit trying to wrangle whole dead heifers into Manhattan and instead moved out West where the cows were. Still, more than a few have stuck around to serve the city's large Jewish community, since kosher meat can be kept only three days after butchering. Wholesale meat markets—fragrant enough to make your nose quiver even if you've never read anything by Upton Sinclair—can still be found sandwiched along the cobblestone streets west of Washington Street and south of 12th Street. (The men you see lingering at corners here work a different kind of meat market.) Photographers love the grit and rawness (no pun intended) of the meat-packing district, and if you stroll around you're bound to see a few fashion shoots in progress. Quite a few late-night restaurants and clubs have sprung up here in recent years. *Subway: A, C, E, or L to W. 14th St.*

Much to the chagrin of its stuffy parishioners, the February 10, 1863, marriage of "General" Tom Thumb to Lavinia Warren, orchestrated by P. T. Barnum, temporarily turned Grace Church into a circus—literally.

EAST VILLAGE AND ALPHABET CITY

The East Village, originally considered part of the Lower East Side, was colonized by the young artists and intellectuals of the 1950s and '60s who'd abandoned Greenwich Village because it was too expensive. Beats like Jack Kerouac, Allen Ginsberg, and William S. Burroughs, jazz greats Charlie Parker and Charles Mingus, and artists like Willem de Kooning and Mark Rothko cruised these streets for inspiration or, sometimes, drugs. Which is not to say the East Village didn't exist before these artists got here: In 1925 George Gershwin penned "I'm Something on Avenue A," and prior to the Civil War rich folks like the Vanderbilts made **Astor Place** (*see below*) one of the city's most exclusive addresses.

Following reluctantly—kicking and screaming even—on the heels of neighborhoods like the West Village, SoHo, and TriBeCa, which morphed into overpriced yuppielands, the scruffy East Village—bounded to the west by 4th Avenue and Lafayette Street, to the north by 14th Street, to the south by Houston Street, and to the east by the East River—is slowly becoming too expensive for the misfits and characters who made it famous. For decades the area miraculously remained the domain of nihilists, starving artists, and people with lots of dyed hair, pierced body parts, and tattoos. All the weird folks are still hanging around, but since the police cleared out Tompkins Square park in 1988 they just don't rule the neighborhood like they used to. Main drags in the East Village are **St. Marks Place** and **Avenue A,** littered with bars, clubs, cafés, avant-garde galleries, hole-in-the-wall theaters, and purveyors of secondhand kitsch. Along the East River is the busy, soccer- and softball-crazy **East River Park** (*see* Parks and Gardens, *below*), where the views of the Brooklyn Bridge can't be beat.

Add to the mix a few thriving ethnic enclaves: **Little Ukraine** (1st and 2nd Aves., near E. 7th St.) has a handful of Ukrainian diners, a few Eastern Orthodox churches, the **Ukrainian Museum** (*see* Museums and Galleries, *below*), and a bunch of dives where elderly Ukrainian women tend bar. **Little India** (6th St. between 1st and 2nd Aves.) is jam-packed with restaurants vying to serve you the cheapest tandoori in the most garish surroundings. For more on neighborhood restaurants, *see* Chapter 4.

EAST VILLAGE AND ALPHABET CITY

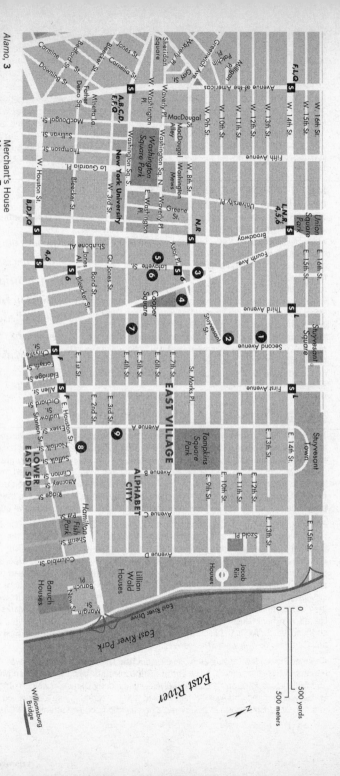

ASTOR PLACE

At the intersection of 4th Avenue and Lafayette Street, Astor Place is the gateway to the East Village: Teen skateboarders hang out; and the occasional band sets up to grind out a few Eagles oldies. The subway entrance here is a green cast-iron replica of the beaux arts original. Next to it is *Alamo,* a huge black steel cube sculpted in 1967 by Bernard Rosenthal. It balances on one corner and was designed to pivot, but, alas, pivots no more. *Subway: 6 to Astor Pl.*

The street's namesake, John Jacob Astor, made his first millions by trading furs in the Pacific Northwest (bas-relief beavers on the tiles at the Astor Place subway station are fuzzy little reminders). Once settled in New York City he degenerated into a human Jabba the Hut, amassing enough land and wealth to be considered the richest man in America by 1840—all with a girth too great to get out of bed and on a steady diet of human milk. On his deathbed he expressed the desire to buy every foot of land in Manhattan.

One of the bloodiest riots in New York history occurred on Astor Place in 1849, over a disparaging remark made by Charles Macready, an English tragedian (popular with the city's Anglophilic elite), about the abilities of Edwin Forrest, an American actor worshiped by the working classes. Hundreds of protesters armed with rotten eggs, fruit, and rocks interrupted Macready's performance of *MacBeth* at the Astor Place Opera House. The ensuing riot left 31 dead, over 150 injured, and painfully underscored the chasm between New York's classes.

The Corinthian columns fronting the town houses at Colonnade Row were built by talented inmates of Sing Sing Penitentiary.

COLONNADE ROW

These days, Colonnade Row's four remaining town houses resemble Greek ruins more than Greek Revival masterpieces. The original 1833 development of nine homes—named "La Grange Terrace" after the country estate of the Marquis de Lafayette—was derided as tacky by New York elites until bigshots like John Jacob Astor, Cornelius Vanderbilt, and Charles Dickens moved in. Current tenants are much less impressive. On the street level of two of the houses are the popular **Indochine** restaurant and the **Astor Place Theatre,** whose present tenant *Blue Man Group* may run forever. *428–434 Lafayette St., between Astor Pl. and E. 4th St. Subway: 6 to Astor Pl.*

JOSEPH PAPP PUBLIC THEATER • The imposing Italian Renaissance–style building across the street began life as the city's first free library (a gift from the usually miserly John Jacob Astor in 1854), then became offices for the Hebrew Immigrant Aid Society (HIAS) before being renovated in the '60s to serve as the New York Shakespeare Festival's Joseph Papp Public Theater. Under the leadership of the late Joseph Papp, the Public's five playhouses built a reputation for innovative performances: The Aquarian hippie-fest *Hair* started here, as well as *A Chorus Line,* and it helped launch the careers of Meryl Streep, Raul Julia, Kevin Kline, James Earl Jones, and David Mamet. For more information, *see* Chapter 7. The theater is most famous for its New York Shakespeare Festival, which has produced every one of the Bard's plays over the last two decades. Today the Public is overseen by producer-director George Wolfe, who directed the big Broadway hit, *Bring in 'Da Noise, Bring in 'Da Funk.* The new bar, "Joe's Pub" has become a trendy theater hangout. *425 Lafayette St., at Astor Pl., tel. 212/260–2400. Subway: 6 to Astor Pl.*

COOPER UNION AND COOPER SQUARE

If self-made millionaire, railroad industrialist, and inventor Peter Cooper were still alive, every year he'd probably get 1,000 big wet kisses from the engineers, artists, and architects in training at the Cooper Union, a totally *tuition-free* college. Cooper himself came from a poor family and learned to read late in life, so he plowed his big bucks back into an institute of higher learning for working folks, opened in 1859. Lectures in its **Foundation Building** (the city's first internal steel-frame building, which was Cooper's own invention) helped launch the NAACP and catapulted Abraham Lincoln to the presidency—Abe gave his famous "Might Makes Right" speech here in 1860. The building has two free galleries presenting changing art shows during the academic year. Call or check the paper for the current lecture and concert schedule. *41 Cooper Sq., between 3rd and 4th Aves., tel. 212/254–6374. Subway: 6 to Astor Pl.*

Cooper Union stands, logically, on **Cooper Square** (bordered by St. Marks Place, 3rd and 4th Aves., and the Bowery), an immaculate—and locked—park with a regal-looking statue of Peter Cooper at its center. The **offices of the *Village Voice*** (36 Cooper Sq.), New York's famous radical weekly, stands to the west of the square.

ST. MARKS PLACE

St. Marks Place, as 8th Street is called between 3rd Avenue and Avenue A, is still one of the liveliest streets in the East Village. Hippies and acid heads tripped here in the '60s, and disco fever found its first NYC outlet here in the '70s at a club called Get Down. White techno kids listening to Tricky now make up the scene. You can buy just about anything in the string of cluttered shops or at the de facto flea market that appears daily along the sidewalk, from vintage clothes to a new guitar. Unfortunately, there's even a Gap. *Subway: 6 to Astor Pl.*

ST. MARK'S-IN-THE-BOWERY CHURCH

This 1799 fieldstone country church was built over the family chapel of Peter Stuyvesant (who is buried here), and is the city's oldest continually used church. Its liberal clergy has sponsored voter-registration drives, preached for civil rights, and opened the nation's first lesbian health-care clinic. In the '20s, one pastor livened up the boring Episcopalian ceremonies with American Indian chants, Greek folk dancing, and recitation of Eastern mantras. It currently hosts dance, poetry, and musical performances; call for a schedule. Their small theater has gleaned a reputation for experimental work. *2nd Ave. at E. 10th St., tel. 212/674–8194. Subway: L to 3rd Ave.*

The stretch of 2nd Avenue next to St. Mark's Church was known as the "Jewish Rialto" at the turn of the century because its eight Yiddish theaters presented the best in comedy, melodrama, and musicals from the Old World. On the sidewalk in front of the **Second Avenue Deli** (*see* East Village and Alphabet City *in* Chapter 4) are Hollywood-style squares commemorating luminaries of the Yiddish stage.

TOMPKINS SQUARE

Tompkins Square Park is the physical, spiritual, and political heart of the radical East Village. It's a good-size park, and you can always find a drum circle or game of Rollerblade basketball or whatever. Look for two monuments: **Temperance Fountain,** oddly out of place given the number of people drinking beers out of brown bags, and the **General Slocum Memorial,** which commemorates 1,021 German immigrants from the East Village who perished on the way to a church picnic when their ship caught fire and sank.

The square takes its name from four-times governor Daniel Tompkins, an avid abolitionist and vice president under James Monroe who once owned this land from 2nd Avenue to the East River. Its history is long and violent: The 1874 Tompkins Square Riot involved some 7,000 unhappy laborers and 1,600 police. The police gained control by beating bystanders and demonstrators indiscriminately. The 1988 Tompkins Square Riot involved police on horseback charging homeless-rights and anti-gentrification protesters armed with sticks and bottles—Mayor David Dinkins had ordered the square cleared of proliferating refrigerator-box castles and tent mansions. The park did not reopen until 1992, midnight curfew in place (it still is). In between the tumultuous events, activist Abbie Hoffman and his New Left Yippies held a few rallies at the square in the '60s. Between 1950–1954, jazz great Charlie Parker lived east of the park at 151 Avenue B; a block of that avenue bears his name. *E. 7th–10th Sts. between Aves. A and B. Subway: 6 to Astor Pl.*

ALPHABET CITY

As you head toward the East River to the blocks along Avenues A, B, C, and D you enter Alphabet City. It was predominantly a Puerto Rican community, once known as the heroin capital of New York. Gentrification and a police crackdown on drugs have made it a much safer place—**Avenue A** has been annexed by East Village hipsters and is crowded with bars, cafés, and cheap restaurants. But avenues C and D are still places to use caution (or avoid) after dark. On buildings throughout the neighborhood look for graffiti murals, sometimes beautiful and poignant. Many eulogize members of the community who have fallen to gang violence. A 30-ft-tall sculpture, of welded-together children's toys, stands on Avenue C between East 5th and 6th streets. Other landmarks to look for: **Red Square** (Houston St. between Aves. A and B) is a redbrick high-rise with a gloriously beaming statue of Vladimir Lenin (plundered from Russia after the fall of Communism) on its roof. The bland, blocklike **First Houses** (E. 3rd St. at Ave. A), built in 1935, have the dubious distinction of being the first public-housing projects in the entire country.

Despite Alphabet City's years of economic troubles and the invasion of the monied crowd, there's still a sense of community here that many other neighborhoods in the city totally lack.

LOWER EAST SIDE

In the century before the Beats carved out their own urban utopia, the East Village, for radical politics and experimental art, everything east of Broadway and from 14th Street south to Canal Street was considered the "Lower East Side." Today it's roughly confined by Houston Street to the north, the Bowery to the west, and Canal Street to the south. Almost every ethnic group to arrive in America has spent some time here: Irish, Italians, Eastern-Europeans, Jews, Russians, Ukrainians, and Poles in the 1880s, and more recently Africans, Puerto Ricans, Chinese, Dominicans, Filipinos, Indians, and Koreans. Wander its streets and you can find octogenarian Sengalese playing dominoes, overhear a heated argument about the meaning of a particular verse in the Talmud, or purchase Spanish-language comics at a corner newsstand.

Although waves of immigrants fresh from Ellis Island made this the most crowded neighborhood in the world around 1915, until recently it had grown nearly deserted. Club kids, Kurt Cobain mourners, and adventurous yuppies have started drifting south from the East Village in search of cheaper rents and bigger thrills; they're responsible for the hipster bars and cafés that have sprung up along **Ludlow Street** and **East Houston Street.** Pinch me bubbi, I think I'm in a Calvin Klein ad! Seriously, though: Recent additions aside, the historically minded will enjoy an afternoon stroll though this fascinating neighborhood. *Subway: F to 2nd Ave.*

Around the turn of the century, the few square blocks along Orchard Street could attract as many as 25,000 pushcart salesmen in a single day. Eventually the city declared pushcarts a nuisance and banished them for good.

ESSEX STREET AND THE JEWISH COMMUNITY

In the '20s a half million Jews comprised one of the largest enclaves on the Lower East Side. Many Jewish shops, delis, and temples still line Essex Street, particularly its intersection with **Hester Street.** An unparalleled junk shop, **Israel Wholesale** (21 Essex St., at Hester St., tel. 212/477–2310) supplies the diaspora with menorahs 'n' more. Buy your yarmulkes at **H&M Skullcap Company** (46 Hester St., near Essex St., tel. 212/777–2280) or some hamentaschen (apricot- or prune-filled pastries) at **Gertel's Bakery** (53 Hester St., at Essex St., tel. 212/982–3250). **Guss' Lower Eastside Pickle Corp.** (35 Essex St., between Grand and Hester Sts., tel. 212/254–4477) sells its vinegary delicacies straight from the barrel and is an essential New York experience.

SCHAPIRO'S WINERY • Also worth a visit is America's first kosher winery. Though it's been around since 1899, Schapiro's will never steal the thunder from France's Châteauneuf-du-Pape; the original Schapiro's slogan was SO THICK YOU CAN CUT IT WITH A KNIFE. The dusty store doles out free samples (Sunday 11–5) and offers free half-hour tours of its cellars on Sundays from September to Passover; call for exact times. *126 Rivington St., between Essex and Norfolk Sts., tel. 212/674–4404. Subway: J, M, or Z to Essex St.*

ELDRIDGE STREET SYNAGOGUE • Built in 1887 for the newly arrived Eastern-European Jewish community, the Eldridge Street Synagogue is one of the Lower East Side's largest and grandest remaining synagogues. Although years of neglect have taken their toll, its intricate carvings and masonry remain intact, as well as its overwhelming sense of history and sanctity. The temple is currently being restored as a cultural heritage center and remains open for guided tours ($4), given every Sunday on the hour noon to 4 and by appointment Tuesday–Thursday. *12–16 Eldridge St., at Canal St., tel. 212/ 219–0888. Subway: J, M, or Z to Essex St.*

ESSEX STREET MARKET • Taking up most of a block between Rivington and Delancey Street, this feisty market is worth a visit for the prices—some of the lowest for fresh produce, fish, and meat in the city—but also for the mainly Dominican and Puerto Rican and other Caribbean characters who man the stalls. *Essex St. between Rivington and Delancey Sts. Subway F to Delancey or J, M, or Z to Essex St.*

FIRST SHEARITH ISRAEL GRAVEYARD • t's hard to believe some of the folks buried hear escaped the Inquisition! The U.S's oldest Jewish Graveyard is home to Spanish Jews from as early as 1690. *57 St. James Place, btw. Oliver and James Sts. Subway B or D to Grand St.*

ORCHARD STREET BARGAIN DISTRICT

Orchard Street is lined with old-time mom-and-pop stores selling ersatz leather goods, linens, bootleg tapes, fabrics, "designer" watches, clothing, housewares, and just plain junk. A spillover of bars from Trendy Ludlow Street threatens to change the bazaarlike character of the street. Originally, immigrants

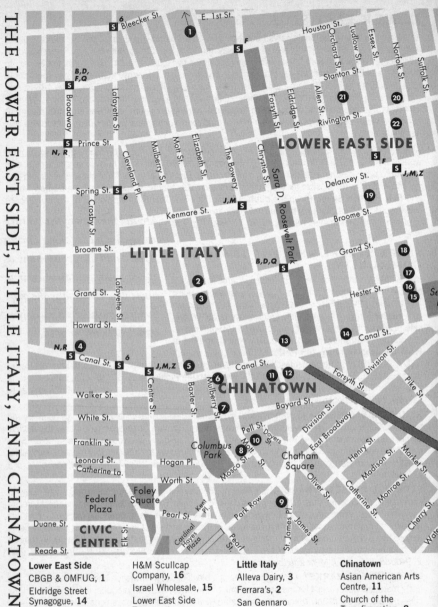

Lower East Side

CBGB & OMFUG, **1**

Eldridge Street Synagogue, **14**

Essex Street Market, **22**

First Shearith Israel graveyard, **9**

Gertel's Bakery, **17**

Guss' Lower Eastside Pickle Corp., **18**

H&M Scullcap Company, **16**

Israel Wholesale, **15**

Lower East Side Tenement Museum, **19**

Orchard Street Bargain District, **21**

Schapiro's Winery, **20**

Little Italy

Alleva Dairy, **3**

Ferrara's, **2**

San Gennaro Church, **5**

Chinatown

Asian American Arts Centre, **11**

Church of the Transfiguration, **8**

Confucius Plaza, **12**

Kam Man, **6**

Mahayana Temple, **13**

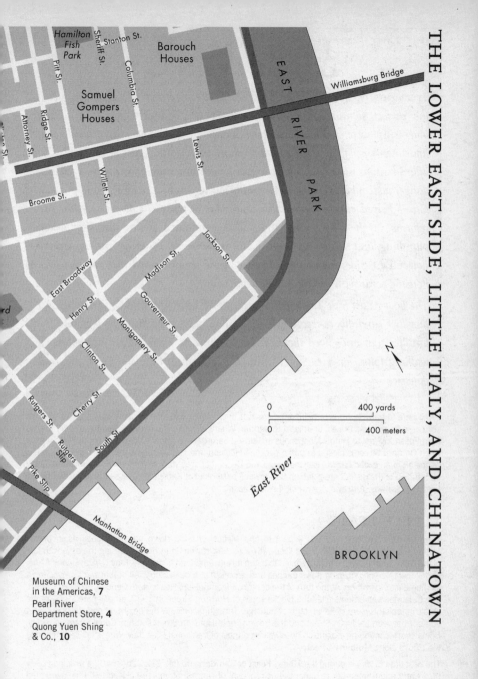

Hamilton Fish Park

Pitt St.

Sheriff St.

Stanton St.

Columbia St.

Barouch Houses

EAST

RIVER

PARK

Williamsburg Bridge

Samuel Gompers Houses

Attorney St.

Ridge St.

Lewis St.

Broome St.

Willett St.

Jackson St.

Madison St.

East Broadway

Gouverneur St.

Henry St.

Montgomery St.

Clinton St.

Cherry St.

Rutgers St.

Rutgers Slip

South St.

Pike Slip

Manhattan Bridge

East River

N

0   400 yards
0   400 meters

BROOKLYN

Museum of Chinese in the Americas, **7**

Pearl River Department Store, **4**

Quong Yuen Shing & Co., **10**

TENEMENT BUILDINGS

Tenements, cheap to build and easy to maintain (or neglect), were considered the perfect solution to the city's 19th-century immigration boom. Early tenements were typically six-story buildings with four tiny, windowless apartments per floor and no indoor plumbing, heating, gas, or electricity. To afford rent, as many as 20 people would cram into each apartment—crowded, dangerous, and depressing. Muckraking journalists like Jacob Riis and Stephen Crane helped expose the squalid conditions of tenement dwellers, leading to reforms in the 1870s and 1900s that mandated basics like ventilation, plumbing, and electricity. You can still see tenement buildings throughout the Lower East Side; notice that the style of the time dictated that even low-cost housing come with ornate Italianate facades.

The Lower East Side Tenement Museum (see Museums and Galleries, below) has two carefully re-created tenement buildings with displays depicting the families that once lived there. The museum also offers weekly neighborhood walking tours for $10–$15, a must if you're into the history of immigrant America.

came here to hawk buttons or heirloom diamonds or whatever else they owned. Scores of New Yorkers still come for cut-rate prices, or at least to wander: Where else can you hear bargaining in every tongue from Polish to Farsi to Hindi? Most shops are closed Saturday—but that's okay. The big deal is Sunday, when Orchard Street is closed to traffic between Houston and Hester streets and the whole area takes on the air of an exotic bazaar. Between April and December, free **walking and shopping tours** (tel. 212/995–8258) of the district are given on Sunday at 11 AM; meet at Katz's Delicatessen (Ludlow and Houston Sts.). *Subway: F to 2nd Ave.; walk 4 blocks east.*

LITTLE ITALY

Welcome to Little Italy. Did you expect to find Mafiosi chasing down narrow streets, as in Martin Scorcese's *Mean Streets*? Or stoops filled with wizened old women in black, passing the days with talk of the Old Country? Maybe you expected to catch Italian-American actors like Tony Danza, Danny Aiello, and Robert De Niro slurping down cannoli and espresso at a café? Sorry. All of that went *arrivederci* a long time ago, *bambino*. At the turn of the century, Piedmontese, Neapolitan, Genoan, Sicilian, Tuscan, and Calabrian settlements filled the blocks south of Houston Street; in 1932, an estimated 98% of the area's inhabitants were of Italian birth or heritage. Though technically the neighborhood still occupies a corridor between Lafayette Street and the Bowery, from Houston Street south to Canal Street, in reality, Chinatown's continuing expansion has swallowed most of traditional Little Italy. What's left is confined to the blocks along **Mulberry Street.**

The best time to visit is during the 10-day **Feast of San Gennaro** (tel. 212/226–9546), a rollicking party held every mid-September to honor the patron saint of Naples. Streets are closed to traffic, decorated with tinsel, then packed with game booths and vendors of Italo-snacks. It's officially sponsored by the **San Gennaro Church** (113 Baxter St., near Canal St.). In June is the smaller **Feast of St. Anthony of Padua.** For more on both, *see* Festivals *in* Chapter 1.

What you get on Mulberry Street are souvenir shops sandwiched between tourist-filled trattorias and sidewalk cafés; looming above are the tenement buildings into which immigrant families once crowded. It's a street for strolling, gawking, and inhaling the aroma of garlic and olive oil, but you'll need an appetite to explore. Off Mulberry at 195 Grand Street, **Ferrara's** (tel. 212/226–6150) is a 100-year-old pastry shop. It's a truly wonderful place to eat tiramisu and sip cappuccino, even if you're sitting next to some bloke who thinks the Grand Canal is a sewage treatment plant in the Bronx. Also on Grand Street, the **Alleva Dairy** (188 Grand St., at Mulberry St., tel. 212/226–7990) has been selling its homemade mozzarella for over a century. *Subway: 6 to Spring St.*

If you want to see a thriving Italian-American community populated by Italian Americans, not tourists, hop a subway to Carroll Gardens in Brooklyn or Arthur Avenue in the Bronx.

CHINATOWN

It looks like New York, but not quite. The streets of Chinatown are crowded, bustling, and vibrant as crowds gather at sidewalk markets, offering buckets of live fish, stacks of alien-looking vegetables, and bundles of refrigerated chicken feet. But the words you hear spoken and see on the shopkeepers' signs are most often Chinese. Even the smells are different, courtesy of street vendors serving up steaming chow mein and conch dumplings. Around half of the city's population of 300,000 Chinese live here; some 55% of its residents speak little or no English. In recent years, a flood of immigrants from Thailand, Korea, Vietnam, Taiwan, and especially Hong Kong have settled beyond the traditional boundaries of Chinatown and swallowed parts of Little Italy and the Lower East Side.

CANAL STREET

Formerly Chinatown's northern barrier, Canal Street (which was once really a canal) is now one of the busiest streets in the neighborhood and lined with interesting shops. Check out the **Pearl River Department Store** (277 Canal St., at Broadway, tel. 212/431–4770) for porcelain teacups and Maoist postage stamps and **Kam Man** (200 Canal St., between Mulberry and Mott Sts., tel. 212/571–0330) for Chinese food items. Just south of Canal Street on the Bowery, you'll find the **Asian American Arts Centre** (*see* Museums and Galleries, *below*). At the eastern end of Canal, across the Bowery and near the entrance to the Manhattan Bridge, is the Buddhist **Mahayana Temple** (133 Canal St., tel. 212/925–8787), with a bright yellow facade, red columns, and golden dragons at the entrance; inside incongruous crystal chandeliers hang above the 15-ft tall golden Buddha. *Subway: J, M, N, R, Z, or 6 to Canal St.*

Be sure to stop at the **Museum of Chinese in the Americas** (*see* Museums and Galleries, *below*), a block south of Canal Street. Other streets great for wandering include **Mott Street, Pell Street,** and **Bayard Street**; the intersection of Mott and Pell streets is the heart of Chinatown. On Mott Street you can visit the ancient curio shop **Quong Yuen Shing & Co.** (32 Mott St., near Pell St., tel. 212/962–6280); and, across the street, the **Church of the Transfiguration** (25 Mott St., at Mosco St., tel. 212/962–5157), an 1801 Georgian structure with Gothic windows and a Chinese Catholic congregation. Mass is said in Cantonese, Mandarin, and English. If you're looking for a place to relax, check out **Columbus Park** (Bayard St. between Baxter and Mulberry Sts.). This tiny, paved park was once the site of a tough, 19th-century slum of Irish and German immigrants. Nowadays you can watch early rising Chinese practicing the graceful movements of tai chi.

CHATHAM SQUARE

Ten different roads converge at Chatham Square, causing vehicular and pedestrian nightmares aplenty. On the center island is the **Kim Lau Arch,** a memorial to the Chinese Americans who died defending the United States in foreign wars (good luck getting across the street to take a closer look). The area north of the square, where Bowery and Canal Street come together, is called **Confucius Plaza,** possibly because a spectacular bronze statue of Confucius stands guard. At the statue's base you'll see a long, thought-provoking quote from the 2,000-year-old wise man's treatise, *The Chapter of the Great Harmony (Ta Tung).*

SOHO

SoHo (so-named because it's the area SOuth of HOuston Street), formerly industrial and now high-wattage hip, shed its working-class roots not so long ago. In the mid-19th century this was a light-industry district, with makers and sellers of goods like china, furs, textiles, glass, and lace; shops and factories and even sweatshops were housed in grand **cast-iron buildings.** Unfortunately, the overcrowded area caught fire so frequently it was dubbed "Hell's Hundred Acres"; as late as 1962 a City Club of New York

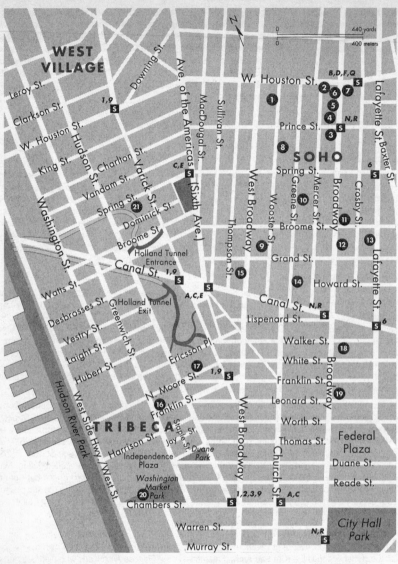

WEST VILLAGE

Leroy St.
Clarkson St.
W. Houston St.
King St.
Hudson St.
Washington St.
Charlton St.
Vandam St.
Spring St.
Dominick St.
Broome St.
Watts St.
Desbrosses St.
Vestry St.
Laight St.
Hubert St.

Downing St.
Varick St.
MacDougal St.
Ave. of the Americas (Sixth Ave.)
Sullivan St.
Thompson St.
West Broadway

Holland Tunnel Entrance
Canal St. 1,9
Holland Tunnel Exit
Ericsson Pl.
N. Moore St. 1,9
Franklin St.
Harrison St.
Independence Plaza
Washington Market Park
Chambers St.
Warren St.
Murray St.

West Side Hwy./West St.
Hudson River Park
Greenwich St.
Staple St.
Jay St.
Duane Park

TRIBECA

W. Houston St.
Prince St.
Spring St.
Greene St.
Wooster St.
Mercer St.
Broadway
Crosby St.
Broome St.
Grand St.
Howard St.
Canal St. N,R
Lispenard St.
Walker St.
White St.
Franklin St.
Leonard St.
Worth St.
Thomas St.
Duane St.
Reade St.

SOHO

Lafayette St.
Baxter St.
Lafayette St.

B,D,F,Q
N,R
C,E
A,C,E

Federal Plaza
Church St.
West Broadway
City Hall Park

Alternative Museum, 7
Children's Museum of the Arts, 13
Ghostbusters' headquarters, 17
Guggenheim Museum SoHo, 4
Haughwout Building, 11
Institute for Contemporary Art/Clocktower Gallery, 19

King of Greene Street, 10
Museum for African Art, 6
New Museum of Contemporary Art, 5
New York City Fire Museum, 21
Queen of Greene Street, 14
SoHo Grand, 15
Tribeca Film Center, 16

Tribeca Performing Arts Center, 20

Art Galleries
Art in General, 18
The Drawing Center, 9
Holly Solomon, 2
Howard Greenberg, 8
Leo Castelli, 3
New York Earth Room, 1

Thread Waxing Space, 12

study called it "commercial slum number one." In the '70s, the city's restless population of artists—always looking for large, cheap, well-lit spaces—defied zoning laws to move into SoHo's run-down and abandoned warehouses. By the '80s it was all over: Zoning laws changed, art-collecting debutantes moved in, and loft prices soared into the millions. Today the smallish, walkable neighborhood (which encompasses only 40 blocks from Houston Street south to Canal Street and from Lafayette Street west to 6th Avenue) is the epitome of postmodern chic. An amalgam of black-clad art dealers, models, artists, celebrities, and other Beautiful People rush in and out of galleries, bistros, and boutiques all day long. Some New Yorkers have lately taken to referring to the area as "like a shopping mall." This is not a compliment. To help orientate yourself in SoHo, picture busy, store-lined West Broadway as its spine, off of which lie the smaller, more interesting, side streets.

The city's longest stretch of redbrick town houses preserved from the 1820s and 1830s runs along the north side of Charlton Street, west of 6th Avenue and south of West Houston Street. The classic houses have high stoops, paneled front doors, lead-glass windows, and narrow dormer windows. Stroll down parallel King and Vandam streets for even finer Federal housing whose past owners have included George Washington, John and Abigail Adams, and that rascal Aaron Burr.

Naturally, SoHo is packed with zillions of galleries (*see* Museums and Galleries, *below*), which look intimidating and in fact sell paintings you will never, ever be able to afford. Relax. No one's going to object to your looking, and much of the art complements whatever's currently on view at the Guggenheim, MoMA, or Met. Here's the best part: The galleries are free. Not surprisingly, artsy SoHo also brims with artsy museums: The **New Museum of Contemporary Art**; the **Guggenheim Museum SoHo**; the **Alternative Museum**; and the **Museum for African Art.** For more information on each, *see* Museums and Galleries, *below.*

Several of SoHo's streets have been spiffed up with quaint Belgian cobblestones, just like Europe. Or Disneyland.

In SoHo's shops hang clothing and furnishings and even toothbrushes for sale so beautiful they could qualify as objets d'art, too. Of course they're priced accordingly. Great for wandering and window-shopping are the blocks along **Prince Street, Spring Street, West Broadway, Wooster Street,** and **Greene Street,** where you'll find hip Euro-style boutiques like **Agnès B.** (116 Prince St., tel. 212/925–4649). But don't max out your credit cards just yet: There are a few affordable things to buy in SoHo, provided you find the right corner. On **Broadway** south of Spring Street you'll find vintage- and secondhand-clothing stores, while vendors at the small vacant lot on the corner of Wooster and Spring streets sell cheapie clothes and trinkets. For more information, *see* Chapter 5.

In 1996 the 15-story **SoHo Grand** (310 W. Broadway, at Grand St., tel. 212/965–3000) became the first major hotel to open in the neighborhood since the 1880s. Be sure to take a look at its chicly designed second-floor lobby; after pounding the pavement, you can relax in one of the oversized sofas or chairs and admire all the well-groomed guests; many of them work in the film, fashion, and design industries. The inviting Canal Room restaurant, serving regional American cuisine, is not as pricey as most other hotel restaurants.

TRIBECA

As Manhattan neighborhoods go, TriBeCa (the name that savvy real-estate developers dreamed up for the TRIangle BElow CAnal Street) is fairly laid back. The area's development shares many similarities with nearby SoHo. This was historically a commercial neighborhood, once filled with fish-packing plants and chemical manufacturers. Its warehouses and factories were all but abandoned in the 1960s; they were recolonized as residential lofts by artists in the '70s, grew trendy in the '80s, and are now affordable only to investment bankers. Like SoHo, TriBeCa still has its share of hip art galleries (*see* Museums and Galleries, *below*) and artsy shops, even if many of the artists have moved elsewhere. Unlike SoHo, TriBeCa (bounded to the north by Canal Street, to the east by Broadway, to the south by Chambers Street, and to the west by the Hudson River) has a tendency to shut down entirely on weekends. But you can still have some fun.

You can cover TriBeCa's attractions in an afternoon, really: Along Broadway, White Street, and Thomas Street are cafés, restaurants, and some shops, many housed in charmingly detailed cast-iron buildings from the late 1800s. Follow White Street across West Broadway to Moore Street; the firehouse (114 Moore St.) you'll see was **Ghostbusters' headquarters** in the two movies of the same name. (Do not disturb the firemen.) A bit farther west is Robert De Niro's **Tribeca Film Center** (375 Greenwich St., at N.

CAST-IRON BUILDINGS

You know how used-car lots put out lots of flags and balloons to attract customers? Well, the shop and factory owners of the 19th century wanted big, showy buildings with large windows for that exact same reason. Between 1860 and 1890 most of these four- to six-story buildings were made of cast iron, which was cheaper, stronger, and easier to work with than brick. Cast iron could be molded to mimic any style—Italianate, Victorian Gothic, neo-Grecian, Second Empire, Star Wars, whatever. Even buildings that housed sweatshops had beautiful facades with fantastic embellishments. Kind of a depressing thought, isn't it?

Some of the finest remaining cast-iron buildings in the world are on Greene Street between Canal and Grand streets: The "Queen of Greene Street" (28–30 Greene St.) is only surpassed by its colossal neighbor the "King of Greene Street" (72–76 Greene St.). The "Parthenon of Cast Iron," the Haughwout Building (488 Broadway), was originally a china and glassware business with an exterior inspired by a Venetian palazzo. Inside, it contained the world's first commercial passenger elevator, a steam-powered device invented by Elisha Graves Otis.

Moore St.), a movie-production complex housed in an old coffee-and-tea warehouse. You might even see De Niro himself dining at his restaurant downstairs, **Tribeca Grill** (*see* Chapter 4). Farther south, interesting residential areas to explore include **Staple Street** (barely an alley) and **Jay Street.** Nearby **Duane Park** (Duane St. between Staple and Hudson Sts.) has been preserved since 1800 as a calm, shady triangle; it is still surrounded by cheese, butter, and egg warehouses.

In contrast, **Independence Plaza** (Greenwich St. near Harrison St.) is a bunch of nondescript '70s high-rises. If it weren't for a bunch of building-hugging preservationists, the entire neighborhood would now look like this apartment complex. At the southern edge of TriBeCa on Greenwich Street is **Washington Market Park** (*see* Parks and Gardens, *below*). On Saturdays a dozen or so vendors gather to sell fresh flowers, vegetables, fish, and baked goods (*see* Greenmarkets *in* Chapter 4). Of course, it's not the same as Bear Market, which flourished around these parts in the early 19th century. Then, you could buy wild game and caviar. Just north of the park off Chambers Street, you can take in a music, dance, or theatrical performance at the **Tribeca Performing Arts Center** (*see* Arts Centers *in* Chapter 7) at the Borough of Manhattan Community College. And farther north of the arts complex, across the West Side Highway, you can enter **Hudson River Park** (*see* Parks and Gardens, *below*).

LOWER MANHATTAN

In Lower Manhattan, behemoth glass-and-steel skyscrapers lie mere blocks from ancient churches and cobblestone alleys. Walk a few blocks and it will seem like every building has a plaque recalling some event from the past quarter of a millennium. It was here, after all, that the Nieuw Amsterdam colony was established by the Dutch in 1625; the city did not really expand much above Canal Street until the middle of the 19th century. Today, this tiny section of Manhattan is a global financial center, and swarms of businesspeople clutching cellular phones crowd its sidewalks on weekdays. You can practically hear the wheels of commerce grinding, and the spirit of the place is pretty infectious—you might get struck with the urge to put on a power tie and renounce socialism if you stay too long. On evenings and weekends, however, the streets are eerily empty of everyone except tourists (and the handful of crazy New Yorkers who come down to Rollerblade the empty streets). Don't expect to find open restaurants, bars, bodegas, or even hot-dog vendors after 5 PM or on weekends.

Streets in Lower Manhattan were laid out back when heavy traffic was defined as a dozen yoked oxen pulling wagons. So, besides **Broadway,** which ends its 17-mi run down the length of Manhattan at **Bowling Green** (*see* Parks and Gardens, *below*), there really isn't a main drag. The most famous of lower Manhattan's labyrinthine streets is Wall Street (*see box,* Wonder Wall, *below*). **Pearl Street** was actually a shoreline drive before more land was reclaimed from the harbor. **Fulton Street** is named for Robert Fulton, whose steam ferry (the first in the world) carried passengers and cargo between Manhattan and Brooklyn.

At the very tip of Lower Manhattan is **Battery Park** (*see* Parks and Gardens, *below*), named for the battery of cannons that was originally placed along the shore to scare off those nasty Brits. It offers awe-inspiring views of the harbor. Stop by the visitors center at **Castle Clinton National Monument** to look at historical exhibits or pick up ferry tickets to Ellis Island and the Statue of Liberty (*see* Major Attractions, *above*). Castle Clinton has also held jobs as an island fort (landfill has now made it part of Manhattan) and an immigration depot (nearly eight million immigrants passed through here).

The best way to see Lower Manhattan's sights is to follow the Heritage Trail. This self-guided tour winds through the streets of Lower Manhattan, passing important stuff like the New York Stock Exchange, Tweed Courthouse, and Castle Clinton. You can pick up the maps and brochures you'll need to start your tour at City Hall, the South Street Seaport, or Castle Clinton in Battery Park; just look for Heritage Trail kiosks. City Hall also offers free interactive video machines that dispense info on Lower Manhattan sights, City Hall history, and mass transit options. For more info on the Heritage Trail, call 212/269-1500.

Besides being the place where Michael Milken types sell their soul to the devil for pocket change and golden parachutes, Lower Manhattan is home to some fascinating museums: the **National Museum of the American Indian, New York Unearthed, Fraunces Tavern,** the **South Street Seaport Museum,** and the **Museum of American Financial History.** For more info, *see* Museums and Galleries, *below*. And don't forget to check out that massive magnet to terrorists and tourists alike, the World Trade Center (*see* Major Attractions, *above*).

NEW YORK STOCK EXCHANGE (NYSE)

Don't be surprised if all the traders you see on the floor of the New York Stock Exchange have a certain skip to their step; these are heady days at the temple of high finance. A five-year bullish market has more than doubled the market value of most stocks, though fears of a crash looms anxiously in the minds of many of these traders.

This hoary hall of high finance, the largest securities exchange in the world, had humble beginnings: Originally Wall Street traders were not tasseled-loafer types, but local merchants who gathered to buy and sell stocks under the shade of a nearby buttonwood tree (which has long since become firewood). In its earliest incarnation, stocks were called out and bid on one at a time. These days, the "Big Board" is capable of handling up to one trillion shares of stock per day, and when the NYSE sneezes, prime ministers in far-off countries murmur nervous "bless you"s. The NYSE's current home is a grand 1903 building with an August Corinthian entrance—a fitting temple to the almighty dollar. Don't miss a trip to the glass-enclosed **visitors' gallery** overlooking the immense trading hall, from which you can peer down at the chaos of video monitors and 1,500 madly gesticulating brokers some 50 ft below. (A free multilingual tape explains all the action.) The glass was installed in 1967 after members of Students for a Democratic Society staged a protest here, throwing $1 bills onto the trading floor. Same-day visitors tickets are issued from 8:45 AM on a first-come, first-served basis; to get one, arrive before 1 PM. *20 Broad St., at Wall St., tel. 212/656-5165. Subway: 4, 5, 1, or 2 to Wall St.; also J, M, or Z to Broad St. Admission free. Open weekdays 9–4.*

TRINITY CHURCH

The Trinity Church you're looking at now was built in 1846 on the site of the 1697 original. For 50-odd years it was the tallest building in the city, but today it's like a dollhouse in the shadow of the World Trade Center's towers. Trinity's medieval-looking sanctuary doesn't hold a candle to the dark Gothic ambience of Grace Church (*see* West Village, *above*) or the colossal grandeur of St. Pat's (*see* Midtown, *above*), but the 2-acre graveyard's a fascinating jumble of crumbling headstones. At rest here are notable dead

LOWER MANHATTAN

Harrison St.
Jay St.
Staple St.
Hudson St.
Worth St.
Thomas St.
TRIBECA

Duar
CI
Read

Chambers St.
A,C, S
S
Chambers St.
1,2,3,9

Warren St.
Warren St.

West Broadway

Park Pl. W.
Murray St.
Broadway
City Pa

Greenwich St.

Park Pl.

Murray St.
Church St.
N,R
6

Barclay St.
2,3 S

Ar

North End Ave.

West St.

Vesey St.
Vesey St.
C,E S
5
Fulton St.
4,5 S

Hudson River Park

World Trade Center
1,9 S

Dey St.
John St.
S
N,R

3 i 4
Cortlandt St.

North Cove Yacht Harbor

AE

Liberty St.

Cedar St.
Cedar St.
Thames St.

BATTERY PARK CITY

West Side Highway

Albany St.
Carlisle St.

Trinity Pl.

20

South St.
Albany St.
Rector St.
4,5 S
AE

1,9 S N,R
Exchange P

South End Ave.

Rector Pl.

West Thames St.

Hudson River

24
23
25 Bowling Green
Bea

Third Pl.

Battery Pl.

Second Pl.
Battery Pl.
4,5 S
State St.
28

First Pl.

Battery Park City Esplanade

South Cove

31

Robert F. Wagner Jr. Park

Bridge
29

Battery Park

N

30

0   440 yards
0   400 meters

32 33

94

Brooklyn Bridge, **14**

Castle Clinton National Monument, **30**

Charging Bull Statue, **23**

City Hall, **7**

Commodities Exchange, **4**

Criminal Courts Building, **13**

Ellis Island, **32**

Federal Hall National Memorial, **21**

Federal Reserve Bank, **19**

Fraunces Tavern, **26**

Fulton Fish Market, **15**

A Living Memorial to the Holocaust—Museum of Jewish Heritage, **31**

Municipal Building, **10**

Museum of American Financial History, **25**

National Museum of the American Indian, **28**

New York City Police Museum, **24**

New York County Courthouse, **12**

New York Stock Exchange (NYSE), **22**

New York Unearthed, **29**

Pier 16, **17**

Pier 17, **16**

St. Paul's Chapel, **5**

Statue of Liberty, **33**

South Street Seaport Museum, **18**

Surrogate's Court, **9**

Trinity Church, **20**

Tweed Courthouse, **8**

U.S. Courthouse, **11**

Vietnam Veterans Memorial, **27**

Winter Garden Atrium, **2**

Woolworth Building, **6**

World Financial Center, **1**

World Trade Center Observation Deck, **3**

KEY

AE American Express Office

i Tourist Information

WONDER WALL

Back in the 1640s, when hostile Indian territory started around 40th Street, Dutch settlers built a protective wooden stockade around the northern outskirts of their settlement. The colony grew so quickly they bagged the wall in 1699, but the name stuck to the street that followed. Wall Street is both an actual street and a shorthand name for the vast, powerful financial community that clusters around the New York and American stock exchanges. While captains of industry, robber barons, and social Darwinists have long revered this street, radicals have cursed it as the heart of capitalist wrongdoing. Not surprisingly, when a horse-drawn wagon loaded with explosives detonated on September 16, 1920, in front of what is now Federal Hall, it was quickly blamed on anarchists bent on disrupting world financial markets. The noontime blast killed 30 and wounded 100, making it the deadliest American bombing of the century—until Oklahoma City in 1995. However, several bystanders (perhaps with cooler heads) testified that the wagon belonged to an explosives company who carelessly abandoned it. No culprits were found, and the explosion remains a mystery to this day.

The real Wall Street, you might be surprised to know, is only ¹/₃ of a mile long and not much wider than an alley. On all sides it's surrounded by unbelievably tall buildings. To best experience this trippy Grand Canyon effect, stand at the corner of Wall Street and William Street. Then look up. Subway: 4 or 5 to Wall St. (at Broadway). Also: 2 or 3 to Wall St. (at William St.).

folk like Alexander Hamilton (laid to rest by Aaron Burr) and Robert Fulton. A free 45-minute tour of the church is given daily at 2 PM. *74 Trinity Pl., at corner of Broadway and Wall St., tel. 212/602–0800. Subway: 4 or 5 to Wall St. Open weekdays 7–6, Sat. 8–4, Sun. 7–4.*

ST. PAUL'S CHAPEL

Six blocks north of Trinity Church on Broadway, St. Paul's Chapel is the oldest (1766) surviving church in Manhattan; it was modeled after London's St. Martin-in-the-Fields. George Washington said his prayers here immediately after being sworn in as America's first president (look for his pew in the north aisle). Both Trinity and St. Paul's offer live music at lunchtime (*see* Music *in* Chapter 7). *Broadway at Fulton St., tel. 212/602–0874.*

VIETNAM VETERANS MEMORIAL

On a large brick plaza near the eastern end of Battery Park, you'll find a 70-ft-long, 16-ft-high wall of greenish glass. It's etched with letters, diaries, and poems written by servicemen and servicewomen during the Vietnam War, as well as excerpts from news dispatches and public documents. *End of Coenties Slip between Water and South Sts. Subway: N or R to Whitehall St. (South Ferry).*

FEDERAL HALL NATIONAL MEMORIAL

Federal Hall, built as a Customs House in 1842, is a mishmash of Europe's greatest hits: Its Doric-columned entrance is modeled after the Acropolis in Athens, and its rotunda is modeled after the Pantheon in Rome. Add to that a statue of George Washington (who was sworn in as president on this spot in 1789) that would look more at home in Washington, D.C. Inside, you'll find a few exhibits on New York and Wall Street. The original building served as our nation's great capitol building until the whole bureaucracy packed off to Philadelphia in 1790. *26 Wall St., at Nassau St., tel. 212/825–6888. Subway: 2, 3, 4, or 5 to Wall St.; also J, M, or Z to Broad St. Admission free. Open weekdays 9–5.*

FEDERAL RESERVE BANK

Shakespeare may have said "all that glitters is not gold," but when you're in a room with enough gold to buy most medium-sized nations, you may beg to differ. The Federal Reserve Bank's got over 10,325 tons of the stuff (equal to one-seventh of the gold ever mined) in a vault carved from solid bedrock 80 ft below street level. Most of it belongs to foreign nations, but the United States lets them store it here for free. They won't talk about the recent World War II gold controversy. Yes, this is the bank that Jeremy Irons's character robbed with such ease in *Die Hard with a Vengeance*. No, such a thing would not be possible in real life. You can take the fascinating, free, 40-minute tour, however, if you call for a reservation at least one week in advance. Tours are given weekdays four times daily and end at the new visitor center with its interactive computer displays explaining the workings of the Bank. *33 Liberty St., between Nassau and William Sts., tel. 212/720–6130. Subway: 2 or 3 to Wall St. Admission free. 1-hr tour by advance (at least 5 days) reservation, weekdays at 10:30, 11:30, 1:30, and 2:30.*

THE CHARGING BULL STATUE

Soon after the stock-market crash of 1987, playful Italian artist Arturo DiModica dumped a 3½-ton bronze statue of a charging bull in front of the New York Stock Exchange under cover of night. It dismayed stockbrokers (who didn't need reminding that the bull market of the '80s was over), but it irked city officials even more. So the statue was "temporarily" parked just north of **Bowling Green** (*see* Parks and Gardens, *below*) until a buyer could be found. And there it stands. Facing north, up Broadway, the Bull menacingly crouches, nostrils flared, large enough to gore a city bus. Some feel the city's cool reception to this fine piece of public art has to do with the bull's gargantuan genitals—tourists seem to take more pictures of the rear of the bull than the front. The ultimate irony is that DiModica's joke has proven true, as the late 1990s' market has been the most bullish in history. *Broadway near Beaver St. Subway: 4 or 5 to Bowling Green.*

Herman Melville was born at 6 Pearl Street and worked as a customs officer on the Gansevoort Street pier while writing Moby Dick.

SOUTH STREET SEAPORT

The closest thing Manhattan has to Disneyland is the 11-block South Street Seaport Historic District, with its snapping, brightly colored flags, smartly painted colonial-style buildings, and tethered flock of tall ships festooned with twinkling lights. If you think it looks a bit like Boston's Quincy Market, you're right; the same corporation "restored" them both. Over 12 million tourists from all over the world come to the Seaport annually to find they've been snookered into shopping at mall standards like the Gap, Sharper Image, and J. Crew, and eating at overpriced, bland restaurants. That said, there are a few reasons to spend an hour or two here: The **South Street Seaport Museum** (*see* Museums and Galleries, *below*) and the **Fulton Fish Market** (*see below*) both give fascinating glimpses into the area's illustrious past. This was, after all, a throbbing zone of brothels, boardinghouses, gambling parlors, and saloons during the era of the clipper ship, and its cobblestone streets were once filled with randy sailors. Now, of course, it's the haunt of pimpled teens looking for the virtual-reality game center (hint: It's at Pier 17). As you walk along Fulton Street—closed to cars east of Water Street—look out for the historic 19th-century buildings of **Cannon's Walk Block** and **Schermerhorn Row.** The tiny white lighthouse you'll notice is the **Titanic Memorial** (Fulton and Water Sts.), commemorating the 1912 sinking of the "unsinkable" ocean liner. Check out **Pier 17** if you have a hankering for souvenir T-shirts and cheese fries, or **Pier 16** to see the tall ships, including the *Peking,* the second-largest sailing ship in existence. For info on boat tours that depart from Pier 16, *see* Guided Tours, *above. Tel. 212/732–7678. Subway: J, M, Z, 2, 3, 4, or 5 to Fulton St.; also A or C to Broadway–Nassau St.*

FULTON FISH MARKET

Strolling by, you might think that this is the smelliest place on earth. And you'd almost be right. Opened in 1831, Fulton is the oldest and largest fish market in the United States—but somewhere out there (we won't tell you where) there's a fish market that's *bigger* and *smellier.* Fishmongers at Fulton deal in a pungent 600 species of fish and shellfish, annually hauling in over eight million pounds. You'll need to arrive early (between 3 and 8 AM) to catch the action; after that, the whole place shuts down. Behave nicely (i.e., don't gawk or ask fishmongers to take a picture of you with their fish) and you can some-times score the catch of the day at wholesale prices. Fascinating tours ($10) are given of the market, though guides will not answer questions about the fish market's alleged ties to the mob, or the suspicious fire a few years back that crippled some of the market. They also suggest you don't wander around alone here before dawn. *South St. between Fulton St. and Peck Slip, tel. 212/748–8600. Subway: J, M, Z, 2, 3, 4, or 5 to Fulton St.; also A or C to Broadway–Nassau St. Market open daily midnight–9 AM. Tours given Apr.–Oct. on 1st and 3rd Thurs. at 6 AM; reservations required.*

CIVIC CENTER

New York City's civic center, just north of the financial district, is so filled with grand buildings it puts most of the nations' *state* capitals to shame, including the one in Albany, New York. But considering most New Yorkers' unshaken belief that their city is vastly superior to all others, does this really surprise you? You can spend a few hours wandering around the stately government and justice buildings, most of which have appeared in countless movies and TV shows like *Wall Street* and "Law and Order." Besides those mentioned below, worth a quick look-see are the **New York County Courthouse** (40 Centre St.), backdrop for Henry Fonda's tirades in *12 Angry Men*; the spectacular beaux arts **Surrogate's Court** (31 Chambers St.); and the towering **U.S. Courthouse** (Foley Sq.). Though these buildings are all crowded together, it's easy to identify each: The U.S. Courthouse has imposing marble steps and a golden pyramid on top. The New York County Courthouse has imposing marble steps and a hexagonal shape (its pediment reads "The true administration of justice is the firmest pillar of good government"). Meanwhile, the grim-looking art deco **Criminal Courts Building** (100 Centre St.) got a bit part in Tom Wolfe's *Bonfire of the Vanities*. This is also where you'll find the entrance to the **Brooklyn Bridge** (*see* Major Attractions, *above*). *Subway: N or R to City Hall; also 4, 5, or 6 to Brooklyn Bridge/City Hall.*

New York's most important federal court, housed in the U.S. Courthouse, is where the creator of the Lone Ranger sued for copyright infringement; where Julius and Ethel Rosenberg were tried for espionage; where the owners of the *Titanic* were sued for gross negligence; where D. H. Lawrence's *Lady Chatterley's Lover* was declared obscene (and James Joyce's *Ulysses* was not); and where hotel queen Leona Helmsley was tried for tax evasion.

CITY HALL • Refreshingly, New York's City Hall looks more like a pastoral New England courthouse than a Politboro. Its exterior columns reflect the classical influence of Greece and Rome, while its crowning statue of Lady Justice seems a nod to positive thinking. The whole thing was built between 1803 and 1812 and touched up a bit in 1858, after fireworks launched from its roof set the top half aflame. At some point the back side was finished off with nice white limestone—city fathers originally assumed New York would never grow north of Fulton Street and had skimped on the part that wouldn't "show." Inside are the Victorian-style city council chambers and the offices of the mayor. Some rooms, including the Governor's Room, brimming with official tchotchkes (including George Washington's writing desk), are open to the public. The Blue Room, traditionally the mayor's office, is on the ground floor; it is now that most important of the modern mayor's functions, the press-conference room. On either side of City Hall are free interactive video machines that dispense information on area attractions and City Hall history. *Broadway, at Park Row. Subway: N or R to City Hall. Admission free. Open weekdays 9–5, reservations required for tours, given at 10, 11, and 12.*

CITY HALL PARK • The triangular park surrounding City Hall started life as the town common and has seen its share of hangings, riots, and demonstrations. Look for the statue of Nathan Hale (hanged as a spy by the visiting Brits) on the Broadway side. **Park Row,** the street bordering the hypotenuse side of the triangle, is itself pretty historic. From the mid-19th to early 20th century it was dubbed "Newspaper Row" because most of the city's 20 or so daily papers had their offices here. A statue of Benjamin Franklin (who was, after all, a printer) stands in tribute across the street from the park near Pace Plaza.

TWEED COURTHOUSE • The Tweed Courthouse, named after legendary "Boss" William Magear Tweed, stands north of City Hall in City Hall Park (*see above*). The swaggering, 300-pound Tweed, who wore an enormous diamond in his shirtfront and seemed preternaturally disposed to the modern-day school of spin control, was adored by the poor as a do-no-wrong Robin Hood. This while he was apparently embezzling some $10 million of the $14 million budgeted to build the courthouse. The truth eventually caught up with Tweed and he died, ironically, in a jail that had earlier been a pet construction project. Peek inside the courthouse (which now houses municipal offices) to see its magnificent seven-story rotunda. *52 Chambers St., between Broadway and Centre St. Subway: N or R to City Hall. Admission free. Open weekdays 9–4:30.*

WOOLWORTH BUILDING • Rising 792 ft above the street like a Gothic church on steroids, the so-called Cathedral of Commerce was the world's tallest building when it opened in 1913. The finest in

Gothic design is what Frank W. Woolworth wanted and got when he ponied up $13.5 million in cash to have architect Cass Gilbert build a suitable headquarters for his Woolworth Company. It's got gargoyles. It's got flying buttresses. It's also got one of the most ornate entryways ever constructed by a perfectly sober man. As you enter, notice on your left the two sculptures set into arches in the ceiling: One is of elderly F. W. Woolworth pinching his pennies, and the other is of Cass Gilbert holding a model of the building you are standing in. *233 Broadway, at Park Pl. Subway: N or R to City Hall.*

MUNICIPAL BUILDING • This was the city government's first skyscraper, and if you've been paying any attention at all to this book, you know something of such monumental importance could only be entrusted to the architectural firm of McKim, Mead & White. And so, in 1914, it was. In the world of *Batman,* the Municipal Building was stunt double for "Gotham City Police Headquarters." In the real world, it's where New Yorkers go to pay parking fines, obtain marriage licenses, and get hitched in civil ceremonies. You can make a quick buck if you hang around on weekdays with a Polaroid camera and offer to capture the moment for ill-prepared newlyweds. *1 Centre St., near entrance to Brooklyn Bridge. Subway: 4, 5, or 6 to Brooklyn Bridge/City Hall.*

BATTERY PARK CITY

Battery Park City is connected to the World Trade Center (*see* Major Attractions, *above*) by a pair of pedestrian walkways spanning West Street. There's another, deeper connection, too: Developers needed someplace to stick all the extra dirt (about 1 million cubic yards of it) they had lying around after they dug the foundation for the World Trade Center's whopping twin towers. Rather than filling a barge and floating it to Jersey, they added landfill to lower Manhattan, and, voilà, Battery Park City was born. Battery Park City *is* like a separate city, sort of, with over 5,000 residents and 20,000 workers. It's just not a very exciting one to visit. The best thing about it is the ever-growing **Battery Park City Esplanade,** which runs along the Hudson River. It offers those rarest of rare things in lower Manhattan, sunsets, trees, and open space, plus stellar views

The city's lights are beautiful at night, aren't they? Imagine the sight when the world's first electrical generating station lit up Manhattan like a birthday cake on September 4, 1882. A plaque marks the spot of the former station at 40 Fulton Street.

of the Statue of Liberty and New Jersey's "Gold Coast." The **World Financial Center** (West St. between Vesey and Liberty Sts., tel. 212/945–0505) dominates the rest of the landscape with its five geometric-capped towers, each 16 to 51 stories high. They're some of the least-offensive modern architecture in the city and serve as world headquarters for companies such as American Express, Merrill Lynch, and most recently, The Mercantile Exchange. On the concourse level you'll find shops and restaurants, plus the gorgeous, glass-walled **Winter Garden Atrium** (open daily 7 AM–1 AM). The 120-ft-tall vaulted atrium is filled with giant palms and hosts free concerts, dance recitals, and art exhibits. *Subway: 1 or 9 to Cortlandt St.; also C or E to World Trade Center.*

A LIVING MEMORIAL TO THE HOLOCAUST—MUSEUM OF JEWISH HERITAGE

Moored in one of the city's most enviable waterfront settings, at the north end of Robert F. Wagner Jr. Park just below Battery Park City, is this new downtown museum. Kevin Roche's Star of David–shape building has three floors of exhibits focusing on the dynamism of 20th-century Jewish culture around the globe; Hitler's war against the Jews, using firsthand recollections; and Jewish life after the Holocaust. *40 1st Pl., Battery Park City, tel. 212/968–1800. Subway: 1 or 9 to Cortlandt St.; also C or E to World Trade Center. Admission $7. Open Sun.–Wed 9–5, Thur. 9–8, Fri. and eve of Jewish holidays 9–2.*

THE OUTER BOROUGHS

When most people think of New York, they think of Manhattan as "The City," and Brooklyn, Queens, the Bronx, and Staten Island as one big peripheral blob—the sticky, brown caramel surrounding the real Big Apple. While Manhattan Island admittedly contains most of the sights that the city is known for, it's only one of the five **boroughs** (counties) that comprise New York City. Almost 80% of New York City's population *doesn't* live in Manhattan, and if you want to rub shoulders with a native New Yorker, you've got a much better chance meeting one in the boroughs than in any up- or downtown hangout. Nothing better illustrates the city's ethnic diversity (and divisions) than a subway ride out of Manhattan; take the N or R from Queens, through Manhattan, and to Brooklyn, and you'll witness the ebb and tide of nations.

Most sights in Brooklyn, Queens, and the Bronx are less than 40 minutes away by subway, and the 20-minute, free ferry ride to Staten Island is a treat in itself. Even the most distant destinations, like **City Island** in the Bronx (an hour away), are definitely worth the schlep if you're feeling boxed in by the asphalt grid. What can be so cutthroat and stressful about a city where you can spend the morning at the high-tech New York Stock Exchange, and an afternoon out in a sleepy Bronx fishing village, where shop owners leave signs saying GONE TO THE BEACH in their windows?

Many museums, parks, and historical sights in the outer boroughs warrant a special trip: the Bronx Zoo, Coney Island, the Brooklyn Museum of Art, the Brooklyn Botanic Garden, Yankee Stadium, and the American Museum of the Moving Image, to name a few. Lesser-known gems include Wave Hill estate (where Franklin Roosevelt, Mark Twain, and Toscanini each lived); the Steinway & Sons Piano Factory (where you can watch a single piece of wood being shaped into a grand piano); the Jacques Marchais Museum (home to the largest private collection of Tibetan art outside Tibet, personally blessed by the Dalai Lama); and the Russian neighborhood of Brighton Beach. Additionally, the outer boroughs are where you'll find New York City's only **beaches**; for more info, *see box* Land of Skyscrapers and Beaches?!, *below.*

BROOKLYN

Hardly Manhattan's wimpy sidekick, Brooklyn is a metropolis in its own right, full of world-class museums, spacious parks, landmark buildings, five-star restaurants, and lively ethnic neighborhoods. In fact, it's the most populous of all the boroughs, with 2.3 million residents; even if it were sheared from the rest of New York, it would still be among the 20 largest cities in the United States. It's no wonder that an intense and long-standing rivalry has existed between Brooklyn and Manhattan ever since the 1898 unification of Brooklyn with the rest of the city.

Not only does Brooklyn have more residents, but more people visit it than any of the other outer boroughs, particularly the charming 19th-century neighborhoods of Brooklyn Heights, Cobble Hill, and Carroll Gardens. Don't listen to dyed-in-the-wool Manhattanites who think you need a visa to cross the Brooklyn Bridge. Those who know better make the trip to take in the Egyptian treasures at the Brooklyn Museum of Art, cycle or rollerblade around Prospect Park, nap in the Botanic Garden's Cherry Orchard, attend some can't-see-that-anywhere-in-Manhattan performance at the Brooklyn Academy of Music (a.k.a. BAM), or head to Coney Island for a stroll along the beach boardwalk and a ride on the Cyclone roller coaster. Its major attractions aren't the only reason to come here, though. Brooklyn is a city of neighborhoods, most of which are more intimate in scale and considerably more family-oriented than any of those across the East River. People (you'll even see kids and senior citizens!) make up the communities here, not the bars, shops, and restaurants. The quarterly *Meet Me in Brooklyn* (30 Flatbush Ave., Suite 427, Brooklyn, NY 11217, tel. 718/855–7882, ext. 51, fax 718/802–9095) has listings of Brooklyn's cultural events, museum and gallery exhibits, street fairs and festivals, and walking and bike tours. Write for a copy, or pick one up at the New York Convention and Visitors Bureau (*see* Visitor Information *in* Chapter 1). Covering neighborhood characters and community developments as well as restaurant and art listings, the monthly *Brooklyn Bridge Magazine* is sold at Brooklyn newsstands.

BROOKLYN HEIGHTS

"All the advantages of the country, with most of the conveniences of the city." So ran the ads for a real-estate development that sprang up in the 1820s just across the East River from downtown Manhattan. Brooklyn Heights (named for its enviable hilltop position) was New York's first suburb, linked to the city first by ferry and later by the mighty Brooklyn Bridge. In the 1940s and 1950s, the neighborhood was said to be home to the city's largest number of writers outside the Village. Among the scribes who've lived here then and in the decades since are Carson McCullers, W. H. Auden, Hart Crane, Arthur Miller, Truman Capote, Richard Wright, Alfred Kazin, and Norman Mailer (still a resident). The Heights deteriorated in the 1930s, but thanks to the vigorous efforts of preservationists in the 1960s, much of the neighborhood was designated as New York's first historic district. Today some 600 buildings more than 100 years old, representing a wide range of American building styles, are lovingly preserved on quiet, tree-lined streets, none more than a few blocks from the Heights' best attraction, the **Promenade.**

Cafés, shops, and plenty of dry-cleaners for Wall Street commuters line the main thoroughfare of **Montague Street.** On a sunny day the inside of **St. Ann and the Holy Trinity Church,** lit through 60 of the first stained-glass windows made in America, is truly inspiring. First installed in 1849, two-thirds of the windows have been restored to date—to see the results up close, visit Monday–Friday, from 10 AM–2 PM. The afternoon light creates colorful spotlights on the dark pews and brings the vaulted ceiling into startlingly clear relief. In 1980 the church created its own performing arts center, "Arts at St. Ann's," where you can hear a wide variety of nonclassical music—jazz, blues, world and new music; musical theater; and experimental opera—March through May and October through December. The 4,718-pipe organ, the largest in Brooklyn, is played by Gregory Eaton; free concerts are given Wednesdays at 1:10 PM. *157 Montague St., at Clinton St., tel. 718/875–6960. Subway: 2 or 3 to Clark St.; M, N, or R to Court St.; or 2, 3, 4, or 5 to Borough Hall.*

Just north of Brooklyn Heights and melding into Dumbo is the up-and-coming Fulton Ferry landing area, where Robert Fulton's steam ferry once shuttled passengers to and from Manhattan. A Walt Whitman ode to Brooklyn, Manhattan, and the river is cut into the fencing bordering the landing. From old tieing posts that now serve as benches, you get the same view that diners at the adjacent River Café pay through the nose for. Though the ferry is gone, life on **Old Fulton Street** still flickers with restaurants, cafés, and bars. The area is dotted with old warehouses and Federal-style row houses, all watched over by the towering Brooklyn Bridge. In the vaults under the bridge look for the **Brooklyn Anchorage** (Hicks and Old Fulton Sts., no phone), a funky art gallery/performance space with a medicinal herb garden out front. More open greenery is hidden around the bend; walk past the entrance to the River Café and behind the anchorage to the **Empire Fulton Ferry State Park** (*see* Parks and Gardens, *below*). *Subway: A or C to High St./Brooklyn Bridge.*

BROOKLYN HEIGHTS PROMENADE • From any one of the benches along this ⅓-mi, paved waterfront promenade, you have spectacular views of the Lower Manhattan skyline, the South Street Seaport, and the majestic Brooklyn Bridge. The small island to your left is Governors Island, a recently deaccessioned military installation, and the Statue of Liberty is

A few blocks north of Montague Street are streets with unusual names like Cranberry, Pineapple, and Orange. Not a citrus promotion, the names were bestowed by a Miss Sarah Middagh, who objected to the practice of naming streets for the town fathers.

visible just to its right. Mornings and after dusk are the best times to come. The rising sun's rays reflect off the thousands of windows on the skyscrapers opposite. During the day, the drab granite colors of towering finance buildings and their repetitive windows can present an anonymous, soulless picture of the city, but at night, light through the same glass creates the most vibrant, tantalizing skyline imaginable. If you're nursing a broken heart, stay far away on moonlit summer nights when lovey-dovey, liplocked couples fill the benches. On the 4th of July, fireworks aficionados head here for inimitable views of the annual show over the East River. *Subway: M, N, or R to Court St.; walk 1 block south to Remsen St., then west to waterfront.*

COBBLE HILL AND CARROLL GARDENS

A few blocks south of Brooklyn Heights, Cobble Hill is a slightly less manicured version of its northern neighbor, with equally charming old town houses. Virtually all of the neighborhood's commercial establishments are confined to Court Street, leaving the rest of the tree-lined streets as quiet as you'll find anywhere in the city. **Atlantic Avenue** (which separates Cobble Hill from the Heights) has amazing Middle Eastern spice and produce shops and, heading toward the Williamsburgh Savings Bank tower, antique stores packed with clunky furniture. A good snack block is between Clinton and Court streets, where you can pick up olives and dried fruits at **Sahadi Importing** (187–189 Atlantic Ave., tel. 718/624–4550), spinach pie at **Damascus Bread & Pastry** (195 Atlantic Ave., tel. 718/625–7070)—whose pita bread is distributed nationwide—and homemade ice cream and pastries at **Peter's Ice Parlor and Coffee Shop** (185 Atlantic Ave., tel. 718/852–3835). Picnic tables are nearby at Cobble Hill park (Clinton St., between Congress St. and Verandah Pl.). Among the tidy carriage houses bordering the small park is **40 Verandah Place,** former home of novelist Thomas Wolfe. To get a look at some Brooklyn-made gift items, check out the **Brooklyn Artisan Gallery** (221A Court St., tel. 718/330–0343), *Subway: F or G to Bergen St.*

Still farther south, below Degraw Street, is the steadfastly Italian neighborhood of **Carroll Gardens.** Here you'll find octogenarians playing boccie in the parks or smoking and chatting on their stoops. On streets

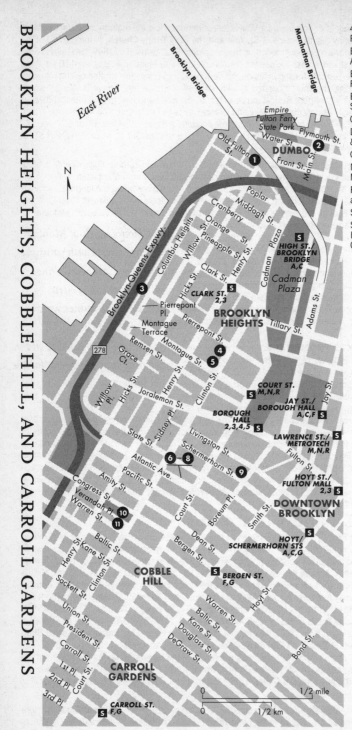

BROOKLYN HEIGHTS, COBBLE HILL, AND CARROLL GARDENS

40 Verandah Place, **11**

Brooklyn Anchorage, **1**

Brooklyn Heights Promenade, **3**

Brooklyn Historical Society, **4**

Cobble Hill Park, **10**

Damascus Bread & Pastry, **8**

Gale Gates et al., **2**

New York Transit Museum, **9**

Peter's Ice Parlor and Coffee Shop, **6**

Sahadi Importing, **7**

St. Ann and the Holy Trinity Church, **5**

like **First Place, Carroll Street,** and **President Street,** houses have front yards (tiny by suburban standards, but nothing to laugh about in front-yard-deficient New York). They're best seen around Christmas, when everyone puts out glow-in-the-dark nativity scenes and giant, plastic Virgin Marys. *Subway: F or G to Carroll St.*

DUMBO

Dumbo—not Disney's flying pachyderm, but down under the Manhattan Bridge overpass—is the place to see how a Soho or Chelsea arts scene gets started. Since the mid-1980s this has been a true struggling-artists' community, with turn-of-the-century brick warehouses, cobblestone streets crisscrossed with old railroad tracks, and the ever-present rumble of subway cars (the B, the D, and the Q) rattling across the Manhattan Bridge above. Needless to say, TV and film crews come here when they want "atmosphere." Dumbo is also the international headquarters for the Jehovah's Witnesses—strange bedfellows for bohemian artists. The best blocks to explore are north of **Front Street,** between Main Street and Hudson Avenue. **Gale Gates et al.** (37 Main St., tel. 718/522–4597) is creating a buzz with its performance/visual art gallery. Judging by the spacious **Le Gamin** bistro (1 Main St., tel. 718/722–2979), someone's expecting a big influx of gallery-goers. An entrance to the **Empire Fulton Ferry State Park** (*see* Parks and Gardens, *below*) is right across from the bistro by the abandoned warehouse smelling of coal. Your only chance for a pint of Guinness and some delicious bar food is **Between the Bridges Pub** (63 York St. at Adams St., tel. 718/237–1977). Check out the view down Jay Street, where the Empire State Building is framed within the bridge anchorage. Walking these quiet streets is both stepping back in time and witnessing a neighborhood taking off into the future. *Subway: F to York St. or A or C to High St.*

FORT GREENE AND CLINTON HILL

Bounded by the East River, Vanderbilt Avenue, Atlantic Avenue, and Flatbush Avenue, Fort Greene is a neighborhood of brownstones and row houses, home to many of the city's African-American professionals, musicians, and artists. Among Fort Greene's residents is director Spike Lee. To get a firsthand look at Fort Greene's artists at work, check out **Urban Glass** (647 Fulton St., entrance on 57 Rockwell Pl., tel. 718/625–3685), the only studio/gallery in New York devoted to glassblowing. In the same building and on the second floor, pick up a **Brooklyn Community Access Television** (BCAT, tel. 718/935–1122) program schedule so you know when to catch shows like "Strange Fruit," a drag queen soap opera, and "The African Village Unsigned," showcasing unsigned artists. Friday nights are devoted to spoken-word performances ($5 cover) at **Moon Café** (745 Fulton St., tel. 718/243–0424).

Beyond tiny, eclectic galleries, Fort Greene is home to a world-class avant-garde performance venue, **Brooklyn Academy of Music (BAM)** (*see* Arts Centers *in* Chapter 7), built in 1905. Adjoining BAM, the **Williamsburgh Savings Bank Tower** (1 Hanson Pl., at Flatbush Ave.) is Brooklyn's tallest building at 512 ft. and a perfect landmark to orient yourself in both time and space (its clockface on four sides can be read from many blocks away). Completed in 1929, the tower was meant to signal Brooklyn's emergence as a commercial superpower. A few months later the Black Tuesday stock market crash flattened that drive, leaving most floors standing empty for decades. Peek in before 3 PM to see the spectacular Republic National Bank's vaulted ceilings, silhouetted windows, mosaic murals, and marble floors. The lobby's blue-tiled arches lead to elevators rising 20-some floors to mostly dentist offices. The 16th floor has a panoramic view of Brooklyn (and out of a smaller wire-mesh window, Manhattan's financial district and midtown). If you haven't had your piece of New York Cheesecake yet, grab it now at **Junior's** (386 Flatbush Ave., tel. 718/852–5257). *Subway: D, Q, 2, 3, 4, or 5 to Atlantic Ave.*

Fort Greene's boundary with Clinton Hill isn't so distinguishable, but when you walk east on DeKalb Ave. and hit the turn-of-the-century mansions on Clinton Ave., you've reached Brooklyn's "Gold Coast," now the Clinton Hill Historic District. Charles Pratt, partner to John D. Rockefeller, built three mansions on Clinton (besides his own) as wedding gifts for his children. The **Caroline Ladd Pratt House** is at 229 Clinton; other Pratt homes are numbers 232 (Pratt's Italianate home), 241, and 245. Washington Avenue is also full of wealthy merchant houses. The Pratt Institute of Art campus is farther east, between Hall St. and Emerson. On Lafayette Avenue, between Clermont and Vanderbilt, are two imposing structures in an otherwise simple neighborhood: the **Masonic Temple** (317 Lafayette Ave.), and **Queen of All Saints Church** (300 Vanderbilt Ave.). The French-Gothic church was built in 1913 and is modeled after the Sainte Chapelle in Paris. *Subway: G to Clinton-Washington Aves. or Classon Ave.*

PRISON SHIP MARTYR'S MONUMENT • A macabre chapter in Fort Greene's and America's history is forever remembered at this 148-ft-tall monument, the world's tallest freestanding Doric column, which stands in shady **Fort Greene Park** (*see* Parks and Gardens, *below*). During the American Revolution, the Brits crowded their colonial prisoners into cattle ships moored in the bay just north of here;

some 11,500 died. The corpses were dumped in trenches and continued, horribly, to wash ashore until 1792. *Subway: D, M, N, Q, or R to DeKalb Ave.*

WILLIAMSBURG

Alternately an Orthodox Jewish neighborhood, a Latino community, and the home of hip young artists, the northern neighborhood of Williamsburg is evolving from a low-rent, best-kept-secret to a scene of restaurants, bars, and galleries that draws those who consider the Lower East Side "mainstream." The neighborhood around the **Bedford Avenue** subway station feels positively small college town, with an eclectic mix of eateries, thrift shops, Polish butcher shops, and the **Clovis Press Bookstore** (229 Bedford Ave., tel. 718/302–3751). One of the more popular watering holes is **Mug's Ale House** (125 Bedford Ave., at N. 10th St.). For a real taste of local brew, take a 45-minute Saturday tour—including tastings—of the **Brooklyn Brewery** (79 N. 11th St., tel. 718/486–7422), formerly the site of a matzoh bakery. Just north of Broadway is a cluster of Latino bodegas and cheap Puerto Rican and Mexican restaurants and coffee shops. Take note: Broadway runs underneath the elevated subway line and isn't a very pleasant place at night. *Subway: L to Bedford Ave.*

If you follow Broadway west to the water you're entering Williamsburg's artist quarter—often called the **"Right Bank."** Artists and writers who've fled gentrified SoHo have been colonizing the industrial buildings near the water and under the ugly gray Williamsburg Bridge for the last 20-odd years. If you double back to Bedford Avenue and follow it south, you'll come to the heart of the second-largest Orthodox Jewish community in Brooklyn (the largest is farther east, in Crown Heights). **Lee Avenue,** which runs parallel to Bedford Avenue, is Jewish Williamsburg's main street; grab something to nosh on at any of the kosher bakeries. You'll see Hebrew-speaking men in black suits, prayer shawls, long beards, and black hats, and women in carefully groomed conservative dress, with children and baby strollers in tow. For a deeper look into Hasidic culture, though in a different Brooklyn neighborhood, contact **Tours of Hasidic Crown Heights** (tel. 718/953–5244).

GREENPOINT

The Polish community of Greenpoint (north of Williamsburg and just a stone's throw south of Queens) is one of the most thriving ethnic enclaves in the city, today home to immigrants not only from Poland but also Puerto Rico, the Dominican Republic, Guyana, Colombia, Pakistan, and China, among elsewhere. Thanks to the Polish, Russian, and Italian immigrants who settled here in the 19th and early 20th centuries, there are lots of beautiful old churches; the 1916 **Cathedral of the Transfiguration of Our Lord** (N. 12th St. and Driggs Ave.), a Russian Orthodox church with five huge copper-clad onion domes, is the finest. The main drag, **Manhattan Avenue,** is lined with Polish bakeries; Polish coffee shops serving up kielbasa, stuffed cabbage, and flan; and even a few Polish curio shops and clothing stores. Drop by **Zakopone** (714 Manhattan Ave., between Norman and Meserole Sts.) for carved eggs, simple wooden toys and painted boxes, and framed photos of the Pope. **Stodycze Wedel** (772 Manhattan Ave., at Meserole St., tel. 718/349–3933) has sparkling clean shelves full of imported Polish candies, crackers, and other gourmet items. The redbrick, 1873 **Sts. Anthony and Alphonsus Church** (Manhattan Ave. at Milton St.) looks like it belongs on a pristine New England hilltop. It does look to the water, its view blocked only by warehouses used for film shoots. *Subway: G to Greenpoint Ave.*

PARK SLOPE

With street after tree-lined street of gorgeous, meticulously maintained brownstone, limestone, and brick row houses, Park Slope is a little like Brooklyn's Upper East Side (in fact, for a short time in the late 19th century, just as it was coming of age, it was the wealthiest neighborhood in America). Thanks to its handsome layout and its proximity to three of Brooklyn's major assets—

Prospect Park (*see* Parks and Gardens, *below*), the Brooklyn Museum of Art, and the Brooklyn Botanic Garden—today the Slope is one of Brooklyn's most sought-after places to live for professionals of all stripes, both straight and gay, married and single.

On weekends the stroller traffic along the sidewalks on **7th Avenue,** the neighborhood's main strip, can be as heavy as the BQE at rush hour, but amid all the real estate agents, churches, dry cleaners, and mediocre restaurants, a number of stores make a stroll down 7th worthwhile. You'll see plenty of stoop sales advertised, and you can buy old costume jewelry to Kilim rugs fresh out of Afghanistan at the weekend flea market between 1st and 2nd streets. **Leaf 'n Bean** (83 7th Ave., at Union St., tel. 718/638–5791) sells lots of hard-to-find tea and coffee accoutrements, plus just what the name promises. The **Clay Pot** (162 7th Ave., between 1st St. and Garfield Pl., tel. 718/788–6564) carries a changing slate of crafts and jewelry by leading American craftspeople—couples shop for wedding bands, others

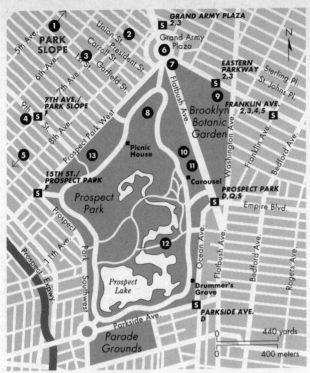

9th Street Bandshell, **13**

Brooklyn Museum of Art, **9**

Brooklyn Public Library, **7**

Coolectibles, **1**

Clay Pot, **3**

Green-Wood Cemetery, **5**

Holy Cow, **4**

Wollman Memorial Rink, **12**

Leaf 'n Bean, **2**

Lefferts Homestead, **11**

Long Meadow, **8**

Soldiers' and Sailors' Memorial Arch, **6**

Prospect Park Wildlife Conservation Center, **10**

for wedding gifts, designer nightlights, and refrigerator accoutrement. **Holy Cow** (442 9th St., at 7th Ave., tel. 718/788–3631) has plenty of old vinyl and new review copies of CDS—mostly pop, rock, and jazz. **Lucky Bug** (438 7th Ave., between 14th and 15th Sts., tel. 718/832–6601), the silliest shop in the Slope, carries plastic doodads and schtick from 10 ¢ and up. Nearby, the artful cupcakes at **Two Little Red Hens Bakery** (1112 8th Ave., tel. 718/499–8108) beg to be tucked into a basket and taken on a picnic in Prospect Park.

Down the slope of the neighborhood, 6th Avenue is almost all residential, and **5th Avenue** is where the brownstones end and a solidly Latino community begins. Joining mom-and-pop shops and bodegas, 5th Avenue is becoming the boho version of 7th Avenue, with a hodgepodge of tchotchke stores and cafés. Most of the new spots and highly praised restaurants are on the five blocks between DeGraw and Garfield streets. **Coolectibles** (217 5th Ave., between Union and President Sts., tel. 718/638–5770) has collectibles of all kinds; their black and white photos of old Brooklyn include streetscapes and Coney Island's long-gone, fantastical Luna Park. *Subway: D or Q to 7th Ave. (at Flatbush Ave.); F to 7th Ave. (at 9th St.); or N, R, or M to Union St.*

Grand Army Plaza (Flatbush Ave. at Eastern Pkwy.) is at one of the main entrances to Prospect Park. The fantastic 80-ft-tall **Soldiers' and Sailors' Memorial Arch** is Brooklyn's post–Civil War answer to the Arc de Triomphe. On Saturday a farmers' market sets up across from it. Also on the plaza is the impressive, "open-book-style" entrance to the **Brooklyn Public Library** (tel. 718/780–7700), which has an informal café inside. The stately **Brooklyn Museum of Art** (*see* Museums and Galleries, *below*), and the lovely **Brooklyn Botanic Garden** (*see* Parks and Gardens, *below*) are about 200 yards down Eastern Parkway. On weekends and holidays from noon to 5 PM, you can ride free on the old-fashioned trolley (tel. 718/965–8967) that runs between the Public Library, the Brooklyn Museum, the Botanic Garden, and several points in Prospect Park. *Subway: 2 or 3 to Grand Army Plaza.*

BAY RIDGE

Bay Ridge, south of Sunset Park's growing Chinese community, is characterized by posh circa-1915 homes and a large Scandinavian population. Before the subway ended the neighborhood's exclusivity,

SLEEPING WITH THE FAMOUS

The 478 idyllic acres and monuments of the prestigious Green-Wood Cemetery, between Park Slope and Sunset Park, became the inspiration for public parks in New York. Commissioned in 1838, by the 1860s the New York Times reported: "It is the ambition of the New Yorker to live upon the 5th Avenue, to take his airings in the (Central) Park, and to sleep with his fathers in Green-wood." So rest here notable figures like Louis Comfort Tiffany, FAO Schwarz, Jean-Michel Basquiat, and Leonard Bernstein. The most popular way to visit is via a walking tour, which can cover only a small portion of the cemetery at a time (call 718/788-8500 for details).

Brooklyn's wealthiest lived in Bay Ridge, and a few of their spectacular waterfront mansions remain: the **Gingerbread House** (82nd St., near Narrows Ave.), in the style of a thatch-roofed English cottage, and the **Fontbonne Hall Academy** (9901 Shore Rd., near 99th St.), a huge mansion turned private girls' school. Your best bets for shopping and eating in Bay Ridge are along **3rd Avenue** and **5th Avenue,** between 70th and 90th streets. Try **Nordic Delicacies** (6909 3rd Ave., at 69th St., tel. 718/748–1874) for authentic Scandinavian deli food. On the Sunday nearest May 17, the whole 'hood parties down at the annual **Norwegian Constitution Day Parade,** which runs along 5th Avenue between 67th and 90th streets. Hugging the shoreline to the east and south is narrow **Shore Park,** a breezy Verrazano Narrows Bridge vantage point, shared by bikers, bladers, joggers, and kite-flyers. *Subway: R to 77th St.*

CONEY ISLAND

During the late 1800s the sandy beach of Coney Island (not actually a separate island) was New York City's golden riviera, and the resort hotels lining its 2-mi-long boardwalk were patronized by presidents and captains of industry. With the introduction of the 5¢ elevated line in the early 20th century, fancy hotels were replaced by penny arcades, roller coasters, and oddities like a hotel built in the shape of an elephant. During this period as many as one million people (nearly 20% of New York's population at the time) would flock to Coney Island and amusement extravaganza Steeplechase Park on hot summer Sundays. After World War II, as more people were able to afford cars and head elsewhere, Coney Island began its decline. In what is now a no-man's-land opposite the boardwalk between 15th and 16th streets, ghosts of Steeplechase Park linger: Look for the vine-covered skeleton of the Thunderbolt roller coaster and the towering Parachute Jump (which once lured gung-ho postwar riders with the claim that it was used to train GIs). Fishers try their luck at the sole boardwalk pier nearby. How far do you feel from Manhattan? Just look down 16th Street and you'll see the familiar World Trade Towers.

Coney Island is still a fun adventure, albeit with a seamy edge. Largely within the **Astroland Amusement Park** (tel. 718/372–0275), rides are open weekends between Palm Sunday and Memorial Day and September, and daily in between. Between 12–3 PM you can buy a $12.99 "pay one price" ticket to the rides. Video arcades, go-carts, merry-go-rounds, and kiddie rides dominate the Midway, at the heart of which towers the 70-year-old **Cyclone** (Surf Ave. at W. 10th St., tel. 718/266–3434), a legendary roller coaster ($4; $3 for that irresistible re-ride) You could attribute a portion of the fright factor to the fact that the coaster's newly replaced but rickety-sounding tracks sound ready to fall apart with every carload of screaming passengers. Near the Cyclone, the **Astrotower** ($2.50) is a Seattle Space Needle wanna-be, providing panoramic views of Coney Island and Brighton Beach. The circa-1920s **Wonder Wheel** can give you the delicious feeling that you're about to fall to a certain death. For a demolition-derby disco experience, take $3 to the **Eldorado Auto Skooter** (Surf Ave. between W. 12th and Hendrickson Sts.).

Freak shows are another big attraction along the Midway. If you're gonna give in to curiosity, the **Coney Island Circus Sideshow** (W. 12th St., at Surf Ave., tel. 718/372–5159) gives you the best value for your $3, with acts like the human blockhead and the sword-swallowing bearded lady. The performers are friendly and kid-conscious, if a bit jaded. Finally, visit Dick D. Zigun's humble **Coney Island Museum** (208 Surf Ave., Admission 99¢) and gawk at his a growing collection of Coney Island memorabilia.

In June, glittering mermaids, from wide-eyed infants to scantily clad sirens (and a barely vintage car motorcade), make up the rambling and rowdy **Mermaid Parade.** Watch the judges encourage bribes from prize-seeking participants at 12th Street. In 1998 David Byrne was the celebrity King Neptune. North and west of the boardwalk is quite dodgy after dark, so stick to the well-lit Midway. And do beware of the glass shards and chipped shot glasses littering the beach between Coney Island and Brighton Beach. *Subway: B, D, F, or N to Coney Island.*

NEW YORK AQUARIUM FOR WILDLIFE CONSERVATION • New York City's only aquarium is Coney Island's major sightseeing attraction, apart from the beach and the boardwalk with its fun and games. You can get upclose and personal with sharks and stingrays in their 90,000-gallon habitat; explore **Sea Cliffs,** a coastal California habitat with playful sea otters; touch slimy and spiky sea critters at **Discovery Cove**; or, at the **Beluga Whales** exhibit, see that even intelligent marine mammals have trouble finding a decent pad in this city (theirs: a cramped 400,000-gallon tank). The first Beluga whale born in captivity was conceived in this love nest. During the week, come after 1 PM to avoid the masses of school groups. *Surf Ave. and W. 8th St., tel. 718/265–3474. Subway: D or F to W. 8th St. Admission $8.75. Open daily 10–5 (Memorial Day–Labor Day, weekends until 7).*

BRIGHTON BEACH

Long before Brighton Beach was immortalized in the Neil Simon play-turned-movie, *Brighton Beach Memoirs,* it was just an old-fashioned Jewish community east of Coney Island, with lots of high-rise retirement towers lining the shore. These days, a flood of Russian, Ukrainian, and Georgian émigrés have earned it the nickname "Little Odessa." **Brighton Beach Avenue** (which runs under the rattling, rusting, elevated D and F subway line) is more interesting than the beach itself. Russian merchants hawk 50¢-knishes, bargain-priced caviar, lingerie, and Russian-language videotapes—it's an other-worldly scene. The **Bread Basket** (307 Brighton Beach Ave.) sells incredibly cheap loose nuts, candies, and dried fruits of ridiculous variety. On weekends thumb through the old and new Russian books sold at 3rd and 5th streets and browse through **M & I International Food** (249 Brighton Beach Ave.), where people are serious about buying their meats. Cut to the beach when you come to Ocean Parkway. At nightfall, many of the Russian restaurants (*see* Outer Borough Restaurants *in* Chapter 4) along the avenue and on the boardwalk push their tables to the wall for a frenzied night of dancing and vodka drinking. *Subway: D or Q to Brighton Beach.*

SHEEPSHEAD BAY

While Brighton Beach is Russian, neighboring Sheepshead Bay is an authentic Italian fishing community with a small-town, 1940s flavor. To get a real feel for the place, walk down **Emmons Avenue** (which runs parallel to the bay) and over the Ocean Avenue footbridge. Here you'll find old salts hunched over the sea wall, diligently fishing up tonight's dinner. Head to the north end of the pier to discover dozens of deep-sea fishing boats ready and willing to take you out for the day (if you can rally by around 7 AM) for the absurdly low price of $25, equipment and advice included. If you've literally missed the boat, you can sometimes purchase fish at the end of the day (lucky fishermen sell their catch from their boats). *Subway: D or Q to Sheepshead Bay.*

QUEENS

Most Manhattan residents only set foot in Queens en route to La Guardia or J.F.K. airport, but those who manage to get past the area's dull appearance will discover a few surprises. According to estimates, approximately 179 nationalities coexist in Queens (including people from Afghanistan, China, Colombia, the Dominican Republic, the Philippines, India, Pakistan, Bangladesh, Korea, Mexico, Uruguay, Argentina, Peru, Romania, Thailand, and Ireland), and the area's strong ethnic flavor is perhaps its main draw. Named for Queen Catherine of Braganza, wife of Charles II, Queens was an independent British outpost until it joined with New York City in 1898. Today it's the largest of the city's five boroughs, accounting for a full third of the city's entire area. It's also the second most populous, surpassed only by Brooklyn.

Almost all of the sights in Queens are accessible by subway. Train rides take between 15 and 45 minutes from midtown Manhattan; the ride to the Rockaways takes more than an hour. The Greek community of Astoria lies over the Triborough Bridge from Manhattan, at the northwestern tip of Queens. Just south of here is the industrial center of Long Island City, a vital artists' community. To the east is the

ASTORIA

giant Flushing Meadows–Corona Park, site of two World's Fairs, in 1939 and 1964; you can't miss the 380-ton *Unisphere*—the largest known model of the earth—as you drive to La Guardia or J.F.K. Flushing, in the northeastern corner of Queens, is predominantly Asian. Near the center of the borough you'll find ritzy residential neighborhoods filled with Tudor-style houses and tree-lined streets, as well as stunning **Forest Park** (*see* Parks and Gardens, *below*). East of the park is the primarily African-American neighborhood of Jamaica, and beyond that is **Alley Pond Park** (*see* Parks and Gardens, *below*). To the south lies the uninhabited Jamaica Bay Islands, site of the 9,155-acre **Jamaica Bay Wildlife Refuge** (*see* Parks and Gardens, *below*), and the narrow, beach-lined Rockaway Peninsula.

ASTORIA

Astoria, home to one of the largest Greek communities this side of the Adriatic, is packed with sidewalk cafés, family-run stores, and Greek tavernas with live music and dancing. Though Colombian greasy spoons and characterless chain stores are now almost as ubiquitous as Greek-owned establishments, the Greek community still thrives in isolated pockets along the old-fashioned blocks between **Broadway** and **Ditmars Boulevard,** from 21st Street to Steinway Street. Stroll along Broadway between 31st and 36th avenues: Here *xaxaroplasteion* (Greek pastry shops) and coffee houses abound, and the elevated subway brings a constant stream of activity. Farther up, 30th Avenue has every kind of food store imaginable; between 35th and 36th streets alone you'll find a salumeria, a meat market, a bakery, a wholesale international food store, and more. The largest orthodox community outside Greece worships at **St. Demetrios Cathedral** (30-11 30th Dr.), at the corner of 31st Drive. *Subway: N to Broadway.*

You probably won't find the Marx Brothers or Bill Cosby walking down the streets of Astoria today—but in fact they have all done time here, along with many other big names in the American motion-picture industry. Before Hollywood, in the 1920s and '30s, the **Kaufman-Astoria Studios** (36–11 35th Ave., at 36th Ave.) were the hub of American movie-making: The likes of Gloria Swanson, Rudolph Valentino, and Claudette Colbert got their starts here. The studios are still used for major films and television shows—*Scent of a Woman, The Cotton Club,* "The Cosby Show," and even "Sesame Street" have all been filmed here. Though most of the studios are closed to the public, between August and April, "Cosby," the '90s spin-off of "The Cosby Show," is videotaped before a live studio audience. To request tickets, call 718/706–5389. You can also visit the excellent **American Museum of the Moving Image** (36th Ave. at 35th St., tel. 718/784–0077), where interactive exhibits give you an in-depth and entertaining view of how movies and television are made. *Subway: R to Steinway St.*

With the sale of its first home in 1924, Sunnyside Gardens presented working-class Queens with a respite from the urban jungle. The 77-acre enclave of moderate-income houses were modeled after England's noted 19th-century garden cities. In 1984, Sunnyside Gardens joined the National Register of Historic Places, becoming the city's largest historic district.

FLUSHING

Flushing is a curious mix of American history and ethnic diversity. To walk down Main Street today, with its staggering number of Asian restaurants and markets, you'd never guess that this was one of the first settlements of the Dutch, dating back to 1645. But venture north of the subway station into the historic area bounded by Northern and Parsons boulevards, Roosevelt Avenue, and Main Street, and you'll find several remnants of a 17th-century Quaker village. There's a fascinating history here: Having been forbidden to worship in public, the Dutch Quakers of *Vlissingen,* as Flushing was then called, found a loophole in the governing patent that granted all villagers liberty of conscience—a finding that not only ended their plight, but also served as the basis for the religious freedom that is granted in the U.S. Constitution.

THE FLUSHING FREEDOM MILE • The Queens Historical Society does a great job of preserving the area's historical buildings and providing information for curious visitors. Their headquarters are at the **Kingsland Homestead** (143–35 37th Ave., west of Parsons Blvd., tel. 718/939–0647)—a 1785 house where you can pick up maps and a self-guided tour brochure. While you're here, check out the **Weeping Beech Tree** in the garden out back: With a 14-ft-round trunk and an 85-ft branch spread, this hulking green giant planted in 1847 is the granddaddy of all American beech trees and one of two living landmarks in New York. (The other is not Ed Koch, but a magnolia tree in Brooklyn.) The nation's first nursery stood on this site, and today you'll still find rare trees throughout Flushing—golden larch,

SCRABBLE, ANYONE?

In the early 1930s, Alfred M. Butts, an out-of-work architect living in Jackson Heights, began experimenting with word games that combined features of anagrams and crossword puzzles. By analyzing the front page of the New York Times, Butts determined the frequency of letters, and assigned different values to each letter. Though Butts' initial patent application for "Lexico" was rejected, he persevered, adding a game board that he hand-drew with his architectural drafting equipment and reproduced by blueprinting and pasting on folding checkerboards. Butts organized games for the neighborhood at the Community Methodist Church, still on 35th Avenue. In 1948, Butts copyrighted his revised game board, Scrabble, which is today sold in 29 languages in more than 120 countries.

cedar of Lebanon, sassafras, mulberry, boxwood bush, and more. At the **Bowne House** (*see* Museums and Galleries, *below*), you can get a feel for life in the 1600s and pay homage to John Bowne, the key player in the establishment of freedom of religion. Three blocks away on Northern Boulevard, the shingled **Friends' Meeting House** (137–16 Northern Blvd., tel. 718/358–9636), in service since 1719, is the oldest house of worship in New York City. Across the street, the **Flushing Town Hall** (137–35 Northern Blvd., tel. 718/463–7700) houses a small art gallery/café, with live jazz ($20) on every other Friday night. *Subway: 7 to Main St.*

THE BRONX

Burned-out tenement buildings, drug crimes, and general urban decay are what most people associate with the Bronx. While these images are true to some extent, New York City's northernmost borough is also home to some of the grandest mansions and greenest parks around, not to mention the much-loved **Yankee Stadium** (*see* Chapter 9), the famous Bronx Zoo, and the stunning **New York Botanical Gardens** (*see* Parks and Gardens, *below*). The city's only mainland borough (the others are all on islands), the Bronx was first settled by Jonas Bronck, a Dane, in the 17th century. Legend has it that the Bronx got its name because other settlers would say, "Let's go see the Broncks." (In fact, the Bronx River had its name long before the Bronck family came along.) Wealthy New Yorkers maintained rural retreats in the Bronx in the 19th century, when the area consisted of a picturesque patchwork of farms, market villages, and country estates. In the 1920s, the Bronx experienced a short-lived golden age: The new elevated subway line attracted an upwardly mobile population, and the **Grand Concourse** was fashioned as New York City's Champs-Elysées. But the Bronx declined as quickly as it had boomed; today, vestiges of its glory days are few and far between.

Aside from the Grand Concourse and the **Bronx Museum of the Arts** (*see* Museums and Galleries, *below*), the southwestern part of the Bronx is not the best place to be . . . unless, of course, you're a Yankee fan. Major attractions—the zoo, the botanical gardens, and the Italian community of Belmont—are clustered in Central Bronx. Riverdale, in the hilly, northwest corner of the Bronx, is a wealthy community of estates, including Wave Hill (*see* Museums and Galleries, *below*). To the east, City Island is a quaint, slightly bohemian fishing community packed with boat-repair shops and fish restaurants. The northern half of the Bronx is dominated by the vast **Van Cortlandt** and **Pelham Bay** parks (for both, *see* Parks and Gardens, *below*). And, if you're a big fan of the man who penned "The Raven," take a peek at the **Edgar Allan Poe Cottage** (*see* Museums and Galleries, *below*). Most Bronx sights are no more than 45 minutes from midtown Manhattan; Yankee Stadium is just a 15-minute ride. Within the Bronx, stick to subways and buses; this is not a place where you'd want to get lost on foot.

NORTH BRONX

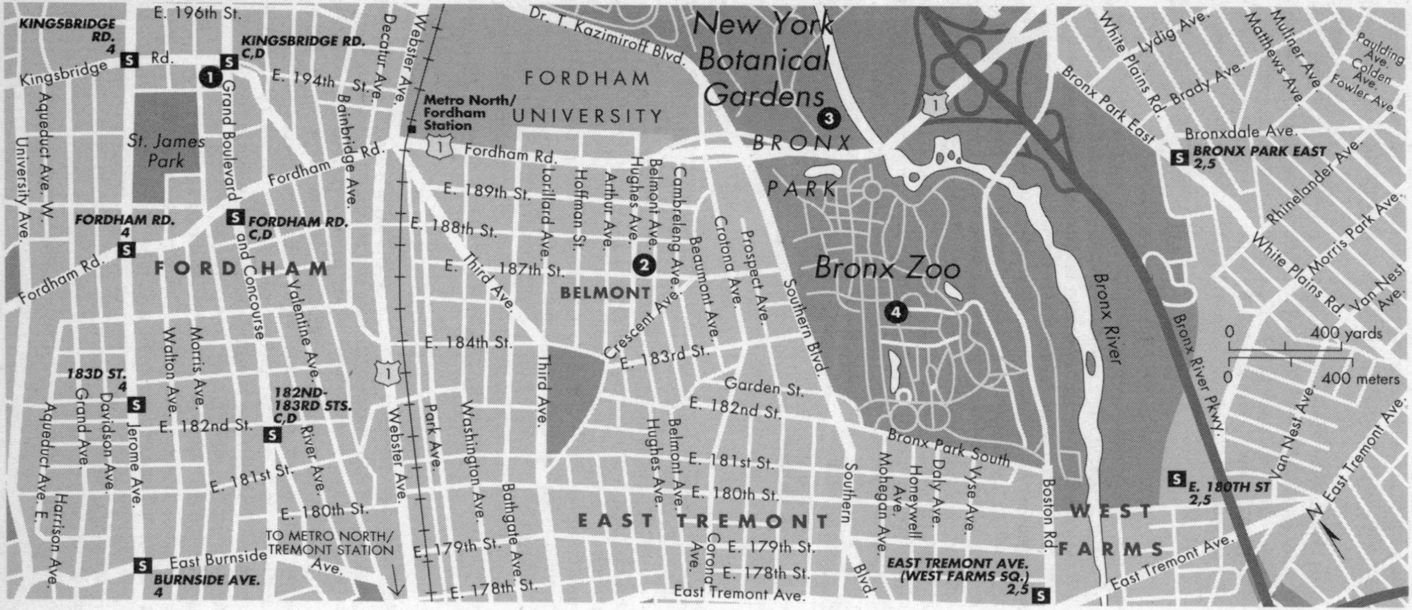

Bronx Zoo, **4**

Church of Our Lady of Mount Carmel, **2**

Edgar Allan Poe Cottage, **1**

New York Botanical Gardens, **3**

BRONX ZOO

With 265 acres and more than 4,000 animals, this is the largest and most interesting of New York City's wildlife conservation centers. Most of the exhibits rely on moats rather than cages to keep animals (and humans) in their proper places, and are landscaped like natural habitats. Be sure to see **Jungle World,** an indoor tropical rain forest complete with five waterfalls; and **Wild Asia,** where tigers, elephants, and rhinos roam freely through 40 acres of open meadows and forest; you can view them from the lofty vantage point of a monorail. Bus and tram tours are also available at certain times of the year. The zoo's trippiest offering? The **Butterfly Zone** (open June–October, weather permitting), where you walk through a caterpillar-shaped tent, populated by almost 1,000 butterflies. Also don't miss the **World of Birds,** where you can walk among your winged friends, and **World of Darkness,** a windowless building that reverses day and night so that you can see bats, leopard cats, and other nocturnal creatures in action. The newest permanent exhibit, the **Congo Gorilla Forest,** is home to the zoo's 19 gorillas. Free walking tours of the zoo are offered on weekends and daily in summer; call 718/220–5141 for reservations. *Bronx River Pkwy. at Fordham Rd., tel. 718/367–1010. Subway: 2 to Pelham Pkwy., then walk 3 blocks west. Bus: Liberty Lines BXM11 Express Bus from midtown Manhattan; call 718/652–8400 for schedule and fares. Admission $7.75; free Wed. Open Apr.–Oct., weekdays 10–5, weekends and holidays 10–5:30; Nov.–Mar., daily 10–4:30.*

BELMONT

Though today's Belmont is populated mostly by African Americans and Latinos, the short stretch of **Arthur Avenue** between 187th Street and Crescent Avenue remains the heart of an old Italian neighborhood, once home to more than 25,000 Italian Americans. The best time to visit is on a Saturday afternoon (the whole place shuts down Sunday). Arrive hungry because numerous bakeries, trattorias, and cafés (*see* Outer Borough Restaurants *in* Chapter 4) line the streets, and tiny markets sell cured olives and giant slabs of salami. You can atone for your gluttony at the **Church of Our Lady of Mount Carmel** (627 E. 187th St., between Hughes and Belmont Aves.) or drop by the **Catholic Goods Center** (630 E. 187th St., tel. 718/733–0250) for religious statuettes and Bibles in every tongue—Nigerian, Serbian, Albanian, and Creole, to name a few. *Subway: D to Fordham Rd. (20 mins), then walk 1 mi east on E. Fordham Rd. to Arthur Ave., turn right and walk 3 blocks to E. 187th St. Train: Metro-North to Fordham Rd. (10 mins).*

CITY ISLAND

City Island is probably the only place in New York where shop owners hang signs reading GONE TO THE BEACH. This mile-and-a-half-long, half-mile-wide spit of land (connected by bridge to the rest of the Bronx) feels like a cross between ye olde New England fishing village and a California hippie commune from the '60s. First settled in the 1760s, the whole place might have dried up and blown away if it weren't for its highly profitable yacht-building industry (the Astors and Vanderbilts have shopped here) and dozens of boat-repair businesses. Today there's not much else going on here, precisely City Island's charm. Spend the day strolling along the marina, poking around the funky, ramshackle little shops, or feasting on fried seafood at seagull-infested picnic tables. Afterward, take a peek inside the **North Wind Undersea Institute** (610 City Island Ave., tel. 718/885–0701), open weekdays 10–5 and weekends noon–4, whose ragtag collection includes whaling artifacts, scrimshaw art, and deep-sea diving gear (ask to see the video of Physty, the rescued sperm whale). At **Mooncurser Antiques** (229 City Island Ave., tel. 718/885–0302), you'll find a collection of 50,000 used LPs presided over by a bearded old eccentric. At the **Boat Livery** (663 City Island Ave., tel. 718/885–1843) you can grab a beer or bait and tackle (they're sold over the same counter), or rent a four-person dinghy ($20 per day) and row out into Pelham Bay. *Subway: 6 to Pelham Bay Park (45 mins); also Bus BX29 to City Island Ave. (20 mins).*

STATEN ISLAND

If you ask a few New Yorkers what's fun to do in the Big Apple for free, they will either shake their heads and tell you to stop dreaming, or they'll brightly mention the ferry ride to Staten Island. Of course, if you ask them *what's on Staten Island,* they'll stare blankly and shove off. This ignorance is infectious: Every day, hordes of tourists join commuters on the Staten Island Ferry (*see below*) for panoramic views of the Statue of Liberty, Ellis Island, and Lower Manhattan. Once there, most get right back on the next boat to Manhattan.

Staten Island is truly the forgotten borough. Though it's twice the size of Manhattan Island, its claims to fame (if it has any) are as the city's official garbage dump, and as the borough that is perpetually agi-

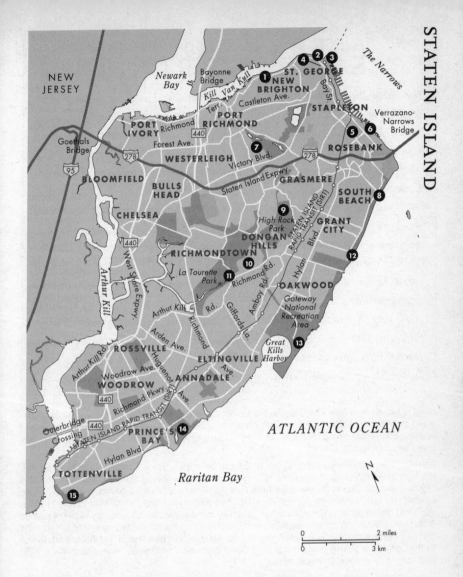

NEW JERSEY

Newark Bay

Bayonne Bridge

Kill Van Kull

Terr.

Castleton Ave.

ST. GEORGE

NEW BRIGHTON

STAPLETON

The Narrows

Bay St.

PORT IVORY

Richmond

PORT RICHMOND

440

Forest Ave.

Goethals Bridge

I-95

278

WESTERLEIGH

Victory Blvd.

BLOOMFIELD

BULLS HEAD

Staten Island Expwy.

ROSEBANK

Verrazano-Narrows Bridge

Verrazano-Narrows Bridge

GRASMERE

SOUTH BEACH

CHELSEA

440

High Rock Park

DONGAN HILLS

GRANT CITY

West Shore Expwy.

RICHMONDTOWN

La Tourette Park

Richmond Rd.

STATEN ISLAND RAPID TRANSIT (SIRT)

Hylan Blvd.

OAKWOOD

Arthur Kill

Arthur Kill Rd.

Richmond

Rd.

Giffords La.

Amboy Rd.

Gateway National Recreation Area

ROSSVILLE

Arden Ave.

Huguenot

ELTINGVILLE

Great Kills Harbor

Woodrow Ave.

WOODROW

Richmond Pkwy.

440

ANNADALE

Ave.

ATLANTIC OCEAN

Outerbridge Crossing

440

STATEN ISLAND RAPID TRANSIT (SIRT)

PRINCE'S BAY

Hylan Blvd.

TOTTENVILLE

Raritan Bay

N

0   2 miles

0   3 km

A TRIP TO THE SOUTH BRONX

The south Bronx, once a well-to-do neighborhood, has a sad history. After World War II industries began drifting out of New York City, forcing the many Bronx residents who depended on high-wage jobs in Manhattan to pick up and haul their possessions elsewhere. By the 1960s and '70s, as immigrants and laborers poured into the city, cheap housing projects were built in the Bronx— a comfortable distance from Manhattan. Crime flourished, buildings rotted, and some landlords even took to torching their empty, run-down apartment buildings to collect the insurance money. Only recently have grass-roots programs started to pull the south Bronx out of its long depression. Today the Grand Concourse (its main drag) shows remnants of its former appeal, with its grand (albeit decaying) art deco buildings housing a lively community of immigrant families. At one end of a four-block span (161st to 165th streets) you'll find the great "House that Babe Ruth Built," better known as Yankee Stadium; at the other is the Bronx Museum of the Arts. On Sunday afternoon, Joyce Kilmer Park (at 162nd Street) fills with salsa dancers and sellers of crafts for the Bronx Sunday Market.

tating to secede from New York City. The two are not unrelated: Islanders resent being dumped on (literally) and fear the environmental ramifications of having the world's largest landfill in their backyard. In addition, they resent paying New York City taxes, which they feel benefit Manhattan and the other boroughs far more than themselves.

Garbage dumps notwithstanding, Staten Island can be a lovely place to visit. It has more natural, unpaved areas than any of the other boroughs, including the 8-acre Staten Island Zoo, coastline beaches, and the hiker's paradise, **High Rock Park** (*see* Parks and Gardens, *below*). It also has a whole lot fewer people: The island's population in the late 1980s was comparable to Manhattan's in 1845. You'll find it's still got an old-time, rural feel, especially in the re-created 18th-century village of Historic Richmond Town and in the 19th-century sailors' haunt of Snug Harbor. Oddly enough, Staten Island is also home to an excellent museum of Tibetan art, the **Jacques Marchais Museum of Tibetan Art,** as well as the **Conference House,** onetime meeting place of Benjamin Franklin and his revolutionary crew (for both, *see* Museums and Galleries, *below*).

If you do disembark the ferry on Staten Island, plan on spending at least half a day there, since the island is vast and the sights spread apart. Brochures detailing the borough's many attractions, including restaurants, may be picked up at a newly erected tourist information office at the Whitehall Ferry Terminal in Manhattan. From the **Staten Island Ferry Terminal** (*see below*) you can catch a bus directly to Snug Harbor (20 min), Richmond Town (40 min), and most other sights. At the Ferry Terminal you can also pick up the Staten Island Railway (SIRT), which makes limited stops on its way to Tottenville, at the south end of the island. Pick up bus maps and train schedules inside the terminal (this information can also be picked up at the Whitehall terminal).

COMING AND GOING BY FERRY • The fact that the Staten Island Ferry is free is almost as stunning as the trip itself. Ferries run 24 hours, departing every 15 minutes during morning and evening rush hours, hourly after 11 PM and on weekend mornings, and every 30 minutes most other times; call for current schedules. In Manhattan the ferry departs from the **Staten Island Ferry Terminal** in Battery Park (South St., near State St., Lower Manhattan; Subway: 1 or 9 to South Ferry). Passengers disembark in Staten Island at the Ferry Terminal in St. George, on the northeastern tip of the island (from there it's easy to catch a bus or train to all of the island's attractions). The trip is 20–30 minutes one-way. A tip: The newer boats are super-fast, but try to get a ride on one of the older ones, which have big open-air decks that are great for snapping photos of the Manhattan skyline and the Statue of Liberty. *Tel. 718/727–2508 or 718/390–5253.*

SNUG HARBOR CULTURAL CENTER

Once home to a colony of "aged, decrepit and worn-out sailors," Snug Harbor is now an 83-acre cultural center full of landmark Greek Revival and Victorian buildings, artists' workshops and studios, a pleasant **Botanical Garden** (tel. 718/273–8200; free), including the newly erected Chinese Scholar's Garden; a **Children's Museum** (tel. 718/273–2060; $4); the **Newhouse Center for Contemporary Arts** (tel. 718/448–2500, ext. 260; $1 donation); and the **Music Hall,** the second-oldest music hall in New York City—after Carnegie Hall (call the general number, *below,* for performance information). The colony was founded in 1831 at the bequest of wealthy shipowner Robert Richard Randall, and for the next 140 years it served as the nation's first maritime hospital and home for retired seamen. Free weekend tours (departing from the Harbor Gift Shop daily at 2 PM) will fill you in on the history of the colony. *1000 Richmond Terr., tel. 718/448–2500. From Ferry Terminal, take Bus S40 (10–15 mins). Museums open Wed.–Sun. noon–5; grounds open daily dawn–dusk.*

HISTORIC RICHMOND TOWN

Sure, it sounds hokey: A living history museum with a bunch of people dressed in silly costumes and lots of 18th-century buildings. But Historic Richmond Town is so well done it's cool. Many of the buildings in this 100-acre village are over 200 years old; one you won't want to miss is the **Guyon-Lake Tysen House,** one of the best surviving examples of Dutch Colonial architecture anywhere in the country (stick around in summer to see folks in period costume whip up snacks in a beehive oven). The **Voorlezer's House,** built in 1695, is thought to be the oldest elementary school in the country. Here the voorlezer, or lay minister, conducted church services and taught children how to read the Bible. You can also watch the tinsmith practicing his craft at the **Tinsmith's Shop,** or drop by an old print shop and a restored general store. Also in Richmond Town, the **Staten Island Historical Society Museum** (*see* Museums and Galleries, *below*) is worth a quick stop. Tours of the village depart from the visitors center on the hour. *441 Clarke Ave., tel. 718/351–1611. From Ferry Terminal, take Bus S74 (40 mins). Admission $4. Open Sept.–June, Wed.–Sun. 1–5; July–Aug., Wed.–Fri. 10–5, weekends 1–5.*

ROSEBANK

The Italian community of Rosebank, centered around Tompkins and Bay streets near the Verrazano Bridge, has been around since the late 1800s. Among the well-tended houses you'll find the **Garibaldi–Meucci Museum** (*see* Museums and Galleries, *below*), which commemorates Rosebank's most famous residents; **Alice Austen House** (*see* Museums and Galleries, *below*), full of works by this photographer of the early 20th century; and the fabulously gaudy shrine to **Our Lady of Mount Carmel** (Amity St. at White Plains Ave.), studded with garishly painted plaster statuettes of various saints, strings of light bulbs, and eternally burning candles. Reach it from Tompkins Avenue by following St. Mary's Street to White Plains Avenue and then turning right onto Amity Street. *From Ferry Terminal, take Bus S78 Tompkins Ave. (15 mins).*

MUSEUMS AND GALLERIES

Despite the recent rise of high-art quotients in metropolises like Los Angeles and Chicago, New York City is still the museum capital of the United States. And, New York being New York, overkill is key. Most cities would be ecstatic just to host the likes of the **Metropolitan Museum of Art** or the **MoMA** (*see* Major Attractions, *above*), but that's not nearly enough for New Yorkers. From the unabashedly Eurocentric Pierpont Morgan Library to the downright esoteric Jacques Marchais Museum of Tibetan Art, New York's museums and galleries successfully enshrine every imaginable object of human and nonhuman contrivance. Throw in an aircraft carrier, a preserved early-19th-century tenement, a giant collection of Fabergé eggs, and dozens of other collections large and small, and you'll begin to see why New York can rightly be considered the United States' museum capital. By some estimates, there are more than 150 museums in the city of New York. This chapter covers more than 70 of 'em.

Many of the city's blockbuster museums are conveniently clustered on 5th Avenue between 82nd and 104th streets, also known as **Museum Mile** (*see* Upper East Side *in* Manhattan Neighborhoods, *above*). These include the **Solomon R. Guggenheim Museum, Frick Collection, National Academy of Design, Cooper-Hewitt National Design Museum, El Museo del Barrio, Goethe House, International Center of Photography (ICP)–Uptown, The Jewish Museum,** and the **Museum of the City of New York.**

In addition to pretty pictures and fascinating artifacts, you'll find that museums offer guided tours, lectures, films (*see* Movie Houses *in* Chapter 7), concerts (*see* Music *in* Chapter 7), dance performances, and more. Often, these activities are free with museum admission, a deal that can turn even the most dedicated museum-hater into a true devotee. For info on current shows and events, check listings in one of the city's weeklies, like *The New Yorker* or *Time Out,* or the "Weekend" section of the Friday *New York Times.* In case your cultural pursuits span lunch hour, most major museums have attractive cafeterias and/or cafés, where you may or may not get a decent value for your dollar—the one at the American Museum of Natural History is called the Diner Saurus. If you keep your admission ticket (or button), however, you can always pop outside for a cheap slice of pizza and reenter the museum. Some museums, like the Met, the MoMA, the Frick, and the Cloisters, offer stunning courtyards and gardens to relax in. And, of course, all museums have gift shops.

Almost all of the city's museums are closed on Mondays. Otherwise, museum hours vary greatly; many major ones offer extended hours on Tuesday or Thursday, and further tempt weekday visitors by making admission free after 6 PM on those evenings. As you would expect, museums are closed on New Year's Day, Independence Day, Thanksgiving, and Christmas. If you want to visit a museum on other holidays, you should call ahead and confirm hours. Keep an eye out for copies of *Museums New York* in your hotel lobby or by museum information desks; this glossy not-quite-a-magazine has a great coupon section as well as rundowns on current exhibits.

AMERICAN MUSEUM OF NATURAL HISTORY

The American Museum of Natural History, established by scientist Albert Bickmore in 1868, is one of the largest and most important museums of its kind. All of the "-ologies" are represented here—zoology, anthropology, vertebrate paleontology, ornithology, and evolutionary biology, to name a few—in a collection of more than 36 million artifacts and specimens enclosed in 40 halls and galleries. If you're expecting just a bunch of dead, stuffed elk displayed in stale, airless rooms, you're in for a big surprise. There's something here for everyone, from the world's largest collection of insects (17 million and counting) to the world's biggest sapphire (563 carats). Of course, there are also plenty of dead, stuffed elk. But the museum has long been on the cutting edge of research in its fields, and is constantly changing its exhibits to jive with the times: During the first decades of the 20th century, the museum president arranged exhibits in the Hall of the Age of Man to reflect his racist belief in the supremacy of northern Europeans, but curators in the 1960s completely revamped the displays and renamed them the Hall of the Biology of Man. More recently, the museum completed a much-needed $34-million overhaul of its world-famous **dinosaur halls** (*see below*).

The museum and the attached Planetarium (*see below*) dominate a four-block tract on the Upper West Side. Originally, architects Calvert Vaux and Jacob Wrey Mould (who both also designed the Metropolitan Museum of Art) were determined to make this the largest building in the United States. They finished one wing and, from 1892 to 1936, other architects finished the rest. The last and most grandiose section, the work of John Russell Pope, is the neoclassical facade that borders Central Park West. It's quite a striking backdrop for the giant statue of Teddy Roosevelt. *Central Park W at W. 79th St., Upper West Side, tel. 212/769–5100. Subway: B or C to W. 81st St. Suggested donation $10. IMAX or Planetarium tickets, including museum admission, $9–$13. Open daily 10–5:45 (Fri.–Sat. until 8:45).*

PRACTICALITIES

Free tours of the museum's highlights are given daily at 10:15, 11:15, 1:15, 2:15, and 3:15, beginning at the African Mammals Hall on the second floor. They provide an excellent overview if you've never been here before, or if you've only got one afternoon to explore. Year-round, the museum offers a number of special performances, films, and lectures; call for the schedule.

COLLECTION HIGHLIGHTS

If you're pressed for time, skip everything else and head directly to the museum's famed **dinosaur halls** (*see below*). Otherwise, most of the good stuff is on the first floor, including the 94-ft-long (that's actual whale size) fiberglass model of a blue whale, which is suspended from the ceiling of the **Ocean Life Room.** In the **Hall of Minerals and Gems** you'll find the famous 563-carat Star of India sapphire, the largest in the world, while the adjoining **Hall of Meteorites** contains the Cape York Meteorite, smaller than a Volkswagen but so heavy that its supporting pillars go through the museum's floor and straight down into the bedrock below the building. The **Hall of Human Biology and Evolution** is all about man's favorite subject, namely, him- or herself; don't miss the "Visible Woman" hologram, a spooky life-size display that flashes from skeleton to internal organs to veins, arteries, and nerves to flesh-and-blood person, depending on the angle you look at her from. To see what a slice of a 1,300-year-old giant sequoia tree looks like, check out the **Hall of North American Forests.**

Also on the first floor is the brand-new **Gottesman Hall of the Planet Earth,** the museum's newest permanent exhibition. Spanning some 8,830-square feet, the collection includes 82 tons of rock and ore ranging from granite and sandstone to gold and platinum (the oldest, a zircon from Australia, is nearly 4.3 billion years old; the youngest, a chunk of sulfur, was picked up the same day it solidified in an Indonesian volcano).

The American Museum of Natural History's fossilized dinosaur embryo on display is thought to be 70 to 80 million years old. Jurassic Park, anyone?

On the second and third floors, you'll find rooms devoted to the peoples of the world. Look for the **Chinese Wedding Chair** (Hall of Asian Peoples); the 3,000-year-old giant jade **Kunz Axe** and the silver-and-gold **Royal Llama of the Inka** (Hall of Mexico and Central America); and the amazing model of an **African Spirit Dancer** wearing a costume made of real snail shells (Hall of African Peoples). Sharing these floors are dioramas of animals in their natural habitats, many bagged by wealthy American taxidermist Carl Akeley in the 1920s—it's hard to think of Akeley as a hero while you're staring at a whole herd of stuffed African elephants in the **Akeley Hall of African Mammals.** You'll have to admit, however, that the Hall of Reptiles and Amphibians' display of three **Komodo dragons** eating a large wild boar is a little titillating.

THE DINOSAUR HALLS • In 1995, after four years and $34 million worth of work, the museum opened two spectacular new dinosaur halls: the **Hall of Suarischian Dinosaurs** and the **Hall of Ornithischian Dinosaurs,** both on the fourth floor. Then, in 1996, they opened the **Hall of Vertebrate Origins,** with displays of primitive fishes and pterodactyls. In these halls, interactive computer displays feature animated footage of how these monstrous beasts got around. More to the point, you'll find the single largest collection of real dinosaur fossils in the world: approximately 100 skeletons, 85% of which are real fossils (not that you would ever notice the difference). During the renovation process some of the skeletons were taken apart and rebuilt according to scientists' improved understanding of how the animals moved; for example, the **Apatosaurus,** previously known as Brontosaurus, got a new skull, additional neck bones, and a tail that has been lengthened by 20 ft. Other highlights include the **Warren Mastodon,** which was discovered in a bog less than 100 mi from New York City and is one of the most complete skeletons of the hairy prehistoric elephant ever found; a **Dinosaur Mummy,** important because it shows the skin and other soft tissues of a duck-billed dinosaur; the **Glenn Rose Trackway,** a series of 107-million-year-old fossilized dinosaur footprints; and last but certainly not least, the mighty, meat-eating **Tyrannosaurus Rex,** reset in a stalking (as opposed to a standing) posture. The rest of the museum's dinosaur collection is on the second floor, and has also been recently restored.

HAYDEN PLANETARIUM • The old Hayden Planetarium is undergoing an extensive renovation and will tentatively reopen in early 2000 as the Earth and Space Center. It will feature a state-of-the-art Sky Theater for stellar views of the constellations and two new exhibition halls.

IMAX THEATER • Films on the IMAX Theater's 40-ft-high, 66-ft-wide screen are usually about nature, whether it's a jaunt through the Grand Canyon, a safari in the Serengeti, or a journey to the bottom of the sea to the wreck of the *Titanic.* If you've never watched a flick on a giant IMAX screen before, you're in for an awe-inspiring experience. *Tel. 212/769–5650 for show times. Admission $10. Purchase tickets at IMAX ticket counter in museum's W. 77th St. lobby.*

BROOKLYN MUSEUM OF ART

You took the subway all the way up to 86th Street and then walked three avenues and four blocks to the Met, right? Well, the Brooklyn Museum of Art should also make it onto your itinerary and the subway stop's right outside its doors. It's the seventh-largest museum in the United States (and the second-largest in New York), with a 1.5-million item collection that runs the gamut from Egyptian mummy cases to Rodin sculptures to elaborately beaded African crowns to an entire 17th-century Brooklyn house.

Now housed in an elephantine, turn-of-the-century beaux arts monument by McKim, Mead & White, the Brooklyn Museum (the "of Art" in the name was added in 1997) was founded in 1823 as the Brooklyn Apprentices' Library Association (Walt Whitman was one of its first directors). Initial plans made this the largest art museum in the world—larger even than the Louvre in Paris—although Brooklyn's 1898 annexation to Manhattan thwarted those plans (only five years after the building opened). The museum keeps renewing itself with more space, reinstalled galleries, extended Saturday hours, film screenings, readings, and musical performances. Exhibits scheduled for 2000 include William Merritt Chase, Maxfield Parrish, and Scythian gold treasures (7th–2nd century BC) from ancient Ukraine. *200 Eastern Pkwy., Park Slope, Brooklyn, tel. 718/638–5000. Subway: 2 or 3 to Eastern Pkwy./Brooklyn Museum. Admission $4; free first Sat. of month 5–11PM. Open Wed.–Fri. 10–5, Sat. 11–6, Sun. 11–6.*

COLLECTION HIGHLIGHTS

The Brooklyn Museum pioneered the collection and study of non-Western art, and its **African and Pre-Columbian Art** galleries are outstanding. Make sure you view the 2,000-year-old *Paracas Textile*, which is considered by many to be the most important ancient Andean textile in the world. The museum's collection of **Asian Art** (second floor) includes pieces from Afghanistan, China, Korea, India, the Islamic world, and much more. You'll also find an impressive number of European and American paintings and sculpture here: The galleries of **Old Masters and French Impressionists** (fifth floor) show works by Hals, Monet, Degas, Pissarro, Cassatt, Toulouse-Lautrec, and others. On the first floor, the **Grand Lobby installations** feature work created by contemporary artists specifically for this grandiose space.

AMERICAN COLLECTION • This collection, which rivals that of the Met, chronicles American art from its origins to the present with paintings by Copley, John Singer Sargent, William Merritt Chase, Winslow Homer, and Thomas Eakins. Don't miss *Brooklyn Bridge* by Georgia O'Keeffe. *5th floor.*

THE EGYPTIAN GALLERIES • The **Schapiro Wing** houses the museum's Egyptian art, considered the finest collection outside London and Cairo. In addition to massive Assyrian wall reliefs, the galleries contain incredible treasures from ancient Egyptian tombs and royal cities dating from the Predynastic period (4,000–3,000 BC) to the Muslim conquest (7th century AD). Besides mummies in glorious sarcophagi, you'll see jewelry; pots; tools; solemn statues of queens, kings, cats, and dogs; and lots of small precious objects made from alabaster or ivory. *3rd floor.*

FRIEDA SCHIFF WARBURG MEMORIAL SCULPTURE GARDEN • This zany outdoor garden features relics from the "lost New York," such as a lion's head from Coney Island's old Steeplechase Park and the white goddess that once cradled the Penn Station clock. You'll find lots more cherubs, lions, scrolls, capitals, Medusas, and Greek-looking columns rescued from 19th-century buildings before they were torn down.

IRIS AND GERALD CANTOR GALLERY • This attractive gallery showcases 58 sculptures by Auguste Rodin, including works related to *The Gates of Hell, The Burghers of Calais,* and *Balzac. 5th floor.*

PERIOD ROOMS • Twenty-eight period rooms—parlors, sitting rooms, and dining rooms, from plantation mansions and New England cottages—show how New Yorkers lived from 1675 to 1830. Viewing the Jan Martense Schenck House, the oldest, is like stepping into a painting by a Dutch master, and the somber, exotic Moorish Room from John D. Rockefeller's town house is a tycoon's Alhambra. Costume galleries and decorative arts displays complement the period rooms. *4th floor.*

THE CLOISTERS

Perched atop a wooded hill near Manhattan's northernmost tip, the Cloisters houses the medieval collection of the Metropolitan Museum of Art (*see* Major Attractions, *above*) in an appropriately medieval monasterylike setting. Colonnaded walks connect authentic French cloisters, a Spanish Romanesque chapel, a 12th-century chapter house, and a Romanesque apse. The whole complex is spectacularly set overlooking the Hudson River, at the high point of Fort Tryon Park; for more on Fort Tryon Park itself, *see* Parks and Gardens, *below.* The galleries that display the collection are organized chronologically, starting with pieces from AD 1200, continuing through the Gothic period, and ending around 1520. Featured are chalices, altarpieces, sculptures, precious illuminated manuscripts, and works in stained glass, metal, enamel, and ivory. An entire room is devoted to the richly woven and extraordinarily detailed 15th- and 16th-century Unicorn Tapestries—a must-see. Just as noteworthy as the art on the walls are the museum's three **formal gardens**: In the central courtyard you'll find a splashing fountain, flowering plants, and piped-in choir music; the herb garden is full of strangely named greens once employed in medieval cures; and the Unicorn garden blooms with flowers and plants depicted in the famous Unicorn Tapestries. The Cloisters also frequently hosts special concerts of medieval music; for more info, *see* Music *in* Chapter 7. *Fort Tryon Park, Washington Heights, tel. 212/923–3700. Subway: A to 190th St.; also Bus M4 to last stop. Suggested donation $8 (includes same-day admission to Metropolitan Museum of Art). Open Mar.–Oct., Tues.–Sun. 9:30–5:15; Nov.–Feb., Tues.–Sun. 9:30–4:45.*

PIERPONT MORGAN LIBRARY

Both a museum and a center for scholarly research, the Morgan Library was originally built in 1906 as the private library for Pierpont Morgan, an immensely influential banker, philanthropist, and collector. This outstanding treasury has a renowned collection of rare books, manuscripts, and drawings that focus on the history and culture of Western civilization from the Middle Ages to the 20th century. Collection highlights include letters penned by Thomas Jefferson and John Keats; handwritten music by Beethoven and Mozart; a summary of the theory of relativity in Einstein's own elegant handwriting; three Gutenberg Bibles; drawings by Dürer, da Vinci, Rubens, and Degas; and original manuscripts by Mark Twain and Charlotte Brontë. The galleries at the museum's main entrance have changing exhibitions; beyond these rooms, you'll find the opulent period rooms of Morgan's original library. The **East Room** (the main library) houses a portion of the Library's collection of rare books. The **West Room,** Morgan's personal study, contains a remarkable selection of mostly Italian Renaissance carvings, furniture, paintings, and other marvels. (The room, however, is so dark and sullen with red damask walls and heavy furniture that you may wonder if Morgan ever actually *read* here.) The **Rotunda,** with its marble columns and Raphael-esque ceiling mosaics, is one of the grandest small spaces in New York. When you get hungry or tired, linger awhile at the museum's delightful glass-roof garden court, which offers salads and sandwiches ($8–$12) and a proper afternoon tea ($17). Free guided tours of the museum take place weekdays at noon. Since it became a public institution in 1924, the Library has grown to half a city block, including the adjacent 1852 Italianate brownstone that belonged to Morgan's son, J. P. Morgan, Jr. Here you'll find the exceptional Morgan Library Shop. The library is slightly off the beaten tourist track, so if you've had enough of fighting crowds in the city's major museums, you'll enjoy the relative silence and privacy of this undervisited gem. *29 E. 36th St., at Madison Ave., Murray Hill, tel. 212/685–0008. Subway: 6 to E. 33rd St. Suggested donation $7. Open Tues.–Thurs. 10:30–5, Fri. 10:30–8, Sat. 10:30–6, Sun. noon–6.*

> *On the first Saturday of the month, the best eclectic party in town is thrown by the Brooklyn Museum of Art. The entire museum is free from 5–11 pm, and you can mingle over drinks amongst totem poles, or groove in the packed lobby to the headline band.*

WHITNEY MUSEUM OF AMERICAN ART

Gertrude Vanderbilt Whitney founded the Whitney Museum in 1930 with the noble notion of celebrating artists while they were still alive; the result is one of Manhattan's most dynamic institutions. Mrs. Whitney's own collection is the nucleus of the permanent collection of some 12,000 20th-century paintings, sculpture, and works on paper by more than 1,500 artists, including George Bellows, Stuart Davis, Jasper Johns, Willem de Kooning, Alex Katz, Ellsworth Kelly, Roy Lichtenstein, Georgia O'Keeffe, Maurice B. Prendergast, Jackson Pollock, Mark Rothko, John Sloan, Frank Stella, and Andy Warhol. Edward Hopper fans will be delighted to find a small room dedicated to the artist, with classics like *Early Sunday Morning,* and his long-in-hiding early work *Soir Bleu.* Other galleries focus on the urban landscape and American social realism.

In addition, there are always lively special exhibits; the 2000 lineup includes Barbara Kruger (mid July through October), Alice Neil (July through September), Edward Steichen (October), and Sol LeWitt

(November). In 2000 the museum will also showcase more of its permanent collection, which will be displayed on the 2nd floor in addition to the fifth. Pause for a moment before entering the museum and size up this granite-clad building (1966), designed by the great Bauhaus/modernist architect Marcel Breuer. If you peer into the surrounding "moat," you'll see the busy hive of Sarabeth's; East-Siders have been known to skip the museum entirely and just come here for brunch. One of the biggest regular events at the Whitney is the **Biennial Exhibition,** which is held in the spring of every odd-numbered year and highlights what the museum considers the greatest creations by American artists during the previous two years. Biennial shows are a blast; they're always wildly controversial and usually generate some wicked banter within the art community. The Whitney also offers a film and video series; dial 212/570–3676 for more info.

If you still haven't had your fill, visit the Whitney's small (and free) Midtown outpost, the **Whitney Museum of American Art at Philip Morris** (120 Park Ave., at E. 42nd St., Midtown, tel. 917/663–2453), which has galleries and a sculpture court. *945 Madison Ave., at E. 75th St., Upper East Side, tel. 212/570–3676. Subway: 6 to E. 77th St. Admission $9; free Thurs. 6–8. Wed. and Fri.–Sun. 11–6, Thurs. 1–8.*

MORE ART MUSEUMS

Alternative Museum. As the sign outside says, this two-room gallery SEEKS TO EXHIBIT THE WORK OF THOSE ARTISTS WHO HAVE BEEN DISENFRANCHISED BECAUSE OF IDEOLOGY, RACE, GENDER, OR ECONOMIC INEQUALITY. It boasts some of the most interesting and engaging (and occasionally offensive or confrontational) art in SoHo. *594 Broadway, between Houston and Prince Sts., SoHo, tel. 212/966–4444. Subway: N or R to Prince St. Suggested donation: $3. Open Tues.–Sat. 11–6.*

American Craft Museum. Across the street from the Museum of Modern Art (MoMA), this small museum showcases contemporary American crafts in clay, fabric, glass, metal, wood, and even chocolate. Stop worrying about the distinction between "crafts" and "high art" while you're here—most of this stuff is just fun to look at. *40 W. 53rd St., between 5th and 6th Aves., Midtown, tel. 212/956–3535. Subway: E or F to 5th Ave. Admission $5. Open Tues.–Sun. 10–6, Thurs. until 8.*

Asian American Arts Centre. This space may not be as slick as galleries farther uptown, but it does showcase contemporary works by talented Asian-American artists not easily seen elsewhere in the city. It also hosts annual Chinese folk-art exhibitions during the Chinese New Year and performances by the Asian American Dance Theater. The center sells a small selection of singular art objects from China. There's no sign out front; the door reads "KTV-City"; ring buzzer No. 1. *26 Bowery, between Bayard and Canal Sts., Chinatown, tel. 212/233–2154. Subway: N, R, J, M, or 6 to Canal St.; also B, D, or Q to Grand St. Admission free. Open Tues.–Fri. 1–6, Sat. 4–6.*

Bronx Museum of the Arts. Don't expect pretty paintings in this progressive museum. The exhibits, by artists of African, Asian, and Latin American descent, range from "The Body in Contemporary Photography" (in which striking black-and-white photos depict cultural and religious practices associated with the body) to "Urban Mythologies: The Bronx Represented Since the 1960s." The museum is in a former synagogue, and the three-story, glass-enclosed atrium gives it an airy, unstuffy feel. *1040 Grand Concourse, at 165th St., Bronx, tel. 718/681–6000. Subway: C, D, or 4 to 161st St./Yankee Stadium. Admission $3; free Wed. Open Wed. 3–9, Thurs.–Fri. 10–5, weekends 1–6.*

Children's Museum of the Arts. A hip, bi-level space in SoHo is not the place you'd expect to find a hands-on children's museum. But kids 1–10 can come here for an introduction to the visual and performing arts (luckily they don't yet have classes in wearing black or looking rich). *182 Lafayette St., between Grand and Broome Sts., SoHo, tel. 212/274–0986. Subway: 1 or 9 to Canal St. Admission $5. Open Wed. 12–7, Thurs.–Sun. 12–5.*

Dia Center for the Arts. This facility arrived in Chelsea several years before the most recent gallery craze. Here artists can develop new work or mount an organized exhibit or installation on a full floor for extended periods. Works from Dia's permanent collection may also be on view, including art by Joseph Beuys, Walter De Maria, Dan Flavin, Blinky Palermo, Cy Twombly, and Andy Warhol, among others. Up on the roof there's a coffee bar and an inspired exhibition by Dan Graham—a two-way mirror glass cylinder inside a cube. Exhibits are also mounted in an annex across the street at 535 W. 22nd St.; hold onto your ticket for admission. *548 W. 22nd St., Chelsea, tel. 212/989–5566. Subway: E to W. 23rd St. Suggested donation $4. Open Thurs.–Sun. noon–6.*

Grey Art Gallery. New York University's main building on Washington Square's east side contains this unpretentious street-level museum with changing exhibitions usually concentrating on contemporary artists. The gallery also houses two major art collections: the NYU art collection, which includes a few works by Picasso, Miró, and Matisse; and the Abbey Weed Grey Collection, which showcases contemporary Asian and Middle Eastern art. *100 Washington Sq. E, West Village, tel. 212/998–6780. Subway: N or R to E. 8th St./NYU. Suggested donation $2.50. Open Sept.–July, Tues.–Fri. 11–6 (Wed. until 8), Sat. 11–5.*

Guggenheim Museum SoHo. The SoHo outpost of the world-renowned Solomon R. Guggenheim Museum (*see* Upper East Side *in* Manhattan Neighborhoods, *above*) has struggled to define itself since its 1992 opening in a landmark redbrick warehouse on one of the city's chicest blocks. It displays contemporary art and works from the permanent collection and, increasingly, cutting-edge multimedia, design, and electronic exhibits. The large gift shop is certainly appealing, but you'll have to look hard to find any bargains. *575 Broadway, at Prince St., SoHo, tel. 212/423–3500. Subway: N or R to Prince St; 6 to Spring St.; or B, D, F, or Q to Broadway/Lafayette St. Admission $8. Open Wed.–Sun. 11–6 (Sat. until 8).*

The Institute for Contemporary Art/Clocktower Gallery. Ride up to the 13th floor to visit this gallery of avant-garde art and sculpture by resident artists (whose studios are closed to the public, except by appointment). The building, which once housed the New York Life Insurance Company, is an 1895 design by McKim, Mead & White. *108 Leonard St., TriBeCa, tel. 212/233–1096. Subway: A or C to Chambers St. or E to Canal St. Suggested donation $2. Open Wed.–Sun. noon–6.*

At the Whitney Museum, look for artist Charles Simonds's tiny, overlooked model based on an Indian pueblo, tucked into a corner of the stairwell.

The Institute for Contemporary Art/P.S. 1 Museum. What do you get when you take an 85,000-square-ft former public school and invite emerging and international artists to fill it up with their avant-garde works? Add to that a gritty location in the midst of the factories and warehouses of Long Island City, and a phenomenal view of the Manhattan skyline, and you have the P.S. 1 Museum. Newly opened after a three-year renovation, P.S. 1 challenges traditional mores about how to present art. You'll find installations in the most unusual spaces—in the attic, the boiler room, the closets—even the bathrooms. If you're in the mood to meditate, look for "Meeting," a room with uniquely colored lights from Sweden and a motorized ceiling that opens to reveal the sky. *22–25 Jackson Ave. at 46th Ave., Long Island City, Queens, tel. 718/784–2084. Subway: 7 to 45th Rd./Court House Sq. Suggested donation $5. Open Wed.–Sun. noon–6.*

Isamu Noguchi Garden Museum. More than 300 works by the famous late Japanese-American sculptor Isamu Noguchi are on display here, from abstract bronzes inspired by Brancusi (a mentor to Noguchi during the '20s) to traditional Japanese ceramic and cast-iron sculpture to surrealist-inspired works in marble, slate, and wood. The peaceful outdoor garden is graced by a traditional *tsukubai* (fountain). *32–37 Vernon Blvd., between 33rd Rd. and 10th St., Long Island City, Queens, tel. 718/721–1932. Subway: N to Broadway. Admission $4. Open Apr.–Oct., Wed.–Fri.10–5, weekends 11–6.*

Museum for African Art. This is one of only two museums in the United States devoted exclusively to the arts of Africa. Its impressive exhibitions, which change every six months, may include wooden sculptures, masks and headdresses, jewelry, and religious relics; items on display are usually accompanied by printed narratives and photographs showing how the artifact was actually used. The museum shop carries African musical instruments, textiles, pottery, jewelry, and children's books. There's a free guided tour every Saturday at 2. *593 Broadway, between Houston and Prince Sts., SoHo, tel. 212/966–1313. Subway: N or R to Prince St.; also B, D, F, or Q to Broadway/Lafayette St. Admission $5. Open Tues.–Fri. 10:30–5:30, weekends noon–6.*

Museum of American Folk Art. A trip to this museum would be a lot like a foray into your grandmother's attic, assuming she hoarded paintings, quilts, carvings, dolls, wooden decoys, furniture, silver pieces, altars, copper weather vanes, and a beautiful collection of carousel horses. You can read all about how these pieces were made, and which immigrant groups brought them here. *2 Lincoln Sq., on Columbus Ave. between W. 65th and 66th Sts., Upper West Side, tel. 212/595–9533. Subway: 1 or 9 to W. 66th St. Suggested donation $3. Open Tues.–Sun. 11:30–7:30.*

Museum of American Illustration. The Society of Illustrators, founded in 1901, mounts exhibits of the commercial arts, such as children's book illustrations, book and magazine covers, postal stamps, cartoons, and print advertisements. The museum's small galleries are in an 1875 carriage house. *128 E. 63rd St., between Park and Lexington Aves., Upper East Side, tel. 212/838–2560. Subway: B or Q to Lexington Ave. Admission free. Open Sept.–July, Tues. 10–8, Wed.–Fri. 10–5, Sat. noon–4.*

New Museum of Contemporary Art. What you'll see here is experimental, often radically innovative work by unrecognized artists—and none of it is usually more than 10 years old. *583 Broadway, between Houston and Prince Sts., SoHo, tel. 212/219–1222. Subway: N or R to Prince St.; also B, D, F, or Q to Broadway/Lafayette St. Admission $5; free Thurs. 6–8. Open Wed., Fri., and Sun. noon–6 (Sat. and Thurs. until 8).*

Nicholas Roerich Museum. Housed in a beautiful Upper West Side town house (built in 1898), this small, eccentric museum displays the work of the prolific Russian artist who was also author, philosopher, explorer, archaeologist, and set designer (he designed sets for Diaghilev ballets). His vast paintings of the Himalayas are suffused with such a trippy mysticism that they give the whole place a cultish appeal. Also displayed are Roerich's books and travel treasures. Drop by on a winter weekend for poetry readings and classical-music performances. *319 W. 107th St., between Broadway and Riverside Dr., Upper West Side, tel. 212/864–7752. Subway: 1 or 9 to W. 110th St. Donations appreciated. Open Tues.–Sun. 2–5.*

Queens Museum of Art. If there's one reason to make the trek to Flushing Meadows–Corona Park, it's to see the knock-your-socks-off **New York City panorama** in the Queens Museum of Art. The 9,335-square-ft model, constructed for the 1964 World's Fair, faithfully replicates all five boroughs of the city, building by building, on a scale of 1 inch per 100 ft. The model's tiny brownstones and skyscrapers are updated periodically to look exactly like the real things. The museum's other exhibits examine the history of the World's Fair, and its frequent art exhibitions often reflect the cultural diversity of Queens. The park's New York City Building, which houses the museum, was also the site of several United Nations meetings between 1946 and 1952. *Flushing Meadows–Corona Park, tel. 718/592–9700. Subway: 7 to Willets Point/Shea Stadium. Admission $4. Open Wed.–Fri. 10–5, weekends noon–5.*

Studio Museum in Harlem. The museum's extensive collection of artifacts and art from the African diaspora includes sculptures, masks, headdresses, delicately beaded clothing, and religious tokens from Guinea, Tanzania, the Ivory Coast, Nigeria, Zaire, Ghana, Cameroon, Angola, and the Zulu people of South Africa. Look for works by the Studio Museum's artists-in-residence, who come from all over the world. *144 W. 125th St., between Adam Clayton Powell Jr. and Malcolm X Blvds., Harlem, tel. 212/864–4500. Subway: B, C, D, 2, or 3 to W. 125th St. Admission $5. Open Wed.–Fri. 10–5, weekends 1–6.*

MUSEUMS ABOUT NEW YORK

Brooklyn Historical Society. The Historical Society has been collecting weird and wonderful artifacts about the borough and its citizenry since 1863. The building was the first major structure in New York to feature terra-cotta ornamentation, which includes lifelike busts, capitals, and friezes. Although the elegant redbrick museum and library are closed for renovations through spring 2001, some of its exhibits will be relocated. The Brooklyn Walks, Brooklyn Talks series led by Brooklyn historians and authors is ongoing ($12 nonmembers); reservations are recommended. *128 Pierrepont St., at Clinton St., Brooklyn Heights, tel. 718/624–0890. Subway: 2 or 3 to Clark St. Closed for renovations. Call for information about walking tours.*

Lower East Side Tenement Museum. This is the only museum in the country devoted to re-creating and remembering the urban squalor of the tenements (no-frills apartment buildings that opportunistic landlords constructed on the Lower East Side during the mid-1800s immigration boom). For $2 a month, destitute Jewish, Italian, and Irish immigrants crowded into one-room tenement apartments; they typically lived in dark, cramped, unventilated, and waterless quarters, and shared a single outdoor privy and water pump with up to 400 other residents. At the museum, you can take a fascinating guided tour of four restored apartments in a 19th-century tenement building (97 Orchard St.). Apartments include those of Natalie Gumpertz, a German-Jewish dressmaker (1878) and Adolph and Rosaria Baldizzi, Catholic immigrants from Sicily (1935). If the tour doesn't interest you, you can watch a slide show about the tenement building's history and a video of interviews with Lower East Side natives. The free gallery has displays relating to Lower East Side history. *90 Orchard St., between Delancey and Broome Sts., Lower East Side, tel. 212/431–0233. Subway: F to Delancey St. Admission $8; includes tenement tour, slide show, and video. Open Tues.–Fri. noon–5; weekends 11–5. Tenement tours Tues.–Fri. 1, 2, and 3, weekends every 45 mins 11–4:15. Neighborhood walking tours weekends 1:30 and 2:30. Walking tour $8; tenement and walking tour $12.*

New York City Fire Museum. It may not be as exciting as a three-alarm blaze, but the nifty collection of ornate old fire carriages and engines is a kick to look at—so are its photos of the horse-drawn fire wagons that once raced around New York, dousing flames and saving babies. There are exhibits devoted to all kinds of lore, including why firehouses have always favored black-and-white-spotted Dalmatians rather than, say, toy poodles. The museum itself is housed in a quaint old fire station that was active from 1904 to 1959. *278 Spring St., between Varick and Hudson Sts., SoHo, tel. 212/691–1303. Subway: C or E to Spring St. Suggested donation $4. Open Tues.–Sun. 10–4.*

New York City Police Museum. "NYPD Blue" this isn't. The city's new police museum doesn't celebrate lurid crimes but instead exhibits historical items such as antique firearms, badges, and uniforms. There are intriguing collections of old mug shots—including ones of Al Capone—and drugs and funny money found on New York's mean streets. Don't miss playing cops and robbers with the Firearms and Tactics Simulator; it's actually used by cops in training. You'll need to show your photo ID to visit. *25 Broadway, between Morris and Beaver Sts. Lower Manhattan, tel. 212/301–4441. Subway: 4 or 5 to Bowling Green, 2 or 3 to Wall St., N or R to Rector St., Admission free. Open daily 10–6; groups by appointment only.*

New-York Historical Society. Since its founding in 1804, the Historical Society has collected over one million artifacts of the city's past, including Ben Franklin's glasses; the Louisiana Purchase contract, complete with Napoléon's signature; the first English Bible published in America; hundreds of busts and statues; 250 Tiffany lamps (the largest such collection in the world); and the remains of a leaden King George statue that had been melted down for bullets during the Revolutionary War. Concerts and walking tours are also part of the Society's program. *2 W. 77th St., at Central Park W, Upper West Side, tel. 212/873–3400. Subway: B or C to W. 81st St. Suggested donation $5. Open Tues.–Sun. 11–5.*

Curators at the New Museum of Contemporary Art feel that art, like fish and house guests, starts to smell if it hangs around too long.

New York Transit Museum. You don't have to be enraptured by public transportation to find this museum fascinating. Housed in a decommissioned 1930s subway station, it shows off 20 retired subway cars (some with ceiling fans and wicker seats), a couple of funky elderly city bus cabs, and exhibits on how the subway tunnels were built, or sometimes dynamited. Two-hour kids' workshops take place on Saturdays and historian-led tours tunnel through lines throughout the boroughs. *Boerum Pl. at Schermerhorn St., Brooklyn Heights, tel. 718/243–3060; 718/243–8601 for tour information. Subway: A, C, or F to Jay St./Borough Hall. Admission $3. Open Tues.–Fri. 10–4, weekends noon–5.*

New York Unearthed. Whenever they start raising a new glass-and-steel monstrosity in Manhattan, New York Unearthed's crack team of urban archaeologists sifts through the dirt. At this museum/laboratory, you'll see artifacts from the prehistoric days right up through the 1950s (interestingly, tobacco pipes seem to be the one artifact common to all eras)—and learn what lies where under New York's pavement. There's some pretty astounding stuff, including 200-year-old oyster shells, each more than a foot long. *17 State St., between Bridge and Pearl Sts., Lower Manhattan, tel. 212/748–8628. Subway: 4 or 5 to Bowling Green. Admission free. Open Mon.–Fri. 12–6.*

South Street Seaport Museum. In the middle of yuppified South Street Seaport stands this great museum, dedicated to New York's early history as an international port. You'll find a working 19th-century printing press, scrimshaw art, model ships, and temporary exhibits on lively topics such as 19th-century sailors' tattoos. Your ticket also lets you board six historic ships, including the *Peking,* a four-masted barque from 1911; the *Wanetree,* an 1885 three-masted tall ship; and the *Ambrose,* a 1908 lightship once used to guide other ships into port. *12–14 Fulton St., between Front and South Sts., Lower Manhattan, tel. 212/748–8600. Subway: J, M, Z, 2, 3, 4, or 5 to Fulton St. Admission $6. Open Apr.–Sept., daily 10–6 (Thurs. 10–8); Oct.–Mar., Wed.–Mon. 10–5.*

Staten Island Historical Society Museum. This excellent little museum, in Staten Island's Historic Richmond Town, displays tools, furniture, toys, photos, fishing paraphernalia, and other objects that shed light on New York's forgotten borough. Bet you never knew that Staten Island was the principal source of beer in the 1850s. Also featured are over 200 best-loved toys from the 1840s through the 1990s. Another room displays a full-size oyster-fishing boat—a reminder of the humble origins of Staten Island's economy. *Tel. 718/351–1611. For directions and admission see Staten Island in the Outer Boroughs, above. Open Sept.–June, Wed.–Sun. 1–5; July–Aug., Wed.–Fri. 10–5, weekends 1–5.*

Staten Island Institute of Arts and Sciences. Located spitting distance from the Ferry Terminal, the Institute houses over 2 million artifacts in exhibits devoted to the art, science, and cultural history of Staten Island. The nearby St. George Ferry Terminal, adjacent to the Staten Island Ferry Terminal, is where the SIIAS operates the Staten Island Ferry Collection, which explores the history of the Ferry line and New York Harbor. *75 Stuyvesant Pl., tel. 718/727–1135. Admission $2.50. Open Mon–Sat. 9–5, Sun. 1-5.*

ETHNIC AND CULTURAL MUSEUMS

The Asia Society. John D. Rockefeller III, great-grandson of the original gajillionaire Rockefeller, founded the Asia Society in 1956 to further the understanding of Asia in America. The Society's modest galleries display art from all reaches of Asia, as well as New Zealand, Australia, and the Pacific Islands; the gift shop has a fantastic book selection and all kinds of reasonably priced knickknacks. Free gallery talks are given Tuesday–Saturday at 12:30 (also at 6:30 on Thursday) and Sunday at 2:30. Shows change several times a year. *725 Park Ave., at E. 70th St., Upper East Side, tel. 212/288–6400 or 212/ 517–6397. Subway: 6 to E. 68th St. Admission $4; free Thurs. 6–8. Open Tues.–Sat. 11–6 (Thurs. until 8), Sun. noon–5.*

Black Fashion Museum. The recently renovated Black Fashion Museum has more than 3,000 pieces in its collection, including all the costumes from *The Wiz*, a few Michael Jackson outfits, a slave girl's original gingham dress, and a copy of Mary Todd Lincoln's second inaugural gown. A few of the designers featured include Lenny Varnadoe (creator of a number of Bobby Brown's getups), Anne Lowe (whose credits include Jacqueline Kennedy's wedding dress), and Willi Smith (the creative force behind WilliWear). *157 W. 126th St., between Adam Clayton Powell Jr. and Malcolm X Blvds., Harlem, tel. 212/ 666–1320. Subway: 2 or 3 to W. 125th St. Admission $3. Open by appointment only.*

China House Gallery. A pair of fierce, fat stone lions guard the doorway to the China Institute. Inside, you'll find a few small galleries where two to three museum-quality shows are mounted yearly, generally on historical topics. The Institute also offers film programs, lectures, and classes in language, calligraphy, and painting (classes are organized by semester). *125 E. 65th St., between Park and Lexington Aves., Upper East Side, tel. 212/744–8181. Subway: B or Q to Lexington Ave. Suggested donation $3 (free Tues. 6–8). Open Mon.–Sat. 10–5 (Tues. until 8), Sun. 1–5.*

Hispanic Society of America. Relics and paintings from the 10th through the 15th centuries are displayed at this 90-year-old museum, housed in a Spanish-style building. Don't miss the giant wall paintings by Joaquin Sorolla y Bastida, which colorfully depict pain in the 1860s–1920s. You'll also find three giant oil paintings by Spanish masters Goya, El Greco, and Velasquez and a bunch of altars and nifty marble sarcophagi. The library houses more than 200,000 books about (surprise, surprise) Spain and Portugal. *Audubon Terr., Broadway at W. 155th St., Washington Heights, tel. 212/926–2234. Subway: 1 to W. 157th St. Admission free. Open Tues.–Sat. 10–4:30, Sun. 1–4.*

Jacques Marchais Museum of Tibetan Art. Find nirvana among the *bodhisattvas* (religious deities), *tankas* (ritual paintings used to aid meditation), *mani* stones (slates inscribed with Tibetan prayers), and other Tibetan artifacts at this hilltop temple museum, seeming totally out of place in Staten Island. It's the brainchild of Jacques Marchais, an Asian art dealer from the Midwest, who indulged her passion for a country she never visited by building this Tibetan center next door to her home. Outside, you'll find a serene garden filled with ponds, statues, and strings of prayer flags. If you're taking the bus, be prepared for a steep uphill walk to the museum. *338 Lighthouse Ave., Staten Island, tel. 718/987–3500. From Ferry Terminal, take Bus S74 to Lighthouse Ave. Admission $3. Open Wed.–Sun. 1–5 (Dec.–Mar., by appointment only).*

Japan Society. Not far from the United Nations is the headquarters of the Japan Society, which produces a range of cultural events, including occasional gallery exhibits, film series, and lectures. In its lobby you'll find a touch of Kyoto: a pond, bamboo trees, and shoji screens. *333 E. 47th St., between 1st and 2nd Aves., Midtown, tel. 212/832–1155. Subway: 4, 5, 6, or 7 to Grand Central. Admission free. Lobby open weekdays 9–5; gallery open Tues.–Sun. 11–6.*

Museum of Chinese in the Americas (MCA). In a century-old schoolhouse once attended by Italian-American and Chinese-American children, MCA is the only museum in America devoted to preserving the history of the Chinese people throughout the Western hemisphere. The permanent exhibit—"Where's Home? Chinese in the Americas"—delves into the Chinese-American experience through displays of artists' creations and personal and domestic artifacts alongside of historical commentary. Slippers for binding feet, Chinese musical instruments, and items from a Chinese laundry are just some of the unique objects on view. Changing exhibits fill a second room; recent shows focused on sights around Chinatown and Brooklyn's Sunset Park Chinese community. *70 Mulberry St., 2nd floor, Chinatown, tel. 212/619–4785. Subway: N, R, J, M, or 6 to Canal St.; also B, D, or Q to Grand St. Admission $3. Open Tues.–Sat. noon–5.*

National Museum of the American Indian. This incredible museum, a branch of the Washington, D.C.–based Smithsonian Institute, houses George Gustav Heye's collection of more than one million American Indian artifacts. Wealthy and passionate collector Heye spent the first half of the 20th century traveling the world, gathering jade ornaments from the ancient Mayans, stone carvings from the peoples of the Pacific Northwest, and even a shrunken head or two. Whether you consider his activities grossly exploitative, you'll find the artifacts—games, clothing, religious items—displayed intelligently, each accompanied by an explanation written by a member of the tribe or group of its origin. The museum is in the former **Alexander Hamilton U.S. Custom House,** one of the most spectacular examples of beaux arts architecture in New York: The first row of statues atop the pediment represents the various continents, while the second row symbolizes the major trading cities of the world. *1 Bowling Green, between State and Whitehall Sts., Lower Manhattan, tel. 212/668–6624. Subway: 4 or 5 to Bowling Green. Admission free. Open daily 10–5 (Thurs. until 8).*

Schomburg Center for Research in Black Culture. Arturo Alfonso Schomburg, black scholar and bibliophile, dedicated his life to collecting evidence of and denouncing white prejudice. At his death in 1938 he had amassed some 100,000 items, including books, photographs, political cartoons, paintings, oral histories, and even the white robe and hood of a KKK member—it's an amazingly powerful collection. In addition to gallery space, the center (part of the New York Public Library system) holds a research library and the renovated **American Negro Theatre,** where Sidney Poitier, Ruby Dee, and Harry Belafonte have performed. *515 Malcolm X Blvd., at W. 136th St., Harlem, tel. 212/491–2265. Subway: 2 or 3 to W. 135th St. Admission free. Open Mon.–Wed. noon–8, Thurs.–Sat. 10–6, Sun. 1–5.*

In 1991 the Dalai Lama blessed the Jacques Marchais Museum, and since then, Buddhists have journeyed from around the world to worship here.

Ukrainian Museum. The exhibitions in the two small rooms were put together by Ukrainian Americans, obviously with much pride in their rich cultural heritage. On permanent display are Ukrainian ceremonial costumes, jewelry, and footwear. Seasonal exhibits include Christmas decorations and fabulously ornate Easter eggs (the latter are worth a special trip). *203 2nd Ave., between E. 12th and 13th Sts., East Village, tel. 212/228–0110. Subway: 4, 5, 6, N, or R to Union Sq./E. 14th St.; also L to 3rd Ave. Admission $1. Open Wed.–Sun. 1–5.*

HISTORICAL HOUSES

Abigail Adams Smith Museum. Back when the Upper East Side was nothing but farmland, Abigail Adams Smith, daughter of President John Adams, set up a nifty 23-acre estate on the East River. Today, her 1799 house (originally a carriage house) is hemmed in by massive brick buildings and auto shops. Tours show off the *in situ* collection of Federalist and Empire furniture, art, and household implements; the nine period rooms appear largely as they did when the house was the Mount Vernon Hotel, a popular day resort for wealthy downtowners. *421 E. 61st St., between 1st and York Aves., Upper East Side, tel. 212/838–6878. Subway: N, R, 4, 5, or 6 to E. 59th St./Lexington Ave. Admission $3. Open Sept.–May, Tues.–Sun. 11–4; June–July, Tues. 11–9, Wed.–Sun. 11–4.*

Alice Austen House. Whoever said that the Victorians were a repressed lot was not accounting for Alice Austen, a woman who was out photographing city life during an age when most sat around doing needlepoint. Here at "Clear Comfort," the harborfront cottage where Austen lived luxuriously (until she lost her fortune in the 1929 stock market crash), you'll see her striking and vivid photos. Changing exhibits also feature the works of other contemporary photographers. *2 Hylan Blvd., at Bay St., Rosebank, Staten Island, tel. 718/816–4506. From Ferry Terminal, take Bus S51 to Hylan Blvd. (15 mins). Admission $2. Open Thurs.–Sun. noon–5; grounds open daily until dusk.*

Bowne House. New Yorkers can thank Mr. John Bowne, the architect of this 1661 house, for their freedom of religion. The defiant Bowne held Quaker meetings here despite the Dutch governor's ban on the sect, and was eventually thrown in jail. At his trial, Bowne successfully argued that the colony's patent granted its new colonists the right "to have and enjoy liberty of conscience"—a principle that was later consecrated by the Bill of Rights. Besides being incredibly old, this house (a stop on the Flushing Freedom Mile), with its slanting floors and low ceilings, is also considered one of the finest examples of Dutch–English architecture in the United States. Guided tours available. *37–01 Bowne St., Flushing, Queens, tel. 718/359–0528. Subway: 7 to Main St. Admission $4. Open Tues. and weekends 2:30–4:30.*

Conference House. This place couldn't be more out-of-the-way, but if you're up for the long bus ride to the tip of Staten Island, you'll rewarded with a neat history lesson. On one fateful day in 1776, Benjamin Franklin, John Adams, and Edward Rutledge met at this Staten Island house with British Admiral

Lord Howe. The rabble-rousing revolutionaries pooh-poohed the Lord's offer of "clemency and full pardon to all repentant rebels," and the rest, as they say, is history. The Conference House's rooms have been fixed up to look the same as they did when American insurgents used them to talk war over "good claret, good bread, cold ham, tongues, and mutton." Outside, in Conference House Park, the small beach where Franklin allegedly took his post-lunch naps, is a prime spot for watching the sailboats in Raritan Bay. *7455 Hylan Blvd., Tottenville, Staten Island, tel. 718/984–2086. From Ferry Terminal, take Bus S78 to Craig Ave., walk 1 block south. Admission $2. Open Apr.–Nov., Fri.–Sun. 1–4.*

Dyckman House. This 1784 Dutch farmhouse-turned-museum is the only attraction in Inwood, the teeny neighborhood north of Washington Heights. Not surprisingly, Dyckman House is the last farmhouse remaining in Manhattan. Surprisingly, there's more to see here than a few rusty hoes: The Relic Room features a Revolutionary War uniform and musketry. In the garden is a replica of a Revolutionary War military hut. *4881 Broadway, at W. 204th St., Inwood, tel. 212/304–9422. Subway: A to W. 200th St. Admission free, donations accepted. Open Tues.–Sat. 11–4.*

Edgar Allan Poe Cottage. In the hope that the fresh, clean country air of Fordham Village might improve the health of Virginia, his tuberculosis-stricken wife, the 37-year-old Poe moved to this cottage in 1846. Alas, Virginia soon passed away, leaving Poe alone with his mum-in-law until 1849, when he, too, succumbed. Not exactly a happy history, but at least fans of Poe's "Annabel Lee," "Ulalume," and "The Bells" can admire the room in which they were written. There's a small collection of manuscripts, a seedy surrounding park, and no rest rooms. *Grand Concourse and Kingsbridge Rd., Fordham, Bronx, tel. 718/881–8900. Subway: D to Kingsbridge Rd. Admission $2. Open Sat. 10–4, Sun. 1–5.*

Fraunces Tavern. So central was Fraunces Tavern to the American Revolution, you'd think the entire insurrection was plotted here over a few pints and tavernkeep Samuel Fraunces's fancy desserts. During the war, the Sons of Liberty met at the tavern, and George Washington bid his officers farewell here in 1783. Later, it housed the fledgling U.S. government's departments of the Treasury, Foreign Affairs, and War. The whole thing was restored in 1904, patched up a bit in 1975 (when it was bombed by a Puerto Rican nationalist organization), and today contains a collection of 18th- and 19th-century paintings, decorative arts, prints, and documents. Downstairs is a re-creation of the original tavern, where you can eat an overpriced meal or down a pint yourself. *54 Pearl St., at Broad St., Lower Manhattan, tel. 212/425–1778. Subway: J, M, or Z to Broad St. Admission $2.50. Open weekdays 10–4:45, weekends noon–4.*

Garibaldi–Meucci Museum. General Giuseppe Garibaldi, the man who established Italy as a nation, took refuge here in 1850 as the guest of Antonio Meucci, argued to be the true inventor of the telephone. This museum is full of informative exhibits about both men—you'll get to see a chair that clever Meucci carved out of tree branches, and the shirt and dagger that Garibaldi used in battle. A guided tour and video tell the sad tale of Meucci's invention of electromagnetism (he died before he was able to renew the costly patent, and Alexander Graham Bell sucked up all the glory). *420 Tompkins Ave., between Vanderbilt and Hylan Aves., Staten Island, tel. 718/442–1608. From Ferry Terminal, take Bus S78 (15 mins) to Tompkins Ave. $3 donation requested. Open Tues.–Sun. 1–5; group tours by appointment.*

Lefferts Homestead. One of several surviving Dutch Colonial farmhouses in Brooklyn, Lefferts Homestead (built between 1777 and 1783) in Prospect Park is the easiest to reach. The house is between the carousel and the Wildlife Center. *Prospect Park, Flatbush Ave. and Empire Blvd., tel. 718/965–6505. Admission free. Open Thur.–Fri. 1–4, weekends 1–5.*

Louis Armstrong House and Archives at Queens College. For nearly 30 years, Louis Armstrong lived in a modest frame house at 34–56 107th Street in Corona, where he played the trumpet for local kids and bought them ice cream. In 1994, the homemade tape recordings, scrapbooks, photographs, and autobiographical manuscripts found in his home became catalogued by Queens College in its Louis Armstrong Archives. The college is also in the process of converting Armstrong's house into a museum and educational center, scheduled to open to the public on Aug. 4, 2001, in honor of Satchmo's centennial. *Benjamin Rosenthal Library, 65–30 Kissena Blvd., Flushing, Queens, tel. 718/997–3670. Subway: 7 to Main St., Flushing. Bus: Q17 bus to Queens College. Open Mon.–Fri. 10–5, Sat. noon–5.*

Merchant's House Museum. This museum is a fully restored Federal- and Greek revival–style town house, built with red bricks and marble trim in 1831–32. Retired merchant Seabury Treadwell and his descendants lived here from 1835 right up until it became a museum in 1933. All of the family's furniture remains, along with personal items such as clothing, needlepoint, and photographs. Concerts, lectures, readings, and cooking demonstrations are held throughout the year. For a free guided tour, come on Sunday afternoon. *29 E. 4th St., between Bowery and 2nd Ave., East Village, tel. 212/777–1089. Subway: 6 to Astor Pl. Admission $5. Open Sun.–Thurs. 1–4.*

Morris-Jumel Mansion. This Palladian-style mansion, built in 1765, is the oldest standing house in Manhattan, and a lot has happened here in the last 200 years. During the Revolutionary War, it was used by the Brits, the Hessians, and George Washington and troops (not all at once, of course). Eliza Bowen Jumel—a former prostitute who in 1832 became the wealthy widow of French wine merchant Stephen Jumel—lived here during her short (1834–1836), unhappy marriage to former Vice President Aaron Burr. Since 1906, the mansion has been a museum of exquisitely refurbished rooms, some of Burr's desks, and a chaise rumored to have once belonged to Napoleon. The gorgeous rose garden offers spectacular views of the Harlem River, and the surrounding **Jumel Terrace Historic District** (W. 160th–162nd Sts. between St. Nicholas and Edgecombe Aves.) encompasses blocks of beautiful 19th-century brownstones. *65 Jumel Terr., between W. 160th and 162nd Sts., Washington Heights, tel. 212/923–8008. Subway: B to W. 163rd St./Amsterdam Ave. Admission $3. Open Wed.– Sun. 10–4.*

Theodore Roosevelt Birthplace. The building now standing isn't the actual house where the Bull Moose was born, but instead a brick-by-brick re-creation (1923). The original brownstone was purchased for Teddy's father by Cornelius Roosevelt, who at the time was the fourth-richest man in New York. House tours, spiced up with anecdotes about Teddy's childhood in New York, look at five rooms filled with authentic furniture. Two galleries are filled with the former president's personal effects (the "big stick" is nowhere to be found). From Labor Day to Memorial Day, you can catch concerts Saturday at 2 PM. *28 E. 20th St., between Broadway and Park Ave. S, Gramercy, tel. 212/260–1616. Subway: N or R to W. 23rd St.; also 4, 5, or 6 to E. 23rd St. Admission $2. Open Wed.–Sun. 9–5; tours given on the hr until 4.*

> *The bayberry candles you see in Bowne House were sort of like colonial chastity insurance. According to lore, when a bayberry candle burned out, all visiting males were supposed to pick up immediately and leave.*

Wave Hill. This lavish estate, in the exclusive Bronx neighborhood of Riverdale, was home at various times to Teddy Roosevelt, Mark Twain, and Arturo Toscanini. It consists of two houses—the 1843 gray-stone Wave Hill House (where you'll find an open-air café) and the newer, neo-Georgian Glyndor House (which has an art gallery)—and 28 acres of beautifully landscaped gardens. The Pergola Overlook, a gazebo with a river view, is the ultimate spot for romance seekers. Garden tours (free) convene Sundays at 2:15 PM. On-site dance performances take place Wednesday evenings in July. *675 W. 249th St., at Independence Ave., Bronx, tel. 718/549–3200. Subway: 1 or 9 to W. 231st St. (45 mins), then Bus BX 7 or 10 (10 mins). Train: Metro-North to Riverdale Station (30 mins). Admission $4; free Tues. and before noon Sat. (free mid-Nov.–Mar.). Open Apr.–mid-Oct., 9–5 daily (Wed. until dusk); mid-Oct.–Mar. 9–4:30.*

MUSEUMS OF MOVIES AND TELEVISION

American Museum of the Moving Image. Housed in what were the historic Paramount-Astoria studios, this museum of movies is absolutely worth the trip to Astoria, Queens. You can play with all kinds of high-tech gizmos to create your own special effects; dub your voice over Robert "are you talkin' to me?" De Niro's; produce and play back your own animated shorts; or pose while a camera makes a video flip-book (the same kind that's used in cartoon animation) of you. Check out one of the vintage film serials or shorts shown regularly in Tut's Fever Movie Palace, a garish re-creation of an Egyptian-style picture palace of the 1930s. The museum's **Riklis Theater** shows new and old films, with famous actors and directors as guest speakers. Most films are free with museum admission. *36th Ave. at 35th St., Astoria, Queens, tel. 718/784–0077. Subway: R to Steinway St. Admission $5. Open Tues.–Fri. noon–5, weekends 11–6.*

Museum of Television and Radio. In this museum it's okay to lounge in cushy chairs watching old episodes of "The Brady Bunch" instead of traipsing past peeling paintings of Christs-on-the-cross and haloed Madonnas-with-Child. In fact, this museum has *60,000* of the best and most significant television and radio programs—from *Howdy Doody* to CNN broadcasts of Princess Di's wedding. And you're free to fast-forward, pause, rewind, whatever. All you have to do is stroll in, select up to four programs at a time from a computer index, then settle down at one of the unbelievably comfortable state-of-the-art viewing consoles (is this the greatest museum you've ever been to, or what?). The museum, which opened in 1991, also offers gallery exhibitions, lectures, and group screenings. *25 W. 52nd St., between 5th and 6th Aves., Midtown, tel. 212/621–6600 or 212/621–6800. Subway: E or F to 5th Ave. Admission $6. Open Tues.–Sun. noon–6 (Thurs. until 8; screening rooms until 9 on Fri.).*

MUSEUMS OF THE SCIENCES

American Numismatic Society. The study of money is what goes on at this 130-year-old organization. Even if you don't have *mucho dinero* yourself, it's a pretty interesting place. They've got more than one million pieces of currency representing every period of history, from ancient Egypt to the Elizabethan age right up through the present. *Audubon Terr., Broadway at W. 155th St., Washington Heights, tel. 212/234–3130. Subway: 1 to W. 157th St. Admission free. Open Tues.–Sat. 9–4:30, Sun. 1–4.*

Sony Wonder Technology Lab. This Sony product–filled place will really wow you, especially if you're one of those who can't program a VCR or considers the microwave oven cutting-edge technology. All the exhibits are interactive and hands-on: Start in the lobby by recording your name, image, and voice on a plastic chip, which acts as your "key" to other exhibits too weird and astounding to describe here. One of the best is the High Definition Theater, where you and other audience members orchestrate a video adventure from your seats—you actually get to determine the outcome of the movie by voting with a futuristic joystick attached to the arm of your chair. *550 Madison Ave., between E. 55th and 56th Sts., Midtown, tel. 212/833–8100. Subway: 4, 5, or 6 to E. 59th St.; also E or F to 5th Ave./53rd St. Admission free. Open Tues.–Sat. 10–6, Thurs. 10–8, Sun. noon–6.*

NONE-OF-THE-ABOVE MUSEUMS

Forbes Magazine Galleries. While millionaires Gertrude Vanderbilt Whitney and Henry Clay Frick collected oil paintings, sculpture, and drawings, magazine magnate Malcolm Forbes gathered items that excited his boyhood fancy. On the ground floor of the Forbes Magazine headquarters you'll find his whimsical collections; they include: "Ships Ahoy," a flotilla of over 500 toy boats; "On Parade," an army of more than 10,000 toy soldiers arranged in battle; "Monopoly," many early versions of Forbes's favorite board game; "Presidential Papers," an impressive assembly of historical presidential correspondence; and "Fabergé," the world's second-largest private collection of the famous jeweled Imperial Russian Easter eggs. Exhibits change regularly in the large painting gallery. *62 5th Ave., between 12th and 13th Sts., West Village, tel. 212/206–5548. Subway: F to W. 14th St.; also 4, 5, 6, N, or R to Union Sq./E. 14th St. Admission free. Open Tues.–Wed. and Fri.–Sun. 10–4.*

***Intrepid* Air, Sea, and Space Museum.** Maximum war glorification is yours for the asking at this World War II aircraft carrier–cum–floating museum. More than two dozen warplanes and helicopters are parked on the deck and inside, including a Grumman Avenger painted for World War II pilot George Bush (look for "Barbara" calligraphed near the cockpit window). Other exhibits cover this century's plentiful wars, outer-space exploration, and aircraft and nautical history. Docked alongside, and also part of the museum, are the *Growler,* a strategic-missile submarine and the *Edson,* a Vietnam-era destroyer. For an extra $5 you can try the Navy Flight Simulator and "land" an F-18 aircraft on board the carrier. *12th Ave. and W. 46th St. at the Hudson River (Pier 86), Midtown, tel. 212/245–0072. Subway: A, C, or E to W. 42nd St. Admission $10. Open May–Sept., Mon.–Sat. 10–5, Sun. 10–6; Oct.–Apr., Wed.–Sun. 10–5.*

Museum of American Financial History. In the former Standard Oil Building, the tiny Museum of American Financial History displays odd Wall Street–related memorabilia such as a bond certificate owned by George Washington; "Wall Street" brand cigars from the 19th century; and ticker tape from the day of the crash. The paper's weather reports, which read "SECtional Showers" or "Wet, Followed by Hangover," prove once and for all that some people should keep their day jobs. *28 Broadway, at Bowling Green, Lower Manhattan, tel. 212/908–4110. Subway: 4 or 5 to Bowling Green. Admission free. Open weekdays 11:30–2:30.*

ART GALLERIES

Is New York the capital of the art world? Draw your own conclusions. It's been home to some of the 20th century's most famous and acclaimed artists and photographers, like Andy Warhol, Jackson Pollock, Keith Haring, Jasper Johns, Willem de Kooning, Mark Rothko, Roy Lichtenstein, Cindy Sherman, Alfred Stieglitz, and Diane Arbus to name a few. And it's probably got more art galleries than any other

city in America: Approximately 500 fill Manhattan, mainly in SoHo and on 57t[...]
neighborhoods of TriBeCa, the Upper East Side, and increasingly, Chelsea. Upt[...]
a bit more snobbish, especially to people who aren't looking to buy, while dow[...]
be more laid-back affairs showing experimental art or just stuff that is way out[...]
is happy to be there. That said, keep in mind that many artists and gallery ow[...]
recent years, claiming it's morphed into one big bland yuppie fantasyland. If y[...]
edge, head to grittier neighborhoods like west Chelsea, or even Long Island City,[...]
Boroughs, *above*).

Despite the high pretensions of many galleries, they're a great way to see art. [...]
And many coordinate their shows to complement special exhibitions at the big museums like the Met,
MoMA, or the Guggenheim. For work that isn't normally accessible to the public, whether it's masterworks that are in private hands or work by contemporary artists who haven't made it into the museums
yet, art galleries are your ticket. Most galleries open between 10 and 11 AM and close by 5 or 6 PM, Tuesday through Saturday. July through early September (the months when their customers leave New York
for their summer châteaus), they're typically open by appointment only. On average, shows change
every six to eight weeks, often less frequently during summer. For info on current shows, check *Time
Out, New York,* or *The New Yorker;* they list many, but hardly
all, galleries and their current exhibitions. The *Village Voice*
and *New York Press* also list galleries, with an emphasis on
downtown and experimental stuff. At galleries and major
museums, you can pick up a copy of **Art Now Gallery Guide**
(free), the most complete reference to the art scene you'll find.
It lists addresses, phone numbers, and open hours of practically all the city's galleries and provides maps for gallery-hop-
pers. "Chelsea Art," a free pamplet available at most galleries
in the Chelsea area, provides a walking tour map and points
out the stops of the free Art Shuttle (tel. 212/769–8100),
which runs on Saturdays from noon to 7.

*At the Ferry Terminal in Staten
Island is a small museum of ferry
paraphernalia, including antique
ships' wheels, scale models of
ferries, and black-and-white
vintage photos of commuters from
the 1950s. Check it out if you have
a few minutes to kill.*

SOHO AND TRIBECA

SoHo possesses the lion's share of the city's art galleries. Quite a few are clustered along Broadway
between Houston and Spring Streets, but you can wander almost anywhere and find dozens lining its
blocks. Several of SoHo's newest galleries can be found on or near Grand Street. TriBeCa, just south of
Houston, has fewer galleries, but they're also less commercial.

Art in General. This gallery, founded by a group of artists, shows experimental work with a heavy political
message. It's got six floors of space and sometimes installs works in the elevator and windows, too. *79
Walker St., between Broadway and Lafayette Sts., TriBeCa, tel. 212/219–0473. Subway: 6 to Canal St.*

The Drawing Center. The Drawing Center, as you may've guessed from the name, shows exclusively
drawings—an art form long neglected by the rest of the world. Recent (and fascinating) shows have
included tattoos, cartoons, and even drawings by sidewalk artists. *35 Wooster St., between Broome and
Grand Sts., SoHo, tel. 212/219–2166. Subway: 1 or 9 to Canal St.*

Holly Solomon. Solomon has been an art-world heavyweight since the '70s, though the gallery moved
downtown only recently. Among the artists whose careers got a boost here are Robert Mapplethorpe
(this was the first gallery to show his photos) and William Wegman. *172 Mercer St., at Houston St.,
SoHo, tel. 212/941–5777. Subway: B, D, F, or Q to Broadway/Lafayette St.*

Howard Greenberg. Vintage 19th- and 20th-century photography is the main focus at this stellar gallery,
which also showcases contemporary artists. Count on seeing retrospectives of the work of such
respected photographers as Walker Evans, Dorothea Lange, Harry Callahan, André Kertész, Roman
Vishniac, and Imogen Cunningham. The emphasis tends toward street and documentary photography.
120 Wooster St., 2nd floor, SoHo, tel. 212/334–0010. Subway: N or R to Prince St.

Leo Castelli. One of the most famous of all New York galleries, Castelli was where many pop-art and
abstract-expressionist artists got their start. Jasper Johns's one-man show in 1958 is recognized by
many as the birth of pop art and minimalism. *578 Broadway, at Prince St., 3rd floor, SoHo, tel. 212/431–
6279. Subway: N or R to Prince St. 420 Broadway, between Prince and Spring Sts., SoHo, tel. 431–
5160. Subway: E to Spring St.*

Room. Come here for something completely different and oddly comforting. Thanks to ˌ artist Walter de Maria, 140 tons of sculpted dirt (22 inches deep) take up 3,600 square ft of a second-floor gallery. *141 Wooster St., between Houston and Prince Sts., SoHo, tel. 212/ ˌ072. Subway: N or R to Prince St.; also B, D, F, or Q to Broadway/Lafayette St.*

ˌread Waxing Space. Video installations and, occasionally, performance art take place at this esteemed nonprofit gallery. Past artists include Nam June Paik, Hiroshi Teshigahara, and Robert Rauschenberg. *476 Broadway, between Grand and Broome Sts., SoHo, tel. 212/966–9520. Subway: A, C, or E to Canal St.*

57TH STREET
Midtown's 57th Street, between 6th and Park avenues, is chock-a-block with galleries trying to retain a ritzy image while standing next to mall staples like the Warner Brothers Studio Store. A few buildings are devoted entirely to art galleries: **41 East, 20 West, 24 West,** and **50 West 57th Street.**

Pace Wildenstein. One of the city's top galleries, Pace is the place where you'll find all those million-dollar Dubuffets, as well as solo shows by the hottest contemporary artists. Separate fiefdoms under the same roof include **Pace Editions** for prints, **Pace Primitive** for "primitive" art, and **Pace/MacGill** for photography. *32 E. 57th St., at Madison Ave., tel. 212/759–7999. Subway: N or R to W. 57th St.*

UPPER EAST SIDE
With few exceptions, the Upper East Side's galleries are clustered along Madison Avenue between 65th and 86th streets—which makes for convenient gallery-hopping if you're exploring the Museum Mile (*see* Upper East Side *in* Manhattan Neighborhoods, *above*). One of the most venerable galleries in the neighborhood is **M. Knoedler** (19 E. 70th St., between Park and Madison Aves., tel. 212/794–0550), which you can count on for famous contemporary artists from Europe and America. **Stone** (113 E. 90th St., between Park and Lexington Aves., tel. 212/987–4997), features works by artists from the New York School of Abstract Expressionism (Willem de Kooning, Franz Kline, Arshile Gorky, John Graham, and Joseph Cornell). If you're looking for art by someone other than the usual cast of Dead (and Living) White Males, visit **Throckmorton** (153 E. 61st St., between Lexington and 3rd Aves., tel. 212/223–1059), which specializes in Latin American photography, as well as tribal and pre-Columbian art (the photographic work is on public display, but to see the rest of the gallery's collection, you'll have to make an appointment). For an excellent selection of 19th- and 20th-century photography, visit **James Danziger Gallery** (851 Madison Ave., between 70th and 71st Sts., tel. 212/734–5300); many of the names here are also in the MoMA, the Whitney, and the Met.

CHELSEA
Galleries in Chelsea almost uniformly show emerging and on-the-edge art, photography, sculpture, and multimedia work, which makes it one of the best places in the city to get in touch with the current vibe. Stretching from 20th to 29th streets between 10th and 11th avenues, the Chelsea art scene really took off in late 1996 and 1997. Several of the recent additions to the neighborhood are big and upscale in the contemporary industrial mode: white-painted, columnless open exhibition spaces, concrete floors, and garage-door exteriors. But you can also find some modest offbeat galleries as well. The easiest place to begin your gallery-hopping is on 22nd Street, which has the **Dia Center for the Arts** (*see* More Art Museums, *above*) and more than a dozen other galleries, including **Jessica Fredericks Gallery** (504 W. 22nd St., tel. 212/633–6555); **Matthew Marks Gallery** (522 W. 22nd St., tel. 212/243–0200); **Pat Hearn Gallery** (tel. 212/727–7366); and **Annina Nosei** (tel. 212/741–8695). On 24th Street, you can stop at three major players—**Barbara Gladstone** (515 W. 24th St. tel. 212/206–9300), **Metro Pictures** (519 W. 24th St., tel. 212/206–7100), and **Matthew Marks**'s second Chelsea gallery space (523 W. 24th St., tel. 212/243–0200).

Paula Cooper Gallery. You don't get much more exclusive than this, a gallery revered even by other snobby gallery owners. After 28 years in SoHo, Paula Cooper moved to Chelsea in 1996; this is an awesome 5,000-square-ft exhibition and office space, perfect for multiple exhibitions, large-scale sculpture shows, and site-specific installations. The main gallery has 2,500 square ft of columnless space, a 27-ft-high beamed vaulted ceiling, and skylights; the other, more intimate 500-square-ft space can be opened to the street. Shows here have been devoted to such international artists as Carl Andre and Andres Serrano. *534 W. 21st St., tel. 212/255–1105. Subway: E to W. 23rd St.*

PARKS AND GARDENS

While there's no ignoring New York's soaring skyscrapers, concrete canyons, and yellow-cab pileups, you'll find that the city offers much more than an urban jungle. It's got some 29,000 acres of park land, playgrounds, gardens, forests, nature reserves, and even beaches—in fact, New York boasts the largest urban forest in the nation—no doubt you've already noticed **Central Park** (*see* Major Attractions, *above*), the 843-acre wonderland that occupies a large chunk of upper Manhattan. But you probably haven't yet discovered the enormous, pristine parks of Brooklyn, Queens, the Bronx, and Staten Island, where you can hike for miles without seeing another human being. You can get info on all the city's parks by calling the **City Parks Department hot line** (tel. 888/NY–PARKS). Additionally, the city's **Urban Park Rangers** (tel. 212/360–1406 or 800/201–PARK in Manhattan, 718/287–3400 in Brooklyn, 718/885–3466 in the Bronx, 718/353–2460 in Queens, and 718/667–6042 in Staten Island) have a wealth of info on the parks in their home boroughs. They also offer free guided park tours and nature walks.

The **Gateway National Recreation Area** and the **Staten Island Greenbelt** offer some of the best destinations in the city for would-be tree huggers and bird-watchers. Gateway encompasses 26,000 acres of beach, marsh, and woodlands in New Jersey and the New York boroughs of Staten Island and Queens; the most accessible portions are Jacob Riis Park (*see box* Land of Skyscrapers and Beaches?!, *below*) and the Jamaica Bay Wildlife Refuge (*see below*). For info on other parks contact the National Park Service, Fort Tilden, New York, NY 11695, tel. 718/318–4300. The Staten Island Greenbelt is a 2,500-acre expanse of undeveloped land with 28 mi of trails winding through woods, meadows, wetlands, and beachfront. For particulars, contact the main Greenbelt office (200 Nevada Ave., Staten Island, tel. 718/667–2165).

If you're pining for just a few trees and a breath of fresh air, Manhattan has some unusual alternatives. Besides the decent-sized parks listed below, don't overlook the dozens of **"vest-pocket" parks,** less than a city block in size, that pepper its neighborhoods. In Midtown, you'll find these little parks at West 46th Street (between 6th and 7th Aves.), East 53rd Street (between 5th and Madison Aves.), and East 51st Street (between 2nd and 3rd Aves.). Other great places to kick back with a book and a brown-bag lunch are office building **atriums,** products of the 1980s building boom (you see, something good did come out of the Decade of Greed). In exchange for "giving" the public some open space at ground level, developers got to build even taller skyscrapers, from which they could garner more rent. Waterfalls, foliage, abundant benches, and a small café often complement the scene, and keep in mind that these indoor atriums are invariably air-conditioned. Most are open daily 8 AM–6 PM. Some of the most spectacular include the **Harkness Atrium** (Broadway between W. 62nd and 63rd Sts., Upper West Side), **IBM Garden Plaza** (E. 56th St. at Madison Ave., Midtown), and **Olympic Tower** (51st St. at 5th Ave., Midtown). In a class by itself is the 120-ft-tall, glass-walled Winter Garden Atrium at the **World Financial Center** (*see* Lower Manhattan *in* Manhattan Neighborhoods, *above*), which also hosts art exhibits and live music.

MANHATTAN

In addition to the parks listed below, don't forget **Union Square** and **Madison Square** (for both, *see* Gramercy and Union Square *in* Manhattan Neighborhoods, *above*), **Washington Square** (*see* West Village *in* Manhattan Neighborhoods, *above*), **City Hall Park** (*see* Lower Manhattan *in* Manhattan Neighborhoods, *above*), and **Tompkins Square** (*see* East Village and Alphabet City *in* Manhattan Neighborhoods, *above*)—the latter two are arguably the liveliest parks in the city. If you're sick to death of competing for a patch of green with yuppies in Central Park, their newborns strapped on in some expensive papoose, buy a bumper of Bud, lean up against a tree, and watch the zany characters parade by in one of Manhattan's smaller parks. For flower gardens, don't overlook the formal beds at **The Cloisters** (*see* Museums and Galleries, *above*).

Battery Park. At the southernmost tip of Manhattan, skyscrapers and taxi-filled streets give way to green fields, trees, and footpaths filled with camera-toting tourists. Battery Park (so named because a battery of 28 cannons was placed along its shore in colonial days to fend off the nasty British) is built on landfill and has gradually grown over the centuries. In fact, its main structure, **Castle Clinton National Mon-**

ument, originally stood on an island some 200 ft from shore—like the mountain coming to Mohammed, the island of Manhattan has gradually snuck up and encompassed it. Since its construction around 1810, Castle Clinton has been a defensive fort, entertainment hall (where P. T. Barnum presented the "Swedish Nightingale" Jenny Lind to an enchanted New York audience), immigration depot, and aquarium. It now holds a **visitor center** and the ticket booth for ferries to the Statue of Liberty and Ellis Island (for info on ferry service and tickets, *see* Statue of Liberty *in* Major Attractions, *above*). The park is loaded with various other statues and monuments, some impressive, some downright obscure. The **East Coast Memorial,** a granite structure topped by a fierce-looking eagle, was dedicated by President Kennedy in 1963 to the American servicemen who died in the Atlantic during World War II. The **Netherlands Memorial Flagpole,** near Castle Clinton, bears a plaque that describes (in English and Dutch) a bead exchange that procured from American Indians the land used to establish Fort Amsterdam in 1626. Also look for a romantic statue of Giovanni da Verrazano, the Florentine merchant who piloted the ship that first sighted New York and its harbor in 1524, and the extraordinary **Hope Garden,** whose 100,000 rosebushes were planted in 1992 as a living memorial to people with AIDS. After wandering past these monuments, head for the waterfront to get unparalleled views of the New York harbor, including Lady Liberty and the onion-domed brick buildings of Ellis Island. *Broadway at Battery Pl., Lower Manhattan. Subway: 4 or 5 to Bowling Green; also 1 or 9 to South Ferry.*

Bowling Green. The benches at this tiny park, just north of Battery Park (*see above*), fill with brown-bagging business types on sunny weekday afternoons. Colonial lawn-bowling enthusiasts once leased this oval of green from the governor for the annual fee of one peppercorn; it became New York's first public park in 1733. Look closely at the iron fence around parts of the Green and you'll notice the height is uneven. That's because rioters stormed the place on July 9, 1776, after learning about the signing of the Declaration of Independence; they toppled a statue of King George III that had occupied the spot for 11 years and then melted most of its lead into bullets. *Lower Manhattan. Subway: 4 or 5 to Bowling Green.*

Bryant Park. For 20 years Bryant Park, Midtown's only major green space, was abandoned to crack addicts and muggers. An incredible $9-million renovation, however, has transformed it into one of the best-loved and most beautiful parks in all the city. (It also boasts New York's cleanest public bathrooms.) Century-old shade trees and formal flower beds line the perimeter of its grassy central square, scattered with hundreds of smart green folding chairs. The chairs aren't bolted down, and no one steals them; like we said, it's a pretty miraculous place. During summer, it draws thousands of lunching office workers; hosts live jazz and comedy concerts; and presents a free, summer-long, outdoor film festival (*see* Movies and Video *in* Chapter 7) on Mondays at dusk. Several times each year giant tents spring up when New York designers hold their "Seventh of Sixth" fashion shows here (forget trying to sneak in, but you can look for supermodels hailing cabs on 6th Avenue). Year-round it's home to a chic, expensive restaurant, the **Bryant Park Grill** (tel. 212/840–6500); and a semi-affordable open-air restaurant, the **Bryant Park Café** (tel. 212/575–0733; open April 15–October 14), which is packed with young Midtown workers on warm evenings. When money is tight, go west to the 6th Avenue edge of the park, where kiosks sell sandwiches and salads for $5–$6. *From W. 40th to 42nd Sts. between 5th and 6th Aves., Midtown. Subway: B, D, F, or Q to W. 42nd St.*

Carl Schurz Park. When Upper East Siders want fresh air and river views, they head for Carl Schurz Park. Once known as East End Park, it was renamed in honor of a German revolutionary and founder of the Republican party, who served as a U.S. senator, cabinet secretary, and editor of *Harper's Weekly* in the late 1800s. Joggers and dog walkers pace along the pleasant **John Finley Walk** (named for an editor of the *New York Times* who was also an avid stroller), while traffic rumbles just below on the FDR Drive. The large, fenced-off home near 88th Street is **Gracie Mansion,** the mayor's residence. Built for Scottish merchant Archibald Gracie, the mansion housed the Museum of the City of New York until the early 1940s, when Parks Commissioner Robert Moses commandeered the mansion for political buddy (and mayor) Fiorello La Guardia. Tours ($4 suggested) are offered Wednesdays at 10, 11, 1, and 2, from the end of March through mid-November. Call 212/570–4751 for reservations, which are required. *East River Dr. between E. 82nd and 90th Sts., Upper East Side. Subway: 4, 5, or 6 to E. 86th St.*

Columbus Park. This Chinatown park isn't the nicest in Manhattan, but if you can deal with the somewhat large homeless population, it's one of the best places in the city to people-watch. Mornings bring groups of elderly Chinese practicing the graceful movements of tai chi. During afternoons, the park's tables fill for heated games of mah-jongg; games are so intense that despite crowds, the only sounds you can hear are the clicking of the mah-jongg tiles. *Bayard St. between Baxter and Mulberry Sts., Chinatown. Subway: J, M, N, R, Z, or 6 to Canal St.*

East River Park. This 1½-mi stretch of green is perfect for running, biking, or just watching the garbage scows toil slowly up the East River. The park is a magnet for sportsters of all varieties (the park includes baseball diamonds and tennis courts), but especially soccer. The views of Brooklyn Heights, Williamsburg, and the Brooklyn Bridge are unparalleled. *East River Dr. between E. 14th St. and Delancey St., Lower East Side. Subway: F to 2nd Ave.*

Fort Tryon Park. This phenomenal 62-acre spread of terraced walks and riotous gardens was another of Olmsted's landscape creations (*see box* They Built This City, *above*). Though it's a long haul north on the subway, it's definitely worth the trip. On a hill at the northern end of the park is **The Cloisters** (*see* Museums and Galleries, *above*), which houses the Metropolitan Museum of Art's collection of medieval art. The central plaza honors Revolutionary War heroine Margaret Corbin. Nearby are the remains of Fort Tryon, used during the Revolutionary War. Walk west along its meandering pathways for spectacular views of the Hudson River or take a breather at the Fort Tyron Park Cafe (tel. 212/923–2233) near the park's entrance. *Entrance on Fort Washington Ave. at W. 190th St., Washington Heights. Subway: A to W. 190th St.; also Bus M4 to last stop.*

Fort Washington Park. This northern Manhattan park is difficult to reach, but worth the trouble: From the foot of the Washington Bridge (179th St. and Fort Washington Ave.), walk north to 181st Street, then west across a pedestrian overpass. Once across, follow the path through a tunnel and over some railroad tracks to eventually reach a shady, pleasant rest area. Here you'll find the **Little Red Lighthouse** (of storybook fame), which once guided ships away from this rocky outcrop, plus a few desolate remains of the old Fort Washington. You can also stare up into the steel framework of the mighty Washington Bridge. You can follow the footpath south from here to tennis courts a quarter mile away or theoretically hike down to the island's southern tip although you'll probably drop dead from exhaustion first. *Riverside Dr. between 170th and 181st Sts., Washington Heights. Subway: A to W. 181st St.*

> *Of the approximately 500 galleries in New York, half are in SoHo and one quarter are along 57th Street.*

Hudson River Park. If you can ignore the blitzkrieg on 'blades and bikes coming at you from all directions, this welcoming park is just right for a stroll along the water. Or grab one of the dozens of benches and enjoy the spectacle of Lycra-clad weekend warriors huffing and puffing up and down the park's length. The northern end of the park is in the West Village, across the West Side Highway; it extends southward for miles along the Hudson River and eventually connects with the 1.2-mi-long Battery Park City Esplanade (*see* Lower Manhattan *in* Manhattan Neighborhoods, *above*). In Lower Manhattan, you can easily reach Hudson River Park from the corner of Chambers and Greenwich streets; if you continue walking west on Chambers Street toward the Hudson River, you'll need to cross the West Side Highway. Behind the Stuyvesant High School building, you'll find the park. *On the Hudson River, from Gansevoort St. to Battery Park City, West Village/SoHo, tel. 212/353–0366. Subway: A, C, E, or L to W. 14th St.; also 1, 2, 3, 9, A, C, or E to Chambers St.*

Inwood Hill Park. The 196-acre Inwood Hill Park covers the northern tip of Manhattan, an area once inexplicably dubbed *Spuyten Duyvil* ("Spitting Devil") by Dutch colonists. The whole place actually looks much as it did centuries ago, its thick forest a tangle of overgrown brambles. The handful of hilly trails provide an afternoon's escape from car horns and exhaust fumes. *Entrance at Dyckman St. and Seaman Ave., Inwood. Subway: A to Dyckman St. (200th St.).*

Lotus Garden. This small garden on the rooftop of an Upper West Side apartment complex has been kept up for over 20 years by a group of dedicated volunteers. It's a flower- and tree-filled oasis in the sky where you can enjoy a few moments of quiet. Look for the iron entrance gate marked LOTUS GARDENS on West 97th Street at Broadway, next to The Wiz music store. *W. 97th St. and Broadway, Upper West Side. Open Sun. 1–4 and by appointment.*

Riverbank State Park. Riverbank is a park with a dark past. In the early 1990s city officials announced plans to build an enormous sewage plant along the Hudson River in Harlem, then flinched in surprise when Harlem residents protested. Then-governor Mario Cuomo brokered a truce by ordering that a park be built atop the sewage plant, and 28-acre Riverbank State Park opened for business in 1993. Amazingly, it's a lovely and stench-free stretch of grass and trees, with striking views of the Hudson River and athletic facilities, including a hockey rink, Olympic-size pool, weight room, basketball courts, and track. *Riverside Dr. between W. 137th and 145th Sts., Harlem, tel. 212/694–3600. Subway: 1 or 9 to W. 145th St.*

Riverside Park. Stretching along the Hudson River from the heart of the Upper West Side north into Harlem, this narrow cliff-top park is a favorite of runners, dog-walkers, bicyclists, and Rollerbladers. Its picturesque terraces, rustic stone walls, and rambling paths were designed at the turn of the century by Frederick Law Olmsted and Calvert Vaux to look like a snippet of English countryside. The park's **Promenade** begins at 72nd Street—with a statue of Eleanor Roosevelt—and continues north for more than a mile, past formal gardens, statues, and a few lofty monuments. At 83rd Street, look for **Mt. Tom,** a boulder Edgar Allan Poe often climbed to ponder the passing river scene. You'll also find a memorial to firemen at 100th Street and a **Joan of Arc Statue** at 93rd Street, the first monument in New York dedicated to a woman when it was put up in 1915. At 121st Street is **Grant's Tomb** (if you want to find out who's buried in Grant's Tomb, *see* Columbia University and Morningside Heights *in* Manhattan Neighborhoods, *above*). Just beyond that at 123rd Street is the **Grave of an Amiable Child,** marking the spot where a five-year-old girl fell to her death in 1797. Though the Henry Hudson Parkway runs alongside most of the park, a pedestrian underpass at 79th Street will take you to the **Boat Basin,** where you can walk right along the river's edge. North of 100th Street the park gets a bit wild and woolly (as you might guess from the number of crack vials scattered under park benches), and isn't the best place to linger alone or at dusk. *Riverside Dr. between W. 72nd and 135th Sts. Subway: 1, 2, 3, or 9 to W. 72nd St.; also 1, 2, 3, or 9 to W. 96th St.*

Washington Market Park. TriBeCa's only park is a 1½-acre former vacant lot turned attractive public square, with a luxurious lawn, children's playground, and Victorian gazebo. It's close to some of TriBeCa's best restaurants and the Tribeca Performing Arts Center (*see* Chapter 7). The park is also a great place to stop for a picnic lunch, especially if you time your visit to coincide with the farmer's market (*see* Greenmarkets *in* Chapter 4) held here every Saturday. *Greenwich St. between Chambers and Duane Sts., TriBeCa. Subway: 1, 2, 3, or 9 to Chambers St.*

THE OUTER BOROUGHS

One of the most romantic gardens in the city can be found in the Bronx at **Wave Hill** (*see* Museums and Galleries, *above*), while awesome views of Manhattan can be had from the **Brooklyn Heights Promenade** (*see* Brooklyn Heights *in* the Outer Boroughs, *above*).

Alley Pond Park. In northeast Queens you'll find 635 acres of woodlands, meadows, fresh- and saltwater marshes, and kettle ponds (a type of lake created 21,000 years ago by melting glaciers). Though the park is crisscrossed by several busy expressways, you'll still find quiet, tree-shaded hiking trails that stretch for miles. Pick up free trail maps and check out the hodgepodge collection of wild animals at the Alley Pond **Environmental Center** (228–06 Northern Blvd., Douglaston, tel. 718/229–4000), at the north end of the park near Little Neck Bay. *Douglaston, Queens. Subway: 7 to Main St. (Flushing), then Bus Q12 to Northern Blvd. (25 mins).*

Brooklyn Botanic Garden. At 52 acres, the Brooklyn Botanic Garden is only one-fifth the size of the stunning New York Botanical Garden in the Bronx. Still, its collection of more than 12,000 different plants constitutes one of the finest botanic gardens in the United States and should be at the top of the list of things to do out here, especially between April and June. Eighty plants immortalized by the bard grow in the intimate **Shakespeare Garden.** The beguiling and serene **Japanese Garden** takes you out of Brooklyn and into Kyoto with winding paths around a lake shaped in the Japanese character for "heart"; its Japanese cherry arbor turns into a heart-stopping cloud of pink in late April. More than 5,000 bushes, representing 1,200 varieties of the thorny plants, grow in the neatly laid-out **Cranford Rose Garden,** one of the most romantic picnic spots in the city. The **Celebrity Path** is Brooklyn's answer to Hollywood's Walk of Fame, with the names of dozens of homegrown stars inscribed on stepping-stones. Placards written in English and Braille identify plants in the **Fragrance Garden,** designed especially for people who are blind. Don't skip a peek into the $25 million **Steinhardt Conservatory,** a greenhouse encompassing 24,000 square ft. Its Trail of Evolution shows how plant life developed from the mosses of billions of years ago to the plants of present-day deserts, temperate lands, and the tropics. In winter the steamy Tropical Pavilion is almost as good as a trip to Hawaii. The **C. V. Starr Bonsai Museum** in the Conservatory exhibits about 80 miniature Japanese specimens. Excellent free tours of the gardens depart weekends at 1 PM from the lily pools in front of the conservatory. *900 Washington Ave., at Carroll St., Park Slope, Brooklyn, tel. 718/623–7200. Subway: 2 or 3 to Eastern Pkwy./Brooklyn Museum. Admission $3; free Tues. and 10–12 on Sat. Open Apr.–Sept., Tues.–Fri. 8–6, weekends 10–6; Oct.– Mar., Tues.–Fri. 8–4:30, weekends 10–4:30. Steinhardt Conservatory open Apr.–Sept., Tues.–Sun. 10– 5:30; Oct.–Mar., Tues.–Sun. 10–4.*

Empire Fulton Ferry State Park. New York's ultimate waterfront lawn is hidden between the Brooklyn and Manhattan bridges on the East River. The views of Manhattan are spectacular and the park itself immaculate. Few people venture here besides sculptors from nearby warehouse studios, who bring their works out onto the grass on sunny days. *Water St. west of Washington St., Dumbo, Brooklyn. Subway: A or C to High St./Brooklyn Bridge.*

Flushing Meadows–Corona Park. Once a city dump so desolate that F. Scott Fitzgerald referred to it as "a valley of ashes" in *The Great Gatsby*—and later the site of two world's fairs—the 1,200-acre park is now a major hub of professional sports and casual recreation. Located in central Queens (and the site of the Unisphere), the park is a microcosm of Queens diversity, where remnants of British India play cricket, Spanish and Italians play soccer, and Ecuadorians roast guinea pigs on barbecues. Here, the annual U.S. Open is held at the U.S.T.A. National Tennis Center, and the Mets attract crowds at Shea Stadium (for more on both, *see* Chapter 8). *Subway: 7 to Flushing Meadows/Corona Park.*

Forest Park. The high hills of this 538-acre park in central Queens offer great views of Long Island Sound and the Atlantic Ocean. Its southwestern half has athletic fields, an antique carousel, a golf course, and a bandshell that hosts frequent Sunday concerts June through September. The northeastern half of the park has nature trails winding through stands of 150-year-old oaks. You can rent horses ($20 per hour) to explore the park at nearby **Dixie Drew Riding Academy** (70th Rd. and Sybilla St., tel. 718/263–3500). *Forest Hills/Kew Gardens, Queens, tel. 718/520–5911 for summer concert info. Subway: J to Woodhaven Blvd.; also E or F to Union Turnpike/Kew Gardens; take Bus Q37 to Union Turnpike and Park La. (1 hr).*

> *In Prospect Park, dogs frolic free and their owners chat over coffee until 9 AM, when leashes become mandatory. After 5 PM, you can unleash your best friend at the Nethermeads section of the park.*

Fort Greene Park. This large, simple park—another product of Olmsted and Vaux—is just waiting for your lazy picnics. Its towering hill has views of both Manhattan and Brooklyn and a long, smooth slope, if you want to make use of your trash-can lid after a good snowfall. The two monuments you'll see are the Prison Ship Martyrs Monument (*see* Fort Greene *in* the Outer Boroughs, *above*) and a memorial to the 126 Spanish soldiers who died during the American Revolution and were buried in Brooklyn. *DeKalb Ave. between Green Pl. and Cumberland St., Fort Greene, Brooklyn. Subway: D, M, N, Q, or R to DeKalb Ave.*

High Rock Park. At only 80 acres, High Rock is one of the smallest but prettiest parts of Staten Island's Greenbelt (*see* Staten Island *in* the Outer Boroughs, *above*). Trails meander through hardwood forest and lush wetlands dotted with glacial ponds; check out the ¼-mi loop around Marsh Pond for spring wildflowers, or take the arduous trek up **Todt Hill** for an eagle-eye view of the Greenbelt, the bay, and Sandy Hook, NJ. At the visitor center (open weekends 10–4) you can pick up a trail map. Call the Staten Island Rangers office to find out about special ranger-led ecology walks, usually run on weekends at 2 PM. *200 Nevada Ave., Staten Island, tel. 718/667–6042. From Ferry Terminal, take SIRT to New Dorp. Also Bus S74 to Rockland Ave.*

Jamaica Bay Wildlife Refuge. You might spot any one of 325 bird species, plus butterflies, box turtles, and small mammals like muskrats and raccoons among the salt marshes, fields, woods, and mud flats of this 9,155-acre wildlife preserve just south of JFK International Airport. Spring and fall are the best times to catch migrating birds, and the wildflowers are tremendous in spring. In summer you'll need insect repellent or a giant fly swatter. Pick up a map and mandatory free permit at the **visitor center** (open daily 8:30–5) before hitting the trails. *Broad Channel, tel. 718/318–4340. Subway: A (make sure it's marked "Rockaways" and not "Lefferts Blvd.") to Broad Channel; walk west to Cross Bay Blvd., turn right and walk ¾ mi north.*

New York Botanical Garden (NYBG). Considered one of the world's leading botany centers, this 250-acre botanical garden built around the dramatic gorge of the Bronx River is reason enough to make a trip to the Bronx. The garden's founders, Lord Hawthorne and his wife, Elizabeth, patterned it after Britain's Royal Botanical Gardens in 1891. In the Enid A. Haupt Conservatory, you can stroll among ferns, tropical flora, and Old and New World deserts. Or step outside and smell the roses—250 different varieties—in the formal rose garden. The 40-acre tract of virgin hemlock forest—the largest remnant of the forest that once covered New York City—is the perfect place to ponder deep thoughts. Guided forest tours are offered on weekends at noon and bird-watching tours take place weekends at 12:30. As you stop to watch the Bronx River churn by, note the Lorillard Snuff Mill—built in 1840 to power the grinding of tobacco for snuff—a monument to days when nicotine was king. Snacks can be found at the

LAND OF SKYSCRAPERS AND BEACHES?!

Beaches in New York? It's not as strange as you'd think. Though you'd need to venture out to Long Island to find really great beaches, there are some decent stretches of sand in Brooklyn, the Bronx, Queens, and Staten Island. Just prepare yourself for 48° water, even in June, and lots of crowds.

Brighton Beach. At Brighton Beach, a.k.a. "Odessa by the Sea," boardwalk café waiters hawk their tables to passersby, and older folks swap news from the old country on the benches. Waves are small enough to let grandma get in the water. Brooklyn. Subway: D or Q to Brighton Beach.

Coney Island Beach and Boardwalk. There's nothing quite like Coney Island in summer, with its Cyclone roller coaster, carnival side shows, pier fishing, and savvy entrepreneurs covertly peddling cans of ice-cold beer. Brooklyn. Subway: B, D, F, or N to Coney Island.

Jacob Riis Park. Besides a full mile of beachfront, Jacob Riis Park offers softball fields, paddle ball courts, and a pitch-and-putt golf course, all free (except pitch-and-putt, $8.50–$11.50). At the eastern end of the park is a gay (formerly, nude) beach. Gateway National Recreation Area, Rockaway, Queens, tel. 718/474–1623. Subway: 2 or 5 to Flatbush Ave./Brooklyn College, then Bus Q35 (1 hr).

Manhattan Beach. Though less than half a mile long, this is one of the city's nicest beaches for sunning and swimming. It's just east of Brighton Beach, off Oriental Boulevard, Brooklyn. Subway: D or Q to Brighton Beach.

Rockaway Beach and Boardwalk. New York City's longest beach faces the Atlantic Ocean. That means decent-size waves and a minimum of pollution. Of course, this is no secret, and in summer it can be difficult to find a spot to spread your towel. Follow the boardwalk past the last subway stop (116th Street) to the area where wealthy residents have tacked up NO PARKING signs. This spot is actually public and much less crowded. Queens, tel. 718/318–4000. Subway: A (make sure it's labeled "Rockaway Park") to Broad Channel, then switch to the C and get off at 105th St./Seaside or 116th St./Rockaway Park.

Staten Island beaches. The entire southeast shore is lined with some of New York City's most undiscovered beaches. There are lifeguards on duty at Wolfe's Pond Park and Beach (tel. 718/984–8266), Great Kills Beach (tel. 718/351–6970), South Beach, and Midland Beach (tel. 718/390–8000 for both). For information on transport, see Staten Island in the Outer Boroughs, above.

Garden Café, near the Conservatory. *200th St. and Southern Blvd., Bronx, tel. 718/817–8500. Subway: D or 4 to Bedford Park Blvd. Train: Metro-North to Botanical Gardens. Admission $3; free Wed. and Sat. 10–noon. Open Apr.–Oct., Tues.–Sun. and Mon. holidays 10–6; Nov.–Mar., Tues.–Sun. and Mon. holidays 10–4.*

Pelham Bay Park. Though the highlight of New York City's largest park is Orchard Beach, this 2,764-acre wooded sprawl has a handful of other attractions, including the **Bartow-Pell Mansion** (895 Shore Rd., tel. 718/885–1461), an elegant 1840s country estate built by Thomas "Lord of Pelham" Pell; two golf courses; miles of hiking trails; and the **Thomas Pell Wildlife Refuge and Sanctuary,** whose wetlands attract thousands of birds in spring and fall. To see the entire park, follow the 6-mi Siwanoy Trail starting on Shore Road at the north side of Pelham Bridge. Or you can rent horses at **Pelham Bit** (tel. 718/885–0551) for $20 per hour. *Bronx, tel. 718/430–1890. Subway: 6 to Pelham Bay Park. Admission to Bartow-Pell Mansion: $2.50 (free 1st Sun. of month).*

Prospect Park. Brooklyn's answer to Central Park, Prospect Park is a 526-acre playground-cum-backyard for the tens of thousands of Brooklyn residents whose neighborhoods abut its periphery. The arrowhead-shape park is regarded by Frederick Law Olmsted aficionados as among his very best creations, superior to Central Park (being completed as work started here in 1866) because no streets divide it and no skyscrapers infringe on its borders. The park is a bit more feral than its more famous Manhattan cousin (fallen trees, overgrown shrubs, untended piles of dirt and woodchips, and uncut grass are everywhere), but that's English-style landscaping for you. There are weekend tours of the newly relandscaped, wooded ravine, complete with waterfalls and gorges (enter at 9th street).

The best way to experience the park is to travel its 3.3-mi circular drive and make detours off of it as you like. On summer evenings and weekends year-round the drive is closed to vehicular traffic when a high-energy parade of joggers, skaters, and bicyclists have it to themselves. One of the best places to kick off your shoes is on the 75-acre **Long Meadow,** near the Grand Army Plaza entrance. If you can believe it, this is the largest open space in an urban park in the entire United States. The 60-acre Prospect Lake dominates the opposite (south) end of the park. On weekends and holidays from mid-May through the end of October you can tool around the lake in pedal boats ($10 per hour). Between November and March at the **Wollman Memorial Rink** (tel. 718/287–6431) you can do the Hamill Camel and your other favorite skating moves ($4 admission, plus $3.50 skate rental). The rink, picnic tables, and grills are directly across the circular drive from the **Drummers Grove,** an officially recognized gathering spot for Caribbean and African-American musicians, drummers, chanters, dancers, and other revelers who cook up a storm here on Sunday afternoons through all but the coldest months.

Don't be fooled by the PC name of the **Prospect Park Wildlife Conservation Center** (450 Flatbush Ave., tel. 718/399–7339); it's really a zoo, with a tiny collection of sea lions, baboons, prairie dogs, wallabies, and red pandas. Admission is $3. The park's 1912 **carousel,** with its 56 horses, chariots, lions, and giraffes, was created by a Russian immigrant. Rides are 50¢ and if you're lucky, you'll hear the organ grinder remake of "Welcome Back, Kotter." During summer, Prospect Park's 9th Street Bandshell (at Prospect Park West) is home to the wonderful **Celebrate Brooklyn** festival (*see* Summer Arts *in* Chapter 7). *West of Flatbush Ave. and south of Grand Army Plaza, Park Slope, Brooklyn, tel. 718/965–8999. Subway: D or Q to Prospect Park; F to 15th St./Prospect Park; or 2 or 3 to Grand Army Plaza.*

Less wellknown than its zoological brethren in the Bronx, Manhattan, or Brooklyn, the **Staten Island Zoo** is formidable in its own right. This 8-acre park is home to a tropical forest habitat, an aquarium and a children's center. If you're around at dusk, check out the baboons, leopards, and other indigenous beasts hanging out at the zoo's African Savannah at Twilight exhibit. *614 Broadway, Staten Island, tel. 718/442–3100. Admission: free Wed. 2–4:45. Open 10–4:45 daily. From Ferry Terminal: Bus S48. Exit at the intersection of Forest Ave. and Broadway, turn left on onto Broadway, and walk 2½ blocks.*

Socrates Sculpture Park. Venture past rows of abandoned factories, and you'll come to this strange but peaceful 4-acre park on the East River. Formerly an illegal dump site, it's now filled with mammoth abstract sculptures made from scrap metal, broken pipes, and used tires—the perfect spot to contemplate weighty themes like Man vs. Nature, Man vs. Machine, and, of course, Art. The views of Manhattan are superb. *Vernon Blvd. at Broadway, Long Island City, Queens, tel. 718/956–1819. Subway: N to Broadway, walk 8 blocks west to river. Open daily 10 AM–sunset.*

Van Cortlandt Park. With 1,146 acres of forest and wetlands, this park offers much more than lots of green space and hiking trails. On the park's Parade Grounds stands the oldest building in the Bronx (1748), the chock-full-of-antiques **Van Cortlandt House Museum** (tel. 718/543–3344). It was twice used by George Washington as headquarters during the Revolutionary War. You can sometimes catch

YOUR OWN 15
MINUTES OF FAME

In New York you can not only watch TV, you can be on it. Numerous shows tape in New York, and they all need studio audiences to laugh, applaud, and answer embarrassing questions. To score a free ticket or two you'll need to plan ahead: Most shows require that you send a postcard (with number of tickets requested) weeks or months in advance. If you missed the boat, you can still land standby tickets if you're willing to spend a morning standing in line.

Fox TV. Fox always has a handful of shows open to studio audiences; call for the latest. Tel. 212/452–3600.

Late Night With Conan O'Brien. Same-day standby tickets are available at the NBC Page Desk in the lobby of 30 Rockefeller Center. NBC Tickets, "Late Night With Conan O'Brien," 30 Rockefeller Plaza, New York, NY 10112, tel. 212/ 664–3055.

The Late Show With David Letterman. Standby tickets are available weekdays at noon in front of the Ed Sullivan Theater. Arrive early. Ed Sullivan Theater, 1697 Broadway, New York, NY 10019, tel. 212/975–1003.

Live With Regis and Kathie Lee. Standby tickets are available at 8 AM weekdays from the ABC headquarters; line up at the corner of 67th Street and Columbus Avenue. Live Tickets, Asonia Station, Box 777, New York, NY 10023, tel. 212/ 456–3537.

Politically Incorrect with Bill Maher. Tapings of this funky and irreverent show are Tuesdays and Thursdays year-round. Tel. 212/512–8959.

Saturday Night Live. Tickets for performances and dress rehearsals are available by lottery, and postcards are accepted only during the month of August. Standby tickets are available at 8 AM on the day of show on the mezzanine of Rockefeller Center (50th Street side). NBC Tickets, "Saturday Night Live," 30 Rockefeller Plaza, New York, NY 10112, tel. 212/664–3055.

Anglophiles playing cricket on the Parade Grounds. Also here is the country's oldest municipal golf course—people have been putting around these greens since 1885. If you like to hike, follow the forest-lined **Old Croton Aqueduct Trail,** the **Cass Gallagher Nature Trail,** or the tracks of the **Old Putnam Railroad line,** which once linked New York and Boston. The **John Kieran Nature Trail** circles Van Cortlandt Lake—New York City's largest—and offers great bird-watching. *Bronx, tel. 718/430–1890. Subway: 1 or 9 to 242 St./Van Cortlandt Park.*

CHEAP THRILLS

In summer, it's impossible not to stumble across some sort of free concert, play, or dance performance in the course of a day's exploration; check one of the city weeklies like the *New York Press* or *Time Out* to see what's going down, where. For more info, *see* Summer Arts *in* Chapter 7. If you plan to visit New York repeatedly, you might want to invest in a yearly subscription of *Free Time* (20 Waterside Plaza, Suite 6F, New York, NY 10010; $13.50), a monthly guide that lists about 450 free concerts, lectures, dance recitals, and plays per issue. You can buy (nope, it's not free) a single copy at most newsstands and some bookstores for $1.

COOL VIEWS

Once you've seen all the obvious cool views—from the **Empire State Building,** the **World Trade Center,** and inside the head of the **Statue of Liberty** (for all, *see* Major Attractions, *above*)—you're ready for the advanced stuff. If you want to work for it, consider the 14-floor climb up the building housing the **Clocktower Gallery** (*see* Museums and Galleries, *above*) in TriBeCa; in Brooklyn, you can climb up the inside of the 80-ft-tall **Soldiers' and Sailors' Memorial Arch** (*see* the Outer Boroughs, *above*); it's open to climbers weekends in warm weather. If you're feeling lazy, take the elevator ($1) to the top of the 22-story, 356-ft tower of **Riverside Church** (*see* Columbia University and Morningside Heights *in* Manhattan Neighborhoods, *above*) to spy on the Hudson River below. If you're just looking to stroll along, sopping up all the New York atmosphere, try one of these less-obvious spots: The 1.2-mi **Battery Park City Esplanade** (*see* Lower Manhattan, *above*) offers stellar views

> *There's something magical about standing in a marsh watching snowy egrets at the Jamaica Bay Wildlife Refuge, the World Trade Center visible in the distance through sepia-hued smog.*

of the Statue of Liberty and New Jersey's "Gold Coast"; the ½-mi **Brooklyn Heights Promenade** (*see* the Outer Boroughs, *above*) is packed on summer evenings with New Yorkers whose gaping mouths and reverent stares at the skyline contradict their world-weary cynicism. In the very un-touristy neighborhood of Long Island City, Queens, you'll find breathtaking waterfront views of the Manhattan skyline at the quirky **Socrates Sculpture Park** (*see* the Outer Boroughs *in* Parks and Gardens, *above*).

HIGH CULTURE: THE FINE ARTS

Unless you're planning to buy that Joan Miró instead of just admiring it, visiting **art galleries** is always free (*see* Art Galleries, *above*). For a taste of shopping, museum-going, people-watching, and high drama all rolled into one, New York's famous auction houses **Sotheby's** (1334 York Ave., at 72nd St., Upper East Side, tel. 212/606–7000) and **Christie's** (502 Park Ave., at 59th St., tel. 212/546–1000) are just the ticket. You can attend both the previews (where they display all the stuff about to be sold) and the auctions themselves for free; call for details. The most famous auctions are those for paintings, which happen in fall and spring.

Many of the city's churches and museums bring string quartets and such into their courtyards and gardens for free performances. One of the best freebies is at the **Metropolitan Museum of Art,** which holds concerts Friday and Saturday evenings on its Great Hall balcony. For info on all your options, *see* Music *in* Chapter 7. And what could be more civilized than free Shakespeare in Central Park? *See* Summer Arts *in* Chapter 7 for details on finagling free tickets to the yearly **New York Shakespeare Festival.**

LOW CULTURE: MOVIES AND TV

You've a bunch of ways to get your daily fix of Low Culture for little or no cash. During summer, classic flicks are shown at dusk on a giant outdoor screen in **Bryant Park** (*see* Movies and Video *in* Chapter 7), so pack the picnic basket. All shows at all times are only $3 at **Worldwide Cinemas** (*see* Movies and Video *in* Chapter 7). The **Museum of Television and Radio** (*see* Museums and Galleries, *above*) offers 60,000 episodes of radio- and TV-land for your viewing pleasure; admission is $6. To satisfy your TV itch with a twist, turn off the tube and go join the studio audience (*see box,* Your Own 15 Minutes of Fame, *below*) for one of the many shows taped in the city.

JOY RIDES

One of the best ways to see the Lower Manhattan skyline and New York Harbor is from the deck of the **Staten Island Ferry** (*see* the Outer Boroughs, *above*), made free in 1997. If you're looking for altitude, climb aboard the **Roosevelt Island Tram** (*see* Upper East Side *in* Manhattan Neighborhoods, *above*), which runs high in the air over the East River, parallel to the Queensborough Bridge. The trip is $1.50. The subway ride to **Rockaway Beach** (*see box,* Land of Skyscrapers and Beaches?!, *above*) is about an hour from mid-Manhattan, and for $1.50 pretty spectacular—the train emerges from below ground to run on elevated tracks through the borough of Queens and finally over the sandy marshes of the Rockaways.

TOTAL KITSCH-O-RAMA

Freak shows are a big thing at the **Coney Island Beach and Boardwalk** (*see* Brooklyn *in* the Outer Boroughs, *above*) and they've all got a "two-headed" baby and the "world's largest" rat. Don't miss the **Sideshows by the Seashore** ($3) acts like the human blockhead, the sword-swallower, and the bearded lady.

Chinatown Fair. This sleazy arcade has all your favorite old video games, like PacMan, Galaxian, Frogger, and Space Invaders, plus a smattering of modern ones. Depending on your feelings about animal rights, you can also "play" tic-tac-toe (50¢ per game) against a pathetic-looking chicken. This genius fowl was once featured on "That's Incredible." *8 Mott St., near Mosco St., Chinatown. Subway: J, M, N, R, Z, or 6 to Canal St.*

THE SPORTING LIFE

Believe it or not, Central Park boasts a lovely public **croquet grounds** (*see* Major Attractions, *above*) where you and your friends can gather together to act out your own version of *Heathers*. You must have a permit ($30) to play, good for an entire year; call 212/360–8133 for more info. If your sport of choice is **disco roller skating**, go to the **Roxy** (*see* Dance Clubs *in* Chapter 6) on Tuesday (gay) or Wednesday (mixed).

Fishing in Central Park. Central Park's Harlem Meer has recently been spruced up and stocked with 50,000 bluegills, largemouth bass, and catfish. You can rent poles for free from the adjacent Charles A. Dana Discovery Center, then catch-and-release to your heart's content. *Near 5th Ave., between E. 106th and 110th Sts., Central Park, tel. 212/860–1370. Subway: 6 to E. 110th St. Open Tues.–Sun. 11–5; shorter hrs in winter.*

Hashing. The New York Hash House Harriers is the club for self-described "drinkers with a running problem." Basically, it's a jolly group of folks who meet weekly to run around the city playing an alcohol-intensive version of the British children's game Hounds and Hares. *Tel. 212/427–4692 for recorded info.*

Moonlight Bike Rides. On the last Friday of each month, **Time's Up** (tel. 212/802–8222) offers moonlight group rides through Central Park; for the October ride everyone's encouraged to come in Halloween costume.

TRIPPING THE LIGHT FANTASTIC

If you've ever had a hankering to swing, waltz, fox-trot, salsa, two-step, lindy, or rumba under the stars, here's your chance. Show up at Lincoln Center's central plaza July 10–August 10 at 6:00 (it starts at 6:30, but the line is long) Wednesday through Saturday for a free hour of instruction; afterward, you'll have several hours to whirl around practicing your new moves during the **Midsummer Night Swing Dance Extravaganza.** Saturdays the dancing starts at 8:15 (with no prior lesson). Admission is $9. Look for a printed schedule in the Center's concert halls, or call 212/875–5102 for a schedule update. *Lincoln Center, W. 66th St. between Columbus and Amsterdam Aves., tel. 212/546–2656. Subway: 1 or 9 to W. 66th St.*

WHERE TO SLEEP

UPDATED BY DORI FERN

here's no way around the fact that lodging in New York City is pricier than a Pentagon hammer. In 1999 the *average* daily hotel room rate was close to $300, and the ritziest places cost hundreds more. If you can afford spending $100 a night, you won't have too much of a problem finding a room in a modest hotel or bed-and-breakfast; but if you define "splurge" as $50 a night, you'll have to look a bit harder. In fact, if it weren't for hostels (*see* Hostels, YMCAs, and Student Housing, *below*) the lodging situation might force you to skip New York City entirely. Hostels are a big success here and are actually growing in number—and beds in hostels usually cost around $25 a night. Another penny-wise option, especially if you're staying in New York for more than a few weeks during summer, is university dormitory lodging (*see* University Housing, *below*). January through April is usually the cheapest time of the year to stay in New York, with prices creeping skyward into the summer and peaking during the fall and winter holiday season. Price categories listed in this book refer to the price of the hotels' least expensive rooms, excluding the 13½% hotel tax and $2 occupancy tax.

HOTELS

When it comes to hotels, wouldn't you know that the pickings are slim in hipper parts of Manhattan, like the East and West villages, SoHo, and TriBeCa. In fact, the majority of New York's hotels are in Midtown—which means that to reach the offbeat gems scattered all around the city, you'll have to get very familiar with the subways.

Even if you don't want to go with a rock-bottom option, there are plenty of ways to save money. Groups of three or four can opt for triples and quads, always priced lower than singles and doubles. (Even if these larger rooms are not publicized, many hotels have them; just ask.) Rooms without private baths often have at least a sink, which makes shared baths bearable. When checking in or making reservations, ask for a cheaper room than what you were offered; hotels often have some unlisted rooms below the published rates, and you may get one if you pry a bit. And remember that many budget hotels offer major discounts for week-long stays; just talk to the management.

A few final notes: If you're traveling with valuables (never a great idea), stow them in the safe-deposit box at the front desk; virtually all the hotels listed below have them (a few also have in-room safes). Wherever you stay, reservations are a good idea—especially in summer, around Christmas, and during any of the city's major festivals (*see* Festivals *in* Chapter 1).

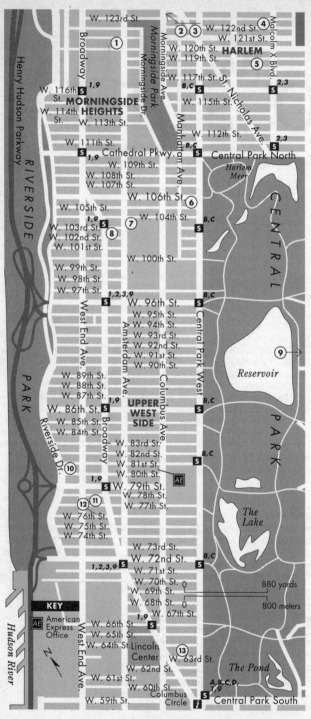

UPTOWN LODGING

W. 123rd St.
W. 122nd St.
W. 121st St.
W. 120th St.
W. 119th St.
HARLEM
W. 117th St.
W. 116th St.
MORNINGSIDE HEIGHTS
W. 115th St.
W. 114th St.
W. 113th St.
W. 112th St.
W. 111th St.
Cathedral Pkwy.
W. 109th St.
W. 108th St.
W. 107th St.
W. 106th St.
W. 105th St.
W. 104th St.
W. 103rd St.
W. 102nd St.
W. 101st St.
W. 100th St.
W. 99th St.
W. 98th St.
W. 97th St.
W. 96th St.
W. 95th St.
W. 94th St.
W. 93rd St.
W. 92nd St.
W. 91st St.
W. 90th St.
W. 89th St.
W. 88th St.
W. 87th St.
W. 86th St.
W. 85th St.
W. 84th St.
UPPER WEST SIDE
W. 83rd St.
W. 82nd St.
W. 81st St.
W. 80th St.
W. 79th St.
W. 78th St.
W. 77th St.
W. 76th St.
W. 75th St.
W. 74th St.
W. 73rd St.
W. 72nd St.
W. 71st St.
W. 70th St.
W. 69th St.
W. 68th St.
W. 67th St.
W. 66th St.
W. 65th St.
W. 64th St.
Lincoln Center
W. 63rd St.
W. 62nd St.
W. 61st St.
W. 60th St.
Columbus Circle
W. 59th St.

Henry Hudson Parkway
Broadway
Morningside Ave.
Morningside Park
Morningside Dr.
Manhattan Ave.
Malcolm X Blvd.
St. Nicholas Ave.
Central Park North
Harlem Meer
RIVERSIDE PARK
Riverside Dr.
West End Ave.
Amsterdam Ave.
Broadway
Columbus Ave.
Central Park West
CENTRAL PARK
Reservoir
The Lake
The Pond
Central Park South
Hudson River

880 yards
800 meters

KEY
AE American Express Office

Hotels and B&Bs
Malibu Studios Hotel, 8
The Milburn, 12
New York Bed-and-Breakfast, 5
Riverside Tower, 10

Hostels and Dormitories
Banana Bungalow, 11
Blue Rabbit International House, 2
De Hirsch Residence at the 92nd Street YMHA, 9
Hostelling International–New York, 7
Jazz on the Park, 6
Sugar Hill International House, 3
Uptown Hostel, 4
Columbia University, 1
YMCA–West Side, 13

UPPER WEST SIDE

Forget about finding a budget hotel on the **Upper East Side**: the pickings are slim indeed. If you really must stay in this neighborhood, your best bet is a room at the **De Hirsch Residence at the 92nd Street YMHA** (*see* Hostels and YMCAS, *below*). Choices on the Upper West Side are few and fairly pricey, but if you can score a room here you'll be able to frolic in Central Park or hop a crosstown bus to the museums on 5th Avenue. The Upper West Side also has an abundance of good bars and restaurants.

UNDER $75 • Malibu Studios Hotel. This recently refurbished hotel did away with its tacky West Coast decor and replaced it with sleek black and white modern detailing, but the budget prices are largely the same, a boon to the young and loud crowd of student interns who summer here. Clean, shared-bath singles are $49, doubles $59; for each additional person the rate goes up $10. Rooms with private bath start at $79. A nice perk: in addition to cable TV, rooms are also equipped with CD players. Continental breakfast is also free. *2688 Broadway, at W. 102nd St., Upper West Side, tel. 212/222–2954 or 800/647–2227, fax 212/678–6842; www.malibuhotelnyc.com. Subway: 1 or 9 to W. 103rd St. 150 rooms, 70 with bath. Air-conditioning, laundry.*

UNDER $100 • Riverside Tower. If your room's above the sixth floor, you'll enjoy sweeping views of Riverside Park, the mighty Hudson River, and—don't get too excited—the New Jersey skyline. A liberal policy toward smoking (heartily embraced by the European backpackers who flock here) means that singles ($85), doubles ($90), and suites for two, three, or four people ($100, $110, and $120) are not only small and dark, they're also occasionally smoke-singed. But it's cheap, and the staff is young and easy to like. *80 Riverside Dr., at W. 80th St., Upper West Side, tel. 212/877–5200 or 800/724–3136, fax 212/873–1400. Subway: 1 or 9 to W. 79th St. 120 rooms, 116 with bath. Air-conditioning, refrigerators, laundry.*

Over the course of the next few years, some 40 projects currently in the works will add another 13,000 hotel rooms to the city.

UNDER $150 • The Milburn. Convenient to Lincoln Center and Central Park, this bohemian little hotel has a lobby inspired by a small Bavarian castle. The homey, spacious studios cost $145 ($10 for a second person); suites that accommodate up to four people cost $175 ($10 for the second, third, and fourth guests). Some rooms are accessible for guests with disabilities. All have kitchenettes, a bonus since Zabar's—the ultimate Manhattan food bazaar—is only five blocks away. Eat with abandon, since you can burn off those calories at the on-site gym. *242 W. 76th St., Upper West Side, tel. 212/362–1006 or 800/833–9622, fax 212/721–5476; www.milburnhotel.com. Subway: 1, 2, 3, or 9 to W. 72nd St. 111 rooms. Air-conditioning, kitchenettes, laundry.*

MIDTOWN

Midtown has the largest selection of hotels, and while the number of flea-infested, smelly joints in the area have decreased with Wall Street gains, prices have—with quality—risen. Hotels around **Times Square** and in the **Theater District** will put you in prime tourist territory—meaning lots of ugly souvenir T-shirts and bad, expensive food. Thanks (or no thanks) to a crackdown by Mayor Rudy Giuliani and the corporate buildup of Disney, 42nd Street has bid adieu to rampant sleaze and embraced a shinier, happier Mickey Mouse aesthetic. **Chelsea** is a hip and happening neighborhood with a few good hotels. In the primarily residential Midtown neighborhood of **Murray Hill** and the no-man's-land around the Empire State Building, you'll find another cluster of budget hotels, though you'll want to catch a subway or cab to somewhere more interesting at night.

UNDER $75 • Carlton Arms. What do you get when you cross a pack of artists with a down-and-out hotel? You get the decades-old Carlton Arms, where each room is done up with a way funky motif, from Astroturf to tropical to hip-hop to faux Grecian. Shared-bath singles run $63, doubles $80, triples $99, and quads $105. Rooms with bathtubs are $75 (singles), $92 (doubles), $111 (triples), and $117 (quads). Students, foreigners, and those who pay up-front for a week or more get a 10% discount. The place has an international cult following, so reserve far in advance. *160 E. 25th St., near 3rd Ave., Gramercy, tel. 212/679–0680; www.carltonarms.com. Subway: 6 to E. 23rd St. 54 rooms, 20 with bath.*

UNDER $100 • Arlington Hotel. The Arlington has signs in both English and Chinese, plus mediocre Asian art on the walls—a bow to the Chinese businesspeople who frequent the place on trips to Chelsea's warehouses. The rooms themselves are large but unspectacular; singles and doubles are $99, triples $119, suites $139. International students get a 10% discount. *18 W. 25th St., between*

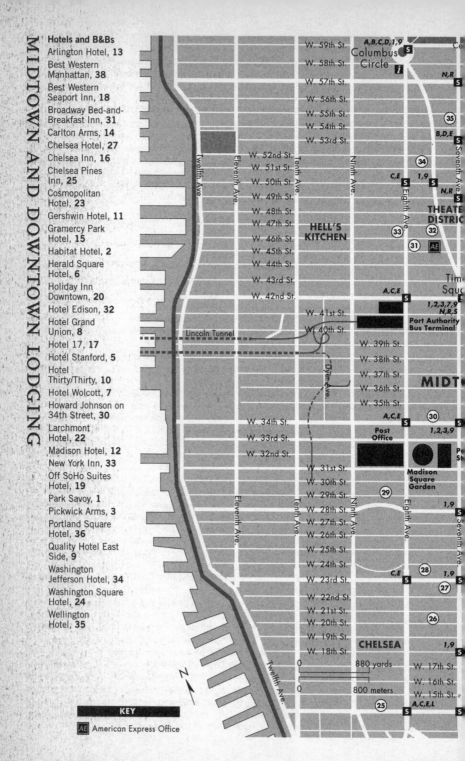

Hotels and B&Bs

Arlington Hotel, **13**
Best Western Manhattan, **38**
Best Western Seaport Inn, **18**
Broadway Bed-and-Breakfast Inn, **31**
Carlton Arms, **14**
Chelsea Hotel, **27**
Chelsea Inn, **16**
Chelsea Pines Inn, **25**
Cosmopolitan Hotel, **23**
Gershwin Hotel, **11**
Gramercy Park Hotel, **15**
Habitat Hotel, **2**
Herald Square Hotel, **6**
Holiday Inn Downtown, **20**
Hotel Edison, **32**
Hotel Grand Union, **8**
Hotel 17, **17**
Hotel Stanford, **5**
Hotel Thirty/Thirty, **10**
Hotel Wolcott, **7**
Howard Johnson on 34th Street, **30**
Larchmont Hotel, **22**
Madison Hotel, **12**
New York Inn, **33**
Off SoHo Suites Hotel, **19**
Park Savoy, **1**
Pickwick Arms, **3**
Portland Square Hotel, **36**
Quality Hotel East Side, **9**
Washington Jefferson Hotel, **34**
Washington Square Hotel, **24**
Wellington Hotel, **35**

KEY

AE American Express Office

144

Hostels and Dormitories

Big Apple Hostel, **37**

Chelsea Center Hostel, **29**

Chelsea International Hostel, **26**

New York University, **21**

YMCA–McBurney, **28**

YMCA–Vanderbilt, **4**

Broadway and 6th Ave., Chelsea, tel. 212/645–3990, fax 212/633–8952. Subway: F, N, or R to W. 23rd St. 96 rooms. Air-conditioning.

Habitat Hotel. The women-only Allerton Hotel may be gone, but its replacement—near Midtown's museums, art galleries, and ritzy boutiques—is a strikingly sophisticated and fairly priced alternative, serving a complimentary Continental breakfast to boot. Welcoming details like a lobby filled with colorful flowers afford a lavish impression. The beige-and-black color scheme, gleaming pedestal sinks, and photos of city sites give the small rooms a hip, downtown feel. Shared-bath singles start at $75, doubles at $85. There aren't many, but the private-bath rooms ($120 singles, $130 doubles) are a good deal for this high-rent area. *130 E. 57th St., between Lexington and Park Aves., Midtown East, tel. 212/753–8841 or 800/255–0482, fax 212/829–9605; www.habitathotel.com. Subway: N, R, 4, 5, or 6 to E. 59th St. 370 rooms, 81 with bath. Restaurant, air-conditioning.*

Herald Square Hotel. This hotel, in the former *Life* magazine building, pays homage to the pre-MTV era with lots of framed *Life* covers. Rooms are bright, clean, and even equipped with telephone voice mail. Singles are $80, doubles $110–$125, triples $140, and quads $150. Singles with shared bath are $55. Lockers are available ($1). *19 W. 31st St., between 5th Ave. and Broadway, Midtown West, tel. 212/279–4017 or 800/727–1888, fax 212/643–9208; www.heraldsquarehotel.com. Subway: B, D, F, N, Q, or R to W. 34th St. (Herald Sq.). 120 rooms, 109 with bath. Air-conditioning, in-room safes.*

Hotel 17. This trendy Euro-style hotel—with its colorful mélange of slackers, club kids, and European funksters—is reason enough to visit New York. Most rooms are small and share a bath, but there's plenty of space to ogle fashion victims or the parade of fabulous guests (among them, Liv Tyler and Busta Rhymes). Be prepared to look pouty and glamorous, and be sure to reserve far in advance. Singles cost $75, doubles $110, and large triples are $200–all with shared baths. *225 E. 17th St., near 3rd Ave., Gramercy Park, tel. 212/475–2845, fax 212/677–8178. Subway: L, N, R, 4, 5, or 6 to E. 14th St. (Union Sq.). 120 rooms. Air-conditioning, laundry.*

Hotel Stanford. The impeccably renovated Stanford is in the center of Midtown's dynamic Korean enclave, its three lobby clocks set for London, New York, and Seoul/Tokyo time. The tidy rooms range from mini to monstrous: Singles are $90, doubles $120, triples $150, and suites $180. Continental breakfast is included. And your craving for a little karaoke can be satisfied, thanks to the hotel cocktail bar. *43 W. 32nd St., between 5th Ave. and Broadway, Midtown West, tel. 212/563–1500, fax 212/629–0043. Subway: B, D, F, N, Q, or R to W. 34th St. (Herald Sq.). 130 rooms. Bar, air-conditioning.*

Hotel Thirty/Thirty. Due to be open in January '00, this hotel will offer the same kind of swanky detailing as its sister property, the Habitat Hotel, for a similarly low price. Singles with shared bath are $75, shared-bath doubles $85. A plus here: rooms with private bath (from $165) will be double the size, and all rooms will be equipped with data ports for Internet access. *30 E. 30th St., between Park Ave. S and Madison Ave., Murray Hill, tel. 212/689–1900, fax 212/689–0023. Subway: 6 to E. 28th St. 300 rooms, 200 with bath. Air-conditioning.*

Hotel Wolcott. This place has a gilded lobby to rival Versaille's Hall of Mirrors, though the medium-size rooms are sterile as a city hospital. Singles start at $99, doubles at $115, and four-person suites at $150. The three shared-bath single rooms are $90. *4 W. 31st St., between 5th Ave. and Broadway, Midtown West, tel. 212/268–2900, fax 212/563–0096; www.wolcott.com. Subway: B, D, F, N, Q, or R to W. 34th St. (Herald Sq.); also 6 to E. 33rd St. 200 rooms, 197 with bath. Air-conditioning, laundry.*

Madison Hotel. The no-frills Madison adds a little touch of its own: An amazing reproduction of Jasper Johns's *Three Flags* hangs behind the bulletproof reception counter. Rooms are dingy but big and all have private baths. Singles run $86, doubles $105, triples and quads $126. Telephones are available with a deposit ($40). *21 E. 27th St., at Madison Ave., Gramercy, tel. 212/532–7373, fax 212/686–0092; www.madison-hotel.com. Subway: 6 to E. 28th St. 75 rooms. Air-conditioning.*

New York Inn. This small, shabby hotel straddles an uncomfortable corner—one where the ersatz glamour of Restaurant Row meets a sleazy stretch of 8th Avenue. Rooms are decent but nothing more, and to reach them you need to deal with creaky, narrow stairs (there's no elevator). Singles cost $87, doubles $97. Continental breakfast is free. *765 8th Ave., between W. 46th and 47th Sts., Theater District, tel. 212/247–5400 or 888/450–5555, fax 212/586–6201. Subway: A, C, or E to W. 42nd St. 50 rooms. Restaurant, air-conditioning.*

Pickwick Arms. The Pickwick's homogenized rooms are clean and reasonably spacious, and on a nice day you can chill on the rooftop patio. Shared-bath singles cost $65–$75, private singles $95, and doubles $120. Studios with double beds and sofas are a good deal at $140, plus $15 for each additional person. The French café next door, Le Bateau Ivre, is a nice place to relax with a glass of wine and a plate of killer frîtes. *230 E. 51st St., between 2nd and 3rd Aves., Midtown East, tel. 212/355–0300 or 800/742–5945, fax 212/755–5029. Subway: 6 to E. 51st St.; E or F to E. 53rd St./3rd Ave. 350 rooms, 250 with bath. Restaurant, air-conditioning.*

Portland Square Hotel. Though the lobby of this renovated 1904 hotel has the besieged feel of a Tel Aviv airport, the Portland's small, antiseptic rooms offer welcome extras such as in-room safes and phones with voice mail. Guests also have access to a small laundry room and a closet-size exercise room. A final bonus: You're not too far from the Theater District's bars and restaurants. Shared-bath singles run $60, private singles $95, doubles $109–$119, triples $130, quads $140. Small and large lockers are available ($1–$2). *132 W. 47th St., between 6th and 7th Aves., Theater District, tel. 212/382–0600 or 800/388–8988, fax 212/382–0684; www.citysearch.com/nyc/portlandsquare. Subway: N or R to W. 49th St. 144 rooms, 112 with bath. Air-conditioning, laundry.*

Quality Hotel East Side. American-eagle wallpaper trumpets the theme of this hotel, open since 1997. Single and double rooms cost $99, while large triples jump in price to $219. Rooms are stocked with phones, TVs, hair dryers, and irons and ironing boards. Checkered curtains and prints of American quilts add to the Americana motif. *161 Lexington Ave., at E. 30th St., Murray Hill, tel. 212/532–2255 or 800/567–7720, fax 212/481–7270. Subway: 6 to E. 28th St. or E. 33rd St. 110 rooms. Air-conditioning, exercise room.*

T-shirts bearing the logo, "It Ain't No Holiday Inn," are sold in the lobby of the Carlton Arms hotel.

Washington Jefferson Hotel. The narrow beds are shoved up against walls and the windows look out over the street—but rooms are spotless and all have cable TV. Plus you can't beat the low prices at this place, which also houses 125 permanent residents: $79 for a single or double with shared bath, $99 with bath. A triple with private bath is $149. *318 W. 51st St., between 8th and 9th Aves., Midtown, tel. 212/246–7550 or 800/567–7550, fax 212/246–7622; www.citysearch.com/nyc/washingtonjeff. Subway: E or C to W. 50th St. (8th Avenue); 1 or 9 to W. 50th (7th Ave.); N or R to W. 49th St. 260 rooms, 35 with bath. Air-conditioning.*

UNDER $150 • Best Western Manhattan. Rooms here are decorated in one of two themes: 5th Avenue (ritzy) or Central Park (lots of florals). Whether you find this corny or cool, at least the rooms are brand-new and equipped with hair dryers, irons, and coffeemakers. There's even a tiny exercise room with a couple of aerobic machines and some weights. In the summer, have a cocktail at the rooftop bar overlooking the Empire State Building and the bustling Korean neighborhood below. Singles and doubles are $109, triples and quads are $139. Two- to five-sleeper suites—with microwaves, refrigerators, and lots of space—cost $199. *17 W. 32nd St., between 5th Ave. and Broadway, Midtown, tel. 212/736–1600 or 800/567–7720, fax 212/790–2760. Subway: B, D, F, or Q to W. 34th St. (Herald Sq.). 178 rooms. Café, restaurant, air-conditioning.*

Chelsea Hotel. The Victorian-era Chelsea is one of the city's most famous residential hotels, home to innumerable artists and other creative folk over the last century: Thomas Wolfe, Arthur Miller, Sarah Bernhardt, Robert Mapplethorpe, Bob Dylan, Dylan Thomas, Eugene O'Neill, Willem de Kooning, and, more recently, Jon Bon Jovi and Matt Damon. Some of the artists who called the Chelsea Hotel home left paintings and sculptures, and there's a gallery of these works in the lobby. The giant guest rooms vary widely in personality; some are regal and others are time capsules from the shag-carpet '70s. This isn't the cheapest option, with singles with bath starting at $150, but if legend is a payoff, this place is worth raiding the piggy bank for. Doubles start at $175 and suites run $265–$310. Naturally, the people who've lived here for decades pay a lot less. *222 W. 23rd St., between 7th and 8th Aves., Chelsea, tel. 212/243–3700, fax 212/675–5531; www.chelseahotel.com. Subway: 1 or 9 to W. 23rd St. (7th Ave.); also C or E to W. 23rd St. (8th Ave.). 330 rooms, 310 with bath. Air-conditioning, kitchenettes.*

Chelsea Inn. This quaint old brownstone is just a couple blocks from the Union Square farmers' market and surrounded by tempting restaurants. Rooms start at $109 for shared bath ($149 with bath), are clean and inviting, with dark-wood furniture, country-style quilts, big TVs, sinks, refrigerators, and hot plates; the white-tiled bathrooms are spic-and-span. Foursomes should ask for the four-person suite ($179). Those who stay seven days or more get $10 taken off each additional day. *46 W. 17th St., between 5th and 6th Aves., tel. 212/645–8989, fax 212/645–1903; www.chelseainn.com. Subway: F to 14th St. (6th Ave.); 2 or 3 to 14th St. (7th Ave.); 1 or 9 to 14th St. or 18th St.; 4, 5, 6 to Union Sq. 25 rooms, 3 with bath. Air-conditioning, refrigerators.*

Hotel Edison. This mondo art deco hotel gets major business from big (and big-haired) tour groups. A relic from the Roaring '20s, it's got some over-the-top extras like a cool hotel bar, a dramatic mural-filled lobby, and a pink-plaster coffee shop that attracts show-business types. There's no room service, but you'll want to check this restaurant out for yourself anyhow (the matzo-ball soup is to die for). The prime Theater District locale and plush rooms make the Edison a great find. Singles are $125, doubles $140, triples $155, and quads $170. *228 W. 47th St., between Broadway and 8th Ave., Theater District, tel. 212/840–5000 or 800/637–7070, fax 212/596–6850; www.edisonhotelnyc.com. Subway: 1 or 9 to W. 50th St. (7th Ave.); also C or E to W. 50th St. (8th Ave.) 790 rooms. Restaurant, coffee shop, bar, air-conditioning.*

Gershwin Hotel. This place caters to a younger and more cosmopolitan clientele than most budget places, offering impromptu barbecues and occasional live music. You can schmooze with fellow GenX-ers at the rooftop wine and beer bar, or over lattes in the hip little café. A bed in one of the sparkling four- to eight-person dorm rooms costs $27. Standard doubles are $125, triples $135. A handful of newly renovated rooms are $139 (double) or $149 (triple). Models who have yet to reach "super"-status can stay in the Gershwin's uniquely fabulous model dorms ($33), four-person rooms equipped—unlike dorms for regular folks—with TVs and phones. Lockers are often available ($5). *7 E. 27th St., between Madison and 5th Aves., Gramercy, tel. 212/545–8000, fax 212/684–5546; www.gershwinhotel.com. Subway: 6 to E. 28th St. (Park Ave.); or N or R to 28th St. (Broadway) 350 beds. Cafeteria, bar, air-conditioning.*

Hotel Grand Union. Though little distinguishes this hotel from others in Murray Hill, at least the newly renovated rooms are clean and spacious. Singles and doubles run $110, triples and quads $125–$150. Students with an ISIC card get a 10% discount. *34 E. 32nd St., between Park Ave. S and Madison Ave., Murray Hill, tel. 212/683–5890, fax 212/689–7397. Subway: 6 to E. 33rd St. 95 rooms. Coffee shop, air-conditioning, refrigerators.*

Howard Johnson on 34th Street. A major rehab by HoJo hoteliers turned the dumpy Penn Plaza Hotel into a spiffy business hotel, complete with data ports on all telephones. Singles cost $109, doubles $139, and large quads are $199, plus $15 for each additional person. Students and AAA members get a 10% discount. *215 W. 34th St., between 7th and 8th Aves., Midtown, tel. 212/947–5050 or 888/651–6111, fax 212/268–4829. Subway: A, C, E, 1, 2, 3, or 9 to W. 34th St. (Penn Station). 111 rooms. Air-conditioning.*

Park Savoy. This inexpensive hotel is just a block south of Central Park and only a few blocks from the Museum of Modern Art—and if you think that's no big deal, try strolling into the glittering lobby of the Plaza Hotel and asking for something "budget." Needless to say, the Park Savoy is a good find, even if the clean rooms are minuscule. Singles run $117, doubles $126, quads $145—*and* you get a 10% discount at the Italian restaurant next door. There's no safe-deposit box here, so don't bring valuables. *158 W. 58th St., between 6th and 7th Aves., Midtown West, tel. 212/245–5755, fax 212/765–0668. Subway: B, Q, N, or R to W. 57th St. 98 rooms. Restaurant, air-conditioning.*

Wellington Hotel. This large, old-fashioned property's main advantage is its location near Carnegie Hall—a big draw for budget-conscious Europeans—though unusual amenities like an in-house hair salon and a concierge who sells theater tickets are also welcome distinctions. Rooms are small but clean; ongoing refurbishment promises a spiffier look throughout. Singles and doubles cost $135; suites that accommodate up to four people with no extra charge are a bargain at $165. For a splurge, try the fine Greek food at Molyvos downstairs. *871 7th Ave., at 55th St., Midtown, tel. 212/247–3900 or 800/652–1212, fax 212/581–1719; www.wellingtonhotel.com. Subway: N or R to W. 57th St. 700 rooms. Restaurant, coffee shop, air-conditioning.*

DOWNTOWN

When the World Trade Center opened a hotel in 1982, it was Lower Manhattan's first new lodging in over a century. Now that the super-fabulous, super-expensive Mercer Hotel and the SoHo Grand have recently opened in SoHo, moneyed visitors have somewhere to stay, but it is still difficult to find affordable hotels below 14th Street. Village-bound hipsters are better off finding a bed in one of the dozens of cheap hotels filling Midtown. One relative bargain is the Holiday Inn Downtown (138 Lafayette St., near Canal St., tel. 212/966–8898, fax 212/966–3933), just outside Chinatown: Doubles start at $139, suites are just a bit more.

UNDER $100 • Cosmopolitan Hotel. This former SRO has been magically transformed into a terrific new hotel. The decor is nothing special, but the rooms are clean and appealing and proximity to Wall Street, Tribeca, and even Soho, is ace. Then there's the cost incentive: singles are $99 and doubles,

$129. All have private baths. *95 W. Broadway at Chambers St., Tribeca, tel. 212/566–1900 or 888/895–9400, fax 212/566–6909; www.cosmohotel.com. Subway: A, C, E, 1, 9, 2 or 3 to Chambers St.; N or R to City Hall. 104 rooms. Air-conditioning.*

Larchmont Hotel. This West Village hotel is hard to beat for location and price—and it occupies an atmospheric beaux arts brownstone complete with geranium-filled window boxes. Inside there's a funky safari theme: Rooms have rattan furniture, ceiling fans, and framed animal or botanical prints. Singles run $70–$80, doubles $90–$109. There are two bathrooms on each floor (six rooms per floor), but every room has its own private sink. Continental breakfast is included, and there's also a communal kitchen for guests. *27 W. 11th St., West Village, tel. 212/989–9333, fax 212/989–9496. Subway: A, C, E, B, D, Q or F to W. 4th St. 55 rooms, all with shared bath. Air-conditioning.*

Off SoHo Suites Hotel. Amidst the urban decay of the Bowery, this self-described European hotel, replete with gleaming brass and mirrors, definitely stands out. The two-person suites ($98) share a kitchen and bath, and the four-person suites ($179) are completely private. All are extremely clean, if totally generic. Because of its small size, reserve well in advance. *11 Rivington St., between Chrystie St. and Bowery, Lower East Side, tel. 212/979–9808 or 800/633–7646, fax 212/979–9801; www.off-soho.com. Subway: J or M to Delancey St.; F to 2nd Ave. 40 suites, 28 with bath. Air-conditioning, kitchenettes.*

UNDER $150 • Best Western Seaport Inn. If you're set on staying near the South Street Seaport and willing to shell out the bucks, head for this chain hotel with the feel of a Colonial sea captain's home. You can spend as little as $139 for a single, $149 for a double, and rooms with a terrace and whirlpool tub start at $159; all come with a VCR. Rates are significantly lower on weekends. *33 Peck Slip, at South St. Seaport, Lower Manhattan, tel. 212/766–6600 or 800/468–3569, fax 212/766–6615; www.bestwestern.com/seaportinn. Subway: 2, 3, or A to Fulton St. 72 rooms. Air-conditioning, in-room safes, refrigerators.*

> *The Gershwin Hotel keeps a Campbell's Soup can in the lobby, but it's not for emergency snacking—this one is signed by Andy Warhol.*

Washington Square Hotel. This turn-of-the-century hotel has a prime West Village location and an irresistible bohemian mood—especially in the tiny lobby, where details like wrought-iron benches and gleaming brass evoke Parisian charm. An ongoing renovation has spruced up many of the small rooms: Singles cost $116, doubles $136–$146, and quads $167. Extras include complimentary beer or wine on arrival, free breakfast, Tuesday night jazz jams at the on-site C3 restaurant, use of the small gym, and unlimited jazz tips from the savvy manager. Lockers can be rented for $1 per day. Be sure to book at least two months in advance. *103 Waverly Pl., at MacDougal St., West Village, tel. 212/777–9515 or 800/222–0418, fax 212/979–8373; www.wshotel.com. Subway: A, B, C, D, E, F, or Q to W. 4th St. (Washington Sq.). 170 rooms. Restaurant, bar, air-conditioning.*

BED-AND-BREAKFASTS

Most of the bed-and-breakfast establishments in New York City are residential apartments with some (or all) of their rooms reserved for guests. These are booked through reservation services that charge no fee but often require a deposit equal to 25% of the total cost. (Ask about weekly rates if you plan to stay for a while.) There are also a handful of independent B&Bs where you book directly. These places are more likely to have the traditional comforts, such as a complimentary (and often gourmet) breakfast, and a desirable location—quite a few are in Brooklyn, near Prospect Park and other scenic neighborhoods. Wherever you stay, rates average $100 a night. But be warned: Not all places do serve breakfast, and many do not accept credit cards.

B&B RESERVATION SERVICES

You have two options when you use a B&B reservation service: a hosted or an unhosted apartment. A hosted apartment is simply an extra room or two in someone's apartment. Your host or hostess will probably feed you a Continental breakfast, let you come and go as you please, and give you access to amenities such as a TV, phone, and private bath. Best of all, hosts are happy to offer the lowdown on where to dine, shop, or drink, and what to see. The more expensive unhosted apartment is unoccupied (but furnished), often with an owner out of town. Here you'll have the run of the place, including full kitchen privileges. Apartments range in size from tiny walk-up studios to expensive penthouses with full-time doormen. Reservation services list hundreds of apartments, so they can set you up in almost any neighborhood. Make reservations as far in advance as possible; refunds (minus a $25 service charge) are given up to 10 days before arrival.

Abode Bed-and-Breakfast. These 30 or so unhosted apartments throughout Manhattan start at $135. Minimum stay is four nights. *Box 20022, New York, NY 10021, tel. 212/472–2000 or 800/835–8880; www.abodenyc.com.*

All Around the Town. This service mostly offers unhosted apartments, which cost $85–150 for two people ($10–20 for each additional person). The three hosted singles or doubles run $80–90. *150 5th Ave., Suite 711, New York, NY 10011, tel. 212/675–5600 or 800/443–3800, fax 212/675–6366.*

Bed-and-Breakfast in Manhattan. The friendly woman who runs this service has hosted singles and doubles for $90–$110, and unhosted apartments for $130 and up. *Box 533, New York, NY 10150-0533, tel. 212/472–2528, fax 212/988–9818.*

Bed-and-Breakfast Network of New York. This service lists more than 300 apartments throughout Manhattan, Queens, and Brooklyn. Hosted singles run $70–$100, doubles $100–$150. Unhosted apartments start at $120. *134 W. 32nd St., Suite 602, New York, NY 10001, tel. 212/645–8134 or 800/900-8134.*

City Lights Bed-and-Breakfast. Many of this service's hosts are gay friendly and are located around the city or on Long Island. Hosted doubles are $80–$130. Unhosted studios and one-bedrooms start at $130. *Box 20355, Cherokee Station, New York, NY 10021, tel. 212/737–7049, fax 212/535–2755.*

Urban Ventures. The oldest of the reservation services, Urban Ventures lists more than 900 locations throughout Manhattan and the outer boroughs. Hosted doubles cost $85–$125. Unhosted apartments start at $110. Full payment by credit card is required at least 10 business days in advance. *38 W. 32nd, Suite 1412, New York, NY 10001, tel. 212/594–5650, fax 212/947–9320; www.nyurbanventures.com.*

INDEPENDENT B&BS

MANHATTAN

Broadway Bed-and-Breakfast Inn. This cozy inn, opened in 1995, musters country charm in the middle of Manhattan's Theater District. Rooms are small but immaculate, and the lobby—with brick walls and stocked bookshelves—is the setting for your Continental breakfast. The staff seem too friendly and helpful to be native New Yorkers. The ground-floor restaurant, Jr's, gives Broadway guests a 20% discount. Singles run $95–$105, doubles $125–$180, suites $210. *264 W. 46th St., between Broadway and 8th Ave., Theater District, tel. 212/997–9200 or 800/826–6300, fax 212/768–2807; www.broadwayinn.com. Subway: N, R, 1, 2, 3, 7, or 9 to W. 42nd St. (Times Sq.); also A, C, or E to W. 42nd St. (Port Authority). 40 rooms. Air-conditioning.*

Chelsea Pines Inn. It may not be Aspen or even Fire Island, but for many gay and lesbians the Chelsea Pines ranks among the best B&Bs anywhere (straights are welcome, too). The tidy rooms are filled with kitsch items and vintage movie posters. The delicious breakfasts include fresh fruit and homemade bread. Doubles start at $89 for a shared bath, $109 for one with private bath. Each extra person pays $20. In summer and fall you should reserve at least a month in advance. *317 W. 14th St., between 8th and 9th Aves., Chelsea, tel. 212/929–1023, fax 212/645–9497; www.qnet.com/chelseapines. Subway: A, C, E, 1, 2, 3, 9 or L to W. 14th St. 23 rooms, 15 with bath. Air-conditioning, refrigerators.*

New York Bed-and-Breakfast. This beautiful old Harlem brownstone is owned by Gisele, a friendly Canadian who also runs the Uptown Hostel (*see* Hostels, YMCAs, and Student Housing, *below*). It's got an ardent fan club of French and German tourists who return annually to enjoy its five rooms with one shared bath. Singles cost $40, doubles $55. There's a Continental breakfast to boot. And if you're planning to stay in town for longer than three months, Gisele will help you find a hosted room in the neighborhood (about $125 weekly), which is relatively safe despite Harlem's iffy reputation. *134 W. 119th St., between Lenox Ave./Malcolm X and Adam Clayton Powell Jr. Blvds., Harlem, tel. 212/666–0559, fax 212/663–5000. Subway: 2 or 3 to W. 116th St. 5 rooms, all with shared bath. Cash only.*

BROOKLYN

Bed-and-Breakfast on the Park. This spectacular brownstone is a great reason to leave Manhattan. Every detail is exquisite, from the rooms appointed with 19th-century antiques and oil paintings to the

Finally, a travel companion that doesn't snore on the plane or eat all your peanuts.

When traveling, your MCI WorldCom Card is the best way to keep in touch. Our operators speak your language, so they'll be able to connect you back home—no matter where your travels take you. Plus, your MCI WorldCom Card is easy to use, and even earns you frequent flyer miles every time you use it. When you add in our great rates, you get something even more valuable: peace-of-mind. So go ahead. Travel the world. MCI WorldCom just brought it a whole lot closer.

You can even sign up today at www.mci.com/worldphone or ask your operator to make a collect call to 1-410-314-2938.

EASY TO CALL WORLDWIDE

1 Just dial the WorldPhone access number of the country you're calling from.
2 Dial or give the operator your MCI WorldCom Card number.
3 Dial or give the number you're calling.

Australia ◆	
To call using OPTUS	**1-800-551-111**
To call using TELSTRA	**1-800-881-100**
Bahamas/Bermuda	**1-800-888-8000**
British Virgin Islands	**1-800-888-8000**
Costa Rica ◆	**0-800-012-2222**
Denmark	**8001-0022**
Norway ◆	**800-19912**
India	**000-127**
For collect access	**000-126**
United States/Canada	**1-800-888-8000**

For your complete WorldPhone calling guide, dial the WorldPhone access number for the country you're in and ask the operator for Customer Service. In the U.S. call 1-800-431-5402.

◆ Public phones may require deposit of coin or phone card for dial tone.

EARN FREQUENT FLYER MILES

AmericanAirlines®
AAdvantage®

Continental Airlines
OnePass

▲Delta Air Lines
SkyMiles®

✈ MILEAGE PLUS®
United Airlines

U·S AIRWAYS
DIVIDEND MILES

MCI WorldCom, its logo and the names of the products referred to herein are proprietary marks of MCI WorldCom, Inc. All airline names and logos are proprietary marks of the respective airlines. All airline program rules and conditions apply.

gourmet breakfasts. And if you ever manage to leave your bedroom, there's a kitchen open to guests. Two shared-bath doubles cost $125 and $135; doubles with private bath start at $195. *113 Prospect Park W, between 6th and 7th Sts., Park Slope, tel. 718/499–6115, fax 718/499–1385; www.bbnyc.com. Subway: F to 7th Ave. (Park Slope). 9 rooms, 7 with bath. Air-conditioning. Cash only.*

HOSTELS AND YMCAS

On the whole, hostels are most popular with students and foreign backpackers and are great for hooking up with other travelers. But you'll need to be able to tolerate lots of noise and a complete lack of privacy. Independent hostels and those affiliated with Hostelling International (HI) (*see* Students *in* Chapter 1) are similar in price and style: They almost always have private rooms as well as dorms that sleep four to 12 people. The three private hostels in Harlem charge $15–$25 per dorm bed, while Midtown joints generally cost $25 or more. From this, clever readers may draw the conclusion that the farther uptown a hostel is, the cheaper the rates. There are no hostels south of 14th Street. Unlike hotels, not all hostels have lockers or safety-deposit boxes—when in doubt, leave your gems at home. All the hostels listed below provide free linens.

Contrary to popular belief, YMCAs (it stands for Young Men's Christian Association, though these places are quite secular) are not always cheaper than hotels. They do offer one big bonus, however: free use of their usually extensive gym facilities with a night's stay. And the atmosphere at most is fairly subdued, thanks to the preponderance of families, older single travelers, and long-term elderly residents. All the Ys listed below have safety-deposit boxes.

The general rule about reservations is to make them at least two weeks in advance (more around Christmas and in late summer). Both hostels and YMCAs often charge a $5–$10 key deposit, so be sure to carry some extra cash. One final note for Americans only: Many private hostels have an unadvertised policy of refusing Americans. Why? Well, it seems that Americans have an ugly reputation for being demanding and for destroying hostel property. If you can politely convince a private hostel that you're an exception, you may be allowed in.

UPTOWN

The hostels in Harlem are usually the least crowded, and the cheapest, of any type of lodging in New York City. Contrary to a somewhat popular belief, Harlem can be a perfectly safe place to stay, as long as you stick to the better neighborhoods such as Sugar Hill. Though, if you plan on coming and going late at night, be sure to travel with company. Hostels on the Upper West Side are more expensive but are within walking distance of more snazzy restaurants, lots of bars, Central Park, the Museum of Natural History, Lincoln Center, and more. Hostels throughout upper Manhattan are usually only a block or two from a subway station; from Harlem it's a 20- to 30-minute subway ride to downtown (the same trip may or may not be shorter by taxi—depending on traffic—but also costs $10–$20—as opposed to $3 round-trip by subway).

Banana Bungalow. A foreign passport is your ticket to the magic Banana kingdom, where a bed in one of the six-person coed dorms costs $24 ($1 off with an ISIC, Rucksacker's, or Backpacker's card). You have easy access to Upper West Side sights, plus all the beer you can drink at the hostel's Wednesday- and Saturday-night parties held on its fabulous rooftop garden: Pay $5 for a stein, then keep refilling. Americans can stay, but only if they can produce an out-of-state ID or a plane ticket to prove that New York's merely a pit stop on their journey. *250 W. 77th St., between Broadway and West End Ave., Upper West Side, tel. 212/769-2441 or 800/646–7835, fax 212/877–5733; www.bananabungalow.com. Subway: 1 or 9 to W. 79th St. 100 beds. Air-conditioning. Reception open 24 hrs, check-in anytime, checkout 11 AM. Kitchen.*

Blue Rabbit International House. Ride the C train to its end in the well-to-do Sugar Hill section of Harlem to this clean, comfortable, refurbished hostel, under the same management as the adjacent Sugar Hill International House (*see below*). Coed and women-only dormitory-style rooms sleep four to eight and cost $20 per night; giant doubles are $25 per person. There are friendly pet cats (and a barking dog), a communal kitchen, and European tourists galore (a passport is required of all guests for check-in). Reservations—for dorms only—are essential in summer and fall. *730 St. Nicholas Ave., between W. 145th and 146th Sts., Harlem, tel. 212/491–3892 or 800/610–2030, fax 212/283–0108; www.hostelhandbook.com/bluerabbit. Subway: A, B, C, or D to 145th St. 25 beds. Reception open 9 AM–10 PM, check-in 9 AM–6 PM, checkout 9–11 AM. Kitchen. Cash only.*

De Hirsch Residence at the 92nd Street YMHA. Stay in the Upper East Side's only affordable lodging and you'll be able to see every Degas, Arbus, and Giacometti on Museum Mile, no prob. Despite the name (Young Men's Hebrew Association), this is a nonsectarian hostel with immaculate dorms and a kitchen, laundry, and shared bath on every floor. You'll also have access to the superb fitness facilities, library, community room, and all sorts of cultural and social events. Here's the catch: You must fill out an application in advance, and you must stay a minimum of three nights. Singles cost $75, doubles $48 per person (they will pair you with someone if you're traveling alone). *1395 Lexington Ave., at 92nd St., Upper East Side, tel. 212/415–5650 or 800/858–4692, fax 212/415–5578; www.92ndsty.org. Subway: 4, 5, or 6 to E. 86th St. 350 beds. Reception open Mon.–Thurs. 9 AM–7 PM, Fri. 9 AM–5 PM, Sun. 10 AM– 5 PM, check-in 1 PM, checkout noon. Air-conditioning, laundry.*

Hostelling International–New York. Despite the barbed wire, this monstrous landmark building (designed by big-deal 19th-century architect Richard Morris Hunt) is the largest youth hostel in North America. The neighborhood is safe and filled with great bars, and the Big House itself boasts an entire city block's worth of clean airy rooms, a garden, and an upper-level outdoor terrace. Beds in 4- to 12-person dorms run $25–$28 ($27–$30 in summer), while a handful of private rooms that accommodate up to four people (with bath) cost $100, or (without bath) $75. Flash a Hostelling International card for a $3 discount. *891 Amsterdam Ave., at W. 103rd St., Upper West Side, tel. 212/932–2300, fax 212/ 932–2574; www.hinewyork.org. Subway: 1 or 9 to W. 103rd St. 602 beds. Reception open 24 hrs, check-in anytime, checkout 11 AM. Air-conditioning, kitchen, laundry.*

Jazz on the Park. Owner Jazz Jordan turned this old brothel into a new hostel serving up good clean fun and pleasant accommodations on a quiet, residential Upper West Side block. Dorms with bunk beds run $25 (10–12 people), $26.50 (6–8 people), and $29 (4 people). Double rooms are $35 per person. Perks abound, like in-room lockers (25¢), free breakfast, and a terrace for sunning or smoking. Lobby phones have data ports for Internet hookups. The party really gets started Friday and Saturday nights when live jazz (what else?) bands play. June through September stays require a two-week advance reservation. Bring a foreign passport or non–New York City photo ID. *36 W. 106th St. at Central Park W., Upper West Side, tel. 212/932–1600, fax 212/932–1700; www.jazzhostel.com. Subway: B or C to 103rd St. and Central Park W. 220 beds. Open 24 hours. Check-in after 11 AM, checkout 11 AM. Coffee shop, air-conditioning, laundry.*

Sugar Hill International House. This hostel, brought to you by the same cheery folks as the Blue Rabbit International House (*see above*), is clean, comfortable, and friendly, with easy subway access and a sunny communal kitchen. Coed and women-only dorms (four to eight beds each) are $20. Or try to score the Sugar Hill's only double ($25 per person). *722 St. Nicholas Ave., at W. 146th St., Harlem, tel. 212/926–7030 or 800/610–2030, fax 212/283–0108; www.hostelhandbook.com/sugarhill. Subway: A, B, C, or D to 145th St. 20 beds. Reception open 9 AM–10 PM, check-in 9 AM–6 PM, checkout 9–11 AM. Kitchen. Cash only.*

Uptown Hostel. Sure, you're a traveler and you're tired, but think of poor Gisele: The hardworking owner of this beautiful brownstone has labored for months to refurbish it, so don't go messing it up with your smelly ol' socks and sad lack of personal hygiene. Coed dorms (four to six beds) are $15 per night. A private double is $23 per person. Gisele—who will help you find long-term lodging if you need it—also operates the slightly more expensive New York Bed-and-Breakfast (*see above*), about three blocks away. *239 Lenox Ave./Malcolm X Blvd., at W. 122nd St., Harlem, tel. 212/666–0559, fax 212/663– 5000. Subway: 2 or 3 to W. 125th St.; walk 3 blocks south on Lenox Ave./Malcolm X Blvd. 30 beds. Reception open 9 AM–7 PM, check-in 10 AM–7 PM, checkout anytime. Kitchen. Cash only.*

YMCA–West Side. Live like a sultan in this attractive, vaguely Middle East–inspired building mere blocks from Lincoln Center. Clean, comfortable singles are $95 with bath, $68 without, doubles are $110 with bath or $80 without, and triples without bath are $110. This princely sum entitles you to use the Y's gym, sauna, pool, indoor track, and squash courts (you packed your racquet, right?). If you get hungry, drop by the cafeteria. There are also shuttles to LaGuardia ($12), J.F.K. ($15), or Newark ($15) airports. Now the caveats: You must be at least 18 years old and can stay no longer than 25 days. Reservations (credit-card number required) are best made two weeks in advance. *5 W. 63rd St., between Central Park W and Broadway, Upper West Side, tel. 212/875–4100 or 800/348–9622, fax 212/875–1334; www.ymcanyc.org. Subway: A, B, C, D, 1, or 9 to W. 59th St. (Columbus Circle). 526 rooms, 27 with bath. Reception open 24 hrs, check-in after 2 PM, checkout noon. Air-conditioning, laundry.*

MIDTOWN

Conveniently, several hostels are in the heart (or at least on the fringe) of the myriad Midtown tourist attractions. Of them, the Chelsea International Hostel (*see below*) is the most "downtown"—in other words, it's the closest to good bars and restaurants and is only a short walk to the West Village. Another good option are the $27 dorms at the hip Gershwin Hotel (*see* Midtown *in* Hotels, *above*).

Big Apple Hostel. The Big Apple takes up seven floors of an old hotel with not a single air conditioner in sight—but who cares when you've got all of Times Square lying at your feet like a lathered, drooling beast? You'll also get brisk service, bathrooms that sparkle, and a big outdoor patio. Four-person dorms are $28, private doubles $75. A non-New York City driver's license or foreign passport is required to stay here. *119 W. 45th St., between 6th and 7th Aves., Theater District, tel. 212/302–2603, fax 212/302–2605; www.travel.to/bigapple. Subway: N, R, 1, 2, 3, 7, or 9 to W. 42nd St. (Times Sq.). 106 beds. Reception open 24 hrs, check-in after 11 AM, checkout 11 AM. Café, kitchen, laundry.*

Chelsea Center Hostel. You can take your shower in the bathroom—or, oddly enough, in the kitchen—at this compact, homey hostel on the northern edge of Chelsea. There are also two coed dorms and a lush back patio to enjoy. The friendly multilingual staff prefers foreigners but will accept Americans during the off-season. Beds are $25; Continental breakfast is included. *313 W. 29th St., between 8th and 9th Aves., Chelsea, tel. 212/643–0214, fax 212/473–3945. Subway: A, C, or E to W. 34th St. (Penn Station). 22 beds. Reception and check-in 8:30 AM–11 PM, checkout 11 AM. Kitchen. Cash only.*

Advertisements in many hostels plug the cheap happy hours and theme parties of nearby bars and clubs, so stay on the lookout.

Chelsea International Hostel. This hostel compensates for cramped rooms with a decent near-downtown location, comfortable bedding, and free pizza 'n' beer parties Wednesday nights. It's a favorite with boisterous young Europeans. Space in a four–six person dorm costs $23; doubles are $55. A $10 deposit and international passport are required. *251 W. 20th St., between 7th and 8th Aves., Chelsea, tel. 212/647–0010, fax 212/727–7289. Subway: C or E to W. 23rd St. (8th Ave.); also 1 or 9 to W. 23rd St. (7th Ave.). 300 beds. Reception open 8 AM–9 PM, check-in anytime, checkout 1 PM. Air-conditioning, kitchen.*

YMCA–McBurney. Many of McBurney's residents are long-term and mildly unsavory. And, depending on your point of view, the security guard and glassed-in reception are either reassuring or depressing. Still, you get free use of the Y's gym, a small but decent room, and a bathroom down the hall. Singles cost $57–59, doubles $69, triples $89, and quads $100. A one-night deposit is required unless you arrive before 6 PM. *206 W. 24th St., between 7th and 8th Aves., Chelsea, tel. 212/741–9226, fax 212/741–8724; www.ymcanyc.org. Subway: C or E to W. 23rd St.; also 1 or 9 to W. 23rd St. 270 rooms, none with bath. Reception open weekdays 7 AM–11 PM (weekends from 8 AM), check-in anytime, checkout noon. Air-conditioning.*

YMCA–Vanderbilt. This popular Y packs in backpackers like the 42nd Street Shuttle at rush hour. The tiny and linoleum-floored rooms share baths; the immaculate building itself is mere blocks from Grand Central Station. Best of all, a stay here entitles you to free use of the vast health facilities (pools, cardiovascular equipment, Nautilus machines, even a roving trainer) and airport shuttle service ($12 to La Guardia, $15 to J.F.K. and Newark). Singles are $68, doubles $81, triples $98–$105, and quads $130. *224 E. 47th St., between 2nd and 3rd Aves., Midtown East, tel. 212/756–9600, fax 212/752–0210; www.ymcanyc.org. Subway: 6 to E. 51st St.; also E or F to Lexington/3rd Aves. 377 rooms, none with bath. Reception open 24 hrs, check-in 1 PM, checkout noon. Air-conditioning.*

UNIVERSITY HOUSING

For those who need longer-term budget housing, a handful of colleges and universities open their dormitories to nonstudents during summer. The catch: You must call or send away for an application far in advance (usually during spring), then wait for a reply—which should come a week or two later. The best choice is **New York University (NYU)** (New York University Summer Housing Office, 14A Washington Pl., NY 10003, tel. 212/998–4621, fax 212/995–4097; www.nyu.edu/housing/summer), whose dormitories are ideally situated in the East and West Villages, smack in the middle of the city's coolest clubs, bars, cheap restaurants, and cafés. Housing is available mid-May through mid-August; for traditional halls (which include five meals per week), weekly rates are $145–$270 (depending on whether or not your room is air-conditioned); apartment-style halls—all with kitchens and air-conditioning but no meals, run $180–$245. The *minimum* stay is three weeks.

Other options: **Teachers College,** the graduate school at **Columbia University** (Residential Life Office, 525 W. 120th St., Morningside Heights, Box 312, NY 10027, tel. 212/678–3235, fax 212/678–3222; www.tc.columbia.edu/administration/res-life) offers small, clean single rooms at its Amsterdam Avenue dormitory for $45–$55 (with shared bath) or $55–$65 (private bath). Double rooms with kitchen and bath are $70–$80, $50–$70 with shared bath. One-bedroom apartments are also available for $80–$95. Maximum stay is six nights, with year-round availability.

FOOD 4

UPDATED BY JENNIFER D'ANGELO, DORI FERN, ANTO HOWARD,

MELISSA KLURMAN, CHRISTINA KNIGHT, ANDREA LAWLOR, HEATHER LEWIS,

LAUREN MYERS, HELAYNE SCHIFF, AND KRISTEN SCHURR

Dining out is an intensely important part of experiencing New York City, and something of a sport among New Yorkers. If you need proof, consider this: William Grimes, the restaurant critic for the *New York Times,* checks out something like 500 restaurants a year. If you like challenges, you can consider that a gauntlet. Go forth and eat! Besides the high-end experiences like Le Cirque 2000, Chanterelle, La Côte Basque, Gramercy Tavern, and Union Square Cafe with five-star chefs and waiters so utterly obsequious they'd probably take a bullet for you, there are many thousands of humbler establishments serving affordable and highly imaginative fare, as well as New York staples like pizza-by-the-slice and bagels—old-world creations perfected over the centuries in America's numero uno melting pot. It's impossible not to be impressed by the city's countless immigrant groups—Irish, Latin American, Eastern European, Italian, Asian, and more—who've proudly introduced their respective culinary secrets to New York: pub grub, burritos, pierogi, dim sum, pad thai, tandoori chicken, and killer cannoli. Live a little while you're here; if you don't know what *feijoada* is, or have never tasted Burmese cuisine before, this is the only place in the world where you can give both a try merely by crossing the right street.

The recession of the early 1990s caused restaurant owners to lower prices and improve the quality of their food and often the size of their portions in order to win back the hearts of jaded diners. Happily, you'll find that this trend has continued unabated—as long as you know where to look. For here, you can easily spend $100 for mediocre food in a trendy restaurant; you could also spend $15 on the best meal of your life in some totally obscure family-run joint. And another important tip: You should try to sample some of New York's finer restaurants during the week, when most offer reduced-price lunch specials. This is especially true in Midtown, where a $15 lunch entrée could easily fetch $50 at dinner.

Throughout New York, it's difficult to define a place strictly as a bar, café, or restaurant—many spots tend to function as all three. Cafés often pour beer and mix cocktails, while plenty of restaurants have very popular bars. Likewise, lots of bars have extremely active kitchens. The point is that you're never far from a decent meal in New York City. And you'll often find that the cheaper the establishment, the longer the hours. In fact, many places that charge less than $10 for a filling feast stay open until the wee hours—good news for bar crawlers who need a food fix after the bars close at 4 AM.

So after you've exhausted the reviews in this book, you're still left with those 15,917 other restaurants to explore—and well over 8,000 of those are in Manhattan alone. Zealous New Yorkers who dine out often refer to **The Zagat Survey** ($11.95), an annual guide to some 1,800 restaurants in all price ranges, mostly in Manhattan. Look for its slim, rectangular, maroon cover at all bookstores and most news-stands. And there is an extremely useful Web site—www.cuisinenet.com/restaurant/new_york/—that provides very complete menus and vital statistics for hundreds of restaurants in New York. The site is definitely worth a visit before you set out for the city; you can download a dozen menus and drool all the way in. And remember that, because of the city's uniquely plentiful foot traffic, virtually every restaurant in Manhattan posts its menu(s) in the front window, near the entrance, where you'll occasionally encounter a gathered crowd. A poorly kept secret: This is a splendid place to meet people, if only to get or share sage gustatory advice. But you might also find a lunch or dinner companion by lingering near an enticing menu and smiling carefully.

The allegedly make-or-break restaurant reviews in the **New York Times** are worth considering, especially since their beats more regularly include affordable places. The **Village Voice** and the **New York Press** tend to review and list restaurants that are affordable, and even include places of interest in the outer boroughs. Strict vegetarians visiting New York should invest in **The Vegan Guide to New York City** (updated annually), available for $5.75 from Rynn Berry (159 Eastern Pkwy., Apt. 2H, Brooklyn, NY 11238). If you're still not sure where to eat, your best bet is to cruise the streets of the East or West Village, 8th Avenue between 14th and 30th streets, or one of the city's many ethnic enclaves, and seek out a place overflowing with locals.

Some final notes: The price categories in this chapter refer to the cost of a main course, including a non-alcoholic drink. If you insist on drinking lots of wine or finishing your meal with a flaming bananas Foster, all bets are off. Also, in our reviews we won't mention a restaurant's credit-card acceptance policy unless it doesn't accept credit cards at all, in which case we'll say "Cash only"; otherwise, you can assume that the establishment takes some or all major cards. Likewise, unless otherwise indicated, all establishments are open seven days a week.

MANHATTAN RESTAURANTS

UPPER WEST SIDE

Restaurants are plentiful along the Upper West Side's three main north–south avenues: **Columbus Avenue, Amsterdam Avenue,** and **Broadway.** All three (and their surrounding side streets) offer just about anything your stomach might desire. Columbus Avenue has the most swank, expensive options, while Amsterdam Avenue draws a crowd that's semi-hip. On Broadway you'll discover an awful lot of nondescript diners offering cheapie Greek gyros and Italian hero sandwiches. If you're looking to dine before catching a performance at **Lincoln Center** (see Chapter 7), be warned: The restaurants in this area are pricey. After all, they're catering to people who think nothing of paying $115 for a single opera ticket.

UNDER $5 • Good Earth Natural Foods Inc. Everything here seems to contain brown rice or tab-bouleh. But given the name, did you expect cubed Spam? The half-dozen tables upstairs draw a crowd that looks more familiar with fluorescent lighting and cigarettes than organic gardening and soy milk. *167 Amsterdam Ave., between W. 67th and 68th Sts., tel. 212/496–1616. Other location: 1330 1st Ave., between E. 71st and 72nd Sts., Upper East Side, tel. 212/472–9055.*

Gray's Papaya. In this enlightened city the natural accompaniment to a couple of dogs is a big frothy cup of papaya juice. Total cost for two hot dogs, a drink, and a taste of a New York institution whose sign reads enticingly WE ARE POLITE NEW YORKERS: $1.95. *2090 Broadway, at W. 72nd St., tel. 212/799–0243. Open 24 hrs. Other location: 402 6th Ave., at W. 8th St., West Village, tel. 212/260–3532. Cash only.*

New York City Bagels. Top your circular sandwich with a stunning variety of shmears, including chocolate chip, raisin-carrot, and four flavors of tofu cream cheese. For lunch, try a bagel with tuna salad or salami. *164 Amsterdam Ave., between W. 67th and 68th Sts., tel. 212/799–0700. Cash only.*

Zabar's. The Zabar's cafeteria, part of the city's famous gourmet food emporium (see Markets and Specialty Shops, *below*), dispenses quality eats at everyman prices: Bagels with lox, salmon chowder, and sandwiches are all about $4. Counter service is quick, though you'll suffer a long line of cranky New Yorkers. *2245 Broadway, at W. 80th St., tel. 212/787–2004.*

UNDER $10 • Ayurveda Café. This Indian vegetarian restaurant, "dedicated to health and well being," uses no animal products and offers a daily prix fixe menu. Lunch is $5.95, dinner $9.95. Highlights include *mattar paneer,* a spicy dish of peas cooked with fresh cheese. *706 Amsterdam Ave., at W. 94th St., tel. 212/932–2400.*

Big Nick's Burger/Pizza Joint. Customers are urged to "confide their ultimate pizza fantasy," and the menu features hard-to-swallow combinations like Gyromania (gyro strips, onions, tomatoes, and cheese), Farmer's Pizza (fresh tomatoes and hard-boiled eggs), and Reuben, Reuben (pastrami, sauerkraut, cheese, and tomato sauce). Of course, there are burgers, too. *2175 Broadway, at W. 77th St., tel. 212/362–9238 or 212/724–2010. Open 24 hrs. Other location: 70 W. 71st St., at Columbus Ave., tel. 212/799–4444. Cash only.*

Café con Leche. This cheery restaurant blends Dominican, Cuban, and Spanish cuisines to produce wildly popular dishes like *arroz con pollo y chorizo* (rice, chicken, and Spanish sausage), *camarones en salsa de coco* (shrimp in coconut sauce), and *filete de pollo al ron* (sautéed chicken in spicy red sauce). Their paella features the special Spanish stew of rice, chicken, sausage, and seafood. *424 Amsterdam Ave., between W. 80th and 81st Sts., tel. 212/595–7000.*

The Cottage. This recently remodeled Chinese restaurant has a loyal following among young Upper West Siders, mainly because of its reasonably priced chef's specialties and the "all the wine you can drink—free" policy at dinner. *360 Amsterdam Ave., at W. 77th St., tel. 212/595–7450.*

La Caridad. The crowds keep coming back to this Cuban-Chinese eatery—despite the high grease factor—because portions are huge and prices cheap. A small roasted chicken or side of beef with a mountain of fried rice is $5–$7; seafood dishes are $5 and up. Expect to wait for a table (or show some initiative and snag a counter seat). *2199 Broadway, at W. 78th St., tel. 212/874–2780. Cash only.*

Monsoon. Join Upper West Siders casually dining on skillfully prepared Vietnamese delicacies like *bun xao* (stir-fried noodles with shrimp, egg, and chopped peanuts), spicy curries, and vegetarian dishes. Though large portions make an appetizer unnecessary, the *cha gio chay* (spring rolls) are first class. *435 Amsterdam Ave., at W. 81st St., tel. 212/580–8686.*

New Yorkers have a staggering 16,000 restaurants to choose from. Do three a day and you'd finish in around 14 years—at which point you'd have to start all over, because by then, thousands of new restaurants will have flung open their doors.

UNDER $15 • Gabriela's. An authentic *taquería* cherished for its generous portions and zesty *mole* (that famously rich and complex sauce), Gabriela's is about as good as it gets in a town where Mexican cuisine is still angling for a foothold. The tamales are fresh and cheap (only $2.95 for chicken, pork, or vegetarian), or get a traditional platter-size dish like the *pozole*, a hominy stew, for $8. Fresh grilled cactus is $9. *685 Amsterdam Ave., at W. 93rd St., tel. 212/961–0574.*

Gennaro. Gennaro Picone, the former chef at downtown hot spot Barolo, now has his own restaurant-in-miniature in the heart of uptown Amsterdam Avenue funk. Small it may be (tables for two are best), but the remarkable food would overshadow any setting: The grilled Italian sausage is delectable while the handmade potato gnocchi has won accolades from tough critics. *665 Amsterdam Ave., at W. 92nd St., tel. 212/665–5348.*

Josie's. This hip, earth-friendly restaurant does hearty food the organic way. We really like the sweet-potato ravioli with gulf shrimp, the grilled-chicken salad with hearts of palm and mango, and the free-range hamburger on focaccia bread. Wash it down with a kiwi-strawberry lemonade. *300 Amsterdam Ave., at W. 74th St., tel. 212/769–1212.*

Luzia's. Your gregarious hosts Luzia and Murray serve up filling Portuguese-influenced fare like white-bean salad and salmon poached in champagne, all accompanied by (heavenly) fresh Portuguese bread. The brunch menu includes omelets and Portuguese sausage. *429 Amsterdam Ave., between W. 80th and 81st Sts., tel. 212/595–2000. Closed Mon.*

UNDER $20 • City Grill. The Upper West Side greasy-spoon diners of yore have been reborn as "grills" serving cholesterol-conscious burgers and sandwiches laden with arugula. So it is with this place, which has made room for wok-charred tuna next to Mom's Meatloaf, and scores just about every patron imaginable. The dozen salad options are unusually fresh and ample. *269 Columbus Ave., between W. 72nd and 73rd Sts., tel. 212/873–9400.*

Fujiyama Mama's. This slick, loud sushi hot spot rocks nightly with young professionals doing the groove-and-food thing while a DJ spins tunes. Sushi à la carte averages $4.75 per roll but it's well worth the splurge. *467 Columbus Ave., between W. 82nd and 83rd Sts., tel. 212/769–1144.*

DINNER, FAMILY STYLE

The family-style Italian restaurant is a special New York institution—it's the perfect setting for celebrating a birthday, graduation, suspended sentence, whatever. If you've got a big, hungry group of people who want lots of vino and garlicky food in a festive atmosphere, reserve a table at one of the following: Carmine's (2450 Broadway, between W. 90th and 91st Sts., Upper West Side, tel. 212/362–2200; 200 W. 44th St., between Broadway and 8th Ave., Midtown, tel. 212/221–3800), Sambuca (20 W. 72nd St., between Columbus Ave. and Central Park W, Upper West Side, tel. 212/787–5656), or Osso Buco (88 University Pl., between E. 11th and 12th Sts., East Village, tel. 212/645–4525).

Good Enough to Eat. On weekends, Volvo-deprived West Side couples pack this Manhattan substitute for a rustic Vermont farmhouse to feast on delicious blueberry pancakes, Mexican scrambled eggs with tortillas, or the formidable Lumber Jack special (two eggs, two strips of bacon, and two giant pancakes). Hearty dinners include roast chicken, meat loaf, or stuffed brook trout. Just up the street, **Popover Cafe** (551 Amsterdam Ave., at W. 87th St., tel. 212/595–8555) also does a mouth-watering country brunch with fantastic popovers, of course. *483 Amsterdam Ave., between W. 83rd and 84th Sts., tel. 212/496–0215.*

Les Routiers. The name means "truck stop" in French, but you won't find any local teamsters inside. The new chef has shot up the usual bistro fare with some Indochine flavor, resulting in such delicacies as marinated flank steak with wasabi horseradish mashed potatoes and pan-seared sea scallops with sweet-pea sauce and curry oil. *568 Amsterdam Ave., between W. 87th and 88th Sts., tel. 212/874–2742.*

Rain. With its wicker furniture, Oriental rugs, and Asian vases, you might think you've retreated into colonial Saigon when stepping into this beautiful restaurant. This kind of attention to detail is conspicuous in such dishes as *kanom jeab*, dumplings filled with pork and shrimp, and the *pla bing*, roasted salmon with pepper and garlic served in a banana leaf. The friendly service is a bonus. *100 W. 82nd St., at Columbus Ave., tel. 212/501–0776.*

COLUMBIA UNIVERSITY AND MORNINGSIDE HEIGHTS

Morningside Heights, the neighborhood surrounding **Columbia University** and **Barnard College,** caters to students who love to eat but hate spending all their hard-earned loan money on food. You'll find dozens of cheap snack shops and 24-hour diners on **Broadway** and **Amsterdam Avenue,** between West 110th and 116th streets. When that gets boring, head north along Broadway to the blocks around 125th Street (a.k.a. Martin Luther King Jr. Boulevard) to find some terrific West African eateries.

UNDER $5 • Amir's Falafel. Everything at this relaxed student hangout is pretty darn cheap. For less than $5 you can eat your fill of falafel, stuffed grape leaves, and baba ghanoush. Sandwiches, loaded with tahini and marinated chicken or beef, are also a steal. *2911-A Broadway, between W. 113th and 114th Sts., tel. 212/749–7500. Cash only.*

The Bread Shop Cafe. Come to this hole-in-the-wall pizza shop–bakery to scarf down heavenly hot 'n' greasy slices or any one of the dozens of exotic delicacies like Chilean potato cake or chocolate-covered rum balls. *3139 Broadway, at La Salle St., tel. 212/666–4343. Cash only.*

Tamarind Seed Health Food Store. If you don't mind being surrounded by vitamin bottles and cans of soy milk, you'll learn to love this health-food store/deli. Sandwiches (tuna, tabbouleh, soy corned beef) are $3.50, and everything at the bountiful salad bar (chow mein, tofu, pasta, plenty of raw vegetables) is $3.99 per pound. Tofu dogs are $1.75. *2935 Broadway, between W. 114th and 115th Sts., tel. 212/864–3360.*

UNDER $10 • Bengal Cafe. Count on this classy, little restaurant for delicious Indian dishes like shrimp curry, chicken tandoori masala, beef vindaloo, and *aloo gobi motar* (sautéed cauliflower with tomatoes and onion), accompanied by big helpings of basmati rice, cabbage, and a half dozen other relishes. *1028 Amsterdam Ave., between W. 110th and 111th Sts., tel. 212/662-7191.*

La Rosita. This Cuban joint's breakfast specials (rice, beans, eggs, juice, and toast) are served around-the-clock, along with *chuletas* (pork chops) and Cuban sandwiches ($2.95–$3.95). The crowd, all cab drivers and unemployed intellectuals, stream in for the tasty (and cheap: $1.10) café con leche. *2809 Broadway, at W. 108th St., tel. 212/663-7804. Cash only.*

Obaa Koryoe. Tease your senses with African techno music and West African cuisine. The traditional chicken, tripe, fish, cow foot, oxtail, and lamb dishes come with *wachey* (rice and black-eyed peas) or *jolloff* (rice with tomato sauce); both are delicious. *3143 Broadway, at 125th St., tel. 212/316-2950. Cash only.*

Riverside Church Cafeteria. Students from the Manhattan School of Music, Columbia University, and Riverside Church's own theological school flock here for the $5.50 lunch platter (chicken, meat loaf, or fish, with greens and bread or potatoes). Breakfast costs even less. *490 Riverside Dr., at W. 120th St., tel. 212/222-5900. Cash only. Closed weekends.*

Tom's Restaurant. A mixed crowd of old-timers and Columbia students come here to chow on cheeseburgers ($3), salads ($5), triple-decker sandwiches ($5.10–$5.50), and thick brain-freezing milk shakes. Curious "Seinfeld" fans just come in to gawk at the blown-up photo of the gang, complete with their signatures. *2880 Broadway, at W. 112th St., tel. 212/864-6137. Open Thurs.–Sat. 24 hrs., Sun.–Wed. 6–1:30 AM. Cash only.*

For those who worship at the house of Jerry (Seinfeld, not Garcia), Tom's Restaurant is a sacred place; its neon sign is featured at some point in every show.

V&T Italian Cuisine & Pizzeria. Heavenly oil-drenched garlic pizza, a good wine selection, and white-aproned waiters make up this simple Italian diner. Standard pasta dishes ($6–$8.50) and pizzas ($10–$13) are consistently good. *1024 Amsterdam Ave., between 110th and 111th Sts., tel. 212/663-1708.*

UNDER $15 • The Mill. It's the side of *kimchee* (spicy pickled cabbage and hot pepper sauce) that adds a little peppery tingle to Korean dishes like *dak bokum* (stir-fried chicken), *haemul dolsott bibimbob* (seafood and rice in a hot earthen bowl), and *bulgogi* (barbecued beef). The decor is upscale and understated; you're more likely to see a Ph.D. holder here than a starving student. *2895 Broadway, between W. 112th and 113th Sts., tel. 212/666-7653.*

HARLEM

You'll find East African, West African, Creole, Caribbean, and Southern restaurants aplenty along Harlem's main commercial arteries: **Malcolm X Boulevard** (Lenox Avenue), **Adam Clayton Powell Jr. Boulevard** (7th Avenue), **Martin Luther King Jr. Boulevard** (125th Street), and **138th Street.** Many of the West African restaurants double as community centers for African immigrants—you can enjoy a really good meal while soaking up a little foreign culture. In **East Harlem** there are dozens of Latino restaurants on Lexington Avenue between East 116th and 125th streets that serve *pupusas* (fried tortillas) and tacos for a few bucks apiece. As a tourist, you'll have no problem visiting Harlem or East Harlem during the day. At night use caution and stay on main thoroughfares or take a cab.

UNDER $5 • Joseph's Food Basket. Everything here is free of additives, preservatives, and chemicals (and sometimes free of dairy, wheat, and cholesterol). Breakfast is an unbelievable $2.50, while lasagna, stir-fried vegetables, macaroni pie, and savory stews are all $1.50–$3. There's also a wide selection of gourmet coffees and fresh organic juices. *471 Malcolm X Blvd., between W. 133rd and 134th Sts., tel. 212/368-7663. Cash only. Closed Sun.*

Uptown Juice Bar & Vegetarian Food. This tiny café serves vegetarian dishes like curry "duck" and shepherd's pie (made from a smattering of soy products from beans to textured soy protein) and barbecue soy chunks. Choose four sides from the lengthy list of daily specials, including okra and collard greens, to make up a $6 plate. Soy cheese pizza, veggie burgers, and freshly made juices are $2 and $3. *54 W. 125th St., between 5th Ave. and Malcolm X Blvd., tel. 212/987-2660. Cash only.*

UNDER $10 • The Reliable. This ramshackle Sugar Hill favorite serves some fine, authentic Southern food: smothered chicken, barbecued ribs, sweet curried chicken, and salmon cakes, served with

PRIX-FIXE MADNESS

When you're on a shoestring budget, a $70 meal at a world-class restaurant might seem like a sick joke. Happily, impoverished gourmets can score big-time at more than 100 of New York's top restaurants during the annual New York Restaurant Week (mid-June). It all started with $19.92 meals offered during the 1992 Democratic National Convention, which the city hosted. Some restaurants now offer these prices (generally priced at the current year) even year-round. Past participants have included such way-outta-your-league joints as Lutèce, the Rainbow Room, and the Four Seasons; for more info, check the city's weekly magazines in June. And make reservations far in advance.

tasty cooked greens and corn bread. Next door and under the same ownership, **Copeland's** (547 W. 145th St., tel. 212/234–2356) is a bit more upscale, with great Southern breakfasts and brunch. *547 W. 145th St., between Broadway and Amsterdam Ave., tel. 212/234–2357. Cash only.*

Singleton's Bar-B-Que. Singleton's claims to have the only brick-oven barbecue in the entire city, and the product is outstanding soul food. Try the hickory-smoked chicken slathered with barbecue sauce and paired with collard greens or yams. The $5 breakfast includes omelets, pancakes, and plenty of meat. *525 Malcolm X Blvd., between W. 136 and 137th Sts., tel. 212/694–9442. Cash only.*

UNDER $15 • Sylvia's. The most famous soul-food restaurant in New York remains popular with locals, despite having fed celebs like Dan "potatoe" Quayle. Dinner favorites are deep-fried fish, smothered steak, and barbecued ribs. On Sunday there's a gospel brunch with live music. Look for matronly Sylvia presiding over the two large dining rooms and outdoor seating area. *328 Malcolm X Blvd., at W. 126th St., tel. 212/996–0660.*

WASHINGTON HEIGHTS

Washington Heights, at the very northern tip of Manhattan, is so far from most tourist attractions that you wouldn't want to make the trip just to get something to eat. But if you're in the neighborhood you can enjoy kosher bagels and lox, Salvadoran fried plantains, or a cup of syrupy Cuban coffee—at prices far lower than in the rest of Manhattan. The main thoroughfares—**St. Nicholas Avenue** and **Broadway**—are chockablock full of street carts and cheap, divey eateries offering Dominican, Salvadoran, Cuban, and other Latin fare. (It helps if you speak Spanish, though you'll find most places serve familiar stuff like tostadas and burritos. And you can always point.) The blocks around **Yeshiva University** (Audubon Ave., near 186th St.) cater to the Jewish student population with dozens of kosher restaurants. Another cluster of diners and bodegas lies a few blocks from **Fort Tryon Park,** around 204th Street. Remember, this isn't the most heavily touristed of neighborhoods, so use your street smarts and don't wander the streets alone after dark.

UNDER $10 • La Cabaña Salvadoreña. At $1.25 apiece, it's easy to fill up on à la carte Salvadoran snacks like *pupusas con queso* (fried tortillas, folded and filled with cheese), enchiladas, and tacos. Or get a combination plate of *carne asada* (grilled steak) or *chuletas de cerdo* (pork chops); both come with fries or rice and beans. *4384 Broadway, at W. 187th St., tel. 212/928–7872. Cash only.*

Caridad IV Restaurant. If you're a monolingual American, this place can be bewilderingly foreign; the waitstaff speaks *solamente español*. It's worth bridging the language barrier, though, because the food is excellent, especially the paella marinera ($35.95 for two), *filete pescado* (fried fish with bananas), and omelets. The coffee, brewed Latin American–style, is strong enough to melt your spoon. *554 W. 181st St., between St. Nicholas and Audubon Aves., tel. 212/927–9729. Open 24 hrs. Cash only.*

UPPER EAST SIDE

Many Upper East Siders have a lot of money to blow on grub, and it shows. For what you'd pay to eat in one of the schmancy restaurants lining 5th and Madison avenues (where, naturally, all the museums are), you could probably buy one of the smaller OPEC countries. That said, there are plenty of affordable options east of Lexington Avenue, along **3rd Avenue** and **2nd Avenue**.

UNDER $5 • H&H East. If you've come in search of the authentic New York bagel, this is the place for you. At this bustling little bagel shop they serve 'em straight from the oven—crispy on the outside, soft on the inside, and melt in your mouth delicious. Go traditional (plain old cream cheese please!) or venture into the realm of tofu and lox spreads. On weekend mornings be prepared to wait, and when it's your turn, bark out your order fast and frenzied—in true New York fashion. *1551 2nd Ave., between E. 80th and 81st Sts., tel. 212/734-7441. Other location: 2239 Broadway, between W. 79th and 80th Sts., Upper West Side, tel. 212/595-8003.*

Soup Burg. A few mirror tricks and a long counter constitute this tiny coffee shop, the quintessential greasy spoon. Order a fat chunk of cow meat with fries (the beef burger de luxe) and an old-fashioned milk shake and don't worry about tomorrow. *1150 Lexington Ave., between E. 79th and 80th Sts., tel. 212/737-0095. Cash only.*

UNDER $10 • Candle Cafe. Earth-friendly dining (at least an upscale version of it) means low-on-the-food-chain vegetarian and macrobiotic dishes. If you need a roughage boost, try a Seasonal Harvest salad (romaine lettuce, vegetables, sprouts, and sesame seeds topped with carrot ginger dressing). Wash it down with a glass of wheat-grass juice or some organic coffee. *1307 3rd Ave., between E. 74th and 75th Sts., tel. 212/472-0970.*

If you don't want to be branded a tourist in Washington Heights, eat your Salvadoran "pupusas" (fried, filled tortillas) with your hands.

EJ's Luncheonette. Good comfort food beckons at this amped-up '90s diner, where the young and the restless love to snuggle into its leather booths, especially for weekend brunch. Flapjacks and waffles are done 14 ways, and the milk shakes are the good, old-fashioned kind. Expect a wait. *1271 3rd Ave., at E. 73rd St., tel. 212/472-0600. Other locations: 447 Amsterdam Ave., between W. 81st and 82nd Sts., Upper West Side, tel. 212/873-3444; 432 6th Ave., between 9th and 10th Sts., West Village, tel. 212/473-5555.*

Patsy's Pizzeria. The Upper East Side branch of this classic Manhattan pizzeria is much more than a place to grab a slice. Sit at the spiffy polished-wood booths and enjoy some of the city's best brick oven–fired pizzas, along with massive family-size salads packed with everything but the kitchen sink. *1312 2nd Ave., at 69th St., tel. 212/639-1000. Other locations: 61 W. 74th St., between Central Park W and Columbus Ave., Upper West Side, tel. 212/579-3000; 509 3rd Ave., at E. 34th St., Midtown, tel. 212/689-7500; 67 University Pl., between E. 10th and 11th Sts., East Village, tel. 212/533-3500.*

Pintaile's Pizza. If you like designer pizza, this eatery hits the spot: No heavy sauce, no goopy cheese—just paper-thin crust topped with fresh ingredients. If you're feeling tame, stick with tomatoes and mozzarella; otherwise, try Cajun spice pizza (with sausage), shiitake-mushroom, or pesto. *1443 York Ave., between 76th and 77th Sts., tel. 212/717-4990. Other locations: 1577 York Ave., between E. 84th and 85th Sts., tel. 212/396-3479; 26 E. 91st St., between 5th and Madison Aves., tel. 212/722-1967.*

Samalita's. There's nothing factorylike about this colorful Cal-Mex hole-in-the-wall squeezed among the Upper East Side's chichi restaurants. The soft tacos and burritos are subtly spiced, and so is the decor. *1429 3rd Ave., between E. 80th and 81st Sts., tel. 212/737-5070.*

Taco Taco. One of the few outposts of authentic Mexican food in Manhattan, this festive little taquería is decked out with piñatas and candles everywhere. As the name implies, soft tacos are the specialty: Try a few different kinds, since you get two for less than $5. Or go for a house special—pork loin with smoked jalapeños and cabbage, or shrimp marinated in garlic and lemon heaped with flavorful beans and rice. *1726 2nd Ave., between E. 89th and 90th Sts., tel. 212/289-8226. Cash only.*

UNDER $15 • Barking Dog Luncheonette. The snazzy tiled dog bar (filled with water) out front is only a precursor to what lies inside. At this retro diner with a twist, the waitstaff wears shirts that say "Sit. Stay." The menu is as silly: There are hefty and inventive salads and sandwiches, and classic hot plates with gussied-up gourmet touches—try salmon fillet with potato-fennel purée and white truffle oil. *1678 3rd Ave., at E. 94th St., tel. 212/831-1800. Cash only.*

Benjarong. Bring someone special to swoon over at this quiet Thai restaurant—the lighting is soft and the music exotic. Whet your appetite with a sampling of delightfully peanutty steamed Thai dumplings, and then move on to pad thai or one of the other noodle dishes; you can have them spiced to taste— sweet and mild or spanking hot. *1485 1st Ave., between E. 77th and 78th Sts., tel. 212/249–5700.*

Caffé Buon Gusto. Head and shoulders above the other trattorias on the Upper East Side, this unpretentious place on a cheerful little side street is always crowded at night and on weekends. Warm foccacia to dip in pepper-infused olive oil starts your meal of homemade pastas and nightly specials like swordfish livornese (with black olives, tomatoes, and capers). *236 E. 77th St., between 2nd and 3rd Aves., tel. 212/535–6884. Cash only. Other locations: 1009 2nd Ave., at E. 53rd St., tel. 212/755–1476; 337 3rd Ave., at E. 25th St., tel. 212/532–2929.*

Good Health Cafe. If you don't mind eating in a health-food store, you'll get a bang for your buck here— and a healthy one at that. Entrées range from standard vegetarian fare like nutty soy burgers and crunchy salads, to more inventive dishes like vegan meat loaf (texturized vegetable protein topped with mushroom gravy, and served with grilled veggies and beans). For weekend brunch (10–4:30), there are wild-rice pancakes, blue-corn waffles, and hefty omelets. And there's a juice bar to boot. *324 E. 86th St., between 1st and 2nd Aves., tel. 212/439–9680.*

Pamir. Tantalize your taste buds at this cozy, family-friendly Afghan restaurant, decorated with Oriental rugs. The lamb here is superb, as are the sauces; try the *norange palaw,* delicately seasoned pieces of lamb under a bed of saffron rice, topped with almonds, pistachios, orange strips, rosewater, and cardamom. Those who go the spicy route will be thankful for the soothing complimentary custard served at the end of the meal. *1437 2nd Ave., between E. 74th and 75th Sts., tel. 212/734–3791. No lunch. Closed Mon.*

UNDER $20 • East Japanese Restaurant. Despite its rather bland name, this place serves some of the zestiest Japanese cuisine on the East Side. Let the house sake warm your cockles, and if you're the indecisive sort (or happen to love smorgasbords) try one of the combination boxes—your choice of chicken teriyaki, beef, or sashimi, complete with mixed green salad, California roll, crispy tempura, *hijiki* (seaweed salad), rice, and miso soup. For a quiet, relaxed evening out, get here early; the place fills up quickly. *1420 3rd Ave., between 80th and 81st Sts., tel. 212/472–3975. No lunch.*

MIDTOWN WEST OF 5TH AVENUE

West of 5th Avenue, Midtown can seem rather charmless. This is where cabs pile up, where skyscrapers tower, and where hundreds of hole-in-the-wall diners and delis feed working stiffs as cheaply and unoriginally as possible. However, all hope is not lost. Though it can be a bit gritty, the neighborhood of **Hell's Kitchen** is where you should go to seek relief: 9th Avenue in the 30s, 40s, and 50s is loaded with ethnic restaurants offering some of the cheapest meals in Manhattan. One weekend every May, Hell's Kitchen is also home to an **International Food Festival** (*see* When to Go *in* Chapter 1). **West 32nd Street** between 5th Avenue and Broadway is referred to as "Little Korea," thanks to its cheap and prolific Korean eateries: Try **Won Jo** (23 W. 32nd St., between Broadway and 6th Ave., tel. 212/695–5815), open 24 hours, for table-top barbecues and traditional dishes such as *bibimbop* and *kimchee*. **West 46th Street** around Broadway boasts a cluster of Brazilian restaurants, cafés, and markets.

Sadly, the **Theater District** is heavy on tourist traps boasting overpriced and often mediocre food. Do you really want to blow $20 or more on a substandard pre-theater dinner, especially if you've already paid $35 for restricted-view seats? **Virgil's Real BBQ** (152 W. 44th St., between Broadway and 6th Ave., tel. 212/921–9494) or the Midtown branch of **Carmine's** (*see box* Dinner, Family Style, *above*) aren't particularly cheap, but the food at both is good and the servings are obscene. The district's **Restaurant Row**—West 46th Street between 8th and 9th avenues—gets a lot of hoopla, and you can eat here without breaking the bank, particularly at a place like tiny **Hourglass Tavern** (373 W. 46th St., tel. 212/265–2060). Its prix-fixe meals are $12.75, after your table's 59-minute hourglass has run out, you are asked to move on.

Finally, there's **West 57th Street** between 5th and 8th avenues. Over the last few years it's undergone a Kafkaesque transmogrification—from plain ol' thoroughfare to one embraced by Disney and bland theme restaurants. As a tourist you may feel obliged to check it out, although real New Yorkers prefer to ignore **Planet Hollywood** (140 W. 57th St., tel. 212/333–7827), **Hard Rock Cafe** (221 W. 57th St., tel. 212/459–9320), **Jekyll and Hyde Club** (1409 6th Ave., at W. 57th St., tel. 212/541–9505), **Brooklyn Diner U.S.A.** (212 W. 57th St., tel. 212/581–8900), and **Harley-Davidson Cafe** (1370 6th Ave., at W. 56th St., tel. 212/

245–6000). The point to all these places is never the food (typically $7–$20), but rather the stuff on the walls. Jekyll and Hyde has an electronically animated Great Sphinx and flapping gargoyles, while Harley-Davidson has a revvable motorcycle upon which you can get your picture taken ($7).

UNDER $5 • Lemon Tree Cafe. Middle Eastern delights at this tiny eatery include giant hummus, babagounash, and falafel pita sandwiches. *769 9th Ave., between W. 51st and 52nd Sts., tel. 212/245–0818.***Manganaro's Hero-Boy.** Come for fast-food Italian dishes, most notably the biggest and best sub sandwiches in the entire city. *492 9th Ave., between W. 37th and 38th Sts., tel. 212/947–7325.*

Tachigui-Soba. A large Japanese lantern hangs in front of this Times Square nosh spot, the only indication of the cheap cafeteria-style food that lies within (there's no sign in English). Chicken tempura is $3, chicken teriyaki $4, and *udon* and *soba* soups $3–$5.50. Seating is upstairs in a zero-decor room. *732 7th Ave., between W. 48th and 49th Sts., tel. 212/265–8181. Cash only.*

UNDER $10 • Chantale's Cajun Kitchen. Looking weirdly out of place (it's next door to the Port Authority Bus Terminal), this homey New Orleans eatery serves authentic Cajun and Creole dishes as well as meal-size salads. The house special, Chantale's Gumbo, is a stew of shrimp, sausage, scallops, fish, and chicken served in small and large portions. *510 9th Ave., between W. 38th and 39th Sts., tel. 212/967–2623. Cash only. Closed Sun.*

Cupcake Cafe. The Cupcake seems trapped in one of those sleepy Twilight Zones where things never seem to age, where pert wanna-be actresses pick daintily at their sandwiches, and where Billie Holiday drifts from the scratchy stereo. Indulge in lusciously frosted baked goods or fill up on decent lunch fare, such as soup and salad. *522 9th Ave., at W. 39th St., tel. 212/465–1530. Cash only.*

What do Madonna and Martha Stewart have in common? They both love cakes from the Cupcake Cafe.

Mitchel London Foods. Everything at this small café is made from scratch, from the garlic aïoli for the amazing fries to the decadent Belgian hot-fudge on the vanilla-bean ice cream. Sink your teeth into a perfect burger or roasted chicken for lunch or an early dinner (they close at 7). Try the bottomless stack of light-as-a-feather pancakes for Saturday brunch. *542 9th Ave., at W. 40th St., tel. 212/563–5969. Closed Sun.*

Sapporo. At Sapporo, a big bowl of *hiyashi chuka* (cold noodle soup) is perfect on hot summer days. Or try any of the filling ramen noodle and teriyaki dishes that keep this place packed with a mostly Japanese clientele. *152 W. 49th St., between 6th and 7th Aves., tel. 212/869–8972. Cash only.*

Soul Fixin's. This small restaurant cranks out an enormous, outstanding country lunch: your choice of barbecued, fried, baked, or smothered chicken; barbecued spare ribs or fried whiting fish; plus corn bread and two side dishes, such as candied yams or black-eyed peas. Vegetarians can get four meatless side dishes. *371 W. 34th St., near 9th Ave., tel. 212/736–1345. Cash only. Closed weekends.*

Soup Kitchen International. Soup Man Al Yeganeh, who came to the States to study physics, probably never could have guessed that Jerry Seinfeld would be his rocket ride to fame. New Yorkers and tourists alike now line up willingly for a take-out taste (small $6, large $8, or extra large $13) of his excellent vegetable, bean, nut, seafood, or meat soups (about 15 daily varieties, both hot and cold). Know what you want (ask no questions and speak quickly) and have your money ready. Don't loiter and *don't* call him the Soup Nazi. *259-A W. 55th St., near 8th Ave., tel. 212/757–7730. Cash only. Closed Sun.*

Westside Cottage II. The Westside Cottage's menu could be considered the Good Book of Asian food, because it lists more than 200 Hunan, Szechuan, and Cantonese dishes. On top of this are about 50 three-course lunch specials and, at dinner, several dozen chef's specials. *689 9th Ave., between W. 47th and 48th Sts., tel. 212/245–0800.*

UNDER $15 • Arroz y Feijão. White or yellow rice? Black or red beans? Once you've decided, sit back and enjoy a Brazilian feast. Try *feijoada,* a stew of black beans, pork loin, sausage, bacon, and spare ribs, or the *peixe amazonas,* a fish stew with onions, tomatoes, green peppers, and coconut milk. For dessert, the Romeo & Juliet (guava paste and cheese) is a mere $2.50. *744 9th Ave., between W. 50th and 51st Sts., tel. 212/265–4444.*

Film Center Café. Sandwiches, soups, and salads all prepared quick and well make this a great pre-theater stop. The accommodating staff will have you in and out lickety split; then come back post-show for a drink or dessert at the friendly bar. *635 9th Ave., between W. 43rd and 44th Sts., tel. 212/262–2525.*

UNDER $20 • Amarone. There are as many Italian restaurants in Midtown as there are guys named Vinny delivering pizza, but don't let that deter you from visiting this gem of a trattoria in Hell's Kitchen.

Delicious housemade pastas change daily and are presented on a platter at your table—try the "priest stranglers," a thick spaghetti, or the saffron fettuccine. Items on the "Classics" menu are an extremely good value ($10 and under). *686 9th Ave., between W. 48th and 49th Sts., tel. 212/245–6060.*

MIDTOWN EAST OF 5TH AVENUE

Unless you have an AmEx Corporate Card, the food situation can be fairly grim east of 5th Avenue. Most of Midtown East is prime big-business country, and nearly all its restaurants are slavishly devoted to the power lunch. On the upside, even the "nice" restaurants offer cheap weekday lunch specials—a good way to sample some of Manhattan's finer eateries without paying $45 for a dinner entrée. One solution is to eat like the working stiffs in the area: there are decent food courts with plenty of seating and unique vendors in the basement levels of 875 3rd Avenue, at East 52nd Street, and the Crystal Pavillion building at East 50th Street and 3rd Avenue. Or pick up some gourmet sandwiches and salads to go at **Mike's Take-Away** (160 E. 45th St., between 3rd and Lexington Aves., tel. 212/856–6453) or **Spoons** (235 E. 53rd St., between 2nd and 3rd Aves., tel. 212/371–3111). Another option is to head for the **Cosi** Sandwich chain where Roman flatbread is baked continuously in wood-fired ovens and filled with an inventive array of meats and veggies.

UNDER $5 • Fresco Tortilla Grill. Despite its ghastly resemblance to Mickey D's, this place produces fresh, wholesome, tasty Cal-Mex food. Big burritos in homemade tortillas, tostada salads, and steak tacos are all fresh and free of nasty additives. *546 3rd Ave., near E. 36th St., tel. 212/685–3886. Cash only.*

Prime Burger. Conveniently located next to St. Patrick's Cathedral, the Prime may look a little worn, but give it a break—it's been in this location since 1938. The decor is also a bit odd: single diners are seated at old-fashioned wood school desks with fold-down arms. The Prime specializes in, what else, burgers, which are perfectly cooked and incredibly tasty. Homemade pies and cakes are worth saving room for. *5 E. 51st St., between Madison and 5th Aves., tel. 212/759–4729. Closed Sun.*

UNDER $10 • Comfort Diner. Homestyle favorites are served up in slick '50s-style retro surroundings. Chicken potpie with a buttermilk biscuit crust and "mom's meatloaf (on her best day)" share menu space with salads, blue-plate specials, thick milk shakes, and delectable desserts. Weekend brunch is packed but worth the wait. *212 E. 45th St., between 2nd and 3rd Aves., tel. 212/867–4555.*

UNDER $20 • Houston's. The dependable American food and a warm clubby atmosphere keep Houston's hopping with a young business crowd who devour the awesome spinach dip, excellent burgers, giant salads, and juicy ribs. Expect to wait since reservations aren't accepted, but the bar is a great place to hang out—there's even a pianist during happy hour. *153 E. 53rd St., at 3rd Ave., tel. 212/888–3828.*

Les Sans Culottes. There's always a festive crowd at this prix-fixe French restaurant enjoying one of the best deals in the city. For $19.99 a person, your table first starts off with a rack of sausages, a pot of pâté, and a giant bowl of crudite. Eat as much as you like and then order a main course from a classic menu (duck à l'orange is a good choice). But wait, there's more: Dessert is also included, as is a shot of the house schnapps. *1085 2nd Ave., between E. 57th and 58th Sts., tel. 212/838–6660.*

CHELSEA

Chelsea was not long ago a warehouse wasteland; nowadays it's truly trendy, rivaling the East Village as a magnet for hip twentysomethings and the hangout of choice among many gays and lesbians. As a result, **8th Avenue,** between West 30th and 14th streets, and **West 18th Street,** between 6th and 9th avenues, are crammed with stylish bistros, cafés, revamped diners, natural-food restaurants, bakeries, and juice bars. On 9th Avenue, between 15th and 16th streets, is **Chelsea Market,** a renovated warehouse now home to more than a dozen food vendors and wholesalers. Some of the best include decadent FatWitch brownies, Amy's Breads, Sarabeth's Bakery, Buonitalia (for delicious Italian picnic makings), and the Chelsea Wine Vault for a well-priced beverage to take along. A good morning jumping-off place is the reasonably priced and friendly **Taylor's** (228 W. 18th St., between 7th and 8th Aves., tel. 212/378–2895;West Village branch, 523 Hudson St., between W. 10th and Charles Sts., tel. 212/378–2890; East Village branch, 175 2nd Ave., between E. 11th and 12th Sts., tel. 212/674–9501)— scope out the scene from the front porch while enjoying a mouth-watering muffin or donut, three dozen types of salads, or sandwiches.

UNDER $10 • Bendix Diner. The menu here is exotic, to say the least, blending American comfort food with Thai dishes. Translation: You can have meat loaf while your date chows on *yaki meshi* (stir-fried chicken teriyaki with soybean sprouts, broccoli, zucchini, and brown rice). The crowd is hip and gay, the servings are huge, and the music kicks. *219 8th Ave., at W. 21st St., tel. 212/366–0560. BYOB. New Bendix Diner, with the same menu: 167 1st Ave., between E. 10th and 11th Sts., East Village, tel. 212/260–4220.*

Uncle Mo's. A family of Sasquatches could feed for a week on one of Uncle Mo's monstrous burritos, stuffed with *barbacoa* (slow-cooked shredded beef), *pollo verde* (chicken in a mild green chile sauce), or *carne asada* (marinated steak). Less massive but still filling are the tacos and quesadillas. This is best for a late lunch, when you're famished: In friendly weather, do it take-out and hop over to Union Square to dine alfresco. *14 W. 19th St., between 5th and 6th Aves., tel. 212/727–9400. Cash only. Closed Sun.*

UNDER $15 • Cafeteria. While Cafeteria may seem a little too cool for school in the attitude department, the restaurant does an amazing juggling act for New York: a hip clientele, good food, decent prices, open 24 hours, with a Dolce & Gabbana–clad staff that is actually friendly *and* efficient. The tasty menu offers American standards with a twist, such as pastrami-cured salmon on rye. Croissant French toast with caramelized bananas is just one of the reasons weekend brunch is so popular. *119 7th Ave., at W. 17th St., tel. 212/414–1717.*

James. Here's a funky little French-influenced Thai bistro right on the hot strip of new galleries in West Chelsea. Try steak au poivre with lemon-chili sauce or succulent salt-and-pepper shrimp fried whole in the shell and eaten in one crunchy bite. Late nights are often hopping with a young hip crowd. *205 10th Ave., at W. 22nd St., tel. 212/741–7925. Cash only.*

Regional Thai Taste. The interesting thing about this Thai joint is that in addition to serving the same old pad thai, it explores recipes from around the country: Try *kow pad rot fie* (fried rice with shrimp and chicken), traditionally sold on Thai trains; *yum ta lay* (marinated seafood salad), from the island of Phuket; or the Bangkok favorite *kow mun som tum* (shredded beef with coconut rice and green papaya). Prices are $2–$4 cheaper before 4 PM. *208 7th Ave., at W. 22nd St., tel. 212/807–9872.*

UNDER $20 • El Cid. A little bit of Spain right on the edge of Chelsea, El Cid is tiny, but worth the cramped conditions for tapas such as garlic shrimp, spicy chorizo, and grilled steak with potatoes. If you sit at the bar (which comprises half the seats here), ask the bartender what he recommends; he'll make sure you get the most for your money. And definitely go for the sangria, easily the best in the city, but be careful getting off that bar stool—this is *really* potent stuff. *322 W. 15th St., between 8th and 9th Aves., tel. 212/929–9332.*

Mesa Grill. Not to be missed, though you will easily drop more than $20. But celebrity chef Bobby Flay is on the cutting edge, and this is your chance to find out why. Highlights of the southwestern menu include shrimp with a roasted garlic and corn tamale, the day's special quesadilla, and some of the best margaritas in town. The food can be spicy, but never overwhelmingly so. *102 5th Ave., between W. 15th and 16th Sts., tel. 212/807–7400.*

Trois Canards. Charming, comfortably elegant, and relaxingly eccentric, this scrupulous French bistro does some of the best duck you'll find at the moment: Each part of the fresh halved duck is prepared according to its precise needs. Homemade ravioli is smashing, service is gracious, and desserts leave you panting. *184 8th Ave., between W. 19th and 20th Sts., tel. 212/929–4320.*

GRAMERCY AND UNION SQUARE

Some of New York's finest five-star restaurants are tucked between the million-dollar town houses that line the blocks surrounding Gramercy Park and Union Square. If you have money to burn, get thee to the enormously and justifiably popular **Union Square Cafe** or **Gramercy Tavern** (*see box* Serious Splurges, *below*), which enjoy the same ownership and management. Both are truly New York experiences. Don't have the cash? Then meander over to the amiable **Union Square Greenmarket** (*see* Greenmarkets, *below*), a great place to pick up snacks and fresh produce—delightfully packed on summer and fall Saturdays.

Your best bet for cheap eats is along **3rd Avenue,** lined with no-frills ethnic restaurants and pubs, pizzerias, bagel shops, and delis. **Irving Place** between East 19th and 14th streets is lined with moderately priced restaurants and sweet shops like **Mio Pane, Mio Dulce Bakery** (77 Irving Pl., at 19th St., tel. 212/677–1905). **Park Avenue South** in the East 20s and 30s has a hyperactive dinner scene. The hot spots of the moment include **Patria** (250 Park Ave. S, at E. 20th St., tel. 212/777–6211), which brandishes Miami/Cuban cuisine at its very finest and most whimsical, and **Lemon** (230 Park Ave. S, between E. 18th and 19th Sts., tel. 212/614–1200), which boasts some of the hottest looking people on the strip, possibly because its investors include the Ford modeling agency and David Lee Roth.

UNDER $5 • City Bakery. In this very high-tech, minimalist space, you'll find simply the best croissants, lemon tarts, hot chocolate (in season), gazpacho (likewise), and lemonade (ditto). The proprietor, Maury Rubin, is the author of the all-important *Book of Tarts,* and he's usually on hand to autograph a copy for you, when he isn't too busy flaming the tops of his crème brûlée tartelettes. Savvy New Yorkers come here often, as well they should. *22 E. 17th St., between 5th Ave. and Broadway, tel. 212/366–1414. Closed Sun.*

Ess-a-Bagel. Pretty much everyone agrees that these are the best bagels in Manhattan—fighting words, to be sure, but the lines at peak hours attest. Just ask for a shmear of cream cheese on whatever bulging bagel is freshest, and you'll never really be the same. Believe it. Then get back on line and try an onion bagel with cream cheese and Nova. The accommodations are slightly grubby, but the bagels are so good you wouldn't mind eating them sitting outside on the curb. *359 1st Ave., at E. 20th St., tel. 212/260–2252. Other location: 831 3rd Ave., between E. 50th and 51st Sts., Midtown East, tel. 212/980–1010.*

UNDER $10 • America. Been inside Madison Square Garden yet? This noisy restaurant seems just as vast, and the food is better (but no Knicks). Dishes are painstakingly regional, and named accordingly. Try one of 25 salads—we like the Omaha, which comes with warm bacon and spinach—or one of about 20 sandwiches; our fave is the Berkeley, with avocado, sprouts, and cucumber. *9–13 E. 18th St., between 5th Ave. and Broadway, tel. 212/505–2110.*

Friend of a Farmer. New Yorkers willingly endure Friend of a Farmer's ultracute gingerbread decor to indulge their hankerings for country cooking (even though they can look unusually sheepish doing so). Entrées are steamed or broiled, never fried. Menu highlights include the old-fashioned chicken potpie and the hefty Farmer's Sandwich. *77 Irving Pl., between E. 18th and 19th Sts., tel. 212/477–2188.*

Galaxy. This smallish, loopy, friendly place with its throwback (1967) decor and eclectic menu will win you over the moment you taste Michael Lipp's utterly unpretentious take on fusion cuisine, always served with a smile. The fresh water chestnuts with Bolivian quinoa, hijiki, grilled pineapple, and asparagus will leave you swooning. So will the West Indian callaloo pancake with salted baked coconut curry-agave sauce. He's also found several ways to cook with, well, hemp—from hemp nut–crusted catfish to hemp-crusted apple pie. Nothing on the menu is over $9.95, and most of the offerings are a good deal cheaper. *15 Irving Pl., corner of E. 15th St., tel. 212/777–3631.*

Heartland Brewery. Heartland is one of the city's most popular microbreweries, which means it's the latest watering hole for big, meaty Wall Street guys and their pulchritudinous ilk. There are eight microbrews ($4.75 per pint) on tap and a menu full of inventive pub grub, especially an eight-item "pu-pu platter" for two that features jalapeño poppers, buffalo wings, and enough other beerish flotsam and jetsam to keep you happy for about 45 minutes. *35 Union Sq. W, between E. 16th and 17th Sts., tel. 212/645–3400.*

Madras Mahal. A letter posted outside this kosher and 100% vegetarian Indian restaurant—part of Lexington Avenue's "Little India"—informs doubting customers that VEGETABLES ARE CLEANED UNDER SUPERVISION. NO BUGS OR INSECTS. How reassuring. Curries and such are fine, but the real deal is the all-you-can-eat lunch ($7). *104 Lexington Ave., between E. 27th and 28th Sts., tel. 212/684–4010.*

Old Town Bar. A zillion people—from cops to picky newspaper food critics to David Letterman—claim that this 1892 saloon serves some of the best burgers in the city. Just beware the weekend crowds. Salads and fancy grilled sandwiches are about $7. *45 E. 18th St., between Broadway and Park Ave. S, tel. 212/529–6732.*

Pete's Tavern. A zillion other people—from tipsy Irish regulars to families of ten to O. Henry, who wrote one of his most famous stories here, no doubt with the hiccups—claim that this even older saloon serves the best burgers in town. There are also nightly special offerings, and prime rib night (currently Tuesday) will quicken your heartbeat sure, and put quite a bounce in your step. *129 E. 18th St., at Irving Pl., tel. 212/473–7676. Subway: L, N, R, 4, 5, or 6 to Union Sq.*

Sam's Noodle Shop & Grill Bar. Attitude and atmosphere are minimal here; at least you get plenty of well-priced food like Mandarin noodle soups and sizzling platters like panfried tofu with vegetables. You can also pick your own vegetables, meat, or seafood to skewer and grill. *411 3rd Ave., at E. 29th St., tel. 212/213–2288.*

UNDER $15 • Chat 'n' Chew. Simply put: sassy home cookin' with no sense of propriety. Gorge yourself on Roseanne-size portions of macaroni and cheese "with the crunchy top," Not Your Mother's Meatloaf, or Thanksgiving on a Roll (roast turkey, stuffing, cranberry sauce, and mayo on ciabatta bread). And enjoy that trailer-park milieu. *10 E. 16th St., between 5th Ave. and Union Sq. W, tel. 212/243–1616.*

Park Avalon. From the outside, the Avalon looks like all the other overpriced restaurants on Park Avenue South. Happily, its new American/Mediterranean cuisine with an Italian flair is surprisingly affordable. And the startlingly beautiful clientele is included at no extra charge. *225 Park Ave. S, between E. 18th and 19th Sts., tel. 212/533–2500.*

Add a Ted Danson look-alike to the Old Town Bar and you'd have "Cheers."

Zen Palate. You're more likely to see a banker than a Buddhist in this starkly beautiful restaurant. The tone is set with Asian-influenced, strictly vegetarian dishes like the Harvest Delight (vegetables in sesame sauce), Sweet and Sour Sensation (fried soy protein and steamed broccoli) and Moo Shu Mexican style (kidney beans and soy gluten served in spinach crepes with a guacamole sauce). Note that there is a café on the street level, and a fancier dining room upstairs (enter on E. 16th Street). *34 Union Sq. E, at E. 16th St., tel. 212/614–9345. BYOB. Other locations: 663 9th Ave., at W. 46th St., Midtown West, tel. 212/582–1669; 2170 Broadway, between W. 76th and 77th Sts., Upper West Side, tel. 212/ 501–7768.*

WEST VILLAGE

The restaurants on the West Village's narrow tree-lined streets can be so tiny that their tables often spill onto sidewalks or into tranquil back gardens. If you think that's romantic, you're absolutely right. While the scene in the West Village proper has gotten a bit stale in recent years (gays prefer Chelsea, and hipsters have drifted over to the East Village), the neighborhood has plenty of reasonably priced options, especially on noisy **6th Avenue** and **7th Avenue South.** The cheapest eats, though, tend to be on the blocks around **New York University (NYU),** and in regions farther east. If you want "charming" and "romantic," try wandering along **West 4th Street, Bleecker Street,** or **Greenwich Avenue.** To sample a few of the cool crowd's hangouts, check out the **meat-packing district,** way off to the west by the Hudson River. If you find you need an oasis, you can linger at **Anglers and Writers** (420 Hudson St., at St. Luke's Pl., tel. 212/675–0810). Also, on **Washington Street,** south of West 12th Street, trendy bistros exist alongside refrigerated meat lockers. This can be a fairly rough area, so use caution at night.

UNDER $10 • Aggie's and **Aggie's Too.** The great Aggie herself says the AA fresh eggs are the main reason why breakfasts taste so good at this hip double-diner. Order those unbelievably wonderful eggs (and any other breakfast food) daily until 3 PM. Or maybe you'd like one of the scrumptious sandwiches. Or, well, Aggie has something for everyone, you'll see. *146 W. Houston St., at MacDougal St., tel. 212/673–8994.*

Benny's Burritos. Hip Benny's makes Cal-Mex tacos, enchiladas, and, above all, burritos the size of a beefy infant's arm. If you must, you can request nondairy tofu sour cream and whole-wheat tortillas, but what fun is that? Nearby, **Harry's Burritos** (76 W. 3rd St., at Thompson St., tel. 212/260–5588) does practically the same thing with a little less flair. *113 Greenwich Ave., between Jane and W. 12th Sts., tel. 212/ 633–9210. Other (original) location: 93 Ave. A, at E. 6th St., East Village, tel. 212/254–2054. Cash only.*

Chez Brigitte. This French bistro may be the size of a closet, but the neighborhood regulars agree that it's very big on charm. Sit at the counter and choose from deliciously spiced sandwiches as well as savory entrées like beef bourguignonne. Save room for a slice of homemade pie. *77 Greenwich Ave., at 11th St., tel. 212/929–6736. Cash only.*

SERIOUS SPLURGES

When your rich uncle and aunt accompany you to town with an empty stomach and a fat wallet, suggest one of the following restaurants, but make reservations well (did we say well?) in advance. What you're getting isn't just fancy food, but a piece of the True New York Experience: stunning decor, impeccable service, and true elbow rubs with the rich-and-famous. Such pampering costs about $65. Per person.

Chanterelle. One of the most enchanting dining experiences in America: contemporary French cuisine at its very finest and freshest, truly elegant service, and a magnificent room to enjoy it in. 2 Harrison St., at Hudson St., TriBeCa, tel. 212/966–6960.

Four Seasons. Its Grill Room has been the deal makers' power-lunch destination for decades. The Pool Room is relentlessly fabulous. 99 E. 52nd St., between Lexington and Park Aves., Midtown East, tel. 212/754–9494.

Gramercy Tavern. Unsurpassedly reliable new American cuisine, from watchfully sautéed foie gras with roasted spring onions, mission figs, and a balsamic reduction to roasted monkfish with pancetta, braised red cabbage, caraway, Jerusalem artichokes, and truffle vinaigrette to, well, you get the idea. 42 E. 20th St., between Broadway and Park Ave. S, Gramercy, tel. 212/477–0777.

Le Cirque 2000. The decor of the new setting is cirque de soleil on LSD, and some complain about blatant favoritism in the way you're treated. Reservations are snapped up faster than tenth-row center seats for "Rent," but the succulent French cuisine and celebrity-ogling justify it all. 455 Madison Ave., between E. 50th and 51st Sts., Midtown East, tel. 212/794–9292.

Nobu. TriBeCa Japanese, and most agree that it's the best in America. Certainly it's the most imaginative. Practice saying "Omikase" before you go— it means you're ordering the chef's pick of the day. 105 Hudson St., at Franklin St., TriBeCa, tel. 212/219–0500.

Peter Luger Steak House. Though it's in a sketchy neighborhood, this is widely and justifiably regarded as the best steak house in the country. Bring cash or a check. 178 Broadway, between Driggs and Bedford Aves., Williamsburg, Brooklyn, tel. 718/387–7400.

Union Square Cafe. The new American cuisine is somewhat less expensive than at other five-star restaurants, but it's no less thrilling—and every bit as popular—and the service is universally rated the very best in Manhattan. 21 E. 16th St., between 5th Ave. and Union Square W, Union Sq., tel. 212/243–4020.

John's Pizzeria. You should probably sample New York's Finest, and by hotly debated general consensus, this is it: If you live for thin-crusted pizza, topped by only the finest ingredients and blazed by a brick oven that's stoked up hours before the first pie goes in, get thee hence to John's, and accept no substitutes. *278 Bleecker St., between 6th Ave. and 7th Ave. S, tel. 212/243–1680.*

Moustache. You'll find some excellent Middle Eastern food at this very busy, tiny restaurant on a beautiful residential street. Try the house specialty pizza, a large pita bread dressed up like a pizza for one, with mushrooms, chicken, lamb, capers, artichokes, eggplant, and other toppings. *90 Bedford St., at Grove St., tel. 212/229–2220.*

Taquería de México. This small eatery proudly gives you a $5.95 lunch special: soup, mixed salad, and rice and beans; or a chicken burrito, rice and beans, and soda. The regular menu won't break the bank, either. The emphasis on authenticity is unusual and most welcome. *93 Greenwich Ave., between Bank and W. 12th Sts., tel. 212/255–5212. Cash only.*

UNDER $15 • French Roast. You'd think you were on the Left Bank by the French decor and very cool international-looking folk. It's laid back, often packed and open all night serving good bistro fare including steak frîtes and mussels Provençale. *458 6th Ave., at W. 11th St., tel. 212/533–2233.*

Home. This appropriately named little treasure features comfort food: chicken dumplings, fresh grilled trout, and hearty french toast breakfasts. Inside it's cozy and warm, and the garden patio out back is glorious. *20 Cornelia St., between W. 4th and Bleecker Sts., tel. 212/243–9579.*

Pink Tea Cup. Fans of Southern diner food will appreciate this shameless emporium, which will whip up the best smothered pork chops in town. Dinner entrées come with a pride of two vegetables, soup, salad, hot bread, and dessert. Breakfasts (from 8 AM) are just as good as you'd expect. And yes, the decor is quite pink. *42 Grove St., between Bedford and Bleecker Sts., tel. 212/807–6755. Cash only.*

Rio Mar. One reason to make the trek into the meat-packing district is Rio Mar's giant portions of traditional Spanish dishes, such as paella or *mariscade en salsa verde* (seafood in green sauce); another is the potent sangria and lively bar scene. *7 9th Ave., at Little W. 12th St., tel. 212/243–9015.*

Salam Cafe. This intimate Middle Eastern favorite featuring Syrian specialties is located on the ground floor of a brownstone. Big on atmosphere, the food is always terrific whether it's curry, couscous, or kebabs. *104 W. 13th St., at 6th Ave., tel. 212/741–0277.*

Tartine. Delicious dishes with a vaguely French accent, like *bouchée à la reine* (chicken potpie), quiche, and grilled polenta Provençale are served with a bit of French surliness at this tiny, attractive restaurant. Local hipsters don't mind waiting up to an hour for a table, especially for weekend brunch. *253 W. 11th St., at W. 4th St., tel. 212/229–2611. BYOB. Cash only. Closed Mon.*

Tortilla Flats. Come play some bingo or take the hula hoop for a spin at this loco diner. It's loud, tipsy fun (the pitchers of margaritas don't hurt). Filling the menu are basic enchiladas, tacos, burritos, and tostadas, not to mention shrimp fajitas and chicken mole. Plastic fruit garlands and Elvis paintings clutter the walls. *767 Washington St., at W. 12th St., tel. 212/243–1053.*

Village Natural Health Food Restaurant. Everything about the Village Natural is simple, from the wood furnishings to the organic, unprocessed entrées (many of which are dairy- and wheat-free). Try spaghetti with "wheatballs" or shiitake mushrooms sautéed with tofu. Omelets are served daily 11–4. *46 Greenwich Ave., between Charles and Perry Sts., tel. 212/727–0968.*

UNDER $20 • Florent. This endlessly hip meat-packing-district diner-cum-bistro with a mind of its very own remains the late-night favorite of a surreal mix of drag queens, truckers, club kids, and stray couples from Jersey. Maps (some of nonexistent places) and French flags cover the walls while reasonably priced French–American food fills the menu. For the true Fellini-esque experience, arrive after midnight; Florent is open around the clock on weekends. *69 Gansevoort St., between Washington and Greenwich Sts., tel. 212/989–5779. Cash only.*

Pò. By all means, treat yourself to a meal at this airy Northern Italian bistro. The people are pretty and the food is scrumptious, under the watchful eye of TV Food Network star (Molto) Mario Batali. Go hearty with grilled pork sausage and grilled baby octopus, or keep it light with white-bean ravioli tossed with balsamic vinegar. The menu changes constantly, but everything works. *31 Cornelia St., between Bleecker and W. 4th Sts., tel. 212/645–2189. Closed Mon.*

BEYOND MICKEY D'S

A number of citywide chains keep New Yorkers coming back for great, reliable, affordable eats. At the places listed below (many of which have additional locations) you can eat well for less than $10.

Burritoville. Some of the best burritos in town—including tons of veggie options. 451 Amsterdam Ave., between W. 81st and 82nd Sts., Upper West Side, tel. 212/787–8181. 141 2nd Ave., between E. 8th and 9th Sts., East Village, tel. 212/260–3300. 144 Chambers St., at Hudson St., TriBeCa, tel. 212/571–1144. 36 Water St., at Broad St., Lower Manhattan, tel. 212/747–1100.

Daikichi Sushi. These take-out shops serve some of the freshest and cheapest sushi in town. 2345 Broadway, between W. 85th and 86th Sts., Upper West Side, tel. 212/362–4283. 1156 6th Ave., at 45th St., Midtown West, tel. 212/ 719–0576. 45 E. 45th St., between Madison and Vanderbilt Aves., Midtown East, tel. 212/953–2468. 35 E. 8th St., at University Pl., West Village, tel. 212/ 254–1987. 32 Broadway, between Beaver St. and Exchange Pl., Lower Manhattan, tel. 212/747–0994.

Dallas BBQ. Hungry carnivores come here to gorge on heaping plates of cheap barbecue and warm corn bread. 27 W. 72nd St., between Columbus Ave. and Central Park W, Upper West Side, tel. 212/873–2004. 21 University Pl., at E. 8th St., West Village, tel. 212/674–4450. 132 2nd Ave., at St. Marks Pl., East Village, tel. 212/777–5574.

John's Pizzeria. Many New Yorkers claim John's makes the best pizzas in the city, bar none. 48 W. 65th St., between Columbus Ave. and Central Park W, Upper West Side, tel. 212/721–7001. 278 Bleecker St., between 6th Ave. and 7th Ave. S, West Village, tel. 212/243–1680.

Mary Ann's. The "especials de la casa" (house specials) at these kitschy Mexican joints are excellent. 2452 Broadway, at W. 91st St., Upper West Side, tel. 212/877–0132. 116 8th Ave., at W. 16th St., Chelsea, tel. 212/633–0877. 80 2nd Ave., at E. 5th St., East Village, tel. 212/475–5939.

EAST VILLAGE AND ALPHABET CITY

Once a Shangri-la for cost-conscious diners, everything in the East Village is steadily getting pricier. Still, the fact remains, nowhere in Manhattan will you find as many funky and cheap restaurants as in the East Village, be they Italian, Middle Eastern, Cambodian, Tibetan, Korean, Mexican, Filipino, Cuban, Burmese, Jewish, Creole, Japanese, Spanish, or plain old American. Farther east, you'll find the strange emergence of quality dining (mostly French) on Avenue B. Even better, most places stay open until the wee hours, especially in summer when the sidewalks are packed at all hours.

East 6th Street between 1st and 2nd avenues is known as "Little India" for its dozens of savory Indian, Bangladeshi, and Pakistani joints—many of which offer live, free traditional music in the evenings. Walk down the block and you'll score a handful of coupons worth up to 30% off your next meal. Most places here allow you to bring your own beer or wine, though a couple will charge a small corkage fee—even if you're drinking King Cobra. Eastern European (particularly Ukrainian) coffee shops are plentiful on **2nd Avenue** from East 7th to 9th streets. **Avenue A** overflows with all sorts of interesting options, including a number of sushi bars just north of Houston Street. For superior people-watching, pick one of the sidewalk cafés lining **Tompkins Square Park**—try Café Pick Me Up or Life Cafe (*see below*). One practical note: The East Village is not easy to reach on the subway unless you take the L line to 1st or 3rd avenues, or the F to 2nd Avenue and Houston. You're better off riding a bus or catching a cab, especially late at night.

UNDER $5 • Dojo. The hordes of East Villagers who favor this vegetarian snack shack don't seem to mind that most of the burgers and salads arrive smothered in "Japanese-style tahini" dressing (actually a carrot-based vinaigrette with not a hint of tahini). Neither should you: You can definitely chow here for less than $5. *24 St. Marks Pl., between 2nd and 3rd Aves., tel. 212/674–9821. Cash only.*

Kai Kai. With only three tables inside and three out, tiny Kai Kai is not the place to bring your extended Italian family. But you can order the $4.50 lunch special (Pad Thai or Curry and a soda) and take it across the road to the park. Thai iced coffee and tea are perfect for summer. *131 Ave A., between E. 8th and 9th Sts., tel. 212/420–5909. Cash only.*

Elvie's Turo-Turo. Get in line at this tiny Filipino cafeteria and "turo" (point) to whatever looks good, from *lumpia* (a cousin to the Chinese egg roll) to *ginisang gulay* (shrimp and pork stir-fried with seasonal vegetables) to *adobo* (grilled meat marinated in soy sauce, vinegar, garlic, and bay leaves). It's $3.75 for one entrée, $5 for two. *214 1st Ave., between E. 12th and 13th Sts., tel. 212/473–7785. Cash only.*

Odessa. Sure, they've got omelets and cheeseburgers at this 24-hour Eastern European diner. But what really make this place famous are the *latkes* (potato pancakes), *pierogi* (dumplings stuffed with a combination of meat, cheese, cabbage, and mushrooms), and giant cheese- or fruit-filled blintzes. Just down the street, **Leshko's Coffee Shop** (111 Ave. A, at E. 7th St., tel. 212/473–9208) serves up similar, but not quite as gratifying, gut-busting Eastern European home-cooking. *117 Ave. A, between St. Marks Pl. and E. 9th St., tel. 212/473–8916. Open 24 hrs. Cash only.*

A food critic once described the Ukrainian borscht soup at 24-hour Veselka (144 2nd Ave., at E. 9th St., tel. 212/228–9682) as "tasting like something your grandmother would make if you came home with a black eye."

UNDER $10 • ACME Bar and Grill. A self-proclaimed "okay place to eat," ACME serves Southern faves like chicken-fried steak, fried chicken, and po'boy sandwiches—all better than "okay." Spice things up with the house hot sauce, labeled ALMOST FLAMMABLE. The rock venue Under ACME (*see* Live Music *in* Chapter 6) lies—surprise—under ACME. *9 Great Jones St., between Broadway and Lafayette St., tel. 212/420–1934.*

Angelica Kitchen. What's the vegan definition of heaven? Probably a place like this, where the food is 100% organic and free of animal products. They even serve a funky barley brew in place of regular coffee. Try the Dragon Bowl, a plate of steamed seasonal veggies with rice, beans, and tofu. *300 E. 12th St., between 1st and 2nd Aves., tel. 212/228–2909. Cash only.*

Esashi. At Esashi, visibly excited East Villagers sit next to visiting Japanese businessmen for superb and inexpensive sushi à la carte, both nigiri and in rolls. Dinner specials (5–8 PM) include udon noodle soups ($7) and big sushi combos ($10). It's not very fancy, but then neither is a Zen garden. *32 Ave. A, between E. 2nd and 3rd Sts., tel. 212/505–8726.*

Frutti de Mare. Savvy New Yorkers usually pass on the *frutti de mare* (seafood) in favor of tasty terrestrial entrées, notably the chicken with balsamic sauce and the homemade pumpkin ravioli in pesto cream sauce. Though the decor is classy, the attitude is very low-key. *84 E. 4th St., at 2nd Ave., tel. 212/979–2034. Cash only.*

Kiev. According to a rough-and-tumble crew of regulars, Kiev's got the best Eastern European cooking west of the Volga. It serves breakfast round-the-clock and has a veggie dinner special (potato pancake, kasha varnishkes, and steamed vegetables) that's bigger than a Yugo. *117 E. 7th St., at 2nd Ave., tel. 212/674–4040 or 212/674–4041. Open 24 hrs. Cash only.*

Life Cafe. On Sunday, slip on your shades and stumble over to Life Cafe for the huge breakfast, coffee and mimosa or Bloody Mary included. Even on days when you don't feel like hell, their Tex-Mex grub tastes pretty damn good. The outdoor tables are great for pondering the action in adjacent Tompkins Square Park. *343 E. 10th St., at Ave. B, tel. 212/477–8791. Other location: 1 Sheridan Sq., between W. 4th St. and Washington Pl., West Village.*

Panna. It's a toss-up between most of the homogeneous Indian restaurants on 6th Street, but the humorous, helpful staff in brightly decorated Panna inch it ahead of the pack. They won't moan if you mix and match your order, varying a little from the set menu of classic tandoori and curry dishes. The Bombay chicken sautéed in the chef's secret spices is the owner's favorite. They even have a separate room for smokers, a rarity in the big brother apple these days, and you can bring in your own beer or wine to complete a triumvirate of simple vices. *330 E. 6th St., between 1st and 2nd Aves., tel. 212/475–9274.*

Sahara East. If you think couscous can only be bought in small cardboard boxes marked "instant," you'll sit up and slap yourself after a spoonful from this upscale Middle Eastern restaurant. It's fluffy, soft, and delicious, and it comes with vegetables, grilled lamb, chicken, or fish. *184 1st Ave., between E. 11th and 12th Sts., tel. 212/353–9000. Cash only.*

Village Mingala. You're greeted with the words *min ga la ba* ("pleasant day") at this Burmese restaurant, then served succulent southeast Asian specialties like squid salad, duck with green and hot red peppers, or Burmese chicken curry with potatoes. The wood-paneled dining room is a bit dark, but not unpleasantly so. *21–23 E. 7th St., between 2nd and 3rd Aves., tel. 212/529–3656 or 212/260–0457.*

Yaffa Café. If you've been given only one meal on Planet Earth, and you happen to be in the East Village, eat it here. The kitschy decor is cool, the patrons are cool, and the waiters and waitresses bedecked in black are just too cool. Filling the five-page menu are cool foods like Berber chicken (with spicy lemon-basil sauce) and the prodigious Yaffa Salad. In summer, grab a seat in the huge, leafy back garden. *97 St. Marks Pl., between 1st Ave. and Ave. A, tel. 212/674–9302. Open 24 hrs.*

UNDER $15 • Avenue A. This is not your typical sushi joint. In addition to the standard Japanese tempura and teriyaki dishes, it's got whacked-out sushi rolls like the Panic (softshell crab tempura and plum paste) and the Dragon (eel, roe, and avocado). Best of all, it sports the ambience of a Tokyo nightclub, including black walls, a DJ spinning house music, and an achingly hip crowd. *103 Ave. A, between E. 6th and 7th Sts., tel. 212/982–8109.*

Great Jones Cafe. It's got a jukebox with one of the best selections in the world and only 10 tables, so you can bet your weight in okra that this Cajun diner is always crowded. A summer favorite is the Crayfish Boil, a pound of the spicy crustaceans that you shell yourself. *54 Great Jones St., between Lafayette St. and Bowery, tel. 212/674–9304. Cash only.*

John's. Possibly the best cheap Italian food outside of Italy, this classy eatery has been around since 1908, when the Belgium mosaic floor and delicate wall murals were finished. Specials like the Portobello mushrooms marinated and grilled and the rollintina of veal and chicken stuffed with a multiple-cheese sauce look and taste great. The elegant, candlelit white-linen tables make you feel like you must be spending a ton of money, until you get your bill, that is. *302 E. 12th St., between 1st and 2nd Aves., tel. 212/475–9531.*

La Gould Finch. One of a cluster of new, quality restaurants to open on Ave. B, this French/Cajun eatery is already getting a name for its savory and sweet crepes; try one filled with sautéed leeks and goat cheese, or another with banana praline. It looks a little like a whorehouse inside (no bad thing), with red feathers on the ceiling, thick rugs, and ornate, high-back chairs. *93 Ave. B, between E. 6th and 7th Sts., tel 212/253–6309.*

La Paella. If you're unfamiliar with Spanish cuisine, here's what you need to do: (1) Arrive with a large group of friends; (2) drink several pitchers of sangria; (3) order up a mess of hot or cold tapas; and (4) come back another day for paella (smallest serving feeds two for $20–$32), a traditional stew of rice, saffron, garlic, sausage, and seafood. *214 E. 9th St., between 2nd and 3rd Aves., tel. 212/598–4321.*

Lavagna. Here's another example of the new spirit of cuisine springing up on once-barren Avenue B. The striking red exterior masks an exposed-brick decor with classic white tablecloths and an original tin ceiling. The Italian menu can be a little pricey, but the adventurous pastas are affordable and very good. If you want to splash out, go for the oven-roasted halibut with grilled eggplant and truffled summer pea coulis. *545 5th St. between Aves. A and B, tel. 212/979–1005.*

Second Avenue Deli. Though it's completely charmless, this has long been one of the city's premier spots for kosher noshes. Try Jewish favorites like gefilte fish and Chicken in the Pot (noodles, carrots, and a matzoh ball), or sink your teeth into a mammoth pastrami sandwich. *156 2nd Ave., at E. 10th St., tel. 212/677–0606.*

St. Dymphna's. Part of the Irish renaissance on St. Marks, this welcoming nouvelle-Gaelic eatery with a sun-splashed garden and full bar is rapidly becoming a top spot on the ever-popular strip. The beef-and-Guinness casserole, with vegetables and mashed potatoes, is a perfect panacea for the New York snows. In summertime, try the crab cakes with vegetable succotash and green pepper sauce. The huge, fry-up Irish breakfast is just right to kickstart your morning. By the way, Dymphna was the patron saint of mental illness; perfect for the Village. *118 St. Marks Pl., between Ave. A and 1st Ave., tel. 212/254–6636.*

Two Boots. This popular spot (with some truly ugly plastic decor) mixes Cajun and Italian cuisines to produce delicious dishes like pizza with andouille sausage and barbecued shrimp ($18 for large) or Linguine Dominique (blackened chicken with spinach linguine). It's popular with families as well as with cool Village types; arrive early on weekend nights. The "boots" in question are Louisiana and Italy, if you hadn't already guessed. See below for Brooklyn location. *37 Ave. A, between E. 2nd and 3rd Sts., tel. 212/505–2276.*

LOWER EAST SIDE

The Lower East Side is an awkward mix of old and new, of kosher eateries unchanged for decades and conspicuously trendy bars and cafés. Some areas have remained largely unchanged since the first Jewish immigrants settled here around the turn of the century, though bagel shops and delis are becoming scarce. **Ludlow** and **Houston streets** represent the epicenter of the Lower East Side, as a parade of East Village colonialists expand their drinking and posing territory. Fortunately, **Moshe's** (181 E. Houston St., tel. 212/475–9629), an old-world Jewish bakery, is still turning out delicious bagels and bialys. The Puerto Rican community has a Lower East Side toehold, a cluster of super-cheap take-out stands near the intersection of **Delancey** and **Clinton streets.** If you crave doner at 4 AM, **Bereket** (187 E. Houston St., at Orchard St., tel. 212/475–7700, open 24 hrs) sells kebabs and other Turkish goodies "just like the ones in Istanbul" for less than $5.

UNDER $5 • F. Restaurant. This is the most popular of the Puerto Rican take-out stands crammed onto the corner of Clinton and Delancey streets—the owner is actually Cuban but don't tell a soul. Everything (except roasted cow tongue and blood sausage) is deep fried and costs $1. And even if you have no idea what *alcapurria* or *pastelillo* are, you'll find them mighty tasty. *105 Clinton St., at Delancey St., tel. 212/475–3029. Cash only.*

Yonah Shimmel's Knishery. The Shimmel family has been making knishes (fried or baked turnovers; $1.35) for more than 100 years; some even claim that they invented 'em. Choose from 12 varieties, including potato, mushroom, kasha, and chocolate cream cheese. *Fressers* (Yiddish for "gluttons") should start with a bowl of cold borscht (85¢) and a half-dozen latkes (potato pancakes; $1 each). *137 E. Houston St., at 2nd Ave., tel. 212/477–2858. Cash only.*

UNDER $10 • Baby Jupiter. Definitely new Lower East Side, Jupiter is a faux '50s diner with an austere metallic exterior, and booths, bar, and rock 'n' roll on the inside. The menu is more daring than the average diner; try the eggs Adolf—poached on salmon cakes with sautéed spinach, served on an English muffin with chipotle hollandaise sauce. *170 Orchard St., at Stanton St., tel. 982–2229.*

Cibao. Rice and beans are the basics of Dominican cuisine, and nobody does this dish better than Cibao. But if you feel like something more exotic, try one of the hearty stews or the mysterious (as in not quite sure what's in it) beef tripe soup. The ear-splitting Latin music and bright plastic decor somehow add to the charm of it all. *72 Clinton St., at Rivington St., tel. 212/228–0703. Cash only.*

El Sombrero (The Hat). In the days before the great East Village migration, The Hat existed as a beloved neighborhood dive. Times change, though: not only has The Hat attracted the young and the pierced, but it's now a magnet for fun-seekers from the entire tri-state area. However, it serves some of the best Mexican-style food on the Lower East Side. Try a burrito accompanied by a pedestrian-yet-potent margarita. *108 Ludlow St., at Stanton St., tel. 212/254–4188. Cash only.*

Festival Mexicana. A more sedate alternative to its Ludlow St. neighbor, The Hat, this authentic, above-average bean slinger serves Mexican favorites like chile rellenos, quesadillas, and burritos, plus novelties like lamb tacos (3 for $5.50). *120 Rivington St., between Essex and Suffolk Sts., tel. 212/995–0154. Cash only.*

Katz's Delicatessen. Katz's has been serving knishes and hefty deli sandwiches to Lower East Siders—including magician Harry Houdini, a regular—since 1888. You'll need to shout your order, since the

BAGELS: THE HOLE STORY

Most cafés and corner stores sell plastic-wrapped bagels, but these are usually too tough or just plain stale. For the real deal, visit one of the popular bagel bakeries listed below. Just don't ask which one is best—no two New Yorkers can agree on how to eat a bagel or where to buy one.

TRADITIONAL BAGELS: H&H Bagels (2239 Broadway, at W. 80th St., Upper West Side, tel. 212/595–8003 or 800/692–2435 for U.S. deliveries; 639 W. 46th St., tel. 212/595–8000).

BIGGEST BAGELS: Ess-a-Bagel (831 3rd Ave., at E. 50th St., Midtown, tel. 212/980–1010; 359 1st Ave., at E. 21st St., Gramercy, tel. 212/260–2252).

24-HOUR BAGELS: Columbia Hot Bagels (2836 Broadway, between W. 110th and 111th Sts., Morningside Heights, tel. 212/222–3200).

BAGELS OF MANY FLAVORS: Bagels on the Square (7 Carmine St., between Bleecker St. and 6th Ave., West Village, tel. 212/691–3041).

LARGEST SELECTION OF SHMEARS: Bagels on Amsterdam (see Upper West Side, above).

BEST SHOP NAME: Kossar's Bialystoker Kuchen Bakery (367 Grand St., between Essex and Norfolk Sts., Lower East Side, tel. 212/473–4810).

staff is usually bickering behind the counter in thick New Yawk accents. It's Bill Clinton's favorite deli, and his photo gawks at you from every wall. *205 E. Houston St., at Ludlow St., tel. 212/254–2246.*

Ratner's. This dairy (no meat) kosher restaurant is a Lower East Side institution. The food is generally overrated, but the blintzes and vegetarian noshes are good. There's a bar in back called **Lansky Lounge,** in honor of Depression-era gangster and Ratner's patron Meyer Lansky; it opens at 8 PM. *138 Delancey St., between Suffolk and Norfolk Sts., tel. 212/677–5588. Closed Fri. 3 PM–Sat. sundown.*

LITTLE ITALY

If you think that Little Italy is the best place in town for Italian food, you need to wake up, stop reading Mario Puzo, and smell the garlic. True, the *ristoranti* here serve authentic—if often pricey—Italian food. It's just that you're paying to sit with a bunch of tourists gushing about how "Olde Worlde" Little Italy is—when, actually, it isn't. Chinatown continues to boom and encroach, and Little Italy has shrunk to just one lonely little avenue, **Mulberry Street.** Walk its length and you'll be accosted by a jacket-wearing waiter at the door of every virtually interchangeable restaurant, bidding you *buon giorno* and tempting you inside with discounts or unbelievably cheap lunch specials—which, come to think of it, is precisely what you'd encounter all over Italy. At some point you'll probably give in, and suck down a plate of spaghetti, order a cappuccino and tiramisu, squint your eyes, and imagine you're in Rome. A couple of glasses of Chianti will certainly help. For something a tad cheaper, try one of Little Italy's many coffee-houses (*see* Cafés and Coffee Bars, *below*).

UNDER $10 • Il Fornaio. This is just about the only place in Little Italy where you can dine like a Mafia don without needing the fortune of a Carlo Ponti. Dive into a generous plate of chicken parmesan or *rigatoni con zucchini*. *132A Mulberry St., between Hester and Grand Sts., tel. 212/226–8306.*

Luna's. The peeling murals of Sicily and the sagging floorboards make it clear this ain't Brunelleschi's Duomo. Despite all that, the food is good and the line often snakes out the door and around the corner. Come early or wait it out. *112 Mulberry St., near Canal St., tel. 212/226–8657.*

Puglia. People come to Puglia in large groups for two reasons: to gorge on decent pastas and to drink prodigious quantities of vino at one of the communal tables. By the end of the night, most folks are sloshed and singing along with Jorge (a man with a serious Elvis fixation), who croons in Italian while noodling on a cheesy Casio keyboard. *189 Hester St., between Mott and Mulberry Sts., tel. 212/966–6006.*

UNDER $15 • Umberto's Clam House. Umberto's is famous for being the place where mobster Joey "Crazy" Gallo had his last supper in 1973: He was whacked by the mob while eating a birthday dinner of scungili. Pastas are pricey, all things considered, but good. *129 Mulberry St., at Hester St., tel. 212/431–7545.*

CHINATOWN

Ask a handful of New Yorkers what their favorite Chinatown restaurant is, and you'll get as many different answers. This is a crowded, bustling, vibrant neighborhood, and restaurants come and go at a manic pace. But don't be deterred: Hit the streets, ponder the boxes of dried what-have-you stationed outside the live-fish markets, and search out your very own favorite pork-bun or custard pie bakery. And know that Chinatown is more diverse than the name suggests: You'll find dishes from Hong Kong, Shanghai, Bangkok, Seoul, Hanoi, and Taipei, all within walking distance of one another. Whatever else you can say about it, Chinatown ain't dull.

The waiters at Luna's are famously rude: Don't be startled if you're greeted with a snarl and told to "quit fooling around and order some food."

Though Chinatown's restaurants often aren't much to look at and rarely cater to tourists, they do offer phenomenally cheap lunch specials. Most are clustered around the intersection of **Bayard** and **Mott streets.** Just off The Bowery, Doyer Street is a little treasure trove of Vietnamese and Thai eateries. For a quick snack (like yummy coconut rolls), try bakeries **New Lung Fung** (41 Mott St., between Pell and Bayard Sts., tel. 212/233–7447) or **Manna 2** (87 E. Broadway, near Forsyth St., tel. 212/267–6200). Both offer a dizzying array of delectable Chinese pastries, cakes, and sweet breads for under $1. The **Chinatown Ice Cream Factory** (65 Bayard St., between Mott and Elizabeth Sts., tel. 212/608–4170) has old standbys like vanilla and chocolate, as well as more exotic flavors like red bean, lychee, ginger, green tea, and taro.

UNDER $5 • Bo Ky. At this spartan joint you can select from over 25 Vietnamese and Chinese soups, all loaded with tasty morsels like shrimp balls, squid, roast duck, and various noodles. Service is speedy and polite. *80 Bayard St., between Mulberry and Mott Sts., tel. 212/406–2292. Cash only.*

Excellent Dumpling House. The green tile walls give it the look of a public rest room, but get over it— the dumplings really are excellent. So are the Shanghai-style noodle soups and stir-frys. At lunchtime the place is packed, with good reason. *111 Lafayette St., between Canal and Walker Sts., tel. 212/219–0212. Cash only.*

Sweet 'n' Tart Cafe. Restore your inner harmony at this crowded snack shop with a few *tong shui* (Chinese sweets believed to have healing properties). The most popular are double-boiled Chinese pears with almonds, licorice-infused gelatin, and walnut broth. The delicious dumplings and noodle soups have no curative properties; they simply taste great. *76 Mott St., at Canal St., tel. 212/334–8088. Cash only.*

UNDER $10 • 31 Division Dim Sum House. You need to be sociable at this spartan dim sum diner: Waiters will lead you to the first open seat, often at an already occupied table. On weekend afternoons expect long lines of locals eager for *har gow* (steamed shrimp dumplings). Dim sum is served daily 7:30–4. *31 Division St., between Bowery and E. Broadway, tel. 212/431–9063.*

House of Vegetarian. The devilish chefs here concoct faux animal flesh out of vegetable gluten, which allows vegetarians to keep their karma intact while tearing into Chinese dishes like lemon "chicken" or Peking "spareribs." Most entrées are $7–$9. *68 Mott St., between Canal and Bayard Sts., tel. 212/226–6572. Cash only.*

Nha Trang. You can make a complete meal from Nha Trang's Vietnamese rice-noodle soups, called *pho.* But then you'd miss out on all the zesty, unusual entrées made with barbecued beef, pork, curry chicken, or frogs' legs. *87 Baxter St., between Bayard and Canal and Sts., tel. 212/233–5948. Cash only.*

Thailand Restaurant. Why bother flying to Bangkok when the chef right here is a genius, producing authentic Thai curries, and prodigiously seasoned noodle and rice dishes? The dining room—decorated with dolls and masks from Thailand—is one of the most elegant in Chinatown. *106 Bayard St., at Baxter St., tel. 212/349–3132.*

Triple Eight Palace. Chinatown's most popular place for dim sum is a chaotic restaurant the size of a football field, crowded from 8 AM on with Cantonese-speaking customers. Rolling by on squeaky carts are 45 varieties of dim sum, from which you'll select *without* the aid of an English menu (just smile and nod and point politely). Only tourists come here for dinner. Dim sum served daily 8–4. *88 E. Broadway, near Market St., tel. 212/941–8886.*

Vietnam. O.K., so the name won't win any originality awards, but this might just be the best Vietnamese restaurant in town. The decor is simple, basic even, with linoleum floor and plain wood tables. But the menu reads like an encyclopedia of classic Vietnamese cuisine. The ultrafresh summer rolls alone make the trip worth while. And the frog's legs in black-bean sauce don't taste like chicken. *11 Doyer St., at Bowery, tel. 212/693–0725.*

UNDER $15 • Joe's Shanghai. The menu's huge and everything's pretty good, but this place is usually packed for one reason: steamed buns. Select from a number of fillings like shrimp, pork, or vegetables, it doesn't really matter, they all taste just about perfect. Joe's soups are also worth a try. *9 Pell St., between Mott St. and Bowery, tel. 212/233–8888.*

Pho Viet Huong. The *bo la nho* (barbecued beef wrapped in grape leaves) at this Vietnamese restaurant is extraordinarily delicious. Entrées like *com tom cari dau que* (curry shrimp and rice) or *ca chien chua ngot* (sweet-and-sour fish) are equally succulent. Save room for guava ice cream. *73 Mulberry St., between Bayard and Canal Sts., tel. 212/233–8988.*

SOHO

Many of the restaurants in glamorous, gallery-filled SoHo are too expensive for travelers on moderate budgets. After all, if you're closing a deal on an $85,000 Stella, you'd look gauche taking your prospective buyer to a greasy spoon. Your options? You can join the Beautiful People and damn the costs. Or you can forsake ambience for a good feed at the smattering of delis and health-food stores in SoHo, notably **Whole Foods** (117 Prince St., between Greene and Wooster Sts., tel. 212/982–1000). SoHo also has two of the city's favorite fancy marketplaces—**Gourmet Garage** (453 Broome St., at Mercer St., tel. 212/941–5850), open daily 8 AM–8:30 PM, and **Dean & Deluca** (*see* Markets and Specialty Shops, *below*)—which offer affordable take-out sandwiches. The most cogent SoHo scene is found along **West Broadway,** especially on late-summer evenings: A sophisticated, often European crowd packs every sidewalk table between Houston and Canal streets.

UNDER $10 • Bell Caffe. Many people describe Bell Caffe as "relaxed." After all, the couches sag and the tables are battered—and it's one of the few places in SoHo where you can simply hang out. But ever since Drew "Firestarter" Barrymore was spotted here it's been in danger of being upgraded to "trendy." Besides serving an eclectic menu of steamed mussels, gazpacho, and chicken dumplings, it's got live music nightly, cover-free. *See also* Bars *in* Chapter 6. *310 Spring St., between Hudson and Greenwich Sts., tel. 212/334–2355.*

Fanelli's Cafe. This 1872 relic is also a classic, unpretentious pub, with its dark wood, tiled floors, chummy barflies, and permanent reek of spilled ale. Join the crowd with a brew and a burger or a snack: chicken wings, stuffed potato skins, or Cuban black-bean salad. *94 Prince St., at Mercer St., tel. 212/226–9412. $50 minimum on credit cards.*

Jerry's. At lunch, loudly dressed art connoisseurs and upwardly nubile teenage models nibble tuna salad on greens or sliced chicken breast with roasted-tomato mayonnaise. The decor— red vinyl booths, zebra-striped walls, and glaring green-framed mirrors—exudes as much attitude as the patrons. *101 Prince St., between Greene and Mercer Sts., tel. 212/966–9464.*

Stock up on heavenly fresh bread ($2) at SoHo's charming, 75-year-old Vesuvio Bakery (160 Prince St., between Thompson St. and W. Broadway, tel. 212/925–8248), a favorite backdrop of fashion photographers.

Kelley and Ping. All day long, black-clad artists and vintage-clothing store clerks pop into this chaotic noodle house/Asian grocery/tea shop for stir-fry, spring rolls, and Vietnamese, Japanese, Cantonese, or Thai noodles. Stacked sacks of Thai black rice and huge jars of tea enhance the *feng shui*. It's packed to burst at lunch time. *127 Greene St., between Houston and Prince Sts., tel. 212/228–1212.*

Lupe's East L.A. Kitchen. Okay, so it's no longer a secret—but this laid-back, divey little Mexican joint is still an un-SoHo haven for luscious quesadillas with rice, beans, and salad or large burritos, all served with killer salsa. *110 6th Ave., at Watts St., tel. 212/966–1326.*

Moondance Diner. Rod Serling could have filmed a "Twilight Zone" in this renovated railroad car on a desolate block. Inside is a 1950s diner with sparkly, blue plastic booths and a big selection of glorious greasy food. Thick milk shakes and root-beer floats complete matters. *80 6th Ave., at Grand St., tel. 212/226–1191.*

UNDER $15 • Abyssinia. At this Ethiopian restaurant, adventurous patrons sit on traditional tiny woven stools and enjoy authentic dishes like ye'beg alitcha (lamb in ginger-garlic sauce), which you scoop up with sweet and spongy *injera* bread. Combination plates are made for two or more to share. *35 Grand St., at Thompson St., tel. 212/226–5959.*

Chez Bernard. Bernard is no common butcher but rather an artiste, a man in a spotless smock who saws sides of beef into perfect sculpture. His restaurant serves everything from basic sandwiches to magnificent pâtés and full-blown French meals. *323 W. Broadway, between Grant Ave. and Canal St., tel. 212/343–2583.*

Félix. This moderately priced little bistro reeks of the Left Bank. Whether you dine inside or alfresco, the service is friendly and the contemporary fare is presented with panache. Try the steak with thin, crunchy french fries. *340 W. Broadway, at Grand St., tel. 212/431–0021.*

Helianthus Vegetarian. Tuck into that Lamb of Happiness or Sweet and Sour Delight without guilt, because all the food at this happy, happy, happy vegetarian café is 100% meat-free. Amazing what you can do with soy protein, wheat gluten, a Chinese wok, and considerable ingenuity. *48 MacDougal St., between W. Houston and Prince Sts., tel. 212/598–0387.*

Jean Claude. It's smaller than a Left Bank apartment, but somehow this elegant bistro puts out affordable platefuls of truly inspired French cooking. Check out the Atlantic salmon in fennel broth; pan-seared monkfish with potato purée and eggplant rounds; or roast Cornish game hen with herb risotto. *137 Sullivan St., between Prince and Houston Sts., tel. 212/475–9232. Cash only.*

Liam. Another moderately priced bistro in overpriced SoHo. The chef (William Prunty) used to work at Jean Claude before going it on his own. The lamb and exotic ravioli dishes are favorites with the mixed, relatively casual crowd (no one's ever really casual in SoHo). *170 Thompson St., between Bleecker and Houston Sts., tel 212/387–0666.*

SoHo Kitchen and Bar. People don't come here for the gourmet pizzas with toppings like Thai chicken, or even for the salads and grilled specialties. The main draw is wine: 110 vintages sold by the glass ($4.50 and up). *103 Greene St., between Prince and Spring Sts., tel. 212/925–1866. Subway: B, D, F, or Q to Broadway–Lafayette St.; also 6 to Spring St.*

Spring Street Natural Restaurant and Bar. Lousy name, great grub. A big, open, wood-floor room with a long bar makes a casual setting for some seriously healthy dining. Two vegetarian dishes are standouts: corn-fried, organic *seitan* (also known as wheat meat), in two dipping sauces, and a crispy tempeh. *62 Spring St., at Lafayette St., tel. 212/966–0290.*

UNDER $20 • L'Ecole. You're dying for a grossly extravagant French meal. You can't afford Lutèce or Chantarelle (where dinner will run you a good $75). Luckily there's L'Ecole, the 100% student-run restaurant at the French Culinary Institute, where aspiring chefs are taught by masters from New York's top restaurants. L'Ecole's prix-fixe lunches (three courses; $18) and dinners (four courses; $25) are worth every penny. And New Yorkers have figured that out: Note that same-day reservations are required Monday–Thursday; for Friday and Saturday reserve at least one week in advance. *462 Broadway, at Grand St., tel. 212/219–3300. Closed Sun.*

Penang. This place follows a simple recipe: Take traditional Malaysian dishes—from *tuland gunung api* (fried pork ribs) to *ikan bakar* (sea bass wrapped in banana leaves)—and combine them with over-the-top ding-dong Tiki decor, including a waterfall and waving palm fronds. Then stir in a hip crowd that's heavy on drag queens. *109 Spring St., between Greene and Mercer Sts., tel. 212/274–8883. Subway: C or E to Spring St. Other location: 240 Columbus Ave., at 71st St., tel. 212/769–8889.*

TRIBECA

TriBeCa residents have conflicting feelings about their neighborhood's paucity of restaurants: After all, there are only so many times you can eat in Bob De Niro's posh **Tribeca Grill** (375 Greenwich St., at Franklin St., tel. 212/941–3900). On the other hand, people here don't want SoHo's trendy bistros and high prices. The end result is that on nights and weekends, TriBeCa's streets are empty and . . . even a little creepy. **Broadway** is the place to go if you're looking for fast food. For snacks and such, **Greenwich Street** offers some interesting options, notably **Bazzini's** (339 Greenwich St., at Jay St., tel. 212/334–1280), which has been selling mixed nuts, candy, and ice cream since 1886. The **Pennsylvania Pretzel Co.** (295 Greenwich St., at Chambers St., tel. 212/587–5938) does nothing but hot pretzels, topped with garlic, cinnamon, cheese, or chocolate.

UNDER $10 • Bubby's. If you can overlook the trendiness and the ridiculous name, Bubby's offers great people-watching and an eclectic menu of fine food. It's totally laid-back in a stylish (read: Gen-X) way and the price is right. *120 Hudson St., at N. Moore St., tel. 212/219–0666.*

Yaffa's Bar and Restaurant. At this sprawling boho lair—furnished with vintage couches and weird abstract sculptures, rather like a Southern whorehouse—the food is a multiethnic medley of Spanish tapas, sandwiches, and Mediterranean entrées. They offer a big and highly popular bargain brunch ($10) on weekends. Next door, **Yaffa's Tea Room** (tel. 212/966–0577) serves the same fare in addition to high tea ($15 per person) weekdays 2–5; for this treat, reservations are required a day in advance. *353 Greenwich St., at Harrison St., tel. 212/274–9403.*

UNDER $15 • Franklin Station Cafe. Nothing in the name would lead you to expect a warehouse-turned-bistro that plays French rock, pours café au lait, and serves Malaysian dishes like satay chicken and eggplant curry fish, along with more prosaic sandwiches. For breakfast, go ahead and try a curry chicken puff and mango milk shake to get your day off to a peculiar start. *222 W. Broadway, between Franklin and White Sts., tel. 212/274–8525. BYOB.*

Odeon. Yes, this is the restaurant featured on the cover of *Bright Lights Big City*. Established in 1980, this was one of the neighborhood's first restaurants; it's still one of its best. Neon, vinyl banquettes, and Formica tables make for a striking art deco setting. Top-notch fare includes crab-and-potato fritters with soy-daikon sauce, and a grilled lamb and leek sandwich on country bread. *145 W. Broadway, at Thomas St., 212/233–0507.*

LOWER MANHATTAN

This is Manhattan's mighty financial district, and something about its skyscrapers and canyonlike streets makes good restaurants wither and die (either it's the lack of sun or the superabundance of bond traders). While high-rolling types motor uptown for their two-martini lunches, regular working stiffs simply saunter over to **Broadway** between Pine and Liberty streets to pick up a $1.25 hot dog or $2.75 take-out carton of chow mein from the weekday-only jumble of street carts. There's an amazing variety of cuisines represented, and all the chefs are pretty talented with their mobile steam trays. When the weather is fair, take your lunch over to **Liberty Park** (Liberty St., between Trinity Pl. and Broadway). Keep in mind that most people flee Lower Manhattan right after work, and that restaurants tend to close early.

UNDER $5 • McDonald's. If you're enthused because the McDonald's at the Spanish Steps in Rome has a waterfall and salad bar, you're gonna flip when you check out this Wall Street branch. It's got a tuxedoed doorman, table service, a coffee bar, an orchid-filled dining room, and even a pianist at a baby grand. You'd think that all this swank would make your Happy Meal taste like steak frîtes. *160 Broadway, at Liberty St., tel. 212/385-2063. Cash only.*

Seaport Soup Company. One of the best kept secrets downtown is this wondrous little place on Fulton Street. You won't find a cleaner restaurant in the area, with quiet jazz and a slender counter that runs under sparkling picture windows that gaze onto a busy corner. This place has a repertoire of 60 soups, and they serve 8–10 of them daily, all of which come with beautiful homemade bread and seasonal fruit. *76 Fulton St., at Gold St., tel. 212/693-1371. Cash only. Closed weekends in summer.*

Fans of Ronald McDonald and his hamburger friends will of course want a McDonald's tie ($15–$30), T-shirt, or stuffed animal from the Wall Street branch gift boutique.

UNDER $10 • Pearl Street Diner. Professionals who fiddle around with other people's millions but don't want to waste a penny of their own come here for tasty and cheap diner food. You'll pay less than $6 for charbroiled burgers and big breakfast specials. *212 Pearl St., near Maiden La., tel. 212/344-6620. Closed weekends.*

UNDER $15 • Carmine's. Whatever wriggling fresh seafood they're hawking at the historic Fulton Fish Market (just around the corner) will probably show up as dinner at Carmine's, which has been offering Italian seafood specialties since 1903. The service is rude and the food average, but locals still prefer it to the touristy restaurants at South Street Seaport. *140 Beekman St., at Front St., tel. 212/962-8606.*

UNDER $20 • Bridge Café. This cozy bistro in a 19th-century town house is in the very shadow of the majestic Brooklyn Bridge. Seasonal entrées include fresh black squid-ink linguine with shrimp ($16) and roast duck in red-wine sauce ($17). *279 Water St., at Dover St., tel. 212/227-3344.*

OUTER BOROUGH RESTAURANTS

BROOKLYN

Restaurants in Brooklyn Heights, Cobble Hill, Fort Greene, and Park Slope cater to residents who may have to cross a bridge to make their living, but sure as well want to spend their meal money in their own neighborhood, whether at a dirt-cheap falafel stand or a pricey French bistro. In Brooklyn Heights, on Atlantic Avenue, you'll find dozens of Middle Eastern and Moroccan restaurants. Just south of Brooklyn Heights begins the very Italian neighborhood of Carroll Gardens. Farther afield, Williamsburg has kosher bakeries and a number of cheap joints catering to its artist community. When in Sheepshead Bay, think "clam bars" and "pasta shops." Meanwhile, Greenpoint is rife with Polish coffee shops serving very cheap kielbasa and borscht, and Brighton Beach supports thriving (and expensive) dinner theaters for Jewish/Russian immigrants.

BROOKLYN HEIGHTS, COBBLE HILL, AND CARROLL GARDENS

UNDER $10 • Fatoosh Barbecue. This Syrian joint serves two things, both of which taste terrific: barbecued meats ($7.65 a platter) and a vegetarian combination platter ($7.50) with choices like hummus, baba ghanoush, and puréed red pepper with walnuts. *311 Henry St., between State St. and Atlantic Ave., tel. 718/596–0030. Subway: M, N, or R to Court St.; also 2, 3, 4, or 5 to Borough Hall. Cash only.*

Moroccan Star. If you stayed awake during history class, you would know that the French gave Moroccans a fondness for seafood crepes and their pesky, difficult-to-speak Romance language. But for a taste of something truly Moroccan, try the *patella* (spicy chicken pie) or *glaba* (sautéed lamb with okra), both big enough for two. Be warned: This family-run place looks more like a Kansas City pool hall than anything from Casablanca. *205 Atlantic Ave., between Clinton and Court Sts., tel. 718/643–0800. Subway: 2, 3, 4, or 5 to Borough Hall. BYOB.*

UNDER $15 • Patsy Grimaldi's Pizza. While all those cheesy pizza joints in Manhattan scramble to call themselves "the original" and "number one," Patsy's keeps pulling the crispiest, best-tasting pizza pies in New York City out of their coal-fired oven. Go with friends, because they sell by the pie, not slice. *19 Old Fulton St., between Water and Front Sts., tel. 718/858–4300. Subway: A or C to High St. (Brooklyn Bridge). No credit cards. Closed Tues.*

Tripoli Restaurant. There are a good handful of vegetarian dishes here, but the Lebanese menu is mostly variations on lamb, such as *ajhi* (an omelet with herbs, onions, pine nuts, and lamb) and *ma'ani* (a spicy lamb sausage). *156 Atlantic Ave., at Clinton St., tel. 718/596–5800. Subway: 2, 3, 4, or 5 to Borough Hall.*

UNDER $20 • Harvest. A 3-ft-high red neon sign proclaims EATS from the brick wall, just what you'll want to do when you're not drawing on the brown butcher paper that covers the dozen tables (crayons supplied). Chef David Schneider has been dishing up Southern comfort food here since late 1996, including crab cakes with tarragon tartar sauce and a grilled marinated trout with sautéed broccoli rabe and sweet potato pancakes. In fair weather you can eat in the garden out back. *218 Court St., between Baltic and Warren Sts., tel. 718/624–9267. Subway: F to Bergen St. Closed Mon.*

La Bouillabaisse. Devotees of this tiny restaurant put up with waits that sometimes extend an hour or more. The crowds return again and again for the eponymous signature dish, prepared in modestly different ways but always chockablock with a half-dozen different fish, including lobster, flounder, snapper, and shrimp. If your idea of a fine time has never included gorging yourself for less than $17, wine included (provided that you bring a bottle from the liquor store up the street), stay away from here. *145 Atlantic Ave., between Henry and Clinton Sts., tel. 718/522–8275. Subway: 2, 3, 4, or 5 to Borough Hall. BYOB. Cash only.*

FORT GREENE AND CLINTON HILL

UNDER $5 • Tillie's of Brooklyn. Stock up on flyers, caffeine, and light meals at this community coffeehouse and find out what's going on in the Pratt Institute art scene and environs. Thursday is open mike night and there's music on Saturday night. *245 De Kalb Ave., at Vanderbilt Ave., tel. 718/783–6140. Subway: D, Q, N, R to DeKalb or A, C to Clinton–Washington Aves. No credit cards.*

UNDER $10 • Cambodian Cuisine. Although it has zero atmosphere, it's only a couple of blocks away from BAM and a good place to eat before a performance. The menu has more than 150 items bearing ingredients such as curry, lemongrass, and coconut milk; we suggest you cut straight to the Cambodian curry on vermicelli: the chicken is white and tender, the bamboo shoots keep their crunch, and the broth is both sweet and spicy. For $2, the tiny spring rolls come with a clear, vinegar-peanut sauce. *87 S. Elliot Pl., between Lafayette Ave. And Fulton St., tel. 718/858–3262. Subway: D, Q, 2, 3, 4, 5, to Atlantic Ave. No credit cards.*

Keur N' Deye. The crowd here has taken to this husband-and-wife team's Senegalese food like natives. The *yassa dieun* is a filling portion of tangy bluefish, and the Mafe peanut sauce, served with chicken, fish, or lamb, is deliciously balanced with a tomato sauce thinner. Fresh Jamaican hot peppers do more than cut the sweetness of the fried plantains. Too bad there's no beer, but there are drinks like sorrel and ginger juices. *737 Fulton St., between S. Elliot Pl. and S. Portland Pl., tel. 718/875–4937. Subway: D, Q, 2, 3, 4, 5, to Atlantic Ave. Closed Mon.*

UNDER $20 • Chez Oskar. This richly colored, French-owned restaurant is the peacock of the block, and pulls a similarly appealing crowd. You'll get away under $15 for brunch or appetizers. Jazz sets entertain all day Sunday and July 14 marks the house's anniversary—Bastille day fête. Expect "leisurely" service. *211 DeKalb Ave., tel. 718/852–6250. Subway: A, C to Lafayette.*

PARK SLOPE AND PROSPECT HEIGHTS

UNDER $5 • La Taqueria. The flamed rotisserie chicken turns daily in the window and all of the California-influenced Mexican dishes are excellent. Daily specials range from $4.75–$5.75. The restaurant's motto "We don't serve fast food, we serve fresh food as fast as we can" draws plenty of commuters grabbing take-out on their way home. *72 7th Ave., between Lincoln and Berkeley Sts., tel. 718/398–4300. Subway: D or Q to 7th Ave.*

UNDER $10 • Lemongrass Grill. There's always a line of folks outside this little restaurant with a back garden, where not much separates your table from the steam and scents emanating from clattering woks. Menu highlights here include *gaiton krai* (Siam chicken), *kae-panang* (lamb with green curry sauce), and the lemongrass pork chops. *61A 7th Ave., at Lincoln Pl., tel. 718/399–7100. Subway: D or Q to 7th Ave; also 2 or 3 to Grand Army Plaza.*

Olive Vine. A fusion of Middle Eastern spices tease the tongue and a lemony tang embellishes every freshly prepared meal here, from the Olive Vine pizza to the marinated chicken sandwich with tahini. *131 6th Ave., at Sterling Pl., tel. 718/636–4333. Subway: 2 or 3 to Bergen; D, Q to 7th Ave. Cash only.*

Park Slope Brewing Company. A dozen brews are the main event at this spot on a quiet residential stretch. Even if the food preparation is inconsistent, sometimes you just want the familiarity of standard pub food (but the fish-and-chips are wonderful). *356 6th Ave., at 5th St., tel. 718/788–1756. Subway: F, N, R to 4th Ave. Other location: 62 Henry St., Brooklyn Heights, tel. 718/522–4801.*

Tom's Restaurant. If you make the trip to the Brooklyn Museum of Art or Botanic Gardens without taking in a lime rickey, egg cream, or brunch here, you've missed the heartbeat of Brooklyn. The Vlahavas family has been sharing its contagious goodwill and diner fare with neighbors since 1936. Gus will apologize for the wait on busy Saturdays, but that's when you'll see the staff's true grace under fire—they even pass around bowls of fresh orange wedges and cookies. *782 Washington Ave., at Sterling Pl., Prospect Heights, tel. 718/636–9738. Subway: 2 or 3 to Eastern Parkway/Museum. Closed dinner and Sun.*

UNDER $15 • Two Boots. Both singles and young families with precocious tots come here for a relaxed meal of Cajun/Italian food. It's got the same menu as the Two Boots in the East Village (*see above*), plus live music on Friday and Saturday nights. Kids love the open-view kitchen, and the patio makes Two Boots one of the best places in Park Slope for an outdoor brunch. *514 2nd St., between 7th and 8th Aves., tel. 718/499–3253. Subway: F to 7th Ave.*

UNDER $20 • Al di là. The most talked about Brooklyn restaurant in 1999 had to be this small, Italian charmer. Most of the diners who congregate on the sidewalk while waiting for a seat will order the *malfatti*—balls of spinach pasta, steamed pork shoulder, or braised rabbit. It's best to arrive by 6 PM if you want to be seated quickly, and expect the crooning over the food to create quite a din in this colorful restaurant. *248 5th Ave., at Carroll St., tel. 718/783–4555. Subway: M, N or R to Union St.*

Cucina. Cucina's airy, elegant dining room, with its painted tin ceiling, warm Tuscan colors, and comfortable armchairs, is easily one of Brooklyn's loveliest. Italian cuisine is beautifully prepared and presented (especially the small antipasto plates), but it's not cheap. If you're on a shoestring, the half portions of the pasta ($8.50–$12) are a good deal. Reservations are required. *256 5th Ave., between Carroll St. And Garfield Pl., tel. 718/230–0711. Subway: M, N, or R to Union St. Closed Mon.*

WILLIAMSBURG

UNDER $10 • bean. California transplants usually get very tense and huffy when New York restaurants claim to serve "authentic" Cal-Mex food. But it's not so bad at bean, a funky Williamsburg eatery that serves huge, delicious burritos, enchiladas, and quesadillas. Most dishes are vegetarian and cost $6–$11. *172 N. 8th St., near Bedford Ave., tel. 718/387–8222. Subway: L to Bedford Ave. Cash only.*

Plan Eat Thailand. The lines can be long at Williamsburg's favorite restaurant, so consider taking a seat at the kitchen's counter, if you can even get that. The food—as spicy as you want it—is fast, cheap, and clean. If you trail fellow patrons out the door on weekend nights (at a respectful distance, of course), you just might find your way to a gallery opening or warehouse party. *184 Bedford Ave., tel. 718/599–5758. Subway: L to Bedford Ave.*

Right Bank Café (RBBQ). A barbecue pit, bar, and art gallery—just what you'd expect in Williamsburg. Baby-back ribs, half-pound hamburgers, and shrimp are all cooked on the outdoor grill in spring and summer; in winter the menu changes to heartier baked dishes. Sunday brunch is $8.95 and includes a pint-sized alcoholic beverage. *409 Kent Ave., at Broadway, tel. 718/388–3929. Subway: J, M, or Z to Marcy Ave. Cash only.*

UNDER $15 • Diner. At a nowheresville crossroads, this tiny, sunny diner looks like it could hook up to the back of a truck and rattle away with its stylish patrons on another casting call. The owners, schooled at Manhattan's Balthazar and Odeon, have given the well-prepared dishes the price and quality they deserve: the $6.50 burger was recently rated best burger in a *Time Out* poll. Bottles of alcohol, not cream puff pies, are displayed behind the marble counter top. *85 Broadway, at Berry St., tel. 718/486–3077. Subway: J, M, or Z to Marcy Ave.*

UNDER $20 • Oznot's Dish. Local hipsters are devoted to the exquisite renditions of brunch standards here, as well as the seafood wrap with lentil salad. Bring extra cash at dinner to appreciate the "new Near Eastern" dishes like Yemen duck confit, sautéed skate, or grilled loin of lamb. Much of the cuisine has a French base and is spiced up with remembrances of India and North Africa. Come Monday–Wednesday for the 3–course $20 prix fixe steal. *79 Berry St., at North 9th St., tel. 718/599–6596. Subway: L to Bedford Ave.*

CONEY ISLAND, BRIGHTON BEACH, AND SHEEPSHEAD BAY

UNDER $5 • Nathan's Famous. Yup, these are the same Nathan's Famous Hot Dogs that live in the freezer at your local supermarket. Nathan Handwerker started selling these franks back in 1916 for 5¢ each (undercutting competitors who charged a dime); today they're $2.11 with tax. Shockingly, there's no sauerkraut, but the delicious fries make up for it. *Surf and Stillwell Aves., Coney Island, tel. 718/946–2202. Subway: B, D, or F to Coney Island (Stillwell Ave.).*

UNDER $10 • Aiello's. This family-run Italian eatery whips up unbelievable pizzas with homemade mozzarella cheese and imported Italian tomato sauce. Also try the hearty pastas and hero sandwiches. *1406 Neptune Ave., at Stillwell Ave., tel. 718/373–1155. Subway: B, D, or F to Coney Island (Stillwell Ave.). Cash only. Closed Sun.*

UNDER $15 • Primorski. Hordes of Russian immigrants flock to this restaurant/nightclub to feast on food from the Motherland, toss back some ice-cold vodka, and dance to a big band fronted by a Russian Sinatra. Entrées like *salyanka* (lamb stew) are great, but those in the know just fill up on appetizers. *282 Brighton Beach Ave., between Brighton 2nd and Brighton 3rd Sts., tel. 718/891–3111. Subway: D or Q to Brighton Beach.*

Randazzo's Clam Bar. The best Italian seafood restaurant in Sheepshead Bay serves monster-size oysters on the halfshell (6 for $7.50), not to mention Little Neck clams ($12 per dozen) so fresh they were probably living off the coast of Long Island only hours before hitting your plate. Pastas are also available. *2017–2023 Emmons Ave., 1 block from Ocean Ave., tel. 718/615–0010. Subway: D or Q to Sheepshead Bay.*

QUEENS

If you're committed to finding authentic ethnic food, chances are you'll be much happier in Queens than Manhattan, where thriving local immigrant communities support a staggering variety of Chinese noodle shops, Latin American taquerías, and everything in between. Though you can find exotic eating adventures virtually anywhere in Queens, a handful of neighborhoods are especially visitor-friendly: Try **Astoria,** known for its Greek tavernas and cafés as well as an increasing number of Latin American eateries; **Flushing,** a virtual mini-Asia; or **Jackson Heights,** where South American, Caribbean, and East Indian cooking reign supreme.

ASTORIA

Walk down **Broadway** or **30th Avenue** between 31st and 36th streets and you'll find more Greek restaurants, cafés, and food stores than you can count on two hands and an abacus.

UNDER $5 • La Espiga. This tiny bakery churns out some of the best Mexican food north of the Rio Grande. Besides the usual tacos and burritos, they make *huaraches* (giant tacos) and *tortas* (grilled sandwiches made with sliced jalapeños, avocados, beans, and your choice of 13 different fillings—including fried pork and head cheese). Eat at the counter and watch Spanish TV, or take your grub to go. *32–44 31st St., at Broadway, tel. 718/777–1993. Subway: N to Broadway. Cash only.*

UNDER $10 • La Fonda Antioqueña. A mere $7.50 buys you a big plate of broiled beef, cornmeal cakes, rice-and-beans, fried pork, fried plantains, and fried egg at this tiny Colombian restaurant. If that makes your arteries shriek, plunk down $5 for a bowl of oxtail, chicken, vegetable, or tripe soup, served with rice and avocado. *32–25 Steinway St., at Broadway, tel. 718/726–9857. Subway: R to Steinway St.*

Omonia. In the center of Astoria's Greek community, Omonia always has a crowd lingering over its sweet coffee drinks and authentic Greek pastries—try *kadaifi* (shredded wheat with nuts and honey), or sticky, sweet baklava. (You can also get light meals here, but they're nothing special.) Sit by the glassed-in wall and watch the street life of Broadway. *32–20 Broadway, at 33rd St., tel. 718/274–6650. Subway: N to Broadway.*

Uncle George's. Legs of lamb, chicken, and suckling pigs turn slowly on spits near the door at this 24-hour Greek taverna, where locals sit elbow-to-elbow with wide-eyed tourists at family-style tables. The menu runs the gamut from authentic Greek entrées—like the juicy roast lamb with lemon-drizzled potatoes, or octopus sautéed with lemon, vinegar, and oil—to lamb burgers and "Greek-style" spaghetti with meatballs. Madonna is a most-famous customer. *33–19 Broadway, at 34th St., tel. 718/626–0593. Subway: N to Broadway. Cash only.*

UNDER $15 • Zenon. On a quiet side street, this place attracts many Greek-speaking locals. Make that annoying friend of yours, the one who always agonizes over the menu for hours, order *meze*, a $14 sampler with 16 different salads, cheeses, and grilled meats. If you're not in the mood to gorge, try the more-manageable Cyprus meatballs or spinach pie. On Wednesdays, Greek singers and dancers entertain with traditional folk tunes on electric guitar. *34–10 31st Ave., between 34th and 35th Sts., tel. 718/956–0133. Subway: N to 30th Ave. Cash or check only.*

On Jackson Heights streets, look for East Indian stands selling "pan" (rhymes with lawn), a mystery concoction of seeds and herbs rolled in a betel nut leaf. Locals swear the stuff aids digestion; some folks claim it's psychoactive.

UNDER $20 • Piccola Venezia. This fine northern Italian eatery specializes in homemade pastas, fresh seafood, top quality meats, and excellent wines. Everything's made to order. Don't pass up *fusi*, a bowtie-shaped pasta, served in veal or garlic sauce. The great food and warm, friendly service comes at a price—at $16.95 for a typical pasta dish, Piccola is among Queens's more expensive restaurants. *42–01 28th Ave., at 42nd St., tel. 718/721–8470. Subway: N to 30th Ave.*

FLUSHING

The blocks around the **Main Street** subway station are crowded with wall-to-wall Asian restaurants, including Hunan, Szechuan, Cantonese, Japanese, Korean, Taiwanese, Vietnamese, and Malaysian. Farther south on Main Street (near the Queens Botanical Gardens), a handful of cheap Indian restaurants rounds out the cultural stew.

UNDER $15 • Joe's Shanghai. This place did so well in Queens that a Manhattan branch has since opened in Chinatown, where it's now all the rage. If you want the more authentic experience, make the trek out to Flushing, where you'll be packed like sardines at family-style tables and hustled through an incredible sequence of hearty dishes such as crispy pork chops with "salt-and-pepper" sauce, sautéed shredded beef, and smoked fish coated with a sugary varnish. Start with the famous soup dumplings— yes, dumplings with soup inside; they're Joe's claim to fame. *136–21 37th Ave., between Main and 138th Sts., tel. 718/539–3838. Subway: 7 to Main St. Cash only.*

Penang. Long before the pan-Asian craze started in Manhattan, this Malaysian mecca had a loyal following in Flushing. Now there are two more ultratrendy branches in Manhattan, but the Flushing original has by far the best Malaysian food: Its flavors and cooking styles are a melting pot of Chinese, Thai, and Indian influences, all combined in a menu that reads like exotic poetry. Best dishes: *roti cani* (flat bread served with a chicken-and-meat curry sauce), Buddhist yam pot (an actual pot made of fried taro root and filled with chicken, cashews, and vegetables in a savory sauce), and clay-pot noodles with baby corn, black mushrooms, and bean sprouts. *38–04 Prince St., between Main St. and Roosevelt Ave., tel. 718/321–2078. Subway: 7 to Main St. Cash only.*

UNDER $20 • Master Grill International. Jumping on the recent Brazilian *churrascaria* trend, Master Grill offers 16 different kinds of meat—at your command! Just turn the "spool" on your table from red to green, and before you get back from the international salad bar, any (or all) of 16 meats are on your plate. For $18.95, you can gorge yourself, and hear live Latin music, too. Prepare to see everything from suits to tank tops. *34–09 College Point Blvd., between 34th and 35th Ave., tel. 718/762–0300. Subway: 7 to Main St., then Q65 bus to College Point Blvd.*

JACKSON HEIGHTS

Around **Roosevelt Avenue** and **82nd Street,** Colombian, Cuban, Brazilian, Puerto Rican, Argentinean, and Peruvian restaurants churn out chorizo, tripe stew, and other South American fare. Just a few blocks down, at **74th Street,** chile peppers give way to cumin and curry, and cheap Indian food abounds.

UNDER $10 • Delhi Palace. This reasonably priced restaurant offers the best of northern and southern Indian cuisine surrounded by hand-painted canvases, intricate sandalwood statues, and handicrafts. For appetizers, try the *iddly* (steamed lentil and rice patties), or the *medu vada* (fried lentil donuts served with chutney). Recommended entrées are the *masala dosai* (rice crepes filled with potatoes, carrots, onions, and nuts), *uthappam* (southern Indian–style rice pancakes filled with onions, chilies, and vegetables), and anything from the tandoori oven. Come for lunch, when the buffet runs just $7.95. *37–33 74th St., between Roosevelt Ave. and 37th Ave., tel. 718/507–0666. Subway: E, F, G, or R to Roosevelt Ave.*

Jackson Diner. Order tandoori or anything cooked in a *kadai* (a type of earthenware pan) and you will understand how a restaurant with pink walls and fake crystal chandeliers can do such booming business. Go for the lunch buffet ($5–$7) weekdays from 11:30 to 4. *37–47 74th St., at 37th Ave., tel. 718/672–1232. Subway: 7 to 74th St. BYOB. Cash only.*

Tierras Colombianas. Arrive hungry if you're planning to tackle a "mountain plate" of South American staples like stewed beef, fried pork, rice-and-beans, plantains, or cassava. Finish up with a thick, sweet juice. *82–18 Roosevelt Ave., near 82nd St., tel. 718/426–8868. Subway: 7 to 82nd St./Jackson Heights. Cash only.*

UNDER $20 • Park Side Restaurant. Epitomizing old Queens, Park Side is a must-hit when you're in town. Take it from Robert De Niro, Dolly Parton, Hugh Grant, and Frankie Valli, all of whom have visited Park Side (and subsequently had tables named after them). In its five rooms (two gardens, an atrium, a wood-paneled dining room, and an entire room dedicated to Marilyn Monroe), Park Side serves up 180 wines and 15 different pastas. Try a meal of hot antipasto, followed by a veal entrée, lobster tails, or calamari. Even the house wine is good. *107–01 Corona Ave., at 51st Ave., tel. 718/271–9276. Subway: 7 to 103rd St.*

LONG ISLAND CITY

UNDER $10 • Buzzeo. Bring your own wine to this authentic Italian restaurant for bang-for-your-buck cappellini, shrimp, and crab cakes for less than $10. *31–36 36th Ave. at 32nd St., tel. 718/392–1747. Subway: N to 36th Ave.*

THE BRONX

Not many Bronx-bound tourists get beyond the zoo, but those who do will find some rewarding restaurant choices. In the Italian-American neighborhood of **Belmont,** trattorias, pizzerias, caffès, pastry shops, salumerias, fish markets, and cheese stores line the streets. Across the Long Island Sound on **City Island,** you can gorge yourself to the gills on deep-fried seafood—and worry about your health later.

BELMONT

For a truly gluttonous experience, stroll Bronx's "Little Italy" around **Arthur Avenue** and **187th Street,** stopping at **Madonia Brothers Bakery** (2348 Arthur Ave., tel. 718/295–5573), where uncountable loaves of fresh bread have been baked since 1918. **Cosenza's Fish Market** (2354 Arthur Ave., tel. 718/364–8510) has an outdoor fish stand that sells six clams on the half shell for $3.25. At **Calabria Pork Store** (2338 Arthur Ave., tel. 718/367–5145), dried meats hang from the ceiling and huge blocks of cheese chill on the sidelines. Don't miss the cheese menagerie at **Calandra's Cheese Shop** (2314 Arthur Ave., tel. 718/365–7572), where cacicavollo giraffes, rhinos, and elephants cavort in the window.

UNDER $10 • Cafe al Mercato. Snack on tasty pizzas and crusty-bread heroes while admiring a tiny fleet—the Nina, the Pinta, and the Santa Maria. *2344 Arthur Ave., at Crescent Ave., tel. 718/364–7681 Subway: D to Fordham Rd. Train: Metro-North to Fordham station.*

Dominick's. This place is about as unpretentious as it gets, with communal tables, jugs of wine, and a point-and-shout approach to ordering. Locals love it, and on weekends the line stretches out the door. A big Italian dinner costs $8–$15. *2335 Arthur Ave., near 187th St., tel. 718/733–2807. Subway: C or D to Fordham Rd. Train: Metro-North to Fordham station. Closed Tues.*

Ristorante Egidio. Everything at this snazzy lunch spot costs less than $10, so indulge in one of the hearty pastas, soups, or sandwiches. For dessert and espresso, head next door to **Caffè Egidio** (tel. 718/ 295–6077), which has outlasted two World Wars and the Great Depression and is still Belmont's favorite Italian café. Dig into the gelato or one of 55 kinds of pastries. *622 E. 187th St., at Hughes Ave., tel. 718/ 295–7203. Subway: D to Fordham Rd. Train: Metro-North to Fordham station.*

UNDER $15 • Ann and Tony's. They've been making mean plates of spaghetti carbonara, veal Parmesan, and chicken marsala at this family-owned restaurant since 1927. *2407 Arthur Ave., at E. 187th St., tel. 718/364–8250. Subway: C or D to Fordham Rd. Train: Metro-North to Fordham station. No dinner Mon.*

Pasquale's Rigoletto. You want authenticity? A visiting tenor bursts into an impromptu aria, local politicians hold court next to First Communion parties, and Yankees fans stop by before games. This is Belmont by way of a Billy Joel song. Sample the penne with eggplant, or the veal *valdostana,* an irresistible festival of prosciutto, fontina cheese, and porcini mushrooms. Leave room for the homemade cheesecake. *2311 Arthur Ave., at Crescent Ave., tel. 718/365–6644. Subway: C or D to Fordham Rd. Train: Metro-North to Fordham station. Reservations required.*

CITY ISLAND

UNDER $10 • Johnny's Reef Restaurant. So what if Johnny's is an empire of fried things? You sit by the sea with your piña colada, groove to the salsa from your fellow diners' portable radios, and munch on broiled lobsters, fresh-shucked oysters on the halfshell, and yes, the savory fried things—shrimp, clams, and other sea critters. Virtually greaseless. *2 City Island Ave., tel. 718/885–2086. Subway: 6 to Pelham Bay (25 mins), then Bus BX29 to end of City Island Ave. (25 mins). Cash only.*

Rhodes. Around the turn of the century, Rhodes was a sailors' home, inn, and whorehouse. Now it's a pub with live music, good burgers, and pub grub. There's even a moose head on the wall. *288 City Island Ave., at Fordham Rd., tel. 718/885–1538. Subway: 6 to Pelham Bay, then Bus BX29 to City Island Ave.*

RIVERDALE AND MORRIS HEIGHTS

UNDER $10 • African and American Restaurant. Ever had Ghanian food? If not, here's the scoop: Ghanian mashes are bricklike blocks of steamed *fufu* (mashed cassava), *gari* (fermented cassava), or *emu-tuw* (kneaded glutinous rice), spiced with toasted melon seeds, peanut, ginger, or garlic and eaten with the right hand. Get in line and point to whatever looks good: There's southern-style grub for the less brazen palate. *1987 University Ave., at Burnside Ave., Morris Heights, tel. 718/731–8595. Subway: 4 to Burnside Ave. BYOB. Open 24 hrs. Cash only.*

An Bēal Bocht. This Irish pub ("The Poor Mouth" in Gaelic) has a funky, bohemian spirit and hosts poetry readings (Tuesday) and live Irish bands on the weekends. The crowd's a cool mix of Irish folk and students from nearby Manhattan College. Foodwise, fill up on Irish stew and soda bread or chicken potpie. Pints of Guinness and Harp are $4. On Sunday they serve a traditional Irish breakfast for $7, with black-and-white pudding, sausage, rashers, eggs, and fried tomatoes. *445 W. 238th St., between Greystone and Waldo Aves., Riverdale, tel. 718/884–7127. Subway: 1 or 9 to 238th St.; walk up 238th St. to steep flight of stairs and start climbing.*

STATEN ISLAND

Though you won't find crowds rushing across the Verrazano-Narrows bridge to dine in Staten Island, there's still decent food to be had in this outer borough. In Rosebank, **Aesop's Table** (1233 Bay St., tel. 718/720–2005) is a big draw for its American-Mediterranean fare—which includes many fish and vegetarian options—as well as for its intimate bistro setting and backyard garden (entrées cost $14–$24). At Richmond Town, the **Parsonage** (74 Arthur Kill Rd., tel. 718/351–7879) serves sophisticated Continental cuisine in a historic home from 1885 (entrées cost $14–$27).

UNDER $15 • Adobe Blues. There are plenty of reasons to come to this Southwestern hangout three blocks from Snug Harbor: good food (try the chili con carne or Drunken Mexican Shrimp, made with tequila and lime juice), a huge beer selection (200-plus), and a cozy setting—there's even a fireplace. If you happen to be on the Island at night, stop by for live blues on Wednesday. From Snug Harbor, walk three blocks on Fillmore Street to Lafayette. *63 Lafayette Ave., New Brighton, tel. 718/720–2583. From ferry terminal, take Bus S44 to Lafayette Ave. (5 mins).*

Cargo Café. Just a few blocks' walk from the ferry terminal, this spot is a good choice for eclectic fare, from burgers and beer to higher-end Continental dishes like panfried sea bass and roasted pork loin. The setting, with its black walls, pool table, and life-size paintings of Hedy Lamar, is equally eclectic. There's an open mike Monday nights, so come prepared to perform. *120 Bay St., St. George, tel. 718/876–0539.*

Gibb's Southern Bar-B-Que. If seeing the Statue of Liberty somehow gave you a hankering for chicken-fried steak, ribs, or fried catfish, then you're in luck. Located up the street from the ferry terminal, Gibb's is a fine place to fill up after the ride over or before returning back to Manhattan. It's not likely to confuse anyone with a last trip to Tennessee, but it is a cute and convenient place to rest your bones and fuel up for the rest of the day. On Wednesday nights there's live acoustic music and bluegrass Saturday nights. *40 Bay St., St. George, tel. 718/815–3366.*

CAFÉS AND COFFEE BARS

Excluding the West Village and Little Italy, decent coffee—much less café au lait and triple cappuccinos—didn't exist in Manhattan until the early '90s. Around that time a few New Yorkers noticed they'd missed the boat on the whole Seattle coffee craze, and imitation Left-Coast cafés started cropping up like pay-per-view wrestling matches. By 1994, the *New York Times* was moved to explain to its poor, confused readers that these new **coffee bars** were not to be confused with the old **coffee shops.** The distinction is subtle but real, so keep this axiom in mind: At coffee shops the grease is on your plate, while at coffee bars the grease is in the hair of the slacker employees.

While it's now impossible to go a single block without bumping into some sort of espresso bar (or three), not all are the kind of place you'd want to hole up with a pack of smokes and a David Foster Wallace novel. Some, the Type-A cafés, are sterile outlets where the furniture is uncomfortable and the lighting fluorescent. These are sadly common in Midtown. The others, more common in the East Village and Chelsea, are cool and funky and often furnished with comfy thrift-store couches. Many do a lot more than just crank out coffee, like displaying the works of neighborhood artists, holding poetry and fiction readings, hosting live music, or providing access to the Internet. And unlike the Type A's, they won't go ballistic if you decide to linger all afternoon over your $1 purchase. You can count on either kind of café to fill you up with a menu of sandwiches, salads, soups, and desserts when you're down to your last $5. Some even serve beer or wine. Typically, a regular coffee costs $1, fancy caffeine brews $2–$4.

COFFEE-BAR CHAINS

A few coffee-bar chains are worth checking out. If you need a CNN fix or want to browse a rack of 450 (yes, 450) foreign and domestic publications, try **News Bar** (2 W. 19th St., near 5th Ave., Chelsea, tel. 212/255–3996; 107 University Pl., between 12th and 13th Sts., West Village, tel. 212/260–4192). The ubiquitous **Barnes & Noble** (4 Astor Pl., between Broadway and Lafayette St., East Village, tel. 212/420–1322) has cafés in all its Manhattan superstores; they've become legendary cruising zones for literary types who feel most glib and chatty when they're clutching a copy of *Sansho the Bailiff.* And finally, the Seattle chain that started it all is regarded by many as having New York's Best-Tasting Cuppa Joe: **Starbucks** (2379 Broadway, at 87th St., Upper West Side, tel. 212/875–8470; Waverly Pl., at E. 6th St., East Village, tel. 212/477–7776; and many, many more).

UPPER WEST SIDE

Café Mozart. Pound out your own *Requiem* on this funky café's baby grand piano, right beneath an incredibly ugly framed likeness of its Austrian namesake. The café is a hangout for foreign journalists and literary types who enjoy decent sandwiches. *154 W. 70th St., between Broadway and Columbus Ave., tel. 212/595–9797.*

Drip. Eyes are roving as twentysomethings scan the questionnaire-filled binders strewn about the couches and tables for a potential blind date. If you can't chat up someone actually sitting next to you, Drip provides a free dating service by arranging meetings for people interested in each other's write-ups. The music is hip, the crowd clean-cut, and the atmosphere charged. *489 Amsterdam, between 83rd and 84th Sts., tel. 212/875–1032.*

The Hungarian Pastry Shop. Columbia University's alternative crowd comes here to think Deep Thoughts while refueling their physical beings with a selection of sugary confections. *1030 Amsterdam Ave., between W. 110th and 111th Sts., tel. 212/866–4230. Cash only.*

Levain Bakery. Measuring more than an inch high and fresh out of the oven, the buttery chocolate chip cookies are worth tripping down the steps of this tiny side-street bakery, whether you're in need of enough calories to keep you exploring the Upper West Side for another few hours or not. *167 W. 74th St., at Amsterdam Ave., tel. 212/874–6080.*

Muffin Man. On warm days they throw the French doors wide open at the popular Muffin Man. Besides sandwiches ($3–$6) and cheap breakfasts ($3), they have a vast array of sinful baked goodies. *1638 3rd Ave., between E. 91st and 92nd Sts., tel. 212/987–2404. Cash only.*

Positively 104th Street. This place is whatever you want it to be: gourmet coffee emporium, art gallery, or café. And they offer free coffee refills—try finding that anywhere else in Manhattan. *2725 Broadway, at W. 104th St., tel. 212/316–0372.*

MIDTOWN

Coffee Pot. Mix-matched overstuffed couches and chairs, mirrors, odd chandeliers, and a twentysomething crowd make this feel more like the East Village than Hell's Kitchen. This is a super-comfortable spot to while away the day. *350 W. 49th St., at 9th Ave., tel. 212/265–3566.*

Columbus Bakery. Under baguette-shape lamps, sip coffee, nibble at buttery pastries, or tuck into sandwiches on homemade bread. Lots of moms with strollers. *957 1st Ave., between 52nd and 53rd Sts., tel. 212/421–0334.*

Manhattan Espresso. This Euro-friendly stand-up coffee bar pulls the perfect espresso with just the right touch of *crema.* Baked treats from Bouley bakery make this a great spot for a treat on the go. Limited weekend hours. *146 E. 49th St., between 3rd and Lexington Aves., tel. 212/832–3010.*

CHELSEA

Big Cup Tea & Coffeehouse. Sip coffee or slam a triple cappuccino with a hip, gay crowd. Lavender flowers blossom with psychedelic radiance on the Big Cup's lime-green walls—very Alice in Wonderland. *228 8th Ave., between W. 21st and 22nd Sts., tel. 212/206–0059. Cash only.*

Eureka Joe. Part dentist's office, part Pee Wee's Playhouse, Eureka Joe has gigantic stuffed chairs and couches strewn randomly around a characterless room. Literary hipsters come for the usual café fare as well as beer and wine. *168 5th Ave., at 22nd St., tel. 212/741–7500. Cash only.*

Paradise Cafe. Hip Chelseans crowd Paradise—while their pooches wait dutifully outside. There's a super-friendly staff here as well as live music on occasion. *139 8th Ave., at W. 17th St., tel. 212/647–0066. Cash only.*

Wild Lily Tea Room. An oasis of calm and serenity right in the heart of Chelsea's burgeoning gallery scene. A koi fish pond welcomes you into the Zen-like sanctuary where you can have a simple cup of Oolong, assorted tea sandwiches, or one of their innovative tea-infused Asian dishes. There's also classical music on Friday night. *511 W. 22nd St., at 10th Ave., tel. 212/691–2258.*

WEST VILLAGE

Bleecker Street Pastry Shop. This Italian bakery and café, opened in 1947, doubles as a social club for Sicilian matriarchs. Try the Lobster Tail, an Italian sweet with rum-flavored filling. *245 Bleecker St., at Leroy St., tel. 212/242–4959. Cash only.*

Bruno Bakery. The international set can smell a good thing–and that would be the wonderful pastries and espresso. This café, close to New York University, offers seasonal sidewalk seating, prime for Village people watching. *506 LaGuardia Pl., between Houston and Bleecker Sts., tel. 212/982–5854.*

Cafe Borgia. The students of NYU come here in droves for delicious Italian desserts and free-flowing cappuccinos. *185 Bleecker St., at MacDougal St., tel. 212/674–9589. Cash only.*

Cafe Mona Lisa. You may wish your date were as gorgeous as this café. Arrive in the evening, when the lights are low and some singer's rich baritone is turned on high. *282 Bleecker St., between Jones St. and 7th Ave. S, tel. 212/929–1262.*

Cafe Reggio. In the '50s this was a favorite hangout of the Beats (at the time, it had the only espresso machine in the Village). Today it's a great place to watch tourists dorking along MacDougal Street. *119 MacDougal St., between W. 3rd and Bleecker Sts., tel. 212/475–9557. Cash only.*

Caffe Dell Artista. Caffe Dell Artista is a terrific place for a tête-à-tête—if you don't mind shouting a bit to be heard over the French show tunes. Salads, sandwiches, and delicious desserts are less than $8. *46 Greenwich Ave., between Charles St. and 7th Ave., tel. 212/645–4431. Cash only.*

Caffe Rafaella. The Village bohemian days are definitely over with the arrival of the nearby gourmet supermarket and latest greatest gym. But never fear, you can still get an awesome piece of strawberry cheesecake while you nurse your cappuccino in this very warm and classic setting. *134 7th Ave. S, between 10th and Charles Sts., tel. 212/929–7247. Cash only.*

EAST VILLAGE AND THE LOWER EAST SIDE

Café Pick Me Up. What could be better than slurping coffee while watching the skate punks, flannel-clad nihilists, hippies, and vinyl fetishists do their thing in Tompkins Square Park? Well, perhaps a $2.25 breakfast that's served until noon. *145 Ave. A, at E. 9th St., tel. 212/673–7231. Cash only.*

First Street Cafe. In size it's somewhere between "closet" and "shoe box," but this is the café of choice for East Village slackers looking to ponder life's meaning over coffee and cheap, tasty eats. Check out the Elvis bathroom. *72 1st St., between 1st and 2nd Aves., tel. 212/420–0701. Cash only.*

Internet Cafe. E-mail an Armenian bass-fishing expert or chat with foot worshipers from around the globe while sipping espresso. Computers here cost $4 per half hour ($75 for 10 hours). The café even sponsors classes; peruse the listings at their Web site (www.bigmagic.com). *82 E. 3rd St., between 1st and 2nd Aves., tel. 212/614–0747.*

Limbo. All-black-clad intellectuals smirk, smoke, and drink cappuccino at the city's most hyped café, run by Vassar grads and founded by a Bergdorf-Goodman heiress. Daytime is for book reading, nighttime for loud conversations about Flaubert and cybersex. On Wednesday evening big-name and upcoming writers alike read their prose and poetry. *47 Ave. A, between E. 3rd and 4th Sts., tel. 212/477–5271. Cash only.*

Ninth Street Market. The best thing about this tiny spot is the fireplace. Also, on weekends they serve a fine prix-fixe brunch for $7.25. And did we mention that they have a fireplace? *337 E. 9th St., between 1st and 2nd Aves., tel. 212/473–0242. Closed Mon.*

LITTLE ITALY

Caffé Roma. More Italian than Michelangelo or World Cup soccer, this Old World transplant has marble-topped tables, an ancient brass espresso machine, and killer cannoli. *385 Broome St., at Mulberry St., tel. 212/226–8413. Cash only.*

Farriery. Your plan of attack at this century-old institution is simple: Keep eating desserts. We recommend the *tartufo* (chocolate-covered Bavarian cream puff) and cannoli (fried pastry roll with sweet cream filling). In fact, actor Tony Danza (think "Taxi") liked the cannoli so much that in return he left a few nice framed photos of himself. *195 Grand St., between Mott and Mulberry Sts., tel. 212/226–6150.*

SOHO AND TRIBECA

Basset Coffee and Tea Co. A genuinely relaxed atmosphere and pleasant outdoor patio make this TriBeCa coffee and tea emporium a fine place to enjoy a light sandwich or salad. *123 W. Broadway, at Duane St., tel. 212/349–1662.*

Cyber Café. SoHo's Cyber Café, spacious and slick, offers organic foods, gourmet coffees, and all-fruit "Cyber Shakes," plus full Internet access, e-mail, and Web surfing ($12 per hour). Their Web address is www.cyber-cafe.com. *273A Lafayette St., at Prince St., tel. 212/334–5140.*

Duane Park Patisserie. Hidden among TriBeCa's warehouses is a bakery/café selling the kind of cheesecakes, chocolate tortes, and custard tarts for which you'd gladly hock your trousers. *179 Duane St., between Greenwich and Hudson Sts., tel. 212/274–8447. Closed Mon.*

In the Black. Come to this lushly appointed café to confirm all those clichés about SoHo people . . . like their fondness for all-black clothing, neatly clipped goatees, and incisive comments about art. *180 Varick St., between King and Charlton Sts., tel. 212/807–8322. Closed Sun.*

Le Gamin. Just as you'd expect from a French café, Le Gamin serves superb crepes and magnificent crème brûlée. And the café au lait comes European-style, in a great big bowl. *50 MacDougal St., between Houston and Prince Sts., tel. 212/254–4678. Other location: 183 9th Ave., at W. 21st St., Chelsea, tel. 212/243–8864.*

Scharmann's. This spacious, loftlike café is decorated with mismatched Victorian furniture and populated by well-manicured SoHoers. *386 W. Broadway, between Spring and Broome Sts., tel. 212/219–2561.*

MARKETS AND SPECIALTY SHOPS

Most New Yorkers treat their kitchens with the same sort of kindly, solicitous dread that St. Augustine extended to leper colonies. They really don't like to deal with cooking, and why should they? The pizza and Thai guys will always deliver—even in a blizzard at 4 AM. That said, there are tons of places to buy the fixings for a do-it-yourself gourmet meal or a glorious but hassle-free picnic. If the selection below leaves you wanting, pick up **New York Eats** by Ed Levine (St. Martin's Press, $16.95); it lists every lox shop and knishery in the five boroughs, and more.

The lox at Russ and Daughters routinely wins praises as "best in New York." Which is nothing to sneeze at in a city where smoked salmon is, to some, more important than national defense.

GENERAL MARKETS

Dean & Deluca. SoHo's epicurean fantasyland isn't really a market—it's an art gallery for food. They sell the best in produce, fresh fish, breads, cheeses, desserts, candies, and strangely beautiful kitchen utensils. *560 Broadway, at Prince St., SoHo, tel. 212/431–1691.*

Eli's Vinegar Factory. Though the Vinegar Factory is notoriously expensive, it's worth making the trip here to check out what some think is New York's highest-quality market, housed in what was once a vinegar factory. Best of all, on weekends only, you can feast on a huge selection of the store's best prepared dishes—all you can eat for less than $15—while peering down at the shoppers. *431 E. 91st St., at York Ave., tel. 212/987–0885.*

Fairway. This suburban-style warehouse/megamarket (complete with a 200-car parking lot) is a one-stop shopper's dream. In addition to a large, cheap selection of produce and baked goods, it abounds with fresh meats, poultry, fish, and dairy products—all displayed in a 38°F former meat-packing room. They even supply jackets so you won't catch cold while picking out the perfect flank steak. The other location, at 74th and Broadway, is practically a night out on the town for Upper West Siders. *2328 12th Ave., between 132nd and 133rd Sts., Harlem, tel. 212/234–3883. Other location: 2127 Broadway, at W. 74th St., Upper West Side, tel. 212/595–1888.*

Russ and Daughters. Although many neighboring stores are run-down or boarded up, Russ and Daughters is spit-shined and orderly. Just about everything here is made on the premises, from barrels of pickled cucumbers, onions, tomatoes, and peppers to the variety of smoked fishes and spreads. *179 E. Houston St., between Orchard and Allen Sts., Lower East Side, tel. 212/475–4880 or 800/787–7229.*

Zabar's. A real New York institution, Zabar's is a crowded and popular food emporium with, among other things, delicious fresh breads, meats, smoked fish, and candy. If you're shopping for housewares, browse the huge selection upstairs. Prices are surprisingly good and often downright cheap. Next door is Zabar's café (*see* Manhattan Restaurants, *above*). *2245 Broadway, at W. 80th St., Upper West Side, tel. 212/787–2000.*

ETHNIC FOODS

Italian Food Center. They have Italian flags on the walls and a great selection of olive oils, salamis, prosciuttos, focaccia breads, and hero sandwiches. The food here is delizioso, but not exactly low-cal—notice that the employees are prone to overindulgence, too. *186 Grand St., at Mulberry St., Little Italy, tel. 212/925–2954.*

Kam Man. This Chinese food and housewares emporium is unparalleled in the city. The main floor has foodstuffs—from ginseng to dried eel to hard candies—while downstairs there's a wide variety of teas, porcelain, noodles, and pots and pans. *200 Canal St., at Elizabeth St., Chinatown, tel. 212/571–0330.*

M & I International. This is the Brighton Beach community's equivalent to Zabar's—a gourmet store and supermarket with a decidedly Russian flavor (note the jaunty Russian pop blaring from the P.A. system). Browse the vast deli cases filled with sausages, salads, and smoked fish and have lunch on the nearby beach. *249 Brighton Beach Ave., between Brighton 2 and Brighton 3 Sts., tel. 718/615–1011. Subway: D to Ocean Pkwy.*

Sahadi Importing Company. This is New York's best Middle Eastern market. In addition to exotic spices, Sahadi's sells grains, olives (nearly two dozen varieties), dates, dried apricots, nuts, and standbys like hummus and leban. *187 Atlantic Ave., between Court and Clinton Sts., Brooklyn Heights, tel. 718/624–4550. Subway: M, N, or R to Court St. Closed Sun.*

SPECIALTY SHOPS

East Village Cheese. Signs proclaiming ROCK-BOTTOM PRICES cover the entire front window of this dairy mecca. The gimmick is low prices on more cheese than you can shake a stick at, including Camembert and fontina for $2.99 per pound. It also sells fresh breads and low-cost pâtés ($5.99 per lb). *40 3rd Ave., between 9th and 10th Sts., tel. 212/477–2601.*

Essex Street Pickles. If you can't imagine why anyone would trek to the sticks of the Lower East Side for a pickle, you've never been to this 80-year-old institution, which regulars still call Guss Pickles (its original name). Coming here is a quintessential New York experience—you can watch old men stand about gabbing in the doorway while you browse the pickles, sauerkraut, and other vinegar-cured treasures all displayed in brawny wooden barrels. *35 Essex St., between Hester and Grand Sts., Lower East Side, tel. 212/254–4477. Closed Fri. 2 PM–Sat.*

Joe's Dairy. Pungent wafts of smoked mozzarella lure unsuspecting passersby into Joe's, an old-world emporium packed floor to ceiling with wheels of cheese. *156 Sullivan St., between Prince St. and Houston St., tel. 212/677–8780. Closed Sun.–Mon.*

WINE AND SPIRITS

Astor Wines & Spirits. A wide selection of wines, spirits, liqueurs, and sake at very nice prices. Astor stocks "good" wines for less than $10, and the prices on hard liquor are some of the best in the city. There's little reason to shop anywhere else. *12 Astor Pl., at Lafayette St., East Village, tel. 212/674–7500. Closed Sun.*

GREENMARKETS

Open-air farmers' markets in New York City? Though it sounds like an oxymoron, it's true. And it comes as no surprise that they are the best places to stock up on organic vegetables and fruit, baked goods, fresh fish, flowers, and wine—all sold by real, honest-to-goodness farmers from New Jersey and upstate New York. A few of the best and most centrally located greenmarkets are listed below; unless indicated otherwise, their hours are 8 AM–5 PM rain or shine. For more info contact the city's **Greenmarket Program** (130 E. 16th St., NY 10003, tel. 212/477–3220).

MANHATTAN MARKETS

Union Square. This is the largest of New York's greenmarkets, a place where epicureans (including some of Manhattan's best chefs) swarm around stalls filled with fresh fruit, vegetables, meat, fish, bread, and flowers. Look for **Tweefontein Herb Farm** (Saturday), which makes sorbets from lavender, lemon verbeno, and rosemary. Special events on Saturday afternoons between April and October include star chef cookbook signing, cooking demonstrations, and free samples. *E. 17th St. at Broadway. Open Mon., Wed., Fri., and Sat.*

Abingdon Square. *W. 12th St. at 8th Ave., West Village. Open June–Dec., Sat. 8–3.*

City Hall. *Chambers St. at Centre St., Lower Manhattan. Open Tues. and Fri. 8–3.*

I. S. 44. *W. 77th St. at Columbus Ave., Upper West Side. Open Sun. 10–5.*

Minisink Townhouse. *W. 143rd St. at Lenox Ave., Harlem. Open mid-July–Oct., Tues. 8–4:30.*

St. Mark's Church. *E. 10th St. at 2nd Ave., East Village. Open June–Nov., Tues. 8–5.*

Sheffield Plaza. *W. 57th St. at 9th Ave., Midtown. Open Wed. and Sat.*

Washington Market Park. *Greenwich St. at Reade St., TriBeCa. Open Sat.*

World Trade Center. *Church St. at Fulton St., Lower Manhattan. Open Thurs. (also Tues. June–Nov.).*

OUTER BOROUGH MARKETS

Albee Square. *Fulton St. and De Kalb Ave., Downtown Brooklyn. Subway: D, Q, M, N, or R to De Kalb Ave. Open July–Oct., Wed.*

Borough Hall. *Court St. at Remsen St., Brooklyn Heights. Subway: 2, 3, 4, or 5 to Borough Hall. Open Tues. and Sat.*

Grand Army Plaza. *At entrance to Prospect Park, Park Slope, Brooklyn. Subway: 2 or 3 to Grand Army Plaza. Open Sat.*

Lief Erikson Park. *66th St. and 4th Ave, Bay Ridge, Brooklyn. Subway: N or R to 59th St. Open mid-July–Nov., Tues., 8–3.*

McCarren. *Lorimer St. and Driggs St., Greenpoint, Brooklyn. Subway: L to Bedford Ave. Open mid-July–Nov., Tues., 8–3.*

Poe Park. *E. 192nd St. at Grand Concourse, Bronx. Subway: C or D to Fordham Rd. Open mid-July–Nov., Tues. 8–3.*

St. George. *St. Marks Pl. at Hyatt St., St. George, Staten Island. From ferry terminal, walk 3 blocks inland on Hyatt St. Open June–Nov., Sat. 8–2.*

Williamsburg. *Havemeyer St. and Broadway, Williamsburg, Brooklyn. Subway: J, M, or Z to Marcy Ave. Open Thurs. mid-July–Oct.*

Windsor Terrace. *Prospect Park W. and 15th St., Windsor Terrace, Brooklyn. Subway: F to 15th St. Open Wed. July–Nov.*

REFERENCE LISTINGS

EAST EUROPEAN

Under $5
Odessa (*East Village*)

Under $10
Kiev (*East Village*)

Under $15
Primorski (*Brooklyn*)

FRENCH

Under $15
Chez Bernard (*SoHo*)
Chez Brigitte (*West Village*)
Felix (*SoHo*)
French Roast (*West Village*)
Jean Claude (*SoHo*)
La Gould Finch (*East Village*)
Liam (*SoHo*)
Tartine (*West Village*)

Under $20
Chez Oskar (*Brooklyn*)
Florent (*West Village*)
La Bouillabaisse (*Brooklyn*)
L'Ecole (*SoHo*)
Les Routiers (*Upper West Side*)
Les Sans Culottes (*Midtown East*)
Trois Canards (*Chelsea*)

GREEK

Under $10
Omonia (*Queens*)
Uncle George's (*Queens*)

Under $15
Zenon (*Queens*)

HEALTH FOOD

Under $5
Fresco Tortilla Grill (*Midtown East*)
Good Earth Natural Foods Inc. (*Upper West Side*)
Tamarind Seed Health Food Store (*Columbia University*)

Under $10
Angelica Kitchen (*East Village*)

Candle Cafe (*Upper East Side*)
Friend of a Farmer (*Gramercy*)

Under $15
Good Health Cafe (*Upper East Side*)
Josie's (*Upper West Side*)
Spring Street Natural Restaurant and Bar *(SoHo)*
Village Natural Health Food Restaurant (*West Village*)

HOME COOKIN'

Under $10
Aggie's and Aggie's Too (*West Village*)
Friend of a Farmer *(Gramercy)*

Under $15
Chat 'n' Chew (*Gramercy*)
Home (*West Village*)

Under $20
Good Enough to Eat (*Upper West Side*)

INDIAN

Under $10
Ayurveda Café (*Upper West Side*)
Bengal Cafe (*Columbia University*)
Delhi Palace (*Queens*)
Jackson Diner (*Queens*)
Madras Mahal (*Gramercy*)
Panna (*East Village*)

ITALIAN/PIZZA

Under $5
The Bread Shop Cafe (*Columbia University*)
Manganaro's Hero–Boy (*Midtown West*)

Under $10
Aiello's (*Brooklyn*)
Big Nick's Burger/Pizza Joint (*Upper West Side*)
Buzzeo (*Queens*)
Cafe al Mercato (*Bronx*)

Dominick's (*Bronx*)
Il Fornaio (*Little Italy*)
John's Pizzeria (*West Village*)
Luna's (*Little Italy*)
Patsy's Pizzeria (*Upper East Side, Upper West Side, Midtown, and East Village*)
Pintaile's Pizza (*Upper East Side*)
Puglia (*Little Italy*)
Ristorante Egidio (*Bronx*)
V & T Italian Cuisine & Pizzeria (*Columbia University*)

Under $15
Ann and Tony's (*Bronx*)
Caffe Buon Gusto (*Upper East Side*)
Carmine's (*Lower Manhattan*)
Gennaro (*Upper West Side*)
John's (*East Village*)
Lavagna (*East Village*)
Pasquale's Rigoletto (*Bronx*)
Patsy Grimaldi's Pizza (*Brooklyn*)
Randazzo's Clam Bar (*Brooklyn*)
Two Boots (*East Village and Brooklyn*)
Umberto's Clam House (*Little Italy*)

Under $20
Al di là (*Brooklyn*)
Amarone (*Midtown West*)
Cucina (*Brooklyn*)
Parkside Restaurant (*Queens*)
Piccolo Venezia (*Queens*)
Pò (*West Village*)

JAPANESE/KOREAN

Under $5
Tachigui-Soba (*Midtown West*)

Under $10
Esashi (*East Village*)
Sapporo (*Midtown West*)

Under $15
Avenue A (*East Village*)
The Mill (*Columbia University*)

Under $20

East Japanese Restaurant (*Upper East Side*)

Fujiyama Mama's (*Upper West Side*)

KOSHER/JEWISH

Under $5

Ess-a-Bagel (*Gramercy and Midtown East*)

H & H East (*Upper East Side*)

New York City Bagels (*Upper West Side*)

Yonah Schimmel's Knishery (*Lower East Side*)

Under $10

Katz's Delicatessen (*Lower East Side*)

Madras Mahal (*Gramercy*)

Ratner's (*Lower East Side*)

Under $15

Second Avenue Deli (*East Village*)

LATIN AND SOUTH AMERICAN

Under $10

Caridad IV Restaurant (*Washington Heights*)

Cibao (*Lower East Side*)

La Cabaña Salvadoreña (*Washington Heights*)

La Fonda Antioqueña (*Queens*)

Tierras Colombianas (*Queens*)

Under $15

Arroz y Feijão (*Midtown West*)

Under $20

Master Grill Internationall (*Queens*)

MEXICAN/TEX-MEX

Under $5

Fresco Tortilla Grill (*Midtown East*)

La Espiga (*Queens*)

La Taqueria (*Brooklyn*)

Under $10

bean (*Brooklyn*)

Benny's Burritos (*West Village*)

El Sombrero (The Hat) (*Lower East Side*)

Festival Mexicana (*Lower East Side*)

Life Cafe (*East Village*)

Lupe's East L.A. Kitchen (*SoHo*)

Samalita's (*Upper East Side*)

Taco Taco (*Upper East Side*)

Taquería de México (*West Village*)

Uncle Mo's (*Chelsea*)

Under $15

Adobe Blues (*Staten Island*)

Gabriela's (*Upper West Side*)

Tortilla Flats (*West Village*)

Under $20

Mesa Grill (*Chelsea*)

MIDDLE EASTERN

Under $5

Amir's Falafel (*Columbia University*)

Lemon Tree Cafe (*Midtown West*)

Mamoun's (*West Village*)

Under $10

Fatoosh Barbecue (*Brooklyn*)

Moroccan Star (*Brooklyn*)

Moustache (*West Village*)

Olive Vine (*Brooklyn*)

Sahara East (*East Village*)

Under $15

Oznot's Dish (*Brooklyn*)

Salam Cafe (*West Village*)

Tripoli Restaurant (*Brooklyn*)

PUB GRUB

Under $10

An Béal Bocht (*Bronx*)

Fanelli's Cafe (*SoHo*)

Heartland Brewery (*Gramercy*)

Old Town Bar (*Gramercy*)

Park Slope Brewing Company (*Brooklyn*)

Pete's Tavern (*Gramercy*)

Rhodes (*Bronx*)

Under $15

St. Dymphna's (*East Village*)

SEAFOOD

Under $10

Frutti de Mare (*East Village*)

Johnny's Reef Restaurant (*Bronx*)

Under $15

Carmine's (*Lower Manhattan*)

Randazzo's Clam Bar (*Brooklyn*)

Under $20

La Bouillabaisse (*Brooklyn*)

SOUTHEAST ASIAN

Under $5

Bo Ky (*Chinatown*)

Cambodian Cuisine (*Brooklyn*)

Elvie's Turo-Turo (*East Village*)

Kai Kai (*East Village*)

Under $10

Bendix Diner (*Chelsea and East Village*)

Galaxy (*Gramercy*)

Kelley and Ping (*SoHo*)

Lemongrass Grill (*Brooklyn*)

Monsoon (*Upper West Side*)

Nha Trang (*Chinatown*)

Plan Eat Thailand (*Brooklyn*)

Thailand Restaurant (*Chinatown*)

Vietnam (*Chinatown*)

Village Mingala (*East Village*)

Under $15

Benjarong (*Upper East Side*)

Franklin Station Cafe (*TriBeCa*)

James (*Chelsea*)

Penang (*Queens*)

Pho Viet Huong (*Chinatown*)

Regional Thai Taste (*Chelsea*)

Zen Palate (*Gramercy, Midtown West, and Upper West Side*)

Under $20

Rain (*Upper West Side*)

Penang (*SoHo*)

SOUTHERN AND BBQ

Under $10

ACME Bar and Grill (*East Village*)

La Caridad (*Upper West Side*)

Chantale's Cajun Kitchen (*Midtown West*)

Right Bank Café (RBBQ) (*Brooklyn*)

The Reliable (*Harlem*)

Singleton's Bar-B-Que (*Harlem*)

Soul Fixin's (*Midtown West*)

Under $15

Gibbs Southern Bar-B-Que (*Staten Island*)

Great Jones Cafe (*East Village*)

La Gould Finch (*East Village*)

Pink Tea Cup (*West Village*)

Sylvia's (*Harlem*)

Two Boots (*East Village and Brooklyn*)

Under $20

Harvest (*Brooklyn*)

SPANISH/PORTUGUESE

Under $10

Café con Leche (*Upper West Side*)

Yaffa's Bar and Restaurant (*TriBeCa*)

Under $15

La Paella (*East Village*)

Luzia's (*Upper West Side*)

Rio Mar (*West Village*)

Under $20

El Cid (*Chelsea*)

VEGETARIAN

Under $5

Dojo (*East Village*)

Good Earth Natural Foods Inc. (*Upper West Side*)

Joseph's Food Basket (*Harlem*)

Tamarind Seed Health Food Store (*Columbia University*)

Uptown Juice Bar & Vegetarian Food (*Harlem*)

Under $10

Angelica Kitchen (*East Village*)

Ayurveda Café (*Upper West Side*)

bean (*Brooklyn*)

Candle Cafe (*Upper East Side*)

House of Vegetarian (*Chinatown*)

Madras Mahal (*Gramercy*)

Ratner's (*Lower East Side*)

Under $15

Good Health Cafe (*Upper East Side*)

Helianthus Vegetarian (*SoHo*)

Spring Street Natural Restaurant and Bar (*SoHo*)

Tripoli Restaurant (*Brooklyn*)

Village Natural Health Food Restaurant (*West Village*)

Zen Palate (*Gramercy*)

SPECIAL FEATURES

ALL YOU CAN EAT

Under $10

Madras Mahal (*Gramercy*)

BRUNCH

Under $10

31 Division Dim Sum House (*Chinatown*)

Aggie's (*West Village*)

An Bēal Bocht (*Bronx*)

Bubby's (*TriBeCa*)

Life Cafe (*East Village*)

Triple Eight Palace (*Chinatown*)

Under $15

Good Health Cafe (*Upper East Side*)

Home (*West Village*)

Eli's Vinegar Factory (*Upper East Side*)

Sylvia's (*Harlem*)

Tartine (*West Village*)

Under $20

Good Enough to Eat (*Upper West Side*)

EATING AT 4 AM

Under $5

Gray's Papaya (*Upper West Side*)

Odessa (*East Village*)

Under $10

African and American Restaurant (*Bronx*)

Bell Caffe (*SoHo*)

Big Nick's Burger/Pizza Joint (*Upper West Side*)

Kiev (*East Village*)

Moondance Diner (*SoHo*)

Singleton's Bar-B-Que (*Harlem*)

Tom's Restaurant (*Columbia University*)

Uncle George's (*Queens*)

Under $15

SoHo Kitchen and Bar (*SoHo*)

Under $20

Florent (*West Village*)

MUSIC WITH YOUR MEAL

Under $10

ACME Bar and Grill (*East Village*)

An Béal Bocht (*Bronx*)

Bell Caffe (*SoHo*)

Puglia (*Little Italy*)

Rhodes (*Bronx*)

Two Boots (*East Village and Brooklyn*)

Under $15

Avenue A (*East Village*)

Primorski (*Brooklyn*)

Rio Mar (*West Village*)

Sylvia's (*Harlem*)

Zenon (*Queens*)

Under $20

Fujiyama Mama's (*Upper West Side*)

TWIST AND SHOUT (CROWDED, CAMPY, AND LOUD)

Under $15

Tortilla Flats (*West Village*)

Under $20

Florent (*West Village*)

NOODLE BARS

Under $5

Excellent Dumpling House (*Chinatown*)

Sweet 'n' Tart Cafe (*Chinatown*)

Under $10

Kelley and Ping (*SoHo*)

Nha Trang (*Chinatown*)

Sam's Noodle Shop& Grill Bar (*Gramercy*)

Sapporo (*Midtown West*)

OUTDOOR SEATING

Under $10

Bell Caffe (*SoHo*)

Life Cafe (*East Village*)

Yaffa Café (*East Village*)

Under $15

Home (*West Village*)

St. Dymphna's (*East Village*)

Sylvia's (*Harlem*)

Under $20

Harvest (*Brooklyn*)

SWEETS AND DESSERTS

Under $5

The Bread Shop Cafe (*Columbia University*)

City Bakery (*Gramercy*)

Sweet 'n' Tart Cafe (*Chinatown*)

Under $10

Cupcake Cafe (*Midtown West*)

Omonia (*Queens*)

VERY NEW YORK

Under $10

Luna's (*Little Italy*)

Right Bank Café (RBBQ) (*Brooklyn*)

Soup Kitchen International (*Midtown West*)

Tom's Restaurant (*Columbia University*)

Under $15

Avenue A (*East Village*)

Barking Dog Luncheonette (*Upper East Side*)

Tortilla Flats (*West Village*)

Under $20

Florent (*West Village*)

Fujiyama Mama's (*Upper West Side*)

Penang (*SoHo*)

SHOPPING

UPDATED BY MELISSE GELULA

The thrill of a New York shopping experience lies mainly in the pursuit. Ever fashion-conscious, New Yorkers simultaneously grumble and boast about the miles of sidewalk covered on an average shopping day—and they'll hotly defend their ability to do so. Trends have shorter half-life here than anywhere else, so it's almost a full-time job just to keep up.

As styles change, so does the face of the city to accommodate them. To finance a multimillion dollar restoration project, Grand Central Terminal was recently reborn as a mall, rebuilt to house such estimable tenants as J. Peterman, Origins, and LaCrasia Gloves; where only oxfords and suspenders had ventured before, Rockefeller Center now has shops that include the casual-wear giant, J.Crew.

But there's also a new kind of experience slinking to the fore—the total sensory experience. In stores like NikeTown or Giorgio Armani, the merchandise seems to play second fiddle to the event of just *being there*. Atmospheres, potent cocktails of music, special displays, atriums, and videos have become the new sales tools—as *New York Times Magazine* noted, shopping at Calvin Klein "is like being thrust into an Obsession commercial."

Despite the inroads of such hypnotic environments, the small, neighborhood-defining store is far from extinct. And to find that elusive jazz vinyl or out-of-print obscure novel, you'll need to be ready, willing, and able to travel the length and breadth of Manhattan. Don't worry—everybody does it.

Some of the more famous shopping neighborhoods include the **Flower District** (6th and 7th Aves. between W. 25th and 30th Sts.), where shops sell everything from tiny cacti to 20-ft-tall ficus trees; the **Garment District** (*see* Clothes, *below*); the **lamp district** (Bowery between Spring and Hester Sts.); the **restaurant equipment neighborhood** (Bowery between Houston and Delancey Sts.), with great buys on knives and cookware; the **Shoe Street** (*see* Shoes, *below*); the historic **Orchard Street bargain and** (more recently) **boutique district** (*see* the Lower East Side *in* Chapter 2); the **semicheap antiques street** (Bond St. around Lafayette St.); and the **even cheaper antiques street** (Atlantic Ave. between Clinton and Smith Sts., Brooklyn), where prices average 10% less than in Manhattan boutiques.

Tired yet? There's more: **Madison Avenue** between East 57th and 92nd streets is lined with an ever-expanding range of gleaming "flagship" stores of major designers like Giorgio Armani and Prada. This couture phalanx is matched only by that of **East 57th Street** between 5th and Lexington avenues, where, more than ever, the snootier stores must share the sidewalk with megacomplexes like the NBA Store and Warner Bros. Studio Store. **East 7th Street** between 2nd Avenue and Avenue A bursts at the seams with vintage-clothing stores. **SoHo** has become increasingly made over with chain stores like Victoria's Secret and elite cosmetics companies like Helena Rubenstein eating away at the galleries, but there are still plenty of distinctive boutiques, especially for fashion and housewares. Likewise, a bit farther east is the small boutique and home-accessory haven, **Elizabeth Street. Chelsea** is newly aswarm with huge discount emporiums like Old Navy; Bed Bath & Beyond; and Loehmann's. And don't forget the rich ethnic neighborhoods of **Chinatown, Harlem,** and the **Lower East Side** (*see* Chapter 2).

Of course, you'll have to deal with crowds year-round and put up with prices that may be higher than in other American cities (and don't forget to add in that 8¼% sales tax). Nobody said this was going to be easy. But remember the caché ahead, when you return home with all your lovely purchases: "Oh this?" you can say. "I bought it in New York City."

DEPARTMENT STORES

New York City's department stores rival the best in Paris. And they leave those of London, Rome, and Tokyo in the dust. At no other stores in the world can you find window displays more overwhelming, perfume sprayers more determined, or customers (and mannequins) more lavishly dressed. It all began around the time when R. H. Macy opened a shop on 6th Avenue at 14th Street in 1858. By the end of the century, the stretch of 6th Avenue between 14th and 23rd streets, called **Ladies' Mile,** was lined with huge department stores in beautiful cast-iron buildings. Fifteen years later most stores had moved uptown, with Macy's (*see below*) landing at 34th Street and most of the higher-fashion stores drifting up 5th Avenue, but the concept was here to stay.

It's easy to treat an afternoon in the department stores like a visit to the museums. They're excellent for a spell of harmless fawning, especially around the holiday season, when most don outrageous and whimsical window displays—Barneys is especially notorious for these. Year-round, most department stores offer fancy cafés that are great for latte-drinking and people-watching—just like at the Met and MoMA.

Barneys New York (660 Madison Ave., at E. 61st St., Upper East Side, tel. 212/826–8900; World Financial Center, Lower Manhattan, tel. 212/945–1600). News of Barneys' financial woes has quieted since the original Chelsea space, going way back to 1923, was fed to the bankruptcy lions (after being trimmed down to make way for the discounter Loehmann's, no less!) in the fall of 1996. Despite the havoc downtown, though, the Madison Avenue store maintains its glamorous sangfroid. The men's and women's departments stock labels from the designing world's stratosphere; the women's department in particular will pick up some truly gawk-worthy pieces. Even seasonal sales here are far from cheap, so New Yorkers line up around the block for the semiannual warehouse sales (late August and January).

Bergdorf Goodman (754 5th Ave.; men's store: 745 5th Ave., between E. 57th and 58th Sts., Midtown, tel. 212/753–7300). This pair of stores has the hushed atmosphere of Money (the women's and men's stores face each other across 5th Avenue)—but there's a buzz on the fifth floor of the women's store, where plenty of casual clothes have red slashes on their price tags. ("Casual" in this setting indicates linen trousers, not jeans.)

Bloomingdale's (1000 3rd Ave., at E. 59th St., Midtown, tel. 212/355–5900). Occupying an entire city block, Bloomingdale's is an institution—as evinced by the high percentage of out-of-towners clutching Bloomie's shopping bags.

CHEAP • Century 21 (22 Cortlandt St., between Broadway and Church St., Lower Manhattan, tel. 212/227–9092; 472 86th St., between 4th and 5th Aves., Brooklyn, tel. 718/748–3266). It's unlikely that Century 21 can still claim to be "New York's best kept secret," since *Vogue*'s ecstatic article on it a few years back. But you'll still find three vast floors of in-season name-brand and designer fashions for men and women, like beautiful blouses by Paul Smith for $65 (originally $130), or a perfect Calvin Klein men's coat for $300 (originally $900). They also sell shoes, bedding, and cosmetics.

Henri Bendel (712 5th Ave., between W. 55th and 56th Sts., Midtown, tel. 212/247–1100). Chic Henri Bendel is filled with whimsical, expensive clothing. Somehow the dizzying layout of small rooms around a swirling staircase adds to the gracious atmosphere—thank the daylight coming in from the Lalique windows.

Macy's (Herald Sq., Broadway at W. 34th St., Midtown, tel. 212/695–4400). Macy's at Herald Square claims to be the largest department store on earth, and who's going to argue? They've got 2.1 million square ft of selling space on nine floors; fashionwise, they go the middle road. On the Balcony level,

In case you want to see the world.

At American Express, we're here to make your journey
a smooth one. So we have over 1,700 travel service locations in over 130 countries ready to help. What else
would you expect from the world's largest travel agency?

do more

Travel

**Call 1 800 AXP-3429 or visit
www.americanexpress.com/travel**

In case you want to be welcomed there.

We're here to see that you're always welcomed at establishments everywhere. That's why millions of people carry the American Express® Card – for peace of mind, confidence, and security, around the world or just around the corner.

do more **AMERICAN EXPRESS**

Cards

In case you're running low.

We're here to help with more than 190,000 Express Cash locations around the world. In order to enroll, just call American Express at 1 800 CASH-NOW before you start your vacation.

do more AMERICAN EXPRESS

Express Cash

And in case you'd rather be safe than sorry.

We're here with American Express® Travelers Cheques. They're the safe way to carry money on your vacation, because if they're ever lost or stolen you can get a refund, practically anywhere or anytime. To find the nearest place to buy Travelers Cheques, call 1 800 495-1153. Another way we help you do more.

do more AMERICAN EXPRESS

Travelers Cheques

you'll find a visitors center where you can get oriented (and even buy theater tickets). Don't leave before descending to the Cellar marketplace, where the cookware and edibles rival those at Zabar's.

CHEAP • Pearl River Mart (277 Canal St., at Broadway, Chinatown, tel. 212/431–4770). Climb the stairs past the knock-off DKNY bags to the third floor, and you'll discover the low-cost source for Chinese wares priced exorbitantly everywhere else. New Yorkers pack the tiny aisles, vying for beautiful ceramics, such as rectangular sushi plates ($13) and matching soy cups ($4). They also sell Chinese lanterns ($5–$20), slippers ($3–$7), and cartoon-style alarm clocks ($5–$15). The second floor sells imported grocery items from jellied drinks to instant udon noodles.

Saks Fifth Avenue (611 5th Ave., between E. 49th and 50th Sts., Midtown, tel. 212/753–4000). In addition to excellent people-watching, courtly service, and acres of haute couture, you'll find surprisingly good bargains on just-out-of-season clothes.

Takashimaya New York (693 5th Ave., between E. 54th and 55th Sts., Midtown, tel. 212/350–0100). This pristine branch of Japan's largest department store somehow casts a spell of Zen-like peace on its customers; even when the store is crowded, everyone seems preternaturally well-behaved. Look in the gardening-section-as-front-window-display for a little something you can't just live without—such as a lovely glazed pot for around $15.

CLOTHES

Not surprisingly for a city that calls itself the fashion capital of the country, New York has a lot of places to buy clothes. And we're not just talking Jack Kerouac's khakis, here, either; how many cities have stores with "Cross Dressers Welcome" signs in the window?

One way to buy clothes cheaply in New York is to head to the **Garment District** (7th Avenue and Broadway from W. 34th to 42nd streets), where you can sometimes hit a few **sample sales.** Besides selling the samples (worn by models) of next year's fashion hopefuls, they usually offer overstock of stuff already in the stores. The best times for sample sales are April–June and November–December; look for men handing out flyers on Garment District street corners and check the weekly *Time Out* magazine for sale dates and locations. ("Blackbelt shoppers" can buy a weekly sales report on otherwise private sales for $9.95 through Lazar Media Group, tel. 877/579–0222.) Just keep in mind that most sales are cash only, no returns and no exchanges, and that not every designer is the next Miuccia Prada.

A new direction in shopping seems to be the spin-off housewears line, most recently starring Banana Republic Home (128 5th Ave., at W. 16th St., Gramercy, tel. 212/366–4630; 552 Broadway, between Prince and Spring Sts., SoHo, tel. 212/925–0308).

NEW CLOTHES

New York has all the same chain stores as your hometown mall, and a few are actually worth checking out: Midtown's über **Gap** (60 W. 34th St., at Broadway, Midtown, tel. 212/643–8960) is gargantuan—it covers 53,000 square ft. **Banana Republic,** a sort of Gap-goes-to-the-office, has nabbed storefronts in some prime locations (552 Broadway, between Prince and Spring Sts., SoHo, tel. 212/925–0308; 655 5th Ave., at E. 52nd St., Midtown, tel. 212/644–6678; 1136 Madison Ave., at E. 85th St., Upper East Side, tel. 212/570–2465). **Polo/Ralph Lauren** (867 Madison Ave., at E. 72nd St., Upper East Side, tel. 212/606–2100), Madison Avenue's first lifestyle store, occupies a stately mansion. Across the street the **Polo Sport** (888 Madison Ave., Upper East Side, tel. 212/434–8000) store promotes activewear, plus some good-old-boy accessories, like antique pocket watches. **Urban Outfitters** (628 Broadway, at W. Houston St., SoHo, tel. 212/475–0009; 374 6th Ave., Washington and Waverly Pl., Greenwich Village, tel. 212/677–9350; 162 2nd Ave., between E. 10th and 11th Sts., East Village, tel. 212/375–1277; 127 E. 59th St., between Park and Lexington Aves., Midtown, tel. 212/688–1200) sells funky and affordable clothes, accessories, and Pottery Barn–esque home furnishings for twentysomethings.

A/X: Armani Exchange (568 Broadway, between Houston and Prince Sts., SoHo, tel. 212/431–6000). If you can avoid the logo-heavy pieces, Giorgio Armani's comprehensive casual line is a good spot for trickle-down Milanese fashion—particularly for men.

Air Market (97 3rd Ave., between 12th and 13th Sts., East Village, tel. 212/995–5888). Stand back, Hello Kitty: this tiny store sells imported Japanese brands of harder-to-get funwear (lately with wind-

WINDOW-SHOPPING AS AN ART

Madison Avenue, 5th Avenue, and 57th Street are purportedly three of the ten most expensive shopping streets in the world. A half-hour here might be a good time to do as the French do: "lécher les vitrines" (literally, lick the windows). Just consider it part of your aesthetic education. For glittering gems, sidle up to Cartier (2 E. 52nd St., at 5th Ave.) and Tiffany & Co. (727 5th Ave., at E. 57th St.). See what you think of sleek Chanel (5 E. 57th St., at 5th Ave.) versus the rowdier, neon-striped Gianni Versace boutique (647 5th Ave., between E. 51st and 52nd Sts.). Calvin Klein (654 Madison Ave., between E. 60th and 61st Sts.) and Giorgio Armani (760 Madison Ave., between E. 65th and 66th Sts.) seem to be locked in a kind of minimalist one-upsmanship, while Prada (841 Madison Ave., at E. 70th St.) bathes itself in sea-green light. Dolce & Gabbana (825 Madison Ave., between E. 68th and 69th Sts.) is all that Isabella Rossellini could desire. And for a bit of levity, head for Moschino (803 Madison Ave., between E. 67th and 68th Sts.) and Diesel (770 Lexington Ave., at E. 60th St.), for their fabulously creative (albeit quirky) window displays.

breakerlike fabric and lots of drawstrings) like Sabotage, Mr. Friendly, and Lover's House, as well as those hologram wallets from Shin & Co. Don't miss the funky underwater-world window display.

BCBG (770 Madison Ave., at E. 66th St., Upper East Side, tel. 212/717–4225). The language of clothing doesn't always translate well. For example, this Parisian store's name is an acronym for "bon chic bon genre," which is almost equivalent to old-guard preppy, but there's not a collared shirt in sight. Instead well-designed pieces of French urbanwear cost under $100, including light and gauzy dresses in watercolor shades, fitted wool coats, flattering A-line skirts, and the store's delicious house-label shoes.

Canal Jeans (504 Broadway, between Spring and Broome Sts., tel. 212/226–1130, SoHo). This is the place for low-price Levi's, including the dark-dyed variety of late ($39), and discounts on brands like French Connection and CK. Military surplus, some mediocre vintage stuff, and a ton of used Levi's ($10–$30) also fill the racks.

Club Monaco (160 5th Ave., at W. 21st St., Flatiron District, tel. 212/352–0936; 111 3rd Avenue, at E. 65th St., Midtown, 212/355–2949; 2376 Broadway, at W. 87th St., Upper West Side, tel. 212/579–2587). Who was it who said if you can't afford Jil Sander, there's Club Monaco? As you may expect in the Kingdom of Designer-Knockoff, black and beige are king and queen. For unruly subjects, male and female, there's a sporty line in bright colors that favors unnatural fabrics, too.

D&G (434 Broadway, SoHo, tel. 212/965–8000). Aloof, poreless-skin faces of D&G models on phone booths and bus-stop shelters announce the arrival of Dolce & Gabbana's offspring—the first U.S. store devoted to a second line aimed at younger, jeans-wearing hipsters with voluminous wallets. Tops are tiny, pants are skinny, and the styles, not unlike the daddy store, are impeccably sharp.

J. Crew (203 Front St., at Fulton St., Lower Manhattan, tel. 212/385–3500; World Trade Center Mall, Lower Manhattan, tel. 212/839–8378; 99 Prince St., at Mercer St., SoHo, tel. 212/966–2739; 91 5th Ave., between E. 16th and 17th Sts., Gramercy, tel. 212/255–4848). The catalogue giant that invented East Coast chic and gave us the rollneck sweater has 14 labels for men and women, which range from flannels to the Collection, a Calvin Klein–ish women's line. Note: Only the SoHo and Gramercy locations carry shoes.

Label (265 Lafayette St., between Prince and Spring Sts., SoHo, tel. 212/966–7736). This place was doing utility chic long before you'd be caught dead in cargo pants. It's retained its edge for funky clothes in a boutique-y and yet sometimes ironic way—witness Laura Whitcombs' Chairman Mao dresses.

Miu Miu (100 Prince St., between Greene and Mercer Sts., SoHo, tel. 212/334–5156). The darling designs of Miuccia Prada—the fashion heiress currently carrying the Prada-family scepter—exemplify haute-style clothing and shoes with playful airs. This is the stuff of the Condé Nast building's elevator scene, and, no, it's not cheap—just cheaper than most anyplace else.

New Republic (93 Spring St., between Mercer St. and Broadway, SoHo, tel. 212/219–3005). Men who want to look sharp but are allergic to business-as-usual suits and ties can shop here without fear. The fine fabrics and styles translate into steepish prices, so watch for sales.

Old Navy (610 6th Ave., at W. 18th St., Chelsea, tel. 212/645–0663; 503 Broadway, between Spring and Broome Sts., SoHo, tel. 212/226–0838; 625 Atlantic Ave., at Flatbush Ave., Brooklyn, tel. 718/638–2935). This Gap-ish, gleaming, discount superstore first infiltrated Chelsea and then SoHo with cotton knits and cargo pants for all.

O.M.G. (546 Broadway, between Prince and Spring Sts., SoHo, tel. 212/343–1164). Does it stand for "Oh My God" because they've got some of the lowest prices in town on Levi's and other jeans? The laid-back atmosphere makes this a great place to shop for those clothes fashion wags call "wardrobe basics."

Funniest bathroom in the city: Moschino's Lego-walled "Toy-lette" (803 Madison Ave., between E. 67th and 68th Sts., Upper East Side).

Patricia Field (10 E. 8th St., between 5th Ave. and University Pl., West Village, tel. 212/254–1699). This is the essence of the club-kid look—tiny tops, big pants, techno-fabrics, Japanese accessories, and—yes—irony. Labels include Miss Sixty, Label Whore, and Snug. Beware, the clothes aren't cheap. Check out the colorful wig salon upstairs. A SoHo spin-off, Hotel Venus by Patricia Field's (82 Broadway, between Spring and Broome Sts., tel. 212/966–4066), sells more expensive designer lines geared toward club kids with even more money.

Zara (750 Lexington Ave., at E. 59th St., Midtown, tel. 212/754–1120; Broadway, at Prince St., SoHo, tel. 212/343–1725). The multinational price tags at this global chain mean you will have a twin out there somewhere, should you shop here. Fabrics can be flimsy, but the style's always right on and the prices are quite low. Shoes seem to come in a variety of six colors.

DISCOUNT CLOTHES

Some discount outlets are truly the bottom of the city's fashion food chain, the final resting place for three-armed jackets and other designer bombs, where finding that little $25 Calvin Klein dress takes patience and luck; others are less gruesome and have a serious following of discount hounds who arrive early and shop often.

Daffy's (111 5th Ave., at E. 18th St., Flatiron District, tel. 212/529–4477; 135 E. 57th St., between Lexington and Park Aves., Midtown, tel. 212/376–4477; 335 Madison Ave., at E. 44th St., Midtown, tel. 212/557–4422; 1311 Broadway, at W. 34th St., Garment District, tel. 212/736–4477). Often lots of designer labels are crammed in the racks of this always-busy store. At other times, there's more polyester to deal with than anyone should have to. Stock also varies among stores: the Madison location is particularly good for work suits and fashions of the moment; for luggage try the Garment District store.

Filene's Basement (620 6th Ave., between W. 18th and 19th Sts., Chelsea, tel.212/620–3100; 2224 Broadway at 79th St., Upper West Side, tel. 212/873–8000). If you're in search of something fancy to wear, make this department-store's spin-off your first-stop. The really reduced-price designer clothes for men and women also manage to keep up with the seasons and trends. Best find: a same-season Vivian Tam skirt for $40. There's also an abundant women's shoe selection that always seems to have something from DKNY for under $50.

Loehmann's (101 7th Ave., at W. 16th St., Chelsea, tel. 212/352–0856). Bargain hunters throughout Manhattan rejoiced when the legendary discounter finally opened a branch downtown. The highest fashion is concentrated in the "Back Room," but don't let that stop you from looking elsewhere. P.S., there are both communal and private dressing rooms.

Moe Ginsberg (162 5th Ave., at W. 21st St., Chelsea, tel. 212/242–3482). Moe has multiple floors of men's suits, sport jackets, trousers, and formal wear that will make you look very respectable, at prices that won't kill you. Some say it's slicker than Brooks Brothers, and it sure is cheaper.

Syms (400 Park Ave., at E. 54th St., Midtown, tel. 212/317–8200; 42 Trinity Pl., at Rector St., Lower Manhattan, tel. 212/797–1199). Syms is an oddball store in that its men's section dwarfs the women's. The emphasis is on suits and other work-appropriate clothes. The Park Avenue store seems to stock better names, among them Versace and Calvin Klein.

SECONDHAND CLOTHING

In this city, secondhand and vintage clothing options go way, way beyond grubby pairs of corduroys. Many of the to-die-for numbers you'll see on passersby are far from new, and finding them is sort of an art. Of course, the older the clothes the higher the price tag: If it's vintage stuff from the '20s and '40s you covet, you probably already know you're gonna blow some dough. Also, prepare yourself for limited dressing room access; if there does happen to be a dressing room, expect to wait. In late-spring and fall, Lighthouse International (110 E. 60th St., between Park and Lexington Aves., tel. 212/821–9300) orchestrates a fabulous sale (formerly the Armory's Posh on Park sale) to benefit the visually impaired. Racks of donated (new or gently-used) very high-end clothes and accessories sold at incredibly low prices make this one of the prime events of the year. General admission is $25, $10 after 11 AM—you pay a lot more for having first dibs on those uptown threads.

Center for the Dull (216 Lafayette St., between Spring and Broome Sts., SoHo, tel. 212/925–9699). Formerly known as Smylonylon, this is still the land of pleather and polyester: lots of groovy skintight shirts, slinky skirts, and many-zippered, bootcut pants—not a natural fiber in the house. Prices start around $12.

Golden Oldies (96 E. 7th St., between 1st Ave. and Ave. A, East Village, tel. 212/533–8550). Born "Rose is Vintage," this narrow store about the size of a suburban home's walk-in closet promises new daily merchandise, so you won't be revisiting the same ol' unwanted pieces. Best sighting to-date: a short faux-Persian lamb coat for $30. Sales mean major markdowns: everything, even the leather and suede items, can drop to as low as $10.

Housing Works (143 W. 17th St., between 6th and 7th Aves., Chelsea, tel. 212/366–0820; 202 E. 77th St., at 3rd Ave., Upper East Side, tel. 212/772–8461; 306 Columbus Ave., between 74th and 75th Sts., Upper West Side, tel. 212/579–7566). Separate designer sections can yield a $20 Calvin Klein button-down at this darling of New York thrift stores. But don't overlook the cheaper racks or the housewares and books sections. The shops benefit housing services for people with AIDS.

INA (21 Prince St., between Mott and Elizabeth Sts., SoHo, tel. 212/334–9048; 101 Thompson St., between Prince and Spring Sts., SoHo, tel. 212/941–4757; men's store: 262 Mott St., between Houston and Prince Sts., SoHo, tel. 212/334–2210). This is where the rich ladies who wear their Prada shoes twice sell their tired things on consignment. You, the shopper, stand to benefit greatly from this irony, as most of the designer garments for resale (Miu Miu, Betsey Johnson, and friends) are just one- or two-seasons-old, and everything's still in good condition.

The 1909 Company (63 Thompson St., between Spring and Broome Sts., SoHo, tel. 212/343–1658). Revel in luxe items like vintage cashmere sweaters (about $60 and up) and genteel ladies' suits. The sale rack is not to be sniffed at.

Rags-A-GoGo (75 E. 7th St., between 1st and 2nd Aves., East Village, tel. 212/254–4771). You've never seen a store so anally organized: all the pink shirts fade into the red shirts, which fade into the orange shirts, well…you get the picture. And then there's the stuffed animal collection *stapled* to the walls, but that's another story. Things aren't tagged, so look for the price menu in the window. At press time it read: Tees are $6, pants are $18, and everything else is $12.

Reminiscence (50 W. 23rd St., between 5th and 6th Aves., Chelsea, tel. 212/243–2292). A vintage-loving boy's dream, this nerdy-is-nice store sells retro reproductions (including the signature Hawaiian Camp shirt) and originals for double-take cheap. You can get pants and shoes for under $20 and shirts as low as $5.

Resurrection (217 Mott St., between Stanton and Spring Sts., Lower East Side, tel. 212/625–1374; 123 E. 7th St., between 1st Ave. and Ave. A, East Village, tel. 212/228–0063). In spring, this is the sweet spot of lotsa cork-bottom platforms—and, just to keep you on your toes (cough)—one or two pairs of outrageous boots. The suit and dress selection can be particularly good; look for the Peter Max transparent bags and the saucy '70s tube tops and halters hanging on the walls. The Mott Street store is bigger.

Screaming Mimi's (382 Lafayette St., at E. 4th St., East Village, tel. 212/677–6464). Mimi's is stocked with super-cool but overpriced stuff from the '50s to '70s, like narrow capri pants in bright colors ($30), plaid pants ($25 and up), and party dresses ($30 and up). Clamber upstairs to a narrow landing for lost-in-time housewares.

Spooly D's (51 Bleecker St., at Lafayette St., East Village, tel. 212/598–4415). Because everything vintage or new is carefully selected (a.k.a. *fabulous*), you pay a little extra here (dresses and adorable suits for women start at $50) for not having to endure racks of untouchables.

Tokio 7 (64 E. 7th St., between 1st and 2nd Aves., East Village, tel. 212/353–8443). Japanese Kewpie dolls and videos of Euroglam runway shows somehow coexist here. Best finds: Cynthia Rowley and Betsey Johnson picks for under $40 (albeit a few seasons old) are to be found on the wall by the register or on the circular rack in front.

SHOES

New Yorkers know the secret to looking good is wearing a great pair of shoes. Even those whose total ensemble above the ankles costs under $30 will drop three- or four-times that for an outfit-making pair. West 8th Street between University Place and 6th Avenue is the city's **Shoe Street,** with more than 20 shops selling every kind of footwear from the must-have shoes of Christmas Past (or was it the Christmas before that one?) to thigh-high glitter platform boots. Prices range from pretty cheap to "no-way, well, okay." Try **Bootéro** (10 5th Ave., at W. 8th St., West Village, tel. 212/529–7515), **Wheels of London** (55 E. 8th St., between Broadway and University Pl., East Village, tel. 212/254–0453), or **Here & Now** (56 W. 8th St., between 5th and 6th Aves., West Village, tel. 212/979–2142). **Luichiny** (21 W. 8th St., between 5th and 6th Aves., West Village, tel. 212/477–3445) and **Juno** (16 W. 8th St., between 5th and 6th Aves., West Village, tel. 212/995–0162) have sharper styles but steeper prices.

Hate that clothes aren't made with your body in mind? Up-and-coming designers in the East Village, like Megan Kinney *(312 E. 9th St., 212/260–6329) and* Blue *(125 St. Mark's Pl., 212/228–7744) are great places to shop for unique, stylish items, where you can actually have a conversation about how the clothes fit you with the person who made them.*

Aldo (700 Broadway, at E. 4th St., East Village, tel. 212/982–0958; 29 W. 34th St., between 5th and 6th Aves., Midtown, tel. 212/239–4045; 579 Broadway, at Prince St., SoHo, tel. 212/226–7974; 157 E. 86th St., at Lexington Ave., Upper East Side, tel. 212/828–3725). You've seen the glued-together wonders sold here on the feet of every teenager south of Winnipeg: they're typically super-chunky, more synthetic than leather, and fly in the face of everything advanced by your podiatrist. An average pair will run you $80.

David Aaron (529 Broadway, at Spring St., SoHo, tel. 212/431–6022). For under $100 a pair, a regular entourage of stylish clientele walks away in knock-off Pradas and pals. Must-haves are always represented, from those angular-toe Mary-Jane models to teva-inspired sandals with velcro straps. Or was that last season?

Giraudon (152 8th Ave., between E. 17th and 18th/W. Sts. Chelsea. tel. 212/633–0999; 339 W. Broadway, between Grand and Broome Sts., SoHo, tel. 212/334–9867). Some of Alain-Guy Giraudon's imaginative designs for men and women have deliberate perforations in the leather, others have his almost-trademark soles that, like running shoes, come up high over the toe. These modern, largely casual, and well-made shoes (around $100) always anticipate forthcoming styles, which means you'll wear them for years.

John Fluevog Shoes (104 Prince St., between Mercer and Greene Sts., SoHo, tel. 212/431–4484). Inventor of the Angelic sole (protects against water, acid . . . and "Satan"), Fluevog designs chunky shoes and boots, some of which are downright excessive, ie: the wood-bottom geisha sandals; others resemble bowling shoes, funkified loafers, and mod-style creepers. Scramble if you see a sale sign; prices often get cut in half.

Maraolo (782 Lexington Ave., between E. 60th and 61st Sts., Upper East Side, tel. 212/832–8182; 551 Madison Ave., at E. 55th St., Midtown, tel. 212/308–8793; 835 Madison Ave., at E. 69th St., Upper East Side, tel. 212/628–5080; 1321 3rd Ave., between E. 75th and 76th Sts., Upper East Side, tel. 212/535–

6225). Clothing designers' footwear (Armani, Donna Karan) fills these shelves—fortunately sales are lengthy affairs. Even better is the factory outlet (131 W. 72nd St., between Columbus and Amsterdam Aves., Upper West Side, tel. 212/787–6550), which carries mostly Maraolo's own shoe line, with a smattering of other name brands. Prices start at $19 and top out at $99.

NikeTown (6 E. 57th St., between 5th and Madison Aves., Midtown, tel. 212/891–6453). With its high technology and high-school gymnasium architecture, Nike's "motivational retail environment" knows how to push your buttons (and extract your signature). The latest in Nike footwear and wick-away fabrics (that quickly evaporate perspiration) are given the full museum treatment. Expect inspirational quotations in the flooring, computer-driven and 3-D foot sizers, and a heart-pumping movie shown every 20 minutes on an enormous screen in the entry atrium.

Tani (2020 Broadway, between W. 69th and 70th Sts., Upper West Side, tel. 212/873–4361). All the usual suspects in women's fashionable footwear—David Aaron, Charles David, Kenneth Cole—are under one roof. You can easily spend less than $100.

Tootsie Plohound (137 5th Ave., between E. 20th and 21st Sts., Gramercy, tel. 212/460–8650; 413 W. Broadway, between Prince and Spring Sts., SoHo, tel. 212/925–8931; 38 E. 57th, between Park and Madison Aves., Midtown, tel. 212/231–3199). This shop's all about groovy shoes. Most cost over $100, but sale stuff hovers at half that price.

BOOKS

Books are a big deal in New York City. Nearly as many residents write them as those who read them. (Question: the previous sentence was an example of: a) hyperbole, b) onomatopoeia, or c) alliteration?) Many bookstores hold regular **author appearances** and **readings** (listed in city weeklies like *Time Out* and *The New Yorker*), kindly tolerate magazine browsing, and keep really late hours. Practically the only time you need to leave anymore is to eat, although some stores, like **Housing Works Used Bookstore Cafe,** *below,* have anticipated this need, too.

In Chelsea, a half-dozen or so bookstores on West 18th Street between 5th and 6th avenues constitute the city's de facto **Book Row.** The whole island of Manhattan becomes one big book-lovers paradise during the three-day **New York is Book Country** fair (*see* Festivals and Annual Events *in* Chapter 1), held every September.

NEW BOOKS

Mega-chain store **Barnes & Noble** (4 Astor Pl., at Lafayette St., East Village, tel. 212/420–1322; 33 E. 17th St., between Broadway and Park Ave., Union Square, tel. 212/691–3770; 1972 Broadway at W. 66th St., Upper West Side, tel. 212/595–6859; 2289 Broadway, at W. 82nd St., Upper West Side, tel. 212/362–8835; and an exponentially increasing number of other locations) has made its despotic presence known in Manhattan (though the hardcover discount has been cut to 10%). **Borders Books & Music** (5 World Trade Center, Northeast Building, Lower Manhattan, tel. 212/839–8049; 461 Park Ave., at E. 57th St., Midtown, tel. 212/980–6785) is equally overwhelming when it comes to sheer merchandise volume. Since there's probably one of these stores where you live, stray from the superstore's path—there may not be as many couches, and you might pay a few dollars more. On the plus side, you'll find academic, smaller-press, and poetry books, and perhaps a little ambience to boot.

Coliseum Books (1771 Broadway, at W. 57th St., Midtown, tel. 212/757–8381). Scant blocks from the book-free zone of Planet Hollywood and the Hard Rock Cafe is a colossal selection of literature, nonfiction (including lots of music, travel, and gift books), and sundry remainder books.

Rizzoli (31 W. 57th St., between 5th and 6th Aves., Midtown, tel. 212/759–2424; 454 W. Broadway, near Prince St., SoHo, tel. 212/674–1616; 3 World Financial Center, at West St., Lower Manhattan, tel. 212/385–1400). Rizzoli stores mercifully avoid the sterile feel and fluorescent lighting that comes with chaindom. The uptown branch is especially classy, with a marble entrance and chandeliers; the SoHo location has a quirky gift shop. All have a particularly good selection of fine arts books, architecture, and travel, plus fiction and nonfiction.

St. Mark's Bookshop (31 3rd Ave., at E. 9th St., East Village, tel. 212/260–7853). The great selection of scholarly and popular works on art, literature, poetry, and history is available for daily perusal until almost midnight. This makes it a popular place for young intellectuals to check out the well-stocked literary criticism and philosophy sections, as well as each other.

Three Lives & Company (154 W. 10th St., at Waverly Pl., West Village, tel. 212/741–2069). One of the most-beloved little-indies, Three Lives is a tiny general-interest store that resembles your library in Utopia, with its sturdy shelves, books stacked on top of one another, and dim lamps. Stock is strong on new and canonical fiction, travel, and biography, and the staff knows of something that'll be just right.

Tower Books (383 Lafayette St., at E. 4th St., East Village, tel. 212/228–5100). Around the corner from Tower Records (see Records, Tapes, and CDs, below) and just as overwhelming, Tower Books carries tons of books, 'zines, and other word-oriented things. For the insatiable, it's open daily until midnight.

USED AND RARE BOOKS

There's nothing quite like that enticing, mildly musty smell of a used-book shop. Note to the prospective seller: Many of the stores listed below will happily buy any books you've got lying around, albeit at ridiculously low prices. Call ahead for buyers' hours—and try not to draw from the experience any general ideas about the state of literature today. Several dozen sellers of used and rare books are set up on the ninth floor of the **Chelsea Antiques Building** (see Flea Markets, below).

Shops in New York City that close early on weekdays often stay open until 7 or 8 PM on Thursday night.

Academy (10 W. 18th St., between 5th and 6th Aves., Chelsea, tel. 212/242–4848). Books about art, architecture, photography, philosophy, history, and film are the objects of a virtual feeding frenzy here whenever a new shipment arrives. Across the street, **Skyline** (13 W. 18th St., tel. 212/675–4773) deals in out-of-print books and first editions, as well as used LPs.

Argosy (116 E. 59th St., between Park and Lexington Aves., Midtown, tel. 212/753–4455). A literary landmark established in 1921, this store has a friendly, helpful staff to guide you to the low-priced, beautiful prints and maps, scholary books, and autographs.

Gotham Book Mart (41 W. 47th St., between 5th and 6th Aves., Midtown, tel. 212/719–4448). An alluring mythology surrounds New York's "most literary bookstore," due to the late proprietor, Frances Steloff, who opened it in 1920 with just $200 in her pocket, half of it on loan; she later became legendary, selling banned works by James Joyce, D. H. Lawrence, and Henry Miller when no other U.S. bookseller would stock them. In some ways, Gotham's still a relic of these times—there's no computer for check-out or inventory. Check out the cluttered stacks of used literature, poetry, drama, and film books, and pick up a signed print or book by Edward Gorey, gothic cartoonist extraordinaire.

Gryphon (2246 Broadway, between W. 80th and 81st Sts., Upper West Side, tel. 212/362–0706). Practically the width of War and Peace, this slip of a bookstore has inexpensive books of all sorts. Squeeze in among the stacks of art books and fiction; there are some great first and rare editions as well, and if they don't have the one you're pining for, they'll order it for you. It's open daily 'til midnight.

Housing Works Used Book Store Cafe (126 Crosby St., between Houston and Prince Sts., SoHo, tel. 212/334–3324). Altruistic citizens and publishers donate new and used books to this comfy store and café whose proceeds benefits the homeless with AIDS (see Housing Works, above). It's also one of the rare stores in the city that sells advance proofs ($2–$5) and has a scrupulously clean bathroom, an important feature for marathon shoppers.

Strand (828 Broadway, at E. 12th St., West Village, tel. 212/473–1452). Flaunting its 8 miles of books, the claustrophobically small aisles sometimes make it feel like there are 80 miles instead. In addition to rare books, first editions, and just-plain-old-used books, they carry reviewers' copies (downstairs) of hot-off-the-presses stuff for 50% off retail. The carts outside offer selections weird and wonderful, like a 1930s Balzac translation for $2.50. With so many titles it's hard to name the Strand's specialty, but it's become a particularly good spot to buy and sell art books.

SPECIALTY BOOKSTORES

The city has several excellent shops for foreign-language books: **Kinokuniya Bookstore** (10 W. 49th St., at 5th Ave., Midtown, tel. 212/765–1461) stocks books in Japanese; the **Librairie de France** and **Libre-**

BIDDING FOR FUN AND FURNITURE

For an extra adrenaline rush, try New York's auction houses. Sales are advertised in Friday's "Weekend" and Sunday's "Arts & Leisure" or "Classified" sections of the New York Times; most houses hold auctions several times a month. Check out the goods during the preview (a few days before the sale) and set a limit for yourself (in case bidding gets hairy). When bidding, be aggressive, as the pace can be very quick.

Christie's East and Sotheby's Arcade (Christie's East: 219 E. 67th St., Upper East Side, tel. 212/606–0400; Sotheby's Arcade: 1334 York Ave., at E. 72nd St., Upper East Side, tel. 212/606–7908). The second-string divisions of the city's two famous auction houses still have paddles and catalogs—you bring your expert eye and good taste and a full wallet (furniture and decorative arts start around $200).

Tepper Galleries (110 E. 25th St., near Park Ave. S, Midtown, tel. 212/677–5300). This no-frills house deals in "anonymous estate liquidation." Translation: everything from furs to wincingly ugly sculpture. Lots can go for under $30.

William Doyle Galleries (175 E. 87th St., near Lexington Ave., Upper East Side, tel. 212/427–2730). In Doyle's "Treasure Auction" room you can score quality sofas for $50 and '50s dresses for $20.

---

ria Hispanica (610 5th Ave., in Rockefeller Center, Midtown, tel. 212/581–8810) stock books in French and Spanish. For works on fine art, architecture, and photography, **museum bookstores** (particularly those at the Met and MoMA) can't be beat; *see* Major Attractions *in* Chapter 2.

Biography Bookstore (400 Bleecker St., at W. 11th St., West Village, tel. 212/807–8655). Famous artists, rock stars, politicians, dictators, ballerinas, religious figures, and television-show hosts just love to publish their fascinating life stories. This shop sells 'em all.

Books of Wonder (132 7th Ave., at W. 18th St., Chelsea, tel. 212/989–3270). This is the perfect place to buy that copy of *Eloise*. They've also got literary-inspired toys and a wonderful selection of classic and rare children's literature. Story-telling is Sunday at 11:45.

A Different Light Bookstore (151 W. 19th St., between 6th and 7th Aves., Chelsea, tel. 212/989–4850). The East Coast branch of this pioneering gay and lesbian bookstore has the city's best selection of les/bi/gay titles, from Radclyffe Hall's *The Well of Loneliness* to Eve Sedgwick's *Epistemology of the Closet*. There's also a small café and gift shop, as well as regular readings, book signings, and films.

The Drama Bookshop (723 7th Ave., at W. 48th St., Midtown, tel. 212/944–0595). At this little Theater District shop, you'll find books on all-things-theater, TV, film, and dance, and more unemployed actors than you can shake a *Playbill* at.

Hacker Art Books (45 W. 57th St., between 5th and 6th Aves., 5th floor). Once a meeting place for artists and intellectuals, Hacker's is now what has become of lots of specialty bookstores—a dying breed. Expect to find about 500,000 titles—everything from Ghirlandaio to Golub—and a helpful, knowledgeable staff. The store closes at 6:30, but you can always order from Hacker's catalogue.

Labyrinth Books (536 W. 112th St., between Broadway and Amsterdam Ave., Upper West Side, tel. 212/865-1588). This independent academic and scholarly shop has about 100,000 titles, including an excellent selection of worthwhile remainders. Recent releases and literary journals are on the first floor; upstairs new and used copies of philosophy, theory, and fiction are shelved side-by-side, which is perfect if you'd prefer a little interpretative marginalia in your copy of Jameson's *Postmodernism, Or, The Cultural Logic of Late-Capitalism.*

New York Open Center Bookshop (83 Spring St., between Broadway and Lafayette St., SoHo, tel. 212/219-2527). Holistic health and nutrition titles and books on New Age spirituality, ecology, and meditation are sold here. There's also a good music section, and an affiliated learning center has a calendar of workshops and events.

Partners & Crime Mystery Booksellers (44 Greenwich Ave., between 6th and 7th Aves., West Village, tel. 212/243-0440). Offering both new and out-of-print mysteries (and loads of British imports), this bright little shop also has a rental library and spooky fireplace. There's a "radio mystery hour" on Saturday evenings; call ahead for reservations.

Printed Matter (77 Wooster St., between Spring and Broome Sts., SoHo, tel. 212/925-0325). Maybe it's not a gallery, but a lot of the stuff here could qualify as art: handmade and small-press books, text-based objets d'art, and art-related magazines.

RECORDS, TAPES, AND CDS

What is New York City's response to the Astor Place K-Mart Super Store (770 Broadway, at Astor Pl., tel. 212/673-1540)? Many locals lament the infiltration, while others pay it homage. One welcoming aspect, however, is the availability and reliability of the bathrooms—something New Yorkers cannot do without.

New York's club scene supports an endless number of 12" shops, and the city's legions of hipsters and rockers and assorted hangers-on keep CD shops stocked with every imaginable American and European release. On **Bleecker Street** in the West Village and **St. Marks Place** in the East Village you'll find plenty of shops competing to offer the lowest prices and largest selection for stuff new and used. In a pinch, try one of the numerous **HMV**s (57 W. 34th St., at 6th Ave., Midtown, tel. 212/629-0900; 2081 Broadway, at W. 72nd St., Upper West Side, tel. 212/721-5900; 565 5th Ave., at E. 46th St., Midtown, tel. 212/681-6700).

Academy (10 W. 18th St., between 5th and 6th Aves., Chelsea, tel. 212/242-3000). In Academy's well-organized bins of used records and CDs you'll find tons of bargains for classical music, rock, and jazz. You'll walk away shaking your head at the valuable things people throw away and how you got it all for less than $10.

Bleecker Bob's Golden Oldies (118 W. 3rd St., at MacDougal St., West Village, tel. 212/475-9677). A legendary New York record store, this place is cluttered with four decades of rock and roll, punk (including some rare older stuff), and the things that happened in between. On Friday and Saturday nights it's open until 3 AM.

Dance Tracks (91 E. 3rd St., at 1st Ave., East Village, tel. 212/260-8729). The music emanating from this store can make the sidewalk vibrate. There's often quite a crush around the DJ, but you can find your own turntables to sample the wares: 12" soulful house, plus some hip-hop, drum 'n' base, and (Chicago and Detroit) jungle-base.

Etherea (66 Ave. A, between E. 4th and 5th Sts., East Village, tel. 212/358-1126). Those looking for small-label triphop, experimental ambient, drum 'n' base, or underground electronica cruise right over to the stacks of vinyl and CDs—but you don't have to know what you want; you can ask for straight-up advice from the helpful staff at this non-intimidating relatively new store, and listen to it in-store before you buy.

Footlight Records (113 E. 12th St., between 3rd and 4th Aves., East Village, tel. 212/533-1572). Movie and Broadway soundtracks, R&B, jazz, big band, and early rock and roll await at this used vinyl/new CD shop. The good stuff's more than $10. The rest is $2.

Generation (210 Thompson St., between Bleecker and W. Houston Sts., West Village, tel. 212/254-1100). Punk New York City lives on here in regular doses of new vinyl, what those-in-the-know simply call "underground stuff," and other assorted hard-to-get small-labels or imports. They've also got the punk standbys, like the Subhumans and The Clash, to complete your collection, and an assortment of multigeneric rare and imported CDs.

Gryphon (233 W. 72nd St., between West End Ave. and Broadway, Upper West Side, tel. 212/874–1588. You might, understandably, find a room packed with 90,000 LPs (mostly classical) overwhelming. But give the staff a few minutes and they'll unearth that rare recording you've been pining for.

Kim's Underground/Kim's Video & Audio/Mondo Kim's (Underground: 144 Bleecker St., at La Guardia Pl., West Village, tel. 212/260–1010; Video & Audio: 350 Bleecker St., at W. 10th St., West Village, tel. 212/675–8996; Mondo: 6 St. Marks Pl., between 2nd and 3rd Aves., East Village, tel. 212/505–0311). These three shops (attached to the Village's favorite video-rental stores) stock well-priced indie and avant films as well as new and used CDs, LPs, and 7"s. Don't think your taste's too obscure—if you've heard it, they have it. All are open daily until midnight.

Other Music (15 E. 4th St., between Broadway and Lafayette St., East Village, tel. 212/477–8150). As if to drive the point home, Other Music is found right across the street from a Tower Records branch. Browse through rows of various niche alternatives you'd never find there, like indie-label electronica, retro sensations, decadanse, and all manner of experimental alterna-genres. Roughly half the music is new, the other used. In-store performances, concert ticketing, and mail orders also happen here.

Tower Records and Video (692 Broadway, at E. 4th St., East Village, tel. 212/505–1500; 1961 Broadway, at W. 66th St., Lincoln Center, tel. 212/799–2500; 725 5th Ave., basement level of Trump Tower, Midtown, tel. 212/838–8110). These are just like the Tower Records in your hometown, except they're bigger and more crowded. The Lincoln Center branch has a café where you can rest your weary, CD-flipping fingertips. If you get lucky, you can catch a free live performance at any of the branches, as bands come through on promo appearances. The Midtown and Upper West Side stores mostly book classical or jazz artists, while the downtown store gets the rock groups. Check the papers for a tip-off.

Virgin Megastore (1540 Broadway, between W. 45th and 46th Sts., Times Square, tel. 212/921–1020; E. 14th St. and Broadway, Union Square, tel. 212/598–4666). Touted as the largest music-entertainment complex in the world (big enough to house 938 taxis), the glitzy Midtown emporium has a 50-ft DJ tower slicing through three levels of consumer frenzy; the newer Union Square store is the less ostentatious, yet more ambitious twin. Both have a café, an interactive game wall, and an excellent bookstore.

HOUSEHOLD FURNISHINGS

The stores listed below are just a smattering of what New York has to offer in the way of beautiful furniture, linens, and accessories for your home (or crowded apartment). Should none of these tickle your fancy, wander around East 9th Street in the East Village and down Avenue A—or just about anywhere in SoHo—where cool new purveyors of knickknacks are always setting up shop.

For peddlers of homey stuff cheap and used, New York City has several options: Many secondhand clothing places like **Housing Works** (*see above*) and the **Salvation Army** (536 W. 46th St., between 10th and 11th Aves., Midtown, tel. 212/757–2311) also stock housewares. Flea markets (*see below*) are another excellent source; get to the West 26th Street market before 6 AM and cross discerning glances with some of SoHo's hippest furniture dealers. You could also try your luck at an auction (*see box, above*).

ABC Carpet & Home (888 Broadway, at E. 19th St., Gramercy, tel. 212/473–3000). Exquisite (and expensive) new and antique furniture, lamps, linens, rugs, and bric-a-brac are displayed in heaps and jumbles at this vast household emporium masquerading as a dowager queen's attic.

Crate & Barrel (650 Madison Ave., at E. 59th St., Midtown, tel. 212/308–0011). This is the tried-and-true center for moderately priced glassware, kitchen and bath items, and won't-rock-the-boat furniture. If your inner interior designer has yet to be awakened, look to the displays to see how everything matches in that blond-wood way. The sales are more than acceptable.

Fish's Eddy (889 Broadway, at E. 19th St., Gramercy, tel. 212/420–9020; 2179 Broadway, at W. 77th St., Upper West Side, tel. 212/873–8819). Fish's Eddy resells dishes, china, and glassware from all walks of crockery life—from big corporations to gone-under restaurants. There are always some cheap new wares, and lots of oddball pieces like finger bowls and porcelain glove molds.

Museum of Modern Art Design Store (44 W. 53rd St., Midtown, tel. 212/767–1050). There's no getting over how happy well-designed otherwise-ordinary objects can make you feel. Behold, then, some of the functional art here: a glamorous toothbrush with polka dots, an ingenious CD holder strip with little speed bumps to separate and hold them upright, an Alvar Aalto vase, and a Philippe Starck utensil rack.

Surprise! Surprise! (91 3rd Ave., at E. 12th St., East Village, tel. 212/777–0990). A mini-warehouse of "I really need that gorgeous dishtowel" irresistibles, such as chunky Good Grips utensils, cleverly designed Umbra housewares, and Krupps machines of every style and size.

Zona (97 Greene St., between Prince and Spring Sts., SoHo, tel. 212/925–6750). From wrought-iron candlesticks to dining tables, the housewares, furniture, and (suitcase-friendly) accessories at Zona are simply beautiful. You'll buy them even if you don't need them.

SPECIALTY STORES

ACCESSORIES

Kate Spade (454 Broome St., at Mercer St., SoHo, tel. 212/274–1991). Since her bags are everywhere, it's somewhat surprising that this is Kate Spade's only boutique. You'll find a full range of her spare, status-symbol handbags—from the black nylon microfiber model that started all those knockoffs to something more eccentric in a leopard-print plush fabric. Prices start at a steep $70. Or melt some plastic for adorable clothes and pajamas.

Manhattan Portage (333 E. 9th St., between 1st and 2nd Aves., East Village, tel. 212/995–5490). You know you want one, so visit the source of the messenger-bag fad. Although they're a-dime-a-dozen around these parts, they cost real money ($20–$100). But don't let either of these facts stop you from impressing friends back home with your colorful and borough-specific, unisex carry-all.

The Pop Shop (292 Lafayette St., near E. Houston St., East Village, tel. 212/219–2784). World-famous artist Keith Haring had close ties to New York, ever since his days spray-painting subway cars; images from his unmistakable pop-art pieces cover all sorts of paraphernalia.

Swatch Timeship (5 E. 57th St., at 5th Ave., Midtown, tel. 212/317–1100; 640 Broadway, at Bleecker St., SoHo, tel. 212/777–1002). Welcome to the wonderful world of tick-tock land that is the colorful, discotheque-ish Swatch store. For under $70, you can get a stretchy-band scuba style; just $20 gets a little "flick-flack" model with a sparkly pink princess on it.

New Yorkers love their pets so much they even have a high-end store just for 'em. Fetch (43 Greenwich Ave., between 6th and 7th Aves., tel. 212/352–8591) offers gourmet food, mind-stimulating toys, and boar-bristle grooming supplies among its wares. If you've left your pooch or kitty behind at home, the gorgeous gifts here will help alleviate your guilt.

COSMETICS AND BODY PRODUCTS

If this is your first time in New York City, you should know that SoHo was not always the giant cosmetic counter that it now resembles. If lab-coat chic is your thing, these specialty stores and their squadron of make-up artists offer free in-store applications. Note that favorite colors and products go fast; in the end, you may have to traipse over to Bloomingdale's for that lipstick of choice.

5S (98 Spring St., between Mercer and Greene Sts., tel. 212/925–7880 or 877/746–6357). The mantra within this new, very pastel, peaceful place named for the five senses, implores you to "own your senses" and buy something to stimulate them. The multimedia presentation here is intended to awaken your senses, too. Everything revolves around the number five and the possibility that you're a changing woman with many moods and cosmetic needs—well, at least five.

Helena Rubenstein (135 Spring St., between Wooster and Greene Sts., SoHo, tel. 212/343–9963). Like the legend herself nearly 100 years ago, the new SoHo store/spa is modern and trend-setting: behold the omnipresent tan-without-tanning look acquired via Opalescence bronzer. Reinventing itself for the late-century lady, Rubenstein offers a Rush Hour Trio—a manicure, pedicure, and mini-facial for $100.

Kiehl's (109 3rd Ave., between E. 13th and 14th Sts., East Village, tel. 212/677–3171). Makeup artists and fashion editors swear by Kiehl's simply packaged shampoos, soaps, and cosmetics. Try not to choke at the prices; shampoo can easily run $25.

MAC (113 Spring St., between Mercer and Greene Sts., SoHo, tel. 212/334–4641; 14 Christopher St., between 6th and 7th Aves., West Village, tel. 212/243–4150). The ballooning popularity of this line of makeup, championed by the likes of RuPaul and k.d. lang, has drawn more stores to the area. It's more than makeup that's transacted here, darling, it's attitude. And don't be surprised if the staff has more piercings than thought hygienically sound.

KITSCH-O-RAMA

Alphabets (115 Ave. A, between E. 7th and 8th Sts., East Village, tel. 212/475–7250; 47 Greenwich Ave., between Perry and Charles Sts., West Village, tel. 212/229–2966; 2284 Broadway, between W. 82nd and 83rd Sts., Upper West Side, tel. 212/579–5702). These stores are so cute it makes you just wanna squeeze something. Fortunately there's tons to play with right at hand. Rubber lizards, Hello Kitty things, night-glow stars, sheriff's badges, and the like are here for the little kid in you or the little kid you're with.

Forbidden Planet (840 Broadway, at E. 13th St., East Village, tel. 212/473–1576). Come here ye fantasy fans and Star Wars addicts, to the mother of all sci-fi stores. They've got new, used, and foreign comics, plus plenty of sci-fi paperbacks.

Love Saves the Day (119 2nd Ave., at E. 7th St., East Village, tel. 212/228–3802). Some of these lunchboxes may look very, very familiar, not to mention the *Charlie's Angels* board game ($39), the Bionic Woman, and '60s Barbie dolls ($1.95 and up).

Mod World (85 1st Ave., East Village, tel. 212/460–8004). During the 19th century, there were no stores that sold retro postcards, glitter nail polish, plastic jewelry, and other unnecessary objects de junk. And how could we have lived without them?

New York Transit Museum Gift Shop (Grand Central Terminal, E. 42nd St. at Park Ave., Midtown, tel. 212/878–0106; Boerum Pl. and Schermerhorn St., Brooklyn Heights, tel. 718/243–3060). An alternate souvenir stop, everything is somehow linked to the MTA, from "straphanger" ties to the solid old subway tokens. The Brooklyn store is authentic from the ground up; the shop was built mostly by transit employees.

PAPER, CARDS, AND STATIONERY

Kate's Paperie (561 Broadway, at Prince St., SoHo, tel. 212/941–9816; 8 W. 13th St., at 5th Ave., West Village, tel. 212/633–0570). If this store doesn't breed collage fantasies, nothing will. Beautiful handmade papers, from stationery to wrapping, are surrounded by fountain pens, blank books, and other like-minded items.

TOYS AND GAMES

FAO Schwarz (767 5th Ave., at E. 58th St., Midtown, tel. 212/644–9400). The constant tinkle of "Welcome to Our World of Toys" may make adult customers bug-eyed, but this store is an undeniable toy fantasyland.

Dinosaur Hill (306 E. 9th St., East Village, tel. 212/473–5850). Smart kids need smart toys. If your kid fits this demographic, you'll appreciate this collection of mindful globally gathered gadgets from inflatable globes to science kits and handmade wonderments.

Enchanted Forest (85 Mercer St., between Spring and Broome Sts., SoHo, tel. 212/925–6677). The antidote to too much Mattel, this store has old-fashioned tin toys, gizmos, and a small, choice selection of children's books. Dozens of stuffed animals peer out from the stairway to the small overhead loft.

ANTIQUES AND FLEA MARKETS

If you don't know where to look, you could get the impression that antiques are solely for the rich. The stuff of the city's smaller, more affordable dealers, however, are accessible to just about any working stiff. They tend to cluster together in what could affectionately be called antiques minimalls, like the **Manhattan Art & Antiques Center** (1050 2nd Ave., between E. 55th and 56th Sts., Midtown, tel. 212/355–4400).

Just as permanently placed as the antiques stores, the city's **flea markets,** which are good things, are not to be confused with its street fairs. Flea markets are full of stuff that's antique, cool, weird, and kitschy, whereas street fairs pop up randomly, and no matter where they are, sell the same old things— block after predictable block of drooping houseplants and incense burners.

Annex Antiques Fair and Flea Market (6th Ave. between W. 24th and 26th Sts., Chelsea, tel. 212/243–5343; open weekends, sunrise to sunset). The mother of all flea markets takes up two lots on Saturday and four lots on Sunday. More than 400 dealers display wares ranging from vintage wallpaper to chandeliers and Fiestaware to mismatched spoons. This is where Andy Warhol used to show up in his black limousine. Today it's where people like Ralph Lauren and Martha Stewart send their lackeys to find all those old saddles and romantic black-and-white photos they use as props.

Chelsea Antiques Building (110 W. 25th St., between 6th and 7th Aves., Chelsea, tel. 212/929–0909; open daily). Looking for World War II photographs? Russian samovars? Or out-of-print Austrian poetry books? This 12-story building is filled with specialized dealers, though prices can be steep. The best bargaining happens on weekends.

I.S. 44 Indoor/Outdoor Flea Market (Columbus Ave. between W. 76th and 77th Sts., Upper West Side, tel. 212/721–0900; open Sun. 10–6). Over 300 dealers of handmade jewelry, vintage clothing, and bric-a-brac (plus a farmers' market) jam this Upper West Side schoolyard and gym.

Metropolitan Arts and Antiques Pavilion. (110 W. 19th St., between 6th and 7th Aves., tel. 212/463–0200). It's strange to be at a mall where the average age isn't 16. But if the kids knew what great, affordable kitsch, jewelry, and funky furnishings could be found here, they just might migrate.

Soho Antiques Fair & Collectibles Market (Grand St. at Broadway, SoHo, tel. 212/682–2000; open weekends, 9–5). Good deals and a great SoHo location are what make this smallish flea market so popular. It's heavy on household items, records and CDs, old toys, and vintage clothes.

AFTER DARK 6

UPDATED BY JOHN DONOHUE

Manhattan's nightlife is the most garish, brazen, and brilliant show on Planet Earth—and true to every cliché, it never stops. Bars stay open until 4 AM, dance clubs wind down around dawn, and the concept of "weeknight" just doesn't exist. The scene varies by neighborhood. On the **Upper West Side** and **East Side,** you'll find Ivy League grads drinking off another market-driven day. The **West Village** and **Chelsea** are centers of gay nightlife—even if Bleecker Street near Washington Square is typically saturated with straight, horny, beer-guzzling NYU students. **SoHo** is a Beautiful People brew of dance clubs and funky bars, while the **East Village** and **Lower East Side** are populated by less pretentious packs of the young, pierced, and hip. Whether it's jazz in a basement dive, a crowded club throbbing with a house-happy beat, or a spoken-word show in a smoky bar, New York is where it's at.

If you're new in town, get off your butt and find a copy of **Paper** magazine ($3), which has the hippest bar and club listings in town, or grab a weekly events magazine: **Time Out New York** ($2.50), the **Village Voice** (free), **New York** magazine ($2.95), **The New Yorker** ($3), the **New York Press** (free), and the **New York Observer** ($1) all have listings. The most thorough is *Time Out,* though the *Voice* has long been considered the bible of the downtown scene. The *Observer*'s "Eight-Day Week" captures quirky society, fashion, and arts stuff. Note that clubs and bars can draw hugely different crowds on different nights: dykes one day, dweebs the next. To add to the confusion, many bars function as clubs, with live bands and dancing one or two nights a week. And dance clubs frequently showcase live bands. But who's complaining? It sure beats navel-gazing in suburbia. A final note: Wherever you go at night, walk on main streets and use designated off-hour subway platforms, especially if you're alone. Or, better yet, catch a cab.

BARS

In Seattle it may be chic to make coffee into a social event, but this Starbucks-fueled trend has yet to subvert nightlife in the Big Apple. Whether you're going out with friends, a blind date, business associates, or even your family, you're bound to end up at one of New York's bars—especially since they're legally allowed to serve alcohol until 4 AM. Throughout New York you can have a cocktail with glorious drag queens, drink single-malt with exiled IRA supporters, or just have an anonymous beer in a dark corner. If your idea of good drinking company is the cast of "Ally McBeal," try the **Upper West Side.** Stop by the **Upper East Side** if you want memories of college drinking games to haunt you again. If Smashing Pumpkins or Sonic Youth are more your style, try the **East Village** or the **Lower East Side**; if you'd rather hang with a slightly more sophisticated (read: moneyed) crowd, try **SoHo**; a more multicultural version of the same mixes in with the gay scene in **Chelsea** and the **West Village**; nearby Bleecker Street is the place to be if you want to experience New York's version of Collegetown U.S.A.

UPPER WEST SIDE AND AROUND COLUMBIA UNIVERSITY

Theme bars are big with the Upper West Side's post-college crowd. Take a happy-hour crawl along Broadway in the 70s and 80s and you'll visit plenty of alcohol-serving jungle huts, hunting lodges, and surf shacks. Much farther north, the blocks around Columbia University naturally support a number of cheap and divey undergrad and grad student hangouts.

420 Bar & Lounge. Black velvet curtains and flickering candles highlight the decor at this disarmingly simple-looking spot. There's a pool table downstairs and a cooler-than-average crowd—MTV has had more than a few parties here. *420 Amsterdam Ave., at W. 80th St., tel. 212/579–8450. Subway: 1 or 9 to W. 79th St.*

Hi-Life Bar & Grill. This restaurant-bar may be a little rough on the decor (a few kitsch items and a fish tank near the door are the standouts), but the padded black vinyl walls create a pleasant semblance of a big-band-era cocktail den. Its outdoor seating makes it the anchor of Upper West Side nightlife in summer. A DJ spins '70s hits on weekends. *477 Amsterdam Ave., at W. 83rd St., tel. 212/787–7199. Subway: 1 or 9 to W. 86th St.*

On alternate Wednesday evenings, the New York Beer Appreciation Club convenes at Ruby's Taphouse to swill new brews.

Jake's Dilemma. A well-worn dive, this eternally popular watering hole owes its success to a crafty mix of cheap drinks (on Wednesdays draft beer is free for women) and kitsch. Beer is served by the half yard, in tall fluted glasses that make it hard not to spill. *430 Amsterdam Ave., at W. 80th St., tel. 212/ 580–0556. Subway: 1 or 9 to W. 79th St.*

Moonlighting. This multilevel lounge with smoky mirrors and dark corners brings a bit of downtown style—and dancing—to the Upper West Side. *511 Amsterdam Ave., between W. 84th and 85th Sts., tel. 212/799–4643. Subway: 1 or 9 to W. 86th St.*

Raccoon Lodge. Come to observe wild, rugby-striped Upper West Siders who drink beer, think beer-induced romantic thoughts, and drink more beer. The bar itself is an Elks Club knockoff with all the trimmings: stuffed moose head, fireplace, and plenty of scrimmaging for the seats at the bar. *480 Amsterdam Ave., at W. 83rd St., tel. 212/874–9984. Subway: 1 or 9 to W. 86th St.*

1020 Amsterdam. The snip, snip, snip of scissors has been replaced by the thwock of billiard balls at this barbershop turned watering hole (a few old salon chairs remain). Don't lose your shirt to the grad students who shoot pool here; they play to win. *1020 Amsterdam Ave., at 110th St., tel. 212/961–9224. Subway: 1 or 9 to Cathedral Pkwy.*

UPPER EAST SIDE

Here single yuppies troll for Mr. or Ms. Right-Now in the sanitized Irish bars of 2nd and 3rd avenues, like the eternally popular **Pat O'Brien's** (1497 3rd Ave., between E. 84th and 85th Sts., tel. 212/628–7242). West of Lexington Avenue is the land of the $15 martini—don't say we didn't warn you. Also note that during summer weekends, the entire Upper East Side shuts down, mostly because everyone is socializing at their beach houses in the Hamptons. So grab a can of malt liquor and pretend.

American Trash. Though true bikers would rather eat asphalt than party on the Upper East Side, this thrashed bar at least *looks* like a Hell's Angel hangout. Happy hour (weekdays 12–7 PM, weekends 4–7 PM) gets you $2 pints and other cheap drinks. *1471 1st Ave., between E. 76th and 77th Sts., tel. 212/ 988–9008. Subway: 6 to E. 77th St.*

Auction House. Looking to escape the keg-party atmosphere of most Upper East Side bars? Then leave your baseball cap and sneakers behind and step into this vaguely Victorian lounge with gilt mirrors and velvet couches. It's surprisingly grown-up. *300 E. 89th St., between 1st and 2nd Aves., tel. 212/427–4458. Subway: 4,5, or 6 to E. 86th St.*

Ruby's Taphouse. The two frat brothers who got together and opened this joint are proud to be your buds. They've got 26 microbrews on tap and decent pub grub. *1754 2nd Ave., between E. 91st and 92nd Sts., tel. 212/987–8179. Subway: 4, 5, or 6 to E. 86th St.*

MIDTOWN

Midtown bars are a weird (and occasionally overwhelming) mix of last-holdout sleazy Times Square XXX dives, swank hotel bars, and cheesy tourist traps. One small comfort: Virtually every Irish pub you'll see is a winner.

44. You may not be wearing Armani, but the waiter probably is at the Royalton Hotel's outrageously chic cocktail lounge. Must-sees include the padded circular bar (where they serve only vodka and such clear spirits as grappa) and the too-fabulous bathrooms. *44 W. 44th St., between 5th and 6th Aves., tel. 212/ 869–4400. Subway: B, D, F, or Q to W. 42nd St.*

Full Moon Saloon. This tiny Theater District dive boasts a 100% country-and-western video jukebox, which most customers treat as if it were a dispenser of bubonic plague. A laid-back attitude and lotsa local color make it worth a visit, especially now that Disney has taken over the neighborhood. *735 8th Ave., between W. 46th and 47th Sts., no phone. Subway: A, C, or E to W. 42nd St.*

Howard Johnson's. The HoJo cocktail lounge is so tacky it's beautiful. There is no place better to sip highballs with complimentary egg-salad sandwiches. The daily happy hour is 4–7. *1551 Broadway, at W. 46th St., tel. 212/354–1445. Subway: 1 or 9 to W. 50th St.*

Monkey Bar. Take a peek at how the other half drinks at the posh Monkey Bar, which has a big, hairless ape at the door. Jungle murals inside don't bring out much barbarism in the mannered banker-types shooting back Scotch. *60 E. 54th St., between Park and Madison Aves., tel. 212/838–2600. Subway: 6 to E. 51st St.*

Morgans Bar. Supermodels and their kin tuck themselves into this handsome little bar, all gilt mirrors and candles, housed in the basement of Morgans hotel. Call ahead to reserve one of the few tables to avoid the 'tude at the bar. *237 Madison Ave., between E. 37th and 38th Sts., tel. 212/726–7600. Subway: B, D, F, N, Q, or R to 34th St.*

Pen Top Bar and Terrace. Atop the 23rd floor of the Peninsula Hotel you'll find indoor and outdoor seating and wonderful views that make this one of the city's best places for a summertime drink. It's patronized by a youngish cocktail-drinking crowd. *700 5th Ave., between 54th and 55th Sts., tel. 212/903–3902. Subway: E or F to 5th Ave./53rd St.*

Revolution. Even though it's a sign of Hell's Kitchen's gentrification, this lounge somehow manages to make everyone feel welcome (including a strong gay following). There's also a full-service restaurant. Go early to secure one of the comfortable couches. *611 9th Ave., between 43rd and 44th Sts., tel. 212/ 489–8451. Subway: A, C, or E to W. 42nd St.*

Sardi's. Come to this landmark spot if you want to be a tourist in the Theater District: The walls are covered with caricatures of past and present Broadway stars. Sometimes celebs even occupy Sardi's red-leather booths. *234 W. 44th St., near 8th Ave., tel. 212/221–8440. Subway: A, C, or E to W. 42nd St.*

Whiskey Bar. With the purchase of an expensive drink you get hours of people-watching at this hyper-trendy bar in the swank Paramount Hotel. *235 W. 46th St., between Broadway and 8th Ave., tel. 212/ 764–5500. Subway: C or E to W. 50th St.*

CHELSEA AND UNION SQUARE

Take a look at the crowds on **8th Avenue,** particularly around **West 18th Street,** and you'll see that this once blah neighborhood is newly hip—especially among gays and lesbians. The action spills over into the Union Square area, though things here tend more towards the preppy than the fabulous. At revamped warehouse discos on Chelsea's western fringe, bawdy crowds keep things going way past 3 AM.

Chelsea Commons. Construction workers mingle with Chelsea dandies at this longtime neighborhood fave. It's got a lamplit brick courtyard straight out of olde London, as well as live music on Saturday. *242 10th Ave., at W. 24th St., tel. 212/929–9424. Subway: C or E to W. 23rd St.*

Ciel Rouge. Sip titillating cocktails like Lady Love Fizz and Bitches Brew in a wicked all-red room straight out of the Left Bank. Don't miss cool happenings like live jazz and piano evenings Tuesday nights. *176 7th Ave., between W. 20th and 21st Sts., tel. 212/929–5542. Subway: 1 or 9 to W. 23rd St.*

Coffee Shop. Arrive way, way, way after midnight to catch the action at this hip, model-owned bar and diner. Attendance is mandatory for club crawlers. *29 Union Sq. W, at E. 16th St., tel. 212/243–7969. Subway: L, N, R, 4, 5, or 6 to Union Sq.*

g. Toned and tan, the young patrons at this chic boys' bar and lounge down frozen Cosmopolitans. This is Chelsea at its best dressed and best behaved. *223 W. 19th St., between 7th and 8th Aves., tel. 212/929–1085. Subway: 1 or 9 to W. 18th St.*

Lot 61. If you have attitude to burn, this high-ceilinged and high-priced lounge is the place you're looking for. Its vinyl couches and modernist decor will make you feel like your life is a fashion-magazine spread. *550 W. 21st St., between 10th and 11th Aves., tel. 212/243–6555. Subway: C or E to W. 23rd St.*

Rebar. Rebar offers every kind of entertainment except ice-skating polar bears: open-mike nights, stand-up comedy, live bands, and a DJ spinning house and salsa on weekends. *127 8th Ave., at W. 16th St., tel. 212/627–1680. Subway: A, C, E, or L to W. 14th St.*

WEST VILLAGE

On cold, wintry evenings cozy up to the Art Bar's fireplace and luxuriate in the plushness of it all.

Gays and straights, drag queens and rockers, and just plain folks all mix in the West Village's myriad bars and clubs. **Christopher Street,** once the center of New York's gay nightlife has become quietly gentrified, though a few remnants of its former life remain. Christopher Street west of Hudson Street is a center of NYC's gay African-American nightlife. On **West 4th** and **Bleecker streets** there are scores of cheesy, tourist-filled bars—great if you just wanna have fun with buffalo wings and cheap beer. Otherwise, avoid them.

Art Bar. Sip your scotch-and-soda on one of the plush couches by the fireplace at this popular Village bar. It's a great place for a romantic cocktail during the week; on weekends it's really, really crowded. *52 8th Ave., between Horatio and Jane Sts., tel. 212/727–0244. Subway: A, C, E, or L to W. 14th St.*

Bar D'O. At this dimly lit lounge, a friendly, gay and straight crowd cradle large martinis and get cozy on the low-slung couches. On Saturday night top-notch cabaret singers in drag entertain for a $5 cover. *29 Bedford St., at Downing St., tel. 212/627–1580. Subway: 1 or 9 to W. Houston St.*

Bar Six. An idyllic stop for a soft, summer night, with French doors opening onto the street, this elegant bar and restaurant has all the trappings of a New York hot spot without the attitude. Late Sunday the blinds are rolled down to usher in a casual hip-hop and acid jazz dance hour. *502 6th Ave., between W. 12th and 13th Sts., tel. 212/691–1363. Subway: 1, 2, 3, or 9 to 14th St.*

Chumley's. Once a speakeasy, this still-secret pub is great for a civilized pint of ale or a debauched night with old chums. To find the unmarked wooden doorway, listen for boisterous conversation and peals of laughter as you walk past Bedford Street's brick row houses. *86 Bedford St., at Barrow St., tel. 212/675–4449. Subway: 1 or 9 to Christopher St. (Sheridan Sq.).*

Corner Bistro. Founded in 1966, this pub-and-grub-style bar has finally come into its own. The cozy place is so inviting, and the young, professional crowd so friendly, you might think you ducked into a small-town place (if it weren't for the sirens outside). Many consider the Corner's burgers among the best in Manhattan. *331 W. 4th St., between Jane St. and 8th Ave., tel. 212/242–9502. Subway: A, C, E, 1, 2, 3, or 9 to 14th St.*

Hogs and Heifers. Sure, this roughneck bar has seen a few fistfights. But most of the time its crew of wanna-be Harley-riding hardasses is just having a damn good, hard-rockin', Pabst-drinkin' time. *859 Washington St., between W. 13th and 14th Sts., tel. 212/929–0655. Subway: A, C, E, or L to W. 14th St.*

Hudson Bar and Books. Satisfy your hankering for brandy and a big fat stogie at this cigar bar, done up like a billionaire's library. Cigars range from $9 (merely stinky) to $16 (Dominican Allone). *636 Hudson St., between Horatio and Jane Sts., tel. 212/229–2642. Subway: A, C, E, or L to W. 14th St.*

Peculier Pub. From Aass Amber to Zywiec, the Peculier Pub stocks more than 500 beers representing 43 countries, including Vietnam, Nicaragua, and the Ivory Coast. The besotted crowd is half as interesting. *145 Bleecker St., between Thompson St. and La Guardia Pl., tel. 212/353–1327. Subway: 6 to Bleecker St.*

RACK 'EM

The city that never sleeps has a couple of pool halls that never close (literally). It's great for a low-key night out, a low-cost date, or if you find yourself restless at a strange hour. Tables cost $10–$15 per hour and are usually cheaper before 5 PM.

Chelsea Billiards. This classy, crowded joint has 43 pool tables, eight snooker tables, and two billiard tables, all spread over two floors. 54 W. 21st St., between 5th and 6th Aves., Chelsea, tel. 212/989–0096. Subway: N or R to W. 23rd St.

Le Q. It has 32 tables and some of the lowest rates in town: $3 per person per hour, any time of day. 36 E. 12th St., near University Pl., East Village, tel. 212/ 995–8512. Subway: L, N, R, 4, 5, or 6 to Union Sq.

Soho Billiards. This is a good spot to keep a promising date from ending; on the weekends the action on its 28 tables keeps going until 4:30 in the morning. 298 Mulberry St., at Houston St., East Village, tel. 212/925–3753. Subway: B, D, F, or Q to Broadway/Lafayette St. or 6 to Bleecker St.

Rio Mar. This throwback to Spain sits hidden on a corner in the meat-packing district. Though they stop serving tapas around 6 PM, the bar stays open (and packed) into the wee hours. If you're really hungry, check out the adjoining dining room (*see* Chapter 4). *7 9th Ave., at Little W. 12th St., tel. 212/243–9015. Subway: A, C, E, or L to W. 14th St.*

Tortilla Flats. This haven of kitsch (streamers and tacky movie posters plastered to every possible inch) is a popular, after-hours munch fest and party when the 1–4—that's AM—Saturday-night happy hour kicks into gear. There's outdoor seating and killer margaritas. *767 Washington St., at W. 12th St., tel. 212/243–1053. Subway: A, C, or E to W. 14th St.*

White Horse Tavern. Go gentle into this good pub, where Dylan Thomas drank himself to death in 1953. A mix of mournful poets and uncaring yuppies carry on the wake at this historic 110-year-old tavern. But unless you want to booze with Jerseyites, come weeknights for a more authentic feel. *560 Hudson St., between W. 11th and Perry Sts., tel. 212/243–9260. Subway: 1 or 9 to Christopher St. (Sheridan Sq.).*

EAST VILLAGE, ALPHABET CITY, AND THE LOWER EAST SIDE

The East Village and Alphabet City are the most bar-dense areas of a city that generally likes to drink. And whether you wear cowboy boots, wing tips, Doc Martens, platform shoes, or go-go boots, you'll have no problem finding something suitable. The big new scene is currently on the Lower East Side, on **Orchard** and **Ludlow streets.** Bars here are hip and nearly unpretentious, frequented by GenXers with lots of style and little cash. If you fall into this category, two mandatory Alphabet City stops are **7B** (E. 7th St., at Ave. B, tel. 212/473–8840) for cheap Genesee beer on tap, and **Sophie's** (507 E. 5th St., between Aves. A and B, tel. 212/228–5680) for pinball machines, a jukebox heavy into alternative music, and endless cheap beer—not to mention major crowds on weekend nights.

2A. A mismash of boozers, pretty young things, and thinker types in heavy glasses patronize this dark, arty bar. If you get tired of the cruising singles scene downstairs, relax on one of the comfy couches upstairs. *25 Ave. A, at E. 2nd St., tel. 212/505–2466. Subway: F to 2nd Ave.*

B-Bar. Formerly known as the Bowery Bar, this once-upon-a-time hip outpost now has more celebrity stalkers than real-life *Post* "Page Six" bold-face names. But the revamped gas station is still a cool spot to hold court. *40 E. 4th St., between Bowery and Lafayette St., tel. 212/475–2220. Subway: 6 to Astor Pl.*

The Boiler Room. This relaxed and dark gay bar with cheap drinks, a pool table, and an '80's-themed jukebox attracts Village locals rather than Chelsea muscle boys. But that doesn't mean there's a shortage of cute patrons. The girls take over one Sunday each month. *86 E. 4th St., at 2nd Ave., tel. 212/254–7536. Subway: 6 to Astor Place.*

Chez es Saada. You'll think you're in Tangier at this neo-Moroccan supper club, with a name that translates as "place of happiness" in French-Arabic. Stretch out on a hassock in the catatcomblike lower level and sip one of the house cocktails, but watch your step leaving lest you slip on the rose-petal covered stairway. *42 E. 1st St., between 1st and 2nd Aves., tel. 212/777–5671. Subway: F to 2nd Ave.*

d.b.a. The name means "doing business as," a legal term that reflects the owners' inability to choose a name when filing the bar's paperwork at city hall. Employees say it means "don't bother asking" and "drink beer always." Which is easy to do with 60 beers in bottles and 15 on tap. It also has one of the largest collections of single-malt whiskeys outside Scotland. *41 1st Ave., between E. 2nd and 3rd Sts., tel. 212/475–5097. Subway: F to 2nd Ave.*

Decibel Sake Bar. Decibel takes care of business with a small sign outside announcing NO SUSHI, NO KARAOKE. Instead, you'll find 40 kinds of sake and dozens of delicious Japanese appetizers. *210 E. 9th St., between 2nd and 3rd Aves., tel. 212/979–2733. Subway: 6 to Astor Pl.*

Diehard geezers at McSorley's Old Ale House still complain about the decision (under court order) to admit women in 1971.

Fez. Brass tables, pillow-strewn divans, and gorgeous Arabic tiles fill this dark and smoky room beneath Time Cafe. Nightly events include everything from big band to hip-hop to spoken word. For big-name bands you should make reservations in advance. *380 Lafayette St., at Great Jones St., tel. 212/533–2680. Subway: 6 to Astor Pl.*

K.G.B. East Village political diehards boozily discuss the state of the Revolution in this crimson room hung with old CCCP posters. It's a favorite hangout of literary types and frequently hosts readings. *85 E. 4th St., between 1st and 2nd Aves., tel. 212/505–3360. Subway: F to 2nd Ave.*

Lucky Cheng's. Drag queens (and the men and women who love them) fill this gay bathhouse turned trendy pan-Asian bar-restaurant. On weekends, a house DJ takes over the lower level while a glossy drag promenade takes the floor. *24 1st Ave., between E. 1st and 2nd Sts., tel. 212/473–0516. Subway: F to 2nd Ave.*

Ludlow Bar. Part rock club, part dance den, pure funk dive, Ludlow is a bare-bones East Village basement bar favored by a diverse crowd of lesbian pool players and struggling actors. Live bands play during the week, DJs spin soul and acid jazz on weekends. *165 Ludlow St., between E. Houston and Stanton Sts., tel. 212/353–0536. Subway: F to 2nd Ave.*

M & R Bar. You can't find a friendlier place for a chat and a bit of scene than at this comfortable little bar and restaurant favored by a conscientiously understated crowd that'll still talk to you even if you *are* from Wichita. *264 Elizabeth St., between Houston and Prince Sts., tel. 212/226–0559. Subway: 6 to Bleecker St.*

Marion's Continental Restaurant and Lounge. Discover the meaning of *swank* in this fabulous '60s-style cocktail lounge, a onetime fave of Gable and Sinatra. Marion's is still ideal for celeb-watching over a cosmopolitan or Stoli Gibson. The food is tip-top. *354 Bowery, at E. 4th St., tel. 212/475–7621. Subway: 6 to Astor Pl.*

Max Fish. One of the Lower East Side's trendiest bars is always ultracrowded with black-clad slackers, seemingly underaged skaters, and the odd raving bum or two. There's no place to sit, so everyone mills around like it's a junior-high dance. If you want a scene, Max Fish is fine; if you want a quiet drink, go elsewhere. *178 Ludlow St., between E. Houston and Stanton Sts., tel. 212/529–3959. Subway: F to 2nd Ave.*

McSorley's Old Ale House. Not much has changed at this sawdust-carpeted saloon since it opened in 1854. By 11 AM on any given day there's a long line of grizzled regulars and curious tourists waiting to doublefist mugs of McSorley's own brew (two mugs for $3). *15 E. 7th St., between 2nd and 3rd Aves., tel. 212/473–9148. Subway: 6 to Astor Pl.*

RED DEATH AND BUFFALO SWEAT

Did you know that cocktails were invented in New York? Well, according to legend, an 18th-century New York tavern keeper used the tail feather from a rooster to stir drinks, inspiring the name. Two hundred years later, even bars that qualify as "dives" know how to make martinis, Cosmopolitans, and Manhattans. Yet when you need something more exotic and perhaps downright toxic, try one of the following at your own risk.

SoHo's MERCBAR (151 Mercer St., between Houston and Prince Sts., tel. 212/ 966–2727) specializes in Cement Mixers, a combo of Bailey's Irish Cream and Rose's Lime Juice that solidifies after you swish it around in your mouth for a few seconds.

Also in SoHo, NAKED LUNCH (17 Thompson St., at Grand St., tel. 212/343– 0828) makes a mean Red Death: vodka, Rose's Lime Juice, Triple Sec, Southern Comfort, Amaretto, sloe gin, and orange juice, topped with Sambuca.

In the East Village, at MARION'S CONTINENTAL LOUNGE (354 Bowery, between Great Jones and W. 4th Sts., tel. 212/475–7621), dive into a Lime Ricky (vodka, club soda, and lime juice), sweet enough to curl your tongue, but big enough so that after a while you won't notice. They also make the best martini south of 42nd Street.

Mona's. The Ultimate Neighborhood Dive Bar is the place to drink and play pool with low-key East Villagers. Crowds show for live Irish folk music (Monday), and $2.75 pints of Guinness (Thursday). *224 Ave. B, between E. 13th and 14th Sts., tel. 212/353–3780. Subway: L to 1st Ave.*

Orchard. You'd easily miss this slim addition to the Lower East Side bar scene if you didn't know it was here. One hint: look for the glowing terrarium in the front window. It's worth seeking out, though, for the good-looking crowd as well as the great DJs. *200 Orchard St., between, E. Houston and Stanton Sts., tel. 212/673–5350. Subway: F to 2nd Ave.*

Sidewalk Café. Most people come here to fight over a bar stool, down a few beers, and leave, though the kitchen's open 24 hours. East Village barhoppers roll through around 10 PM and again at dawn. *94 Ave. A, at E. 6th St., tel. 212/473–7373. Subway: L to 1st Ave.*

CHINATOWN AND LITTLE ITALY

If you're looking for an Italian-American watering hole à la *Goodfellas*, rent the movie—you won't find it in Little Italy. Opium dens are likewise scarce in Chinatown. Sorry, kids.

Double Happiness Don't bump your head on the way into this swank subterranean lounge where the beautiful people swill green-tea martinis (they're quite good actually). Arrive early and you can take over a small banquette-lined room with a skylit ceiling to the sidewalk above. *173 Mott St., at Broome St., tel. 212/941–1282. Subway: 6 to Spring St.*

Marechiaro Tavern. Sometimes known as Tony's, this gruff no-nonsense bar is Little Italy's only authentic spot for a drink. Note the mural-size photo of Frank Sinatra and the barkeep, looking swell together. *176½ Mulberry St., between Broome and Grand Sts., no phone. Subway: 6 to Spring St.*

SOHO AND TRIBECA

SoHo is the center of glam New York nightlife, and **West Broadway**'s bars and bistros are always packed, especially when they set up outdoor tables in summer. Along **Greenwich** and **Hudson streets** there are some fine places that happily don't charge the steep prices you'll find at bars in SoHo's center (i.e., along Spring and Mercer streets). TriBeCa has more restaurants than bars, though you will find a few watering holes off Broadway above **Chambers Street.**

Bell Caffe. If any struggling artists still lived in SoHo, they would drown their sorrows in this funky pub filled with lumpy couches and weird kitsch items. Sit outside on summer nights or dive on in for some free live music or an art opening. *310 Spring St., between Hudson and Greenwich Sts., tel. 212/334–2355. Subway: C or E to Spring St.*

Café Noir. You'll wonder if you're still in SoHo at this chic French-Moroccan oasis: The waiters, waitresses, and bartenders all speak French (and not much English). *32 Grand St., at Thompson St., tel. 212/431–7910. Subway: A, C, or E to Canal St.*

Those comedians you're paying to watch will seem much funnier if you've cut the cost of the cover charge by checking for coupons in the Village Voice.

Ear Inn. Rumor has it that this used to be the Bear Inn, until the B fell off the sign. Regardless, this self-described "dump with dignity" draws a crowd of friendly folk to its long, old-fashioned bar for leisurely pints of stout. If it's crowded, head across the way to Bell Caffe (*see above*). *326 Spring St., at Greenwich St., tel. 212/226–9060. Subway: C or E to Spring St.*

Lucky Strike. This über-cool bistro has started quieting down now that the supermodels party elsewhere. Even so, its weekend dance parties are still crowded affairs, with DJs playing funky tunes for the young Euro types boozing it up at the cozy back tables. *59 Grand St., between Wooster St. and West Broadway, tel. 212/941–0479. Subway: A, C, or E to Canal St.*

Match. A hip crowd checks in at this beautifully understated restaurant/bar in between gallery openings, AIDS benefits, loft parties, spoken-word performances, sexual dalliances, etc., etc., etc. *160 Mercer St., between Houston and Prince Sts., tel. 212/343–0020. Subway: N or R to Prince St.; also B, D, F, or Q to Broadway/Lafayette St.*

Mercbar. Always crowded, Merc is a staple SoHo scene, with an eclectic clientele of tourists, bankers, actors, and artists lolling on cushy couches at the front. The hostesses are Gestapo recruits: Don't take it personally, they order everybody around. Look for tall French doors; in SoHo fashion, there's no sign outside. *151 Mercer St., between W. Houston and Prince Sts., tel. 212/966–2727. Subway: N or R to Prince St.*

Novecento. A lively crowd and good music (usually acid jazz or salsa) make this Argentinean café-bar an adventure any night of the week. The downstairs is spacious and airy; upstairs it's intimate, with deep couches and dim lighting. *343 W. Broadway, between Broome and Grand Sts., tel. 212/925–4706. Subway: A, C, E, 1, or 9 to Canal St.*

Pravda. Capitalism may be struggling in the home country, but it's flourishing at this pricey Russian-themed restaurant and bar. A truly beautiful space, you had better be beautiful yourself to get in, or go before 10 PM to slide past the stern bouncers. *281 Lafayette St., between Prince and Houston Sts., tel. 212/226–4696. Subway: 6 to Spring St.*

Red Bench. SoHo's trendiest (and tiniest) late-night bar draws downtown scenesters, stockbrokers, street artists, and nouvelle hippie chicks. Definitely a place to be seen. *107 Sullivan St., between Prince and Spring Sts., tel. 212/274–9120. Subway: C or E to Spring St.*

Spy Bar Somehow, SoHo's hottest lounge remains a draw. Perhaps its the strict door code; only the good looking and the better dressed get in. Now you know. *101 Greene St., between Spring and Prince Sts., tel. 212/343–9000. Subway: N or R to Prince St.*

DISCO BOWL

Years ago, there used to be many more lanes to choose from, but bowling is a dying pastime (and cheap date idea) in the city. At one point, many places were replaced with the increasingly popular sanitized pool hall (another cheap date idea). Ah, progress. These two have stuck it out and in the process have moved into "institution" status.

BOWLMOR LANES. A cool Village crowd plays on Bowlmor's busy 44 lanes (try not to think about how many feet have been in your bowling shoes before you); grab a beer at the bar while you wait. The best night is Monday, when you get disco lights, a DJ, and bowling until 4 AM—all for $14. 110 University Pl., between E. 12th and 13th Sts., East Village, tel. 212/255–8188. Subway: L, N, R, 4, 5, or 6 to Union Sq. Open daily 10 AM–1 AM (Mon., Fri., and Sat. until 4 AM).

LEISURE TIME. While you're waiting for a bus outta town, catch a game ($4 per person) at the Port Authority Bus Terminal's 30-lane bowling alley. Once a month (usually on Saturday) they host a "Moonlight Bowl" ($23), which includes food, cheap beer, raffle prizes, a DJ, disco lights, and as many games as you can play until 4 AM. W. 42nd St. and 9th Ave., Midtown, tel. 212/268–6909. Subway: A, C, or E to W. 42nd St. Open daily 10 AM–11 PM (Fri. and Sat. until 2 AM).

WaxBar. One of the trendiest hangouts in Manhattan's trendy heart, this mausoleumlike space packs in a lot of people you guess are good looking, but you can barely see them it's so dark. Not a bad place to lick your wounds if you don't get into the Spy Bar (*see above*). *113 Mercer St., between Spring and Prince Sts., tel. 212/226–6082. Subway: N or R to Prince St.*

Zinc Bar. A perennial favorite in the downtown social scene, this subterranean space oozes sexy ambience (gilt mirrors, flickering candles, and velvet-curtained walls). Catch live jazz Thursday–Saturday and Brazilian music on Sunday. *90 W. Houston St., between W. Broadway and Thompson St., tel. 212/477–8337. Subway: 1 or 9 to Houston St.*

LOWER MANHATTAN

New Yorkers who work on Wall Street don't stick around Lower Manhattan much past 6 PM. As a result, most bars here cater to tourists (and hard-core drunks), close early on weeknights, and shut down completely on weekends. That said, pubs around the **South Street Seaport** keep their doors open relatively late to accommodate the Nikon-toting hordes.

Bridge Cafe. This American bistro is in a woodframe building built in 1794. Close to the Seaport, this romantic spot is a good place for a quiet drink. They stock a load of single malt scotches and a good selection of American wines. *279 Water St., at Dover St., tel. 212/227–3344. Subway: J, M, Z, 2, 3, 4, or 5 to Fulton St.*

Jeremy's Ale House. Enjoy two-pint styrofoam "buckets" of beer and the ultimate in frat-party ambience (e.g., stacked kegs and bras in the rafters). The crowd is heavy on tourists from the Seaport, with a few Wall Streeters nostalgic for their Ivy days. *254 Front St., at Dover St., tel. 212/964–3537. Subway: J, M, Z, 2, 3, 4, or 5 to Fulton St.*

North Star Pub. This snug London-style pub is one of the only places at the South Street Seaport not completely overrun by tourists. Have an Imperial (20-ounce) pint of Guinness, but skip the greasy, expensive bar food. *93 South St., at Fulton St., tel. 212/509–6757. Subway: J, M, Z, 2, 3, 4, or 5 to Fulton St.*

OUTER BOROUGHS

BROOKLYN

Henry's End. Here's a cozy little spot to take a pint after a day's exploration in Brooklyn Heights. They serve a good dinner, too, with entrées around $17. *44 Henry St., at Cranberry St., tel. 718/834–1776. Subway: A or C to High St./Brooklyn Bridge.*

Peter's Waterfront Alehouse. It's not exactly on the waterfront, but the cozy booths, mellow atmosphere, and fine selection of ice-cold beers—60 in bottles, 15 on tap—merit a trip across the East River. *136 Atlantic Ave., between Henry and Clinton Sts., Cobble Hill, tel. 718/522–3794. Subway: 2, 3, 4, or 5 to Borough Hall.*

Primorski. Come to this Brighton Beach joint to toss back iced vodka with old Russian men. *282 Brighton Beach Ave., between Brighton 2 and Brighton 3 Sts., tel. 718/891–3111. Subway: D or Q to Brighton Beach.*

Rightbank Cafe. This is where Williamsburg artists, too smart and too poor to pay Manhattan rents, get together to talk shop. This place serves barbecued everything and has live music in the outdoor garden during the summer. *409 Kent Ave., at Broadway, tel. 718/388–3929. Subway: J, M, or Z to Marcy Ave.*

If Latin and American ballroom dancing is your thing, come to Roseland on Thursday ($8 for DJ music) or Sunday ($11 for live bands).

BRONX

An Béal Bocht. The crowd at this authentic Irish pub (the name means "The Poor Mouth" in Gaelic) is a cool mix of Irish immigrants and students from nearby Manhattan College. Offerings include poetry readings and live Irish bands on Fridays and Saturdays. *445 W. 238th St., between Greystone and Waldo Aves., Riverdale, tel. 718/884–7127. Subway: 1 or 9 to 238th St.; walk up 238th St. to steep flight of stairs and climb 'em.*

QUEENS

Amnesia. Local bohemians gather at this artsy café-bar for occasional live music (European and house) and frequent loud conversation. During summer the tables near the folding glass doors are *the* place to scope out Astoria's street life. *32–03 Broadway, at 31st St., Astoria, tel. 718/204–7010. Subway: N to Broadway.*

STATEN ISLAND

Adobe Blues. Choose from more than 200 international beers and 55 kinds of tequila at this kitschy but cozy Old West–style bar. On Wednesday, Friday, and Saturday nights you also get live jazz and blues free of charge. The adjoining dining room serves up Southwestern and Mexican fare (*see* Chapter 4). *63 Lafayette Ave., at Fillmore St., New Brighton, tel. 718/720–2583. From Ferry Terminal, take Bus S40 to Lafayette Ave. (10 mins).*

COMEDY

There's something sad and a little desperate about people paying upwards of $25 (and don't forget that two-drink minimum!) for a few hours of yuks. But that's the state of comedy in most New York clubs today, so consider yourself warned. Luckily, "alternative comedy" clubs keep the scene from being a total wash. Comics at these clubs perform a manic mix of stand-up comedy, sketch comedy, and performance art, sometimes to hilarious effect, and sometimes, well, not. Best of all, alternative comedy clubs usually impose little or no cover charge and practically never have a drink minimum. Most clubs (unless otherwise noted) offer one show nightly Sunday–Thursday and two or more shows Friday and Saturday nights.

Boston Comedy Club. The young and the raunchy bring their gags to this NYU favorite. (It's named the Boston because the owner likes Boston. Funny, huh?) Monday is open-mike amateur night. *82 W. 3rd*

St., between Thompson and Sullivan Sts., West Village, tel. 212/477–1000. Subway: A, B, C, D, E, F, or Q to W. 4th St. (Washington Sq.). Cover: $8 Sun.–Thurs.; $12 Fri. and Sat. 2-drink minimum.

Caroline's Comedy Club. Manhattan's high-profile comedy venue has showcased well-known funny people for years; Margaret Cho, Jon Stewart, Sandra Bernhard, and Gilbert Gottfried have all held stage here. 1626 Broadway, between 49th and 50th Sts., Midtown, tel. 212/757–4100. Subway: C, E, 1, or 9 to W. 50th St.; B, D, or E to 7th Ave.; N or R to W. 49th St. Cover: $10–$19 Sun.–Thurs.; $21–$25 Fri. and Sat. 2-drink minimum.

Chicago City Limits. The oldest comedy and improvisational theater company in the city busts out with outrageous off-the-cuff skits and skewering of celebrities, based entirely on *your* insane suggestions. Okay, they do pre-write some of their material—but it doesn't make it any less funny. 1105 1st Ave., at E. 61st St., Upper East Side, tel. 212/888–5233. Subway: 4, 5, or 6 to E. 59th St.; also N or R to Lexington Ave. Cover: $10 Mon., $20 Wed.–Sat.

Comedy Cellar. Beneath the Olive Tree Café is this dim and smoky throwback to the Village coffeehouses of the '60s. The nightly lineup features pros from "Letterman," HBO, and "Conan O'Brien." Newer talent slinks in after midnight. 117 MacDougal St., between W. 3rd and Bleecker Sts., West Village, tel. 212/254–3480. Subway: A, B, C, D, E, F, or Q to W. 4th St. (Washington Sq.). Cover: $5 Sun.–Thurs., $12 Fri. and Sat. 2-drink minimum.

Dangerfield's. Rodney "No Respect" Dangerfield and pal opened this kitschy Vegas-style club in '69 so Rodney could become famous. And somehow (don't ask us), he did. It's also served as a springboard to stardom for guys like Jay Leno, Jim Carrey, Andrew Dice Clay, and Sam Kinison (R.I.P.). 1118 1st Ave., between E. 61st and 62nd Sts., Upper East Side, tel. 212/593–1650. Subway: 4, 5, or 6 to E. 59th St.; also N or R to Lexington Ave. Cover: $12.50 Sun.–Thurs., $15 Fri., and $20 Sat. No minimum.

Gotham Comedy Club. This relative newcomer to the Flatiron district in Chelsea, housed in a landmark historic building, is certainly snazzier than the usual club; there's a turn-of-the-century chandelier, custom copper bars, and mahogany furnishings (as well as clean bathrooms). Come here for classic stand-up performed by the likes of Chris Rock and David Brenner. A Latino comedy show happens once a month. 34 W. 22nd St., between 5th and 6th Aves., Chelsea, tel. 212/367–9000. Subway: F, N, R, 1, or 9 to 23rd St. Cover: $8 Sun.–Thurs., $12 Fri. and Sat. 2-drink minimum.

Luna Lounge. On Monday comics both recognizable and obscure try out performance-art comedy skits at this hip club. Expect experimental material that's uproarious or just plain strange. 171 Ludlow St., at Houston St., Lower East Side, tel. 212/260–2323. Subway: F to 2nd Ave. Free.

New York Comedy Club. Friday puts the spotlight on new talent and more seasoned headliners; the late show brings together "New York's Best African-American and Latino Comics." Wednesday and Thursday expect traditional stand-up. 241 E. 24th St., between 2nd and 3rd Aves., Gramercy, tel. 212/696–5233. Subway: 6 to E. 23rd St. Cover: $5 Sun.–Thurs., $10 Fri. and Sat. 2-drink minimum.

Stand-up New York. Robin Williams is known to drop by this swank joint to warm up for his "Letterman" appearances. Unannounced. Maybe you'll get lucky. Otherwise, look for young faces you may have seen on TV. 236 W. 78th St., at Broadway, Upper West Side, tel. 212/595–0850. Subway: 1 or 9 to W. 79th St. Cover: $7 Sun.–Thurs., $12 Fri. and Sat. 2-drink minimum.

DANCE CLUBS

The city's myriad dance clubs encompass every type of music, fashion, sexual orientation, ego, and bank account. Biggies, like **Webster Hall** and **Twilo** (*see below*), are fantasylands with thousands of dollars' worth of strobe lights, lasers, and smoke machines and a cast of characters dressed like space men and dominatrixes. House, techno, and ambient are currently in vogue, although plenty of clubs stick to soul, hip-hop, dance hall reggae, and acid jazz.

To visitors with small-town sensibilities, the city's dance scene might seem more shocking than glamorous: Cover for an A-list club costs up to $20, even more for men (if it's a straight club). At many clubs you'll encounter the cursed Velvet Rope, cordoning off the rabble from celebrities and hard-core club kids; keep in mind that flashy up-to-the-minute style is what really matters here. Age limits and dress codes may be selectively enforced to keep out those whom the bouncer deems undesirable. If you get rejected, don't take it personally.

New York's dance scene is notoriously fickle, and this week's hottest club may get boarded up a month later. Likewise, a place can host completely different crowds depending on the night of the week—drag ball on Tuesday, punk "battle of the bands" on Wednesday—or even shut its doors temporarily to throw a private party. And many places are only open one or two (rotating) nights a week. Call ahead to avoid any nasty surprises. Or check the huge stacks of flyers at one of the city's several dance record stores for upcoming events and—this is key—big discounts (see Records, Tapes, and CDs in Chapter 5). DJs Junior Vasquez and Danny Tenaglia guarantee a massive, throbbing crowd wherever they spin. Finally, turn to the **New York Press,** for decent (but selective) listings and reviews; the **Village Voice** and **Time Out New York** are the most comprehensive. **Homo Xtra** and **Next** are gay rags that list the big gay club events in town (many of which are also mixed or straight-friendly).

The Bank. Wear black—lots and lots of black—to New York's premier industrial and Gothic club. It's the best place in the city to see Trent Reznor look-alikes getting sweaty in a former bank lobby. *225 E. Houston St., at Essex St., Lower East Side, tel. 212/505-5033. Subway: J, M, or Z to Essex St. Cover: $8-$14.*

Don Hill's. This old warehouse has been converted into a hangout for go-go trash; come for one of the cool weekend dance parties. *511 Greenwich St., at Spring St., SoHo, tel. 212/219-2850. Subway: C or E to Spring St. Cover: $10.*

Jackie 60. This party, held at the club Mother, is the famous domain of drag queens who strut their stuff for an appreciative crowd of gays and straights. Expect glitter and spectacle with undercurrents of fetish and bondage. *432 W. 14th St., at Washington St., West Village, tel. 212/929-6060. Subway: A, C, E, or L to W. 14th St. Cover: $10. Open Tues. only.*

At Tunnel, top DJs spin techno on a dance floor the size of a bus terminal, and the bar inside the coed bathroom is its own nonstop scene.

Jet Lounge. One of the best clubs in New York, but unfortunately, everyone knows it. Expect a 45-minute wait to (maybe) get in. The interior, decorated with millions of glass shards stuck in the plaster walls, and the funky groove are worth it. *286 Spring St., between Varick and Hudson Sts., West Village, tel. 212/929-4780. Subway: 1, 2, 3, or 9 to Houston St.*

Key Club. A hot spot for house and techno, this chic club has a sizable dance floor. The liquor available at the two bars near the entrance will help reduce any inhibitions you may feel about your dancing ability. *76 E. 13th St., between Broadway and 4th Ave., Union Sq., tel. 212/388-1060. Subway: L, N, R, 4, 5, or 6 to E. 14th St. (Union Sq.). Cover: $20.*

Life. The most recent aspirant to the title of hottest New York club attracts the usual masses crying to get in. Once you elbow your way past the velvet rope, however, it's a bit of a disappointment. The cavernous, throbbing dance hall is so bare of decor there's little to differentiate it from a community center. The VIP room is upstairs and so is the real action. *158 Bleecker St., between Sullivan and Thompson Sts., West Village, tel. 212/420-1999. Subway: A, B, C, D, E, F, or Q to W. 4th St.*

Nell's. Years ago, this dark and elegant club was *the* haunt of the demimonde. Although it's looking a little shabbier these days, it retains a chic, multiethnic following. *246 W. 14th St., between 7th and 8th Aves., West Village, tel. 212/675-1567. Subway: 1, 2, 3, or 9 to W. 14th St. Cover: $10-$15.*

NV. Upstairs there's an inviting dance floor, and on the main level there are even more beguiling curtained nooks at this thriving SoHo dance club. Look for attractive professional types who want to throw off their chains. *289 Spring St., between Hudson and Varick Sts. tel. 212/929-6868. Subway: C or E to Spring St. Cover: $10-$20.*

Ohm. You'll find techno and house music at this sleek club that's popular with twentysomething professionals. *16 W. 22nd St., between 5th and 6th Aves., Chelsea, tel. 212/229-2000. Subway: N or R to W. 23rd St. Cover: $10-$20.*

Roxy. Cavernous Roxy has cool raves and occasional live bands—and don't miss the roller-skating dance fest on Wednesday nights. Rental skates are $5, blades $10. A DJ spins house music on the weekends (Saturday is gay night). *515 W. 18th St., between 10th and 11th Aves., Chelsea, tel. 212/645-5156. Subway: A, C, E, or L to W. 14th St. Cover: $12-$20.*

Tunnel. For a long time, the Tunnel had achieved the impossible in clubland: perpetual coolness. Fading now, it still manages to attract a hearty ultra-diverse crowd almost every night. The party ends around, oh, 10 or 11 AM the next day. *220 12th Ave., at W. 27th St., Chelsea, tel. 212/695-4682. Subway: C or E to W. 23rd St. Cover: $20. Ages 18 and over.*

Twilo. Gay muscle boys, hip heteros, post-ravers, and club kids fill the wide-open dance floor at Twilo. Music is mostly progressive house with some trance in the wee hours. Sasha and Digweed and other visiting European DJs spin regularly. *530 W. 27th St., between 10th and 11th Aves., Chelsea, tel. 212/268–1600. Subway: C or E to W. 23rd St. Cover: $20.*

Webster Hall. Even the truly jaded will find something to do at this 40,000-square-ft megaclub. All kinds, from rastas to transvestites, hang at Webster Hall's four diversion-filled dance floors. *125 E. 11th St., between 3rd and 4th Aves., East Village, tel. 212/353–1600. Subway: 6 to Astor Pl. Cover: $20.*

LIVE MUSIC

Strike up a conversation with most New Yorkers, and they'll tell you about the time when Bono or Eddie Vedder or Sean McGowan, then totally obscure, cruised into their favorite dump and jammed for six hours straight. This is New York City, and you can see the best of everything here, be it cutting-edge indie bands or arena rockers. Bars also host live bands, usually on weekends, sometimes for a cover and sometimes for free. If you're broke, check the *Village Voice* for listings of free shows. To find out what's going on at venues like Madison Square Garden, Shea Stadium, Giants Stadium, and Roseland, call **Ticketmaster** (tel. 212/307–7171).

Summer is the perfect time for free concerts. Central Park offers its **SummerStage** series (tel. 212/360–2777) from June through August, featuring opera performances, rock, world music, and spoken word by some big names. Past performers have included Patti Smith, the Indigo Girls, Steel Pulse, and Paul Simon. For more on Summerstage, *see* Summer Arts *in* Chapter 7. Coney Island offers its own version of these events every summer at the **Asser Levy Bandshell**; for information call Community Board 13 (tel. 718/266–5064). The best of jazz is showcased at two big festivals, the prestigious **JVC Jazz Festival** (tel. 212/501–1390), held for 10 days in late June at larger venues (with free shows in Bryant Park) and during the **Jazz at Lincoln Center** series (tel. 212/875–5299), which runs from September through May.

Two gigantic annual music festivals give you a chance to scope up-and-comers in every genre. The **Digital Music Festival** (July), playing at clubs around Manhattan, features rock and blues by both little-known and signed bands. Two or three computers are placed at each club so patrons can access the festival Web site (www.digitalclubfest.com) on the Internet for a schedule of performances, as well as constantly updated visuals of the action. The *College Music Journal* hosts a major festival every September, featuring college talent with forums for students and industry people. If you're in town during one of these fests, grab a city weekly for more info.

For big events, purchase tickets in advance from one of two agencies—if you don't mind paying a service charge (a big "if"). **Tele-Charge** (tel. 212/239–6200) deals with most shows and charges $5.50 per ticket. Corporate monster **Ticketmaster** (tel. 212/307–7171) has outlets all over the city and charges $3–$5 per ticket (depending on the show and venue), plus an additional $1.50 if you charge by phone. The moral: Avoid ticket agencies (and their service charges) by purchasing tickets in cash at the venue itself or a record store.

MAJOR VENUES

Beacon. Built in 1928 as a vaudeville theater, the Beacon has an interior to rival Radio City Music Hall. It seats around 3,000 and usually hosts big-name music acts from the Allman Brothers to Sheryl Crow. *2124 Broadway, between W. 74th and 75th Sts., Upper West Side, tel. 212/496–7070. Subway: 1, 2, 3, or 9 to W. 72nd St.*

Bowery Ballroom. The owners of the Mercury Lounge (*see below*) have converted a former carpet showroom into one of the city's best mid-sized venues. Take in the view from the balcony or cut a rug on the floor at this 500–800 capacity gem. *6 Delancey St., at Bowery, Lower East Side, tel. 212/533–2111. Subway: F to Delancey St.*

Carnegie Hall. This landmark music hall, built in 1891, features mostly classical and jazz (October–June). Occasionally, major pop and rock acts like Natalie Merchant or Crosby, Stills, and Nash also fill the hall's 2,800 seats. *154 W. 57th St., at 7th Ave., Midtown, tel. 212/247–7800. Subway: N or R to W. 57th St.; B, D, or E to 7th Ave.; also A, C, 1, or 9 to 59th St./Columbus Circle. Closed Aug.*

Hammerstein Ballroom. Opera impresario Oscar Hammerstein built this magnificently arched venue in 1906. The triple-balconied space, with a capacity of 2,000, was renovated in 1997 and offers some of the best sight lines in the city, as well as a grade A sound system. *211 W. 34th St, at 8th Ave., Midtown, tel. 212/564–4882. Subway: A, C, or E to 34th St.*

Irving Plaza. Once the home of the Polish Army Veterans association, this second-floor ballroom can handle up to 800 fans who tend to make the dance floor shake as they cheer on their favorite up-and-coming acts. Escape to the balcony for a more relaxed, but still packed, vantage point. Sunday nights feature swing dancing. *17 Irving Pl., at 15th St., Union Square, tel. 212/5777–6800. Subway: 4, 5, 6, L, N, or R to Union Square.*

Madison Square Garden. This giant 20,000-seat indoor arena hosts mega-major rock and pop concerts, not to mention Knicks and Rangers games (*see* Spectator Sports *in* Chapter 8). *7th Ave. between W. 31st and 33rd Sts., Midtown, tel. 212/465–6741. Subway: A, C, or E to W. 34th St. (Penn Station).*

Radio City Music Hall. Besides the hokey annual "Christmas Spectacular" and the "Easter Show," Rockefeller Center's stylish music hall puts on national music acts of all kinds. Seating capacity is 6,000. *1260 6th Ave., between W. 50th and 51st Sts., Midtown, tel. 212/247–4777. Subway: B, D, F, or Q to W. 47th–50th Sts. (Rockefeller Center).*

Roseland. Tickets for touring rock shows average $15–$30 at this stellar open-floor hall. Seating capacity is 3,200. *239 W. 52nd St., between Broadway and 8th Ave., Midtown, tel. 212/247–0200. Subway: 1 or 9 to W. 50th St.*

Town Hall. This landmark 1921 auditorium seats 1,500 for every imaginable kind of show, from classical to rock to spoken word. *123 W. 43rd St., between 6th and 7th Aves., Midtown, tel. 212/840–2824. Subway: N, R, 1, 2, 3, 7, or 9 to W. 42nd St. (Times Sq.).*

Take note: Many jazz clubs are not late-night affairs, and bands typically play from 8 PM to around midnight.

CLUBS AND OTHER VENUES

MUSIC MIX

Brownies. Every night there seems to be a different group of people lined up outside this East Village favorite: sometimes grunge kids and New Jersey skate rats, sometimes NYU freshmen, sometimes drunken punks smoking cloves. Needless to say, the music varies from night to night. *169 Ave. A, between E. 10th and 11th Sts., East Village, tel. 212/420–8392. Subway: L to 1st Ave. Cover: $5–$15.*

Knitting Factory. What started as a crude '80s punk venue has grown to include two slick bars and three stages. Shows include everything from jazz to punk to Gothic/industrial, with both big names and local talent. In the front room, pick up a calendar of events or buy a CD of whomever or whatever the hell you just heard. The **AlterKnit Theatre,** downstairs, books folksier artists and cool spoken-word stuff. In the even smaller **Old Office** space, even farther downstairs, you'll be just an arm's length from jazz and world-beat musicians. *74 Leonard St., between Broadway and Church St., TriBeCa, tel. 212/219–3055. Subway: 1 or 9 to Franklin St. Cover: $7–$25.*

Mercury Lounge. Here's yet another reason to head to the Lower East Side for music. The Mercury's reputation has been built on its eclectic music and great sound system. *217 E. Houston St., at Essex St., Lower East Side, tel. 212/260–4700. Subway: F to Delancey St.; also J, M, or Z to Essex St. Cover: $6–$15.*

Tonic. A former Kosher winery, this relative newcomer to the Lower East Side is a sort of alternative Knitting Factory. Avant-garde jazz and late-night rock shows are the norm here. There's also a lounge and bar in the basement where you can sit in converted wine casks. *107 Norfolk St., between Delancey and Rivington Sts., Lower East Side, tel. 212/358–7503. Subway: F to Delancey St.*

Tramps. Tramps's spacious, table-filled floor is one of the better places in the city to catch live bands. Shows range from record-company freebies to big-name, ticketed items ($10–$30). Some shows are all ages, some are 21 and over; call for details. Seating capacity is 700. *51 W. 21st St., between 5th and 6th Aves., Chelsea, tel. 212/727–7788. Subway: N or R to W. 23rd St.*

ROCK, PUNK, AND ALTERNATIVE

CBGB's & OMFUG. CBGB's may be the most famous rock club in the world. During the 1970s and early '80s, it *was* American Punk and post-Punk, with alumni including the Ramones, Blondie, the Talking Heads, and Sonic Youth. It still is a great—if smoky and seriously crowded—place to see a show; there are usually about four or five bands a night. Not to be missed is the graffiti-covered bathroom, which has never, ever been painted. Next door is **CB's 313 Gallery** (313 Bowery, tel. 212/677–0455), serving up more folksy musical offerings. *315 Bowery, at Bleecker St., East Village, tel. 212/982–4052. Subway: 6 to Bleecker St.; also F to 2nd Ave. Cover: $5–$15*

The Cooler. This former meat locker (look for stray hooks on the walls, once used to hang sides of beef) has become a slick, black-and-stainless-steel club. It draws a hip and tattooed crowd for punk, spoken word, and the occasional dance party. *416 W. 14th St., between 9th and 10th Aves., West Village, tel. 212/229–0785. Subway: A, C, E, or L to W. 14th St. Cover: $10–$20.*

Downtime. There are live bands downstairs, a pool room on the second floor, and a steamy industrial dance floor on top. A big drawback: a crowd that takes Goth far too seriously. *251 W. 30th St., between 7th and 8th Aves., Chelsea, tel. 212/695–2747. Subway: 1 or 9 to W. 28th St. Cover: $5–$15.*

Lion's Den. The Den is a great place to catch a ton of rock bands. It's cheap, and the cavernous space means good views and plenty of room for dancing. *214 Sullivan St., between W. 3rd and Bleecker Sts., West Village, tel. 212/477–2782. Subway: A, B, C, D, E, F, or Q to W. 4th St. (Washington Sq.). Cover: $3 and up.*

Under ACME. This basement club offers little-known alternative acts, as well as the rare show by a big-name star. Upstairs there's a trendy restuarant (*see* Chapter 4). *9 Great Jones St., between Broadway and Lafayette St., East Village, tel. 212/420–1934. Subway: 6 to Bleecker St. Cover: $5–$15.*

Wetlands. This joint rock venue and environmental action center has helped launch big names like Phish, Blues Traveler, the Spin Doctors, and Hootie and the Blowfish. "Save the Rainforest" info is posted on an old VW hippie bus parked next to the dance floor. *161 Hudson St., at Laight St., TriBeCa, tel. 212/966–4225. Subway: 1 or 9 to Franklin St. Cover: $5–$20. Ages 18 and over.*

FUNK, BLUES, AND REGGAE

The Bitter End. This prominent blues joint draws a cool, mixed-age crowd. During the '70s it was the place to see folks like Billy Joel, Linda Ronstadt, and Stevie Wonder. *147 Bleecker St., between Thompson St. and La Guardia Pl., West Village, tel. 212/673–7030. Subway: A, B, C, D, E, F, or Q to W. 4th St. (Washington Sq.). Cover: $5–$10.*

Manny's Car Wash. Manny's is your crowded, grungy outpost for blues on the Upper East Side. It's heavy on bridge-and-tunnel types too meek to tackle the downtown scene. *1558 3rd Ave., between E. 87th and 88th Sts., Upper East Side, tel. 212/369–2583. Subway: 4, 5, or 6 to E. 86th St. Cover: $10–$20.*

S.O.B.'s (Sounds of Brazil). After more than 15 years in the business, S.O.B.'s excels at finding African, reggae, Caribbean, Latin, jazz, funk, and soul bands that tear up the night. *200 Varick St., at W. Houston St., SoHo, tel. 212/243–4940. Subway: 1 or 9 to W. Houston St. Cover: $10–$25.*

JAZZ

Arthur's Tavern. This tiny club, once the stomping ground of Charlie Parker, has been hosting Dixieland jazz for almost 50 years. The stage is so small that patrons can mill around right next to the performers. Best of all, there's rarely a cover. *57 Grove St., at 7th Ave. S, West Village, tel. 212/675–6879. Subway: 1 or 9 to Christopher St. (Sheridan Sq.).*

Birdland. The legendary club named for saxophonist Charlie Parker moved from uptown to the Times Square neighborhood in 1996. It continually books top names and is a great place to see a show. *315 W. 44th St., between 8th and 9th Aves., Midtown, tel. 212/581–3080. Subway: A, C, or E to W. 42nd St. (Port Authority). Cover: $5 with a two-drink minimum (free Mon.).*

The Blue Note. Without a doubt, this is one of New York's most famous jazz clubs, showcasing local and big-name talent almost every night of the week. Now the bad news: The cover charge can be as high as $75. Go on Monday nights when a mere $15 will let you see top names during record release parties. *131 W. 3rd St., between MacDougal St. and 6th Ave., West Village, tel. 212/475–8592. Subway: A, B, C, D, E, F, or Q to West 4th St. (Washington Sq.).*

Lenox Lounge. Head uptown to Harlem on Friday and Saturday nights for smoky ambience and smoking jazz from some of the city's top players. *288 Lenox Ave, between 124th and 125th Sts., Harlem, tel. 212/427–0253. Subway: 2 or 3 to 125th St. Cover: $8 with a two-drink minimum.*

Red Blazer Hideaway. Every night of the week, combos play New Orleans or Chicago Dixieland, swing, and traditional jazz to an older audience in the mood for a post-*Phantom* party. *32 W. 37th St., between 5th and 6th Aves., Midtown, tel. 212/947–6428. Subway: A, C, or E to W. 42nd St. (Port Authority). Cover: $5 with a two-drink minimum (free Mon.).*

Smalls. Owner Mitchell Borden (a jazz man from San Francisco, and no relation to Lizzie) keeps the coolest joint in the city: Nonalcoholic beverages are free (BYO stronger stuff), and you get two smokin' sets followed by a jam session stretching into the wee hours. *183 W. 10th St., at 7th Ave. S, West Village, tel. 212/929–7565. Subway: 1 or 9 to Christopher St. (Sheridan Sq.). Cover: $10.*

Sweet Basil. For almost 20 years, Sweet Basil has been winning praises as one of the city's top spots for jazz. Just don't do any talking: Patrons here want to listen to the *music,* okay? Friday and Saturday feature three shows; on other nights there are two. *88 7th Ave. S, between Bleecker and Grove Sts., West Village, tel. 212/242–1785. Subway: 1 or 9 to Christopher St. (Sheridan Sq.). Cover: Mon.–Thurs. $17.50 with a $10 minimum food or drink charge; weekends $20 with a $10 minimum.*

Village Vanguard. The Vanguard isn't a jazz club, it's a jazz institution. Some of the biggest names in the business have played here since it opened in 1935—Miles Davis, John Coltrane, Sonny Rollins, Charlie Mingus, Dexter Gordon, and Thelonious Monk. *178 7th Ave. S, at W. 11th St., West Village, tel. 212/255–4037. Subway: 1 or 9 to Christopher St. (Sheridan Sq.). Cover: Mon.–Thurs. $15 with a $10 minimum drink charge; weekends $20 with a $10 minimum.*

THE ARTS

UPDATED BY STEPHANIE ADLER

From the Five Lesbian Brothers to the Metropolitan Opera, New York City is like no other when it comes to the performing arts. It's got all the big names and about a million small ones, whether you're looking for name-brand or cutting-edge dance, theater, music, or opera. On any given night you'll struggle to choose among the world-famous American Ballet Theatre, the renowned New York Philharmonic, and a few Tony- or Pulitzer Prize–winning plays. Or you can just cruise the downtown arts scene, maybe take in a poetry slam at the Nuyorican or catch an outrageous performance artist at P.S. 122.

Sounds fabulous, right? Can't wait to see it all? Reality check: These days, a pair of tickets to a Broadway show can cost you up to $200. That's right, *$200.* Major concerts and recitals don't come so cheap, either. And of course ticket agencies like **Tele-Charge** (tel. 212/239–6200 or 800/233–3123) and **Ticketmaster** (tel. 212/307–4100), which handle most of the city's big theaters and concert halls, slap a hefty $4–$6 per-ticket surcharge on top of that (and sometimes a $2–$3 per-order fee). There are, thankfully, lots of ways to beat high ticket prices. And lots of the arts centers downtown (particularly on the Lower East Side, in TriBeCa, and the East and West Village) will charge you around $10 to $15 for a full night's entertainment. Many places even have open-house nights when you can enjoy a work-in-progress for free.

Off- and Off-Off-Broadway theaters have their own joint box office called **Ticket Central** (416 W. 42nd St., tel. 212/279–4200). It's open daily between 1 and 8 PM. You won't find discounts here, but tickets to performances in these theaters are usually less expensive than on Broadway. Ticket Central carries a cornucopia of events, including legitimate theater, performance art, and dance. There's a $4 per-order handling charge.

PUBLICATIONS

To find out who or what's playing where, your first stop should be a newsstand. Consult *Time Out New York,* the *New York Times* (particularly Friday's two "Weekend" sections), "Goings on About Town" in *The New Yorker,* the "Cue" listings at the back of *New York* magazine, and the city's free weeklies, the *Village Voice* and the *New York Press.* The most thorough is *Time Out,* though the *Voice* has long been considered the bible of the downtown scene.

HOT LINES

You can get weekly updated info by phone from the **NYC/ON STAGE Hotline** (tel. 212/768–1818), the Theatre Development Fund's (TDF) 24-hour performing arts information service. For wheelchair accessibility information, call Tele-Charge or Ticketmaster (*see above*). Additionally, the TDF runs a **Theatre Access Project** (tel. 212/221-1103) for city residents and tourists with disabilities. Membership (which is free) gives you access to special seating and discount tickets for some of the city's hottest shows.

FINDING A CHEAP SEAT

Getting a good deal on performance tickets doesn't have to be painful. If you know where to look, discounted tickets are there for the taking. The best plan, if not the cheapest, is to buy your tickets at the theater's or concert hall's own box office, where they'll help you choose the best seats and won't stick you with a service charge. You can go the day of the performance, or you can go a few days earlier to avoid crushing disappointment. Since *Rent* began offering $20 rush, or day-of-performance, tickets when it opened in 1996—with the intention of making top seats accessible to a wider audience—many shows have followed suit. Rush-ticket policies vary from production to production, but the tickets are definitely worth the bit of research they require. Playbill Online (*www.playbill.com*) maintains a list of such policies. If you're having a really hard time getting tickets for a particular show, check with the box office for whether they sell same-day standing-room tickets ($10–$20) for sold-out shows.

TICKET AGENCIES • The city's two **TKTS** booths offer day-of-performance tickets for selected Broadway and Off-Broadway shows at 25%–75% off (cash or traveler's checks only), plus a $2.50 per-ticket service charge. TKTS also carries tickets for some opera, symphony, and dance performances, though not every day. The **Times Square** TKTS booth (Duffy Square, W. 47th St. and Broadway) is open Monday–Saturday 3–8 and Sunday 11–8, with additional hours Wednesday and Saturday 10–2. Expect lines to form an hour before the booth opens; during the week, the lines are usually shorter after 4:30 until closing time; on weekends, lines can be long for most of the day, especially when the weather's warm. The TKTS booth at the **World Trade Center** (Mezzanine Level, 2 World Trade Center), open weekdays 11–5:30 and Saturday 11–3:30, is worth the trek downtown: It's indoors, it's rarely crowded, and (unlike the Times Square booth) it sells matinee and Sunday tickets one day in advance. For more info, call the NYC/ON STAGE Hotline (*see above*).

The annual Workshop Performances of the School of American Ballet (tel. 212/877-0600), whose students eventually graduate into the New York City Ballet's prestigious corps de ballet, are held the first week in June. Tickets are $25 and $45.

COUPONS AND VOUCHERS • Look for **"two-fer" coupons**—which offer two tickets for the price of one, or at least some sort of discount—at the New York Visitors and Convention Bureau, at the Broadway Ticket Center (in the Times Square Visitors Center), and in bookstores, department stores, banks, restaurants, and hotel lobbies. They're generally available only for the long-running Broadway extravaganzas that probably came to your hometown several years ago.

Another option is a **Theatre Development Fund (TDF)** voucher, sold in sets of four ($28) and redeemable at Off- and Off-Off-Broadway theaters as well as at many music and dance spaces. They're available to union members and students (and other limited-income types) only. For an application to see if you qualify, send a SASE to: TDF applications, 1501 Broadway, Suite 2110, NY 10036, and allow six to eight weeks for processing. For more information, call the TDF's 24-hour information line (tel. 212/221-0013) or the NYC/ON STAGE Hotline (*see above*).

Finally, before you purchase tickets, check the Web for little-publicized printable discount coupons. You'll often find these at the site for the venue (www.bam.org sometimes has online coupons for BAM Rose Cinemas), or at entertainment-guide sites, like Sidewalk and Citysearch. Also check www.nytheatre-wire.com for theater-ticket coupons. For more on how to exploit the Internet to your best cultural advantage, see *box* Log On, Tune In, *below*.

ARTS CENTERS

At the city's arts centers you can catch performance art, classical and new music, serious drama, modern dance, a lecture, or a literary reading. Whether you're in the mood to see David Byrne or Kathleen Battle, you can probably find the performance you're looking for at one of these cultural clearinghouses.

LINCOLN CENTER

From the moment it opened on the Upper West Side some 30 years ago, the 14-acre Lincoln Center for the Performing Arts has been the undisputed heart of the city's arts scene. This is where you'll find **Alice**

LOG ON, TUNE IN

Trying to keep up with the local arts scene can leave even a seasoned New Yorker dizzy. When the sheer volume of listings in the Village Voice or Time Out overwhelms, user-friendly online city and arts guides can help. And if you're lucky, you might even stumble upon an online-only promotion and wind up saving dough.

newyork.citysearch.com. A general city guide with arts listings and reviews, citysearch tells you what's going on on a given night, and links to a venue's or an event's home page if there is one.

newyork.sidewalk.com. This site's sometimes slow to load, but it's ground zero for NYC arts and entertainment listings online.

www.culturefinder.com. A nationwide guide to visual and performing arts events, the "Get Local" section will take you to city-specific listings and discount-ticket offers.

www.danceonline.com. Here you'll find contemporary dance news and criticism, plus performance listings for the New York metro area.

www.nytheatre.com. You'll get a directory of current and upcoming shows, the lowdown on where to buy tickets and how to find bargains, and a who's who guide to the New York stage.

www.nytheatre-wire.com. This site's dedicated to breaking the latest news about what's on New York City stages. There are columns, reviews, theater specs, and discount coupons here.

www.playbill.com. A useful theater resource, playbill offers a list of discount-ticket policies, theater seating charts, and daily updated theater news.

Tully Hall (*see* Concert Halls, *below*), home to the Chamber Music Society; **Avery Fisher Hall** (*see* Concert Halls, *below*), home to the New York Philharmonic; the acclaimed **Juilliard School** (*see* Music Schools, *below*), which frequently puts on free concerts, theatrical performances, and operas; the grand **Metropolitan Opera House** (tel. 212/362–6000), home to the Metropolitan Opera (*see* Opera, *below*) and the American Ballet Theatre (*see* Dance, *below*); the **New York State Theater** (tel. 212/870–5570), home to the New York City Opera (*see* Opera, *below*) and New York City Ballet (*see* Dance, *below*); and two theaters, the **Vivian Beaumont** and **Mitzi Newhouse.** The Film Society of Lincoln Center organizes several annual film festivals and screens independent, revival, and foreign films at the **Walter Reade Theater** (*see* Film and Video, *below*). Outdoor **Damrosch Park** and the **Bandshell** are frequently incorporated into the Center's many festivals and concerts, such as the **Lincoln Center Festival, Mostly Mozart,** and **Lincoln Center Out-of-Doors** (*see box,* Summer in the City, *below*). Lincoln Center's year-round program, **Great Performers at Lincoln Center,** brings the world's greatest talents, such as Luciano Pavarotti and the Vienna Philharmonic, to Lincoln Center. For more on Lincoln Center, including tours of the grounds, *see* Upper West Side *in* Chapter 2. *W. 62nd to W. 66th St., Broadway to Amsterdam Ave. (mailing address: 70 Lincoln Center Plaza, NY 10023–6583), tel. 212/875–5000. Subway: 1 or 9 to 66th St. (Lincoln Center).*

OTHER VENUES

Brooklyn Academy of Music (BAM). America's oldest performing arts center (opened in 1859) has a reputation for presenting daring and innovative dance, music, opera, performance art, and theater. Its fall festival of new music, theater, and dance, **Next Wave,** brings artists from around the globe. The main performance halls are the 2,000-seat Opera House and the elegantly decrepit 900-seat Majestic Theatre, around the corner at 651 Fulton Street.

A major renovation that began in 1996 brought a new bookstore, **BAMcafé,** and the **BAM Rose Cinemas** (*see* Film and Video, *below*) in 1998. The café is open Tuesday–Sunday from noon to 10 PM; live music performances and readings take place frequently here.

Student rush tickets ($10) are available for some BAM shows; call on the day of performance for information. And lest BAM seems dauntingly far from Manhattan island, bus service is available for a nominal fee from midtown. BAM buses depart an hour before any performance (but not movie screenings); make reservations by phone. *30 Lafayette Ave., between Ashland Pl. and St. Felix St., Fort Greene, Brooklyn, tel. 718/636–4100. Subway: D, Q, 2, 3, 4, or 5 to Atlantic Ave.; walk 2 blocks north to Fulton St. and turn left. Tickets: $10–$75.*

City Center. In 1923, the Ancient and Accepted Order of the Mystic Shrine (whatever that is) built City Center's exotic Spanish dome, under which you'll now find the home stage of Manhattan Theatre Club. Presented here are innovative new dramas; performances by the Alvin Ailey American Dance Theater, the American Ballet Theatre, and the Paul Taylor Dance Company; and concert versions of musicals. *131 W. 55th St., between 6th and 7th Aves., Midtown, tel. 212/581–1212. Subway: N or R to 57th St. Tickets: $15–$50.*

Dixon Place. At the heart of the city's experimental performance community, Dixon Place provides a space for artists to develop their work in front of an audience. Its emphasis on the participation of the audience in the creative process ensures a lively bill of literature, performance art, dance, and theater that you won't soon see elsewhere. Ongoing series include Brand New Dance, the New Play Reading Series, and Open Performance Night. The literary readings are particularly well attended (*see* Spoken Word, *below*). *309 E. 26th St., Gramercy, tel. 212/219–3088. Subway: 6 to 28 St. Tickets: Free–$12.*

The Kitchen. This is *the* Manhattan center for performance art, although video, dance, and music have their moments here, too. The warehouselike space is where unclassifiable artists like Philip Glass, Meredith Monk, and Laurie Anderson first took center stage. *512 W. 19th St., between 10th and 11th Aves., Chelsea, tel. 212/255–5793. Subway: A, C, E, or L to 14th St. (8th Ave.). Tickets: $8–$15.*

New Victory Theater. After a stint as a burlesque house, New York's oldest active theater reopened in 1995 as the city's first performing-arts center for children. Now groups like the Metropolitan Opera Guild and the New Shanghai Circus appear on the bill of dance, circus, comedy, puppet, and dramatic productions. *209 W. 42nd St., between 7th and 8th Aves., Midtown, tel. 212/564–4222. Subway: N, R, 1, 2, 3, 7, or 9 to Times Sq.; also A, C, or E to 42nd St. (Port Authority). Tickets: $10–$25.*

92nd Street Y. The Y's Kaufmann Hall, the city's most prestigious site for readings and lectures by poets, artists, writers, and scholars, also has a lively menu of musical programs. At its Unterberg Poetry Center are tapes dating back to the 1940s of some of the finest writers of this century reading their work for Y audiences. Innovative dance performances are held around the corner at the Y's Playhouse 91. *1395 Lexington Ave., at E. 92nd St., Upper East Side, tel. 212/996–1100. Subway: 4, 5, or 6 to 86th St. Tickets: $10–$45.*

Performance Space 122. Performances at this former public school are so cutting-edge that the *Village Voice* once called it "the petri dish of downtown culture." Experimental dance and music performances, one-man and -woman theater, and multimedia installations all breed here, especially during their February marathon. Check out the informal Hothouse on Sundays at 4; for only $4 you can see P.S. 122–performance-style art as it evolves. Student rush tickets are available for most shows; call for details. *150 1st Ave., at E. 9th St., East Village, tel. 212/477–5288. Subway: L to 1st Ave., 6 to Astor Pl., N or R to 8th St. (Broadway). Tickets: $4–$25.*

Sylvia and Danny Kaye Playhouse. At this pearl of a concert hall, you can see piano recitals, chamber music concerts, opera, and dance. Tickets are discounted for students. *Hunter College, E. 68th St. between Park and Lexington Aves., Upper East Side, tel. 212/772–4448. Subway: 6 to 68th St.–Hunter College. Tickets: $20–$35.*

Town Hall. Designed by McKim, Mead & White, this Georgian Revival structure hosts a diverse program of cabaret performances, readings, opera, chamber, popular, and world music, plus stand-up comedy—all at reasonable prices. Eleanor Roosevelt, Anaïs Nin, and Orson Welles all took the stage at Town Hall in the early days; more recently, Dawn Upshaw, Audra McDonald, and Robert Pinsky have been seen here. *123 W. 43rd St., Midtown, tel. 212/840–2824. Subway: B, D, F, or Q to 42nd St.; also 1, 2, 3, or 9 to Times Sq. Tickets: $10–$45.*

Tribeca Performing Arts Center. On the far west side of TriBeCa, steps away from the neighborhood's trendiest restaurants, is this modern complex. The center, part of Manhattan Community College, presents eclectic theater, dance, and music events for young and adult audiences. *Manhattan Community College, 199 Chambers St., between Greenwich and West Sts., TriBeCa, tel. 212/346–8510. Subway: 1, 2, 3, 9, A, C, or E to Chambers St. Tickets: Free–$50.*

DANCE

The 1990s haven't exactly been the Golden Age of dance in New York. The revered Joffrey Ballet Company (founded here in 1956) relocated in 1995 to the more dance-friendly city of Chicago, and smaller, less established troupes have struggled to amass resources to mount performances. Nonetheless, some 140 dance companies—classic and modern—soldier on. The New York City Ballet, where George Balanchine effectively introduced serious American dance to the world, and the American Ballet Theatre, are still at the heart of the international dance community. The Dance Theatre of Harlem, too, is among the most celebrated troupes in the world. Innovative modern dance companies like those of Merce Cunningham and the late Martha Graham call New York City home. And if that isn't enough, New York continuously attracts ballet troupes from around the globe: the Bolshoi, the Kirov, the Royal Danish, the Stuttgart. While New York's dance fans somewhat anxiously await the next big thing, there remain plenty of talented dancers and choreographers to keep them distracted, at least for the time being.

Note that dance prices are very approximate under company listings. The venue for any given show determines the price; it's quite possible that student or rush tickets will be available once tickets for a performance go on sale.

Many of the dance companies listed below perform at the big performing-arts centers around the city. A few venues whose programs are worth checking out are the **Brooklyn Academy of Music, Lincoln Center, P.S. 122,** the **Sylvia and Danny Kaye Playhouse** (*see* Arts Centers, *above*), and **City Center.**

Alvin Ailey American Dance Theater. Artistic director Judith Jamison, a former dancer under Alvin Ailey, carries on the work of her late teacher, a brilliant choreographer who blended ballet, modern dance, and jazz. The company performs at the Brooklyn Academy of Music and City Center (*see* Arts Centers, *above*). *Tel. 212/767–0590. Tickets: $25–$65.*

American Ballet Theatre. In its 50-plus-year history, the ABT has included some of the greatest dancers of the century: Mikhail Baryshnikov, Natalia Makarova, Rudolf Nureyev, and Cynthia Gregory. It's famous for its dazzling, grand-scale productions of 19th-century classics—*Swan Lake, La Bohème, Don Quixote*—and increasingly for its repertory of 20th-century masterworks by the likes of Balanchine, Robbins, and Tharp. The season runs from April to June. *Metropolitan Opera House at Lincoln Center, Upper West Side, tel. 212/362–6000 (see Arts Centers, above). Tickets: $15–$68.*

Ballet Hispanico. The nation's leading Latin-influenced modern dance company has been delighting New York audiences for more than a quarter-century with works inspired by the cultures of the Caribbean, Latin America, and the land of the flamenco, Spain. Performances are usually at the Joyce Theater or the Tribeca Performing Arts Center (*see* Arts Centers, *above*). *Tel. 212/362–6710. Tickets: $35; standing room $15; students $12.*

Bill T. Jones/Arnie Zane Dance Company. This physically diverse and multiethnic ensemble was founded in 1982 by dancer-choreographers Jones and Zane. Zane died in 1988, and Jones carries on the duo's personal style. The company's provocative works always provoke discussion—whether of sexuality or race—and many of Jones's dancers have become successful choreographers themselves. *Tel. 212/477–1850. Tickets: $30–$50.*

Dance Theater Workshop. The Workshop, on the second floor of a converted warehouse, began in 1965 as a choreographers' cooperative. It now showcases some of the city's freshest dance talent, as well as contemporary music, video, theater, readings, and "Family Matters," a series of dance programs for kids. The Doug Elkins Dance Company, which performs his playful mix of martial arts- and break dance–inspired choreography, takes regularly to the DTW stage. *219 W. 19th St., between 7th and 8th Aves., Chelsea, tel. 212/924–0077. Subway: 1 or 9 to 18th St. (7th Ave.); also C or E to 23rd St. (8th Ave.). Tickets: $12–$15.*

Dance Theatre of Harlem. This company is famous for taking a traditionally all-white art and standing it on its ear. Led by Arthur Mitchell, the first African-American principal dancer in the New York City Ballet, the company has reworked classics ("Giselle" in a Creole setting, for example) and trained several generations of black dancers and choreographers. *466 W. 152nd St., between Amsterdam and St. Nicholas Aves., Harlem, tel. 212/690–2800. Subway: A, B, C, or D to 145th St. Tickets: $25–$60.*

Danspace Project. This organization sponsors a series of contemporary choreography on the pristine wood floor of a church sanctuary, a perfectly intimate environment in which to observe the latest pieces by downtown choreographers. The season runs from September through June. *St. Mark's-in-the-Bowery Church, 10th St. and 2nd Ave., East Village, tel. 212/674–8194. Subway: 6 to Astor Pl.; also N or R to 8th St. (Broadway). Tickets: $15.*

Joyce Theater. This converted art deco movie theater is a major dance center. It's the unofficial permanent home of the Feld Ballet Company (founded in 1974 by Elliot Feld, an upstart ABT dancer) and Feld's younger Ballet Tech company, and a favorite for visiting companies. Year-round programs include tap, jazz, ballroom, and world dance. Don't miss the fringe dance hotshots during the "Altogether Different" festival every January. *175 8th Ave., at W. 19th St., Chelsea, tel. 212/242–0800. Subway: 1 or 9 to 18th St. (7th Ave.); C or E to 23rd St. Tickets: $25–$35.*

If there's a film you're dying to see, plan ahead. New releases sell out quickly, especially on weekends; call MovieFone (tel. 212/777–FILM) or visit www.777film.com to get tickets in advance.

Mark Morris Dance Group. Mark Morris, one of today's most creative choreographers, draws on everything from Roland Barthes and Indian ragas to Yoko Ono and 18th-century opera as he creates musically aware pieces that blend humor with social commentary. As this book went to press, construction was beginning on this group's yet-unnamed permanent home right near BAM. The building will comprise three studios—one convertible to a 50-seat theater—a school, an archive room, a video library, warm-up and dressing spaces, and street-level retail shops. *Tel. 212/219–3660. Tickets: $20–$50.*

Martha Graham Dance Company. For most of its 65 years, this revered company was headed by the icon of modern dance herself, Martha Graham. Former dancers like Merce Cunningham and the late Alvin Ailey went on to form troupes of their own, and the group continues to perform some 200 of Graham's works. The company can be seen in New York at the Joyce Theater. *Tel. 212/838–5886 or 212/832–9166. Tickets: $35.*

Merce Cunningham Dance Company. The unfailingly avant-garde works of Merce Cunningham have included collaborations with John Cage, David Tudor, Jasper Johns, Robert Rauschenberg, and Andy Warhol. Among the New York venues where you might see the company are BAM, Lincoln Center, and the Merce Cunningham Studio. *55 Bethune St., at Washington St., West Village, tel. 212/255–8240. Subway: A, C, E, or L to 14th St. (8th Ave.). Tickets: $20–$60.*

New York City Ballet. With the founding of the NYCB, George Balanchine brought Dance (capital "D") to America. The stellar troupe of more than 80 dancers, started in 1948 by Balanchine and Lincoln Kirstein, has since become one of the most highly praised ballet companies in the world. Currently under the leadership of Peter Martins (formerly one of Balanchine's best dancers), the company presents a wide range of works, from the brand-new to the classics. The beloved production of *George Balanchine's The Nutcracker* plays to sellout crowds every holiday season. The season runs from mid-November to February and late April to June. *New York State Theater, at Lincoln Center (see Arts Centers, above), tel. 212/870–5570. Tickets: $16–$70.*

92nd St. Y Harkness Dance Project. The thoughtful program here focuses on emerging dance troupes with discussion following performances. *Playhouse 91, 316 E. 91st St., Upper East Side, tel. 212/996–1100. Subway: 4, 5, or 6 to 86th St. Tickets: $15.*

Paul Taylor Dance Company. The 1999 documentary *Dancemaker* chronicles a year in the life of this, one of the best modern dance companies in the world. When at home in New York, the company performs at City Center. *Tel. 212/431–5562. Tickets $25–$55.*

Trisha Brown Company. In 1999 choreographer Brown broke into directing opera at BAM (*L'Orfeo*). Like Mark Morris, she seems to love it and who knows what Brown, still experimental after over 30 years on the New York scene, will do next. *Tel. 212/582–4370. Tickets: $25–$45.*

FILM AND VIDEO

New York City is a movie town, and ticket prices here are higher than anywhere else in the country. Movies old, new, big, and small can be found on screens here, if anywhere. And if New Yorkers aren't watching movies, they're making them. Spike Lee, Jim Jarmusch, Ang Lee, and Martin Scorsese all went to school here, and scores of filmmakers use the city each year as a backdrop for their next big release. Walk around Manhattan, particularly during the summer, and you'll eventually stumble upon a camera crew. Not surprisingly, film aficionados will find quite a few small movie houses and museums devoted exclusively to screening independent and foreign films, both new and classic. For philistines, there's a multiplex showing the latest Batman sequel in just about every neighborhood.

FILM FESTIVALS

The New York film community does right by the city's many resident filmmakers by providing a forum in which their work can be shown and appreciated. In March, the often provocative **New Directors/New Films** (tel. 212/708–9500) series at the Museum of Modern Art showcases up-and-coming directors. The **New York Video Festival** (tel. 212/875–5928), featuring video, interactive, and multimedia work, is presented every July by the Film Society of Lincoln Center. If you're in town in late September and early October don't miss the annual **New York Film Festival** (tel. 212/875–5638), held at Lincoln Center, which acts as the premier showcase for dozens of feature films and shorts from around the world; it's also one of your best bets for spotting famous directors and actors. Tickets for both festivals can be tough to come by, so buy in advance.

Dozens of special-interest festivals go on throughout the year, too. A few notables are: the **New York Women's Film Festival** (Apr.; tel. 212/431–9297), **Gen Art Film Festival** (Apr.; tel. 212/290–0312), **Human Rights Watch International Film Festival** (June; tel. 212/290–4700), **Asian American International Film Festival** (Jul.–Aug.; tel. 212/925–6014), and the **Gay & Lesbian Experimental Film Festival** (Nov.; tel. 212/501–2309). Check the *Village Voice*'s "Retro & Beyond" section of film listings for festival announcements.

FIRST-RUN THEATERS

If you're worried you won't be getting your money's worth, keep in mind that most of New York's major movie houses are equipped with the latest sound and projection technology. The newest movie theaters—and they're sprouting up all the time—have stadium seating, digital sound systems, and, of course, coffee bars.

Loews Kips Bay Theatres. Does more mean better? This 15-cinema complex takes up almost an entire city block; unfortunately, it's somewhat far out on the east side. It's not a bad place to catch the latest blockbuster, though—all the theaters are equipped with the latest projection and sound technology, and rocking seats. *2nd Ave. at E. 32nd St., Midtown, tel. 212/447–9425. Subway: 6 to 33rd St.*

Sony Theatres Lincoln Square. Ever seen a 3-D IMAX film? This impressive multiplex has 12 state-of-the-art theaters with huge screens, plus an eight-story IMAX Theater. Though the projection and sound system here can't be beat, the weekend crowds can be exasperating. *1998 Broadway, at W. 68th St., Upper West Side, tel. 212/336–5000. Subway: 1 or 9 to 66th St. (Lincoln Center).*

Ziegfeld. One of the few Manhattan theaters reminiscent of the old movie palaces, the Ziegfeld has a grand screen, bright-red decor, and a sometimes overwhelmingly loud sound system; it's the place to go if you're planning to see a *Star Wars* revival, the latest Steven Spielberg extravaganza, or a restored widescreen classic like *Vertigo*. *141 W. 54th St., west of 6th Ave., Midtown, tel. 212/765–7600. Subway: B, D, F, or Q to 47th–50th Sts. (Rockefeller Center).*

DISCOUNT

Cineplex Odeon Worldwide Cinemas. The going rate for a first-run film is a sky-high $8.50, but this theater shows second-run and non-blockbuster movies on six screens for $3. *340 W. 50th St., between 8th and 9th Aves., Midtown, tel. 212/504–0960. Subway: C or E to 50th St.*

INDEPENDENT, REVIVAL, AND FOREIGN

Film in New York is hardly synonymous with Hollywood. Sure, you can go to the multiplex and pay ten bucks to see the latest catastrophe flick. But here you've also got more exotic options for movie-watching: beyond theaters, museums, cultural societies, bookstores, and even cafés regularly screen flicks that you won't often see on a big screen.

THEATERS

Angelika Film Center. The Angelika is revered among hip New York movie buffs as a mecca of exceptional independent and foreign films (cult classics screen weekends at midnight). The six screens (some tiny) and austere lobby café inspire lines around the block. *18 W. Houston St., at Mercer St., SoHo, tel. 212/995–2000. Subway: B, D, F, or Q to Broadway–Lafayette St.; also 6 to Bleecker St.*

Anthology Film Archives. Anthology's vaults hold more than 10,000 experimental and avant garde films by artists like Cocteau, Flaherty, Eisenstein, and all those other directors whose movies you can't see elsewhere. Its varied, eclectic schedule may include tributes to "auteur" directors like Mike Leigh and Luis Buñuel and thematic programs such as "100 Years of Japanese Cinema." *32 2nd Ave., at E. 2nd St., East Village, tel. 212/505–5181. Subway: F to 2nd Ave.*

Feeling a bit of déjà vu? Even if you haven't been to New York before, chances are you've seen most of it on the big and little screens—more than 200 movies and 100-plus TV series are shot here every year.

BAM Rose Cinemas. The first art house in the outer boroughs opened its doors in 1998, at the tail end of a massive renovation of the Brooklyn Academy of Music (*see Arts Centers, above*). Architects carved four screening rooms out of BAM's little-used Carey Playhouse; the two upstairs theaters have retained the ornate architectural details of the theater's ceiling and proscenium. Films, usually first-run foreign and independent, are sometimes linked to what's playing on BAM's other stages. *Brooklyn Academy of Music (see Arts Centers, above), tel. 718/623–2770.*

Cinema Village. This aging theater shows movies outside the mainstream—indies, documentaries, and animation. It's home to the annual NY Gay and Lesbian Film Festival and a wildly popular annual tribute to the films of Hong Kong. *22 E. 12th St., between 5th Ave. and University Pl., East Village, tel. 212/924–3363. Subway: L, N, R, 4, 5, or 6 to 14th St./Union Sq.*

The Film Forum. The Film Forum can't be beat for recent independents, cult classics, and rare uncut versions of old favorites. There's always some sort of tribute on one of the three screens. *209 W. Houston St., at 6th Ave., SoHo, tel. 212/727–8110. Subway: 1 or 9 to Houston St.*

Lincoln Plaza Cinemas. One of the first art-house multiplexes to open in Manhattan, this six-screen underground theater attracts large numbers of extremely serious film-goers who can't seem to get enough of its award-winning, challenging, and often subtitled fare. *30 Lincoln Plaza, Broadway, between 62nd and 63rd Sts., Upper West Side, tel. 212/757–2280. Subway: A, B, C, D, 1, or 9 to 59th St./Columbus Circle.*

Paris Theatre. Everything about this theater is pure sophistication—its location (next to the Plaza Hotel), its look (luxe old-time movie palace), and its films (the best in classic, foreign, and revival). *4 W. 58th St., between 5th and 6th Aves., Midtown, tel. 212/688–3800. Subway: N or R to 5th Ave.*

Quad Cinema. Expect to see unusual choices on the Quad's four very small screens. Where else can you see a film about phone sex by Vincent van Gogh's great-grandnephew, Theo? *34 W. 13th St., near 5th Ave., West Village, tel. 212/255–8800. Subway: L, N, R, 4, 5, or 6 to 14th St./Union Sq.*

Walter Reade Theater. This gem is part of Lincoln Center, specializing in foreign films and often highlighting the work of a single director. *70 Lincoln Center Plaza, at W. 65th St. and Broadway, Upper West Side, tel. 212/875–5600. Subway: 1 or 9 to 66th St. (Lincoln Center).*

MUSEUMS AND SOCIETIES

American Museum of Natural History. This museum screens awesome science and nature films on its four-story IMAX movie screen. *Central Park W at W. 79th St., Upper West Side, tel. 212/769–5100. Subway: B or C to 81st St.; also 1 or 9 to 79th St.*

American Museum of the Moving Image. The museum is housed in the historic Kaufmann-Astoria studios in Queens. Its main viewing space, the 200-seat Riklis theater, screens Hollywood classics, experimental videos, documentaries, and major retrospectives of artists' works (sometimes with personal appearances). There's also the tiny, quirky, neo-Egyptian Tut's Fever Movie Palace, which shows vintage films and shorts like the 1940 Flash Gordon serials. *35th Ave. at 36th St., Astoria, Queens, tel. 718/784–0077. Subway: R to Steinway St.; also N to Broadway (Queens). For hrs,* see *Museums and Galleries in Chapter 2.*

Asia Society. Screenings here are of little-seen films from India, Hong Kong, China, and Japan. *725 Park Ave., at E. 70th St., Upper East Side, tel. 212/517–2712. Subway: 6 to 68th St.*

French Institute/Alliance Française (FIAF). The Alliance's Ciné-Club (that's "see-nay-cloob" if you don't speak Frog) screens French films contemporary and classic every Tuesday night. The Alliance also cosponsors the annual Avignon/New York Film Festival every April; the program juxtaposes French and American indie filmmakers. *Florence Gould Hall, 55 E. 59th St., between Park and Madison Aves., Midtown, tel. 212/355–6160. Subway: N or R to 5th Ave.*

Japan Society. This cultural institution near the U.N. shows a respectable weekly program of mostly older Japanese films; there's usually a retrospective as well. *333 E. 47th St., between 1st and 2nd Aves., Midtown, tel. 212/832–1155. Subway: 6 to 51st St.; also E or F to Lexington Ave.*

Museum of Modern Art (MoMA). The MoMA is a treasure house of films dating from cinema's earliest days and just about every country that makes 'em. Screenings almost daily are at the Roy and Nina Titus Theater; your movie ticket is free with museum admission. Pick your ticket up at the main desk beginning at 11 AM for the afternoon show and at 1 PM for the evening show. Go early—they disappear quickly. *11 W. 53rd St., between 5th and 6th Aves., Midtown, tel. 212/708–9400. Subway: E or F to 5th Ave./53rd St. For hrs,* see *Major Attractions in Chapter 2.*

Museum of Television and Radio. This bi-coastal museum (there's another branch in L.A.) regularly screens "vintage" TV programs—recent retrospectives have examined the careers of Elvis Presley, Laurence Olivier, Jim Henson, and...Janet Jackson. If you miss the scheduled viewings, episodes and videos can be watched at individual consoles. *25 W. 52nd St., between 5th and 6th Aves., Midtown, tel. 212/621–6600. Subway: E or F to 5th Ave./53rd St. For hrs,* see *Museums and Galleries in Chapter 2.*

Whitney Museum of American Art. The Whitney was the first major museum to establish a department for avant-garde and experimental film. Many of the screenings from its vast collection of American film and video are in this vein; others are the usual classic standards. All are held in the museum's Kaufmann-Astoria Studios Film & Video Gallery. *945 Madison Ave., at E. 75th St., Upper East Side, tel. 212/570–3676. Subway: 6 to 77th St.*

OTHER VENUES • A Different Light. Camp, cult, and other alternaflicks are shown for free on Sunday evenings at this gay and lesbian bookstore. *151 W. 19th St., between 6th and 7th Aves., Chelsea, tel. 212/989–4850. Subway: 1 or 9 to 18th St.*

Ocularis. This is the ultimate "alternative venue"—an independent screening room within the Galapagos Art & Performance Space (formerly a mayonnaise factory) in artsy Williamsburg, where on Sunday nights in fall, winter, and spring, retro and foreign features are coupled with locally made short films and shown for only five bucks. In summer, the screenings move outdoors. *70 N. 6th St., between Wythe and Kent Aves. (look for the blue light), Williamsburg, Brooklyn, tel. 718/388–8713. Subway: L to Bedford Ave.*

The Screening Room. The dinner-and-a-movie date formula was never so user-friendly. The Screening Room is a bar, restaurant, café, and movie theater—for $30 you can eat (well) in the restaurant and then move on to the theater, where you'll see a classic or indie film. *54 Varick St., south of Canal St., TriBeCa, tel. 212/334–2100. Subway: 1, 9, A, C, or E to Canal St.*

MUSIC

Even if you're not a big fan of classical music, you've probably seen *Live at Lincoln Center* on PBS, know that Juilliard is the world's most prestigious music school, and have heard the lame joke about "practice" being the only way to get to Carnegie Hall. If these three institutions were all that New York had going for it, its music scene would still surpass the combined efforts of most major U.S. cities. Luckily, though, they're but the tip of the iceberg. New York City is home to several major orchestras and three of the country's finest music schools; it's also a favorite stop for touring musicians from all over the world.

You absolutely don't need to visit Carnegie Hall or Lincoln Center to take in a virtuoso performance—follow your ears through the city's museums, churches, and parks, which frequently host musical performances both traditional and avant-garde, and often free.

CONCERT HALLS

The stages of New York concert halls are constantly taken by one or another world-class musician. Lincoln Center's 2,700-seat Avery Fisher Hall (*see below*) is one of the grandest venues in the city, though nitpickers will tell you that the 1976 renovations didn't entirely repair the hall's dreadful acoustics. In addition to those listed below, venues noted for classical music include the Brooklyn Academy of Music, City Center, The Kitchen, the 92nd Street Y, and P.S. 122 (*see* Arts Centers, *above*).

> *More than half of the New York Philharmonic's musicians graduated from the Juilliard School.*

Aaron Davis Hall. The World Music Institute stages a wide variety of contemporary and classical concerts and theater productions, including a number of events designed for children. One of their theaters holds 750, another 250. Tickets start at $3 for children's shows. *City College, W. 133rd St. at Convent Ave., Harlem, tel. 212/650–6900. Subway: 1 or 9 to 137th St./City College. Tickets: $8–$20.*

Alice Tully Hall. The Chamber Music Society of Lincoln Center performs at this intimate, acoustically perfect space, along with promising Juilliard students, small ensembles such as the Guarneri and Kronos quartets, musicians using period instruments, famous soloists, and choirs. Seats for the Chamber Music Society's performances are $22–$30. *Lincoln Center (see Arts Centers, above), tel. 212/875–5050 for box office or 212/721–6500 for CenterCharge. Ticket prices vary.*

Avery Fisher Hall. Playing at Avery Fisher is the 150-year-old New York Philharmonic, considered one of the world's premiere symphony orchestras. It's currently led by Kurt Masur; the great Leonard Bernstein was musical director from 1958 to 1970. Weeknight "Rush Hour" Concerts (6:45 PM) and "Casual Saturday" Concerts (2 PM) last one hour and are less expensive than regular concerts. Occasional seats in the orchestra ($25) are available 30 minutes before performances. Weekday rehearsals at 9:45 AM are open to the public for a bargain $10. *Lincoln Center (see Arts Centers, above), tel. 212/875–5030 for box office, 212/721–6500 for CenterCharge, or 212/875–5656 for info on rehearsals. Tickets: $15–$65. Season Sept.–early June.*

Bargemusic. This concert-hall-with-a-view is a 102-ft former Erie Lackawanna coffee barge, now tethered along the East River, that seats 125. Bargemusic's resident artists recruit wonderful soloists from around the world and bring them together to make impromptu chamber groups. Tickets are $23. *Fulton Ferry Landing, Brooklyn, tel. 718/624–4061. Subway: A or C to High St./Brooklyn Bridge.*

Carnegie Hall. This granddaddy of concert halls has hosted some of the greatest orchestras and musicians of all time, including Isaac Stern, Leonard Bernstein, Yo-Yo Ma, Frank Sinatra, Tchaikovsky, and the Beatles (not all at the same time). Though the emphasis is on classical music, it also hosts jazz, cabaret, and folk-music series. The Opera Orchestra of New York puts on concerts of rarely performed works here, and the city's music schools debut their star students in its Weill Recital Hall. *881 7th Ave., at W. 57th St., Midtown, tel. 212/247–7800. Subway: N or R to 57th St. Ticket prices vary.*

Merkin Concert Hall. This relatively new concert hall is doing an admirable job of keeping up with the Joneses, especially considering that the Joneses are the Merkin's near neighbor, Lincoln Center. Lots of famous soloists and chamber groups perform at this 457-seat hall, which also occasionally hosts the New York Philharmonic Ensemble and the Mendelssohn String Quartet. *Abraham Goodman House, 129 W. 67th St., between Broadway and Amsterdam Ave., Upper West Side, tel. 212/501–3330. Subway: 1 or 9 to 66th St. (Lincoln Center). Tickets prices vary.*

OTHER SPACES

Stray outside the city's concert halls and you'll find venues where the sight lines may be imperfect and the acoustics less than ideal, but where the experience is still somehow grand. Nothing can rival a summer evening's concert in the Metropolitan Museum's rooftop garden. And you can't complain about the cost (there's often none) of performances at the city's top-ranked music schools.

CHURCHES

Musical offerings at churches take place during worship services and afternoon vespers, or frequently as separate concerts. During the Christmas holidays every church and cathedral in the city breaks out the Bach.

Cathedral of St. John the Divine. Mammoth St. John has a lively arts calendar, including music and drama. *1047 Amsterdam Ave., at W. 112th St., Morningside Heights, tel. 212/662–2133. Subway: 1 or 9 to 110th St. Ticket prices vary.*

St. Ann's Cathedral. The Arts at St. Ann's series more than merits a trip to the next-best borough. Vic Chesnutt and Jackson Browne have performed here recently. *157 Montague St., Brooklyn Heights, Brooklyn, tel. 718/834–8794. Subway: M, N, R, 2, or 5 to Court St. Ticket prices vary.*

St. Paul's Chapel. Together with nearby **Trinity Church** (Broadway at Wall St., tel. 212/602–0800), St. Paul's offers free lunchtime concerts (at noon, Mondays at St. Paul's; Thursdays at Trinity) of everything from Beethoven's symphonies to the traditional music of Zimbabwe. *Broadway, at Fulton St., Lower Manhattan, tel. 212/602–0874. Subway: 4 or 5 to Fulton St. Tickets: $2 (suggested).*

Theater at Riverside Church. Chamber music concerts, dance productions, drama, and one of the largest organs in the country make this a great place to catch a performance. *490 Riverside Dr., at W. 122 St., Morningside Heights, tel. 212/870–6784. Subway: 1 or 9 to 125th St. Tickets: $10–$20.*

MUSEUMS

For open hours, subway directions, and other info on the museums mentioned below, *see* Museums and Galleries *in* Chapter 2.

The Cloisters. Well-known early music groups perform most Sunday afternoons in the museum's fabulously atmospheric medieval chapel. For tickets send a SASE to: Concerts at the Cloisters, Fort Tryon Park, NY 10040, or charge your order by phone. Traditional Christmas concerts performed by the Waverly Consort sell out fast, so plan ahead. *Fort Tryon Park, tel. 212/923–3700 or 212/650–2290 to order tickets. Tickets: $20–$35.*

The Frick Collection. Sundays bring classical concerts, from Norwegian violinists playing Brahms to quartets performing 16th-century Spanish works. Tickets are only available by mail in advance. Send a SASE to: Concerts Department, The Frick Collection (1 E. 70th St., NY, NY 10021). *1 E. 70th St., at 5th Ave., tel. 212/288–0700. Tickets free.*

Metropolitan Museum of Art. The Met offers a wide variety of classical music concerts weekends at its Grace Rainey Rogers Auditorium. Standing-room tickets are available 30 minutes before most performances and are half price. Additionally, Friday and Saturday evening concerts on its Great Hall Balcony are free (you pay for the wine). On warm summer evenings, head to the museum's roof, where classical guitar accompanies the view. *5th Ave. at E. 82nd St., tel. 212/570–3949. Tickets: Free–$40.*

Museum of Modern Art. The MoMA's Summergarden concert series takes place in its beautiful sculpture garden among the Picassos and Rodins. Performances are Friday and Saturday evenings in July and August. *11 W. 53rd St., between 5th and 6th Aves., tel. 212/708–9480. Tickets: Free.*

MUSIC SCHOOLS

If student recitals bring to mind a bunch of third-graders blowing furiously on plastic recorders, think again. New York City's music schools are the launching pads for many of the nation's most respected musicians. Best of all, performances are usually inexpensive or free.

The Juilliard School. Juilliard offers exceptional orchestral, opera, dance, and theater performances in Lincoln Center's Avery Fisher and Alice Tully halls, as well as in its own Paul Recital Hall (also at Lincoln Center). Many performances are free; those that aren't generally cost $15. *Lincoln Center (see Arts Centers, above), tel. 212/769–7406.*

Manhattan School of Music. Four concert spaces mean hundreds of classical and jazz performances (many free) throughout the year. *120 Claremont Ave., at W. 122nd St., Morningside Heights, tel. 212/749–2802, ext. 428, or 212/749–3300 for concert hot line. Subway: 1 or 9 to 116th St. Tickets: Free–$20.*

OPERA

If you can't leave New York till you've heard the fat lady belt out a few arias, you've got a plethora of operatic options. And for an art that's typically pegged as highbrow, the prices can be shockingly plebian. Small and ethnic opera groups are constantly forming in New York, performing cutting-edge and classical operas for a song (sorry). Check out the **National Opera Ebony** (Aaron Davis Hall, City College, W. 133th St. at Convent Ave., Harlem, tel. 212/650–6900) for performances by up-and-coming African-American, Hispanic, and Asian singers. The students of the Juilliard American Opera Center, the Manhattan School of Music, and the Mannes College of Music (*see* Music Schools, *above*) perform operas—often free—on a par with the pros in other cities. At the other end of the spectrum, even the upscale Metropolitan Opera Company will squeeze you in for as little as $12.

Two additional venues for opera are **Carnegie Hall** (*see* Concert Halls, *above*), where the Opera Orchestra of New York performs, and the **Brooklyn Academy of Music** (*see* Arts Centers, *above*). In the summer, you can catch an opera under the stars for free (*see box,* Summer in the City, *below*).

One unorthodox, but very popular, stage is the World Trade Center Plaza, where pop, classical, jazz, oldies, and R&B concerts are staged at least three days a week at 12:15 and 1:15 during the summer.

Amato Opera Theater. You've never seen *The Marriage of Figaro* performed more passionately than at the Amato, where up to 70 performers at a time (most of them young, unpaid, and yearning to be discovered) have been known to squeeze onto its 20-ft-wide stage. *319 Bowery, at E. 2nd St., East Village, tel. 212/228–8200. Subway: 6 to Bleecker St.; also B, D, F, or Q to Broadway–Lafayette St. Tickets: $23.*

American Opera Projects. Come to this minuscule (75-seat) SoHo loft/theater to hear short, experimental new operas by American composers. *463 Broome St., between Greene and Mercer Sts., SoHo, tel. 212/431–8102. Subway: N or R to Prince St. Tickets: Free–$15.*

Metropolitan Opera Company. One of the most lauded opera companies in the world performs on a stage the size of a football field. Since 1883, it's given more than 16,000 performances of 235 different works, and it continues to crank out four major new productions (with extravagant touches like live horses and falling snow) each season. It attracts the finest singers, like Jessye Norman and Marilyn Horne—and plenty of criticism for a tendency to stick with opera's greatest hits rather than try anything adventurous. Although tickets can cost more than $200, many less-expensive seats and standing room ($12) are available. Weekday prices are lower than weekend prices. Standing-room tickets go on sale (cash only) every day at 10 AM. *The Metropolitan Opera House, at Lincoln Center (see Arts Centers, above), tel. 212/362–6000. Tickets: $12–$250. Season Oct.–mid-Apr.*

New York City Opera. In addition to classics like *Carmen, Madama Butterfly,* and *The Magic Flute,* the renowned New York City Opera has a penchant for unusual and rarely performed works like *The Times of Harvey Milk* and *The Most Happy Fella.* It was one of the first opera houses in the country to introduce "supertitling" (line-by-line English translation displayed electronically over the stage) and has helped start the careers of some of the world's finest singers, including Placido Domingo, Frederica von Stade, and Beverly Sills. Student-rush ($10) and standing-room tickets ($8) are sold on the day of performance starting at 10 AM, cash only (depending on availability). *New York State Theater, at Lincoln Center (see Arts Centers, above), tel. 212/870–5570. Tickets: $8–$230. Season Sept.–Nov. and Mar.–Apr.*

SPOKEN WORD

Only in New York City do novelists, poets, historians, journalists, and other intellectuals get treated with the sort of adulation and respect Americans normally reserve for movie stars and pro-basketball players. Dozens of readings, workshops, and lectures take place nightly at bookstores, museums, universities, galleries, theaters, and cafés around the city; check one of the weeklies for listings or the ***Poetry***

SUMMER IN THE CITY

As faithfully as the swallows of San Juan Capistrano, theater groups, orchestras, and opera companies alight in the city's parks come summer for festivals and free concerts. Many museums, like the Cooper-Hewitt Museum and the Museum of Modern Art, *also hold summertime concerts in their gardens and courtyards. For more info on parks and museums, see Chapter 2, or check the city weeklies. To find out about concerts and other goings-on in the city's parks, you can call the* Parks and Recreation Special Events Hotline *(tel. 212/360–3456). For information on the city's summer jazz festivals, see Live Music in Chapter 6.*

A hint for the uninitiated: Getting a swatch of lawn at a free summer concert— particularly performances by the New York Philharmonic, which are followed by fireworks—can be as fun and easy as scoring a cab in midtown during rush hour in the pouring rain. Arrive at least an hour before curtain time (often sunset) with a bottle of wine and a blanket and you'll do just fine.

Calendar (611 Broadway, Suite 905, 10012, tel. 212/260–7097), published monthly September through June, and available free at several Manhattan bookstores and poetry venues. The Calendar is also available at the Academy of American Poets Web site www.poets.org.

A quick survey of the literary goings-on in this town will tell you that most of the action takes place below 14th Street. Also worth checking into are the many readings and book signings held daily at Borders and Barnes & Noble bookstores throughout the city (*see* Books *in* Chapter 5).

The city's two most distinguished venues for readings and lectures are the **92nd Street Y** (*see* Arts Centers, *above*) and **Symphony Space** (2537 Broadway, at W. 95th St., Upper West Side, tel. 212/864–5400), which hosts the National Public Radio program "Selected Shorts" (short-story readings by notable authors and actors) twice monthly. **Manhattan Theatre Club** (*see* Theater, *below*) hosts "Writers in Performance," a program of readings and discussions with American and foreign writers.

The **KGB Bar** (85 E. 4th St., between 2nd and 3rd Aves., tel. 212/505–3360) used to be the home of the Ukrainian Mens Club. The walls of the second-floor hole-in-the-wall space are still covered with Commie kitsch and period photos, and readings—mostly of fiction and poetry—are free, turning the KGB into the downtown literati's mecca.

Nuyorican Poets Cafe (236 E. 3rd St., between Aves. B and C, Alphabet City, tel. 212/505–8183) is home of the "poetry slam," ground zero for urban poetry. Nuyorican poets—not your typical mush-mouthed, whey-faced spewers of wispy sonnets—have even busted rhyme on MTV. A typical night is packed with in-your-face urban rap and hip-hop jams; performing bards are scored by a panel of judges.

The **Cornelia Street Café** (29 Cornelia St., between Bleecker and W. 4th Sts., West Village, tel. 212/989–9319) schedules readings several times a week. The Alterknit Theater at the **Knitting Factory** (74 Leonard St., TriBeCa, tel. 212/219–3006) holds a weekly poetry series and open-mike Friday ($5). For readings by well-known poets, check out the monthly events at **Dia Center for the Arts** (548 W. 22nd St., Chelsea, tel. 212/989–5566); the **Poetry Project** (St. Mark's-in-the-Bowery Church, 131 E. 10th St., at 2nd Ave., East Village, tel. 212/674–0910); the **Academy of American Poets** (584 Broadway, Suite 1208, SoHo, tel. 212/274–0343); the **Poetry Society of America** (15 Gramercy Park S, Gramercy Park, tel. 212/254–9628); and **Poets House** (72 Spring St., SoHo, tel. 212/431–7920).

Dixon Place and the Kitchen (*for both, see* Arts Centers, *above*) both sponsor readings regularly, several of which border on performance art. At SummerStage (*see box,* Summer in the City, *below*), the Central Park arts festival, big-time authors read from their latest and greatest works.

SUMMER ARTS

Bryant Park Summer Film Festival. Join the hordes of New Yorkers who cram the green behind the New York Public Library on summer Mondays for classic films like *To Kill a Mockingbird, Breakfast at Tiffany's,* and *King Kong.* Screenings are free and films start at sunset, but come early with a picnic and blankets to stake out prime movie-viewing real estate. *6th Ave. at W. 42nd St., Midtown, tel. 212/512–5700. Subway: B, D, F, or Q to 42nd St. Season mid-June–Aug.*

Celebrate Brooklyn. Free Shakespeare, opera, and dance productions and all kinds of concerts at Prospect Park bring Manhattanites across the Brooklyn Bridge in droves. A performance here on a glorious summer evening is *the* best way to enjoy the park and the Slope at their finest. *9th St. Bandshell, Prospect Park, Park Slope, Brooklyn, tel. 718/965–8969. Subway: F to 7th Ave. Season June–Sept.*

Central Park SummerStage. Central Park's free performing arts mega-festival features something different just about every day of the week: Verdi operas performed by the New York Grand Opera, readings and performances by big-name novelists and poets, modern dance performances, and concerts of just about every sort. *Rumsey Playfield, mid-park at 72nd St., tel. 212/360–2777 or 800/201–7275. Subway: B or C to 72nd St. Season mid-June–early Aug.*

Lincoln Center Festival. This international summer performance program includes opera, classical and contemporary music and dance, theater, and non-Western arts. The New York Video Festival (see Film and Video) is part of the larger festival, which makes use of the entire complex, indoors and out. Tickets range from free (for lectures and symposia) to a whopping $120. *At Lincoln Center, (see Arts Centers). Season July.*

Lincoln Center Out-of-Doors. During summer, as many as 300,000 people attend some 100 events at stages set up in Lincoln Center's plaza. Offerings include free performances of theater, modern dance and ballet, symphonic and chamber music, jazz and blues, and even clowns and mimes. *At Lincoln Center, tel. 212/875–5108 (see Arts Centers). Season Aug.*

Mostly Mozart. At this indoor festival it's Mozart, Mozart, Mozart, and when you think you've heard it all, more Mozart, by the world's best music groups as well as the finest solo performers and opera singers. *At Lincoln Center's Avery Fisher Hall, tel. 212/875–5030 (see Concert Halls). Season late July–3rd wk in Aug.*

New York Shakespeare Festival. Each summer brings two plays (at least one by you-know-who), outdoors and under the stars. Pick up tickets from 1 PM onward the day of the show at the Delacorte Theater, or from 1 to 3 PM the day of the show at the Joseph Papp Public Theater box office (*see* Theater). Tickets (free, limit two per person) are notoriously hard to get hold of. Your best bet is to go on a weekday, and head to the Delacorte for tickets, where lines are usually shorter. Performances are at 8. *Delacorte Theater, mid-park at 80th St., tel. 212/861–7277. Subway: B or C to 81st St. Season mid-June to mid-July and Aug.*

THEATER

Theater in New York is broadly defined. At the roughly 250 legitimate theaters, and many more ad hoc venues—lofts, galleries, sidewalks, even parking lots—you can see just about any brand of comedic, dramatic, romantic, musical, classic, or experimental production on a given night.

New York City theaters are divided into three categories—**Broadway, Off-Broadway,** and **Off-Off-Broadway.** The distinctions are based largely on theater size, ticket price, and attitude. Technically, theaters with 100–500 seats are considered Off-Broadway; those with fewer than 100 seats are Off-Off. More than 500 seats and it's Broadway, baby. Some Broadway theaters surpass that figure by far—the Ford Center for the Performing Arts, for example, has more than 1,800 seats.

"Old Broadway" is generally associated with long-running, over-the-top productions that have big casts, big budgets, and big hair-dos. The stereotype is partially, but not entirely true. Big Apple theater has always been democratic, and there is, as ever, something for everyone. Sure, a few Broadway shows are extravagantly commercial, Disney-esque (or actual Disney) productions, and others are the same stale musicals that tour buses have been spilling into for a decade-plus. But you'll also find a broad selection of well-executed classic and reinterpreted musicals and exciting dramatic productions, often starring familiar film and theater actors.

Off-Broadway and Off-Off-Broadway theaters stage performances that can be pretentious, incendiary, or obscure, but rarely boring. To tell the truth, though, there's not much difference anymore between Off- and Off-Off-Broadway. And the professionalism of some productions has reached new heights in recent years. The hit Broadway musical *Rent*, for example, was developed at the New York Theater Workshop, whose output is consistently innovative and outstanding.

For some shows, Broadway tickets can now be had for well over $100 per, red carpet included. (That is, champagne before and during the show and admission to a VIP lounge.) Discount tickets for certain shows are always available (*see box*, log on, tune in, *above*), but needless to say, ticket prices like these are exclusive. If you can't (or don't choose to) cough up the cash for the Broadway "experience," take solace in the fact that a well-chosen non-Broadway production will likely match the quality of the forsaken show.

You can get the latest information about the city's theatrical offerings by calling one of the arts hot lines or checking the city weeklies (*see above*). **The Broadway Line** (tel. 212/302–4111) is an extensive information service that provides plot summaries, theater addresses, and ticket prices for Broadway shows. For reliable reviews and listings of Off-Broadway and Off-Off-Broadway productions, your best bets are the *Village Voice* and *Time Out New York*.

Most theaters are dark on Mondays. Matinees (afternoon shows) are typically staged on Wednesdays, Saturdays, and Sundays. A few Off-Broadway productions have two shows on Friday or Saturday evenings.

BROADWAY

The **Theater District** (West 42nd–53rd streets, between 6th and 9th avenues) is the heart and soul of that state of mind, Broadway. Come here to find marquees emblazoned with Hollywood names like Julie Andrews, Matthew Broderick, Lou Diamond Phillips, and Glenn Close. Broadway theaters typically don't have telephones (possibly to avoid flak about those ticket prices), so for up-to-date show times call a ticket agency, check magazine listings, or visit the box office. Some prominent Broadway theaters are listed below.

Booth. One of Broadway's most intimate theaters, the Booth has hosted four Pulitzer prize–winning productions over the last few decades. Since the theater's so small, sight lines here are prime. David Hare's one-man *Via Dolorosa* played here in 1999. *222 W. 45th St., between Broadway and 8th Ave. Subway: N, R, 1, 2, 3, 7, or 9 to Times Sq.; also A, C, or E to 42nd St. (8th Ave.).*

Broadhurst. Opened in 1917 and named for forgotten playwright George Broadhurst, this mid-size charmer has been home to several Tony winners, including *Amadeus* and *Kiss of the Spider Woman*. *235 W. 44th St., between Broadway and 8th Ave. Subway: N, R, 1, 2, 3, 7, or 9 to Times Sq.; also A, C, or E to 42nd St. (8th Ave.).*

Broadway. *Miss Saigon*, a Vietnam War–era take on Puccini's *Madama Butterfly*, has been parked at this gargantuan theater since 1991. The place tends to book large-scale musicals; it began as a movie house in 1924. *1681 Broadway, at W. 53rd St. Subway: C, E, 1, or 9 to 50th St. (8th Ave.).*

Cort. Some of the most daring shows on Broadway have turned up here, including the Pulitzer prize–winning *Diary of Anne Frank*. Katharine Hepburn had her debut here in *These Days* (1928), a flop. *138 W. 48th St., between Broadway and 6th Ave. Subway: N or R to 49th St.*

Ethel Barrymore. Marlon Brando and Jessica Tandy started their careers here in *A Streetcar Named Desire*, and Sidney Poitier started his in Lorraine Hansberry's *A Raisin in the Sun*. Dame Judi Dench stole the spotlight here in 1999 as the star of *Amy's View*. *243 W. 47th St., between Broadway and 8th Ave. Subway: C, E, 1, or 9 to 50th St. (8th Ave.); also N or R to 49th St.*

Eugene O'Neill. Neil Simon premiered a half dozen of his plays here in the '60s and '70s, when he was its owner. More recently, Brian Dennehy took the Tony for Best Actor as Willy Loman in the theater's revival of *Death of a Salesman*. *230 W. 49th St., between Broadway and 8th Ave. Subway: C, E, 1, or 9 to 50th St. (8th Ave.).*

Ford Center for the Performing Arts. Built on the site of two classic 42nd Street legitimate theaters, the Lyric (1903) and the Apollo (1910), this spectacular 1,839-seat theater opened in December 1997 with a musical production of E. L. Doctorow's novel *Ragtime*. The innovative design incorporates a landmark

43rd Street exterior wall from the Lyric and architectural elements from the Apollo, including its stage, proscenium, and dome. Note the stunning tile work in the lobby and murals on either side of the box seats. *213–215 42nd St., between Broadway and 8th Ave. Subway: N, R, 1, 2, 3, 7, or 9 to Times Sq.; also A, C, or E to 42nd St. (8th Ave.).*

Gershwin. Built in 1972, this is one of the newest, largest, and least attractive theaters on Broadway. It accommodates almost 2,000 people, so avoid sitting in seats upstairs, which are fairly far from the stage and not worth the ticket price. The Gershwin has already had scores of hits—including the acclaimed revival of *Show Boat,* directed by Harold Prince. The Theatre Hall of Fame is here, but its displays are rather stale. *222 W. 51st St., between Broadway and 8th Ave. Subway: C, E, 1, or 9 to 50th St. (8th Ave.).*

Helen Hayes. Among the smallest theaters you'll find along the Great White Way, the Helen Hayes has merely 499 seats, all of which offer a wonderfully intimate view. *240 W. 44th St., between Broadway and 8th Ave. Subway: N, R, 1, 2, 3, 7, or 9 to Times Sq.; also A, C, or E to 42nd St. (8th Ave.).*

Imperial. Shows at the grand Imperial (*Peter Pan, Fiddler on the Roof, Annie Get Your Gun*) rarely flop, earning it the nickname "The Lucky House." *Les Misérables* has been playing here since 1987. *249 W. 45th St., between Broadway and 8th Ave. Subway: N, R, 1, 2, 3, 7, or 9 to Times Sq.; also A, C, or E to 42nd St. (8th Ave.).*

Lyceum. This is the oldest running theater on Broadway. Tony Randall's National Actors Theatre is based at this, the oldest running theater on Broadway. Great views can be had from anywhere but the balcony. *149 W. 49th St., between 6th and 7th Aves. Subway: N or R to 49th St.*

Majestic. The Majestic is famous for having premiered Rodgers and Hammerstein musicals like *Carousel* and *South Pacific.* Its current tenant, *The Phantom of the Opera,* has been going since 1988 and seems like it might be here forever. *245 W. 44th St., between Broadway and 8th Ave. Subway: N, R, 1, 2, 3, 7, or 9 to Times Sq.; also A, C, or E to W. 42nd St. (8th Ave.).*

Marquis. This theater is on the second level of a Marriott Hotel in the middle of Times Square. Step into the revolving penthouse lounge after the show for a tacky-cocktail break. Don't worry; the revolutions are slooooow. *1535 Broadway, at 45th St. Subway: N, R, 1, 2, 3, 7, or 9 to Times Sq.; also A, C, or E to W. 42nd St. (8th Ave.).*

Nederlander. This funky mid-size theater was revitalized when the hit musical *Rent* moved uptown from the New York Theater Workshop (see above) in 1996; *Rent* has played here since. Decorative details in the lobby and in the theater itself—like the wall fixtures and mosaic moldings—serve as an extension of the aesthetic you'll see on stage. *208 W. 41st St., between Broadway and 8th Ave. Subway: N, R, 1, 2, 3, 7, or 9 to Times Sq.; also A, C, or E to 42nd St. (8th Ave.).*

Neil Simon. Named for one of America's most prolific playwrights, this theater recently hosted the mediocre musical *The Scarlet Pimpernel. 250 W. 52nd St., between Broadway and 8th Ave. Subway: C, E, 1, or 9 to 50th St.*

New Amsterdam. Starting in 1903, the likes of Eddie Cantor, Will Rogers, Fanny Brice, and the Ziegfeld Follies packed the crowds into this wonderful art nouveau theater. The current owner, Disney, brought the remarkable theater back from the dead as a venue for its own productions. Julie Taymor's visually stunning staging of the *Th Lion King* opened here in November 1997. *214 W. 42nd St. Subway: N, R, 1, 2, 3, 7, or 9 to Times Sq.; also A, C, or E to 42nd St. (8th Ave.).*

St. James. The St. James is a classic Broadway gem—it is big, but doesn't feel it. Steer clear of the rear orchestra; the mezzanine seems to hang rather low here. *246 W. 44th St., between Broadway and 8th Ave. Subway: N, R, 1, 2, 3, 7, or 9 to Times Sq.; also A, C, or E to 42nd St. (8th Ave.).*

Shubert. *A Chorus Line* had its record-breaking 15-year (1975–1990) run here (though it's since been outdone by the show with nine lives). This is also where Barbra Streisand made her 1962 Broadway debut, and the Tony-winning revival of Kander & Ebb's *Chicago* wowed audiences in 1996. *225 W. 44th St., between Broadway and 8th Ave. Subway: N, R, 1, 2, 3, 7, or 9 to Times Sq.; also A, C, or E to 42nd St. (8th Ave.).*

Walter Kerr. August Wilson's prize-winning *The Piano Lesson* and Tony Kushner's moving two-part epic about gay life, *Angels in America: Millennium Approaches* and *Perestroika,* have played at this lovely theater, renovated and renamed in 1990 for the respected drama critic. *219 W. 48th St., between Broadway and 8th Ave. Subway: C, E, 1, or 9 to 50th St.; also N or R to 49th St.*

Winter Garden. In the Roaring '20s this was *the* place to catch vaudeville extravaganzas by the Shubert brothers. Many hit musicals have played here, including *Funny Girl* and *Mame.* Since 1982 it's been inhabited by singing, dancing, jellicle *Cats. 1634 Broadway, at W. 50th St. Subway: C, E, 1, or 9 to 50th St.; also N or R to 49th St.*

OFF-BROADWAY

Off-Broadway is a good place to catch Broadway smashes in the making—like *A Chorus Line,* which opened at the Public Theater, or Wendy Wasserstein's *The Heidi Chronicles,* which first appeared at Playwrights Horizons—before they relocate to the Great White Way and ticket prices hit the stratosphere. The biggest clusters of Off-Broadway theaters can be found in the West Village (around Sheridan Square) and in Midtown on Theater Row (42nd Street, between 9th and 10th avenues).

Off-Off-Broadway, which came of age when experimental theater began to flourish in the '60s, offers an in-your-face, the-hell-with-it alternative to everything else. Depending on which night you show up, you'll find everything from cabaret and alternative comedy to serious drama and unclassifiable performance at Off-Off-Broadway theaters. They're the birthplace of performance art (a mix of dance, drama, music, and video, usually expressing Very Deep Thoughts). Of the theaters listed below, **La MaMa E.T.C.** is known for its devotion to performance art. So are the **Brooklyn Academy of Music,** the **Joseph Papp Public Theater, The Kitchen,** and **P.S. 122** (*see* Arts Centers, *above*). Ticket prices for Off-Broadway shows typically run $15–$45, for Off-Off-Broadway $10–$25. Most venues also offer some kind of free weekly event.

Actors Studio. This respected drama school has productions open to the public. Tickets are free ($5 donation suggested), but reservations are required. The Actors Studio M.F.A. Program also has a free repertory season (March to May) performed by graduate students (tel. 212/229–5859) at the downtown Circle in the Square. *432 W. 44th St., between 9th and 10th Aves., Midtown, tel. 212/757–0870. Subway: A, C, or E to 42nd St. (Port Authority).*

Atlantic Theater Company. Founded by playwright David Mamet and actor William H. Macy in 1985, this troupe mounts challenging new plays by up-and-coming writers. The space, formerly a parish house, works well for theater—seats are comfortable and acoustics excellent. *307 W. 26th St., between 8th and 9th Aves., Chelsea, tel. 212/633–9797. Subway: C or E to 28th St.; also A, C, or E to 23rd St.*

Classic Stage Company (CSC). Here's a lively showcase for the classics—Beckett or Racine, for example—in new translations and adaptations. Rush tickets at $15 are available a halfhour before the performance. *136 E. 13th St., between 3rd and 4th Aves., East Village, tel. 212/677–4210. Subway: 4, 5, 6, L, N, or R to 14th St./Union Sq.*

Jean Cocteau Repertory. The company specializes in the obscure plays that drama geeks rave about. You can also see classic and contemporary standards here by playwrights such as Ibsen, Ionesco, and Stoppard. *Bouwerie Lane Theatre, 330 Bowery, at Bond St., East Village, tel. 212/677–0060. Subway: 6 to Bleecker St.; also, B, D, F, or Q to Broadway–Lafayette St.*

Joseph Papp Public Theater. The Joseph Papp Public Theater, a complex of five theaters, is the year-round home of the New York Shakespeare Festival. Despite the name, performances are not limited to the bard and are anything but staid: *Bring In 'Da Noise, Bring in 'Da Funk* premiered here in 1995. Each June, the theater moves uptown to its summer home—the Delacorte Theater in Central Park—where free Shakespeare performances are staged. Shakespeare in the Park has become a major cultural tradition for New Yorkers since it debuted in the '60s, and people wait at the box office for hours hoping to snag a pair of the free tix (*see box,* Summer in the City, *above*). Rush tickets at $15 are available a halfhour before curtain time when plays are not sold out. *425 Lafayette St., at Astor Pl., East Village, tel. 212/260–2400. Subway: 6 to Astor Pl.; also, N or R to 8th St./Broadway.*

La MaMa E.T.C. Famous alumni of this "MGM of experimental theater" include Sam Shepard, Bette Midler, Andy Warhol, Nick Nolte, and Meatloaf. In its three performance spaces you can find everything from African fables to new wave operas. *74 E. 4th St., between 2nd and 3rd Aves., East Village, tel. 212/475–7710. Subway: 6 to Astor Pl. or F to 2nd Ave.*

Manhattan Theatre Club. Some of the most talked-about new plays and musicals in town are presented here by such major talents as Terrence McNally, Athol Fugard, and Stephen Sondheim. *City Center, 131 W. 55th St., between 6th and 7th Aves., Midtown, tel. 212/581–1212. Subway: N or R to 57th St.*

National Black Theatre. Come here for new works by contemporary African-American writers. *2031–3 5th Ave., between 125th and 126th Sts., Harlem, tel. 212/722–3800. Subway: 2, 3, 4, 5, 6, A, C, B, or D to 125th St.*

New Dramatists. New Dramatists is a great resource for playwrights—it offers seven-year memberships to talented writers to allow them to develop their craft. And what's in it for you, the audience? You get to come see free readings of works-in-progress, often on their way to the big leagues. Reserve far in advance. *424 W. 44th St., between 9th and 10th Aves., Midtown, tel. 212/757–6960. Subway: A, C, or E to 42nd St. (Port Authority).*

New York Theater Workshop. The mega-hit musical *Rent* exploded at this tiny venue, which produces controversial new theater works by playwrights like David Rabe, Tony Kushner, and Paul Rudnick, and performance groups like the Five Lesbian Brothers. *79 E. 4th St., between 2nd and 3rd Aves., East Village, tel. 212/460–5475.. Subway: 6 to Astor Pl. or F to 2nd Ave.*

Pan-Asian Repertory Theatre. This forum for Asian-American actors and artists presents new work and adaptations of Western plays. *St. Clement's Church, 423 W. 46th St., between 9th and 10th Aves., Midtown, tel. 212/245–2660. Subway: C or E to 50th St. (8th Ave.).*

Pearl Theatre Company. A troupe of resident players concentrates on classics from around the globe; the works of such masters as Molière, Ibsen, Shakespeare, Shaw, and Sophocles find a new life here. *80 St. Marks Pl., between 2nd and 3rd Aves., East Village, tel. 212/598–9802.. Subway: 6 to Astor Pl.*

The Performing Garage. This small space has an uncompromising program of experimental theater, often by up-and-comers. Members of the Performing Garage's resident company, the Wooster Group, include actor Willem Dafoe, director Elizabeth LeCompte, and monologuist nonpareil Spalding Gray. *33 Wooster St., between Broome and Grand Sts., SoHo, tel. 212/966–9796. Subway: A, C, or E to Canal St. Tickets: $15–$25.*

Playwrights Horizons. This theater (and theater school), at the heart of Theater Row, is dedicated to developing the talents of new playwrights. *Driving Miss Daisy* and *Once on this Island* both began here. *416 W. 42nd St., between 9th and 10th Aves., Midtown, tel. 212/279–4200. Subway: A, C, or E to 42nd St. (Port Authority).*

Don't overlook tomorrow's hits and today's flops—there's something special about seeing a show in previews or an already-panned play before it bites the dust.

Primary Stages. The spotlight here is on new creations by American playwrights such as Charles Busch, David Ives, and Donald Margulies. *354 W. 45th St., between 8th and 9th Aves., Midtown, tel. 212/333–4052. Subway: N, R, 1, 2, 3, 7, or 9 to Times Sq.; also A, C, or E to 42nd St. (8th Ave.).*

Repertorio Español. The works shown here are by Latin-American and Spanish playwrights and novelists. Those who can't follow the action *en español* can listen to a simultaneous translation though a nifty cordless headset. *Gramercy Arts Theatre, 138 E. 27th St., between Lexington and 3rd Aves., Gramercy, tel. 212/889–2850. Subway: 6 to 28th St.*

Second Stage Theatre. The company's new Rem Koolhaas–designed space opened in 1999 in what was once a bank. The theater brings a refreshing touch of futuristic minimalism to the otherwise surreal "new" Times Square. *307 W. 43rd St., between 8th and 9th Aves., Midtown, tel. 212/246–4422. Subway: N, R, 1, 2, 3, 7, or 9 to Times Sq.; also A, C, or E to 42nd St. (8th Ave.).*

Signature Theatre Company. Each season, this company devotes its time to the works of one American playwright; past seasons have reexamined the plays of Edward Albee, Horton Foote, Adrienne Kennedy, and John Guare. *555 W. 42nd St., between 10th and 11th Aves., Midtown, tel. 212/967–1913. Subway: A, C, or E to 42nd St. (Port Authority).*

Sullivan Street Playhouse. Here's the home of *The Fantasticks*, the world's longest-running musical. *181 Sullivan St., between W. Houston and Bleecker Sts., West Village, tel. 212/674–3838. Subway: A, B, C, D, E, F, or Q to W. 4th St. (Washington Sq.).*

Vineyard Theatre. Innovative new plays and musicals by established and emerging artists are given stellar productions. Edward Albee's Pulitzer Prize winner *Three Tall Women* had its New York premiere here. *108 E. 15th St., between Union Sq. and Irving Pl., Gramercy, tel. 212/353–3366. Subway: 4, 5, 6, L, N, or R to 14th St./Union Sq.*

York Theatre Company. If you like musicals, check out the well-received revivals and new works presented by this admirable group. *Theatre at St. Peter's Church, E. 54th St. at Lexington Ave., Midtown, tel. 212/935–5820. Subway: E or F to Lexington Ave. or 6 to 51st St.*

SPORTS AND OUTDOOR ACTIVITIES

UPDATED BY HANNAH BORGESON

N ew Yorkers may love dining out and drinking cocktails—but during summer you'll see a flood of rippled hardbodies on bikes and 'blades, slackers whacking around tennis and soccer balls, and old folks speed-walking through Central Park. Many more fill stadiums and line the streets during major annual events like the U.S. Open and the New York Marathon, and to cheer on the city's pro sports teams. If you feel like joining in, *Time Out New York* ($2.50), sold at most newsstands, is a great resource: Its "Sports" section lists upcoming events, times, dates, and ticket info, although it's better for pro sports than the myriad participant opportunities. *MetroSports,* a free monthly newspaper available at many health clubs and sporting goods stores, is better for the latter.

GYMS AND REC CENTERS

There are plenty of private health clubs in town that charge thousands of dollars for the privilege of sweating your extra flesh off on their StairMasters. Thankfully, **Crunch Fitness** (tel. 212/620–7867) has five locations in Manhattan and only charges $22 for the day. That entitles you to as many yoga, kick boxing, aerobics, and karate classes as you can stand. **New York Sports Clubs** (tel. 800/796–6972 for locations) has so many gyms in Manhattan that we stopped counting after twenty; they're all yuppie-infested bastions of fitness with the latest technological gizmos to enhance your workouts; a few locations have tiny lap pools. Day passes are $25. The venerable **YMCA** (tel. 212/630–9600) allows visitors to use the good-quality, down-to-earth facilities at its Vanderbilt, Chinatown, West Side, and Harlem branches (but not at the McBurney branch, in Chelsea). They have a full range of conditioning and strength-training classes and equipment, pools, and reasonable prices ($10–$25 per day, depending on location). Most health clubs, including those listed above, allow members to bring guests for free, so you could try hitting up your athletic friends for passes.

PRIVATE GYMS

Asphalt Green. This 5.5-acre, state-of-the-art facility in a former asphalt plant features an Olympic-size indoor pool (with special features for swimmers with disabilities), indoor and outdoor tracks, basketball courts, an Astroturf field, and all kinds of exercise equipment and classes. The drop-in fee for the pool or gym is $15 ($30 for both); the outdoor field and track are open to the public for free when they're not in use. *York Ave. at E. 91st St., Upper East Side, tel. 212/369–8890. Subway: 4, 5, or 6 to E. 86th St. Open weekdays 5:30 AM–10 PM, weekends 8–8. Pool closed to nonmembers weekdays 3–8.*

Chelsea Piers Sports Center. In this gym the size of three football fields, you'll find the city's longest running track (¼ mi), a boxing ring, volleyball courts, a climbing wall, a swimming pool, plush locker rooms, and just about everything else a sports fiend could want–all indoors. A day pass ($36) gives you access to everything at the Sports Center, but you can purchase only six day passes per year. On the adjacent piers are numerous indoor and outdoor facilities that are open to the public for separate and generally affordable fees: ice-skating rinks (*see* Participant Sports, *below*); a golf driving range; a bowling alley; a kids' climbing wall; basketball courts; Astroturf fields; a kayaking center; and roller rinks. *W. 23rd St. at Hudson River, Chelsea, tel. 212/336–6000 or 212/336–6666 for recorded info. Subway: C or E to W. 23rd St.; walk 3 long blocks or catch M23 crosstown bus. Open weekdays 6 AM–11 PM, weekends 8 AM– 9 PM for Sports Center; varying hours for other activities.*

PUBLIC GYMS

City-operated rec centers are an excellent deal. Pay the $25 annual membership fee at one and you have access to all 12 Manhattan locations. Offerings include swimming pools (outdoor pools are free in summer; at this time the indoor pools at centers with both are closed), basketball and volleyball courts, weight-training equipment, all sorts of exercise bicycles and Nautilus machines, even salsa aerobics and classes in African martial arts; contact the **NYC Parks & Recreation Department** (tel. 212/360– 8111 or 800/201–7275 in NYC) for more info. Two of the best are:

Carmine Street. Here you'll find indoor and outdoor pools, an indoor track, indoor volleyball and basketball courts, two gyms, a dance studio, and weight rooms. Classes include yoga, aerobics, fencing, and self-defense. *3 Carmine St., at 7th Ave. S, West Village, tel. 212/242–5228. Subway: 1 or 9 to W. Houston St. Open weekdays 7 AM–10 PM, weekends 9–5., closed holidays. Hrs vary for courts and pool.*

West 59th Street. Facilities here include an indoor pool, fitness rooms, a gym, and an indoor climbing wall. *533 W. 59th St., between 10th and 11th Aves., Upper West Side, tel. 212/397–3166; 212/974– 2250 for climbing wall. Subway: A, B, C, D, 1, or 9 to W. 59th St. Open weekdays 11–10, Sat. 9–5 (hrs for climbing wall and recreational swimming vary).*

PARTICIPANT SPORTS

There is no lack of sports activities in New York, be it ice-skating at Rockefeller Center or mountain biking in the Bronx. No matter what you're into—jogging, biking, in-line skating, football, soccer, ultimate Frisbee, snoozing by a shady tree—the best place to start is **Central Park** (*see* Major Attractions *in* Chapter 2). Most sports activities are free if you do it yourself or join a pickup game. For info on participant sporting events throughout the city, call the **NYC Parks & Recreation Department** (tel. 212/360– 8111 or 800/201–7275 in NYC) and dial your way through their recorded choices.

BASKETBALL

Yorkville Sports (tel. 212/645–6488) holds open gym starting at 6:30 PM every Friday night from September through November for $10 per person; call for location.

PICKUP GAMES • There are hundreds of outdoor courts all over the city, where competition ranges from inept to life-threatening. Most players are men. Female hoopsters tend to gather at **Tompkins Square Park** (Ave. A at St. Marks Pl., East Village), while the courts on **West 4th Street** at 6th Avenue draw hotshots from around the city (and even an audience). Lively play also takes place on the six halfcourts at **West 76th Street** at Columbus Avenue and at the recently redone courts in **Central Park,** near the northeast end of the Great Lawn. On the Upper East Side, easygoing players fill half-courts at **Carl Schurz Park** (E. 84th St. at East End Ave.) and the courts at the **Armory Building** (E. 94th St. at Madison Ave., Upper East Side).

BIKING

While many New Yorkers swear by bikes for year-round transportation and could talk your ear off about their "locking systems," park riding is generally less stressful than vying for space on city streets. **Central Park, Riverside Park** (Riverside Dr., between W. 72nd and 135th Sts., Upper West Side), or the **Hudson River Park Esplanade/Bike Route 9** (along the Hudson from Chambers St. to 23rd St., and to extend to 59th St. by 2003) are scenic rides. Outside Manhattan, the best spots to explore on two wheels are **Prospect Park,** Brooklyn, where the loop road is never as crowded as Central Park's; **Forest**

Park, Queens, fantastic for BMXers; and **Shore Parkway Path** along the Brooklyn waterfront between Coney Island and Owls Head Park (for more, *see* Parks and Gardens *in* Chapter 2). **Century Road Club Association** (tel. 212/222–8062), which meets Saturday mornings (6 AM) in Central Park, runs three- to eight-lap races around its 6-mi circular drive. Rides over the **Brooklyn Bridge** boardwalk (riders going both directions should keep to the south side) or the **George Washington Bridge** (south sidewalk) are thrilling escapes from or to Manhattan. Mountain bikes are recommended for the Croton Aqueduct trail and the Putnam Rail Trail, both of which start in **Van Cortlandt Park** in the Bronx.

If you prefer to pedal with a group, join **Time's Up** (*see* Cheap Thrills *in* Chapter 2) for one of their evening rides. The **Five Borough Bicycle Club** (tel. 212/932–2300) and the **New York Cycle Club** (tel. 212/828–5711) have the most day rides on weekends year-round; **Fast and Fabulous** (tel. 212/567–7160), a predominantly gay and lesbian club, recommends its "fabulous" (as opposed to "fast") summer rides for casual cyclists.

BIKE RENTALS AND REPAIRS • Plenty of bike shops in the city will rent you a pair of wheels for cruising around. Try **Bicycle Habitat** (244 Lafayette St., between Prince and Spring Sts., SoHo, tel. 212/431–3315), which rents mountain bikes and hybrids for $25 per day (plus $250 deposit); **Metro Bicycles** (332 E. 14th St., between 1st and 2nd Aves., East Village, tel. 212/228–4344; and six other locations citywide) rents hybrids for $7 per hour or $35 per day ($45 to keep bike overnight), plus a $250 deposit. In summer you can rent bikes ($8–$14 per hr, $32–$40 per day) inside Central Park at **AAA Bikes** (Loeb Boathouse, mid-park at 74th St., tel. 212/861–4137).

BOATING

Loeb Boathouse (tel. 212/517–2233, mid-park at E 74th St.) rents rowboats (plus one Venetian gondola for nighttime glides in the moonlight) on the 18-acre Central Park Lake, with its picturesque bridges and remote corners, daily from April through October. The cost is $10 per hour ($30 cash deposit), and the peaceful views of the treeline and skyline are well worth it. The 60-acre Prospect Lake and the connecting Lullwater in **Prospect Park** are no less bucolic, and you can enjoy them in pedal boats rented from **Kate's Corner** (tel. 718/282–7789) at the Wollman Memorial Rink weekends and holidays from mid-May through October for $10 an hour. Kayaking the Hudson is adventurous fun for beginners and experienced paddlers at the **Downtown Boathouse** (Pier 26, N. Moore St. and the Hudson River, tel. 212/966–1852), which shoves you off in a kayak for free on summer weekends.

CLIMBING

Rock climbers intent on climbing in Manhattan, but not ready to scale the Empire State Building, can test their mettle in a converted racquetball court at the **Manhattan Plaza Health Club** (482 W. 43rd St., between 9th and 10th Aves., Midtown, tel. 212/563–7001). Day access is $10, but there are weekly ladies' and men's nights where admission is waived and equipment-rental and belay-test fees are reduced. In Central Park, **Rat Rock** (near the carousel) and **Cat Rock** (near Wollman Rink), both are good for bouldering. **Extravertical Climbing Club** (61 W. 62nd St., at Broadway, Upper West Side, tel. 212/586–5718) has a 50-ft and a 30-ft wall within the indoor/outdoor Harmony Atrium. A day pass is $16; equipment rental and belay tests are extra. Your horizontally inclined friends can admire you from the adjacent atrium café. **Chelsea Piers** and the **West 59th Street** rec centers (*see* Gyms and Rec Centers, *above*) also offer indoor climbing walls and equipment rentals.

CROSS-COUNTRY SKIING

When a heavy snowfall hits New York, Central Park's bridle paths and roadways make for spectacular treks, particularly in the woodsy wonderland above 86th Street. **Eastern Mountain Sports** (20 W. 61st St., near Broadway, Upper West Side, tel. 212/397–4860), just a few strides from Central Park, can set you up with boots, poles, and skis for $15 per day.

HIKING

Though hiking in New York City seems an odd concept, there are plenty of nearby places to worship Mother Nature. The obvious choice is Central Park—literally dozens of trails crisscross its length, most of them rarely crowded, some of them unpaved. In the outer boroughs, enormous parks like **Alley Pond Park** and **Forest Park** (in Queens), **Pelham Bay Park** and **Van Cortlandt Park** (in the Bronx), Staten Island's **High Rock Park,** and the **Gateway National Recreation Area** along the shore in Staten Island, Brooklyn, and Queens (including **Jamaica Bay Wildlife Refuge**) each offer acres of wilderness and plenty of picnic tables; *see* Parks and Gardens *in* Chapter 2, for more info on each.

The **Urban Park Rangers** (tel. 800/201–7275 and ask for the phone number for the borough that interests you) organize guided walks throughout New York City parks; they can also recommend the best spots for bird-watching, dog walking, jogging, you name it. *The **Jamaica Bay Wildlife Refuge** (tel. 718/318–4346) in Broad Channel, Queens, offers moonlight walks, birding workshops, flora and fauna walks, and more, all for free. The **Central Park Conservancy** (tel. 212/360–3444), in Central Park, organizes park history tours, bird-watching expeditions, fishing, and other nature programs. **Shorewalkers** (tel. 212/330–7686) leads weekend tours of New York–area shorelines.

HORSEBACK RIDING

Chelsea Equestrian Center is an indoor facility that's newly open to the public, although at a price: half-hour lessons are $50, and $100 buys you a full hour at the indoor and outdoor arenas. You can choose English or Western, but be sure to book ahead. *W. 23rd St. at the Hudson River, Chelsea, tel. 212/367–9090. 7 AM–10 PM weekdays, 8–7 weekends.*

Claremont Riding Academy is a more than 100-year-old institution on Manhattan's Upper West Side. Experienced English riders can rent horses to explore 6 mi of bridle paths in nearby Central Park for $35 per hour. Reserve far in advance. *175 W. 89th St., at Amsterdam Ave., Upper West Side, tel. 212/724–5100. Rentals weekdays 6:30 AM–1 hr before dusk, weekends 6:30–4.*

All ice-skating rinks offer skate rentals, lockers, tacky music, and snack bars serving steaming cups of cocoa. Hockey players need to bring their own gear.

Lasker Rink. This outdoor rink, at the northern end of Central Park near 106th Street, offers crowd-free skating November–March. Skate rentals are $3.50. *Tel. 212/396–1010. Subway: 2 or 3 to W. 110th St. (Central Park N). Admission: $3. Open daily mid-Oct.–March; call for hours as schedule varies.*

Rockefeller Center Ice-Skating Rink. The rink isn't huge, but there's still something amazing about skating in the heart of Manhattan on a crisp winter evening. Kids love this place. The best deal is the nonholiday lunchtime session (11:30–1), when it's only $4. Skate rentals are $4–$5. *Rockefeller Center, between W. 49th and 50th Sts., Midtown, tel. 212/332–7654. Subway: B, D, F, or Q to W. 47th–50th Sts. (Rockefeller Center). Admission: $7.50–$11. Open Oct.–Apr., Mon.–Thurs. 9 AM–10:30 PM, Fri.–Sat. 8:30 AM–midnight, Sun. 8:30 AM–10 PM.*

Sky Rink. This pair of deluxe indoor rinks (the size of Alaska) is the reason for Chelsea Piers' existence. There's open skating year-round. Rentals are $5. Drop-in hockey play is offered weekdays early mornings, at lunchtime, and in the evenings at a cost of $18, but players must bring their own equipment. *W. 23rd St. at the Hudson River, Chelsea, tel. 212/336–6100. Subway: A, C, or E to W. 23rd St. Admission: $10.50. Opening hours vary.*

Wollman Memorial Rink. Ice-skaters pack this famously beautiful Central Park rink, near 62nd Street, from November through March. Skate rentals are $3.50. *Tel. 212/396–1010. Subway: B or Q to W. 57th St.; also N or R to 5th Ave. Admission: $7. Open mid-Oct.–March, Mon.–Tues. 10–3, Wed.–Thurs. 10–9:30, Fri.–Sat. 10–11, Sun. 10–9.*

IN-LINE SKATING

On weekends, city parks and roadways swarm with 'bladers oblivious to everything but their Walkmans. Evel Knieval types set up obstacle courses and jumps near **Tavern on the Green** (near Central Park W, at 66th St.) in Central Park. During warm months, the park's **Wollman Memorial Rink** (*see* Ice-Skating, *above*) becomes a roller disco Thursday–Sunday; rentals are $6, plus $3 for padding. Other popular outdoor spots include Hudson River Park, Riverside Park, and the concrete canyons and wide-open plazas of **Wall Street** (nearly car-free on weekends). *See* Biking, *above,* for more ideas for skilled skaters.

Chelsea Piers (W. 23rd St. at the Hudson River, Chelsea, tel. 212/336–6200) has two outdoor roller rinks, which offer general skating (admission $5, rentals and padding $13.50); and, on Saturday nights, DJ'd dance parties. The Chelsea Piers Skate Park is set up with ramps, half-pipes, and the like for aggressive skating ($8 per three-hour session). **Riverside Skate Park** (Riverside Dr. at 108th St., Upper West Side, tel. 212/408–0264) is a city-run aggressive skating park; you must have your own equipment and admission is $3.

The **Empire Skate Club of New York** (tel. 212/774–1774) holds instructional sessions and organizes members-only group skates to New Jersey, Long Island, and around New York City. They're your best bet for information about other free group skates, like Tuesday Night Skate and Blade Night Out (Wed.). Skaters, members or not, are welcome on all **Time's Up** Rides (*see* Biking, *above*).

If you need to rent, head to one of the **Blades** branches. Full-day rentals (pads included) are $16 on weekdays, $27 on weekends, plus a credit-card deposit. *120 W. 72nd St., between Columbus Ave. and*

Broadway, Upper West Side, tel. 212/787–3911. Subway: 1, 2, 3, or 9 to W. 72nd St. Open daily 10–8 (Sun. until 6). Call for other locations.

IN-LINE SPORTS • Chelsea Piers (*see above*) offers several levels of league in-line hockey play, year-round. If hockey isn't your fancy, the **National In-line Basketball League** (tel. 888/466–4225) sponsors *basketball* games on 'blades on Saturday from 10 AM–1 PM at Tompkins Square Park in summer. Who'd have thunk it? Although it's a membership organization, drop-ins are welcome for free.

New Yorkers aren't afraid to cross-check, so arrive well-padded wherever you go. The best place to play street in-line hockey is **Robert Moses Playground** (E. 41st St. at 1st Ave., Midtown), where the competition is pretty fierce. In summer you'll also find pickup games at **Riverbank State Park** (W. 145th St. at Riverside Dr., Harlem). Throughout the year on weekends, there are also games at **Tompkins Square Park** (Ave. A, at St. Marks Pl., East Village) and, on Sunday afternoons, at the north end of **Union Square** (E. 17th St. at Broadway, Gramercy).

RUNNING

Though Manhattan streets are crowded with pedestrians, cyclists, skaters, limos, city buses, and curb-jumping taxis, there are plenty of places where you can run safely in New York. Most popular is the **Jacqueline Kennedy Onassis Reservoir** in Central Park (mid-park, between 85th and 96th Sts.); tenacious people in Lycra orbit its 1.6-mi track in every kind of weather; thanks to the recent refurbishment spearheaded by the New York Road Runners Club (*see below*), it's in great shape and no longer resembles a moat in even heavy rains. Roads within the park all have designated runners' lanes and close completely to traffic weekdays 10–3 (except the southeast portion) and 7–10 PM and from Friday at 7 PM until Monday at 6 AM. The entire loop of the park—from 59th Street to 110th Street and around the other side—is 6 mi.

Other favorite Manhattan circuits are: **Riverside Park** (4½ mi), **Washington Square Park** (½ mi), **East River Park** (¼-mi track), and the **Hudson River Esplanade** (3½mi). In Brooklyn, try either the **Brooklyn Heights Promenade** (1 mi), which offers stunning views of the lower Manhattan skyline, or the loop in **Prospect Park** (3½ mi), which, in summer, is closed to traffic longer hours than in Central Park. For park locations, *see* Parks and Gardens *in* Chapter 2.

RUNNING CLUBS • New York has almost a dozen clubs geared exclusively toward runners; most organize group runs, provide safety info, plan races, and sponsor events throughout the year. Most clubs meet weekly in Central Park and welcome drop-in participants. The **Achilles Track Club** (tel. 212/354–0300) is primarily for wheelchair racers and runners with disabilities, although many nondisabled runners act as guides or partners. **Front Runners** (tel. 212/724–9700) is New York's main gay and lesbian running group. The **Hash House Harriers,** "drinkers with a running problem," organize runs with a three-fold purpose: follow a marked route without losing the trail; (2) run as fast as you can; and (3) end up at a bar. There's usually more than one run in New York City per week; call 212/427–4692 for times, "hash cash" fees (usually about $15 for the bar), and locations.

SOCCER

Alexi Lalas aspirants should cruise over to **Soccer Sport Supply** (1745 1st Ave., between 90th and 91st Sts., Upper East Side, tel. 212/427–6050), which can outfit you with cleats and Umbro shorts and get you up-to-date on soccer activities around the city.

PICKUP GAMES • You may have noticed that Manhattan isn't blessed with acres of open fields. Your best bet is to join a weekend game at Central Park's **North Meadow** (mid-park, at 97th St.), which has three soccer fields; groups must have permits to play.

SOFTBALL AND BASEBALL

Between April and mid-September, softball dominates the city's parks on weekends and weekday evenings. Most games are sponsored by a league, either men's, women's, or coed and either fast- or slow-pitch. Most people hook up with a league through their employer or with an organization like **Corporate Sports** (tel. 212/245–4738), **Manhattan Indoor/Outdoor Sports** (tel. 718/712–0342), or **Yorkville Sports** (tel. 212/645–6488), but many gladly accept visitors—especially if they're good players—so ask around to find someone who will bring you to a game. The **NYC Parks & Recreation Permit Office** (tel. 212/408–0234) controls access to the city's hundreds of baseball diamonds, all of which require permits. Sorry.

SWIMMING

If you're too poor to escape to the Italian Riviera—or even the south shore of Long Island—at least you can keep your cool at a city pool or nearby beach (*see box,* New York City, Land of Skyscrapers and

Sunny Beaches?!, *in* Chapter 2). To celebrate the ever-cleaner Hudson River, the **Manhattan Island Foundation** (tel. 888/692–7946) organizes several fun and/or competitive swims—in the Hudson—during summer. Call for dates and prices. The pools at public rec centers (*see* Gyms and Rec Centers, *above*) are free during summer—and crammed with splashing preteens. You're better off at a private pool: The indoor eight-lane, 50-meter Olympic pool at **Asphalt Green** (*see* Gyms and Rec Centers, *above*) is open to nonmembers early in the day on weekdays and all day weekends for $15. A $15 day pass gives you access to the **Midtown YWCA**'s (610 Lexington Ave., at E. 53rd St., Midtown, tel. 212/735–9770) six-lane indoor pool, perfect for rigorous workouts. The **Vanderbilt YMCA** (*see* Gyms and Rec Centers, *above*) is another good lap pool in Midtown. Your cheapest option is **Lasker Rink** (tel. 212/534–7639) in Central Park. In summer this skating rink becomes a swimming pool; a full day of splashing around is entirely free. To reach Lasker Rink, enter the park at 110th Street and Lenox Avenue.

TENNIS

Whenever the weather is good, you'll find dozens of people on the 24 public courts in Central Park (open dusk to dawn). Though pickup games are possible, most people arrive in pairs and aren't in the mood to share. Reservations are a good idea. Also, you must get a permit to play on a city-owned court from April through November: $5 for a single-play permit or $50 for a full-season permit that's valid in all five boroughs. Call the **NYC Parks & Recreation Permit Office** (tel. 212/360–8133) for more info. Or pick up your permit in person at Room 1 in the Arsenal Building (Central Park at 5th Ave., near E. 64th St., Upper East Side). The courts at **East River Park** (East River Dr. at Delancey St., Lower East Side, tel. 212/529–7185) are available on a first-come, first-served basis; they're never as busy as the courts in Central Park. If you don't mind the trek to Queens, reserve one of 45 outdoor/indoor courts at the **U.S.T.A. National Tennis Center** (Flushing Meadows–Corona Park, Queens, tel. 718/760–6200), site of the U.S. Open. You can make reservations two days to an hour in advance; courts cost $28–$40 depending on the time of day. For directions, *see* Queens *in* Chapter 2.

If you've never been on Rollerblades before, proceed slowly and cautiously to one of the Central Park Skate Patrol's "Stopping Clinics." From noon to 6 in late spring to early fall, these quick, free, knee-saving seminars are held daily.

VOLLEYBALL

New York's volleyball scene is dominated by leagues consisting of set teams; most hold open games only during tryouts. Anyone can go to the **New York Urban Professional League** (tel. 212/877–3614) open games on Friday night. They cost $6 for beginners and $10 for everyone else; admission buys you three hours of playing and a beer at a local bar. The games are at Louis D. Brandeis High School (145 W. 84th St., between Columbus and Amsterdam Aves.) starting at 7, and you should be prompt to assure that you'll get a space. If you want to hone that killer serve, try the three nets in Central Park between Sheep Meadow and the Mall, or the two above the northeast end of the Great Lawn, or in one of New York's public rec centers (*see above*).

SPECTATOR SPORTS

Even though they lost their beloved Dodgers to Los Angeles in 1957, sports-crazy New Yorkers still have great pro teams like the Yankees, Mets, Knicks, Islanders, and Rangers. Sure, the *Post* and *Daily News* seem to find more excitement chronicling off-field antics—like Yankee owner George Steinbrenner's bullying (and unending) threats to move his team to New Jersey or Spike Lee's latest courtside outburst—but, hey, a sunny day hanging in the House that Ruth Built (New Yorkers' pet name for Yankee Stadium) while drinking beer with rowdy fans is still a singular New York experience.

The main venues for New York's pro teams are: **Giants Stadium** (*see* Football, *below*); **Continental Airlines Arena** (Rte. 3, East Rutherford, NJ, tel. 201/935–3900), accessible by bus from Port Authority; and **Madison Square Garden** (7th Ave. between W. 31st and 33rd Sts., Midtown, tel. 212/465–6000) at the Penn Station subway stop (A, C, E, 1, 2, 3, or 9). In addition to hosting the Knicks, Liberty, and Rangers, the Garden is the place to catch an endless parade of wrestling, boxing, running, ice-skating, and monster-truck shows. Purchase tickets at a team's box office (where you still can't avoid MSG's pesky surcharge) or through **Ticketmaster** (tel. 212/307–7171), which slaps a service charge (usually about $5 per ticket, depending on the game) on whatever you buy.

RUN FOR YOUR LIFE

New York's marathon is one of the city's most celebrated civic events, a 26.2-mi party that passes through all five boroughs before ending in Central Park. In a single Sunday in early November, over 27,000 runners from 99 foreign countries and all 50 states will have passed approximately 18,000 yards of barricade tape and 2 million spectators; 22,000 gallons of Gatorade, 30 live bands, and 642 tubes of K-Y Jelly will keep the whole thing running smoothly.

The New York Road Runners Club holds free group runs of various distances and paces weekdays at 6:30 PM, Saturday at 10 AM, all starting near Central Park at the club headquarters. They also sponsor classes, races, and "fun runs" year-round, and coordinate the annual New York Marathon (see box). 9 E. 89th St., between 5th and Madison Aves., Upper East Side, tel. 212/860–4455. Subway: 4, 5, or 6 to E. 86th St.

BASEBALL

Nothing's better than hot dogs, beer, and baseball—except all of that *plus* a free pair of plastic Yanks sunglasses. Annual freebie fests include the Mets' Umbrella Night and Kids Jersey (shirts, not cows) Day, and the Yankees' Sunglasses and Bat (the baseball-hitting kind, not the flying rodents) days—you might even score a mouse pad. Regular baseball season runs April–early October.

New York Yankees. In years past, greats like Babe Ruth, Joe DiMaggio, and Lou Gehrig led the Bronx Bombers to championship after championship. These days things are looking up again, after some recent World Championship seasons, and late-season tickets are sometimes hard to come by. Bleachers cost $8, reserved seating is $14–$29. The Yankee Clipper ferry is a fun way to travel from Manhattan's East Side to games (NY Waterway, tel. 800/533–3779). *Yankee Stadium, 161st St. and River Ave., Bronx, tel. 718/293–4300 or 212/307–1212 for Ticketmaster. Subway: B, D, or 4 to 161st St. (Yankee Stadium). Box office open Mon.–Sat. 9–5, Sun. 10–5 and during home games.*

New York Mets. The Mets seem often overshadowed by their Bronx cousins, who have nearly always outplayed them, but games at Shea are still lots of fun—because real Mets fans never give up hope. Tickets cost $10–$30; all seating is reserved. *Shea Stadium, Roosevelt Ave. at 126th St., Flushing, Queens, tel. 718/507–8499. Subway: 7 to Willets Point (Shea Stadium).*

BASKETBALL

The **New York Knickerbockers** (Madison Square Garden, Midtown, tel. 212/465–5867) suffered through several humiliating runs for the championship under Armani-clad coach and personality Pat Riley. Don Nelson (of Golden State Warriors fame) tried his hand as coach from 1995 until he got canned in early 1996, when finally Jeff Van Gundy took over a mismatched crew still hoping to go all the way with aging center Patrick Ewing. Tickets start at $22 and go up sharply from there—but they're *very* hard to get. The **New Jersey Nets** (Meadowlands Arena, tel. 800/765–6387), who migrated from New York to New Jersey in 1977, perennially rank as one of the NBA's worst teams—despite star players like Jayson Williams and Stephon Marbury. A small number of tickets sell for $5 or $10; the next level is $30. The pro-basketball men's season runs late October–early May. Women pick up the slack in the summer, mid-June–August, when the WNBA's **New York Liberty** (tel. 212/964–9622) takes to the court. The atmosphere at the games is less showboating and more finesse; many say players are more skilled than in the NBA. Because the team is so new (founded 1997), tickets are easy to get, starting at $8. Look for Rosie O'Donnell among the fans. Madison Square Garden also hosts college games and the Big East and National Invitational college tournaments in winter.

FOOTBALL

If you've come to town expecting to see some football, try a sports bar. Tickets for both New York pro teams are almost impossible to get: You can scramble for single **New York Jets** (tel. 516/560–8200) tickets when they go on sale in August, join the waiting list for **New York Giants** (tel. 201/935–8222) tix, or hand a scalper your life savings. Both teams play in New Jersey at **Giants Stadium** (Meadowlands Complex on Rte. 3 in East Rutherford, NJ); catch a bus from Port Authority to reach the stadium. Football season runs September–December.

As an alternative of sorts, check out the **Columbia Lions,** the Ivy League's perpetual doormat. Their losing streaks have hit 40-plus in a row, but they continue to strive for that elusive winning record. The Lions play at Columbia University's **Baker Field** (W. 218th St. at Broadway, Inwood, tel. 212/854–2546) September–November. Tickets cost $13–$14.

ICE HOCKEY

Fast paced, brutal, and full of fights, ice hockey is just like the subway at rush hour—no wonder New Yorkers love it. The season runs October–April.

The rabid fans of the **New York Rangers** (Madison Square Garden, Midtown, tel. 212/465–6000), who make the players seem wimpy by comparison, are holding their breath in the wake of Wayne Gretzky's 1999 retirement. Tickets are always tough to come by and cost anywhere from $25–$150. The **New Jersey Devils** (Meadowlands Arena, New Jersey, tel. 201/935–3900) won the Stanley Cup in 1995 after enduring a lifetime as league losers and saw postseason play again in 1999, but their tickets, starting at $20, are no more popular than they ever were. The **New York Islanders** won four consecutive Stanley Cups in the early '80s, but thanks to ugly politics at Nassau Coliseum, you won't have trouble getting cheap tickets starting at $15. The Islanders play at Nassau Coliseum (Hempstead Turnpike, Uniondale, Long Island, tel. 516/794–9300), accessible by train from Penn Station.

Use caution wherever you run or jog, and don't go out alone in deserted areas or after dark. The New York Road Runners Club *(tel. 212/860–4455) can match you with a running partner if you're new in town.*

TENNIS

The prestigious **United States Open Tennis Tournament** (tel. 718/760–6200) takes place late August–early September at the U.S.T.A. National Tennis Center (*see* Tennis *in* Participant Sports, *above*). It's a hugely popular event with New Yorkers, and tickets ($21–$66) to the exciting matches go fast (and can run into hundreds of dollars). You can purchase tickets by phone through **TeleCharge** (tel. 888/673–6849) for a $5-per-ticket service fee. The **WTA Tour Championships** (tel. 212/465–6521), formerly hosted by Virginia Slims, brings together the top 16 women's singles and top eight women's doubles for over a million dollars in prizes. It's held at Madison Square Garden in mid-November, and tickets cost $15–$75.

INDEX